THE WALL STREET JOURNAL.

GUIDE TO UNDERSTANDING MONEY & INVESTING

KENNETH M. MORRIS

VIRGINIA B. MORRIS

LIGHTBULB
PRESS ®

LIGHTBULB PRESS
Project Team

Design Director Dave Wilder
Editors Sophie Forrester, Mavis Morris, Bess Newman, Tania Sanchez
Production Thomas F. Trojan
Illustration Krista K. Glasser
Photography Danielle Berman, Andy Shen

SPECIAL THANKS   *DOWJONES*

Dow Jones & Co. Dan Austin, Joan Wolf-Woolley, Lottie Lindberg and
Elizabeth Yeh at The Wall Street Journal Library
The Wall Street Journal Tom Herman, Douglas Sease, Dave Kansas

PICTURE CREDITS
American Bank Note Company, American Stock Exchange, Bureau of Engraving and Printing,
Chase Manhattan Archives, Chicago Board of Trade, CUC International, Museum of the City of
New York, NASD, New York Stock Exchange, The Nasdaq Stock Market, Pax World, The Options
Industry Council, T. Rowe Price Investment Services, United States Mint

*W*hen *The Wall Street Journal Guide to Understanding Money & Investing* first appeared in 1993, we thought that the book, with its colorful graphics and clear language, would appeal to people who wanted to know about the often-baffling world of the financial markets.

But we had no idea that it would become an indispensable resource in brokerage firms, banks, financial advisers' offices and school classrooms, or that there would be over a million copies in print. Nor did we ever dream it would be recast for the Asian markets and translated into Chinese.

As popular as the guide remains, we felt it was time for a revised editon that recognizes the monumental changes in the financial markets since the second edition was published in 1999, a period that saw the peak of the long bull market and the downturn that followed. We've updated the facts and figures, made the switch to decimal pricing, and included the introduction of the euro, ETFs, and single stock futures. Among the biggest changes we note is the evolution of the electronic markets and its impact on every phase of investing.

But in updating *Money & Investing* we haven't lost sight of our original mission: to unravel the mysteries of the financial markets—the language, the players, the strategies and, above all, the risks and rewards of investing—in a straightforward but lighthearted way. We show (and tell) how the markets work, why money gains and loses value, and what you need to know to make the right investments and measure their performance.

In preparing this revision, we are deeply indebted to The Wall Street Journal for the use of their financial tables and charts, and for the vast information resources and financial expertise they made available to us.

Kenneth M. Morris
Virginia B. Morris

CONTENTS

THE WALL STREET JOURNAL.
GUIDE TO UNDERSTANDING MONEY & INVESTING

MONEY

6 The History of Money

8 Paper Money

10 The U.S. Dollar

12 The Money Cycle

14 Other Forms of Money

16 The Federal Reserve System

18 Controlling the Money Flow

20 The Money Supply

22 Measuring Economic Health

24 Consumer Confidence

26 The Consumer Price Index

28 The Economic Cycle

30 The World of Money

32 The Value of Money

34 Trading Money

STOCKS

36 Stocks: Sharing a Corporation

38 The Right to Vote

40 The Value of Stock

42 The Stock Certificate

44 Selling New Stock

46 Stock Buyers

48 Buying Stocks

50 Selling Short

52 Buying on Margin

54 Getting Stock Information

56 Reading the Stock Tables

58 Sifting Stock Information

60 Evaluating Companies

62 The Stock Market

64 Trading on the New York Stock Exchange

66 Trading on the Nasdaq Market

68 The Evolving Markets

70 Tracking the Markets

72 Market Cycles

74 Crash!

76 Trading Around the Clock

78 Tracking International Markets

80 International Investing

82 Privatization

CONTENTS

BONDS

84 Bonds: Financing the Future

86 The Bond Certificate

88 Figuring a Bond's Worth

90 Rating Bonds

92 Tracking Bond Performance

94 Municipal Bonds

96 U.S. Treasury Notes and Bills

98 A Bond Vocabulary

100 Buying and Trading Bonds

102 Other Bonds, Other Choices

104 A Look at the World of Bonds

MUTUAL FUNDS

106 Mutual Funds: Putting It Together

108 The Mutual Funds Market

110 Targeted Investments

112 Focused Funds

114 Inside a Mutual Fund

116 Mutual Fund Quotations

118 It's All in the Charts

120 Tracking Fund Performance

122 The Prospectus

124 International Funds

FUTURES AND OPTIONS

126 Futures and Options

128 Commodities

130 The Futures Exchanges

132 Trading Futures Contracts

134 Hedgers and Speculators

136 How Futures Work

138 Reading Futures Tables

140 Financial Futures

142 A World of Options

144 Stock Options Tables

146 Using Options

148 Options Trading

150 Tracking Other Options

152 Derivatives Over the Counter

The History of Money

Most money doesn't have any value of its own. It's worth what it can buy at any given time.

The history of money begins with people learning to trade the things they had for the things they wanted. If they wanted an ax, they had to find someone who had one and was willing to exchange it for something of theirs. The system works the same way today, with one variation: Now you can give the seller **money** in exchange for the item you want, and the seller can use the money to buy something else.

IN THE BEGINNING WAS BARTER

Our earliest ancestors were self-sufficient, providing their own food, clothing and shelter from their surroundings. There was rarely anything extra—and nothing much to trade it for.

But as communities formed, hunting and gathering became more efficient. Occasionally there were surpluses of one commodity or another. People with extra animal skins but not enough grain could exchange their surplus with people who had plenty of food but no skins. **Barter** was born.

As societies grew more complex, barter flourished. The most famous example may be Peter Minuit's reputed swap, in 1626, of $24 worth of beads and trinkets for the island of Manhattan. And barter continues to this day.

MONEY FILLS THE BILL

It takes time and energy to find someone with exactly what you want who's also willing to take what you have to offer. And it isn't always easy to agree on what things are worth. How many skins is a basket of grain worth? What happens if the plow you want is worth a cow and a half?

As trade flourished, money came into use. Once buyers and sellers agreed what was acceptable as a means of payment, they could establish a system that assigned different values to coins or other durable and easily transportable items. The term **currency**, another word for money, means anything that's actually used as a means of exchange.

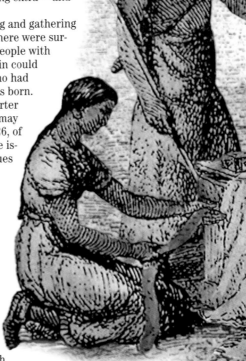

Using money also meant that buying and selling didn't have to happen at the same time. Sellers could wait until they were ready to make a purchase to spend the money they had received. What's more, they could accumulate money from a number of sales to give them more buying power.

Money has taken many different forms over the years. In Rome, for example, soldiers were often paid with sacks of salt—that's sal in Latin, the root of **salary**—and salt was also used in ancient China to pay for small purchases.

The expression "Don't take any wooden nickels" was a common warning for country boys headed for the big city in the 1800s. But there never were any—until 1932, when the bank closed in Tenino, WA, and left people without cash. The money they used was wooden coins worth 25¢, 50¢, and $1.

METAL BECOMES THE STANDARD

As early as 2500 B.C. various precious metals—gold, silver and copper—were used to pay for goods and services in Egypt and Asia Minor. By 700 B.C. the kingdom of Lydia was minting coins made of electrum, a pale yellow alloy of gold and silver. The coins were valuable, durable and portable. Better yet, they couldn't die or rot on the way to market. In addition, using coins permitted payments by **tale**, or counting out the right amount, rather than weighing it. That simplified the exchange process even more. For a long time, the relative value of currencies was measured against precious metals, usually gold or silver. That's where terms like **pound sterling** and **gold standard** originated.

In modern times, though, national economies have moved away from basing their currency on metal reserves. Gold hasn't been a universal yardstick since 1971, when the U.S. stopped redeeming its paper currency with gold.

MONEY BY FIAT

When money was made of gold or silver—or could be exchanged for one of them—it was **commodity currency**. But money that has no intrinsic value and can't be redeemed for precious metal is **fiat currency**. Most currency circulating today is fiat money, created and authorized by various governments as their official currency.

FORMS OF PAYMENT

Stone Money
Yap Island

Salt
China

Ivory (Whale Tooth)
Fiji

Elephant Hair
Africa

Tobacco
Solomon Islands

Brick Tea Money
Siberia

East Indian Money Tree
Malay Peninsula

Copper Money
Alaskan Indian

Gold Stater
Turkey

Owl Coin
Athens

Drachma
Thessaly

Sestertius of Caesar Augustus
Rome

Pine Tree Shilling
Massachusetts

Yen, or Round Money
Japan

Piece of Eight (8 Reals)
Spain

Paper Money

Bills come in different sizes, colors and denominations, but their real value is based on the economic strength of the country that issues them.

THE ORIGINS OF PAPER MONEY

Although the idea of paper money can be found in bills and receipts recorded by the Babylonians as early as 2500 B.C., the earliest bills can be traced to China. In 1282, Kubla Khan issued paper notes made of mulberry bark bearing his seal and his treasurers' signatures. The **Kuan** is the oldest surviving paper money. The currency—about 8½x11 inches—was issued in China by the Ming dynasty between 1368 and 1399.

The first European bank notes were printed in Sweden in 1661, and France put paper money into wide circulation in the 18th century.

The first paper money in the British Empire was in the form of **promissory notes** given to Massachusetts soldiers in 1690, when their siege of Quebec failed and there was no booty to pay them with. The idea became popular with the other colonies, if not with the soldiers who were paid that way.

THE U.S. DOLLAR

The American **dollar** comes from a silver coin called the Joachimsthaler minted in 1519 in the valley (thal) of St. Joachim in Bohemia (Jachymov in the Czech Republic). The coin was widely circulated and called the **daalder** in Holland, the **daler** in Scandinavia and the **dollar** in England.

Joachimsthaler
1519

More than two dozen countries besides the U.S. call their currency dollars.

The U.S. dollar's early history was chaotic until the National Banking Act of 1863 established a uniform currency. Before that, banks used paper money (called **scrip**), but they couldn't always meet their customers' demands for **hard currency** (gold or silver coins, or **specie**). Often the dollar could be exchanged for just a fraction of its stated value.

Dollars were once backed by gold and silver reserves. Until 1963, U.S. bills were called **silver certificates**. Today they are Federal Reserve notes, backed only by the economic integrity of the U.S. You can't exchange them for specie.

DOLLARS AROUND THE WORLD

Australia

Canada

Bermuda

Hong Kong

Antigua & Barbuda
Bahamas
Barbados
Belize
Brunei
Cayman Islands
Dominica
Fiji Islands
Grenada
Guyana
Jamaica
Liberia

Namibia
New Zealand
St. Kitts and Nevis
St. Lucia
St. Vincent
Singapore
Solomon Islands
Taiwan
Trinidad & Tobago
Zimbabwe

THE UPS AND DOWNS OF PAPER MONEY

Paper money has had its ups and downs because its value can change so quickly with changing economic conditions. When there's lots of money in circulation, prices tend to go up and paper money buys less. That's known as **inflation**.

For example, during the American Revolution paper money dropped in value from $1 to just 2.5 cents. In Germany in 1923, you needed 726,000,000 marks to buy what you'd been able to get for 1 mark in 1918.

In 1923, a German housewife burned mark notes in her kitchen stove, since it was cheaper to burn marks than to use them to buy firewood.

MAKING PAPER MONEY

The Bureau of Engraving and Printing prints money at plants in Washington, D.C. and Fort Worth, Texas. The money is printed in large sheets, stacked into piles of 100 and cut into bills that are bundled into bricks for shipping. The engraved plates, which can be used to produce up to three million impressions before they have to be replaced, are designed with intricate patterns of lines and curves to make the money hard to copy. As an added security measure, several different engravers work on each plate.

The Bureau makes the slightly magnetic ink itself from secret formulas. Special paper, made by Crane and Company, has been used for all U.S. currency since 1879.

The content of the paper is a closely guarded secret, although we know the sheets are now about 75% cotton and 25% linen and contain small, faintly colored nylon threads.

You can get back the full value of a torn bill from the Bureau of Engraving and Printing in Washington, D.C.—as long as you turn in at least 51% of the ripped one.

The U.S. Dollar

In 1862, the U.S. government issued its first paper money. The bills were called **greenbacks** because the backs were printed in green ink—to distinguish them from gold certificates.

Each U.S. dollar bill has a distinctively marked green-, black- and cream-colored face. A letter within a seal to the left of the portrait identifies the Federal Reserve Bank that issued the bill. In this case, it's B for New York. A corresponding number—New York's is 2—appears four times on the face. On other denominations, the seal of the Federal Reserve system itself appears.

The back of each denomination is different. On the dollar, it's the **Great Seal of the United States**. Its reverse side, on the right of the bill, features the American eagle and the number 13, representing the country as a whole and the original 13 states. Symbols include: 13 stripes on the eagle's shield, the 13-star constellation above the eagle's head, 13 warlike arrows grasped in one of the eagle's claws and the olive branch of peace, with 13 leaves and 13 olives, grasped in the other.

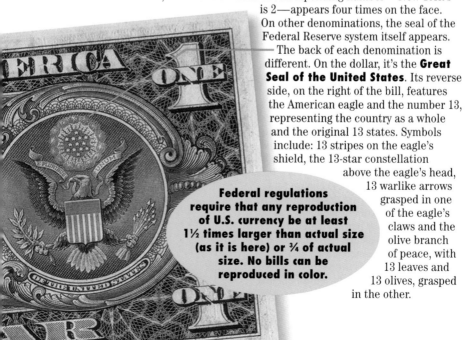

Federal regulations require that any reproduction of U.S. currency be at least 1½ times larger than actual size (as it is here) or ¾ of actual size. No bills can be reproduced in color.

Greenbacks are created in several steps. First the sheets are pressed into intricately designed plates to give the bills their raised feel. The backs are painted with green ink and, when it dries, the black front is printed. Finally, the serial numbers and Treasury seal are added to the front using a process called COPE, or currency overprinting and processing equipment.

Legal tender is money a government creates that must—by law—be accepted as payment of debt. A $100 bill is legal tender, for example, but a $100 check isn't. That's because the check is issued by a bank, not the government.

Bills are numbered two ways. The **eight-digit serial number** is printed on the top right and lower left on the front. The number of every bill of the same denomination in the same series is different. The number begins with a letter (here B) identifying the issuing Federal Reserve Bank.

Each bill also has a **series identification number** engraved between the portrait and the signature of the Secretary of the Treasury. It gives the year the note's design was introduced, usually when a new Secretary or a new U.S. Treasurer has been appointed.

The front of the seal has a 13-letter Latin motto, **ANNUIT COEPTIS**, which means "He has favored our undertaking," a reference to the blessing of an all-seeing deity whose eye is at the apex of the pyramid. The pyramid itself suggests a strong base for future growth. Underneath, in Roman numerals, is the date 1776, the year the Declaration of Independence was signed. The second motto, **NOVUS ORDO SECLORUM**, means "New order of the ages."

DOLLARS BY ANY OTHER NAME...			
	clams	lettuce	simoleons
	dinero	long green	smackers
	dough	loot	spondulics
	gelt	moolah	sugar
	gravy	rocks	the ready
boodle	grease	sawbucks	wad
bread	jack	scratch	wampum
bucks	juice	shekels	wangan

The Money Cycle

Money is a permanent fixture of modern society, but the bills and coins we use have a limited lifespan.

A major redesign of U.S. currency is underway—again. It began in 1996, with the new look for the $100 bill. Gradually, all but the $1 had larger, off-center portraits and more intricate border designs. Now, colors are being added to the front of the bills, there's a random pattern imprinted on the back, the portraits are not framed, and the number in the lower right is a brighter metallic. The goal in both cases: make the bills harder to counterfeit.

Since paper bills wear out from changing hands, replacements are printed regularly to maintain a steady supply. Not surprisingly, dollar bills have the shortest life span, about 13 to 18 months. Other countries have successfully introduced durable coins with lifespans of 30 to 40 years to replace their small bills, though so far that approach hasn't worked in the U.S. What has caught the public imagination is the state quarter program, which began in 1999 and runs through 2008. Five new coins are introduced each year, in the order the states entered the Union.

The Money Cycle

Old money is taken out of circulation and replaced on a regular basis.

The Treasury ships new money to the Federal Reserve Banks.

U.S. TREASURY

FED BANKS

Federal Reserve Banks return the old money to the Treasury. Paper money is shredded and burned into mulch. Coins are sent back to the Mint for melting and recasting.

THE LINCOLN PENNY

The first U.S. coin with the portrait of a president was the 1909 penny honoring Abraham Lincoln. The face of the penny is still the same today, though the back was redesigned in 1959 to include the Lincoln Memorial.

McKinley

Cleveland

Madison

Chase

Wilson

VANISHING AMERICANS

In 1969, bills over $100 in value were eliminated as currency because of declining demand. The faces that disappeared were McKinley on the $500, Cleveland on the $1,000, Madison on the $5,000, Chase on the $10,000 and Wilson on the largest of them all, the $100,000.

THE TWO-DOLLAR BILL

The Treasury from time to time issues $2 bills, but they've never been very popular with the public. The last ones were printed in 1995, but they shared the same rejection as the earlier series, and you rarely see them. A surprisingly large portion of the population is superstitious about using them.

Federal Reserve Banks and branches distribute the new money to individual banks in their regions.

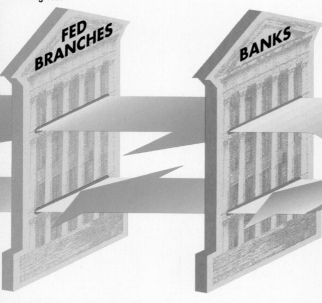

The banks distribute the money to their customers, including businesses and individuals.

The money circulates through the economy and around the world, changing hands many times as people pay in cash and get change back.

Businesses and individuals deposit their cash, including old bills, in their bank accounts.

The banks separate the worn bills and coins they collect from the ones that can stay in circulation. They ship the worn (and very dirty) ones back to their Federal Reserve branch or bank.

HOW COINS COME TO LIFE

In the U.S., new coins are struck at three Bureau of the Mint branches, and each coin carries the mark of the branch where it was minted: **D** for Denver, **S** for San Francisco, and **P** (or no mark at all) for Philadelphia. The process of making coins is called **minting**, from the Latin word *moneta*.

The whole process is a modest profitmaker. For example, it costs about 9/10 of a cent to make a penny. That difference—about a dollar for every thousand pennies—is profit. The Mint prefers the term **seigniorage**. But whatever you call it, it amounts to more than $400 million annually.

Other Forms of Money

Money doesn't always change hands. It's often transferred from one account to another by written or electronic instructions.

Technology has revolutionized the way we use money. The form we're most familiar with—bills and coins—represents only about 8% of the trillions of dollars that circulate in the U.S. economy.

Before 1945, most people paid with cash. By 1990, about $30 trillion was transferred annually by check. Electronic transfers have increased the volume dramatically. In 2003, an average of $7.3 trillion was moved electronically every day through the Federal Reserve System.

NOT CASHLESS—YET

A society that gets along without cash still seems a long way off.

People haven't yet abandoned their pennies, let alone their bills. On the other hand, the money being moved with a checkbook, an ATM card, a credit card, a debit card—or a personal computer—suggests that the story of money is still being written.

Increasingly sophisticated **smart cards**, whose dollar value is imbedded in a microchip that can be debited and replenished electronically, are part of that tale. For example, they're already replacing tickets and tokens to pay for mass transit, highway and bridge tolls, and phone calls.

HOW CHECKS MOVE MONEY

High-speed electronic equipment **reads** the sorting and payment instructions, called **MICR** (Magnetic Image Character Recognition) codes, printed in magnetic ink along the bottom of the check. The money is then **debited**, or subtracted, from the writer's account and **credited**, or added to, the receiver's.

Your bank account number, beginning with the branch number, identifies the account that money will be taken from to pay the recipient.

The check routing number identifies the bank, its location, and its Federal Reserve district and branch. The coded information explains the arrangement for collecting payment from the bank. The same information, in different format, appears in the upper right of the check, under the check number.

The check number and the amount of the check are printed by the first bank to receive the check when it is deposited or cashed. When you actually write the check, the space under your name is blank.

Information written and stamped on the back of the check shows the account the dollar value was credited to, the bank where it was cashed or deposited and the date, plus the payment stamp from your bank.

MAKING THE MOST OF CREDIT

In 2003, an estimated 80% of all U.S. households had one or more credit cards. The majority used their cards regularly. And based on the number of households that pay their bills in full every month—just 39% according to the Cambridge Consumer Credit Index—the companies that issue the cards are collecting a significant amount of interest. Most sellers are happy to accept credit, too, despite the fee they pay the card issuer, because people tend to spend more when they're using a card than they do when they're laying out cash.

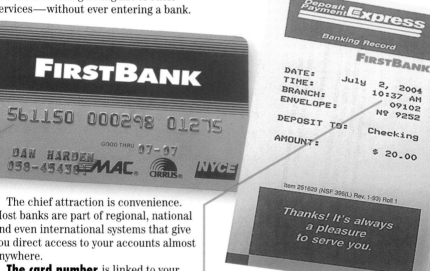

MONEY 'ROUND THE CLOCK

With a **personal identification number (PIN)** or **personal identification code (PIC)** and a bank debit card linked to one or more of your accounts, you can withdraw or deposit money, find out how much you have in an account, pay bills or choose from a growing list of other services—without ever entering a bank.

The chief attraction is convenience. Most banks are part of regional, national and even international systems that give you direct access to your accounts almost anywhere.

The card number is linked to your bank account, though it is not the same as your account number. The magnetic strip on the back identifies the bank and account when the card is inserted in a machine. The PIN number doesn't appear anywhere, for security reasons.

> **Credit and debit card transactions are protected by the government's Regulation E.**

Details of your transactions are printed on the receipt the ATM provides. **The date and location of the ATM** branch may be important if you question certain transactions. Cameras often record the activity at an ATM and can provide evidence in unresolved disputes. There's rarely a limit on the number of transactions you can make on any one visit, or the number of times you can use your card, but there may be a limit on the total amount you can withdraw in one day.

ELECTRONIC TRANSFERS

You can use a telephone or computer to authorize movement of funds among your bank or brokerage firm accounts, and you can pay your bills online, either using commercial banking software or directly through your bank's website. Income from paychecks, Social Security, and investments can be deposited directly to your accounts, and regular payments can be debited on a fixed schedule.

DEBIT AND CREDIT CARDS

Debit cards and credit cards look alike, but work differently. Credit cards let you charge a purchase and pay for it later because you've got a credit arrangement with a bank or other financial institution. Debit cards subtract the amount of your purchase directly from your bank account and credit it to the seller's account.

Usually you sign a credit card receipt to authorize a purchase. When you use a debit card, you may enter your PIN on a keypad or sign a receipt, depending on the vendor.

The Federal Reserve System

The Federal Reserve System is the guardian of the nation's money—banker, regulator, controller and watchdog all rolled into one.

Like other countries, the U.S. has a national bank to oversee its economic and monetary policies. But the Federal Reserve System, known informally as the Fed, isn't one bank. It's 12 separate district banks, with 25 regional branches, spread across the country, so that no one state, region or business group can exert too much control.

Each district bank has a president and board of directors, and the system itself is run by a seven-member board of governors. In addition, there's an Open Market Committee, whose responsibility is guiding day-to-day monetary decisions.

The Federal Reserve's Many Roles

The Fed plays many roles as part of its responsibility to keep the economy healthy.

The Fed handles the day-to-day banking business of the U.S. government. It gets deposits of corporate taxes for unemployment, withholding and income, and also of federal excise taxes on liquor, tobacco, gasoline and regulated services like phone systems. It also authorizes payment of government bills like Social Security and Medicare as well as interest payments on Treasury bills, notes and bonds.

REGULATOR

By authorizing buying and selling of government securities, the Fed tries to balance the money in circulation. When the economy is stable, the demand for goods and services is fairly constant, and so are prices. Achieving that stability supports the Fed's goals of keeping the economy healthy and maintaining the value of the dollar.

BANKER

The Fed maintains bank accounts for the U.S. Treasury and many government and quasi-government agencies. It deposits and withdraws funds the way you do at your own bank, but in bigger volume: Over 80 million Treasury checks are written every year.

LENDER

If a bank needs to borrow money, it can turn to a Federal Reserve bank. The interest the Fed charges banks is called the **discount rate**. Bankers don't like to borrow from the Fed, since it may suggest they have problems. And they can often borrow more cheaply from other banks.

Seattle

Helena

Portland

Salt Lake City

Denve

★ SAN FRANCISCO

Los Angeles

El Paso

HOW THE FED WORKS

Technically a corporation owned by banks, the Fed works more like a government agency than a business. Under the direction of its chairman, it sets economic policy, supervises banking operations and has become a major factor in shaping the economy.

The governors are appointed to 14-year terms by the president and confirmed by Congress, which insulates them from political pressure to some extent. One term expires every two years. However, the chairman serves a four-year term and is often chosen by the president to achieve specific economic goals.

MEMBER BANKS

About half of all the banks in the country are members of the Federal Reserve System. All national banks must belong, and state-chartered banks are eligible if they meet the financial standards the Fed has established.

IT'S NOT THE FDIC!

The Fed is not the same as the **FDIC**, the Federal Deposit Insurance Corporation. The FDIC insures bank depositors against losses if their bank gets into financial trouble. It doesn't regulate the banks.

AUDITOR	CONTROLLER	GUARDIAN	ADMINISTRATOR

AUDITOR

The Fed monitors the business affairs and audits the records of all of the banks in its system. Its particular concerns are compliance with banking rules and the quality of loans.

CONTROLLER

When currency wears out or gets damaged, the Fed takes it out of circulation and authorizes its replacement. Then the Treasury has new bills printed and new coins minted.

GUARDIAN

Gold stored in the U.S. by foreign governments is held in the vault at the New York Federal Reserve Bank—some 10,000 tons of it. That's more gold in one place than anywhere else in the world, as far as anyone knows. Among its many tasks, the Fed administers the exchange of bullion between countries.

ADMINISTRATOR

The Fed is also the national check clearing house. It facilitates quick and accurate transfer of more than $39.3 trillion in 42.5 billion check transactions a year.

BOSTON

Buffalo

MINNEAPOLIS   Detroit

Pittsburgh   NEW YORK

PHILADELPHIA

CHICAGO   CLEVELAND   Baltimore

Omaha   Cincinnati   RICHMOND

KANSAS CITY   ST. LOUIS   Louisville

Charlotte

Nashville

Memphis   ATLANTA

Oklahoma City   Little Rock   Birmingham

DALLAS   Jacksonville

New Orleans

Houston   Miami

San Antonio

Controlling the Money Flow

The money that powers our economy is created essentially out of nothing by the Federal Reserve.

Keeping a modern economy running smoothly requires a pilot who'll keep it from stalling or overaccelerating.

The U.S., like most other countries, tries to control the amount of money in circulation. The process of injecting or withdrawing money reflects the monetary policy that the Federal Reserve adopts to regulate the economy.

Monetary policy isn't a fixed ideology. It's a constant juggling act to keep enough money in the economy so that it flourishes without growing too fast.

HOW IT WORKS

The Fed's Open Market Committee meets about every six weeks to evaluate the economy.

Then it tells the Federal Reserve Bank of New York—the city where the nation's biggest banks and brokerage firms have their headquarters—whether to speed up or slow down the creation of new money.

About 11:15 a.m. every day, the New York Fed decides whether to buy or sell government securities in order to implement the Open Market Committee's policy decisions.

U.S.S. FEDERAL RESERVE

CREATE NEW MONEY TO STIMULATE THE ECONOMY

WITHDRAW MONEY FROM THE ECONOMY

FULL AHEAD SPUR ECONOMIC GROWTH

STOP ECONOMIC GROWTH

STOP GROWTH

FULL ASTERN SLOWER GROWTH

HALF ASTERN SLOW GROWTH

SLOW AHEAD SLOWER GROWTH

HALF AHEAD SLOW ECONOMIC GROWTH

HOW FAST MONEY GOES

Money's velocity is the speed at which it changes hands. If a $1 bill is used by 20 different people in a year, its velocity is 20. An increase in either the quantity of money in circulation or its velocity makes prices go up—and when both increase an even larger jump typically occurs, driving prices significantly higher.

The Fed's reserve requirement makes banks keep a portion, usually 10%,

10% RESERVE

of their deposits in a fund to cover any unusual demand from customers for cash.

REGULATION IS A TOUGH JOB

It isn't easy to regulate the money supply or control the rate of growth. That's because the economy doesn't always respond quickly or precisely when the Fed acts. Typically, it takes about six months for significant policy changes to affect the economy directly.

ADJUSTING THE RATE

Among the tools the Fed uses when it wants the economy to change direction is increasing or decreasing the discount rate, the rate it charges banks to borrow money. If the discount rate is increased, the banks tend to borrow less and have less money available to make loans to their clients. If the rate is decreased, banks tend to borrow more freely and lend money to their clients at attractive rates. The result is that changes in the discount rate have a ripple effect throughout the economy. And if the Fed isn't satisfied with the response, it can lower or raise the rate a second time or a third.

CHANGING THE SUPPLY

The Fed regularly influences the amount of money in circulation when it chooses to buy or sell government securities in the open market.

To slow down an economy where too much money is in circulation, the New York Fed sells government securities, taking in the cash that would otherwise be available for lending. And to give the economy a shot in the arm, it creates money by buying securities.

For all practical purposes, there isn't any limit on the amount of money the Fed can create. The $100 million in the example to the right is only a modest increase in the money supply. In a typical month, the Fed might pump as much as $4 billion or as little as $1 billion into the economy.

CREATING MONEY

To create money, the New York Fed buys government securities from banks and brokerage houses. The money that pays for the securities hasn't existed before, but it has value, or worth, because the securities the Fed has bought with it are valuable.

More new money is created when the banks and brokerages lend the money they receive from selling the securities to clients who spend it on goods and services. These simplified steps illustrate how the process works.

1

The Fed writes a check for $100 million to buy the securities from a brokerage house. The brokerage house deposits the check in its own bank (A), increasing the bank's cash.

2

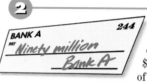

Bank A can lend its customers $90 million of that deposit after setting aside 10%. The Fed requires all banks to hold 10% of their deposits (in this example, $10 million) in reserve. A young couple borrows $100,000 from Bank A to buy a new house. The sellers deposit the money in their bank (B).

3

Now Bank B has $90,000 (the deposit minus the required reserve) to lend that it didn't have before. A woman borrows $10,000 from Bank B to buy a car, and the dealer deposits her check in Bank C.

4

Bank C can now loan $9,000.

This one series of transactions has created $190,099,000 in just four steps. Through a repetition of the loan process involving a wide range of banks and their customers, the $100 million that the Fed initially added to the money supply could theoretically become almost $900 million in new money.

The Money Supply

There's no ideal money supply. The Fed's goal is to keep the economy running smoothly by keeping an eye on the money that people have to spend.

The money supply measures the amount of money that people have available to spend—including cash on hand and funds that can be **liquidated**, or turned into cash.

When the Federal Reserve is following an easy money policy—keeping the rates low and increasing the money supply—the goal is to have the economy grow quickly. If companies hire more workers, consumer confidence tends to increase, boosting spending. But if the Fed adopts a tight money policy—slowing the money supply to combat inflation—the fear is that the economy can bog down, unemployment may increase and spending may slow.

In a strong economy, demand for currency increases without Federal Reserve intervention, and the amount of money in circulation goes up. But in a weak economy, growth stalls.

MEASURING THE MONEY SUPPLY

If you keep careful track of your personal money supply, you know, for instance, how much cash you have in your wallet and how much money is in your checking account. You also know how much salary is coming in and which investments, such as savings accounts and certificates of deposit (CDs), can be turned into cash quickly.

Similarly, economists and policymakers keep careful track of the public money supply using measures called M1, M2, M3 and L.

The three Ms are **monetary aggregates**, or ways to group assets that people use in roughly the same way. M1, for instance, counts **liquid assets**, like cash. The object is to separate money that's being saved from money that's being spent in order to predict impending changes in the economy.

L is a measure of other highly liquid assets, and adds a number of short-term bonds, commercial paper and savings bonds, for example, to M3.

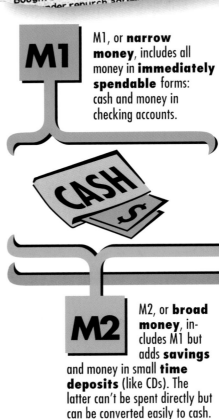

FEDERAL RESERVE DATA

RESERVE AGGREGATES
(daily average in millions)

	Two wee Jan. 27
Total Reserves (sa)	45,072
Nonborrowed Reserves (sa)	45,004
Required Reserves (sa)	44,084
Excess Reserves (nsa)	988
Borrowings from Fed (nsa)-a	68
Free Reserves (nsa)	92C
Monetary Base (sa)	515,87(

a-Excluding extended credit. nsa-Not season
sa-Seasonally adjusted.

	Feb. 3 J 1999
Reserve bank credit:	
U.S. Gov't securities:	
Bought outright	455,061 +
Held under repurch agreemt	3.674 -
Federal agency issues:	
Bought outright	336

M1, or **narrow money**, includes all money in **immediately spendable** forms: cash and money in checking accounts.

M2, or **broad money**, includes M1 but adds **savings** and money in small **time deposits** (like CDs). The latter can't be spent directly but can be converted easily to cash.

READING THE CHARTS

The Federal Reserve reports the financial details of the money supply every week. It's tracked in several different time periods to show both short-term changes and long-term trends. The average daily amounts—in billions of dollars—are provided for each component, M1, M2 and M3, and printed in The Wall Street Journal as Monetary Aggregates. The M3 figure, the most inclusive, is always the largest and the M1 the smallest. In addition, a summary of Reserve Aggregates appears every two weeks, providing additional financial statistics.

Seasonally adjusted (sa) amounts are always computed and compared with non-adjusted numbers (nsa). Seasonal adjustments reflect the varying flow of money into and out of bank accounts. In the spring, for instance, tax refunds tend to swell checking accounts that were depleted in the winter as consumers paid off holiday bills.

CHANGING YARDSTICK

In the early 1990s, the Federal Reserve stopped using its long-standing yardstick for measuring the economy—growth in the M2 money supply. Because people increasingly keep their cash in mutual fund money market accounts, which aren't included in M2, the Fed found that the figure wasn't a reliable indicator of economic growth.

So, instead of adjusting interest rates to control the money supply as a reaction to changes in M2, the new method is to set short-term **real interest rates** (the current interest rates minus the rate of inflation) at a level that the Fed believes will produce growth without inflation.

FEDERAL RESERVE DATA

MONETARY AGGREGATES
(daily average in billions)

	One week ended:	
	Jan. 25	Jan. 18
y supply (M1) sa	1086.8	1087.2
y supply (M1) nsa	1077.9	1090.0
y supply (M2) sa	4434.0	4435.6
y supply (M2) nsa	4407.9	4453.6
y supply (M3) sa	6023.4	6031.9
y supply (M3) nsa	6014.7	6060.6
	Four weeks ended:	
	Jan. 25	Dec. 28
y supply (M1) sa	1091.6	1091.4
y supply (M1) nsa	1106.3	1110.3
y supply (M2) sa	4435.4	4412.0
Money supply (M2) nsa	4447.9	4428.0
Money supply (M3) sa	6031.4	6011.5
Money supply (M3) nsa	6041.7	6031.3
	Month	
	Dec.	Nov.
Money supply (M1) sa	1093.0	1088.8
Money supply (M2) sa	4412.9	4375.2
Money supply (M3) sa	6013.1	5954.7

nsa-Not seasonally adjusted. sa-Seasonally adjusted.
MEMBER BANK RESERVE CHANGES

SAVINGS

INSTITUTIONAL ASSETS

M3 is the broadest measure of the money supply. It includes all of M1 and M2, plus the assets and liabilities of financial institutions, including long-term deposits, which can't be easily converted into spendable forms.

M3

Measuring Economic Health

Economists keep their fingers on the pulse of the economy at all times, determined to cure what ails it.

Intensive care is a 24-hour business. Doctors and nurses measure vital signs, record changes in temperature and physical functions, conduct test after test. That gives you an idea of how thousands of experts—and countless more interested amateurs—watch the economy.

The biggest differences? The vigil never stops—even when the economy seems healthy. And there are usually multiple causes for any sign of weakness, often including a number that can't be cured by treating the U.S. economy alone.

The Index of Leading Economic Indicators is released every month by The Conference Board, a business research group. The numbers rarely surprise the experts, since many of the components are reported separately before the Index is released. But it does provide a simple way to keep an eye on the economy's overall health. Generally, three consecutive rises in the Index are considered a sign that the economy is growing—and three drops, a sign of decline and potential recession.

Ten leading indicators are averaged to produce the Index, with some carrying more weight than others. Taken together, they're designed to predict short-term economic conditions. Among them are the spread between the 10-year Treasury and the federal funds rates, the M2 money supply, the S&P 500-stock Index and housing starts.

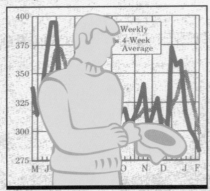

Jobless Claims

Weekly claims in thousands

Weekly 4-Week Average

Unemployment Figures

Weekly reports and monthly summaries of new claims for unemployment insurance provide a sense of how many people have recently lost their jobs, though not the number of people who have exhausted their benefits and are still out of work.

Economists and politicians tend to see continuing high unemployment as a danger signal. While some level of unemployment is the norm even in a robust economy, the higher the rate, the greater the risk that the economy, and the society, have serious problems.

The flip side is that low unemployment rates may carry the potential for higher inflation as employers increase wages to attract new workers.

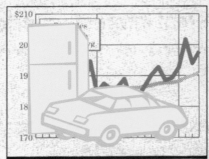

Durable Goods

In billions of dollars

NEW ORDERS received by manufacturers of durable goods rose in March to a

Durable Goods

A backlog of orders for a wide range of manufactured products, from machinery to transportation equipment, signals increasing demand that will keep the economy expanding.

Leading Indicators

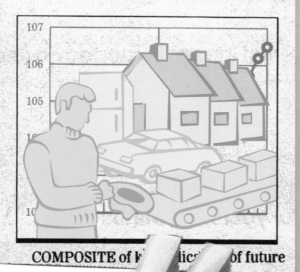

107
106
105
1
10

COMPOSITE of k̶ ̶ ̶d̶i̶c̶ of future

Housing Starts

Annual rate, in millions of dwelling units

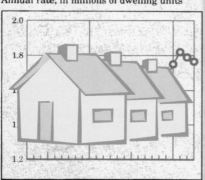

2.0
1.8
1.2

HOUSING STARTS in March fell to a seasonally adjusted annual rate of 1.766

New Factory Orders

In billions of dollars

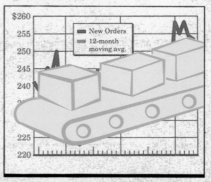

$260
255
250
245
240

■ New Orders
▨ 12-month moving avg.

225
220

NEW ORDERS reported by manufacturers in May fell to a seasonally adjusted

Housing Starts
The number of housing permits being issued is a measure of economic health. A growing economy typically generates increased demand for new housing. But strength in the housing market may also be a bright spot in an otherwise lackluster economy.

New Factory Orders
Rising orders reported by manufacturers for consumer goods and materials affirms confidence in the economy and suggests continued growth. In contrast, falling or flat demand can signal economic problems.

Consumer Confidence

Consumers' attitudes toward the health of the economy are influenced by what they hear. And their confidence—or lack of it—affects how the economy fares.

If consumers feel good about their current situation and about the future, they tend to spend more freely, which boosts economic growth. If they're worried about things like job security, they tend to save more and spend less, slowing economic growth and the economy itself.

Consumers often respond slowly to news of an economic recovery if they don't see an immediate, positive financial impact on their own lives. Their reluctance to start spending helps keep the recovery slow.

But no pattern, however recurrent it has been, predicts future behavior. In some economic downturns continued consumer spending has been credited with preventing a shaky situation from getting worse.

JOB CREATION

The BLS also reports monthly on job creation, or the number of jobs that have been added during the period. Like unemployment, job creation—or the absence of it—has economic and political consequences.

Job creation is actually easier to measure than unemployment, which includes not only people who have lost jobs recently but also those who have stopped looking for work and sometimes those who describe themselves as self-employed.

There's no question that a growing number of jobs, or what is sometimes called net employment growth, makes the economy stronger. Looked at the other way, jobs growth is often used as evidence of economic strength.

Unlike the BLS survey of median income, however, the information on job creation includes part-time as well as full-time jobs. What it doesn't evaluate is whether more part-time jobs is a positive or negative indicator, stimulating or replacing full-time jobs.

WEEKLY EARNINGS

The Bureau of Labor Statistics (BLS), part of the U.S. Department of Labor, tracks the median weekly earnings of full-time workers—just over 100 million of them—by surveying 60,000 households across the country. The median amount is the mid-point, which means that half the workers earn more and half earn less.

This survey reports whether the median income is increasing or decreasing and calculates real earnings by adjusting the current dollar value for changes in the consumer price index (CPI). In addition, it looks at the income patterns of specific groups within the sample, subdivided by gender, ethnicity, age, profession, and education.

MEASURING EMOTIONS

SURVEYING SENTIMENT

Consumer sentiment is measured in several different ways. Two of the principal guides that economists use are the monthly surveys done by the **University of Michigan Institute for Social Research** and **The Conference Board.** The results are intended for specific audiences, but it's only a matter of minutes before Wall Street's information networks make survey results public knowledge.

The surveys can produce different results because the organizations ask different questions.

- **Michigan's poll asks if consumers are confident enough to take on debt for such big-ticket items as cars and appliances.**

- **The Conference Board focuses on consumer worries about job security.**

- **Other surveys measure consumers' income, their views on the economy, and business conditions. Changes in interest rates, increases in energy or food costs, and major political events that consumers believe will affect their financial and job security also have an impact on survey results. However, a strong labor picture can sometimes overshadow those concerns—or the other way around.**

CONSUMER CREDIT

Use of consumer credit, or the extent to which individuals charge their purchases rather than paying cash, is sometimes seen as a measure of confidence in the economy. The logic behind this view is that people are willing to spend more freely when they feel secure about their jobs and good about the future.

On the other hand, some economists worry that easy access to credit in an era of low interest rates may encourage more people to borrow even in a period of economic uncertainty. Rising interest rates could make it difficult for over-extended consumers, especially subprime borrowers who pay higher rates, to meet their payments. That could have a ripple effect on the economy as a whole and on lenders' bottom lines in particular.

GROSS DOMESTIC PRODUCT

The gross domestic product (GDP) reports the output of finished goods and services produced in the U.S. during the year, though numbers are reported and revised monthly and quarterly. It is widely considered the broadest measure of the health of the economy, and usually a higher GDP is the sign of a healthier economy.

There are five components: personal consumption, which accounts for about two-thirds of the total figure, government expenditures, private investment in new assets, inventory growth, and the balance of trade, which is exports minus imports.

What is doesn't include is money spent on goods created in previous years, or invested in stocks or bonds. Nor does it count the value of intermediary products that are used in some final product, such as the steel in cars.

The Consumer Price Index

The Consumer Price Index (CPI) looks at the economy from your perspective: It reports what it costs to pay for food, housing and other basics.

The **Consumer Price Index (CPI)** serves the double role of reflecting economic trends and influencing economic policy decisions. Though its accuracy as well as its urban bias are sometimes questioned, it's the most widely used measure of inflation—and the basis for figuring adjustments to Social Security payments as well as determining cost-of-living increases in wages and pensions.

HOW THE CPI IS FIGURED

The Bureau of Labor Statistics compiles the CPI every month by recording prices for 80,000 goods and services that reflect the current lifestyle of the typical urban American consumer. It includes food, housing, clothing, transportation, healthcare, recreation and education as well as a catchall category called other. The Bureau reports changes from month to month and year to year, using the period 1982-1984 as the **basis**, or starting point, against which the numbers are measured.

The CPI components are adjusted periodically to reflect changes in lifestyle and in the relative cost of living.

CURRENT COMPONENTS OF THE CPI-U	2003	1992
HOUSING • Shelter, rent and homeowners' equivalent of rent • Fuel, including oil, coal, bottled gas, gas, electricity	42.1%	42%
FOOD • Eaten at home and away from home • Beverages	15.4%	17.9%
TRANSPORTATION • Private cars, trucks, other • Public transportation	16.9%	17.1%
MEDICAL CARE	6.1%	6.2%
CLOTHING	3.9%	6.1%
RECREATION	5.9%	4.4%
EDUCATION AND COMMUNICATION	5.9%	*
OTHER	3.8%	6.3%

The cost of each component of this chart is used to figure the CPI. The relative weight of each item is calculated by using the percentage shown.
*The category for education is the most recent addition to the list, covering elements previously grouped in the Other category.

THE CPI
Originally called the cost-of-living index, the CPI can't evaluate the changing quality of things you buy. An appliance that can do more things may cost more—but perhaps doesn't last as long as an older, plainer model. And the CPI doesn't measure the shrinking size of products for which you pay the same price you paid for the larger version.

The Annual Change in the CPI

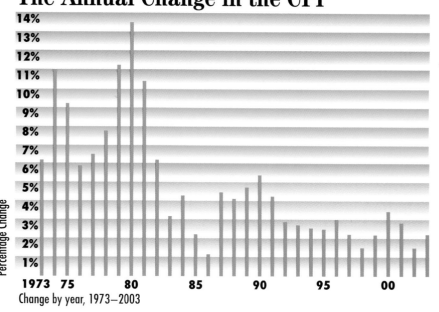

Percentage Change

Change by year, 1973–2003

The Economic Cycle

Inflation and recession are recurring phases of a continuous economic cycle. Experts work hard to predict their timing and control their effects.

Inflation occurs when prices rise because there's too much money in circulation and not enough goods and services to spend it on. When prices go higher than people can—or will—pay, demand decreases and a downturn begins.

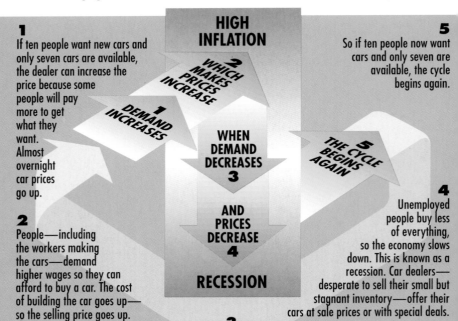

HIGH INFLATION

1 DEMAND INCREASES

2 WHICH MAKES PRICES INCREASE

WHEN DEMAND DECREASES **3**

AND PRICES DECREASE **4**

RECESSION

5 THE CYCLE BEGINS AGAIN

1
If ten people want new cars and only seven cars are available, the dealer can increase the price because some people will pay more to get what they want. Almost overnight car prices go up.

2
People—including the workers making the cars—demand higher wages so they can afford to buy a car. The cost of building the car goes up—so the selling price goes up.

3
When the car costs more than people can afford, they stop buying. Fewer cars are needed, and the factory lays off workers.

4
Unemployed people buy less of everything, so the economy slows down. This is known as a recession. Car dealers—desperate to sell their small but stagnant inventory—offer their cars at sale prices or with special deals.

5
So if ten people now want cars and only seven are available, the cycle begins again.

THE INFLATION STRUGGLE

Since inflation typically occurs in a growing economy that's creating jobs and reducing unemployment, politicians are willing to risk its problems. But the Federal Reserve prefers to cool down a potentially inflationary economy before it gets out of hand. So it sells government securities, which has the effect of raising interest rates and slowing borrowing. But since it also wants to prevent a long-term slowdown, it typically reverses its policy when the economy seems likely to shrink.

CONTROLLING THE CYCLE

Most developed economies try not to let the economic cycle run unchecked because the consequences could be a major worldwide **depression** like the one that followed the stock market crash of 1929. In a depression, money is so tight that the economy virtually grinds to a halt, unemployment escalates, businesses collapse and the general mood is grim.

Instead, most central banks adjust their monetary policy at the first sign of a slowdown, or recession, to ward off more trouble.

TIME AS MONEY

In 1800, you could travel from New York to Philadelphia in about 18 hours by stagecoach. The trip cost about $4.

Today the train costs about $48, but takes 75 minutes. While the trip's price has **inflated** about 1,100%, the travel time has **deflated** about 1,340%. So, if time is money, today's traveler comes out ahead.

THE RULE OF 72

The rule of 72 is a reliable guide to the impact of inflation. You simply divide 72 by the annual inflation rate to find out the number of years it will take prices to double. For example, when inflation is at 10%, prices will double in seven years ($72 \div 10 = 7$) and when it's 3%, they will double in 24 years ($72 \div 3 = 24$).

You can also use the Rule of 72 to estimate how long it will take you to double the money you're saving. If you're earning a 5% return on your investment portfolio, you should double your principal in 14.4 years. But if your return is 10%, it should double in half the time.

INFLATION DESTROYS VALUE

Most economists agree that inflation isn't good for the economy because, over time, it destroys value, including the value of money. If inflation is running at a 10% annual rate, for example, a book that cost $10 one year would cost $20 just seven years later. For comparison's sake, if inflation averaged 3% a year, the same book wouldn't cost $20 for 24 years.

Inflation may also prompt investors to buy things they can resell at huge profits—like art or real estate—rather than putting their money into companies that can create new products and jobs.

CHARTING A RECESSION

Recessions, or periods when unemployment rises, while sales and industrial production slows, occur cyclically though not predictably in the U.S. and around the world. The National Bureau of Economic Research (NBER), which tracks recessions, describes the low point of a recession as a **trough** between two **peaks**—the points at which the recession began and ended. Of course, peaks and troughs can be identified only in retrospect, though the fact there's a slump in the economy is evident.

Recessions are typically substantially shorter than the period of economic expansion they follow, as was the case in 1990-1991 and in 2001—when the economy declined from March until November and then

turned upward. But they can be quite severe even if they're brief, and recovery can be slower from some recessions than from others.

For example, the economy may expand while unemployment rates stay high if there's an increase in **productivity**. That means fewer workers are creating more goods and services.

WHO GETS HURT?

The people hit the hardest by inflation are those living on fixed incomes. For example, if you're retired and have a pension that was determined by a salary you earned in less inflationary times, your income will buy less of what you need to live comfortably. Workers whose wages don't keep pace with inflation can also find their lifestyle slipping.

But inflation isn't bad for everyone. Debtors love it because the money they repay each year is worth less than it was when they borrowed it. If their own income keeps pace with inflation, the money they repay is also an increasingly smaller percentage of their budget.

WHEN THERE'S NO INFLATION

When the rate of inflation slows, it's described as **disinflation**. Several years of 1% annual increases in the cost of living are disinflationary after a period of more rapid growth. Employment and output can continue to be strong, and the economy can continue to grow.

Deflation, though, is a widespread decline in the prices of goods and services. But instead of stimulating employment and production, deflation has the potential to undermine them. As the economy contracts and people are out of work, they can't afford to buy even at cheaper prices.

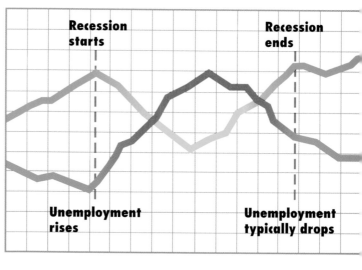

Recession starts

Recession ends

Unemployment rises

Unemployment typically drops

The World of Money

Currencies are **floated** against each other to measure their worth in the global marketplace.

A currency's value in the world marketplace reflects whether individuals and governments are interested in using it to make purchases or investments, or in holding it as a source of long-term security. If demand is high, its value increases in relation to the value of other currencies. If it's low, the reverse occurs.

Some currencies are relatively stable, reflecting an underlying financial and political stability. Other currencies experience wild or rapid changes in value,

the sign of economies in turmoil as the result of runaway inflation, deflation, defaults on loan agreements, serious balance-of-trade deficits or economic policies that seem unlikely to resolve the problems.

Similarly, certain currencies are used widely in international trade while others are not. That's the result of the relative stability of the currencies and the volume of goods and services a country or economic union produces.

Key Currency Cross Rates

	Dollar	Euro	Pound	SFran
Canada	1.3235	1.6206	2.3886	1.028
Japan	110.78	135.65	1989.93	86.05?
Mexico	10.9709	13.4339	19.800	8.522?
Switzerland	1.2873	1.5763	2.3234	...
U.K.	.55410	.6785	...	.4304
Euro	.81670	...	1.4739	.63438
U.S.	...	1.2245	1.8048	.77680

Source: Reuters

NOTHING IS FIXED

Currency values of even the most stable economies change over time as traders are willing to pay more—or less—for dollars or pounds or euros or yen. For example, great demand for a nation's products means great demand for the currency needed to pay for those products.

If there's a big demand for the stocks or bonds of a particular country, its currency's value is likely to rise as overseas investors buy it to make investments. Similarly, a low inflation rate can boost a currency's value, since investors believe that the value of long-term purchases in that country won't erode over time.

HOW CURRENCY VALUES ARE SET

Between 1944 and 1971, major trading nations had a fixed, official rate of exchange tied to the U.S. dollar, which could be redeemed for gold at $35 an ounce. Since 1971, when the gold standard was abandoned, currencies have floated against each other, influenced by supply and demand and by various governments' efforts to manage their currency. Some countries, for example, have sought stability by pegging, or linking, their currency to the value of the U.S. dollar. In Europe, the European Union established the euro as a common currency for participating member nations. At year's end, 1998, their currencies were permanently aligned with one another and the euro has replaced individual currencies for all transactions.

Late New York Trading Wednesday, March 10		
Peso	**Yen**	**CdnDlr**
2063	.01195	...
).097	...	83.704
...	.09903	8.2896
1734	.01162	.9727
5050	.00500	.41866
444	.00737	.61707
115	.00903	.75560

CURRENCY CROSS RATES

Currency cross rates, reported as the late New York trading price of the basic units of seven major currencies in relation to each other, are published daily in The Wall Street Journal. Since these exchange rates apply to bank trades of $1 million or more, they usually reflect a higher unit of foreign currency per dollar than you would get in a retail transaction, such as changing money at a bank.

To find the current exchange rate between two currencies, you find the place on the chart where one country's name (listed on the left) intersects with the other's currency (listed across the top). Here, for example, the Mexican peso is trading at 10.9709 to the dollar.

The chart has a global perspective, providing exchange information for trading partners whose transactions may not be handled in dollars or euros—Japanese yen and U.K. pounds, for example, or yen and Canadian dollars. What it does not reflect is trade between emerging markets or between emerging and developed markets, where currencies such as the Chinese yuan have a major impact.

STABILITY IS A GOAL

Governments usually want their currency to be **stable**, maintaining a constant relative worth with the currencies of their major trading partners. Sometimes they interfere with market forces—buying up large amounts of their own currency or agreeing with trading partners to lower interest rates—to achieve that goal.

If interest rates are lowered, however, fewer foreign investors may want to put money in the country's banks. They'll look for better return elsewhere.

Other times, a currency is deliberately **devalued** if a government decides to lower the value of its currency against those of other countries, often to make its exports more competitive.

EURODOLLARS

are U.S. dollars on deposit in non-U.S. banks. They can earn interest, be loaned or used to make investments in American or international companies. For example, U.S. banks borrow Eurodollars regularly.

The Value of Money

Exchanging dollars for euros, pounds for yen, or rupees for rubles is big business—to the tune of $1.5 trillion a day.

Money flows across national borders all the time, so **foreign exchange**—changing one currency for another—flourishes. But there is no actual physical marketplace where the world's currencies are traded. The global foreign exchange market, or **forex**, is a network of interconnected telephones and computers that operate virtually around the clock.

CURRENCY TRADING

Traders working for big banks and other financial institutions buy and sell currencies in what is by far the largest single financial market in the world. On a typical day, roughly $1.5 trillion in currencies is traded electronically around the world.

There's a pattern to these transactions, though it continues to evolve as computerized links among markets become more sophisticated. Electronic broking systems, which are increasingly the norm, tend to reduce volatility and provide more competitive prices than market makers specializing in particular currencies, who formerly handled most of the forex trading.

EUROPE

16.78 euros*

JAPAN

2283.6 yen*

AUSTRALIA

29.11 dollars*

TRADING FOR BUSINESS

Corporations that do business in more than one country depend on foreign exchange. If a corporation knows it needs Japanese yen to pay for a shipment of electronic equipment, it asks its bank to buy Japanese currency at the best exchange rate possible.

On a smaller scale, when a New York retailer buys sweaters from a Norwegian company, the New Yorker tells his bank to pay his bill. The bank either dips into its own reserves of kroners or buys them in the currency market. Then the bank calculates the current exchange rate between dollars and kroner, deducts the dollars from its client's account, and instructs the Norwegian company's bank in Oslo to credit the seller's account with the appropriate number of kroner.

* As of May 2004

Trading Money

Everybody wants to do business at the best possible exchange rates.

You're unlikely to be involved in having to negotiate what a dollar is worth, since currency exchange is a huge business, handled by traders working for large commercial banks or through electronic broking systems. But you are directly affected by the fact that its value is constantly changing, whether you're traveling abroad or buying imported goods. Basically, a strong dollar means more buying power.

World Value of the Dollar

The table below, compiled by Bank of America, gives the rates of exchange for the U.S. dollar Friday February 12. Unless otherwise noted, all rates listed are middle rates of interbank bid pressed in foreign currency units per one U.S. dollar. The rates are indicative and aren't base basis for particular transactions. BankAmerica International doesn't trade in all the listed foreign currencies.

Country (Currency)	Value 2/12	Value 2/5
Afghanistan (Afghani -c)	4750.00	4750.00
Albania (Lek)	139.70	139.90
Algeria (Dinar)	63.4022	62.7906
Andorra (Peseta -7)	148.0303	146.9971
Andorra (Franc -8)	5.0269	4.9918
Angola (Readjust Kwanza)	257128.00	257128.00
Antigua (E Caribbean $)	2.70	2.70
Argentina (Peso)	0.9999	0.9999
Aruba (Florin)	1.79	1.79
Australia (Australia Dollar)	1.5576	1.5373
Azerbaijan (Manat)	3950.00	3950.00
Bahamas (Dollar)	1.00	1.00
Bahrain (Dinar)	0.38	0.38
Bangladesh (Taka)	48.50	48.50
Barbados (Dollar)	2.00	2.00
Belize (Dollar)	2.00	2.00
Benin (C.F.A. Franc)	502.6868	499.1784
Bermuda (Dollar)	1.00	1.00
Bhutan (Ngultrum)	42.4475	42.4675
Bolivia (Boliviano -o)	5.68	5.67
Bolivia (Boliviano -f)	5.68	5.68
Botswana (Pula)	5.69	5.69
Bouvet Island (Norwegian Krone)	4.5872	4.5455
Brazil (Real)	7.6765	7.6925
Brunei (Dollar)	1.91	1.815
Bulgaria (Lev)	1.6932	1.6874
Burkina Faso (C.F.A. Franc)	1734.30	1726.40
Burma (Kyat)	502.6868	499.1784
Burundi (Franc)	6.1047	6.0989
Cambodia (Riel)	499.95	500.54
Cameroon (C.F.A. Franc)	3775.00	3775.00
Canada (Dollar)	502.6868	499.1784
	1.4927	1.4886
		04 71

Country (Currency)
Lebanon (Pound)
Lesotho (Maloti)
Liberia (Dollar)
Libya (Dinar -21)
Liechtenstein (Franc)
Luxembourg (Lux.Franc)
Macao (Pataca)
Madagascar DR (Franc)
Malawi (Kwacha)
Malaysia (Ringgit)
Maldive (Rufiyaa)
Mali Rep (C.F.A. Franc)
Malta (Lira *)
Martinique (Franc -8)
Mauritania (Ouguiya)
Mauritius (Rupee)
Mexico (New Peso)
Monaco (Franc -8)
Mongolia (Tugrik -o-29)
Montserrat (E Caribb)
Morocco (Dirham)
Mozambique (Metica)
Namibia (Rand -c)
Nauru Islands (Aust)
Nepal (Rupee)
Netherlands Ant'le
New Zealand (N.Z.)
Nicaragua (Gold Co)
Niger Rep (C.F.A.)
Nigeria (Naira -o)
Nigeria (Naira)
Norway (N)
Oman

WHAT A DOLLAR'S WORTH

The chart above provides the approximate rates of exchange for the U.S. dollar against various world currencies. The figures give the amount of foreign currency a dollar would buy. Here, for example, a dollar was worth 1.79 Aruban florins and 0.38 Bahrainian dinar. A few countries with close tourist or political ties to the U.S., like Bermuda, set the value of their currency permanently at $1.

MONEY AWAY FROM HOME

Travelers exchanging money are very minor players in the currency market. But if they're savvy, they can benefit from banks' and credit card companies' large-volume trading. The key is to get the most local currency for their own currency by exchanging where the rate is the best and the **commission**, or charge for the transaction, is the lowest.

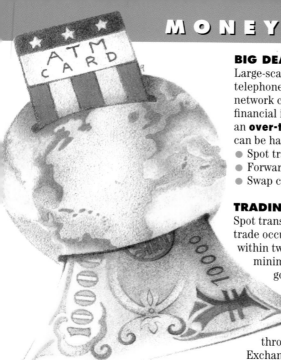

BIG DEALS

Large-scale currency trading is done by telephone or electronically through a network controlled by banks or other financial institutions, in what's known as an **over-the-counter** market. The trades can be handled three different ways, as
- Spot transactions
- Forward transactions
- Swap contracts

TRADING ON THE SPOT

Spot transactions, in which the currency trade occurs immediately and is settled within two days, are big money deals, with minimum trades of $1 million. Trading goes on around the clock, through what is known as the global trading day, which begins when the New Zealand market opens and runs through the end of New York trading. Exchange rates are updated constantly, and traders must pay careful attention, as a good deal typically depends on split-second timing and small price differences.

FORWARDS AND SWAPS

Companies doing business in more than one country need to protect themselves against sudden or dramatic changes in the relative value of currencies, so they hedge commitments to invest, sell or borrow with agreements that have predetermined **forex**, or foreign-exchange, rates. Conventional deals are described as plain vanilla, while others are complex, customized transactions.

Basically, swaps involve converting a cash flow or interest rate in one currency to a cash flow or interest rate in another. Forward transactions mean agreeing on an exchange rate that will apply when currency is traded on a set date in the future.

YOUR MONEY ABROAD

The popularity of credit cards and the growing use of globally linked electronic banking systems has made it easier to handle money matters when you travel in developed countries, especially in large cities.

In many places, you can pay for goods and services with a credit card. When the bills appear on your statement, the value of the transactions is converted to dollars, ususally at favorable rates because the credit card companies do such a huge volume of international business.

With an ATM, American Express or Diner's Club card, you can withdraw cash in local currency directly from your checking account. There's typically a fee for each transaction, but the exchange rate is usually the best that you can get anywhere.

Origins of Currency Names

India
RUPEE
from the root meaning *silver*

Soviet Union
RUBLE
means *to cut*

Sweden
KRONOR
refers to a gold coin that bore the image of a crown

Peru
SOL
means *the sun*

Brazil
CRUZADO
is the Southern Cross

Guatemala
QUETZAL
A bird with golden-green and scarlet plumage, the male with a dramatic long tail

South Africa
RAND
from a South African Dutch word meaning *shield*

Japan
YEN
means *round*, and originated when Japanese money changed from square to round

England
POUND
a pound of silver

Mexico
PESO
means *weight* (of a silver dollar)

Stocks: Sharing a Corporation

Stocks are pieces of the corporate pie. When you buy stocks, or shares, you own a slice of the company.

Stocks are **equity** investments. If you buy stock in a corporation, you own a small part of that corporation and are described as a **stockholder** or **shareholder**. You buy stock because you expect it to increase in value, or because you expect the corporation to pay you dividend income, or a portion of its profits. In fact, many stocks provide both growth and income.

When a corporation issues stock, the company receives the proceeds from that initial sale. After that, shares of the stock are **traded**, or bought and sold among investors, but the corporation gets no income from those trades. The price of the stock moves up or down depending on how much you and other investors are willing to pay for it at the time.

COMMON STOCK

Most stock in the U.S. is **common stock**. If you buy common stock, there are no guarantees you'll make money. You take the risk that the stock won't increase in value or pay dividends. In fact, it's possible that the value of the stock will drop, and you'll lose some or all of your investment if you sell at that point.

In exchange for the risk you take, however, you stand to make money if the company prospers—sometimes a lot of money. Over time, stocks in general, though not each individual stock, tend to increase in value.

PREFERRED STOCK

Preferred stocks are also ownership shares issued by a corporation and traded by investors. They differ from common stocks by reducing investor risk—but they may also limit return. The amount of the dividend is usually guaranteed and paid before dividends on common stock. And preferred stockholders have a greater chance of getting some of their investment back if a company fails. But the dividend isn't increased if the company profits, and the price of preferred stock tends to be stable over time.

COMMON STOCK

- Owners share in success when company profits
- Owners at risk if company falters

CLASSES OF STOCK

Companies may issue different classes of stock, label them differently and list them separately on a stock market. Sometimes a class indicates ownership in a specific division or subsidiary of the company. Other times it indicates shares that sell at different market prices, have different dividend policies, or impose voting or sales restrictions on ownership.

♣ StrwdHtlRsrt	HOT	1.34e	4.2	5	5796	32
StateSt	STT	.56	.6	34	4087	89
StatnlslBcp	SIB	.36f	2.2	15	841	16
StationCno	STN		...	dd	1111	1?
StationCno pf		3.50	7.0	...	82	
Steelcase A	SCS	.44	2.7	11	974	
Steinway	LVB		...	15	.143	
Stepan	SCL	.60	2.6	11	48	
SterisO			...	22	805?	

Classes of stock

Preferred stocks

PREFERRED STOCK

- Dividend payment has priority over common stock dividends
- Dividends don't increase if company prospers

BLUE CHIP

is a term borrowed from poker, where the blue chips are the most valuable. Blue chips refer to the stocks of the largest, most consistently profitable corporations. The list isn't official—and it does change.

SPLIT STOCK

- More shares created at lower price per share
- Stockholders profit if price goes up

STOCK SPLITS

When the price of a stock increases significantly, you and other investors may be reluctant to buy, either because you think the price has reached its peak or because it costs so much. Corporations have the option of splitting the stock to lower the price, which they expect to stimulate trading. When a stock is split, there are more shares available, but the total market value is the same. Say a company's stock is trading at $100 a share. If the company declares a two-for-one split, it gives you two shares for each one you own. At the same time the price drops to $50 a share. If you owned 300 shares selling at $100 you now have 600 selling at $50—but the value is still $30,000.

The initial effect of a stock split is no different from getting change for a dollar. But the price may move up toward the presplit price, increasing the value of your stock.

Stocks can split three for one, three for two, ten for one or any other combination.

REVERSE SPLITS

In a **reverse split** the corporation exchanges more shares for fewer—say ten shares for five—and the price increases accordingly. Typically the motive is to boost the price so that it meets a stock market's minimum listing require-ment or makes the stock attractive to institutional investors, including mutual funds and pension funds, which may not buy very low-priced stocks.

LOVE ME TENDER

Just as it may issue additional shares, a company may choose to **repurchase**, or buy back, shares of its stock, either gradually in the stock market or by **tender offer**, giving shareholders the right to sell at a specific price. The company's motive may be to boost its stock price or to reduce dilution that results from granting stock options. Or it may decide a buyback is a better use for extra cash than investing in a new company, reinvesting in its own business, or paying a dividend.

The Right to Vote

Owning stock gives you the right to vote on important company issues and policies.

As a stockholder, you have the right to vote on major policy decisions, such as whether a company should issue additional stock, sell itself to outside buyers or change the board of directors. In general, the more stock you own, the greater your voice in company decisions. But if you've held shares for more than a year, you may present a proposal to be voted on at the annual meeting, provided it meets the requirements of the Securities and Exchange Commission (SEC).

ALL STOCKS ARE NOT EQUAL

Usually, each share of stock gives you one vote. Some companies, however, issue different classes of stock with different voting privileges. When stocks carry extra votes, a small group of people can control a company's direction while owning fewer than 50% of the shares.

THE WAY YOU VOTE

You can attend the company's annual meeting and vote in person. Or you can cast your vote by mail using a ballot called a **proxy**, vote by telephone, or at the designated website, using an electronic ballot.

Before the annual meeting you receive a **proxy statement**, a legal document that presents information on planned changes in company management that require shareholder approval. By law, it must also present shareholder proposals, even if they are at odds with company policy. The statement also identifies the nominees for the board of directors, and lists the major shareholders.

SEC rules require proxies to show, in chart form, the total compensation of the company's top five executives. The proxy must also report the company's stock performance in relation to comparable companies in the industry and to the S&P 500-stock Index.

The proxy asks shareholders to elect a board of directors and vote on several issues. The directors oversee the operation of the company and set long-term policy goals. You can support them all, vote against them or vote for some but not others.

The proxy lets shareholders vote yes or no or abstain on shareholder proposals and other issues affecting the corporation. The directors want you to vote yes on the issues they support and no on the others. If you don't return your proxy, your vote isn't counted.

X	Please mark your votes as in this example.	

Unless otherwise specified, proxies will be voted FOR the election of the nominees for directors, FOR proposals 2 and 3, and AGAINST proposals 4, 5 and 6.

The Board of Directors recommends a vote FOR election of directors and proposals 2 and 3.

	FOR	WITHHELD			FOR	AGAINST	ABSTAIN
1. Election of Directors (see reverse)	X			2. Approval of Amendments to the 1987 Stock Option Plan	X		
FOR, except vote withheld from the following nominee(s):				3. Appointment of Independent Auditors		X	

The Board of stockholder p

4. Stockholder proposal
5. Stockholder proposal
6. Stockholder proposal

SIGNATURE(S) _John Q. Investor_ DATE _9/11_

NOTE: Please sign exactly as name appears hereon. Joint owners should each sign. When signing as attorney, executor, administrator, trustee or guardian, please give full title as such.

CHANGING ATTITUDES

Investors are increasingly demanding a say in corporate affairs. For example, they may express concern about how effectively the board of directors sets policy and oversees the performance of the company's chief executive. They also want to confirm that current business practices not only provide an acceptable profit but are taking the company in the right direction.

Similarly, socially and environmentally conscientious individual shareholders are becoming more involved in the voting process. Typically they want more information about corporate policies that touch on issues such as the environmental impact of company operations, the working conditions of employees and suppliers, and other ethical concerns. Although individuals may find it difficult to affect corporate policy directly, their inquiries, and their shareholder proposals, can force companies to explain and sometimes alter their business practices.

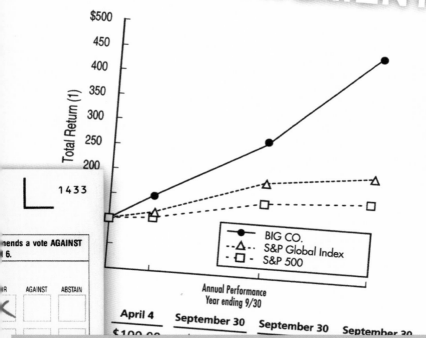

CUMULATIVE VOTING

As a shareholder, you typically get one vote for each share of stock you own. But when you vote for the board of directors in some companies, you may have the opportunity to cast your votes in a nontraditional way. In traditional corporate voting—called statutory voting—you cast the same number of votes for each director running for election. In cumulative voting, on the other hand, you can combine your votes and cast different numbers of votes for different candidates.

For example, if you owned 100 shares and eight directors were running for election, in a statutory vote, you'd cast 100 votes for each of the candidates, for a total of 800 votes. In a cumulative vote, you could still do that, or you could distribute your 800 votes among some of the candidates, assigning no votes to others. You could even cast all 800 votes for a single candidate. The purpose of cumulative voting is to give small shareholders more voice in corporate governance.

The Value of Stock

A stock's value can change at any moment, depending on market conditions, investor perceptions, or a host of other issues.

A stock doesn't have a fixed value, as measured by its price. When investors are buying the stock enthusiastically because they believe it is a good investment, the stock increases in value. But if they think the company's outlook is poor, and either don't invest or sell shares they already own, the value of the stock will fall.

But price is only one measure of a stock's value. **Return on investment**—the amount you earn on the stock—is another. To assess the likelihood of a strong future return, you can look for a history of strong performance and steady growth.

THE BLUES AT BIGCO.

The peaks and valleys in the price of a stock dramatically illustrate how value changes.

Usually a stock climbs in price when the over-all stock market is strong, the company's products or services are in demand and its profits are rising. When the three factors occur together, the increase can be rapid.

A stock's price seldom moves in the same direction for more than a few days, though it may gain or lose a lot over a month or a year. A stock is most likely to decline when the market is weak, a competitor introduces a new product, or if profit growth slows or declines.

Nothing ultimately dictates the highest price a stock can sell for. As long as people are willing to pay more for it, it will climb in value. But when investors unload shares or the market falls, prices can drop rapidly.

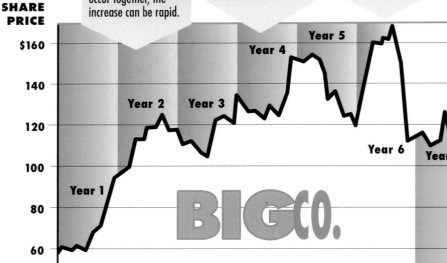

STOCK SHARE PRICE

$160, 140, 120, 100, 80, 60

Year 1, Year 2, Year 3, Year 4, Year 5, Year 6, Year

CYCLICAL STOCKS

All stocks don't act alike. One difference is how closely a company's business is tied to the condition of the economy. **Cyclical stocks** are shares of companies that are highly dependent on the state of the economy. When things slow down, their earnings typically fall, and so does the stock price. But when the economy recovers, earnings rise and the stock price goes up. Airline and hotel stocks are typically cyclical: People tend to cut back on travel when the economy is slow. In contrast, stock prices for companies that provide necessary services and staples, such as food, tend to stay fairly stable.

TIMING IT RIGHT

While you can't accurately predict the future return a stock may provide, you

BETTING WITH THE ODDS

Investing is a gamble, but it's not like betting on horses. A long shot can always win the race even if everyone bets the favorite. In the stock market, the betting itself influences the outcome. If lots of investors bet on Atlas stock, Atlas's price will go up. The stock becomes more valuable because investors want it. The reverse is also true: If investors sell Zenon stock, it will fall in value. The more it falls, the more investors will sell.

MAKING MONEY WITH STOCKS

You can make money with stocks by selling your shares for more than you paid for them or by collecting dividends—or both.

The profit you make on the sale of stock is known as a **capital gain**. Of course, it doesn't all go into your pocket. You owe taxes on the gain as well as a commission on the sale, but if you've owned the stock for more than a year, it's a long-term gain. That means you pay the tax at a lower rate than you pay on your earned income.

If you're buying stocks for the quarterly income, you can figure out the **dividend yield**—the percentage of purchase price you get back through dividends each year. For example, if you buy stock for $100 a share and receive $2 per share, the stock has a dividend yield of 2%. But if you get $2 per share on stock you buy for $50 a share, your yield would be 4% ($2 is 4% of $50).

Purchase Price	Annual Dividend	Yield
$100	$2	2%
$ 50	$2	4%

Qualifying stock dividends are also taxed at your long-term capital gains rate.

Dividends are the portion of the company's profit paid out to its shareholders. A company's board of directors decides how large a dividend the company will pay, or whether it will pay one at all. Usually only large, mature companies pay dividends, while smaller ones reinvest their profits to continue growing.

Following a price collapse, a stock can recoup its value or continue to decline, depending on its internal strength and what the markets are doing. In this example, the price moved up and down for several years at about $100, the level it had reached several years before.

If a company is out of favor with its shareholders, has serious management problems or is losing ground to competitors, its value can collapse quickly even if the rest of the market is highly valued. That's what happened here.

However, strong companies can cope with dramatic loss of value and can rebound if internal changes and external conditions create the right environment and investors respond with renewed interest.

can evaluate its growth potential and the probability of its being a good investment by looking at:
- The rate at which the company's earnings are growing
- Competitiveness of its product or service
- The availability of new markets
- Management strengths and weaknesses
- The overall economic environment in which a company operates

Stocks that pay dividends regularly are known as **INCOME STOCKS**, while those that pay little or no dividend while reinvesting their profit are known as **GROWTH STOCKS**.

The Stock Certificate

The securities called stock certificates are traditional, and often elaborate, records of stock ownership—but they're increasingly rare.

Before the era of electronic record-keeping, written proofs of ownership, called **securities**, were needed to track investments. Today, you often don't get certificates—in fact, some brokerage houses charge a fee to issue them. Instead, the information is stored in computer files.

Like many investors, you may choose to have your stocks registered in **street name**, which means in the name of your brokerage firm. That makes selling stock easier, since you don't have to deliver the certificate to your broker. It's also safer. Billions of dollars worth of security certificates are lost or stolen each year.

Still, the certificates have a charm of their own, and rather than abandoning them as outdated, many companies are redesigning them with new images of their identities.

Each corporation's stock certificate is distinctive, but they all share certain identifying features.

Registration numbers are assigned to all stock certificates by the Securities and Exchange Commission

(SEC) as one way to establish their authenticity and ownership. Stock certificates are negotiable, but they're tracked in several ways to make stolen ones difficult to trade.

The **corporate seal** of the issuer, with the date and place of incorporation, appears along the bottom of the certificate.

Certificates are designed in several shades of color on specially made paper to ensure that they are difficult to forge. The intricate geometric designs that form the borders are created by machines programmed to specific settings to make them hard

SCRIPOPHILY

It isn't a dread disease. It's collecting antique stocks, bonds and other securities. The most valuable ones are the most beautiful and those that have some historical significance because of the role the issuing company played in the economy.

The **name of the issuer** appears prominently on the certificate.

A **human figure** with clearly recognizable facial features must appear with at least a three-quarter frontal view on stocks traded on the New York Stock Exchange. It's these figures—and the scenes around or behind them—that are being updated to project new images for certain corporations. Belching smokestacks, for instance, are disappearing. The replacements often suggest environmental responsibility or contemporary lifestyles.

The **number of shares** the certificate represents appears several times.

SHARES

1

COMMON

PAR VALUE $0.025

SEE REVERSE FOR CERTAIN DEFINITIONS

CUSIP 255555 55 5

INCORPORATED UNDER THE LAWS OF THE STATE OF DELAWARE

© 1988 The Walt Disney Company

ALT DISNEY COMPANY

THIS CERTIFICATE IS TRANSFERABLE IN THE CITY OF BURBANK OR NEW YORK

JANE INVESTOR

*****1***********
******1**********
*******1*********
********1********
*********1*******

ONE

PAID AND NON-ASSESSABLE SHARES OF THE COMMON STOCK OF

...any, transferable on the share register of the Corporation by the holder ...authorized attorney upon surrender of this Certificate properly endorsed ...until countersigned by the Transfer Agent and registered by the Registrar ...Corporation, and the signatures of its duly authorized officers.

Dated: MAY 22, 1992

...MPANY
...sfer Agent and Registrar,

Authorized Signature.

Secretary

Chairman of the Board

to copy. They're also printed on intaglio plates so that the image feels raised. Other printing methods can't reproduce the feel.

The **stockholder** is identified on the face of the certificate. To make any changes in the ownership or to sell the shares, the certificate has to be endorsed on the back and surrendered to the corporation or a broker.

A **CUSIP number** is a nine-digit identification number assigned to every security in the U.S. The Committee on Uniform Securities Identification Procedures was established by the American Bankers Association as a way to safeguard and track all traded securities.

Though the **par value** of a share of stock was once related to its investment value, today the issuing company sets it, typically at between 25 cents and $1 a share, strictly for accounting purposes.

In contrast, a bond's par value, also called its **face value**, is the amount that's repaid at maturity. The interest a bond pays is a percentage of its par value.

Selling New Stock

The first time a company issues stock, it's called **going public**.

Going public, or taking a company public, means making it possible for outside investors to buy the company's stock. To go public, the management registers the stock with the Securities and Exchange Commission (SEC) and makes an **initial public offering (IPO)**.

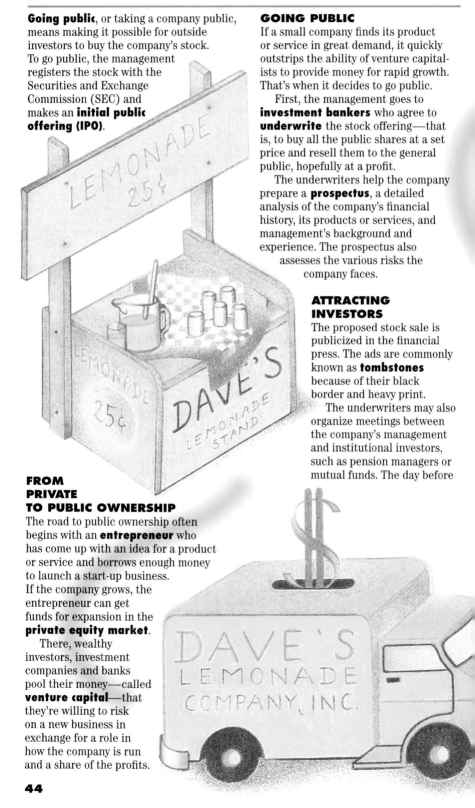

FROM PRIVATE TO PUBLIC OWNERSHIP

The road to public ownership often begins with an **entrepreneur** who has come up with an idea for a product or service and borrows enough money to launch a start-up business. If the company grows, the entrepreneur can get funds for expansion in the **private equity market**.

There, wealthy investors, investment companies and banks pool their money—called **venture capital**—that they're willing to risk on a new business in exchange for a role in how the company is run and a share of the profits.

GOING PUBLIC

If a small company finds its product or service in great demand, it quickly outstrips the ability of venture capitalists to provide money for rapid growth. That's when it decides to go public.

First, the management goes to **investment bankers** who agree to **underwrite** the stock offering—that is, to buy all the public shares at a set price and resell them to the general public, hopefully at a profit.

The underwriters help the company prepare a **prospectus**, a detailed analysis of the company's financial history, its products or services, and management's background and experience. The prospectus also assesses the various risks the company faces.

ATTRACTING INVESTORS

The proposed stock sale is publicized in the financial press. The ads are commonly known as **tombstones** because of their black border and heavy print.

The underwriters may also organize meetings between the company's management and institutional investors, such as pension managers or mutual funds. The day before

A company gets the money only when its stock is issued. All subsequent trading means a profit or loss for the stockholder, but nothing for the company that issued it.

the actual sale, underwriters **price the issue**, or establish the price they will pay for each share.

When the stock begins trading the next day, the price can rise or fall, depending on whether investors agree or disagree with the underwriters' valuation of the new company.

SELLING DIRECT

Some companies are taking a shortcut to an IPO by making a direct offering to investors, or by selling shares on the Internet through an electronic brokerage firm. This type of do-it-yourself offering saves money by eliminating fees paid to underwriters. But the companies still must meet the SEC's filing rules.

One drawback of direct offerings that aren't listed on an exchange or followed by market analysts is that trading is often **thin**, or infrequent. That may limit investor interest in the stock.

SECONDARY OFFERINGS

If a company has already issued shares, but wants to raise additional **capital**, or

money, through the sale of more stock, the process is called a **secondary offering**.

Companies are often wary of issuing more stock, since the larger the supply of stock outstanding, the less valuable each share already issued.

For this reason, a company typically issues new shares only if its stock price is high. To raise money, it may decide to issue bonds, or sometimes convertible bonds or preferred shares.

Stock Buyers

All investors buy stock for the same reason: to make money. But they do their buying differently.

According to an ICI/SIA survey, an estimated 84.3 million adult Americans, or 52.7 million households, own equities. About 49% of them hold shares of stock directly, while 89% own stock mutual funds. Among these equity investors, 66% own stock and stock funds in tax-deferred plans such as IRAs and 401(k)s, and nearly half—48%—made their first equity purchase through an employer sponsored plan.

The average portfolio size is small, just four equities, and the vast majority of investors who own individual stocks buy and sell only infrequently. Just 20% make more than 12 transactions a year.

INSTITUTIONAL INVESTORS

An institutional investor is an organization that invests its own assets or those it holds in trust for others. Typical institutional investors are investment companies (including mutual funds), pension systems, insurance companies, universities and banks.

For example, CalPERS, California's public pension fund, had $109.7 billion, or 68% of its assets, invested in stocks in late 2003. Because they have so much money to invest and are committed to making a profit, institutional investors trade regularly and in enormous volume.

A buy or sell order must be 10,000 shares or more to be considered an institutional trade—a small number for a big mutual fund eager to put its investors' money to work.

PROGRAM TRADING

Program trading means buying or selling a **basket**, or group, of 15 or more stocks with a combined worth of more than $1 million at the same time. Some program trades are triggered automatically when prices hit predetermined levels. Others are initiated to profit from price spreads.

Large-scale program trading can cause abrupt price changes in a stock or a group of stocks, or even dramatic shifts in an entire market. To control potentially negative consequences, exchanges, including the New York Stock Exchange, impose restrictions, called **circuit breakers**, to slow down or halt trading when markets fall too far too fast.

SIZE MAKES A DIFFERENCE

Capitalization

LARGE-CAPS
(Companies with capitalizations of more than $10.9 billion)

MID-CAPS
(Companies with capitalizations of more than $2.3 billion)

SMALL-CAPS
(Companies with capitalizations of less than $2.3 billion)

BUYING STYLES

If you take a long-term view, your investing style may be described as **buy and hold**. That means you keep stock you've purchased in your portfolio through market ups and downs, often over a period of years. You may even buy more shares in market dips.

If you buy stocks and plan to sell them when they have increased a certain per- centage in value—say 15% or 20%—your style may be described as trading. It may take some effort to stick to your strategy if stock markets are booming, since you may feel you're missing out on the potential for greater profits. But the idea is to lock in gains and invest in new stocks.

Day traders, in contrast, attempt to profit by buying and selling rapidly to take advantage of small price changes. This approach, also known as **market timing**, has some serious drawbacks for the individual investor despite access, via the Internet, to volumes of information and sometimes real-time price quotes. Repeated transactions result in higher trading costs, and the probability of executing the right move at the right time is extremely small.

INVESTMENT CLUBS

If you want to participate in the stock market but hesitate to get started on your own, you can join one of the more than 37,000 investment clubs in the U.S. or organize your own.

While investment clubs have many advantages— among them building con- fidence, sharing the burden of investment research and being able to build a diversi- fied portfolio—joining a club doesn't necessarily guarantee stellar returns. One common problem is that investment decisions are typically made by consensus. That could mean agreeing to buy and sell decisions against your better judgment. Another is that many clubs buy small lots of stock, which can result in high commissions.

Most clubs follow guidelines from the National Association of Investment Clubs (NAIC). If you are interested, you can contact them at 877-275-6242 or visit their website (www.better-investing.org).

A company's size, or **market capitaliza- tion**, is one factor to consider when you decide which stocks to buy. Capitalization is calculated by multiplying a company's outstanding shares by its current stock price. For example, a company with 100 million outstanding shares at a current market value of $25 per share has a capitalization, or cap, of $2.5 billion. The chart below summarizes the differences between large-cap, mid-cap and small-cap stocks.

Where to Get Information	Volume of Trading	Ease of Trading	Risks and Rewards
Dow Jones Industrial Average, S&P 500-stock index	Large	Rapid	Often high prices, though little risk of company failure
Extensive media and brokerage attention			Usually regular dividends
Companies provide information			Not always high growth potential
Mid-cap indexes	Large	Rapid	Potential for growth greater than for larger companies
Some media and brokerage attention			
Companies provide information			
Small-cap indexes	Potentially small	Potentially slow	Big gains possible
Limited media coverage			Higher risk from company failure or poor management
Companies provide information			

Buying Stocks

Buying stocks isn't hard, but the process has its own rules, its own language and a special cast of characters.

To buy or sell a stock, you usually have to go through a **brokerage house**, an investment firm that is a member of a **stock exchange** or **market**. Your order is handled by a **stockbroker** who has passed an exam on securities law and has registered with the Securities and Exchange Commission (SEC).

You may also be able to buy stock directly from the company that issues it through a **dividend reinvestment plan (DRIP)**. A number of large companies offer these plans and charge only a minimal fee to handle your transactions. If you sign up, your dividends are automatically reinvested to buy more shares, and you can make additional cash purchases as well.

WHAT'S IN A NAME?

Though you probably use the term broker to describe the professionals who buy and sell stocks, the financial markets use other, more specific titles to describe the ways securities change hands.

Brokers handle buy and sell orders placed by individual and institutional clients in return for a commission. A floor broker handles buy and sell orders on the floor of an exchange.

Dealers buy and sell securities for their own accounts or the firm's account rather than for a client. Dealers make their money on the difference between what they pay to buy a security and the price they get for selling it.

Traders, also called registered or competitive traders, buy and sell securities for their own portfolios. The term traders also describes those employees of broker-dealers who handle the firms' securities trading.

A **broker**, originally, was a wine seller who broached—broke open—wine casks. Today's broker has a less liquid but often heady job as a financial agent.

CUSTOMER

PLACES ORDERS TO BUY AND SELL

When you tell your broker to buy or sell a stock at the current price, called the **market price**, you're giving a **market order**. The price you pay (or get) is usually the same as or close to the quote you're given when you place the order, depending on how quickly it's handled and how actively traded the stock is.

If you think the price of the stock you want to trade is going to change, you can place a **limit order**, which instructs your broker to buy or sell only when the stock is at the price you've named, or better.

A **stop order** instructs your broker to buy or sell at market price once the stock hits a specified target price, called the **stop price**. Stop orders are usually placed to limit losses or protect profits. Their downside is that they may be executed at a price higher or lower than the stop price since the stock trades at the current market price after it hits the stop price.

When you give a stop order or a limit order, your broker will ask if you want a **good 'til canceled (GTC)** or **day order**. A GTC stands until it is either filled, you cancel it, or the firm's time limit expires. A day order is canceled automatically if it isn't filled by the end of the trading day.

WHERE THE COMMISSION GOES

The commission you pay to buy and sell stocks is divided—by prearranged contract—between your broker and the brokerage firm. The commissions and any additional fees are set by the firm, but your broker may be able to give you a break if you trade often and in large volume. Generally, the higher the commission rate the firm usually charges, the more room there is for negotiation.

BROKERAGE FIRM

HANDLES TRANSACTION

STOCK MARKET

REFLECTS ACTIVITY

Some brokers, usually called **full-service brokers**, provide a range of services beyond executing buy and sell orders for clients, such as researching investments and developing long- and short-term investment goals.

Discount brokers carry out transactions for clients but typically offer more limited services. Their fees, however, are usually much lower than full-service brokers'. And for experienced investors who trade often and in large blocks of stock, there are **deep discount brokers**, whose commissions are even lower.

The cheapest way to trade securities, however, is usually with an **online brokerage firm**. Many established full-service and discount brokerage firms offer substantial discounts to their customers who buy and sell securities online.

BROKER-DEALER

A broker-dealer (B/D) is a license granted by the SEC that entitles the licensee to buy and sell securities for its clients' accounts and to trade securities for its own account. B/Ds range in size from independent one-person firms to multi-office brokerage firms.

Up-to-date information is the lifeblood of stock trading. It not only reflects current investment decisions but also influences what happens in the hours and days that follow.

Trading activity in individual stocks and the market as a whole is reported constantly online, on radio and television, and is summarized daily in The Wall Street Journal and other newspapers. Overall movement in the stock markets is tracked by a variety of indexes and averages, such as the Dow Jones Industrial Average and the S&P 500-stock Index.

Access to online information in particular is dramatically changing the way individuals invest. With just a little practice, you can research the financial history of a particular company, take advantage of online software that will help you choose an appropriate stock or access real-time stock quotes. Investors can also use this information to analyze the impact of their buy and sell decisions on their portfolios and plan their future trades.

Selling Short

Some stock investors take added risks in the hope of greater returns.

Not all stock trades are straightforward buys or sells. There are several strategies you can use to increase your gains, though they also increase your risk of incurring losses. Among these strategies are **selling short** and **buying warrants**. Both are based on a calculated wager that a particular stock will change in value, either dropping quickly in price—for a short sale—or increasing, for a warrant.

How Selling Short Works

While most investors buy stocks they think will increase in value, others invest when they think a stock's price is going to drop, perhaps substantially. What they do is described as **selling short**.

To sell short, you borrow shares you don't own from your broker, order them sold and pocket the money. Then you wait for the price of the stock to drop. If it does, you buy the shares at the lower price, turn them over to your broker (plus interest and commission) and keep the difference.

For example, you might sell short 100 shares of stock priced at $10 a share. When the price drops, you buy 100 shares at $7.50 a share, return them to your broker, and keep the $2.50-a-share difference—minus commission. Buying the shares back is called **covering the short position**. In this case, because you sold them for more than you paid to replace them, you made a profit. And you didn't have to lay out any money to do it.

YOU BORROW 100 SHARES AT $10 PER SHARE FROM YOUR BROKER	YOU SELL THE 100 SHARES AT THE $10 PRICE, GETTING $1,000
	Stock Value **$10**
SHARES YOU OWE YOUR BROKER	**100** Shares
YOUR COST TO PAY BACK THE SHARES	
YOUR PROFIT— OR LOSS	

SHORT INTEREST HIGHLIGHTS

Short interest is trading activity in stocks that have been sold short on the New York Stock Exchange and the American Stock Exchange and not yet repurchased. The volume of short interest gives you a sense of how many investors expect prices to fall and the stocks they expect to be affected.

Selling short often increases when the market is booming. Often, short sellers believe that a **correction**, or drop in market prices, has to come, especially if the overall economy does not seem to be growing as quickly as stock values are rising. But short selling is also considered a bullish sign, or a predictor of increased trading, since short positions have to be covered.

The average daily volume, which is the average number of shares sold short each trading day during the month, and the percentage change during the month are reported for each company that has had at least 550,000 shares sold short or a change of short interest of at least 250,000 in the month.

In addition, a Wall Street Journal graph tracks the recent history of short interest and a summary table provides the names of the companies with the largest short positions and the greatest change. There's also a graph and chart showing the short interest ratio. That's the number of days it would take to cover the short interest in selected stocks if trading continued at a consistent pace.

BUYING WARRANTS

Like a short sale, a warrant is a way to wager on the future price of a stock—though a warrant is definitely less risky. Warrants guarantee, for a small fee, the opportunity to buy stock at a fixed price during a specific period of time. Investors buy warrants if they think a stock's price is going up.

For example, you might pay $1 a share for the right to buy DaveCo stock at $10 within five years. If the price goes up to $14 and you **exercise**, or use, your warrant, you save $3 on every share you buy. You can then sell the shares at the higher price to make a profit ($14 − ($10 + $1) = $3), or $300 on 100 shares.

Companies sell warrants if they plan to raise money by issuing new stock or selling stocks they hold in reserve. After a warrant is issued, it can be listed in the stock columns and traded like other investments. A **wt** after a stock table entry means the quotation is for a warrant, not the stock itself.

If the price of the stock is below the set price when the warrant expires, the warrant is worthless. But since warrants are fairly cheap and have a relatively long life span, they are traded actively.

YOU PROFIT IF STOCK PRICE DROPS

| Stock Value $7.50 |
| 100 Shares |
| $750 |
| $250 Profit |

YOU LOSE IF STOCK PRICE RISES

| Stock Value $12.50 |
| 100 Shares |
| $1,250 |
| $250 Loss |

WHAT ARE THE RISKS?

The risks in selling short occur when the price of the stock goes up—not down—or when the drop in price takes a long time. The timing is important because you're paying your broker interest on the stocks you borrowed. The longer the process goes on, the more you pay and the more the interest expense erodes your eventual profit.

An increase in the stock's value is an even greater risk. If it goes up instead of down, you will be forced—sooner or later—to pay more to cover your short position than you made from selling the stock.

SQUEEZE PLAY

Sometimes short sellers are caught in a squeeze. That happens when a stock that has been heavily shorted begins to rise. The scramble among short sellers to cover their positions results in heavy buying, which drives the price even higher.

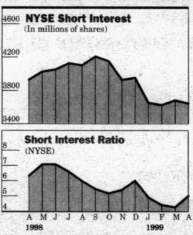

SHORT INTEREST HIGHLIGHTS

rgest Short Positions

	Apr. 15	Mar. 15	Change
	NYSE		
lt-Hldg	63,511,686	64,335,994	−824,308
nline	56,942,532	60,790,757	−3,848,225
	49,809,348	59,237,122	−9,427,774
ot	36,668,829	38,074,018	−1,405,189
HcaHlth	35,752,915	34,662,905	1,090,010
	28,888,180	29,718,508	−830,328
	27,852,884	27,021,119	831,765
	25,282,240	20,819,324	4,462,916
	23,717,412	22,453,817	1,263,595
ne	22,947,745	21,297,003	1,650,742
mputer	22,568,494	24,284,300	−1,715,806
	22,226,674	20,491,643	1,735,031
	22,211,401	20,194,365	2,017,036
	21,857,344	17,341,408	4,515,936
er Hldg	21,020,765	15,942,873	5,077,892
o	20,784,955	20,837,521	−52,566
Group	19,671,144	20,012,545	−341,401
tores	19,439,354	31,144,592	−11,705,238
al	18,427,279	18,238,224	189,055
	397,693	17,196,410	201,283

4600 NYSE Short Interest (In millions of shares)

Short Interest Ratio (NYSE)

A M J J A S O N D J F M A
1998 1999

Largest % Inc

Rank		Apr.
		NYSE
1	Met-Pro	297,3
2	CGI Group	287,0
3	CanadianImpBnkC	396,0
4	Midamr Enrgy Hldg	4,697,3
5	Newhall Land Farm	664,1
6	Enersis S.A. Ads	1,890,1
7	SummitProperties	1,159,2
8	CSK Auto	568,7
9	York Int'l	789,0
10	Empresa NacEl-Chile	897,4
11	SabreGroupHoldings	364,9
12	Toronto-DominionBk	320,6
13	BankofMontreal	310,6
14	CIT Group The	3,428,1
15	WatsonPhrmctcls	3,137,0
16	KansasCitySOInd	1,503,0
17	Jones ApparelGroup	2,597,7
18	Quaker Oats	1,664,3
19	PubSvcNewMexic	
20	Fortune B	

Largest Short Int

Buying on Margin

Buying on margin lets investors borrow some of the money they need to buy stocks.

If you want to increase the potential return on a stock investment, you can **leverage** your purchase by **buying on margin**. That means borrowing up to half of the purchase price from your broker. If you can sell the stock at a higher price than it cost, you can repay the loan, plus interest and commission, and keep the profit. But if the stock drops in value, you still have to repay the loan. And if you must sell the shares for less than you paid, your losses could be larger than if you had owned the stock outright.

MARGIN ACCOUNTS
To buy on margin, you set up a **margin account** with a broker and transfer the required minimum in cash or securities

How It Works

YOU OPEN A MARGIN ACCOUNT WITH YOUR BROKER

YOU PURCHASE 1,000 SHARES AT $10 EACH

YOU PROFIT IF STOCK PRICE RISES

Stock Value **$10**

Stock Value **$15**

THE VALUE OF YOUR INVESTMENT

$10,000

$5,000

YOUR BROKER'S INVESTMENT

$5,000

$5,000

CLOSING THE BARN DOOR
The government and its regulatory agencies are good at figuring out ways to prevent financial disasters—after they happen. The rules and regulations that govern stock trading, for example, were devised in the wake of two major stock market crashes.

STOCKS

LEVERAGING YOUR STOCK INVESTMENT

Leverage is speculation. It means investing with money borrowed at a fixed rate of interest in the hope of earning a greater rate of return. Like the lever, the simple machine for which it is named, leverage lets the users exert a lot of financial power with a small amount of cash.

Companies use leverage—called **trading on equity**—when they issue both stocks and bonds. Their earnings per share may increase because they expand operations with the money raised by bonds. But they must use some of the earnings to repay the interest on the bonds.

to the account. Then you can borrow up to 50% of a stock's price and buy with the combined funds.

For example, if you buy 1,000 shares at $10 a share, your total cost would be $10,000. But buying on margin, you put up $5,000 and borrow the remaining $5,000. If you sell when the stock price rises to $15, you get $15,000. You repay the $5,000 and keep the $10,000 balance (minus interest and commissions). That's almost a 100% profit. Had you paid the full $10,000 with your own money, you would have made a 50% profit, or $5,000.

YOU LOSE IF STOCK PRICE DROPS

Stock Value **$7.00**

YOUR BREAK-EVEN POINT

MARGIN CALL

$5,000

$2,000 MINIMUM

MARGIN MINIMUMS

To open a margin account, you must deposit a minimum of $2,000 in cash or eligible securities (securities your broker considers valuable). All margin trades have to be conducted through that account, combining your own money and money borrowed from your broker.

MARGIN CALLS

Despite its potential rewards, buying on margin can be very risky. For example, the value of the stock you buy could drop so much that selling it wouldn't raise enough to repay the loan.

To protect brokerage firms from losses, the New York Stock Exchange (NYSE) and NASD, formerly the National Association of Securities Dealers, require you to maintain a margin account balance of at least 25% of the purchase price of any stock you buy long, to hold in your account. Individual firms can require a higher margin level, say 30%, but not a lower one.

If the market value of your investment falls below its required minimum, the firm issues a **margin call**. You must either **meet the call** by adding money to your account to bring it up to the required minimum, or sell the stock, pay back your broker in full and take the loss.

For example, if shares you bought for $10,000 declined to $7,000, your equity would be $2,000, or 28.6% of the total value of the shares. If your broker has a 30% margin requirement, you would have to add $100 to bring your margin account up to $2,100 (30% of $7,000).

During crashes, or dramatic price decreases in the market, investors who are heavily leveraged because they've bought on margin can't meet their margin calls. The result is panic selling to raise cash and further declines in the market. That's one reason the SEC instituted Regulation T, which limits the leveraged portion of any margin purchase to 50%.

Getting Stock Information

Up-to-date information is the lifeblood of stock trading. What was once reported on ticker tape is now completely electronic.

Investors—both individual and institutional—can follow the ups and downs of the stock market, and the minute-to-minute changes in the markets, all day long if they wish. That information is featured on dozens of broadcast and cable television programs, on business radio, and on financial websites, some of which provide real-time quotes as well as opinion and analysis.

While current trading information is only part of what you need to make long-term investment decisions, having it readily available lets you fine-tune your decision about when to buy.

ONLINE RESEARCH

Much of the information you need to choose stocks and build a portfolio is available online—some for free and some with a paid subscription. One source is The Wall Street Journal website, www.wsj.com.

Thousands of corporate and financial websites, newsletters, FAQs and online forums provide comprehensive market information, from background reports on virtually every publicly traded stock to economic analyses and vital market statistics. Many online financial publishers send newsletters tailored to your exact specifications and interests, whether you want information on certain companies, particular market indices, or late-breaking news on the stocks in your portfolio.

One of the most reliable resources available for investors is the SEC's website (www.sec.gov).

As part of their effort to educate investors, many financial services websites let you create a hypothetical portfolio and learn while you trade with imaginary money.

SEC filings for every publicly traded company are available from its EDGAR (Electronic Data Gathering, Analysis, and Retrieval system) database.

THE ROLE OF THE SEC

In the wake of the market crash of 1929 and the stock-trading scandals that it exposed, the U.S. government created the **Securities and Exchange Commission (SEC)** in 1934. Its mission is to regulate the securities markets. When necessary, the SEC enforces securities law with various sanctions, from fines to prosecution. Simply put, the SEC's role is twofold:

- To see that investors are fully informed about securities being offered for sale
- To prevent misrepresentations, deceit and other types of fraud in securities transactions

The SEC also monitors **insider trading**, which occurs when corporate officers buy or sell stock in their own company. Their trading decisions are influenced by what they know about the company's inner workings and its prospects.

It is perfectly legal for officers to buy and sell their company's stock as long as they follow certain rules and report their trading activity. In fact, tracking legitimate insider trading can be a valuable indicator of which way a stock price is heading.

But corporate officers—or their legal or financial advisers—can be aware of potential problems or events that could affect the price of the company's stock. If they manipulate trading to profit from the information before it is released to the public, that trading is illegal. So are efforts to hide trading by having a third party—such as a relative—buy or sell for them.

TICKER TAPE

Before the development of computers and electronic media, the ticker tape was the broker's lifeline. (The first one was installed in 1867 and rented for $6 a week.) The tape listed the latest prices and the size of every stock transaction almost as quickly as prices changed. These days, it's tough to find actual ticker tape on Wall Street—or anywhere else—since the information is provided electronically. Even the ticker tape parades in lower Manhattan have crowds tossing shredded computer printouts and confetti.

Reading the Stock Tables

The stock tables keep investors up to date on what's happening in the market.

Highest and lowest prices for the past 52 weeks are reported daily. When there's a new high or low, it's indicated with an arrow in the margin like the one next to Phelps Dodge in the first column of this example. The range between the prices is a measure of the stock's volatility, or price movement. The **year to date (YTD) percentage change** reports gain or loss in each stock's price as a percentage of its price on January 1. For example, Phillips Electric's price has gained 14.5%.

Percent yield is one way to evaluate the stock's current value. It tells you how much dividend you get as a percentage of the current price. For example, the yield on Pfizer is 1.8%.

Percent yield also lets you compare your earnings on a stock with earnings on other investments. But it doesn't tell you your total return, which is the sum of your dividends plus increases (or decreases) in stock price. When there's no dividend, yield can't be calculated, so the column is left blank.

NEW YORK STOCK EXCHANGE

CLOSE	NET CHG	YTD % CHG	52-WEEK HI	LO	STOCK (SYM)	DIV	YLD %	PE	VOL 100s	CLOSE
13.38	0.52	11.8	31.94	10.77	PtrlBras ADS A **PBRA**	1.56e	5.2	...	6291	29.80
37.58	0.28	16.8	43.50	18.75	PfeiffrVac **PV**	.60e	1.5	...	22	40.90
29.38	.31	8.0	38.89	26.95	Pfizer **PFE** x	.68f	1.8	59	153386	38.15
31.37	0.37	-7.6	75.44	31.93	PharmRes **PRX**		...	20	12285	60.18
49.67	1.67	▲ 10.4	80.45	30.11	PhelpDodg **PD**		...	cc	48019	84.04
40.16	0.02	0.2	25.97	25.00	PhilAuthInd **POB**	1.64	6.5	...	186	25.16
17.85	0.63	-2.6	18.60	5.11	PhlpLngDst **PHI**		...	...	547	16.96
31.75	0.05	▲ 14.5	32.75	13.80	PhlpsEl **PHG**	.39e	1.2	...	15153	33.31
15.89	0.13	2.3	18.31	11.16	PhillipsVanH **PVH**	.15	.8	40	542	18.14
16.40	...	13.3	14.25	6.03	PhoenixCos **PNX**	.16e	1.2	dd	7283	13.64
43.38	0.67	11.3	42.50	21.71	PhoenixCos un	1.81	4.3	...	2	42.00
33.05	-0.14	18.4	2.49	0.95	PhosphtRes **PLP**		...	dd	669	2.25
33.21	-0.08	-4.5	43.95	33.22	PidmntNG **PNY**	1.66	4.0	...	813	41.52
14.19	0.05	5.2	26.44	14.42	Pier 1 **PIR**	.32	1.4	17.00	10614	23.00
15.50	-0.28	▲ 29.5	20.91	7.01	PilgrmPr **PPC**	.06	3.	14	5116	21.15
6.30	-0.10	▲ 43.6	12.86	3.92	Pinnacle...					
30.83	0.66	-6.1	40.81							
25.29										
43.85										

DECIMAL PRICING

Markets in the U.S. have converted from pricing stock in dollars and sixteenths of dollars to pricing in decimals, or dollars and cents. That means prices may move up or down by as little as 1 cent rather than 6.25 cents.

Consumer advocates supported the move to decimal pricing as a way to narrow the spread, or gap, between the highest price bid by a buyer and the lowest price asked by a seller. A narrower spread means the buyer pays less and the seller gets more in each trade. From the brokerage firm perspective, however, a narrower spread means reduced profits.

Cash dividends per share is an estimate of the anticipated yearly dividend per share in dollars and cents. Notice that the prices of stocks that pay dividends tend to be less volatile than the prices of stocks with no dividends. Pier 1's yearly dividend is estimated at .32 cents a share. If you owned 100 shares, you'd receive $32 in dividends, probably in quarterly payments of $8.

Corporations are listed alphabetically—sometimes in shortened versions of the actual name—and followed by their trading symbol. Some symbols are easy to connect to their companies, like PNX for the Phoenix Companies, but others can be more cryptic. That often happens when companies have similar names or the logical abbreviation has already been used.

Price/earnings ratio (PE) shows the relationship between a stock's price and the company's earnings for the last four quarters. It's figured by dividing the current price per share by the earnings per share—a number the stock table doesn't provide as a separate piece of information. Here, for example, the St. Paul Companies P/E ratio of 15 means its price is 15 times its annual per share earnings.

Since stock investors are interested in earnings, they use P/E ratios to compare the relative value of different stocks. But the P/E ratio reported in this chart, called a trailing P/E, reports past earnings, not future potential. Two companies with the same P/E may face very different futures: one on its way to posting higher earnings and the other headed for a loss.

Those differences may be revealed in a **forward P/E**, which stock analysts compute by combining earnings reports for the two most recent quarters with the earnings they expect for the next two.

There's no perfect P/E ratio, though some investors avoid stocks if they think the ratio is too high. However, for others, a small, rapidly growing company can have a high P/E yet still be an attractive investment.

Volume refers to the number of shares traded the previous day. Unless a **Z** appears before the number in this column, multiply by 100 to get the number of shares. (The Z indicates the actual number traded.) An unusually large volume, indicated by underlining, usually means buyers and sellers are reacting to some new information.

COMPOSITE TRANSACTIONS

YTD % CHG	52-WEEK HI	LO	STOCK (SYM)	DIV	YLD %	PE	VOL 100s	CLOSE	NET CHG	YTD % CHG
0.4	27.45	24.85	Safeco 8.072Corts **KNH**	2.02	7.5	...	3	27.10	...	-17.7
29.5	**6.25**	**1.16**	SafegrdSci **SFE**		...	dd	75380	**5.23**	**-0.77**	-7.5
-0.5	25.83	16.20	Safeway **SWY**		...	dd	59361	21.79	-0.11	-0.1
1.2	21.84	16.20	SagaCom A **SGA**		...	30	245	18.75	-0.19	2.0
7.2	41.36	26.19	StJoe **JOE**	.48	1.2	31	10567	39.98	-0.87	12.6
22.3	75.60	40.69	StJudeMed **STJ**		...	41	17545	75.03	-0.27	3.9
5.1	30.70	24.32	StMaryLand **SM**	.10	.3	14	305	29.95	0.35	6.2
8.3	43.40	29.00	StPaul **SPC**	1.16	2.7	15	12444	42.93	-0.08	16.0
5.9	78.79	57.97	StPaul un	2.25	2.9	...	788	78.28	-0.08	8.1
14.4	17.30	6.66	Saks **SKS**		...	36	11772	17.20	0.20	12.2
-1.9	15.20	8.13	Salton **SFP**		...	dd	796	12.80	-0.10	27.2
-11.0	22.97	13.50	SanJuanBsn **SJT**	2.05e	10.6	...	1569	19.30	0.01	25.9
-3.3	40.10	22.53	SanofiSnth ADS **SNY**	.46e	1.3	...	850	36.49	0.22	0.3
5.7	28.00	12.65	Sanpaolo ADS **IMI**	.64e	2.3	...	482	27.40	0.25	7.4
10.9	28.47	13.25	SantdrBcp **SBP**	.44	1.6	45	178	27.00	0.08	10.4
	14.23	11.30	Sanni AD				791	13.72	0.23	6.3

Close reports a stock's closing price for the previous day. Usually the daily difference is small even if the 52-week spread is large. For example, Sanofi-Synthelabo moved only 22 cents from the previous close, though its price over 52 weeks shows a spread of $17.57.

Net change compares the closing price with the previous closing price. A minus (–) indicates that the price has fallen, and no minus that it has risen. Here, Saks closed up 20 cents from the day before. Prices that change 5% or more are in **boldface**, as Safeguard Scientifics is here.

OTHER MARKETS, OTHER TABLES

There are similar tables in The Wall Street Journal that report trading information for stocks listed on the American Stock Exchange (AMEX). And, if you're interested in closed-end funds, exchange traded funds (ETFs), and preferred stocks listed on the NYSE, AMEX, and Nasdaq Stock Market, you can find some of the same information—including dividends, yields, and closing prices—for every trading day.

Sifting Stock Information

There are plenty of resources to help you make informed investment decisions.

Stock tables are a smart place to start if you're researching investments. But there is a lot of other information available that you can use to evaluate stocks and the companies that issue them.

WHAT THE NUMBERS TELL

The following figures are good indicators of the shape a company is in—and whether its stock is likely to be a good investment. They are reported regularly in the financial press, on financial websites and online trading firms, and are also available directly from brokers.

- The **book value** is the difference between the company's assets and liabilities. A small or low book value from too much debt, for example, means that the company's profits will be limited even if it does lots of business. However, a low book value may indicate that assets are underestimated, and that the stock is a good value for potential investors.
- The **earnings per share** are calculated by dividing the company's net profit by the number of its outstanding shares. If earnings increase each year, the company is growing.
- The **return on equity** is a percentage figured by dividing a company's earnings per share by its book value.
- The **payout ratio** is the percentage of net earnings a company uses to pay its dividend. The normal range is 25% to 50% of its net earnings. A higher ratio may mean that the company is struggling to meet its obligations.

DARTBOARD ANALYSIS

concludes that you make out just as well if you throw darts at the stock pages and buy what you hit. While ups and downs in the markets do sometimes seem like a game of chance, over the long term most experts agree that a logical, reasoned approach to choosing investments will help you score long-term gains even if you don't hit a bullseye.

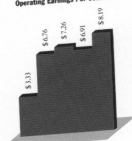

BIGCO.
Consolidated Financial Highlights

For the Year
Revenues
Operating earnings
Operating earnings per common share
Net income
Net income per common share
Dividends paid per common share

At Year-End
Total investments
Total assets
Common shareholders' equity
Book value per common share

Operating Earnings Per Common Share

$3.33 $6.76 $7.26 $6.91 $8.19

Record per share 1999 operating earnings (excluding realized investment gains) exceeded the previous high year by 13%.

Contents

A Profile of BigCo...
A review of our worldwide insurance underwriting, reinsurance and brokerage operations.

Financial Highlights...
Record revenues and operating earnings provide excellent results.
1

Letter to Shareholders...
Insight into success, with a nod toward the future.

Interview with the Chairman...
6
Chairman and Chief Executive Officer Douglas W. Jones addresses long-term issues and strategic outlook.

Gat
cove

Ins
cov

USING THE INFORMATION

Different investment professionals analyze stock in different ways. Those who do **fundamental analysis** study a company's financial condition, management and competitive position in its industry or sector. They may also look at features of the economy at large, such as unemployment and interest rates, in order to estimate the potential stock performance.

Those who do **technical analysis** chart the statistics of past market performance to identify price trends and cyclical movements of particular stocks, industries or the market as a whole.

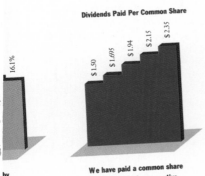

		Percent Change
$ 4,005,237,000	$ 3,788,648,000	5.7
$ 385,458,000	$ 338,267,000	14.0
$ 8.19	$ 6.91	18.5
$ 391,270,000	$ 398,158,000	(1.7)
$ 8.31	$ 8.12	2.3
$ 2.35	$ 2.15	9.3
$ 8,467,668,000	$ 8,106,756,000	4.5
$12,203,990,000	$11,030,066,000	10.6
$ 2,196,371,000	$ 2,349,254,000	(6.5)
$ 52.00	$ 47.65	9.1

Dividends Paid Per Common Share

16.1% $1.50 $1.695 $1.94 $2.15 $2.35

by
ings
ls) by

equity.

We have paid a common share dividend for 119 consecutive years.

Portraits and Profiles...   10
"Insuring the Future": the people and the plans.

Financial Management...   20
Superior capital management, strong dividends and solid investments.

Financial Section...   21
A detailed look at financial results.

Management Group and Board...   50, 51
Our corporate management and board of directors.

Glossary of Insurance Terms...   52
You won't find this in your dictionary.

Inside back

A NOTE OF CAUTION:
Most annual reports are prepared by the company's public relations department and are intended to show the company in the best possible light.

WHAT THE COMPANY TELLS

Companies are required by law to keep shareholders up to date on how the business is doing. That information can be very valuable in keeping tabs on your investment. The most complete information the company provides is in its Form 10K, which must be filed with the SEC. Similar material is outlined in its **annual report** and in **quarterly reports**, which cover the company's current performance.

An annual report summarizes the company's operations for the past year. Often quite elaborately designed and illustrated, it usually begins with a letter from the company's chairman touching on the year's highlights and offering some broad prediction for the coming one.

A typical annual report includes:
- A section outlining the company's **philosophy** of doing business.
- Detailed reports on each segment of the company's **operations**. This information can reveal weaknesses in the management structure, or the products or services the company offers.
- Financial information, including the profit-and-loss statement for the year, and the **balance sheet**, showing the company's assets and liabilities at the end of the year compared to previous years. Footnotes attached to the financial summaries can sometimes reveal problems, such as lawsuits against the company or proposed government regulations that might influence profitability.
- An **auditor's letter** saying that the company's financial statements are in order. Annual reports, along with other details about the company, are usually available both in print and on its website.

Evaluating Companies

A company's earnings and what it has paid in dividends can be useful indicators of what's in store for a particular stock.

Earnings and dividend reports, along with feature stories on particular companies, various industry groups, and the overall economy, give you the background you need to make informed buy and sell decisions. The information is available in the financial press—both in print and online—and on company home pages and the thousands of financial websites, forums, online newsletters and other resources that can provide new perspectives on your existing—and potential—investments.

DIGEST OF EARNINGS REPORTS

The rising prices and big dividends that make investors happy with a stock's performance are tied directly to the financial health of the company. When a company's earnings are up, investor confidence increases and the price of the stock usually rises. If the company is losing money—or not making as much as anticipated—the stock price usually falls, sometimes rapidly.

The Digest of Corporate Earnings Report is printed regularly in The Wall Street Journal. The Digest is a scorecard of company quarterly, and sometimes annual, earnings and profits that covers different companies from day to day. **Losses** are indicated in parentheses.

The **name and symbol** of the company appears, followed by a **code** for the market where the company is traded: **N** for the New York Stock Exchange, **A** for the American Stock Exchange, **Nq** for the Nasdaq Stock Market and **Sc** for the Nasdaq Small Cap.

Gross income **(REV)** is listed in millions of dollars. The **percentage change (% CHG)** refers to the same period of the previous year.

A **P** following the company name indicates a profit in the latest period compared to a loss in the previous year, and the arrows indicate an income increase or decrease of 25% or more. **Net income (NET)** is the company's profit for the current quarter or year.

To find **per share earnings**, or earnings per share, the **net income** is divided by the number of shares, with losses appearing in parentheses.

These figures appear for the **current period (CURR)** and the same period a year before **(PREV)**, along with the **percentage change (% CHG)**.

Year figures, including revenues and net income, are provided, noted by the symbol **Yr**, for companies reporting their cumulative second-, third- and fourth-quarter profits.

The Journal also publishes two earnings summaries: **Highlights**, a selection of the most important and noteworthy figures from the tables, and **Earnings Surprises**, reporting companies whose quarterly profits differed significantly from analysts' estimates.

DIGEST OF EARNINGS REPORTS

- G -

COMPANY	PERIOD	REV (mill)	% CHG	INC CT OP (mill)	NET (mill)	% CHG	PER SHARE CURR	PREV	% CHG
Gateway Finl Hldgs Q9/30		...	...	...	0.15	...	.06	(.20)	...
GBTS (Sc) P 9 mo		...	...	...	0.42	...	.21	(.63)	...
Genesis Microchip Q9/30		36.1	140	...	6.63	238	.29	.10	190
GNSS (Nq) ▲ 6 mo		57.4	106	...	8.23	133	.37	.18	106
Gibraltar Steel Q9/30		161.5	-9.4	...	3.59	-50	.28	.57	-51
ROCK (Nq) ▼ 9 mo		475.6	-9.8	...	11.0	-48	.86	1.66	-48
Gillette Co.................Q9/30		2,362	2.3	...	296.0	-15	.28	.33	-15
G (N) 9 mo		6,243	-2.7	710.0	710.0	49	.67	.45	49
...anc Corp Q9/30		...	...		6.16	72	.18	.10	80
		...	...		18.2	98	.51	.24	113

MY STOCK CHECKLIST

- ☒ **EARNINGS PER SHARE (EPS)**
- ☒ **RETURN ON EQUITY (ROE)**
- ☒ **SALES GROWTH**
- ☒ **PRICE TO EARNINGS (P/E)**

CORPORATE DIVIDEND NEWS

Dividends, like earnings, often have a direct influence on stock prices. When dividends are increased, the message is that the company is prospering. That often stimulates added interest in the stock.

If a dividend has been announced but not yet paid, the stock is said to have gone **ex-dividend**. In most cases, stocks go ex-dividend four business days before the date of record, which is the last day a transaction will settle by the record date. If you own the stock before it goes ex-dividend, you receive the dividend. But if you buy stocks during the ex-dividend period, you don't receive a dividend until the next one is paid—usually three months later.

When dividends are cut, the opposite message is sent. Investors conclude that the company's future expectations have dimmed. One typical consequence is an immediate change in the stock's price.

The names of companies announcing dividends are listed in alphabetical order: A **pf** following the name indicates a dividend on preferred stock, and a **clA** or **clB** shows different classes of stock.

Q indicates a quarterly dividend—the most common type. **M** indicates a monthly dividend. **S** indicates a semiannual dividend. A few stocks pay dividends irregularly.

The **period amount** is the amount of dividend per share, stated in cents. In this example, Hershey Foods is paying a quarterly dividend of 24 cents.

The **record date** is the date by which you must own shares in order to receive the dividend.

The **payable date** is the date the dividend will be paid.

Here Oxford Industries has declared a regular quarterly dividend of 21 cents per share, which will be paid on May 29 to shareholders of record as of May 14.

DIVIDEND NEWS

Dividends Reported April 6

Company	Period	Amt.	Payable date	Record date
REGULAR				
Brenton Banks	Q	.09½	4 – 27 – 99	4 – 15
Claire's Stores	Q	.04	5 – 19 – 99	5 – 5
Cummins Engine	Q	.27½	6 – 15 – 99	6 – 1
First First Corp-RI	Q	.09	5 – 17 – 99	5 – 3
FrptMcMrnCop depSlvr	Q	.2137	5 – 1 – 99	4 – 16
FrptMcMrnCop depGld	Q	.2471	5 – 1 – 99	4 – 16
FrptMcMrnCop dpGldlI	Q	.2294	5 – 1 – 99	4 – 16
FrptMcMrnCop depstp	Q	.43¾	5 – 1 – 99	4 – 21
Greenbrier Cos	Q	.06	5 – 12 – 99	4 – 21
Hershey Foods Corp	Q	.24	5 – 15 – 99	4 – 9
IllinoisPwr4.08%pf	Q	.51	5 – 1 – 99	4 – 9
IllinoisPwr4.20%pf	Q	.52½	5 – 1 – 99	4 – 9
IllinoisPwr4.26%pf	Q	.53¼	5 – 1 – 99	4 – 9
IllinoisPwr4.42%pf	Q	.55¼	5 – 1 – 99	4 – 9
IllinoisPwr4.70%pf	Q	.58¾	5 – 1 – 99	4 – 9
Managed HiYield Plus	M	.12½	4 – 30 – 99	4 – 19
Oxford Industries	Q	.21	5 – 29 – 99	5 – 14
PNC Bank Corp pfC	Q	.40	7 – 1 – 99	5 – 28
PNC Bank Corp pfD	Q	.45	7 – 1 – 99	6 – 15
PugetSoundEnrgy7.45%pfII	Q	.465⅝	7 – 1 – 99	6 – 15
PugetSoundEnrgy8.50%pfIII	Q	.53⅛	5 – 15 – 99	4 – 19
Puget Sound Energy Inc	Q	.46	5 – 30 – 99	4 – 16
RPM Inc		.11¾		

* * *

Stocks Ex-Dividend April 8

Company	Amount	Company	Amount
CNB Bancshares	.24	Mills Corp	.50¼
Carolina P&L	.50	Nevada Power	.25
Cmmnwlth Enrgy	.41½	Pep Boys ManMoeJk	.06¾
Conectiv ClA	.80	Pilgrim Pri	
Conectiv	.38½	Rec	
France C			

MOVING AVERAGE

A moving average is created by graphing 52 weeks of weekly average stock prices. It's moving because the chart is updated every week by dropping the oldest number and adding the newest one. The result is a smoother curve than you would get by recording the daily ups and downs of the market.

The Stock Market

Stocks change hands every trading day on traditional and electronic markets.

The first stock exchange in America was organized in Philadelphia in 1790. But by the time the traders who met every day under the buttonwood tree on Wall Street adopted the name **New York Stock Exchange** in 1817, New York had become the center of market action.

The rival **New York Curb Exchange** was founded in 1842. Its name said it all: Trading actually took place on the street until it moved indoors in 1921. In 1953, the Curb Exchange became the **American Stock Exchange**.

A STREET BY ANY OTHER NAME

Wall Street, which got its name from the stockade built by early settlers to protect New York from attacks from the north, was the scene of New York's first organized stock trading. Now it lends its name to the financial markets in general—though lots of traders never set foot on it.

WALL STREET AND BEYOND

As more and more trading is conducted by telephone and computer, the original stock exchanges that provide centralized facilities for trading, such as the New York Stock Exchange (NYSE) and the American Stock Exchange (AMEX), have come to be known as **traditional markets** to distinguish them from the newer electronic markets that allow brokers to trade from their offices all over the country. However, traditional markets take full advantage of the latest technology to maximize the efficiency and volume of their trading.

OTHER U.S. MARKETS

Stocks listed on the NYSE or AMEX may also be traded in one of the smaller **regional exchanges**, including Chicago, Boston, Philadelphia, and the Pacific Exchange in California. In addition, some smaller, regional companies are listed only on the exchange in their area.

Transactions handled on the regionals can be faster, and sometimes cheaper, than transactions on the larger exchanges, which encourages competition among the exchanges. However, trading results for all of the stocks listed on both the NYSE and the regional exchanges are combined daily into a single statistic in the NYSE **Composite Trading** table.

SEATS, AT A PRICE

The NYSE and AMEX are private associations that sell memberships, or seats, permitting brokers to trade on the exchange. The NYSE currently has 1,366 members, and the AMEX has 864. Generally, the cost rises and falls with the market.

THE ELECTRONIC STOCK MARKET

Unlike traditional exchanges, the Nasdaq Stock Market has no central trading location and no exchange floor. Rather, it's an advanced telecommunications and computer network on which market

makers post prices and execute buy and sell orders from brokers around the country. The Nasdaq umbrella includes several markets, differentiated by market capitalization. The largest, called the National Market, lists a wide range of companies, from small, emerging firms to corporate giants, such as Microsoft and Intel.

A STEADY EVOLUTION

Computer-based, rather than face-to-face, stock trading is assuming an increasingly important role, not only in the U.S. but around the world. Trading in London and Tokyo, for example, is exclusively electronic. The same is true of most of the stock markets in emerging nations.

At the traditional exchanges, including the NYSE and the AMEX, orders are increasing routed, filled, and reported electronically. Clearing and settlement is also electronic, speeding up the process of buyers paying for purchases and sellers delivering securities to their new owners.

OVER-THE-COUNTER TRADING

Stocks in many small and new companies aren't listed on either the Nasdaq or a traditional market. Instead, they're bought and sold **over-the-counter (OTC)**. The term originated at a time when U.S. investors actually bought stock over-the-counter at their local broker's office. Today, transactions are handled over the telephone or by computer.

Many OTC stocks are comparatively inexpensive and infrequently, or **thinly**, traded. There are two quotation services for OTC stocks—the Pink Sheets' Electronic Quotation Service (www.pinksheets.com), and the NASD OTC Bulletin Board (www.otcbb.com). Both quotation services provide online real-time quotations for OTC stocks—the Bulletin Board for the approximately 3,800 OTC stocks that are registered with the SEC, and the Pink Sheets LLC for the OTC stocks that are not registered with the SEC.

REQUIREMENTS FOR STOCK MARKET LISTING

The major U.S. stock markets impose specific requirements that companies must meet before their stock can be listed, or traded on that market. If they qualify for all three, the companies can choose where they wish to be traded.

Exchange	Requirements*	Average daily volume*	Number listed*
NYSE New York Stock Exchange	1.1 million publicly held shares minimum; $100 million minimum market capitalization	±1.5 billion shares	about 2,800
NASDAQ® The Nasdaq Stock Market	There are sets of quantitative and qualitative requirements for companies listed on the Nasdaq National Market and the Nasdaq Small-Cap Market	±1.7 billion shares	about 3,400
AMEX American Stock Exchange	500,000 publicly held shares minimum; $3 million minimum market capitalization	±65 million shares	about 700

*As of April 2004

Trading on the New York Stock Exchange

A stock exchange is both the activity of buying and selling and the place where those transactions take place.

The New York Stock Exchange, like other traditional exchanges, provides the facilities for stock trading and rules under which the trading takes place. It has no responsibility for setting the price of a stock. That is the result of supply and demand, and the trading process.

Trading on the floor of the NYSE is **auction style**: In each transaction, stock is sold for the highest bid and bought for the lowest offer.

THE TRADING FLOOR The NYSE's trading area is known as the **trading floor**.

1 The trading day begins (at 9:30 a.m. EST/EDT) and ends (at 4:00 p.m.) when the bell is rung from **the podium**.

8 **Confirmation** is made when the floor broker sends the successful trade details back to the branch office where the order originated.

7 After every deal, a reporter uses a digital scanning device to record the stock symbol, the price and the initiating broker. The scanner transmits the information within seconds to the Exchange's electronic tape. It also begins an **audit trail** in the event that something about the trade is suspicious.

COMPUTERIZED TRADING
The Super Designated Order Turnaround (DOT) System sends orders to the trading floor. Specialists execute them and return reports to the originating firm's offices via the same electronic circuit.

6 **Post display units** show the day's activity at the post. They report the stocks traded, the last sale price and order size.

Action on the floor often occurs at a furious pace. People wear different colored jackets to indicate they're doing specific jobs:

 light blue jackets with orange epaulets for messengers

 green jackets for floor supervisors or traders

 navy jackets for exchange reporters

2 The Exchange rents **booths** to brokerage houses. Each booth is home base for a firm's floor brokers. When an order is received from one of its brokerage offices, a floor broker takes the order to the appropriate **specialist** post to carry out the transaction.

3 The Exchange rents space to **specialist** firms—the brokers to the brokers. A specialist keeps a list of unfilled orders. As buy and sell orders move in response to price changes, the specialist processes the transactions.

The specialists' other job is to maintain an orderly market in a stock. If the **spread** between the **bid** and **asked** (the gap between the highest price offered by a buyer and the lowest price asked by a seller) becomes too wide, specialists turn into dealers themselves who buy and sell stock. This narrows the spread and stimulates trading—a good thing for the vitality of the Exchange and for the specialists as well, since the more they trade, the more they have the potential to earn.

4 Various stocks or groups of stocks are traded at **trading posts** near the specialists' positions. Each company's stock trades at only one post on the floor of the Exchange so the trading can be tracked accurately. However, the stock of several different companies may be traded at the same post. The number of companies assigned depends on the combined volume of business they generate.

5 Floor brokers can use a specialist if they choose. But many trades actually occur between two floor brokers who show up at the post at the same time.

On a typical day a floor broker walks—or runs— an average of

12 MILES

in crisscrossing the floor.

Trading on the Nasdaq Market

Thousands of stocks are traded electronically—using computers and telephones—on the Nasdaq Stock Market.

The Nasdaq Stock Market was the world's first electronic market when it opened in 1971. Now dozens of markets around the world are screen based, including those in London, Paris, Tokyo and Hong Kong.

Trading on the Nasdaq is through an open market, multiple dealer system, with many market makers competing to handle transactions in each individual stock. That's a contrast to the system used on traditional exchanges, where all the buy and sell orders in a stock must go through a single specialist. And since there are a number of market makers, more transactions can take place at the same time.

A market maker posts buy and sell prices for a guaranteed number of shares—usually one round lot, or 100 shares. When an order arrives, the market maker fills it at the posted price or finds a buyer or seller to complete the trade.

INTRODUCING ECNs
Electronic communications networks (ECNs) are alternative securities trading systems that collect, display, and execute orders electronically without a middle-man, such as a specialist or market maker. Trading on an ECN allows institutional and individual investors to buy and sell anonymously. That may help to reduce the volatility that can be triggered by a bell-wether investor making a major trade.

ECN trade execution can be faster and less expensive than trades handled through screen-based or traditional markets, and ECNs facilitate extended, or after-hours, trading. One limitation is that the trading volume is sometimes thin, which can translate into higher prices. However some ECNs have been approved for official stock exchange status, expanding the number of stocks that can be traded on their systems.

A 55-foot wall of 100 multi-media screens displays the most up-to-date information—from new data to live video.

TRADING SYMBOLS
All securities are represented by trading symbols—one-to-five letter abbreviations used to identify a stock in the market where it trades, and in stock quotations and tables. Originally developed in the 19th century, one-letter symbols were especially presti-gious, since they were given to the most actively traded stocks. Nowadays, trading symbols are assigned according to avail-ability. And no two symbols are alike—even in different markets.

READING NASDAQ TABLES

The largest and most actively traded Nasdaq stocks are listed in the **Nasdaq National Market Issues** and are published every trading day. National Market Issues uses a format similar to the listings for NYSE and AMEX stocks. But the trading symbols in the Nasdaq lists have four or five letters, unlike the NYSE and AMEX exchanges, which use symbols of one to three letters. Because many of the Nasdaq companies are either small or start-up companies, which often prefer to put earnings back into the business, fewer pay dividends.

In the example below, Party City (PCTY) is up 11% in value at this point in the year. Its highest price over the last 52 weeks was 15, and its lowest was 7.17. The closing price quoted was 14.31, a gain of 0.69 cents from the previous trading day.

Trading was 97,035 shares. The boldface type indicates that the volume was up 5% or more from the previous trading day. Unlike some other stocks on the market, Party City has earnings, so it's possible to calculate its P/E ratio of 18. But the company didn't pay a dividend so the ellipsis (…) indicates it has no yield.

NASDAQ NATIONAL MARKET ISSUES

NSE CHG	NET CHG	YTD % CHG	52-WEEK HI	LO	STOCK (SYM)	DIV	YLD %	PE	VOL 100s	CLOSE	NET CHG	YTD % CHG	52-W HI
50	0.01	17.5	4.75	1.80	ParametTch PMTC	…		dd	13242	4.63	0.14	-1.5	40.54
83	0.22	7.3	18.78	11.80	Parexel PRXL	…		27	z65637	17.44	0.19	-6.5	18.22
67	0.38	-21.5	12.30	4.08	ParkerVision PRKR	…		dd	2402	7.69	-0.31	-18.7	15.57
05	-0.05	▲ 11.8	30.00	20.95	ParkvlFnl PVSA	.72	2.4	17	z5198	30.03	0.03	-0.6	14.15
82	-0.10	▲ 19.1	40.44	15.99	PtnrsTr PRTR	.40	1.0	40	z23195	40.50	0.50	0.5	23.50
28	0.19	11.0	15.00	7.17	PartyCity PCTY	…		18	z97035	14.31	0.69	0.2	51.00
			4.40		Pathmark PRMK	…		17	z88406	8.37	0.12	9.5	17.00
								04	z52593	30.25	0.25	22.3	11.74

NASDAQ SMALL-CAP ISSUES

VOL 100s	CLOSE	CHG	STOCK (SYM)	VOL 100s	CLOSE	CHG	STOCK (SYM)	VOL 100s	CLOSE	CHG
3750	3.64	0.10	CentralFed cp GCFC	4	14.35	0.04	DectrnInt DECT	33	4.00	…
20	5.27	…	CentCsno CNTY	z42510	3.05	-0.04	DelcathSys DCTH	z67021	1.59	-0.03
6791	3.46	-0.20	CentRlty CRLTS	z752	11.00	0.03	Deltathree DDDC	2213	3.09	-0.02
312	3.66	0.10	CheviotFnl CHEV	z22446	13.49	0.15	DialysCp DCAI	z66754	5.29	0.47
10	17.45	-0.01	ChldtmLrng CTIM	z2085	2.17	-0.01	DiamndHill Inv DHIL	z1050	8.50	-0.50
525	1.68	-0.02	ChnResDev CHRB	z23162	9.85	0.27	DickyWalker DWMA	z7035	2.02	-0.08
20	2.07	-0.06	Chindex int CHDX	z22214	16.48	-0.37	DgtlRec TBUS	z9350	2.60	0.04
			ChrmysnMed CVSN				DVID			

NASDAQ SMALL-CAP ISSUES

Smaller, emerging companies—the Nasdaq's specialty—are listed in the **Nasdaq Small-Cap Issues**. The table concentrates on current volume and price, since many of the companies are too new to have established a financial track record, including a P/E ratio.

In general, the average price per share of these small-cap stocks is lower than for the companies listed on the National Market.

Trading activity in the different stocks varies from more than a million shares to fewer than 1,000 per day.

The Evolving Markets

There are always new ways to buy and sell investments.

One of the distinguishing features of modern stock markets is the speed at which trading information can be processed and shared. That speed, combined with innovative technology, has made it possible to invest in new ways.

Among the most popular of these techniques are exchange traded funds (ETFs) and personal investment folios.

EXCHANGE TRADED FUNDS

With an ETF, you buy and sell shares in the collective performance of an entire stock portfolio—sometimes described as a basket of stocks—in the same way you buy and sell shares of a single stock. You trade ETFs as you do stock, typically through a brokerage account. And you can use traditional stock trading techniques, such as stop orders, limit orders, margin purchases, and short sales.

While ETFs are listed on a stock exchange—most of them on the American Stock Exchange (AMEX)—and trade like stocks, they also resemble open-end mutual funds in certain ways. For example, in each case you buy shares of the fund, which in turn owns a diversified portfolio of stocks. Each ETF also has a **net asset value (NAV)** determined by the total market capitalization, plus stock dividends and minus fund expenses, of all the stocks in its portfolio divided by the number of existing fund shares.

JUST TICKING ALONG
Though it doesn't make the distinctive ticks of the original ticker tape as it moves across your computer screen, the modern-day electronic ticker provides timely information on market activity.

THE DIFFERENCES

Despite their resemblance to mutual funds, ETFs are different in a number of ways that make them attractive to investors:

- ETFs trade throughout the day at market prices while mutual funds shares trade only once, at the end-of-day price

- ETFs don't have to buy and sell shares to accommodate shareholder purchases and redemptions, minimizing portfolio turnover and the potential tax consequences of capital gains

- ETFs can be bought on margin or sold short, even on a downtick, which is useful in hedging or other risk management strategies

- ETFs have lower expense ratios than most mutual funds

11.66 QCOM ▲3s60 QQQ ▲40.83 RDB ▼22.5

The stock symbol

Whether that price is up or down

The most recent trading price

NAMING CONVENTIONS

Some ETFs attract considerable attention for the cleverness of their names.

- **SPDRs** (or Spiders) track the Standard & Poor's 500-stock Index (S&P 500)
- **Qubes**, designated by a QQQ trading symbol, track the Nasdaq-100 Index
- **Diamonds** track the Dow Jones Industrial Average
- Vanguard **VIPERs** track different MSCI domestic benchmarks

MARKET

INDEX BASED

ARE KEY

At the same time, experts point out that:

- You pay brokerage commissions each time you buy or sell ETF shares, as you do when you trade stock
- You risk potential loss of value if stock prices in general decline or if you sell in a falling market

NOW AND FUTURE ETFs

The ETFs trading in late spring 2004 are passively managed index funds or unit investment trusts. An index fund's goal is to match, as closely as possible, the performance of the index on which it is based. The fund buys or sells stocks only to update its portfolio when the index list is revised.

The Securities and Exchange Commission (SEC) is considering the possibility of approving actively managed ETFs. This would allow actively managed funds, which regularly buy and sell stocks in their portfolio in an attempt to outperform their benchmark index, to be traded throughout the day at market prices rather than just at the close of trading.

THE PRICE PICTURE

The price you pay for ETF shares depends on supply and demand. If other investors are buying when you buy, you'll pay more than if you buy when the majority is selling. That's also what happens with an individual stock.

But with ETFs, the market price is measured against the NAV. If you pay less than the NAV, you're buying **at a discount**, and if you pay more than the NAV, you're buying **at a premium**.

The market price and the NAV are rarely exactly aligned, but the difference is typically small because ETFs feature a unique process that allows institutional investors to buy or redeem large blocks of shares at the NAV with in-kind baskets of the fund's stocks. This helps ensure that ETF prices do not deviate significantly from their NAVs and provides a buffer against the potentially large premiums and discounts often associated with closed-end funds.

MAKE YOUR OWN FOLIO

You can also invest in a personalized stock or bond portfolio—variously called folios, baskets, or personal funds—offered by brokerage firms. You invest a dollar amount, either as a lump sum or in regular increments, and pay a fixed monthly or annual fee.

The folios contain a number of securities, often between 20 and 50. You can choose an existing combination—such as a folio of the 30 stocks in the Dow Jones Industrial Average or a folio structured to provide long-term growth. Or you can modify the folio by adding or deleting specific stocks, or create a portfolio of your choice. And you can choose the way your investment principal is allocated among the components of the portfolio.

Advocates say that folios are an ideal way to get the type of diversification that mutual funds provide while giving you more control over cost and tax consequences. But some people are not convinced that this approach is really workable in the long haul.

MY FOLIO

Tracking the Markets

No single index or average gives you a complete picture of what's up—or down.

Indexes and averages track day-to-day changes in stock and bond prices and longer-term trends in financial markets. In fact, the best known U.S. indicators, such as Standard & Poor's 500-stock Index (S&P 500) and the Dow Jones Industrial Average (DJIA), are sometimes used as snapshots of the country's economic health. They're also benchmarks against which to measure the performance of investment portfolios.

The catch is that each index or average measures something a little bit different.

WEIGHT LIMITATIONS

Weighted indexes can give a skewed picture of the markets by suggesting that most prices are moving in a particular direction when in fact the change is being driven by a relatively small number of stocks.

For example, it's quite possible for the price-weighted DJIA to rise—even though the majority of its stocks are falling in value—provided a handful of its most expensive stocks are gaining. Of course, the opposite could happen as well.

Similarly, the upward trend of the S&P 500 in the late 1990s was driven by the market capitalization of some high-flying stocks. Their momentum overshadowed the fact that many other stocks remained flat or lost value during the same period.

On the other hand, equally weighted indexes don't always produce the same results, and may understate or overstate the combined performance of the stocks they track. The reason for this discrepancy is that indexes are calculated differently. For example, the Value Line

WEIGHTING THE OUTCOME

Some indexes and averages count all of their components equally. Others give more weight to some components than to others on the grounds that price changes in the stock of the biggest companies or in the prices of the most expensive stocks have a greater impact on the economy.

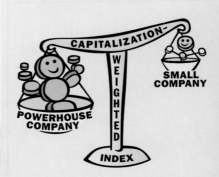

Capitalization-weighted indexes are designed to reflect the significant impact—economically and psychologically—of powerhouse companies: those with lots of stock selling at higher-than-average prices.

Geometric Index increases less in value during any one time period than the Value Line Arithmetic Index—despite the fact that the indexes include exactly the same stocks.

INDEX OR AVERAGE?

Did you ever wonder why some stock market benchmarks are called indexes and others are called averages? Or why one well-known stock benchmark is at 10,600 while another is at 1,362 and a third at 3,055? The difference is based not only on what's included in the average or index, but how each is computed.

Basically, to find an average you add a series of numbers and divide the total by that number of items. For example, you could figure the average net asset value (NAV) of 25 mutual funds by adding their total returns for one year and dividing by 25.

To construct an index, on the other hand, you compare a current average to a baseline value, stating the difference as percentage change. For example, using January 1, 1990, as the starting point, you could track the way that average NAV changed each day or each month over a decade.

The best known financial average, the DJIA, is actually a hybrid. It's initially computed by adding the weighted closing prices of its 30 stocks and then dividing not by 30, but by a number that has been adjusted over the years to account for changes based on additions, deletions, and mergers, as well as stock splits. Then changes in the average are reported in the same way changes in an index would be reported, as a percentage change.

Price-weighted indexes emphasize changes in the value of higher-priced stocks more heavily than changes in the value of lower-priced stocks.

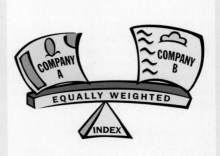

Equally weighted equity indexes count an increase in the value of one stock as much as an increase in the value of another stock, regardless of the opening price of the stocks or how many shares have been issued.

DEFINING FEATURES

A key factor in assessing how much an index or average can tell you about the economy as a whole, or about the performance of your investment portfolio, is whether it's a broad or narrow measure.

Despite its enormous influence, the DJIA is a narrow measure, tracking only 30 large-company stocks. In contrast, the Wilshire 5000 is the broadest of the U.S. indexes and averages, and tracks all of the companies currently being traded on organized exchanges and markets.

Between the narrow DJIA and the broad Wilshire is the S&P 500, which tracks 500 large-company stocks. This index is frequently used as the benchmark for equity mutual fund performance, in large part because it includes so many of the stocks these funds hold in their portfolios.

INDEX INVESTING

If you buy shares in a mutual fund or unit investment trust (UIT) that tracks a particular market index, your investment's performance mirrors the performance of the index. In other words, it gains in value when the index goes up, and declines when the index drops.

Index investing is appealing for a number of reasons, especially when the securities markets are strong. For one thing, you get instant diversification at a much lower price than you'd have to pay to buy a diversified portfolio of individual investments. And the management fees for index mutual funds tend to be low, since the fund changes its holdings only when the index it is tracking changes. For the same reason, index funds are typically tax-efficient. However, index funds tracking the same index may produce different results because of their fees.

Market Cycles

Stock market ups and downs can't be predicted accurately—though they often can be explained in hindsight.

The market goes up when investors put their money into stocks, and it falls when they take money out. A number of factors influence whether people buy or sell stocks—as well as when and why they make decisions.

But most of the time the strength or weakness of the stock market is directly related to economic and political forces. For example, when earnings are strong and unemployment low, prices tend to rise as they did during most of the 1990s. But when corporate earnings fail to meet expectations or investor confidence is shaken, stock prices drop or the market is erratic, as it was in 2001 and 2002.

WHEN PEOPLE INVEST

Economic, social and political factors affect investment. Some factors encourage it and others make investors unwilling to take the risk.

Positive factors	Negative factors
Ample money supply	Tight money
Tax cuts	Tax increases
Low interest rates	High interest rates offering better return in less risky investments
High employment rate	High unemployment rate
Political stability or expectation of stability	International conflicts
	Pending elections

MOVING WITH THE CYCLES

Pinpointing the bottom of a slow market or the top of a hot one is almost impossible—until after it has happened. But investors who buy stocks in companies that do well in growing economies—and buy them at the right time—can profit from their smart decisions (or their good luck).

The DJIA 1992–2003

Closing value of the Dow Jones Industrial Average, weekly data

The DJIA crossed the 4,000 mark and the pace of growth quickened, building a bull market that began in 1992

| 1992 | 1993 | 1994 | 19 |

One characteristic of expanding companies is their ability to raise prices as the demand for their products and services grows. Increased income means more profit for the company and may also mean larger dividends and higher stock prices for the investor.

It's generally difficult to predict which companies will falter during a downturn and which ones will survive and prosper. No economic cycle repeats earlier ones exactly. So the pressures that companies face in one recession aren't the same ones they face in another. In most cases, though, financial success depends more on the internal strength of the company and the goods or services it provides than on the state of the economy.

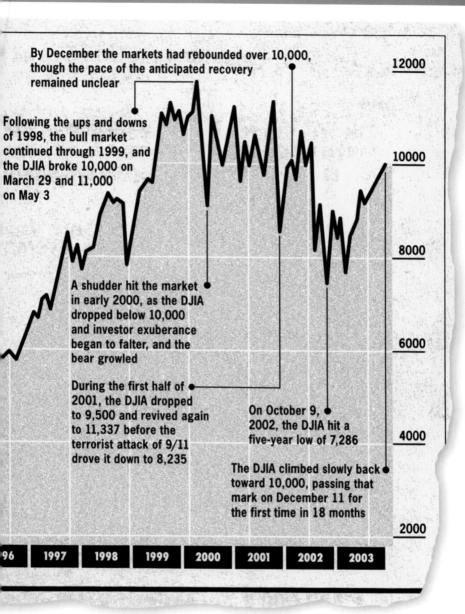

By December the markets had rebounded over 10,000, though the pace of the anticipated recovery remained unclear

Following the ups and downs of 1998, the bull market continued through 1999, and the DJIA broke 10,000 on March 29 and 11,000 on May 3

A shudder hit the market in early 2000, as the DJIA dropped below 10,000 and investor exuberance began to falter, and the bear growled

During the first half of 2001, the DJIA dropped to 9,500 and revived again to 11,337 before the terrorist attack of 9/11 drove it down to 8,235

On October 9, 2002, the DJIA hit a five-year low of 7,286

The DJIA climbed slowly back toward 10,000, passing that mark on December 11 for the first time in 18 months

12000
10000
8000
6000
4000
2000

96 | 1997 | 1998 | 1999 | 2000 | 2001 | 2002 | 2003

BULL AND BEAR MARKETS

The stock market moves up and down in recurring cycles, gaining ground for a period popularly known as a **bull market**. Then it reverses and falls for a time before heading up again. Generally, a falling market has to drop 20% before it's considered a **bear market**. Sometimes market trends last months, even years. Overall, bull markets usually last longer than bear markets.

Historically, the U.S. stock market has risen farther than it has fallen, producing a chain of record levels. But drops in the market tend to happen quickly, while rises tend to take a long time. It's much like the law of gravity: It takes a lot longer to climb 1,000 feet than it takes to fall that distance.

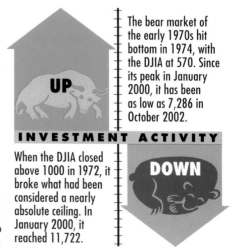

UP

The bear market of the early 1970s hit bottom in 1974, with the DJIA at 570. Since its peak in January 2000, it has been as low as 7,286 in October 2002.

INVESTMENT ACTIVITY

When the DJIA closed above 1000 in 1972, it broke what had been considered a nearly absolute ceiling. In January 2000, it reached 11,722.

DOWN

Crash!

The bottom fell out of the stock market twice in the 20th century: in October 1929, and almost 60 years later in October 1987.

October has a reputation for being the cruelest month for the U.S. stock market. The two great market crashes of the 20th century—in 1929 and 1987—both came in October.

The crashes, or sudden collapses in the value of stocks that sent the DJIA into a tailspin, were triggered by a variety of reasons, including high stock prices and inadequate controls on trading. Afraid of losing everything, investors rushed to sell, compounding the problem by driving the prices lower and lower.

WHICH WAS THE GREATER LOSS?

October 29, 1929

% Loss	**12.8%**
$ Loss	**$14 BILLION**

October 19, 1987

% Loss	**22.6%**
$ Loss	**$500 BILLION**

TRACKING THE COLLAPSE

The dramatic loss of value that characterized both market crashes is illustrated in these graphs, which index the weekly closing prices of the Dow Jones Industrial Average for 1929 and 1987. They use December 31 of 1928 and 1986 as the **index point**, or base, and show a parallel pattern of increasing prices and stunning drops—12.8% in 1929 and 22.6% in 1987.

Using an index, which gives figures in terms of an agreed-upon base, instead of the actual Dow Jones Industrial Average—which closed at 230.07 in 1929 and 1738.34 in 1987—makes it possible to compare the two events.

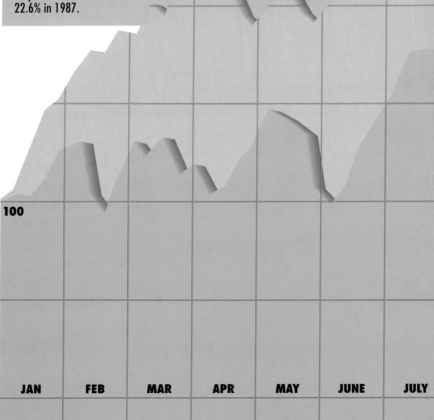

100						
JAN	**FEB**	**MAR**	**APR**	**MAY**	**JUNE**	**JULY**

STOCKS

HOW BLUE CHIP COMPANIES FARED IN THE TWO GREAT CRASHES

1929	opening price	closing price	loss	% loss
AT&T	266	232	−34	12.7
Eastman Kodak	222⅞	181	−41⅞	18.7
Sears Roebuck	127	111	−16	12.5
1987	opening price	closing price	loss	% loss
AT&T	30	23⅝	−6⅜	21.2
Eastman Kodak	90⅛	62⅞	−27¼	30.2
Sears Roebuck	41½	31	−10½	25.3

LEARNING FROM THE PAST

In 1987, in part because of government regulations and trading limitations that had been put in place after 1929, the market recovered much more quickly, and the long-term effect on the economy was modest in comparison to the worldwide depression of the 1930s.

In the wake of 1987, efforts to prevent yet another crash led to restrictions on computer-generated program trading and the introduction of shut-down mechanisms, called **circuit breakers**.

For example, trading on the New York Stock Exchange will be halted if the market, measured by the Dow Jones Industrial Average, drops 10%. But trading could resume, depending on the time of day the drop occurred. If the DJIA drops 30%, trading will end for the day. The actual number of points the DJIA would need to drop is calculated quarterly, based on its average value in the last month of the previous quarter.

Circuit breakers have been set off only once, on October 27, 1997, when the Dow Jones Industrial Average fell 554 points, or 7.2%, and the trigger levels were lower. In fact, the DJIA has dropped as much as 10% only three days since 1915.

That means a crash would almost certainly be drawn out over several days. Since investor panic makes any crash worse, slowing down the pace of the fall may help deter hasty sell decisions.

On March 10, 2000, the Nasdaq Stock Market hit an all-time high of 5,048. By April 14, it was at 3,321 and reached its most recent low—1,423, a 77.8% fall—in September 2001. The parallels with 1929 are striking, though it's impossible to predict if the climb to its precrash high will take the same 25 years.

1987

1929

140

130

120

110

100

90

80

AUG   SEPT   OCT   NOV   DEC   JAN   FEB

Trading Around the Clock

Stock trading goes on around the world, around the clock, in an electronic global marketplace.

Stock trading goes on nearly 24 hours a day, on dozens of different exchanges on different continents in different time zones.

As the trading ends in one city, activity shifts to a market in another city, sweeping the changes in price around the world. The opening prices in Tokyo or Sydney are influenced by the closing prices in the U.S.—just as Asia's closing prices affect what happens in European trading, and what happens in Europe influences Wall Street. Just after the New York markets close, for example, trading begins in Wellington. Two and a half hours after Tokyo closes, London opens. And with two and a half hours to go in London, trading resumes in New York.

The global market explains why a stock can end trading one day at a specific price and open the next day at a different price.

What's still evolving is the extent to which the markets are interrelated. One reason is the growing number of multinational companies that trade on several exchanges. Another is the increasing tendency for investors to buy in many markets, not just their own.

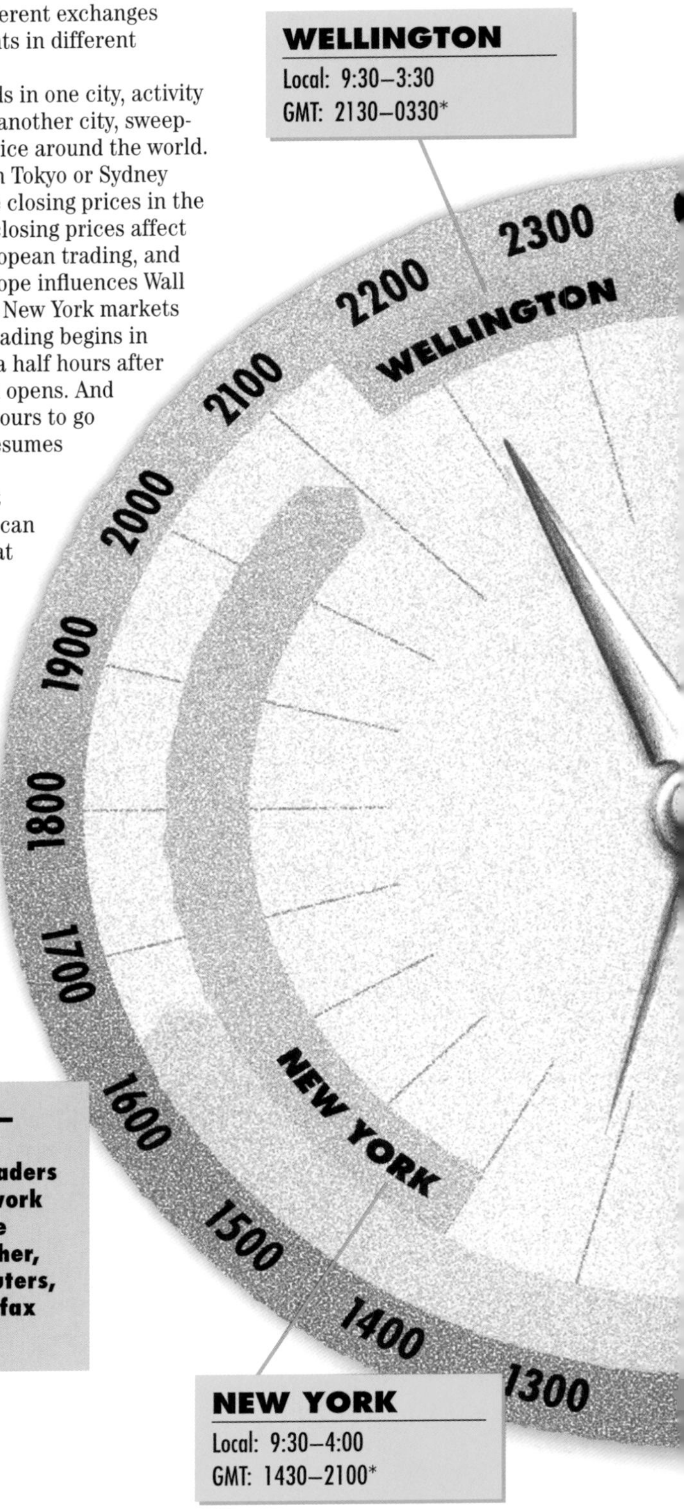

WELLINGTON
Local: 9:30–3:30
GMT: 2130–0330*

ZONING OUT— OR IN
International traders can—and do—work in one time zone and live in another, thanks to computers, telephones and fax machines.

NEW YORK
Local: 9:30–4:00
GMT: 1430–2100*

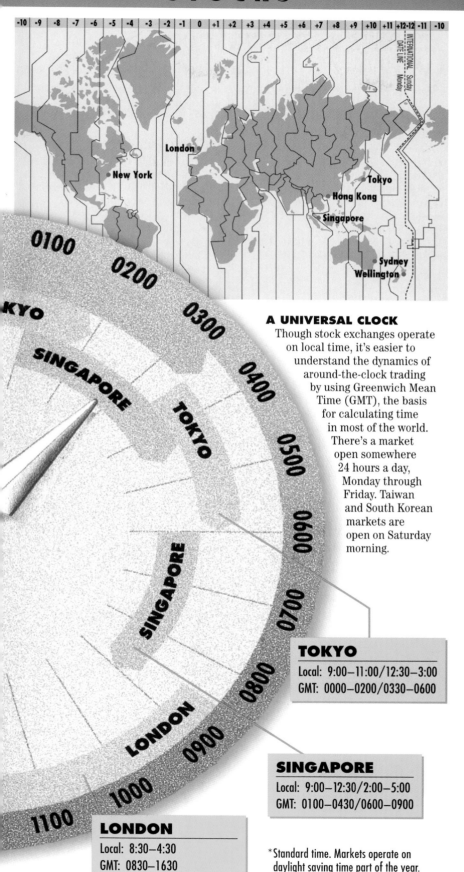

A UNIVERSAL CLOCK

Though stock exchanges operate on local time, it's easier to understand the dynamics of around-the-clock trading by using Greenwich Mean Time (GMT), the basis for calculating time in most of the world. There's a market open somewhere 24 hours a day, Monday through Friday. Taiwan and South Korean markets are open on Saturday morning.

TOKYO
Local: 9:00–11:00/12:30–3:00
GMT: 0000–0200/0330–0600

SINGAPORE
Local: 9:00–12:30/2:00–5:00
GMT: 0100–0430/0600–0900

LONDON
Local: 8:30–4:30
GMT: 0830–1630

*Standard time. Markets operate on daylight saving time part of the year.

Tracking International Markets

As investors buy more global stocks, they want to know more about how those markets are doing.

With global markets increasingly open to all investors, and electronic media capable of providing up-to-the-minute reports on what's happening around the world, investors' appetites are being met with a steady stream of information.

The performances of 36 indexes tracking 26 national stock markets outside the U.S. and four Dow Jones indexes denominated in euros are reported daily in The Wall Street Journal. These statistical composites, which are similar to the S&P 500-stock Index, include the day's close and the net change from the previous day as well as the change expressed as a percentage.

Stock Market Indexes

EXCHANGE	INDEX	CLOSE	YTD PCT CHG
Australia	All Ordinaries	2893.80	+ 2.86
Belgium	Bel-20 Index	3411.59	− 2.93
Brazil	Sao Paulo Bovespa	8172.00	+ 20.46
Britain	London FT 100-share	5896.00	+ 0.23
Britain	London FT 250-share	5024.20	+ 3.49
Canada	Toronto 300 Comp.	6729.05	+ 3.75
Chile	Santiago IPSA	103.03	+ 3.03
China	Dow Jones China 88	120.76	− 0.36
Europe	DJ Stoxx (Euro)	288.31	+ 3.26
Europe	DJ Stoxx 50 (Euro)	3446.25	+ 3.79
Euro Zone	DJ Euro Stoxx (Euro)	308.97	+ 3.55
Euro Zone	DJ Euro Stoxx 50 (Euro)	3547.15	+ 6.13
France	Paris CAC 40	4251.80	+ 7.84
Germany	Frankfurt DAX	5159.96	+ 3.15
Germany	Frankfurt Xetra DAX	5180.29	+ 3.47
Hong Kong	Hang Seng	9506.90	− 5.39
Japan	Tokyo Nikkei 225	14499.25	+ 4.75
Japan	Tokyo Nikkei 300	224.58	+ 3.93
Japan	Tokyo Topix Index	1125.26	+ 3.52

DAILY NUMBERS
The daily numbers on a particular exchange have meaning only in relation to what has happened on that exchange in the past. For example, Japan's Nikkei 225 reports on only its market, as the Australian All Ordinaries, Canadian Toronto 300 Composite and French Paris CAC40 do on theirs.

COMPARATIVE PERFORMANCE
Worldwide stock market performance can be compared by looking at **percentage change**. Knowing that London's Financial Times 100-share index, or FTSE (pronounced *footsie*), is up 0.23% means more to investors than saying it was up 13.40 points.

About four times as many markets are up as down in this illustration, in various places around the world. But don't forget that the political and economic situations at home still do have a major influence on stock performance despite what's happening in the world at large.

PICKING A MARKET

Financial analysts tend to evaluate overseas markets from a top-down perspective, focusing on a country's or a region's financial environment rather than on the prospects of individual companies. Among factors that make a country's stocks attractive to investors are the underlying strength and stability of its economy, the value of its currency and its current interest rate. Growing economies, strengthening currencies and flat or falling interest rates are generally good indicators of economic growth. Conversely, countries whose currencies are weak, interest rates high and economies in recession don't attract equity investors.

INTERNATIONAL MARKETS

MEXICO CITY in pesos

Alfa A	24.25	+	0.25
Apasco A	37.40	–	1.10
Banacci B	11.02	–	0.32
Bimbo A	19.02	–	0.38
Cemex B	28.90	+	0.35
Citra C	11.20	–	0.10
Cifra V	11.12	–	0.18
ComerciUBC	6.52	–	0.28
Femsa B	24.05	–	0.10
Gcarso A1	29.00	–	0.65
GModeloC	22.00		....
Kimber A	29.50	–	0.50
Maseca B	8.24		....
Tamsa	73.50	–	0.50
Telecom A1	38.95	–	0.85
Televisa	130.50	–	2.70

FRANKFURT in euros

Adidas Salmn	85.00	+	2.40
Allianz	287.70	–	16.30
BASF	31.06	–	0.89
Bayer	30.89	–	1.11
Beiersdorf	66.00	+	1.50
BMW	716.50	–	9.99
Byr Vereinsbk	54.96	+	0.77
Commerzbank	25.50	–	0.60
Continental	24.96	–	0.70
Degussa	35.85	–	0.20
Deutsche Bank	48.00	–	1.52
Deutsche Tel	36.10	–	2.35
Dresdner Bank	32.24	–	1.86
Gehe	52.00	–	1.00
Heidlbg Zemnt	55.50		

TOKYO in yen

Aiwa	2400	–	40
Ajinomoto	1245	–	16
Alps Elec	2040	–	30
Amada Co	567	–	23
ANA	343	–	4
Ando Elec	690		....
Anritsu	944	–	1
Asahi Chem	524		....
Asahi Glass	685	+	5
Banyu Pharm	2000		....
Bk of Yokohama	226	–	2
Bridgestone	2490	–	10
Brother Ind	345	–	2
Canon Inc	2275		

FOREIGN MARKETS

Some of the most actively traded stocks on overseas exchanges are listed in the Foreign Markets column. Their closing prices and their previous close are given in local currency. For example, on the Mexico City exchange, Cemex B shares closed at 28.90 pesos, up 0.35%.

For six of the European markets that are included in the chart, the local currency is the euro. Frankfurt is one example.

Many of the corporations whose stocks are listed on a home country's market are also traded on a U.S. stock market as **American Depositary Shares (ADS)**. Examples from this clipping include Bayer on the Frankfurt market and Canon on the Tokyo market.

Because prices are quoted in different currencies, and the markets are influenced by different forces, there's no easy formula to compare the yields on international investments—with the exception of countries trading in the euro.

But stock market performances around the globe are increasingly interrelated, so that a boom or bust in one market affects what happens to prices in all markets. In fact, analysts regularly anticipate opening prices in New York based on prices in Tokyo and London.

International Investing

In the new economy, investors looking for ways to diversify their portfolios have a world of opportunity.

If you want to balance some of the risks of investing in U.S. stocks, you can diversify your portfolio by putting some of your money into equities available on overseas markets. The assumption is that an economic downturn at home could be offset by stronger performances abroad, since the markets would be responding to different economic conditions.

As electronic trading makes investing in overseas markets easier, though, it also emphasizes their interaction. That means that strengths or weaknesses in one market or region tend to carry over into others.

THERE ARE REWARDS

Buying stocks abroad can produce rich returns. In the best of all possible worlds, investors win three ways, in what investment pros call the **triple whammy**:

- The stock rises in price, providing **capital gains**
- The investment pays **dividends**
- The country's **currency rises against the dollar**, so that when investors sell they get more dollars

BUT ALSO RISKS

Buying stocks abroad is no less risky than buying at home. Prices do fall and dividends get cut. Plus, there may be hidden traps that can catch unwary investors. Here are some of the common ones:

- Tax treatments of gains or losses differ from one country to another
- Accounting and trading rules may be different
- Converting dividends into dollars may add extra expense to the transaction
- Some international exchanges require less information about a company's financial condition than U.S. exchanges do
- Giving buy and sell orders can be complicated by distance and language barriers
- Unexpected changes in overseas interest rates or currency values can cause major upheavals
- Political instability in a country or region can affect the value of investments there

ANOTHER PERSPECTIVE

Overseas investors make money in U.S. stocks when the dollar is strong against their currency and stock prices are climbing. If the dollar weakens, though, the value of their investment drops as well.

The Currency Risk—and Its Reward

The greatest variable in calculating the risks and rewards of international investing hinges on changes in currency values. If the dollar shrinks in value, U.S. investors make more when they sell at a profit. But just the opposite happens if the dollar gets stronger.

	STOCK PRICE IN EUROS
BUY • Dollar is stronger than euro	One Share EUR **50**
SELL • Stock rises • Dollar weaker	One Share EUR **60**
SELL • Stock rises • Dollar unchanged	One Share EUR **60**
SELL • Stock drops • Dollar weaker	One Share EUR **45**
SELL • Stock rises • Dollar stronger	One Share EUR **60**
SELL • Stock drops • Dollar stronger	One Share EUR **45**

WAYS TO INVEST

There are several ways for a U.S. investor to buy international stocks:

- Big U.S. brokerage firms with branch offices abroad can buy stocks directly
- Some international and multinational companies list their stocks directly on U.S. exchanges
- Multiple mutual fund firms offer international funds that invest overseas
- The stock of some of the largest companies is sold as **American Depositary Shares (ADS)** on U.S. exchanges. You may also hear them called American Depositary Receipts (ADR)

Although trading information on an ADS, like Glaxo or Mitsubishi, is reported in U.S. stock tables, actually they are certificates representing a set number of shares held in trust for the investor by a bank. The bank converts the dividends it receives into dollars and takes care of withholding taxes, plus other paperwork. It's the method of choice for many investors.

In this example, a U.S. investor buys a German stock for 50 euros per share. A year later, the investor sells for 60 euros per share. Clearly that's a profit, but how much?

Since the price has gone up 10 euros per share, from 50 to 60, there's a gain of 20%. That's also what a German investor would have made on the deal. But the revaluation of the currency also affects the return. If the dollar were worth less—say 90 cents per euro instead of $1.10—an American investor would have a greater gain.

But if the dollar had gained ground against the euro and was worth $1.20 per euro, the U.S. investor would have a net loss despite selling the stock for a profit in euros.

To figure the stock price, divide the price per share by the exchange rate.

$$\frac{\text{Price per share}}{\text{Exchange rate}} = \text{Stock price}$$

To figure the gain or loss, divide the difference between the sale price and the initial cost by the initial cost.

$$\frac{\text{Sale price-initial cost}}{\text{Initial cost}} = \text{Gain or loss}$$

EXCHANGE RATE	STOCK VALUE IN DOLLARS
Dollar = EUR **1.10**	$**45.45**
Dollar = EUR **.90**	$**66.67**
Dollar = EUR **1.10**	$**54.55**
Dollar = EUR **.90**	$**50.00**
Dollar = EUR **1.20**	$**50.00**
Dollar = EUR **1.20**	$**37.50**

GAIN OR LOSS

47% GAIN — The double advantage of a higher stock price and a lower dollar produced a $66.67 sale price, for a $21.22—or 47%—per-share profit.

20% GAIN — Because the stock price increased and there was no change in the exchange rate, the $54.55 sale price was $9.10 more than the purchase price, a 20% gain.

10% GAIN — Investors can make money on a dropping share price if the value of the dollar also drops. In this example the price drops to 45 but there's a $4.55, or 10%, profit.

10% GAIN — U.S. investors often lose money when the dollar increases in value if they bought when it was worth less. Here the 20% gain in euro price means only a 10% gain in dollars.

17.5% LOSS — The biggest losses occur when the value of the dollar increases and the share price drops. Here a loss of 5 euros a share represents a $37.50 loss in dollars.

Privatization

When governments sell their assets or sign contracts to provide public services, it's called privatization.

Privatization, which means either selling part or all of government enterprises to individual and institutional investors, or turning over previously public functions to private firms, is a major economic trend around the world. Other ways to describe it are as a transfer of ownership, called **denationalization**, or as a shifting of responsibility for providing goods and services from the public sector to the private sector.

There are a number of examples of privatizing services in the U.S., on both the national and local level. A number of state prisons are run by private companies, as are some public school systems. And many former federal jobs are outsourced to private firms.

PUBLIC OWNERSHIP
Public ownership means that governments own and operate national enterprises.

WHY PRIVATIZE?

There are many motives to privatize, most of them economic. One theory, for example, is that privately run enterprises are more efficient than public ones, so that private ownership or operation provides better service or superior products at lower cost.

In addition, selling off attractive assets, such as telephone companies and natural resources, can raise substantial amounts of cash to offset financial problems brought on by public debt or provide cash infusions to bolster the economy and attract outside investors.

Another reason to privatize is to dispose of holdings that are a drain on public resources, such as hospitals or transportation systems, because they're expensive to operate and don't produce enough income to offset costs.

Political philosophy sometimes also plays a large role in the decision to privatize, with attitudes toward the role of government and free-market forces shaping action.

PROS AND CONS

In the privatization debate, there are strong arguments on both sides:

Pros
- Provides infusion of capital
- Introduces stronger management
- Eases or eliminates debt
- Brings nations and companies into the economic mainstream

Cons
- Potential loss of jobs and employee benefits
- Redistribution of wealth into fewer hands
- Potential outside control of national resources

NATIONAL TELECOMM

A GOLDEN SHARE

Governments sometimes like to keep a hand in the company being privatized by holding onto a special class of stock, called golden share, with special voting privileges. The New Zealand government, for instance, kept a voice in the country's telecommunications company to insure that coverage remained universal.

TAKING SOME RISKS

In privatization, both governments and investors take some risks. From a government's perspective, there's always a question of whether it will raise enough money to justify the sale, what will happen to citizens if unemployment increases and services cost more, and how private ownership will affect its own power base.

Investors must consider the potential for government interference, especially when it remains a partial owner, and the impact of reserving shares that carry special privileges. They also have to factor in the impact of the enterprise's existing debts as well as the more traditional market and interest-rate risks that any equity purchase involves.

PUBLIC TO PRIVATE

Buying a public company is another form of privatization. Instead of selling shares in a government-held property, a corporation or group of investors accumulates all of the outstanding shares, either gradually or by making a tender offer. The goals are often reduced regulatory oversight and the expectation of increased financial gains.

PRIVATE OWNERSHIP

When governments sell assets, the ownership passes into private hands.

HOW PRIVATIZATION WORKS

Moving government assets into the private sector can be handled three ways, listed in order of popularity:

DIRECT SALES

Direct sales to strategic investors, often through an auction process. The new owners may then offer shares to the public, either domestically or internationally.

PUBLIC OFFERINGS

Public offerings, coordinated through one or more investment banks. In practice, it works much like an IPO in private industry. However, most of the shares sold internationally go to institutional, rather than individual, investors.

OPEN SALES OR GIFTING

Sale or gifting of shares to citizens, who can hold them or sell to investment companies. Singapore, for example, sold shares in its telephone company through bank ATM machines.

One of the key debates in formulating a public offering focuses on the role of international investors, including whether there will be separate **tranches**, or groups of shares, sold domestically or elsewhere, whether or not the separate shares are **fungible**, or interchangeable, and how large a stake international investors can hold.

Among the things privatizing governments have learned are that if they're going to fulfill their goals, they must create a mechanism that allows the transfer to take place smoothly, protect the interests of the workers and strengthen the regulatory framework to prevent abuses. Some governments also offer incentives to make the shares more attractive to domestic investors, including discounts on pricing, the opportunity to buy on an installment plan and bonus shares if the investor holds the stock for a specific period of time.

Bonds: Financing the Future

Bonds are loans that investors make to corporations and governments. The lenders earn interest, and the borrowers get the cash they need.

A bond is a loan that pays interest over a fixed **term**, or period of time. When the bond **matures** at the end of the term, the **principal**, or investment amount, is repaid to the lender, or owner of the bond.

Typically, the rate at which interest is paid and the amount of each payment is fixed at the time the bond is offered for sale. That's why bonds are also known as **fixed-income securities**. That's one reason a bond seems less risky than an investment whose return might change dramatically in the short term.

A bond's interest rate is competitive, which means that the rate it pays is comparable to what other bonds being issued at the same time are paying. It's also related to the cost of borrowing in the economy at large, so when mortgage rates are down, for example, bond rates also tend to be lower.

TYPES OF BONDS

You can buy bonds issued by U.S. companies, by the U.S. Treasury, by various cities and states, and various federal, state and local government agencies. Many overseas companies and governments also sell bonds to U.S. investors. When those bonds are sold in dollars rather than the currency of the issuing country, they're sometimes known as **yankee bonds**. There is an advantage for individual investors: You don't have to worry about currency fluctuations in figuring the bond's worth.

ISSUERS PREFER BONDS

When companies need to raise money to invest in growth and development, they can issue stock or sell bonds. They often prefer bonds, in part because issuing more stock tends to **dilute**, or lessen, the value of shares investors already own. Bonds may also provide some income-tax advantages.

Unlike companies, governments aren't profit-making enterprises and can't issue stock. Bonds are the primary way they raise money to fund capital improvements like roads or airports. Money from bond issues also keeps everyday operations running when other revenues (like taxes, tolls and other fees) aren't available to cover current costs.

ISSUING A BOND

When a company or government wants to raise cash, it tests the waters by **floating a bond**. That is, it offers the public an opportunity to invest for a fixed period of time at a specific rate of interest. If investors think the rate justifies the risk and buy the bond, the issue floats.

THE INDIVIDUAL AS LENDER

INVESTORS WILLING TO LEND MONEY

INVESTOR GETS PAR VALUE AT MATURITY

INVESTOR GETS INTEREST PAYMENT AT SPECIFIC INTERVALS

THE LIFE OF A BOND

The life, or **term**, of any bond is fixed at the time of issue. It can range from **short-term** (usually a year or less), to **intermediate-term** (two to ten years), to **long-term** (more than ten years). Generally speaking, the longer the term, the higher the interest rate that's offered to make up for the additional risk of tying up your money for so long a time. The relationship between the interest rates paid on short-term and long-term bonds is called the **yield curve**.

MAKING MONEY WITH BONDS

Conservative investors use bonds to provide a steady income. They buy a bond when it's issued and hold it, expecting to receive regular, fixed-interest payments until the bond matures. Then they get the principal back to reinvest.

Bonds that are issued when interest rates are high become increasingly valuable when interest rates fall. That's because investors are willing to pay more than the face value of a bond with a 8% interest rate if the current rate is 5%.

That means an increase in the price of a bond, or **capital appreciation**, can produce more profits for bond sellers than holding the bonds to maturity. More aggressive investors **trade** bonds, or buy and sell as they might with stocks, hoping to make money by selling a bond for more than they paid for it.

But there are risks in bond trading. If interest rates go up, you can lose money if you want to sell an older bond, which is paying a lower rate of interest. That's because potential buyers will typically pay less for the bond than you paid to buy it.

The other risk bondholders face is rising inflation. Since the dollar amount you earn on a bond investment usually doesn't change, the value of that money can be eroded by inflation. For example, if you have a 30-year bond paying $5,000 annual interest, the income will buy less at the end of the term than at the beginning.

THE INSTITUTION AS BORROWER

CORPORATE BONDS

Corporations use bonds:
- To raise capital to pay for expansion, modernization
- To cover operating expenses
- To finance corporate takeovers or other changes in management structure

U.S. TREASURY BONDS

The U.S. Treasury floats debt issues:
- To pay for a wide range of government activities
- To pay interest on the national debt

MUNICIPAL BONDS

States, cities, counties and towns issue bonds:
- To pay for a wide variety of public projects: schools, highways, stadiums, sewage systems, bridges
- To supplement their operating budgets

BOND MATURES

HOW BONDS ARE SOLD

For corporations, issuing a bond is a lot like making an initial public offering. An investment firm helps set the terms and underwrites the sale by buying up the issue. In cooperation with other companies, the investment firm then offers the bonds for sale to the public.

When bonds are issued, they are sold at **par**, or face value, usually in units of $1,000. The issuer absorbs whatever sales charges there are. After issue, bonds trade in the **secondary market**, which means they are bought and sold through brokers, similar to the way stocks are. The company gets no money from these secondary trades.

Government issues (U.S. Treasury bills and notes) are available directly to investors through a Federal Reserve Bank program called Treasury Direct or through your broker. Most agency bonds and municipal bonds are sold through brokers, who often buy bonds in large denominations ($25,000 or more) and sell pieces of them to individual investors.

The Bond Certificate

A bond is an IOU, a record of the loan and the terms of repayment.

Unlike stockholders, who have **equity**, or part ownership, in a company, bondholders are **creditors**. The bond is an IOU, or a record of the money you lent and the terms on which it will be repaid.

Until 1983, all bondholders received certificates that provided the terms of the loan. Some of these **bearer bonds** had coupons attached to the certificate. When it was time to collect an interest payment, the investor (or bearer) detached the coupon and exchanged it for cash. That's why a bond's interest rate is known as its **coupon rate**.

Today most new bonds, known as **book-entry bonds**, are registered electronically, the way stock purchases are, rather than issued in certificate form. But there are still thousands of investors holding certificates that haven't yet matured.

BEARERS STILL

Eurobonds, which are bonds issued by borrowers outside their own country, are still bearer bonds. They're not registered with any regulatory authority, and the certificates can be traded or redeemed by the bearer.

You're not likely to own one, however, since they're sold in very large denominations. Typical buyers are corporations and governments.

WHAT THE CERTIFICATE TELLS

Issuers register bonds with an **identifying number** on the face of the bond. The bondholder's name also appears on the bond.

The **issuer** is the corporation, government or agency that sells the bond. It is identified by name and often by a symbol or logo. Its **official seal** authenticates the bond's validity. When a company issues bonds, the documents have the same design as the company's stock certificates. And they are protected against counterfeiting in the same way, with special paper, elaborate borders and intaglio printing.

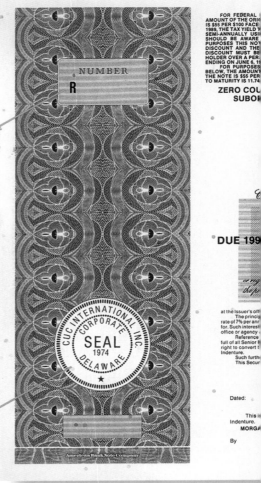

NUMBER

R

FOR FEDERAL
AMOUNT OF THE ORI
IS $55 PER $100 FACE
1989, THE TAX YIELD
SEMI-ANNUALLY USI
SHOULD BE AWARE
PURPOSES THIS NO
DISCOUNT AND THE
DISCOUNT MUST BE
HOLDER OVER A PER
ENDING ON JUNE 6, 1
FOR PURPOSES
BELOW, THE AMOUNT
THE NOTE IS $55 PER
TO MATURITY IS 11.74

ZERO COU
SUBO

DUE 199

CUC INTERNATIONAL INC. CORPORATE SEAL 1974 DELAWARE

at the issuer's off
The principi
rate of 7% per anr
for. Such interes
office or agency
Reference
full of all Senior
right to convert t
Indenture.
Such furthe
This Secur

Dated:

This is
Indenture.
MORG

By

American Bank Note Company

Interest rate is the fixed percentage of par value that is paid to the bondholder annually. For example, a $1,000 bond that pays 6.5% yields $65 a year. If the original buyer holds the bond to maturity, the **yield** (or return on investment) is also 6.5% a year. However, if the bond is traded, the yield could change even though the interest rate will stay the same. For example, if an investor buys the bond for $1,100 in the secondary market, the interest will still be $65 a year, but the yield will be reduced to 5.91% because the new owner paid more for the bond.

Par value, or the dollar amount of the bond at the time it was issued, appears several times on the face of the bond. Par value is the amount originally paid for the bond and the amount that will be repaid at maturity. Most bonds have a par value of $1,000.

A **baby bond** has a par value of less than $1,000. Bonds of $500, or even less, can be issued by municipal governments to involve a larger number of people in the fund-raising process.

Maturity date is the date the bond comes due and must be repaid in full. A bond may be bought and sold in its lifetime and reregistered in the new owner's name. Whoever owns the bond at maturity is the one who gets par value back.

22222
REGISTERED

CUSIP 121212 AA 0
SEE REVERSE FOR CERTAIN DEFINITIONS

CUC INTERNATIONAL INC.

...ional Inc., a Delaware corporation (the "Issuer"), for value received hereby promises to pay to

DUE 1996

DOLLARS

...ose in New York, New York on June 6, 1996 in such coin or currency of the United States of America as at the time of payment shall be legal tender for the payment of public and private debts. ...bear interest except in the case of a default in payment of principal upon acceleration, redemption or at maturity and in such case the overdue principal of this Security shall bear interest at the ...ayment of such interest shall be legally enforceable), which shall accrue from the date of such default in payment to the date payment of such overdue principal has been made or duly provided ...sis of a 360-day year of twelve 30-day months. Interest on any overdue principal shall be payable on demand. Payment of the principal of and any such interest on this Security will be made at the ...r that purpose in New York, New York.

...sions set forth on the reverse hereof including without limitation provisions subordinating the payment of principal of and interest on overdue principal, if any, on the Securities to the payment in ...nture dated as of May 25, 1989 (the "Indenture") between the Issuer and Morgan Guaranty Trust Company of New York, as Trustee (the "Trustee"), and provisions giving the holder hereof the ...Stock, par value $.01 per share ("Common Stock"), of the Issuer on the terms and subject to the conditions and limitations referred to on the reverse hereof, as more fully specified in the

...urposes have the same effect as though fully set forth at this place. ...ligatory until the certificate of authentication hereon shall have been duly signed by the Trustee acting under the Indenture.

...Whereof, the Issuer has caused this instrument to be duly executed under its corporate seal.

CUC International Inc.

...JTHENTICATION
...escribed in the within-mentioned

...COMPANY OF NEW YORK,
as Trustee

Attest:

By:

Authorized Officer

Secretary

Chairman of the Board

The 30-year Treasury bond was popularly known as the long bond. But the longest bonds around are the 100-year corporate bonds that were introduced in 1993 by Disney Corporation. The first ones come due in 2093.

Figuring a Bond's Worth

The value of a bond is determined by the interest it pays and by what's happening in the economy.

In most cases, a bond's interest rate doesn't change, even though other interest rates do. If the bond is paying more interest than is available elsewhere, you, as an investor, will be willing to pay more to own it. If the bond is paying less, the reverse is true.

Interest rates and bond prices fluctuate like two sides of a seesaw. As the table below illustrates, when interest rates drop, the value of existing bonds usually goes up. When rates climb, the value of existing bonds usually falls.

Several factors—including **yield** and **return**—affect whether or not a bond turns out to be a good investment.

PAR FOR THE COURSE

If you buy at par and hold the bond to maturity, **inflation**, or the shrinking value of the dollar, is your worst enemy. The further in the future the bond will mature, the greater the risk that at some point infla-

tion will rise dramatically and reduce the value of the money that you are repaid.

If the bond pays more than the rate of inflation, you come out ahead. For example, if a bond is paying 8% and the annual rate of inflation is 3%, the bond produces real earnings of 5%. But if inflation shoots up to 10%, the interest earnings won't buy what they once did. And the amount you have invested in the bond itself also shrinks in value.

UNDER (AND OVER) PAR

But many bonds, particularly those with maturities of five or more years, aren't held by one investor from the date of issue to the date of maturity. Rather, investors trade bonds in the secondary market. The prices fluctuate according to the interest rate the bond pays, the degree of certainty of repayment and overall economic conditions—especially the rate of inflation—which influence interest rates.

SELLERS

BUYERS

Original bond issuer is selling bond

AT PAR VALUE

Par value:	$1,000
Term:	10 years
Interest rate:	6%

At Issue

6% Prevailing interest rate

BUYING AT PAR VALUE
- Pay par value at issue and keep to maturity
- Receive 10 annual interest payments of $60
- Receive par value—$1,000—at maturity

If bondholder sells two years after issue when interest rates are high, the bond is

SELLING AT A DISCOUNT

Market value	$800
Interest (x2)	+ 120
	920
Less original cost	− 1000
LOSS	**−$80**

2 Years Later

8% Prevailing interest rate

BUYING AT A DISCOUNT
- Pay $200 less than par value
- Receive 8 annual interest payments of $60
- Receive par value—$1,000—at maturity

If bondholder sells three years after issue when interest rates are low, the bond is

SELLING AT A PREMIUM

Market value	$1,200
Interest (x3)	+ 180
	1380
Less original cost	− 1000
RETURN	**$380**

3 Years Later

3% Prevailing interest rate

BUYING AT A PREMIUM
- Pay $200 more than par value
- Receive 7 annual interest payments of $60
- Receive par value—$1,000—at maturity

HOW IT WORKS

Generally, when inflation is up, interest rates go up. And conversely, when inflation is low, so are interest rates. It's the change in market interest rates that causes bond prices to move up or down.

It's also the fluctuations in interest rates, and therefore in bond prices, that produce much of the trading that goes on in the bond market.

If DaveCo Corporation floats a new issue of bonds offering 6% interest, and it seems like a good investment, you buy some bonds at the full price, or par value, of $1,000 a bond.

Three years later, interest rates are up. If new bonds costing $1,000 are paying 8% interest, no buyer will pay you $1,000 for a bond paying 6%. To sell your bond you'll have to offer it at a **discount**, or less than you paid. If you must sell, you might have to settle for a price that wipes out most of the interest you've earned.

But consider the reverse situation. If new bonds selling for $1,000 offer only a 3% interest rate, you'll be able to sell your 6% bonds for more than you paid—since buyers will agree to pay more to get a higher interest rate. That **premium**, combined with the interest payments for the last three years, provides profit.

CHANGING YIELD

Several factors—including yield and return—affect whether or not a bond turns out to be a good investment.

Yield is what you earn, expressed as a percentage. If you buy a 10-year $1,000 bond paying 6% and hold it until it matures, you'll earn $60 a year for ten years—an annual yield of 6%, or the same as the interest rate.

But if you buy in the secondary market, after the date of issue, the bond's yield may not be the same as its interest rate. That's because the price affects the yield.

Most bond charts express current yield as a percentage. For example, if a bond's yield is given as 6%, it means your interest payments will be 6% of what you pay for the bond today—or 6% back on your investment. You can use the yield to compare the relative value of bonds.

Return, on the other hand, is what you make on the investment when the par value of the bond, your profit or loss from trading it, and the interest you've earned are computed.

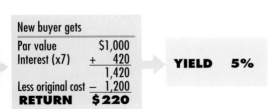

RETURN · YIELD

Original buyer gets

Par value	$1,000
Interest (x10)	+ 600
	1,600
Less original cost	− 1,000
RETURN	**$600**

→ **YIELD 6%**

New buyer gets

Par value	$1,000
Interest (x8)	+ 480
	1,480
Less original cost	− 800
RETURN	**$680**

→ **YIELD 7.5%**

New buyer gets

Par value	$1,000
Interest (x7)	+ 420
	1,420
Less original cost	− 1,200
RETURN	**$220**

→ **YIELD 5%**

HOW TO FIGURE A BOND'S YIELD

$$\frac{\text{Annual interest}}{\text{Price}} = \text{Yield}$$

for example

$$\frac{\$60}{\$1,000} = .06, \text{ or } 6\%$$

YIELD TO MATURITY

There's an even more precise measure of a bond's current value called the **yield to maturity**. It takes into account:

- The interest rate in relation to the price
- The purchase price in relation to the par value
- The years remaining until the bond matures

Yield to maturity is a way to predict return over time, but it is calculated by a complicated formula—and it isn't often stated in bond tables. Brokers have access to the information, and it's available on websites that specialize in bond information or bond trading.

Rating Bonds

Investors want to know the risks in buying a bond before they take the plunge. Rating services measure those risks.

As a bond investor you want to be reasonably sure that you'll get your interest payments on time and your principal back at maturity. It's almost impossible for an individual to do the necessary research. But rating services make a business of it.

The best-known services are **Standard & Poor's** and **Moody's Investors Service, Inc.** These companies carefully investigate the financial condition of a bond issuer rather than the market appeal of its bonds. They look at other debt the issuer has, how fast the company's revenues and profits are growing, the state of the economy and how well other companies in the same business (or municipal governments in the same general shape) are doing. Their primary concern is to alert investors to the risks of a particular issue.

Issuers rarely publicize their ratings unless they are top of the line. So you need to get the information from the rating services themselves, the financial press or your broker or financial adviser.

WHAT BONDS GET RATED?

The rating services pass judgment on municipal bonds, all kinds of corporate bonds and international bonds. U.S. Treasury bonds are not rated. The assumption is that they're absolutely solid, since they're obligations of the federal government, backed by its full faith and credit. This means the government has the authority to raise taxes to pay off its debts.

Rating a Bond:

Moody's	Standard & Poor's
Aaa	AAA
Aa	AA
A	A
Baa	BBB
Ba	BB
B	B
Caa	CCC
Ca	CC
C	C
•	D

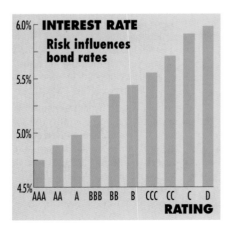

INTEREST RATE

Risk influences bond rates

6.0%

5.5%

5.0%

4.5%

AAA AA A BBB BB B CCC CC C D

RATING

RANKINGS INFLUENCE RATES

As the chart to the left shows, credit ratings influence the interest rate an issuer must pay to attract investors. In comparing bonds with the same maturity, typically the higher the bond's rating, the lower the interest it pays and the lower its yield.

Similarly, lower-rated bonds must typically pay higher rates, providing higher yields, to entice investors who might be concerned about whether their interest will be paid on time or their principal repaid. That's why the lowest-rated bonds are sometimes described as high-yield bonds.

THE RISK OF DOWNGRADING

One danger bondholders face—and one they can't anticipate—is that a rating service may **downgrade** its ratings of a company or municipal government during the life of a bond, creating a **fallen angel**. That happens if the issuer's financial condition deteriorates, or if the rating service feels a business decision might have poor results. If downgrading occurs, investors instantly demand a higher yield for the existing bonds. That means the price of the bond falls in the secondary market. It also means that if the issuer wants to float new bonds, the bonds will have to be offered at a higher interest rate to attract buyers.

The rating systems of the two major services are similar, but not identical, in the ways they label bond quality. Both services also make distinctions within categories Aa/AA and lower. Moody's uses a numerical system (1,2,3) and Standard & Poor's uses a + or −.

Meaning

Best quality, with the smallest risk. Issuers exceptionally stable and dependable

High quality, with slightly higher degree of long-term risk

High-medium quality, with many strong attributes but somewhat vulnerable to changing economic conditions

Medium quality, currently adequate but perhaps unreliable over long term

INVESTMENT GRADE BONDS

Investment grade generally refers to any bonds rated Baa or higher by Moody's, or BBB or higher by Standard & Poor's.

Some speculative element, with moderate security but not well safeguarded

Able to pay now but at risk of default in the future

Poor quality, clear danger of default

Highly speculative quality, often in default

Lowest-rated, poor prospects of repayment though may still be paying

In default

JUNK BONDS

Junk bonds are the lowest-rated corporate and municipal bonds. There's a greater-than-average risk of default. But investors may be willing to take the risk of buying these low-rated bonds because the yields are so much higher than on other, higher-rated investments. However, the prices are volatile as well, exposing investors to additional risk.

TIME IS MONEY

When bonds have the same ranking but different terms, those with longer terms typically pay higher rates to encourage investors to commit their money for an extended period, which means greater potential for inflation risk.

YIELD COMPARISONS

Based on Merrill Lynch Bond Indexes, priced as of afternoon Eastern time.

	8/12	8/11	−52 Week− High	Low
Agencies 1-10yr	5.34	5.34	6.22	5.24
10+yr	6.79	6.78	8.01	6.78
Corporate				
1-10 yr High Qlty	5.79	5.82	7.00	5.72
Med Qlty	6.21	6.24	7.31	6.16
10+yr High Qlty	7.28	7.29	8.31	7.28
Med Qlty	7.64	7.66	8.74	7.64
Yankee bonds(1)	6.73	6.75	7.97	6.73
Current-coupon mortgages (2)				
GNMA 6.50%	6.57	6.61	7.97	6.51
FNMA 6.50%	6.57	6.58	7.98	6.53
FHLMC8.00%	6.25	6.22	7.95	6.14
High-yield corporates	9.81	9.81	11.43	9.80
New tax-exempts				
10-yr G.O. (AA)	4.75	4.85	5.85	4.65
20-yr G.O. (AA)	5.35	5.45	6.60	5.30
30-yr revenue (A)	5.75	5.85	6.80	5.75

AAA-AA; medium quality

Tracking Bond Performance

You can follow day-to-day changes in bond prices and yields.

Trading in corporate bonds listed on the New York Stock Exchange and on the American Stock Exchange is reported for every business day in The Wall Street Journal and online at a number of specialized websites.

In this example, company names, followed by their trading symbols, are listed in descending order by total trading volume for a specific issue. Because they were among the most actively traded on the previous trading day, four Goldman Sachs bonds are in the list, three Sprint Capital and three Ford Motor Credit bonds, and two issues each from several other companies.

The most actively traded list changes regularly, based on a number of factors including current news about the issuer.

The first number in the chart is the **coupon**, or **interest rate**, expressed as a percentage. Bonds issued at different times have different coupons, based on the current market rates at the time of issue and the issuer's credit rating. For example, the first Ford Motor Credit bond in the list has a coupon rate of 7%, the

CORPORATE

COMPANY (TICKER)	COUPON	MATURITY	LAST PRICE	LAST YIELD	EST $ VOL (000's)
Walt Disney (DIS)-c	2.125	Apr 15, 2003	116.362	1.169	223,093
First Data (FDC)-c	2.000	Mar 01, 2008	100.350	1.909	215,525
Ford Motor Credit (F)	7.000	Oct 01, 2013	106.481	6.098	214,802
Goldman Sachs Group (GS)	6.125	Feb 15, 2033	101.390	6.023	196,642
Safeway (SWY)	6.500	Mar 01, 2011	110.317	4.757	127,110
Goldman Sachs Group (GS)	5.150	Jan 15, 2014	101.296	4.982	113,445
Goldman Sachs Group (GS)	3.875	Jan 15, 2009	100.982	3.654	92,104
Wal-Mart Stores (WMT)	6.875	Aug 10, 2009	115.879	3.650	81,885
Ford Motor Credit (F)	6.875	Feb 01, 2006	106.777	3.263	71,475
General Electric Capital (GE)	6.000	Jun 15, 2012	110.217	4.513	68,268
Telefonos de Mexico S.A. de C.V. (TFONY)	8.250	Jan 26, 2006	110.150	2.831	65,471
Wachovia (WB)	4.875	Feb 15, 2014	100.421	4.821	60,937
Walt Disney (DIS)	6.375	Mar 01, 2012	110.889	4.730	60,725
Devon Financing (DVN)	7.875	Sep 30, 2031	112.109	6.193	60,218
Ford Motor (F)	7.450	Jul 16, 2031	102.490	7.239	59,636
Bear Stearns Companies (BSC)	2.875	Jul 02, 2008	97.750	3.433	58,699
BellSouth (BLS)	6.875	Oct 15, 2031	111.133	6.041	57,600
General Motors (GM)	8.375	Jul 15, 2033	114.910	7.153	57,239
General Motors Acceptance (GMAC)	6.125	Sep 15, 2006	10⊡		
Sprint Capital (FON)					

Maturity is the date on which the bond's term ends and the principal is repaid to the bondholder. Corporate bonds mature across the spectrum from fewer than 5 years to more than 30. Callable bonds may be repaid before maturity.

Last price is the price at which the bond closed on the previous trading day. When a bond is traded, it usually sells for more or less than its par value. The price moves in relation to the bond's interest rate, its yield to maturity, and the bond's rating.

Last yield is the percentage of interest an investor would earn if buying the bond at its current price. If the market price is lower than par, the yield is higher than the coupon rate. If the price is higher, the rate is lower than par.

Compare the Bear Stearns Companies 2.875% bond yielding 3.433% and selling at a discount for $977.50, or $22.50 less than par, with the General

UNDERSTANDING BOND PRICES

Corporate bond prices, which were once quoted in increments of points and eight fractions of a point with a par of $1,000 as the base, are now quoted in dollars and cents. The value of each point was $10, and of each fraction $1.25, as the chart shows:

⅛ = $1.25	⅜ = $3.75	¾ = $7.50
¼ = $2.50	½ = $5.00	⅞ = $8.75
	⅝ = $6.25	

So a bond quoted at 85½ would have been selling for $855, and one quoted at 105⅞ would have been selling for $1058.75.

second 6.875%, and the third 7.450%.

Bond interest always refers to a percentage of par value, which is the amount the issuer will repay when the bond comes due. The par value of most corporate bonds is $1,000. So the annual interest payment with a coupon of 7% will be $70.

Convertible bonds, identified with a −c following the company name, may be exchanged for shares of company stock rather than redeemed for cash if the bondholder wishes, based on the conditions of the offer. As a result, convertibles are sometimes considered hybrid investments. The two most actively traded issues in this list are both convertibles.

Corporations also issue **zero coupon bonds**, which pay no periodic interest. Instead principal and interest are paid at maturity.

BONDS

COMPANY (TICKER)	COUPON	MATURITY	LAST PRICE	LAST YIELD	EST $ VOL (000's)
Verizon Global Funding (VZ)	7.375	Sep 01, 2012	117.529	4.843	51,868
Sprint Capital (FON)	6.900	May 01, 2019	106.418	6.239	51,361
Verizon Virginia (VZ)	4.625	Mar 15, 2013	97.481	4.973	50,915
TXU Energy Co. LLC (TXU)	7.000	Mar 15, 2013	112.909	5.197	50,776
Sara Lee (SLE)	6.250	Sep 15, 2011	112.499	4.299	50,402
Safeway (SWY)	7.250	Feb 01, 2031	111.386	6.361	49,375
Goldman Sachs Group (GS)	4.750	Jul 15, 2013	98.609	4.936	48,604
Verizon Global Funding (VZ)	6.875	Jun 15, 2012	113.623	4.864	48,291
Countrywide Home Loans (CFC)	5.500	Aug 01, 2006	107.176	2.466	47,908
Kraft Foods (KFT)	4.625	Nov 01, 2006	105.078	2.664	47,814
General Electric Capital (GE)	5.000	Jun 15, 2007	106.915	2.806	47,217
Sprint Capital (FON)	7.900	Mar 15, 2005	106.416	1.843	46,822
Schlumberger Limited (SLB)-c	1.500	Jun 01, 2023	109.052	0.590	46,382
Kraft Foods (KFT)	5.250	Jun 01, 2007	107.056	2.979	46,000
ConocoPhillips (COP)	4.750	Oct 15, 2012	102.152	4.447	41,507
Kimberly-Clark (KMB)	5.625	Feb 15, 2012	108.706	4.312	41,500

Motors 8.375% bond yielding only 7.153% and selling at a premium for $1,149.10, or $149.10 above par.

Bond volume reports the dollar value of the previous day's trading in individual bonds, in millions of dollars. To find the actual amount, you add three zeros to the number in the chart. So, for example, the $41.5 million in ConocoPhillips

February 2012 bonds is small in comparison to the $127.1 million in Safeway March 2011 bonds.

CORPORATE APPEAL

Investors buy corporate bonds in part because they generally provide a higher **yield** than U.S. Treasury issues with the same maturity. The trade-off is the higher level of default risk, since corporations depend on earnings to

repay their obligations. And, the greater the difference in the yield, the greater that risk is.

Both types of bonds expose you to **market risk**, or the possibility that the bond will trade at a lower price than par value.

One drawback of corporates for individual investors is that there's generally a large minimum investment required.

Municipal Bonds

The not-so-secret charm of municipal bonds is their tax-exempt status. You usually don't have to share your earnings with the IRS—or state taxing authorities.

The interest paid on most corporate bonds is taxed. To encourage investors to lend money to cities and states to pay for public projects—like highways and water systems—Congress exempts municipal bond interest from federal income taxes although it may be subject to the Alternative minimum tax (ATM).

If you were considering both a corporate bond and a municipal bond that paid 6% interest, the obvious choice would be the municipal bond. But the choices are seldom that simple. High-rated municipal bonds usually offer a lower rate than corporate bonds. That's why municipal bonds, commonly called **munis**, usually appeal most to investors in the higher tax brackets, where the exemption can provide the biggest tax savings.

Municipal bond interest is also exempt from state tax (and city tax where it applies) if you live in the state where the bond is issued. An Ohioan, for example, would pay no Ohio income tax on bond interest earned on a Cincinnati bond. But someone from Kentucky who bought the Cincinnati bond would have to pay Kentucky tax on the interest income. Most investors, however, would not have to pay federal tax on the interest.

TAX-EXEMPT BONDS

Representative prices for several active tax-exempt revenue and refunding Changes rounded to the nearest one-eighth. Yield is to maturity. n-New. Sour

ISSUE	COUPON	MAT	PRICE	CHG	BID YLD	ISSUE
Alameda Corr TA Ca	4.750	10-01-25	95⅞	+ ⅛	5.03	Jefferson Parish H
Alameda Corr TA Ca	5.000	10-01-29	99	+ ¼	5.06	LA Stad & Expo Ho
Alaska Intl Arpts	5.000	10-01-24	97⅛	+ ¼	5.21	MA Bay Trans Auth
Ca Hlth Fac Fin Auth	5.350	08-15-28	102½	+ ⅛	5.19	Mass Tpk Auth Ser
CA Hlth Fin Rev 98 Ser	5.000	10-01-20	97⅛	+ ⅛	5.22	Mo. Hlth & Ed Fac
California GO Ser 98	4.750	12-01-28	95⅝	+ ⅛	5.03	Monty BMC Spc Ca
Chgo Ill Sls Tx Rev	5.375	01-01-30	107⅞	+ ⅛	5.25	NJ Hlth Cr Rev Ser
Ctl Pgt Sd Transit WA	4.750	01-01-28	94⅜	...	5.12	NJ Hlth Fin Rev Se
Denver Colo Arpt	5.000	11-15-25	97¼	...	5.19	NJ Trans Trust Fu
Denver Sch Dist #1	5.000	12-01-23	98¾	+ ⅛	5.08	No East Ind Sch Di
Det Cty Sch Dist MI sch	4.750	05-01-28	94⅝	...	5.11	NYC Muni Wtr&Sw
Florida St Bd of Ed	4.500	06-01-23	92⅝	+ ⅛	5.02	Orge Co FL Trst De
Grpvn-Coly Sch TX	5.000	08-15-29	98	+ ⅛	5.13	Phil PA Go Ser 98
Highld Co Hlth FL	5.250	11-15-28	97⅜	+ ⅛	5.43	Phila Sch Dist Pa
Hono HI Wastewtr	5.000	07-01-23	98¼	...	5.12	Pub Hwy Auth Colc
Houstn Ind Sch Dis Tx	4.750	02-15-26	95	+ ⅛	5.09	Puerto Rico Pub In
Houstn Ind Sch Dist Tx	5.000	02-15-24	98⅜	...	5.11	Sacramento Cty Fi
Huston Tx Airport Sys	5.000	07-01-25	97⅛	...	5.20	Wash Hlth Care
Ul Hlth Fac Auth19	5.000	01-01-05	97	+ ⅛	5.21	Wash Hl

READING MUNI STATISTICS

There are hundreds of thousands of munis in the market. The Wall Street Journal quotes price information for some of the largest bonds that are being actively traded.

The **name** of the issuing municipal government or government agency is listed, along with a series number, if it applies.

Coupon rate is the interest rate, given as a percentage of par value. The bond issued by the Denver School District pays 5% of par value in interest, or $50 per $1,000.

Maturity date is the date the bond matures and will be paid off. This Florida Board of Education bond comes due on June 1, 2023.

Munis are often long-term bonds, maturing in 20 to 40 years. All of the ones in this list mature between 2019 and 2038.

Price is the amount the bond sold for at the end of the previous trading day, given as a percentage of par. Here, the Massachusetts Bay Transit Authority's price of 97 1/8 means it closed at $971.25.

MUNICIPAL BOND INDEXES

Each week The Wall Street Journal prints a Municipal Bond Index of the average interest issuers would have to pay to sell investment-quality long-term bonds. In the week ending January 26, for example, the average interest was 4.77%, down 0.05% from the week before.

Specific figures are given for the two main categories of municipal bonds.

Revenue bonds are backed by the revenues a specific project or agency generates. New York State Thruway revenue bonds, for example, are repaid by the money paid for tolls.

General obligation bonds are backed by the **full faith and credit**, meaning the taxing power, of the issuer. Because revenue bonds generally have longer terms and are somewhat riskier, they pay slightly higher rates overall.

Municipal Bond Index

Merrill Lynch Muni Master

Week ended Tuesday, January 26

The following index is based on major municipal issuers having bonds with amounts outstanding of at least $50 million, an investment grade rating and issuance within the last five years. The chart shown displays the market weighted average yield to worst* of each index. The index is calculated by Merrill Lynch, based on pricing obtained from Standard & Poor's J.J. Kenny Co.

— MUNI MASTER BOND INDEX —
4.77 −0.05

— REVENUE BONDS —
Sub-Index 4.91 −0.05

— 22-52 YEAR REVENUE BONDS —	01-26	Change In Week
AAA-Guaranteed....		
Airport	4.86	− 0.05
Power	5.04	− 0.04
Hospital	4.86	− 0.05
Housing- Single Family	4.94	− 0.04
Housing- Multi Family	5.23	− 0.02
Miscellaneous	5.02	− 0.06
Pollution Control/ Ind. Dev.	n.a.	....
Transportation	4.45	− 0.03
Water	4.88	− 0.05
Advance Refunded	4.91	− 0.05
— 12-22 YEAR GENERAL OBLIGATIONS —	3.93	− 0.06
Sub-Index 4.63 −0.05		
Cities	4.68	− 0.05
Counties	3.67	− 0.05
States	4.59	− 0.05
Other Districts	n.a	
The tra...		

MAT	PRICE	CHG	BID YLD
07-01-28	96¾	...	5.22
07-01-26	97⅞	...	5.14
03-01-28	97⅛	...	5.14
01-01-37	97	...	5.18
05-15-38	95⅜	...	5.28
11-15-29	97	+ ⅛	5.19
07-01-24	99	+ ⅛	5.07
07-01-28	95⅜	+ ⅛	5.05
06-15-19	94	+ ⅛	4.97
10-01-28	91⅜	+ ¼	5.0
06-15-31	94⅞	+ ⅛	5.07
10-01-24	95½	+ ⅛	5.
03-15-28	98⅛	+ ¼	
04-01-27			

sed on institutional trades. nd Buyer.

Change is the difference between the price quoted here and the previous day's closing price. Here it is quoted as a fraction of par value. However, bond prices like stock prices may be expressed in dollars and cents rather than in points and fractions of points. Among other things, that means than the smallest change in price can be a few cents rather than $1.25 (1/8), and most day-to-day changes tend to be less than $1.

Bid yield is the rate of return. It's figured using the interest, the amount paid for the bond, its redemption value and the time remaining until it matures.

BOND OFFERINGS

When states, cities or towns want to offer new bonds, there are two ways to get them to market. They can negotiate an arrangement with a securities firm to underwrite the bond, or they can ask for competitive bids.

A competitive bid means the issuer works with the lowest bidder to sell the bonds. A negotiated agreement takes other factors into account.

Since the mid-1980s, most offerings—up to 80% —have been negotiated. The main advantage is a guaranteed presale. The potential problems are the opportunity for manipulating the deal to the advantage of the underwriter at the expense of the taxpayer who foots the interest bills, and the possibility of political kickbacks. Competitive bids are free of those problems but may rule out developing a strong working relationship that could benefit the issuer.

U.S. Treasury Notes and Bills

The U.S. government is a major force in the bond market.

The U.S. Treasury issues three basic types of debt securities. They differ from each other in their maturities, in the frequency with which they are offered, in the interest rates they pay and the way in which the interest is paid. But they share the reputation of being free from default because they are government bonds.

The most common issues are **notes**, available with 2-, 3-, 5- or 10-year terms, and **bills**, available with 4-, 13-, or 26-week terms. The others are Treasury **STRIPS**, which are government zero-coupon bonds offered only by securities dealers in the secondary market.

The Treasury also issues 10-year **inflation indexed notes**, called TIPS—short for Treasury Inflation Protected Securities. The principal is adjusted to reflect changes in the consumer price index (CPI), and at maturity you receive either par value or the adjusted principal, whichever is greater. The notes pay a fixed rate of interest, but, if the principal grows, the interest is paid on the larger base.

Long-term 30-year bonds and inflation-indexed 30-year bonds are no longer being issued, although existing bonds continue to trade in the secondary market.

Treasury issues are sold in $1,000 increments, and you can invest as little as $1,000 or as much as $1 million. You can buy and sell directly, through a program known as Treasury Direct. But like other debt securities, Treasurys are traded in the secondary market after issue, and their prices and yields fluctuate as a reflection of changing demand. Details of those trades, in order of maturity date, are reported regularly in tables like the one below.

TREASURY BONDS

GOVT. BOND & NOTES

RATE	MATURITY MO/YR	BID	ASKED	CHG	ASK YLD	RATE	MATURITY MO/YR	BID	ASKED	CHG
4.625	May 06n	106:02	106:03	2	1.86	3.000	Jul 12i	111:08	111:09	11
6.875	May 06n	111:01	111:02	2	1.85	4.375	Aug 12n	103:15	103:16	7
7.000	Jul 06n	111:27	111:28	2	1.96	4.000	Nov 12n	100:18	100:19	7
2.375	Aug 06n	100:28	100:29	2	2.00	10.375	Nov 12	127:22	127:23	5
6.500	Oct 06n	111:12	111:13	2	2.09	3.875	Feb 13n	99:14	99:15	7
2.625	Nov 06n	101:08	101:09	2	2.14	3.625	May 13n	97:19	97:20	6
3.500	Nov 06n	103:20	103:21	3	2.13	1.875	Jul 13i	101:19	101:20	10
3.375	Jan 07i	109:04	109:05	6	0.23	**4.250**	**Aug 13n**	**101:23**	**101:24**	7
6.250	Feb 07n	111:19	111:20	2	2.23	12.000	Aug 13	138:05	138:06	2
6.625	May 07n	113:09	113:10	3	2.35	4.250	Nov 13n	101:16	101:17	7
4.375	May 07n	106:08	106:09	4	2.36	2.000	Jan 14i	102:10	102:11	11
3.250	Aug 07n	102:17	102:18	4	2.48	13.250	May 14	148:26	148:27	4
6.125	Aug 07n	112:07	112:08	4	2.46	12.500	Aug 14	146:19	146:20	3
3.000	Nov 07n	101:16	101:17	5	2.57	11.750	Nov 14	144:05	144:06	5
3.625	Jan 08i	111:24	111:25	7	0.58	11.250	Feb 15	162:01	162:02	11
3.000	Feb 08n	101:03	101:04	5	2.70	10.625	Aug 15	157:22	157:23	10
								151:04	151:05	10

Rate is the percentage of par value paid as annual interest. The note maturing in May 2006 pays 4.625% interest.

Maturity date is the month and year the bond or note comes due. An **n** after the date, which occurs in most entries, indicates that the issue is a note. An **i** means the bond is inflation indexed.

Prices for Treasury bonds and notes are measured in 32nds of a point rather than dollars and cents. Each 1/32 equals 31.25 cents, but the fractional part is dropped when the price is quoted. For example, if a bond is selling at 100:02 (or 100 and 2/32), the price translates to $1,000.62.

Prices for Treasury issues are quoted as **bid** and **asked** instead of as a closing price. That's because Treasury issues are

STRIPS AND BILLS

Trading in STRIPS and bills is also reported in separate sections of the table. STRIPS prices are always less than par, since they are issued at a **deep discount**. Those closer to maturity trade at higher prices, since they can be redeemed at par value when they come due. Compare the 99.09 bid price of the issue maturing in January 2005 with the 97.07 bid price for one maturing in November 2005. Those with later maturity dates are also more volatile, as the change figures shows.

T-bill bid and asked prices are stated as discount percents rather than price in relation to par value. The bills are sold

originally at discount, and the difference between the price paid and par value is the interest. Full par value is repaid at maturity.

Dealers trade T-bills by bidding and asking discount percents. For example, the highest bid on the bill due February 26 was 0.83, meaning that the price offered was at a 0.83% discount. That is, the offer was to pay $991.70 to buy a

$1,000 bill.

Yield is the **yield to maturity**. As with bonds and notes, it represents the relative value of the issue. The figure that gives the most accurate sense of what an investor makes on a T-bill is the **coupon equivalent yield**, or the percentage return resulting from dividing the dollar return by the amount paid. For example, a $1,000 bill sold for $960 has a coupon equivalent yield of 4.16%.

FIGURING COUPON YIELD

$$\frac{\text{Dollar return on T-bill}}{\text{Cost of T-bill}} = \text{Coupon equivalent yield}$$

for example

$$\frac{\$40}{\$960} = 4.16\%$$

NOTES & BILLS

U.S. TREASURY STRIPS

MATURITY	TYPE	BID	ASKED	CHG	ASK YLD
05	ci	99:09	99:10	1	0.75
05	ci	98:28	98:28	1	1.11
05	np	98:28	98:28	1	1.11
05	ci	98:16	98:17	1	1.18
05	bp	98:15	98:16	1	1.21
05	np	98:13	98:14	1	1.25
05	np	98:13	98:13	1	1.27
05	ci	98:19	98:19	1	0.99
05	ci	97:31	98:00	1	1.35
05	bp	97:28	97:29	1	1.41
05	np	97:28	97:29	1	1.40
05	ci	97:09	97:10	1	1.56
05	np	97:07	97:09	2	1.58
05	np	97:08	97:09	1	1.57
06	ci	97:10	97:11	2	1.41
		96:17	96:18	2	1.75

TREASURY BILLS

MATURITY	TYPE	BID	ASKED	CHG	ASK YLD
Feb 12 04	2	0.80	0.79	...	0.80
Feb 19 04	9	0.81	0.80	...	0.71
Feb 26 04	16	0.83	0.82	...	0.83
Mar 04 04	23	0.87	0.86	0.01	0.87
Mar 11 04	30	0.89	0.88	0.07	0.89
Mar 18 04	37	0.81	0.80	...	0.81
Mar 25 04	44	0.84	0.83	0.01	0.84
Apr 01 04	51	0.86	0.85	...	0.86
Apr 08 04	58	0.86	0.85	...	0.86
Apr 15 04	65	0.88	0.87		
Apr 22 04	72				
Apr 29 04	79				
May 06 04	8				
May 13 04					
Ma					

traded over the counter, in thousands of telephone or electronic transactions instead of on the major exchanges. So it's not possible to determine the exact price of the last transaction. The best information that's available is the highest price being

bid, or offered by buyers, and the lowest price being asked by sellers at 4:00 p.m. Eastern time.

For example, the bond paying 12.5% that matures August 2014 had a bid price of 146:19 and an asked price of 146:20. The :19 in the price refers to 19/32 of a point, or $5.9375 and :20

to 20/32 or $6.25. So the bid price was $1,059.38 and the asked price was $1,062.50.

Change reports the change in the bid price given here and the bid price given in the tables for the previous trading day. The change is stated in 32nds. If the number is preceded by a minus (–), the price is lower. If there is no minus, the price is higher. For example, the bid price on the August 2014 bond is 3/32 higher than it was on the previous day.

A Bond Vocabulary

The words that describe individual bonds have very specific meanings, which can influence your investment decisions.

Like the word **security**, which once meant the written record of an investment, the word **bond** once referred to the piece of paper that described the details of a loan transaction. Today the term is used more generally to describe a vast and varied market in debt securities.

The language of bonds tells potential investors the features of the loan: the time to maturity, how it's going to be repaid and whether it's likely to be **called**, or repaid ahead of schedule.

How Bonds Are Backed Up

Asset-backed bonds are secured, or backed up, by **accounts receivable**, or money owed to the issuers. An asset-backed bond can be created when a securities firm **bundles** some type of debt, such as outstanding credit card debt, and sells investors the right to receive the payments that consumers are making on those loans.

Debentures are the most common corporate bonds. They're backed by the credit of the issuer, rather than by any specific assets. Though they sound riskier, they're generally not. The debentures of reliable institutions are typically more highly rated than asset-backed bonds.

Pre-refunded bonds are corporate or municipal bonds, usually AAA rated, whose repayment is guaranteed by a second bond issue. Proceeds from the secondary issue are usually invested in safe U.S. Treasury issues.

Mortgage-backed bonds are backed by a pool of mortgage loans. They're sold to brokers by government agencies and private corporations, and the brokers resell them to investors. Mortgage-backed bonds are **self-amortizing**. That means each payment you get includes both principal and interest, so that there is no lump-sum repayment at maturity.

Collateralized mortgage obligations (CMOs) are more complex versions of mortgage-backed bonds. Although they are sold as a reasonable alternative to more conventional bonds, evaluating their risks and potential for return may require more specialized skills.

Bonds with Conditions

A subordinated bond is one that will be paid after other loan obligations of the issuer have been met. **Senior** bonds are those with stronger claims. Corporations sometimes sell senior and subordinated bonds in the same issue, offering more interest and a shorter term on the subordinated ones to make them more attractive.

Floating-rate bonds promise periodic adjustments of the interest rate—to persuade you that you aren't locked into what seems like an unattractively low rate.

Convertible bonds give you the option to convert, or change, corporate bonds into company stock instead of getting a cash repayment. The terms are set at issue. They include the date the conversion can be made, and how much stock each bond can be exchanged for. The conversion option lets the issuer offer a lower initial interest rate, and makes the bond price less sensitive than conventional bonds to changes in the interest rate.

A sinking fund, established at the time a bond is issued, is a cash reserve set aside to finance periodic bond calls.

Bonds with Strings Attached

Callable bonds don't always run their full term. The issuer may **call** the bond, which means pay off the debt before the maturity date. The process is called **redemption**. The first date a bond is vulnerable to call is named at the time of issue. Call, or redemption, announcements are published regularly in The Wall Street Journal.

Issuers may want to call a bond if interest rates drop. If they pay off their outstanding bonds, they can float another bond at the lower rate. (It's the same idea as refinancing a mortgage to get a lower interest rate and make lower monthly payments.) Sometimes only part of an issue is redeemed, rather than all of it. In that case, the bonds that are called are chosen by lottery.

Callable bonds can be less attractive for investors than noncallable ones because an investor whose bond has been called is often faced with reinvesting the money at a lower, less-attractive rate. To protect bondholders expecting long-term steady income, call provisions usually specify that a bond can't be redeemed before a certain number of years, usually five or ten.

> ## REDEMPTION NOTICES
>
> The following is a list of securities called for partial or complete redemption during the week ended Jan. 22. The notices are taken from advertisements appearing in editions of The Wall Street Journal and aren't meant to be definitive. Inquiries regarding specific issues should be directed to the paying agent or, if none is listed, the issuer.
>
> **CORPORATES**
> **Fannie Mae** will redeem on Feb. 4, $100 million of its 6.79% MTN issue due Feb. 4, 2002; and on Feb. 21, $200 million of its 7.8% MTN issue due Feb. 21, 2007.
>
> **MUNICIPALS**
> **City of Wheeling** will redeem on March 1, its parking revenue refunding bonds series 1978 with CUSIP number 963235 BX3 in the amount of $5,000 each, due March 1, 2002. Wesbanco Bank Wheeling is trustee.
> **City of Beacon Industrial Dev~**
> on Feb. 1~

Popular Innovations

Zero-coupon bonds are a popular variation on the bond theme for some investors. Since **coupon**, in bond terminology, means interest, a zero-coupon by definition pays out no interest while the loan is maturing. Instead, the interest **accrues**, or builds up, and is paid in a lump sum at maturity.

You buy zero-coupon bonds at a **deep discount**, or prices far lower than par value. When the bond matures, the accrued interest and the original investment add up to the bond's par value.

Bond issuers like zeros because they have an extended period to use the money they have raised without paying periodic interest. Investors like zeros because the discounted price means you can buy more bonds with the money you have to invest, and you can buy bonds of different maturities, timed to coincide with anticipated expenses, such as college tuition bills, for example.

Zeros have two potential drawbacks. They are extremely volatile in the secondary market, so you risk losing money if you need to sell before maturity. And, unless you buy tax-exempt municipal zeros, you have to pay taxes every year on the interest you would have received had it, in fact, been paid.

This announcement is under no circumstances to be construed as an offer to sell or as a solicitation of an offer to buy any of these securities. The offering is made only by the Prospectus.

$575,000,000

e Worldwide Corporation

uid Yield Option™ Notes due 2016
(Zero Coupon – Senior Secured)
angeable for Shares of Common Stock of

Cole

e Cole Company, Inc.

Price 24.067%

obtained in any State or jurisdiction in which this announcement is circulated
lers or brokers as may lawfully offer these securities in such State or jurisdiction.

Buying and Trading Bonds

Investors can buy bonds from brokers, banks or directly from certain issuers.

Newly issued bonds and those trading in the secondary market are available from securities dealers and from some banks. Treasurys, though, are sold at issue directly to investors without any intermediary—or any commission.

The Bureau of the Public Debt handles transactions in new Treasury issues—such as bills and notes. To buy, you establish a **Treasury Direct** account, which keeps records of the transactions and pays interest directly into your bank account. You can pick up the forms you need at most banks, call Treasury Direct at 800-722-2678 or go to the website at www.treasurydirect.gov to download the forms or have any that you need mailed to you. And you can handle your transactions on the phone or online.

Activity in the bond trading room is every bit as intense as a busy day on the floor of the NYSE.

THE PRICE OF BONDS

Price is one factor that may keep individuals from investing heavily in bonds. While par value of a bond is usually $1,000, bonds are often sold in bundles, or packages, that require a much larger minimum investment. The cost of bonds also limits the diversification you can achieve in your bond portfolio. As a result, many people prefer to buy bond funds, and many of the bonds themselves are bought by large institutional investors, including fund companies.

HOW TRADING WORKS

Most already-issued bonds are traded **over-the-counter (OTC)**, a term that really means over the phone or by computer. Bond dealers across the country are connected via electronic display terminals that give them the latest information on prices. A broker buying a bond tries to find the dealer who is currently offering the best price and calls that dealer to negotiate a trade.

Brokerage firms also have inventories of bonds that they want to sell to clients looking for bonds of particular maturities or yields. Sometimes investors make out better buying bonds their brokers already own—or **make a market in**—as opposed to bonds the brokers have to buy from another firm.

The New York Stock Exchange and American Stock Exchange, despite their names, also list a large number of bonds. Their **bond rooms** are the scene of the same level of brisk, constant trading that occurs on the exchange trading floor.

THE COST ISSUE

While many newly issued bonds are sold without sales expense to the buyer—because the issuer absorbs the cost—all bond trades incur sales costs. The amount you pay to buy an older bond depends on the **commission** earned by the stockbroker involved and the size of the **markup** that's added to the bond.

Markups are not officially regulated, and the total amount is not reported on confirmation orders, so charges can be excessive. A broker should reveal the markup if you ask. Or you can figure it out by finding out the current selling price of the bond and subtracting the buying price. The difference is the markup. If you check with two brokers, you may find that you would pay very different prices to buy the same bond. That means you have to be vigilant so that the cost of trading doesn't outweigh your return.

MONDAY

9AM *T-bills offered on Thursday for Monday sale*

10AM

1 The U.S. Treasury offers 13-week and 26-week T-bills for auction every Monday.

2 Across the country, institutional investors (such as pension funds and mutual funds) who want to buy the major part of the issue ready their competitive bids. Their bids must arrive at the Treasury by 1:00 p.m. Monday, the auction deadline.

11AM

Bidders state the rate they are willing to accept on the bills. In a hypothetical example, one fund might bid 2.205%, another, 2.210%, a third, 2.215%, and a fourth, 2.220%.

3 At the same time, individual investors can submit noncompetitive tenders, or offers, through Treasury Direct. Investors decide how much they want to put into T-bills, and either send a check or authorize a debit for that amount. For example, someone might commit $30,000.

NOON

1PM *Deadline for all bids!*

4 The Treasury accepts bids, from the lowest to the highest rate, until the quota is filled.

1:10 – 1:15 Results announced

2PM

5 Within minutes, Treasury announces the auction results, and bidders learn what the auction rate is and the price they will pay to buy the bills. Using the sample bids above, that rate might be 2.215%. All the competitive bidders who bid rates lower than the cutoff bid have their orders filled at the auction rate. However, the fund whose bid is the cutoff, or auction rate, may not be able to invest as much as it had wanted if the quota has already been filled.

3PM

6 Individuals and small institutions that have submitted non-competitive bids get the auction rate that's been determined by the competitive auction. They can invest as much as they wish, up to $1 million.

4PM

7 If an individual has submitted a check for the purchase amount, as might be the case with a first-time investor, Treasury refunds the difference between the par value and the auction price. But if the investor has authorized a debit, the amount of the purchase is taken out of the designated account. For example, if the auction rate on a 26-week bill was 2.028%, the price for each $1,000 investment would be $989.86. Someone who had written a check for $30,000 would get a refund of $304.20, or $10.14 on each $1,000. But if a debit had been authorized, $29,695.80 would have been taken out of the account.

5PM

8 At maturity, noncompetitive bidders with Treasury Direct accounts can roll over their T-bill investment at the new auction rate, or they can redeem their investment at par value.

Other Bonds, Other Choices

Variety is the hallmark of the bond market—there's something for everyone.

Government agencies and government-sponsored corporations issue bonds to fund specific projects or ongoing operations like mortgage lending, economic development or flood control.

Agency bonds have a double appeal to investors in part because they pay higher interest than Treasurys, yet they're considered almost as free from default. They're issued by full-fledged government agencies, like the Federal Home Loan Bank or the Federal Farm Credit Bank, or by former government agencies that are now public corporations, like Fannie Mae.

READING THE TABLES

Government agency and similar issues are reported regularly in tables that resemble those for Treasury issues. Mortgage-backed issues are included, as well as bonds sold by the World Bank, the Inter-America Development Bank and the Tennessee Valley Authority (TVA).

MORTGAGE MONEY

Mortgage-backed bonds play a major role in keeping the U.S. housing market healthy. The corporations Fannie Mae and Freddie Mac and the federal agency Ginnie Mae (GNMA) buy mortgages that meet their individual criteria from lenders across the country who make what are known as conforming loans. The money they pay for the loans is then available to the lenders to make new loans, which are also eligible for purchase.

The money to buy the mortgages is raised by creating and selling bonds backed by the mortgages, a process known as **securitization**. The bond issuers pass through to the bondholders the principal and interest that individual mortgage holders pay on their loans. Using a similar process, Sallie Mae, formerly the Student Loan Marketing Association, helps to provide funding for student loans.

GOVERNMENT AGENCY & SIMILAR ISSUES

Over-the-Counter mid-afternoon quotations based on large transactions, usually $1 million or more. Colons in bid and asked quotes represent 32nds; 101:01 means 101 1/32.

All yields are calculated to maturity, and based on the asked quote.
*Callable issue, maturity date shown. For issues callable prior to maturity, yields are computed to the earliest call date for issues quoted above par, or 100, and to the maturity date for issues below par.

Source: Bear, Steams & Co. via Street Software Technology Inc.

Fannie Mae Issues

RATE	MAT	BID	ASKED	YLD
2.88	10-05	101:30	102:00	1.67
6.00	12-05	107:17	107:19	1.79
5.50	2-06	107:00	107:02	1.91
2.13	4-06	100:04	100:06	2.03
5.50	5-06	107:03	107:05	2.18
2.25	5-06	100:10	100:12	2.07
5.25	6-06	107:00	107:02	2.14
4.38	10-06	105:09	105:11	2.30
2.63	11-06	100:21	100:23	2.36
4.75	1-07	105:29	105:31	2.59
5.00	1-07	107:03	107:05	2.45
7.13	3-07	113:15	113:17	2.55
5.25	3-07*	100:16	100:18	0.29
5.25	4-07*	107:30	10:	
5.00	5-07*	10:		

RATE	MAT	BID	ASKED	YLD
6.00	1-12*	103:13	103:15	2.22
6.13	3-12	112:27	112:29	4.22
6.25	3-12*	104:24	104:26	1.86
5.50	7-12*	103:08	103:10	3.12
5.25	8-12	104:14	104:16	4.60
4.38	9-12	100:14	100:16	4.30
4.75	2-13*	99:23	99:25	4.78
4.63	5-13	99:06	99:08	4.72
6.25	5-29	111:16	111:20	5.40
7.13	1-30	123:19	123:23	5.41
7.25	5-30	125:15	125:19	5.4
6.63	11-30	116:29	11	

Freddie Mac
RATE	MAT	BID	ASKED	YLD
3.75	4-04	1		

RATE	MAT	BID	ASKED	YLD
5.25	1-06	106:10	106:12	1.87
1.88	2-06	99:27	99:29	1.92
2.38	4-06	100:22	100:24	2.03
5.50	7-06	107:22	107:24	2.20
2.75	8-06	101:07	101:09	2.23
4.88	3-07	106:25	106:27	2.56
4.50	7-07*	101:07	101:09	1.65
3.50	9-07	102:12	102:14	2.79
3.25	2-08*	99:24	99:26	3.30
2.75	3-08	98:31	99:01	3.00
3.50	4-08*	100:14	100:16	3.04
5.75	4-08	110:14	110:16	3.05
5.13	10-08	107:31	108:01	3.26
5.75	3-09	110:23	110:25	3.43
5.75	4-09*	100:30	101:00	1.04
4.75	8-09*	101:14	101:16	1.74
6.63	9-09	115:05	115:07	3.6
7.00	3-10	117		

Prices are quoted as **bid** and **asked**. The 2.25 Fannie Mae issue quoted here had a high bid of 100:10 ($1,031.25). The lowest price asked was 100:12 ($1,037.50). Like Treasury issues, the numbers after the colon refer to 32nds.

This bond's **yield** (**to maturity**) is 2.07%, less than the bond's stated interest rate, in part because it is trading at a premium, or above par. But the 4.75 issue due in February 2013 with bid and ask prices at a discount, or less than par, has a yield of 4.78%, slightly higher than its coupon rate.

BONDS

U.S. SAVINGS BONDS

To many people, bonds mean the U.S. savings bonds you buy through a regular savings program at work or to use as gifts. Savings bonds differ from investment bonds in several important ways. Perhaps the most significant is that they're not marketable, which means that, while you can redeem your bonds for cash, you can't sell them to another investor. But they are alike in the sense that they pay interest on your investment principal and can be redeemed for cash at maturity. And because they're issued by the federal government, there's no danger of default.

There are three types of savings bonds: Series EE and Series I, plus Series HH, which were issued through August 2004. There will be no new HH bonds, but existing ones will continue to pay interest until maturity. Series EE and I bonds are sold in eight denominations. Interest is added monthly, and paid for up to 30 years. You can redeem your bonds for cash after 6 or 12 months, depending on the date of issue, but there is an early redemption fee equal to three-months interest if you cash the bonds during the first five years.

Series I bonds, which you buy at their par value, are inflation indexed. That means they guarantee a real rate of return over and above inflation, which will help protect your purchasing power. The interest on Series I bonds is a combination of the percentage change in the Urban Consumer Price Index (CPI-U) and a fixed rate of return that's set for the life of the bond at the time it is issued. Series EE bonds are sold at half their face value and earn interest at 90% of the market yield on five-year Treasury notes. New rates for both I and EE bonds are announced twice a year, in May and November.

BOND RESOURCES

You can find valuable information on how savings bonds work, the interest they pay, the way that interest is taxed, and how to buy them at www.savingsbonds.gov. In addition, the website links you to calculators that help you determine how long it will take to reach a financial goal, such as paying for college. And it explains how you may be able to use interest on Series I and certain Series EE savings bonds to pay post-secondary tuition expenses without owning income tax on those earnings.

Among the rules that apply are that you must be at least 24 when you buy the bonds and must use the money for either your child's education or your own. The full tax exclusion is available to married couples filing a joint return or single filers, provided that their modified adjusted gross income (MAGI) is less than the annual limit for the year when the tuition is paid.

When you buy a **savings bond**, you get a printed certificate. It's registered in your name or the name of the person you buy it for. You need that certificate to cash the bond. If you lose it, you can try to replace the lost bond by writing to The Bureau of Public Debt, Parkersburg, West Virginia 26106-1328.

A Look at the World of Bonds

Type of bond	Par value	Maturity period
CORPORATE BONDS Corporate bonds are readily available to investors. Companies use them rather than bank loans or new stock issues to finance expansion and other activities.	**$1,000**	**Short-term:** **1–5** years **Intermediate-term:** **5–10** years **Long-term:** **10–20** years
MUNICIPAL BONDS More than one million municipal bonds have been issued by states, cities and other local governments to pay for construction and other projects.	**$1,000** (but may vary)	From **1** month to **40** years
T-NOTES These debt issues of the federal government are a major source of government funding to keep operations running and to pay interest on national debt.	**$1,000** (also issued in $5,000, $10,000, $100,000 and $1 million denomina-tions)	**2–10** years
T-BILLS Treasury bills are the largest component of the money market—the market for short-term debt securities. The govern-ment uses them to raise money for immediate spending at lower rates than bonds or notes.	**$1,000** (also issued in amounts up to $1 million)	**4** weeks **13** weeks **26** weeks
AGENCY BONDS The most popular and well known are the bonds issued by **Ginnie Mae**, formerly the Government National Mortgage Association (GNMA). But many federal and state agencies also issue bonds to raise money for their operations and projects.	**$1,000** often sold in lots of **$25,000** and up	From **30** days to **20** years

BONDS

Trading details	Rated	Tax status	Call provisions	Interest and safety
Through brokers, either on an exchange or OTC	Yes	Taxable	Callable	**Riskier** than government bonds, but potentially **higher yields** than government bonds. Very little default risk with highly rated bonds Usually **large minimum investment required**
Through brokers, OTC. Often, investment bankers underwrite whole issues and resell to dealers and brokers	Yes	Exempt from federal taxes Exempt from state and local taxes under certain conditions	Sometimes callable	**Lower interest rates** than comparable corporate bonds **because of tax-exemption** Especially attractive to high-tax-bracket investors, who benefit from tax-exemption feature Usually **large minimum investment required**
New issues: Through Treasury Direct **Outstanding issues**: Through brokers, OTC	Not rated, since considered risk-free	Exempt from state and local taxes	Sometimes callable	**Maximum safety** from default since backed by federal government, but relatively **low** interest rates
New issues: By auction at any Federal Reserve Bank **Outstanding issues**: Through brokers, OTC	Not rated, since considered risk-free	Exempt from state and local taxes	Not callable	**Short-term investments**, with no periodic interest payments. Instead, interest consists of the difference between a discounted buying price and the par amount paid at maturity
By brokers, OTC or directly through banks	Some issues rated by some services	**Ginnie Mae** taxable **Some other federal agencies** exempt from state and local taxes	Sometimes callable	Marginally **higher risk and higher interest** than Treasury bonds Usually **large minimum investment required**

Mutual Funds: Putting It Together

A mutual fund buys investments with money it gets from selling shares in the fund, and manages its portfolio to meet its financial goals.

Most investment professionals agree that it's smarter to own a variety of stocks and bonds than to gamble on the successful performance of just a few. But diversifying can be tough because buying a portfolio of individual stocks and bonds can be expensive. And knowing what to buy—and when—takes time and concentration.

Mutual funds offer one solution: When you put money into a fund, it's pooled with money from other investors to create much greater buying power than you would have investing on your own.

Since a fund can own hundreds of different securities, its success isn't dependent on how one or two holdings do. And the fund's professional managers keep constant tabs on the markets, trying to adjust the portfolio for the strongest possible performance.

How Mutual Funds Work

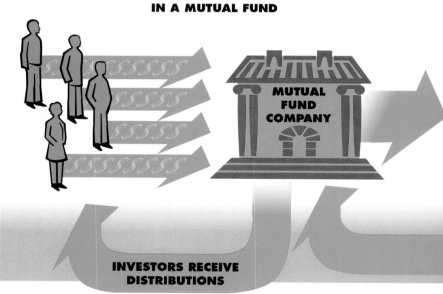

A LARGE NUMBER OF PEOPLE WITH MONEY TO INVEST BUY SHARES IN A MUTUAL FUND

MUTUAL FUND COMPANY

INVESTORS RECEIVE DISTRIBUTIONS

PAYING OUT THE PROFITS

A mutual fund makes money in two ways: by earning dividends or interest on its investments and by selling investments that have increased in price. The fund distributes, or pays out, these profits (minus fees and expenses) to its investors.

Income distributions are paid from the income the fund earns on its investments. **Capital gain distributions** are paid from the profits from selling investments. Different funds pay their distributions on different schedules—from once a day to once a year. Many funds offer investors the option of reinvesting all or part of their distributions to buy more shares in the fund.

You pay taxes on the distributions you receive from the fund, whether the money is reinvested or paid out in cash. But if a fund loses more than it makes in any year, it can use the loss to offset future gains. Until profits equal the accumulated losses, distributions aren't taxable, although the share price may increase to reflect the profits.

HOW A MUTUAL FUND IS CREATED

A mutual fund company decides on an investment concept

Then it issues a prospectus

Finally, it sells shares

CREATING A FUND

Investment companies, also called mutual fund companies, brokerage firms, banks, and insurance companies offer mutual funds for sale to individuals and institutional investors, such as money managers or pension funds. Most fund sponsors offer a range of fund types, while others specialize in one category of funds.

Each new fund has a professional manager, an investment objective, and a plan, or investment program, it follows in building its portfolio. The funds are marketed to potential investors with ads in the financial press, through direct mailings and press announcements, and often with the support of registered representatives who make commissions selling them.

THEIR POOLED MONEY HAS MORE BUYING POWER

THE FUND MANAGER INVESTS THE MONEY IN A COLLECTION OF STOCKS, BONDS OR OTHER SECURITIES

SUCCESSFUL INVESTMENT ADDS VALUE TO THE FUND

OPEN- AND CLOSED-END FUNDS

Most mutual funds are **open-end funds**. That means the fund sells as many shares as investors want. As money comes in, the fund grows. If investors want to sell, the fund buys their shares back. Sometimes open-end funds are closed to new investors when they grow too large to be managed effectively—though current shareholders can continue to invest money. When a fund is closed this way, the investment company often creates a similar fund to capitalize on investor interest.

Closed-end funds more closely resemble stocks in the way they are traded. While these funds do invest in a variety of securities, they raise money only once and offer only a fixed number of shares that are traded on an exchange or over the counter. The market price of a closed-end fund fluctuates in response to investor demand as well as to changes in the value of its holdings.

The Mutual Funds Market

Mutual funds never invest at random. Each shops for products that fit its investment strategy.

There are three main categories of mutual funds:

- **Stock funds**, also called equity funds, invest primarily in stocks
- **Bond funds** invest primarily in corporate or government bonds
- **Money market funds** make short-term investments to keep their share value fixed at $1

THE PART DIVERSITY PLAYS

Most funds diversify their holdings by buying a wide variety of investments that correspond to their category. A typical stock fund, for example, might own stock in 100 or more companies providing a range of different products and services. The charm of diversification is that losses on some stocks may be offset—or even outweighed—by gains on others.

On the other hand, some funds are extremely focused. For example:

- **Precious metal funds** trade chiefly in mining stocks
- **Sector funds** buy shares in a particular industry, such as healthcare, electronics or utilities
- **High-yield bond funds** buy risky bonds to produce high income

The appeal of focused funds is that when they're doing well, the returns can be outstanding. The risk is that a change in the economy or in the sector can wipe out any gains.

FIRST MUTUAL FUND

The first investment trust, a forerunner of modern mutual funds, was put together by Robert Fleming in the 1800s. Fleming collected money from fellow Scots and traveled to the U.S., where he invested—with notable success—in growing enterprises. And he shared the profits with the other investors.

The first U.S. mutual funds, Massachusetts Investors Trust and State Street Research Investment Trust, were established in 1924 and are still doing business. But today there are thousands of mutual funds to choose from.

STOCK FUNDS

The name says it all: Stock funds invest in stocks. But stock fund portfolios vary, depending on the fund's investment objectives. For example, some stock funds invest in well-established companies that pay regular dividends. Others invest in younger, more growth-oriented firms or companies that have been operating below expectation for several years.

Unlike individual investors, who might buy several different types of stocks to diversify their portfolios, a fund typically concentrates in one area, like blue chips or small-company stocks. A fund's prospectus identifies its major holdings and its investment goals—though funds sometimes buy more widely to try to provide stronger returns.

There are several different types of stock funds. A key distinction among them is that some stress growth, some income and some a combination of the two. Some funds involve more risk to capital than others because they buy stock in emerging companies. The profits on all stock fund distributions are taxable (unless held in a qualified retirement account), but no tax is due on the increased value of a fund until you sell it.

BOND FUNDS

Like bonds, bond funds provide income. Unlike bonds, however, these funds have no maturity date and no guaranteed repayment of the amount you invest, in part because the fund's holdings have different terms.

On the plus side, you can automatically reinvest your distributions to buy more shares. And you can buy shares in a bond fund for much less than you would need to buy a bond on your own—and get a diversified portfolio to boot. For example, you can often invest $1,000 to open a fund, and make additional purchases for smaller amounts.

Bond funds come in many varieties, with different investment goals and strategies. There are investment-grade **corporate bond funds** and riskier junk bonds often sold under the promising label of high-yield funds. You can choose long- or short-term **U.S. Treasury funds**, funds that combine issues with different maturities, and a variety of tax-free **municipal bond funds**, including some limited to a particular state.

IT'S ALL IN THE FAMILY

Mutual fund companies usually offer a variety of funds—referred to as a family of funds—to their investors. Keeping your money in the family can make it easier to transfer money between funds, but like most families, some members do better than others.

MONEY MARKET FUNDS

Money market funds invest to maintain their value at $1 a share, so they're often described as cash equivalent investments. Typically, you earn interest on the investments the fund makes. Since these funds are considered stable in value, some investors prefer them to stock or bond funds. But the interest the funds pay is low when interest rates are low. As an added appeal, most money market funds let investors write checks against their accounts. There's usually no charge for check-writing—although there may be a per-check minimum.

The two main categories of bond funds are **taxable** and **tax-free**. Distributions earned on corporate and U.S. government funds (including Treasurys and agency funds) are taxed. There's no federal tax on municipal bond fund distributions, and no state or local taxes for investors who live in the municipality that issues the underlying bonds. New Yorkers, for example, can buy **triple tax-free** New York funds and keep all their earnings.

Money market funds also come in two varieties, **taxable** and **tax-free**. Taxable funds buy the best-yielding short-term corporate or government issues available, while tax-free funds are limited to buying primarily municipal debt. Taxable funds pay slightly higher dividends than tax-free funds, but investors must pay tax on any distributions they receive. In either case, the rate a fund pays is roughly the same as bank money market accounts or CDs.

Targeted Investments

Mutual funds aim at particular targets. To hit them, the funds make certain types of investments.

INVESTMENT OBJECTIVE

Every mutual fund—stock, bond or money market—is established with a specific investment objective that fits into one of three basic goals:

- **Current income**
- **Some income and growth**
- **Future growth**

To achieve its objective, the fund invests in securities it believes will produce the results it wants. To identify those securities, a fund may do a vast amount of research, including what's known as a bottom-up style, which involves a detailed analysis of individual companies. When the objective is small-company growth or the focus is on emerging markets, the process can be more difficult because there's only limited information readily available.

In addition, each fund manager has a buying style, seeking a particular type of investment from the pool that may be appropriate for the objective. Some equity-fund managers, for example, stress **value**, which means buying stocks whose price is lower than might be expected. Other managers may be **contrarians**, buying investments that others are shunning.

THE RISK FACTOR

There is always the risk that a fund won't hit its target. Some funds are, by definition, riskier than others. For example, a fund that invests in small new companies takes the chance that some of its investments will do poorly because it believes that some, at least, will do very well.

FUNDS TAKE AIM

These charts group funds in three categories by investment objective. They also illustrate the correlation between a fund's objective and the risks it may face.

INCOME FUNDS

Kind of fund	Investment objective	Potential risks	What the fund buys
Agency bond	Income and regular return of capital	Value and return dependent on interest rates	Securities issued by U.S. government agencies and related institutions
Corporate bond	Steady income	Interest-rate changes and inflation	Highly rated corporate bonds, with various maturities
High-yield bond	Highest current income	High-risk bonds in danger of default	Low-rated and unrated corporate and government bonds
International money market	Income and currency gains	Changes in currency values and interest rates	CDs and short-term securities
Municipal bond	Tax-free income	Interest-rate changes and inflation	Municipal bonds in various maturities
Short-/inter-mediate-term debt	Income	Less influenced by changes in interest rate	Different types of debt issues with varying maturities, depending on type of fund
U.S. Treasury bond	Steady income	Interest-rate changes and inflation	Long-term government bonds

GROWTH AND INCOME

Kind of fund	Investment objective	Potential risks	What the fund buys
Balanced	Income and growth	Less growth during strong equity markets than all-equity funds, dividend cuts	Part stocks and preferred stocks (usually 60%) and part bonds (40%)
Equity income	Income and growth	Less growth during strong equity markets than all-equity funds, dividend cuts	Blue chip stocks and utilities that pay high dividends
Growth and income	Growth plus some current income	Less growth during strong equity markets than all-equity funds, dividend cuts	Stocks that pay high dividends and provide some growth
Income	Primarily income	Interest-rate changes and reduced interest payments	Primarily bonds, but some dividend-paying stocks

GROWTH FUNDS

Kind of fund	Investment objective	Potential risks	What the fund buys
Aggressive growth, also called capital appreciation	Long-term growth	Very volatile and speculative. Risk of above-average losses to get above-average gains	Stocks of new or under-valued companies expected to increase in value
Emerging markets	Growth	Gains limited to index gains and no protection against index losses	Stocks in companies in developing countries
Equity index	Imitate the stock market	Average gains and losses for the market the index tracks	Stocks represented in the index the fund tracks
Global equity	Global growth	Gains and losses depend on stock prices and currency fluctuation	Stocks in various markets including the U.S.
Growth	Above-average growth	Can be volatile. Some risk of loss to principal to get higher gains	Stocks in mid-sized or large companies whose earnings are expected to rise quickly
International equity	International growth	Potentially volatile, based on currency fluctuation and political instability	Stocks in non-U.S. companies
Sector	Growth	Volatile funds, dependent on right market timing to produce results	Stocks in one particular industry, such as energy or transportation
Small-company growth	Long-term growth	Volatile and speculative. Risk of above-average losses to get higher gains	Stocks in small companies traded on the exchanges or over-the-counter
Value funds	Growth	Often out of step with overall market	Stocks in companies whose prices are lower than they seem to be worth

HEDGING

International fund managers may use a practice called hedging to protect the return on their funds. That's because if a currency gains value in relation to others, investments **denominated**, or sold, in those other currencies have less value when they are converted into the stronger currency. To protect against losses that could result from that situation, mutual funds often buy futures contracts on a currency at preset exchange rates.

Funds that hedge may put up to 50% of their total assets in currency contracts rather than stocks or bonds. But other funds don't hedge at all, figuring that exposure to other currencies is part of the reason for investing overseas.

Focused Funds

Mutual fund companies have expanded their horizons—and the opportunities they offer to investors—by developing specialty funds.

Stock funds are the oldest and still the most popular category of mutual fund. But as investing in funds has grown increasingly popular, fund companies have responded by expanding their offerings in a effort to appeal to people with specific investment goals. Many of the newer funds have narrowly defined objectives and strategies, focusing on previously untapped market segments. Others have been added to compete with popular existing funds.

SPECIAL INVESTMENT OBJECTIVES

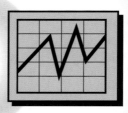

INDEX FUNDS

Index funds are designed to produce the same return that you would get if you owned all the stocks in a particular index—such as the Dow Jones Industrial Average or the S&P 500. While this diversification would be overwhelming for an individual, it's all in a day's work for an index fund. There are index funds tracking almost every known stock index for large, mid-cap and small companies—as well as bond market indexes and several international indexes.

And there are a number of specialty indexes that track narrower segments of the market, some of which are also the basis of an index fund.

Index funds are popular because the performances of the major stock and bond indexes often surpass the returns that professional mutual fund money managers achieve by following a particular investment strategy. Investing in an index fund can eliminate having to decide among specific stock or bond funds. It can also provide a balance to other investments.

In a falling market, however, managed fund performance can outshine index funds. And as a rule, index funds that track small companies have produced spottier results than growth funds that invest directly in specific small companies.

QUANT FUNDS
These funds are named for their quantitative investment style—they aim to beat the index funds they imitate by relying on statistical analysis to decide which securities will top the benchmarks. Instead of buying all the stocks in the S&P 500, they buy selected stocks that their numbers tell them will turn a higher profit.

An **efficient market** isn't one that works quicker or smarter. Rather, it's the object of constant, intensive analysis, and the information is available to everyone almost immediately. **Inefficient markets**, conversely, aren't as widely analyzed and can offer enormous opportunity for profit to savvy fund managers who track them.

MARKET-NEUTRAL FUNDS

Some newer mutual funds follow a controversial investment strategy once the realm of private hedge funds: market-neutral investing, also called zero beta or long/short portfolio investing.

Market neutral funds aren't trying to beat the market but to maintain average annual returns that are a few points above three-month U.S. Treasury bills, regardless of whether the market is going up or down. That means providing a measure of stability within your investment portfolio.

These funds use computer programs to evaluate and rank possible investments quantitatively, analyzing factors such as price/earnings ratios, yield, volatility and earnings growth. The funds then buy the top-ranking stocks and sell short the ones ranked at the bottom.

Some market-neutral funds use multiple managers in an attempt to diversify their risk. Since meeting the fund's goals depends so heavily on accurate assessments of future market movements, a manager's decisions may even be more crucial to overall return than if the fund were following a more conventional trading approach.

TAX-FREE FUNDS

Although the earnings on all stock funds and most bond funds are taxable, it's possible to invest in a variety of mutual funds that pay tax-free distributions. Tax-free income is particularly appealing to people in the highest tax brackets, since they may come out ahead at tax time, even though some interest may be subject to the alternative minimum tax (ATM).

The biggest tax savings occur when a person who lives in a high-tax state—like California—buys a fund that specializes in municipal bonds issued there. The interest is free of both state and federal tax. And when a fund buys bonds issued by a municipality like New York City, the interest is triple tax-free for residents who invest in the fund.

The dilemma that many funds face is finding enough high-quality investments to meet investor demands. This can be especially hard for tax-free funds, and even harder for single-state funds.

SECTOR FUNDS

Sector funds focus on the stocks of a particular industry or segment of the economy, such as technology, healthcare or financial services. In that sense, they are out of step with the underlying principle behind mutual funds—diversification. While a sector fund is more diversified than a single stock, there is nothing in the fund portfolio to offset a downturn in its sector.

Since sectors are highly volatile, they offer an opportunity for big profits to investors who ride the right wave. Often, though, one year's hot sector is slow the next. Technology and emerging markets are just two of the sectors that have had roller coaster rides in recent years.

Precious metal funds

resemble sector funds, since all their money is invested in mining stocks and bullion—but they're more predictable. When inflation is high or there's political turmoil, precious metal funds tend to do well because they're seen as a hedge against instability.

SOCIALLY CONSCIOUS FUNDS

Mutual fund companies have also created funds to attract investors whose strong political, religious or social commitments make them unwilling to invest in companies whose business practices are at odds with their beliefs. A fund might avoid tobacco companies, companies with poor environmental records or those that sell products investors consider unacceptable.

Each fund explains in its prospectus the criteria, called **screens**, that it uses to identify acceptable investments.

Socially responsible funds have been criticized for putting more emphasis on their individual agendas than on solid investment principles. But there's evidence that value-based funds, as a group, provide returns on a par with the broader universe of funds, and that some have strong performance records, according to the research company Morningstar, Inc.

Inside a Mutual Fund

Mutual funds operate virtually around the clock, managing their portfolios and serving their investors.

A mutual fund has two distinct yet intertwined businesses: making a profit and providing services to its clients. Each fund, or closely related group of funds, is run by one or more professional managers responsible for both its day-to-day operations and for its performance. In fact, some experts believe the success of a fund is so closely linked to the skill of its manager that they select funds based almost entirely on their managers—and lose interest when a manager leaves.

A typical fund depends on a battalion of employees, including financial analysts, accountants, traders, sales representatives and support staff. Equally crucial are the software programs, computers and other electronic equipment—and the people who keep them running—that make this kind of operation work.

Operating the Fund

Each fund buys and sells securities in a specific financial market or markets. A stock fund, for example, buys and sells shares through brokers on the exchanges, over-the-counter and in private transactions. Because they trade in large volumes, mutual funds are known as **institutional traders**.

While clients may not be able to talk to a telephone representative at the fund until around 8:00 a.m. local time, reports on the fund's previous day's performance are available in the financial press and online well before then.

Every day the fund's manager and analysts digest how the markets did the day before, where the fund stands in relation to other funds and its benchmark indexes, and what economic news might affect the fund's value.

Servicing the Investor

Funds are never static. Money moves in and out constantly—in staggering amounts. Investors buy and sell shares in response to their expectations for an individual fund or type of fund, or as a reaction to what's happening in the markets as a whole.

Regulators have introduced new rules in response to market timing and late trading abuses that were uncovered in the mutual fund industry in 2003 and 2004.

Mail pours into mutual fund offices by the ton. Each piece must be opened, coded with an account number, and put in the right in basket. Checks are credited to the right client accounts at the day's closing price. Then they're shipped off to the bank.

Checks and confirmations from the previous day's transactions are mailed out to clients, making good on the claim that mutual funds are among the most liquid investments.

OTHER WAYS TO BUY FUNDS

One big question investors face when buying mutual funds is whether to buy directly from the fund—the process that's described here—or through a broker, bank or other financial agent. You may wonder, for example, whether professionals can identify better performing funds than you can on your own.

In fact, the evidence shows that there's very little difference in performance. However, buying through an adviser generally means paying a sales charge, which can reduce what you actually gain on the fund. That charge is offset only if you hold the fund for an extended period. On the other hand, some experts point out that if an adviser gives you the incentive to invest, it's worth the added cost.

A significant portion of mutual funds assets—about one-third of the total—are held in retirement savings plans, including 401(k)s and IRAs, and in other tax-deferred or tax-free accounts according to the Investment Company Institute (ICI).

Fund managers and analysts are always in the market for new securities that meet the fund's investment objectives. Their research staff provides up-to-the-minute price information and analysis.

Trading managers authorize buy and sell orders. Traders, looking for the best price, keep their eyes on the computer screen and their hands on the telephone. Other employees keep a running count of the fund's balance sheet.

In time to meet the press deadline, details of the fund's current value and the change from the day before are calculated by the staff and sent to NASD, formerly the National Association of Securities Dealers.

Investors can open accounts, send checks or have money transferred into their accounts throughout the day. At the close of the trading day, at 4 p.m. in New York, the price is set and the money is invested in shares of the fund. Written confirmations follow all transactions.

Telephone reps keep busy answering client questions and acting on orders. Conversations are recorded to back up the actions the reps take. There are very few transactions that can't be done by phone—as long as you sign up for phone services when the account is opened. Fund transfers, however, have to go to accounts registered in the same name(s).

At most funds, customers can talk to a representative after the exchanges close, placing orders that will be acted on the next day. And they can place orders online. After the people go home, automated phone systems continue to provide details about earnings, balances and recent trades, as well as other account and performance information.

Mutual Fund Quotations

As the popularity of mutual funds has grown, so has the information about them.

As investors have put more money into mutual funds, there's been a revolution in the way that fund performance is reported. The Wall Street Journal, for example, tracks individual funds daily, monthly, quarterly and annually in different formats.

The funds themselves supply the basic information daily to NASD, formerly the National Association of Securities Dealers, and Lipper Inc. calculates the performance, cost and rankings.

A fund must have net assets of at least $100 million to be listed in these tables, by NASD rules. Generally, a family of funds needs assets of $5 billion or so to stay alive. Otherwise, it's vulnerable to a takeover by a larger, more aggressive firm.

M U T U A L

NAV$ 2/28	Fund Name	Inv Obj	Feb	1Yr	3Yr-R	5Yr-R	10Yr-R	Max Init Chrg	Exp Ratio
7.25	US Sht	SE	+3.9	−14.9 C	NS ..	NS ..	NS ..	0.00	1.57
	Price Funds:								
18.44	Balanced	BL	−2.2	+9.3 B	+15.4 B	+14.1 B	+13.7 A	0.00	0.81
30.63	BlChip	GR	−2.8	+18.3 C	+25.6 B	+23.6 A	NS ..	0.00	0.95
10.96	CA Bond	SS	−.6	+5.9 A	+6.9 A	+6.5 A	+7.7 B	0.00	0.58
12.80	CapApp	CP	−2.0	−0.5 D	+10.5 D	+11.9 D	+11.9 D	0.00	0.64
17.44	CapOpp	CP	−3.6	+1.5 D	+11.9 D	NS ..	NS ..	0.00	1.35
9.62	CorpInc	AB	−2.3	−0.3 E	+6.5 C	NS ..	NS ..	0.00	0.80
21.12	DivGro	GI	−1.6	+4.6 D	+20.4 C	+19.5 C	NS ..	0.00	0.80
9.84	DvsfSmGr	SC	−9.5	−15.0 C	NS ..	NS ..	NS ..	0.00	1.25
8.95	EmgMktB	WB	+0.8	−25.9 E	+6.7 B	NS ..	NS ..	0.00	1.25
8.12	EmMktS	EM	−3.0	−29.8 C	−9.7 B	NS ..	NS ..	0.00	1.75
25.46	EqInc	EI	−0.8	+1.5 D	+16.6 C	+17.9 B	+14.4 B	0.00	0.79
33.68	EqIndex	GI	−3.1	+19.5 A	+26.5 A	+23.8 A	NS ..	0.00	0.40
21.14	Europe	EU	−1.8	+10.0 C	+20.0 C	+17.2 B	NS ..	0.00	1.05
10.50	ExtIndex r	MC	−5.1	−.7 C	NS ..	NS ..	NS ..	0.00	NA
16.60	FinSvcs	SE	−0.9	+4.3 A	NS ..	NS ..	NS ..	0.00	1.25
10.86	FL Inter	IM	−0.8	+5.3 B	+5.3 D	+5.6 B	NS ..	0.00	0.60
17.45	ForEq	IL	−1.8	+2.8 C	+9.1 C	+7.6 B	NS ..	0.00	0.75
9.44	GNMA	MG	−0.9	+5.0 C	+6.8 B	+6.8 A	+8.4 B	0.00	0.70
11.03	GA Bond	SS	−0.7	+5.7 A	+6.8 A	+6.5 A	NS ..	0.00	0.65
9.85	GlbBond	WB	−4.2	+4.8 C	+5.4 C	+6.1 B	NS ..	0.00	1.20
14.77	GlbStk	GL	−2.1	+9.6 B	+16.4 B	NS ..	NS ..	0.00	1.20
31.69	Growth	GR	−2.7	+14.8 C	+23.2 C	+20.5 B	+17.1 C	0.00	0.75
25.69	Gr&In	GI	−0.5	+2.6 D	+17.2 D	+16.9 D	+14.2 D	0.00	0.78
15.67	HelSci	HB	−4.0	+11.2 C	+15.4 C	NS ..	NS ..	0.00	1.18
8.39	HiYield	HC	−0.2	+2.8 A	+9.9 A	+7.5 C	+8.6 D	0.00	0.81
8.58	N Inc	AB	−2.4	+2.2 E	+5.5 E	+6.1 D	+8.0 E	0.00	0.71
9.78	IntlBond	WB	−4.3	+6.9 B	+4.8 D	+6.3 B	+8.6 A	0.00	0.86
16.86	IntDis	IL	+2.6	+4.1 B	+4.7 D	+0.7 E	+6.9 D	0.00	1.47
14.53	IntlStk	IL	−1.9	+2.7 C	+8.9 C	+7.5 B	+9.6 B	0.00	0.85
7.72	Japan		−3.1		6.0 B	NS			1.20

NAV$ 2/28	Fund Name	Inv Obj
27.83	StkIdxI	GI
27.82	StkIdxZ	GI
11.23	UtilityZ	UT
17.65	GloZ	GL
9.69	PugetSnd	SE
16.27	Purisima TR p	MP
	Putnam Funds Class A	
8.74	AmGv p	LG
9.34	AZ TE	SS
8.92	Asia p	PR
11.84	AABal p	MP
10.35	AACn p	MP
13.45	AAGr n	MP
10.59	BalRet p	BL
8.77	CATx p	SS
21.90	CapApr p	CP
7.28	CapOp p	SC
19.28	Conv p	MP
13.61	DvrEq p	GL
11.28	Dvrin p	GT
6.97	EmMkt p	EM
15.54	EqIn p	EI
21.64	EuGr p	EU
9.47	FLTx	SS
17.76	Geo p	BL
12.64	GlGv p	WB
12.41	GlGr p	GL
12.87	GlGrInA p	GL
15.14	GlNtRs p	NR
20.39	GrIn p	GI
13.96	GrInIIA p	GI

The **mutual fund company's name** appears first, followed by its different funds listed in alphabetical order.

r after the fund name means the fund charges a fee to redeem shares for cash. This type of charge is also known as a **back-end load**.

p after the fund name means the fund charges a fee for marketing and distribution costs, also known as **12b-1 fees**.

t after the fund name means both r and p apply: You pay back-end loads and 12b-1 fees.

NAV is the fund's **net asset value**. A fund's NAV is the dollar value of one share in the fund, and the price a fund pays you per share when you sell. It's figured by totaling the value of all the fund's holdings and dividing by the number of shares. For example, the NAV of the Price Blue Chip fund is $30.63.

A fund's NAV moves up or down to reflect market conditions, though the short-term changes are rarely dramatic. Those changes are reported for each trading day, as are year-to-date yields.

R stands for ranking. The return each fund has provided is compared with the results for other funds with the same **investment objective**. Investment objectives, expressed as a two-letter abbreviation in the column following the fund's name, identify the type or types of investments the fund makes. A chart identifying each of the categories and what each buys is printed in the monthly, quarterly and annual reviews. The example highlighted here, EU, indicates a fund investing in Europe.

Total return is the percentage of gain (+) or loss (−) the fund has provided, assuming all distributions have been reinvested. This chart reports those figures for 1-, 3-, 5- and 10-year periods as well as for the previous month. An **NS** in a column indicates that the fund wasn't operating at the beginning of the period.

Here, for example, the total return on Putnam Funds' Balanced Return fund is up 4.5% over one year, and an average of 13% over three years and 12.3% over ten years.

Many mutual funds charge a **load**, or sales charge, when you buy shares. Loads are a percentage of the investment amount and may be charged when you buy, when you sell or throughout the period you own the fund. Funds that charge when you buy are often identified as Class A shares, as the Putnam Funds are here. When those charges apply, they are listed in the column labeled **maximum initial charge**. If 0.00 appears, the fund is a **no-load**.

Load charges are not included in the fund's **expense ratio**, but the annual expenses you pay are figured in. The differences in return among funds with the same investment objective can be the result of the fees they charge.

	Total Return			Max Init Chrg	Exp Ratio		NAVs 2/28	Fund Name	Inv Obj	Feb	1Yr	Total Return				Max Init Chrg
r	3Yr-R	5Yr-R	10Yr-R									3Yr-R	5Yr-R	10Yr-R		
5 A	NS ..	NS ..	NS ..	0.00	0.30		9.91	HiQual p	LG	−2.3	+4.1 E	+5.8 D	+6.1 C	+7.7 D	4.7
5 A	+26.2 A	+23.6 A	NS ..	0.00	0.40		7.42	HiYTotP p	HC	−0.4	−8.5 E	NS ..	NS ..	NS ..	4.7
4 E	NS ..	NS ..	NS ..	0.00	0.57		7.78	HiYT il p	HC	−0.5	−4.0 D	NS ..	NS ..	NS ..	4.7
5 B	NS ..	NS ..	NS ..	0.00	1.13		61.65	Hih p	HB	−3.3	+11.2 C	+20.2 B	+25.2 A	+20.5 D	5.7
5 A	NS ..	NS ..	NS ..	0.00	NA		8.12	HYAd p	HC	−0.6	−10.7	+3.8 E	+4.7 E	+8.8 D	4.7
							10.74	HiYd p	HC	−0.6	−9.3 E	+5.5 E	+5.7 D	+9.1 C	4.7
							6.75	Incm p	AB	−2.4	+1.5	+5.4 E	+5.9 D	+8.4 C	4.7
3 C	+6.6 B	+6.6 B	+7.4 E	4.75	1.07		19.54	IntlGr p	IL	−2.4	+10.4 A	+17.3 A	+12.8 A	NS ..	5.7
5 E	+5.7 D	+5.3 D	NS ..	4.75	0.99		10.96	IntGrln p	IL	−1.3	+2.3 C	NS ..	NS ..	NS ..	5.7
3 B	−8.3 B	−4.8 A	NS ..	5.75	1.46		13.42	IntlNop p	IL	−2.9	+11.3 A	+10.7 B	NS ..	NS ..	5.7
4 C	+13.5 B	+13.0 C	NS ..	5.75	1.22		4.92	IntUS p	SG	−1.2	−5.5 B	+6.0 A	+6.2 A	NS ..	3.2
9 C	+10.2 D	+9.7 D	NS ..	5.75	1.39		13.88	IntVoy p	IL	−1.1	+15.9 A	+20.0 A	NS ..	NS ..	5.7
6 C	+15.1 B	+14.5 B	NS ..	5.75	1.31		14.97	Inv p	GR	−3.6	+25.0 A	+28.6 A	+24.2 A	+19.8 A	5.7
2 C	+13.0 D	+12.8 C	+12.3 D	5.75	1.13		9.60	MaTx p	SS	−0.6	+4.9 D	+6.3 C	+6.0 B	NS ..	4.7
	+6.3 C	+6.1 D	+7.8 B	4.75	0.77		9.28	MiTx p	SS	−0.9	+3.9 E	+6.0 C	+5.6 D	NS ..	4.7
5 D	+19.0 C	+18.5 B	NS ..	5.75	1.03		9.19	MNTX p	SS	−0.4	+4.7 D	+5.7 D	+5.5 D	NS ..	4.7
	NS ..	NS ..	NS ..	4.75	NA		9.30	Muni p	GM	−0.9	+5.1 C	+6.3 C	+6.3 C	+6.4 B	4.7
3 D	+12.0 C	+12.0 C	+12.6 B	5.75	0.97		57.68	NwOp p	GR	−6.2	+12.9 C	+16.0 D	+19.8 C	NS ..	5.7
2 D	+19.1 A	NS ..	NS ..	5.75	1.37		13.59	NwValA p	GI	−2.4	+4.4 D	+15.0 E	NS ..	NS ..	5.7
1 E	+4.6 E	+5.2 D	+8.5 C	4.75	0.97		9.32	NJTx p	SS	−0.7	+4.4 E	+6.1 C	+5.6 D	NS ..	4.7
8 B	−7.3 A	NS ..	NS ..	5.75	2.10		8.94	NYTx p	SS	−0.8	+4.8 D	+6.1 C	+5.3 D	+7.5 C	4.7
8 B	+18.6 B	+18.5 A	+13.7 C	5.75	0.99				SS	−0.6	+4.9 D	+6.4 B	+6.4 A	NS ..	5.7
9 B	+21.0 B	+18.2 A	NS ..	5.75	1.32										5.7
8 D	+6.0 D	+5.8 C	NS ..	4.75	0.96										5.7
4 C	+14.9 C	+14.9 B	+13.3 B	5.75	1.00										4.7
4 D	+3.6 C	+3.7 D	+7.4 C	4.75	1.26										4.7
2 C	+17.8 A	+13.5 A	+12.8 A	5.75	1.18										4.7
2 C	+16.5 B	NS ..	NS ..	5.75	1.70										4.7
3 C	+3.4 A	+6.8 A	+8.0 B	5.75	1.20										4.7
3 C	+18.7 C	+18.7 C	+15.7 B	5.75	0.84										4.7
0 C	+13.0 D	NS ..	NS ..	5.75	0.96										4.7

The ranking code assigns an A to funds that rank among the top 20%, a B to the next 20% and so on, with an E indicating the bottom 20%. When a fund with a higher total return gets a lower rating than a fund with a lower return, as with the one-year returns on the Price Balanced and Blue Chip funds, it is because they have different objectives.

Some funds receive similar rankings for all periods, like the Price Balanced fund, while others, like the company's Emerging Markets B, have less consistent returns and rankings.

MUTUAL-FUND OBJECTIVES

Categories compiled by The Wall Street Journal, based on classifications by Lipper Inc.

STOCK FUNDS

Emerging Markets (EM): Funds that invest in emerging-market equity securities, where the "emerging market" is defined by a country's GNP per capita and other economic measures.

Equity Income (EI): Funds that seek high current income and growth of income through investment in equities.

European Region (EU): Funds that invest in markets or operations concentrated in the European region.

Global Stock (GL): Funds that invest in securities traded outside of the U.S. and may own U.S. securities as well.

Gold Oriented (AU): Funds that invest in gold mines, gold-oriented mining finance houses, gold coins or bullion.

Health/Biotech (HB): Funds that invest in companies related to health care, medicine and biotechnology.

International Stock (IL) (non-U.S.): Canadian; International; International Small Cap.

Latin American (LT): Funds that invest in markets or operations concentrated in the Latin American region.

Large-Cap Growth (LG): Funds that invest in large companies with long-term earnings that are expected to grow significantly faster than the earnings of stocks in major indexes. Funds normally have above-average price-to-earnings ratios, price-to-book ratios and three-year earnings growth.

Large-Cap Core (LC): Funds that invest in large companies, with wide latitude in the type of shares they buy. On average, the price-to-earnings ratios, price-to-book ratios, and three-year earnings growth are in line with those of the U.S. diversified large-cap funds' universe average.

Large-Cap Value (LV): Funds that invest in large companies that are considered undervalued relative to major stock indexes based on price-to-earnings ratios, price-to-book ratios or other factors.

Midcap Growth (MG): Funds that invest in midsize companies with long-term earnings that are expected to grow significantly faster than the earnings of stocks in major indexes. Funds normally have above-average price-to-earnings ratios, price-to-book ratios and three-year earnings growth.

Midcap Core (MC): Funds that invest in midsize companies, with wide latitude in the type of shares they buy. On average, the price-to-earnings ratios, price-to-book ratios, and three-year earnings growth are in line with those of the U.S. diversified midcap funds' universe average.

Midcap Value (MV): Funds that invest in midsize companies that are considered undervalued relative to major stock indexes based on price-to-earnings ratios, price-to-book ratios or other factors.

TAXABLE BOND FUNDS

Short-Term Bond (SB): Ultra-short Obligation; Short Investment Grade Debt; Short-Intermediate Investment Grade Debt.

Short-Term U.S. (SU): Short U.S. Treasury; Short U.S. Government; Short-Intermediate U.S. Government debt.

Intermediate Bond (IB): Funds that invest in investment-grade debt issues (rated in the top four grades) with dollar-weighted average maturities of five to 10 years.

Intermediate U.S. (IG): Intermediate U.S. Government; Intermediate U.S. Treasury.

Long-Term Bond (AB): Funds that invest in corporate- and government-debt issues in the grades.

Long-Term U.S. (LU): General U.S. Government; General U.S. Treasury; Target Maturity.

General U.S. Taxable (GT): Funds that invest in general bonds.

High-Yield Taxable (HC): Funds that aim for high current yields from fixed-income securities tend to invest in lower-grade debt.

Mortgage (MT): Adjustable Rate Mortgage; GNMA; U.S. Mortgage.

World Bond (WB): Emerging Markets Debt; Global Income; Int...

It's All in the Charts

You can use a number of benchmarks and time frames to evaluate a fund's performance.

There are a number of tools you can use to evaluate how well individual mutual funds, or mutual funds in general, are performing. The Wall Street Journal regularly prints **benchmark indexes and averages** that track different categories of investments, including stocks and bonds, which are the underlying investments of mutual funds. There are also indexes tracking mutual funds grouped by investment objective.

For example, if the Standard & Poor's 500-stock index reports a gain in large-company stock performance, as it does in the example here, you can reasonably expect that a mutual fund investing in large-company stocks will also have a gain. Similarly, if you're discouraged by the performance of your small-cap stock fund, it may make you more comfortable to know that Vanguard's Small Company Index fund, which tracks the Russell 2000 (a small-cap benchmark), is reporting only a small gain over the last year.

MUTUAL FUND INDEXES

The performance of various categories of mutual funds, each with a different investment objective, is reported in the **Lipper Indexes**. Some of the indexes track funds that invest in stocks and others track types of bond funds. Each index reports the gain (+) or loss (−) for one category of fund, based on the performance of the largest funds in that category.

The numbers in the first column indicate the combined NAVs of all the funds in the sample. That gives you a sense of which categories of fund are the largest, specifically large cap value funds and multi-cap core funds.

The next three columns indicate the percentage the current NAV has increased or decreased from the previous day, for the week and since December 31. These fluctuations in value are shown in percentages, which means you can compare the gains or losses of different fund categories. In most cases, the most relevant information is the change from December 31, though patterns may emerge, such as losses at the previous close but gains over the week, that are related to what happened in the market as a whole.

Benchmarks for Mutual-Fund Investors

	YEAR-TO-DATE	FOUR WEEKS	ONE YEAR	3 YRS (annualized)	5 YR (annual
DJIA (w/divs)	+ 17.37%	+ 11.02%	+ 18.93%	+ 26.75%	+ 26
S&P 500 (w/divs)	+ 10.95	+ 7.19	+ 21.93	+ 30.25	+ 27
Small-Co. Index Fund¹	+ 1.82	+ 11.55	− 11.95	+ 10.23	+ 14
Lipper Index: Europe	+ 0.08	+ 3.23	− 1.51	+ 18.93	+ 16
Lipper Index: Pacific	+ 17.59	+ 11.84	+ 12.79	− 7.43	− 3
Lipper L-T Govt²	− 0.65	+ 0.22	+ 5.48	+ 7.01	+ 6

¹Vanguard's: tracks Russell 2000　　　　²Includes government agenc

PERFORMANCE YARDSTICKS

While recent mutual fund winners and losers tend to make the headlines, a multi-year overview of the various fund categories is a more reliable indicator of how they have performed over time, both individually and in relation to each other, than what has happened in any given year.

During the five-year period that this chart covers, nearly all of the fund categories show significant gains over the past 12 months. But there are differences in the three- and five-year numbers, evidence of the impact of market losses in the funds' underlying investments in 2000-2002. For example, compare the longer-term returns of harder-hit large-cap funds with those of small-cap funds.

LIPPER INDEXES

| | | PERCENT CHANGE FROM | | |
Stock-Fund Indexes	PRELIM CLOSE	PREVIOUS CLOSE	WEEK AGO	DE
Large-Cap Growth	3027.81	-0.62	+2.00	+1.
Large-Cap Core	2204.05	-0.76	+1.23	+1.
Large-Cap Value	9464.37	-0.71	+0.94	+0.
Multi-Cap Growth	2616.59	-0.35	+2.66	+2.
Multi-Cap Core	6864.83	-0.54	+1.65	+1.
Multi-Cap Value	4063.54	-0.39	+1.35	+1.
Mid-Cap Growth	635.49	-0.30	+2.54	+2.3
Mid-Cap Core	634.66	-0.25	+1.91	+1.8
Mid-Cap Value	947.61	-0.28	+1.82	+1.7
Small-Cap Growth	538.53	-0.39	+3.40	+3.6
Small-Cap Core	382.05	-0.46	+1.96	+2.3
Small-Cap Value	608.42	-0.45	+1.57	+2.0
Equity Income Fd	675.00	-0.14	+5.80	+6.2
Science and Tech Fd	675.00	-0.14	+5.80	+6.2
International Fund	785.87	+0.45	+2.52	+3.5
Balanced Fund	4961.01	-0.21	+1.30	+1.07
Bond-Fund Indexes				
Short Inv Grade	254.10	+0.25	+0.46	+0.37
Intmdt Inv Grade	303.00	+0.60	+1.28	+0.94
US Government	400.02	+0.65	+1.26	+0.82
GNMA	435.12	+0.36	+0.89	+0.67
Corp A-Rated Debt	1077.96	+0.64	+1.33	+0.93

Indexes are based on the largest funds within the same investment objective and do not include multiple share classes of similar funds.
Source: Lipper Inc.

Performance Yardsticks
How Fund Categories Stack Up

INVESTMENT OBJECTIVE	FEBRUARY	YEAR-TO-DATE	12 MONTHS	3 YEARS*	5 YEARS*
DIVERSIFIED STOCK and STOCK/BOND FUNDS					
Large-Cap Core (LC)	+1.16%	+2.74%	+34.55%	-3.52%	-1.33%
Large-Cap Growth (LG)	+0.60	+2.36	+33.32	-6.49	-3.83
Large-Cap Value (LV)	+1.90	+3.50	+40.06	+0.63	+3.08
Midcap Core (MC)	+1.52	+3.97	+47.87	+5.40	+10.82
Midcap Growth (MG)	+0.81	+3.58	+44.94	-3.28	+4.13
Midcap Value (MV)	+2.07	+4.61	+54.49	+10.23	+12.83
Small-Cap Core (SC)	+1.13	+4.60	+60.09	+10.01	+13.01
Small-Cap Growth (SG)	-0.45	+3.77	+58.85	+1.41	+7.19
Small-Cap Value (SV)	+1.66	+4.53	+59.16	+14.53	+16.01
Multicap Core (XC)	+1.23	+3.36	+39.91	+0.24	+3.57
Multicap Growth (XG)	+0.63	+3.12	+42.82	-5.23	-0.45
Multicap Value (XV)	+1.85	+3.94	+42.82	+2.99	+5.97
Equity Income (EI)	+1.71	+2.96	+36.88	+1.82	+3.82
S&P 500 Funds (SP)	+1.34	+3.14	+37.59	-1.65	-0.65
Specialty Divers. Equity	+0.16	-0.28	-5.82	-1.06	-1.14
Balanced (BL)	+1.11	+2.44	+24.67	+1.81	+3.05
Stock/Bond Blend (MP)	+0.95	+2.36			
Avg. U.S. Stock Fund [1]	+1.10	+3.40			

CHOOSING BENCHMARKS

The key to using a benchmark effectively in making investment decisions is to be sure that the benchmark you choose correlates as closely as possible with the fund or other investment you want to evaluate. Otherwise what the benchmark reports about its segment of the market may reveal little or nothing about how well your fund has been doing in relation to its peers.

You can get a sense of the problem you'd encounter if you used the return on the small-cap core funds reported in the chart above to evaluate a fund that invested primarily in large-cap stocks. The same would be true if you evaluated the small-cap core fund against the S&P 500, an index of large-company stocks.

It's also important to remember that past performance by itself can't predict future results of either a fund category or an individual fund. That's true in large part because it is impossible to anticipate the timing of ups and downs in the market or how long those periods might last.

THE EFFECT OF FEES

Performance figures for the funds include all asset-based fees the fund charges for management and other expenses. The higher the fees a specific fund charges, the more difficult it may be for its performance to equal or surpass the results for other funds in that category.

You can get a sense of the relative expense of each fund in The Wall Street Journal's monthly mutual fund reviews. That information is provided in the final column of information for each fund, under the heading Expense ratio. Experts point out that even half a percentage point can make a significant difference over time.

The information is most relevant when you compare two funds with the same or similar investment objectives. For example, index funds typically have low fees, and international equity funds have high ones.

One way that fund managers may try to compensate for higher-than-average fund expenses is by increasing the level of risk they take in selecting investments for the fund. That might result in a certain amount of style drift, which may occur when a fund alters its investment strategy while not changing its stated objective.

Tracking Fund Performance

There are several formulas for measuring mutual fund performance. The bottom line is whether the fund is meeting your investment goals.

Whether a mutual fund aims for current income, long-term growth or a combination of the two, there are three ways to track its performance and judge whether or not it is profitable. Investors can evaluate a fund by:

- Following changes in share price, or **net asset value (NAV)**
- Figuring **yield**
- Calculating **total return**

You can compare a fund's performance to similar funds offered by different companies, or you can evaluate the fund in relation to other ways the money could have been invested—stocks or bonds, for example.

Because return is figured differently for each type of investment, there isn't a simple formula for comparing funds to individual securities.

NAV CHANGE

$$\frac{\text{Value of fund}}{\text{Number of shares}} = \text{NAV}$$

for example

$$\frac{\$52,500,000}{3,500,000} = \$15$$

A fund's **NAV** is the dollar value of one share of the fund's stock. It's figured by dividing the current value of the fund by the number of its outstanding shares. A fund's NAV increases when the value of its holdings increases. For example, if a share of a stock fund costs $15 today and $9 a year ago, it means the value of its holdings increased about 66% per share, and you could sell at a profit.

YIELD

$$\frac{\text{Distribution per share}}{\text{Price per share}} = \text{Yield (\%)}$$

for example

$$\frac{\$.58}{\$10.00} = 5.8\%$$

Yield measures the amount of income a fund provides as a percentage of its NAV. A long-term bond fund with a NAV of $10 paying a 58 cent income distribution per share provides a 5.8% yield. You can compare the yield on a mutual fund with the current yield on comparable investments to decide which is providing a stronger return. Bond fund performance, for example, is often tracked in relation to individual bonds or bond indexes.

TOTAL RETURN

$$\frac{\text{Change in value + dividends}}{\text{Cost of initial investment}} = \frac{\text{Total}}{\text{Return (\%)}}$$

for example

$$\frac{\$832}{\$8,000} = 10.4\%$$

A fund's **total return** is the annual amount your mutual fund investment changes in value plus the distributions the fund pays on that investment. It's typically reported as **percentage return**, figured by dividing the dollar value of the total return by the amount of the initial investment. For example, an $8,000 investment with a one-year total return of $832 ($700 increase in value plus $132 in reinvested distributions) has an annual percentage return of 10.4%.

WATCHING RETURN

The most accurate measure of a mutual fund's past and current performance is its **total return**, or its increase in value plus its reinvested distributions. Total return is reported for several time periods, typically for as long as the fund has been in operation. When the figure is for periods longer than a year, the number is annualized, or converted to an annual figure by dividing the total return over the period by the number of years.

Annualized figures reflect the impact of gains and losses over the period that's being tracked. But they don't report whether the return represents a fairly consistent performance from year to year or a seesaw of ups and downs.

Among the key factors that influence total return are the direction of the overall market or markets in which the fund is invested, the performance of the fund's portfolio of investments, and the fund's fees and expenses.

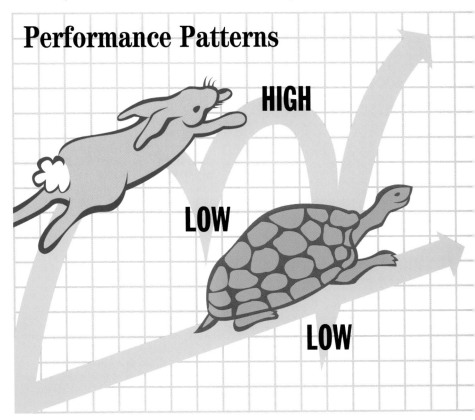

Performance Patterns

HIGH

LOW

LOW

THE IMPACT OF TIME

Most financial experts stress that mutual funds are best suited for long-term investing. They believe you should ignore the short-term peaks and valleys and be unconcerned about finding the top-performing funds of the year. For one thing, the individual fund or fund category that provides the strongest return in one year is unlikely to be in that position the following year.

The experts also point out that you can identify a number of funds in various categories that have provided returns consistent with the appropriate benchmark year after year, though these funds may never make it to the top—or the bottom—of the performance charts.

Holding a fund for an extended period also allows you to amortize the cost of the front-end load if you've purchased Class A shares. In the short term, paying this load reduces your return since the amount of the sales charge is subtracted before your principal is invested. If you stay in the fund, the effect of the sales charge essentially disappears. But if you trade funds frequently, paying repeated sales charges can consume a big share of your potential earnings.

Another argument for maintaining a long-term perspective with a diversified portfolio of funds is that you decrease the risk of missing the periods of growth that often follow depressed or falling markets. It's also true that selling a fund when its NAV has dropped means locking in any losses to that point, though you might decide that is a better choice than taking the chance of having an even greater loss.

The Prospectus

The prospectus provides a detailed roadmap of a fund—covering everything from its objective and fees to its portfolio holdings and manager.

The Securities and Exchange Commission (SEC) requires all mutual funds to publish a prospectus and issue a copy to potential investors before they buy or with the confirmation of an initial investment. The prospectus must explain the fund's objectives, management, fees and past performance, and provide details of its operation. Each fund also issues semiannual and quarterly reports with updated statistics.

LEAPS AND BOUNDS

Mutual funds report their results in a variety of graphs and charts to show historical performance. Funds have the potential to grow in value over the long term when distributions are reinvested, though they can also lose value.

$10,800 — 1 Year
$14,693 — 5 Years
$21,588 — 10 Years
$31,720 — 15 Years

In this example, a hypothetical investment of $10,000 grew at an annualized rate of 8% over 15 years. The results are not based on the return of any specific investment.

A FUND'S OPERATIONS

A fund's prospectus explains the programs and policies the fund's management uses to achieve its investment goals.

As an investor, you have the right to vote on changes a fund proposes in its underlying financial policies, including the amount of money it can **leverage**, or borrow to make additional investments. Since mutual fund investors are actually shareholders of the fund, you vote in the same way corporate shareholders do, either in person at the annual meeting, by proxy or online. And you vote on major issues, not on day-to-day matters like the fee structure.

FEES

A summary of fees and expenses usually appears near the beginning of the prospectus. The fees can range anywhere from a low of 0.2% up to 8.5%, and are the basis of the fund's **expense ratio**. That's the percentage of the fund's assets deducted to cover operating and management expenses. The ratio doesn't include sales charges or **transaction costs**, which are also deducted.

Sales charges, also known as loads, are levied by some, but not all, funds. The charges are typically figured as a percentage of the amount you invest. **Front-end loads**, charged at the time you purchase your shares, are the most common. Or you may pay a **back-end load**, also known as a contingent deferred sales charge, when you sell shares during the first few years after purchase. A third type, known as a **level load**, has no front- or back-end charges. Back-end and level load funds have higher annual fees than front-end load funds.

When a fund offers you a choice of when to pay the sales charge, it typically identifies front-end loads as Class A shares, back-end loads as Class B shares and level-loads as Class C shares.

Redemption charges are a type of back-end load some fund companies charge on certain of their funds to discourage frequent in-and-out trading.

Marketing fees (called **12b-1 fees**) cover marketing and advertising expenses, and are sometimes used to pay employee bonuses. About two-thirds of all mutual funds charge these fees.

Exchange fees can apply when money is shifted from one fund to another within the same mutual fund company.

PORTFOLIO TURNOVER RATE

All open-end mutual funds trade securities regularly—some more regularly than others. A fund's **portfolio turnover rate** reveals how much buying and selling is going on. The range can be enormous, with some funds turning over more than 100% annually. In general, high turnovers mean higher transaction expenses. That means the fund needs higher returns to offset the cost.

THE NUTS AND BOLTS

The prospectus also tells you how to buy and sell shares in the fund, as well as how to use all the fund's services.

Minimum investments exist for most funds. A higher amount is required for opening an account than for adding to it. Sometimes the minimum initial investment is as low as $500, sometimes as high as several thousand dollars.

Investment options let you buy online, over the phone, by mail, through a broker or with automatic direct deposit.

Reinvestment options let you decide what to do with the money you earn. You can plow your distributions back into the fund, take the money in cash or some combination of the two.

Exchange services let you transfer money from one fund to another.

Redemption options provide lots of ways for you to get your money out of the fund. They include checks, wire transfers, electronic transfers and automatic withdrawal plans.

Check-writing privileges let you use checks to redeem your holdings or pay your bills. However, redeeming stock and bond funds by check has tax consequences, since there's always a profit or loss on the investment. Money market funds are the only ones that really work like checking accounts.

BREAKPOINTS

Regulators at the state and federal levels have been examining mutual fund fees, including how clearly the costs of buying and holding funds are explained to investors and whether certain fees are appropriate. An earlier inquiry into **breakpoints** revealed that many investors were not receiving the discounts to which they were entitled on large-volume purchases of front-load fund shares.

PROSPECTUS

PAX WORLD FUND

- Statement of objective
- Investment risk
- Fund fees and expenses
- Fund performance
- Result of $1,000 investment
- List of fund investments
- Shareholder services
- How to redeem shares

While a prospectus provides all the details of a fund's operation, it also tries to portray the fund in the best possible terms. Smart investors carefully sift through all the information.

International Funds

If someone needed to invent a reason for the existence of mutual funds, investing abroad might be the best one.

The number of mutual funds that invest in overseas markets has multiplied rapidly over the past ten years. In addition to diversification, professional management and ease of investing, overseas funds give even small investors access to markets they couldn't enter on their own. There are overseas stock funds, bond funds and money market funds to appeal to a variety of interests. While they're often referred to generically as international funds, there are actually four specific categories of funds: **international**, **global**, **regional** and **country**.

INTERNATIONAL FUNDS

Also known as **overseas funds**, international funds invest exclusively in stock or bond markets outside the U.S. By spreading investments throughout the world, these funds balance risk by owning securities not only in mature, slow-growing economies but also in the more volatile economies of emerging nations.

GLOBAL FUNDS

Also called **world funds**, these funds include U.S. stocks or bonds in their portfolios as well as those from other countries. The manager moves the assets around, depending on which markets are doing best at the time. That means that the percentage invested in U.S. stocks can vary widely, depending on their performance in comparison with others around the world.

Despite what the name suggests, global funds often invest up to 75% of their assets in U.S. companies.

REGIONAL FUNDS

These funds focus on a particular geographic area, like the Pacific Rim, Latin America or Europe. Many mutual fund companies that began by offering international or global funds have added regional funds to capitalize on the growing interest in overseas investing and on the strength of particular parts of the world economy.

Like the more broad-based funds, regional funds invest in several different countries so that even if one market is in the doldrums, the others may be booming.

Regional funds tend to focus on groups of smaller countries or emerging markets, where one country may not issue enough securities to make a single country fund viable.

EUROPE

THE RISK OVERSEAS

When you put money into overseas funds, you don't have to deal with currency fluctuations or calculate taxes—they're handled by the fund. But the value of any fund that invests in other countries is directly affected not only by market conditions but by exchange rates and potential political instability.

Overseas **bond funds** are less dependable than U.S. funds as income producers because changes in the dollar's value directly affect the fund's earnings. If a bond fund is earning high interest, but the country's currency is weak against the dollar, the yield is less. For example, if a fund earns £100 when £1 equals $2, the yield is $200. But if the pound drops in value, and £1 equals $1.50, the yield is only $150.

Equity funds are somewhat less vulnerable to currency fluctuation because they profit from capital gains. So if international markets are paying high dividends, a U.S. investor can make money, especially when the dollar is weak. However, if the dollar strengthened by 10% during a year that an overseas stock fund gained 10%, there would be no profit. And if the dollar strengthened by 20%—which may happen as part of the regular ebb and flow of international markets—you could actually have a loss of 10%.

COUNTRY FUNDS

These funds allow you to concentrate your investments in a single overseas country—even countries whose markets are closed to individual investors who aren't citizens. When a fund does well, other funds are set up for the same country, so that there may be many funds all investing in the same country. Many single-country funds are closed-end funds that are traded on a stock market once they have been established.

By buying stocks and bonds in a single country, you can reap the benefits of a healthy, well-established economy, or profit from the rapid economic growth as emerging markets start to industrialize or expand their export markets. The risk of investing in a single country, however, is that a downturn in the economy can create a drag on fund performance.

GERMANY

Closed-end funds that buy big blocks of shares in a country's industries can influence share prices and sometimes corporate policy—just as institutional investors may when they buy U.S. stocks.

INTERNATIONAL INDEX FUNDS

Like other index funds, international index funds attempt to produce the results you would get if you owned all the stocks in a particular index. The Morgan Stanley Capital International Europe, Australasia, Far East Index (EAFE), for example, follows around 1,000 stocks from around the world.

International index funds are an easy way to start investing in overseas markets. And they generally have smaller management and operating fees than other types of funds that invest abroad. But, particularly in more volatile markets, index funds may not produce results as strong as those funds run by managers who are constantly monitoring their holdings.

Futures and Options

Futures and options are complex and volatile but also useful investments.

FUTURES ARE <u>OBLIGATIONS</u> TO BUY OR SELL a specific commodity—such as corn, gold or Treasury bonds—on a specific day for a preset price.

OPTIONS MAY BE A <u>RIGHT</u> OR AN <u>OBLIGATION</u> TO BUY OR SELL a specific item—such as stocks, precious metals or Treasury bonds—for a preset price during a specified period of time.

[Calendar notations: JUNE — "pchs'd gold options" (Thur 1); "Gold options expire — must trade or let go!" (16 circled); "WHEAT FUTURES EXPIRE — trade or they're mine!" (24)]

DERIVATIVE INVESTMENTS

Futures and options belong to a group of financial products known as **derivatives** because their prices reflect, or are derived from, the value of the item underlying the futures or options contract. For example, the item could be a commodity, such as wheat underlying a futures contract, or a security, such as a stock underlying an options contract.

Buying and selling a futures or options contract does not transfer ownership, as buying or selling a stock does. Rather, the contract spells out the terms of the deal, including the rights and obligations of the buyer and seller, the underlying product—also called the underlying instrument—to be purchased or sold, the quantity and the price.

REDUCING THE RISK

For some, futures and options can be ways to reduce risk. Farmers who commit themselves to sell grain at a good price are protected if prices drop. Investors who sell options on stock they own can offset some of their losses if the market collapses.

Other investors trade futures and options because the risk of a possible loss is offset by the opportunity for a gain. But individual investors are usually small players in the futures markets because the stakes are high and the returns are unpredictable.

LEVERAGE AND RISK

Leverage, in financial terms, means using a small amount of money to control an investment of much greater value.

Futures contracts are highly leveraged instruments because, under most circumstances, you can buy or sell a futures contract with a **good faith deposit** called an **initial margin** of less than 10% of the underlying item's value. For example, if you buy a gold contract worth $35,000 when the futures contract represents 100 ounces of gold and the gold futures price is $350 an ounce, the required good faith deposit might be $3,500. That gives you 10-to-1 leverage since you control the $35,000 investment with your $3,500 deposit.

During periods when the price of gold is volatile, it could change by $30, $40, or even $50 within a short period of time. If the price went up $50, to $400 an ounce, the value of your futures contract on 100 ounces of gold would jump $5,000 ($50 an ounce x 100 ounces = $5,000). That's an almost 150% gain on your $3,500 deposit. But, of course, the opposite could also happen. If the price of an ounce of gold dropped $50, the value of your futures contract would drop $5,000, and you'd have to add $1,500 to your margin account to cover the loss.

So while leverage means that the initial amount required to buy a futures contract, known as opening a futures position, is relatively small, changes in the price of the contract are magnified in relation to your initial deposit.

MAKING A PROFIT

If you buy a futures contract, you make a profit if the price of the underlying item rises above the contract price. That's because you are able to buy the item at the lower contract price rather than at the current, higher price.

If you sell a futures contract, you make a profit if the price of the underlying item falls below the contract price. That's because you are able to sell at a higher price than the current market price.

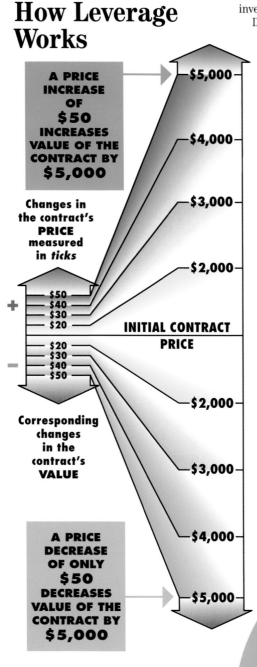

How Leverage Works

BUYS A $35,000 CONTRACT

A $3,500 INVESTMENT

100 oz. GOLD

|← LEVERAGE →|
OF
10 to 1

A PRICE INCREASE OF $50 INCREASES VALUE OF THE CONTRACT BY $5,000

$5,000
$4,000
$3,000
$2,000

Changes in the contract's PRICE measured in ticks

$50
$40
$30
$20

INITIAL CONTRACT PRICE

$20
$30
$40
$50

Corresponding changes in the contract's VALUE

$2,000
$3,000
$4,000
$5,000

A PRICE DECREASE OF ONLY $50 DECREASES VALUE OF THE CONTRACT BY $5,000

Futures contracts and options expire on a specific day each month and are dropped from trading. In the U.S. contracts expire on the third Saturday and can be exercised or offset on or before the third Friday.

Commodities

Modern life depends on raw materials—the products that keep people and businesses going. Anticipating what they'll cost fuels the futures market.

Commodities are raw materials: the wheat in bread, the silver in earrings, the oil in gasoline and a thousand other products. Most producers and users buy and sell commodities in the **cash market**, commonly known as the **spot market** because the full cash price is paid on the spot.

DETERMINING CASH PRICES

Commodity prices are based on **supply and demand**. If a commodity is plentiful, its price will be low. If it's hard to come by, the price will be high.

Supply and demand for many commodities move in fairly predictable seasonal cycles. Tomatoes are cheapest in the summer when they're plentiful (and most flavorful), and most expensive in the winter when they're out of season. Soup manufacturers plan their production season to take advantage of the highest-quality tomatoes at the lowest prices.

But it doesn't always work that way. If a drought wipes out the Midwest's wheat crop, cash prices for wheat surge because bakers buy up what's available to avoid a short-term crunch. Or if political turmoil in the Middle East threatens the oil supply, prices at the gas pumps jump in anticipation of supply problems.

MINIMIZING FUTURE RISK

Since people don't know when such disasters will occur, they can't plan for them. That's why **futures contracts** were invented—to help businesses minimize risk. A baker with a futures contract to buy wheat for $3.20 a bushel is protected if the spot price jumps to $3.70—at least for that purchase.

Farmers, loggers and other commodity producers can only estimate the demand for their products and try to plan accordingly. But they can get stung by too much supply and too little demand—or the reverse. Similarly, manufacturers have to take orders for future delivery without knowing the cost of the raw materials they will need to make their products. That's why they buy futures contracts in the products they make or use: to smooth out the unexpected price bumps.

What's in a Contract and What Can Affect Its Price

PRICES RISE WHEN — Bad weather ruins U.S. wheat crop

WHAT THE CONTRACT IS FOR AND WHAT IT COSTS — ONE WHEAT CONTRACT IS 5,000 BUSHELS. If wheat is $3.20 a bushel, one contract is worth **$16,000**

PRICES FALL WHEN — Russia has bumper crop of wheat

CASH PRICES AS CLUES

The derivative markets watch cash prices closely. The price of a futures contract for next month, or five months from now, is based on today's prices, seasonal expectations, anticipated changes in the weather, the political scene and dozens of other factors, including what the market will bear.

The fluctuation in cash prices provides clues to what consumers can expect to pay in the marketplace for products made from the raw materials.

FINANCIAL COMMODITIES

Though we don't think of dollars or yen or Treasury bonds as commodities, they really are. Money is the raw material of trade, both domestic and international. What the interest rate will be next summer, or what the dollar will be worth against the euro, concerns people whose businesses depend on the money supply, or on what imported materials will cost. They use futures to hedge against sudden changes in rates or currency values.

However, institutional traders, rather than individuals, do the bulk of financial futures trading, both on futures exchanges and in private, over-the-counter transactions.

While the same forces of supply and demand affect the shopper in the supermarket or the driver at the gas pumps, the futures market doesn't deal in five pounds of sugar or ten gallons of gas. Efficiency demands that commodities be sold in large quantities.

Mideast turmoil causes oil shortage

Insects ravage cane crops

Pound gains in value against dollar

ONE GASOLINE CONTRACT IS 42,000 GALLONS

If gasoline is $1.10 a gallon, one contract is worth
$46,200

ONE SUGAR CONTRACT IS 112,000 POUNDS

If sugar is 21.33¢ per pound, one contract is worth
$23,890

ONE STERLING CONTRACT IS 62,500 POUNDS

If a pound is selling at $1.8032, one contract is worth
$112,700

Oil producers increase output

Health fad causes drop in sugar consumption

Falling interest rates in U.K. lower pound's appeal

CASH PRICES

GRAINS AND FEEDS

	Wed	Tues	Yr.Ago
arley, top-quality Mpls., bu	2.00-.55	2.00-.50	2.22½
ran, wheat middlings, KC ton	69.-71.0	67.-69.0	63.00
rn, No. 2 yel. Cent. Ill. bu	bp2.17	2.21	2.20½
rn Gluten Feed, Midwest, ton	66.-89.0	c66.-89.0	100.00
ttonseed Meal, Clksdle, Miss. ton	185.-190.	190-192½	157.50
miny Feed, Cent. Ill. ton	58.00	60.00	71.00
eat-Bonemeal, 50% pro. Ill. ton.	230.00	230.-235.	220.00
s, No. 2 milling, Mpls., bu	1.49¾-64¾	153¼-66¼	1.57
ghum, (Milo) No. 2 Gulf cwt	4.30	4.37	4.3¢
bean Meal, Cent. Ill., 44% protein-ton	195.-197.	197½-201½	
bean Meal, ent. Ill., 48% protein-ton	208.-211.	211½-21⁵	
beans, No. 1 yel Cent.-Ill. bu	bp6.47		
eat, ring 14%-pro Mpls. bu			

As the chart shows, the price range for bran increased Wednesday from the level on Tuesday—and both are higher than last year's price. So cereal lovers might reasonably expect to pay more for raisin bran next fall. But the other prices illustrate that the cash market in each product operates independently of the others.

The Futures Exchanges

Futures are traded on exchanges that offer markets in everything from pork bellies to stock indexes.

Futures contracts linked to a range of commodities and financial products are traded on futures exchanges in the U.S., on exchanges in Europe and Asia, and in hundreds of private, over-the-counter transactions arranged for specific clients through banks, brokerage firms and other financial institutions.

Typically, exchange-traded contracts are traded only on the exchange that issues them, and attract both individual and institutional investors. Private contracts, on the other hand, are almost always commercial arrangements.

Exchanges provide speedy clearing of trades, an accurate record of prices, trading limits to prevent excessive price fluctuations both for floor and electronic transactions, and a system to assure that an investor's obligations to buy or sell are met. However, since over-the-counter trading isn't regulated, those protections can't be guaranteed.

EXCHANGE RULES

Each exchange develops the terms and conditions of the futures contracts that are listed for trading on that exchange. The same or similar futures contracts may be traded on more than one exchange, but normally one exchange's contract on a particular commodity dominates its competitors on other exchanges in terms of trading volume and liquidity.

The major types of futures contracts currently trading are based on agricultural products, metals, energy products, interest-rate instruments, stock indexes, single stocks, and currencies. The last four are referred to as financial futures.

To trade futures, you open an account with a futures brokerage firm known as a **futures commission merchant (FCM)** or an **introducing broker (IB)**, who will execute and record your trades. Your money and assets are held in a separate account, segregated from the firm's own money. You pay a commission and fees to trade futures as you do when you buy or sell stocks and bonds.

When you're ready to trade, you give your broker an order to buy or sell one or more futures contracts, either to open a position or to cancel a position you hold with an offsetting trade. The broker sends your order to an exchange floor or enters it in an electronic trading system.

When an order is filled, the details of the purchase and corresponding sale are matched, recorded, and confirmed.

MARKET REGULATION

The Commodity Futures Trading Commission (CFTC) is the federal agency responsible for monitoring the activity on the exchanges. Its role is comparable to the SEC. The exchanges also scrutinize themselves and enforce regulations through the **National Futures Association (NFA)**. The NFA, like NASD for the securities industry, tests and registers industry professionals and sets financial and customer protection standards.

Where the Exchanges Are

The major U.S. futures exchanges whose trading is reported in The Wall Street Journal specialize in particular commodities:

CHICAGO
CBT Chicago Board of Trade: grains, Treasury bonds and notes, precious metals, financial indexes

CME Chicago Mercantile Exchange: meat and livestock, milk, currency

EUREX US Eurex: fixed income derivative products

KANSAS CITY
KC Kansas City Board of Trade: grains, livestock and meats, food and fiber, stock indexes

MINNEAPOLIS
MPLS Minneapolis Grain Exchange: wheat, corn, soybeans

NEW YORK
NYCE, NYFE, FINEX New York Cotton Exchange and its divisions New York Futures Exchange and Financial Instruments Exchange: cotton, orange juice, foreign currency, Treasurys, stock indexes

CSCE Coffee, Sugar and Cocoa Exchange: coffee, sugar and cocoa

NYM, CMX-COMEX New York Mercantile Exchange and its division the Commodity Exchange: financial futures, precious metals, copper, natural gas

How They Work

Exchange floors are divided into pits where the actual trading occurs. To impose some order, each commodity is usually traded in one specific area on the floor, although pits for soybeans, gold and even stock index futures may stand side-by-side. **Options** on the futures contracts always trade in an area next to the corresponding futures trading area.

A **trading pit** is shaped like a ring and tiered into three or four levels. During **open outcry**, traders jockey for position to see over the heads of the traders in front of them. Some pits are divided into sections so several different commodities can be traded at the same time.

In an electronic system, orders are entered on a computer terminal in a futures broker's office that is connected to the exchange's computer. Orders are filled using an electronic matching system or by open outcry auction, depending on the exchange where the order is executed. Completed trades are reported back to the brokerage firm that originated them. The firm confirms the trade with the customer who placed the order.

Brokerage firm traders and some individual members, called **locals**, can work on the trading floor. While all market players have indirect access to the trading floor through a broker, only members of the exchange can actually trade on the floor.

Large **electronic display boards** circle the trading floor. They're constantly updated with new trade data, which is simultaneously sent out to the rest of the world by quote machine.

Trading Futures Contracts

You don't need to invest much to enter a futures contract, but you need nerve—and luck—to ride this financial roller coaster.

To trade futures, you give an order to buy or sell a commodity on a particular date in the future—such as October wheat, December pork bellies, or June Eurodollars. The price is determined in trading on the exchange where there's a market in that commodity.

But you pay just the **good faith deposit**, or initial margin. Briefly, a futures margin is a performance bond that's available to the futures broker to meet a customer's obligations for potential losses on a futures position. That's different from buying stock on margin, where you must provide at least 50% of the purchase price, and the balance is a loan arranged through the firm.

AFTER THE ORDER

When an order is filled, the contract typically goes into a pool at the exchange's clearing house with all the other filled orders. Buyers and sellers are anonymously paired. Since contracts are traded aggressively, the pairing process is always in motion.

Since the price of a contract changes continually throughout the day, the value of your account changes, too. At the end of each trading day, the clearing house moves money either in or out of its members' accounts, based on the shifting worth of the contracts. The process is called **marking to market**. The member firms then allocate those gains and losses to their investors' accounts.

Winning and Losing with a Futures Contract

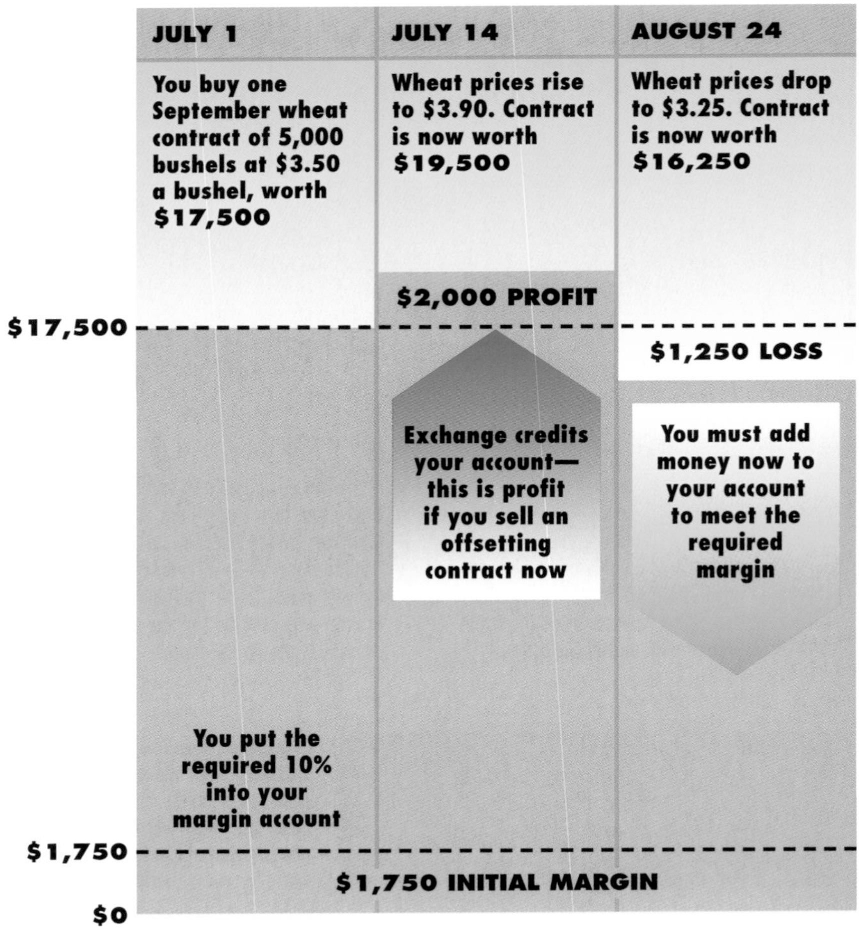

JULY 1	JULY 14	AUGUST 24
You buy one September wheat contract of 5,000 bushels at $3.50 a bushel, worth $17,500	Wheat prices rise to $3.90. Contract is now worth $19,500	Wheat prices drop to $3.25. Contract is now worth $16,250
	$2,000 PROFIT	

$17,500 –

$1,250 LOSS

| | Exchange credits your account— this is profit if you sell an offsetting contract now | You must add money now to your account to meet the required margin |

You put the required 10% into your margin account

$1,750 –

$1,750 INITIAL MARGIN

$0

THE LANGUAGE OF FUTURES

Futures trading involves contracts that cancel, or offset, each other: For every buy there's a sell and vice versa. The language of futures trading reflects this phenomenon.

To Enter the Market	Which Means	To Offset Your Position	Which Means
GO LONG	**ENTER A FUTURES CONTRACT TO BUY**	**GO SHORT**	**ENTER A FUTURES CONTRACT TO SELL**
GO SHORT	**ENTER A FUTURES CONTRACT TO SELL**	**GO LONG**	**ENTER A FUTURES CONTRACT TO BUY**

A TWO-PARTY SYSTEM

There are two parties to every futures transaction—the **buyer**, who is called the long, and the **seller**, who is called the short. If you want to enter the futures market, you can **go long** or **go short**. And if you want to leave the futures market, canceling your obligation under the contract, you offset your position with an equal number of the same futures contract on the opposite side of the market.

For example, if you have purchased, or have a long position, in three September U.S. Treasury note futures and want to leave the market, you would sell, or take a short position, in three September U.S. Treasury note futures.

To offset a futures contract you don't have to find the investor who was on the other side of your original futures contract and hope that person also wants to offset his or her position. That's because once a futures position has been cleared by a futures clearing firm, the clearing firm becomes the buyer for every seller and the seller for every buyer. This means that when you give the order to offset your existing futures position, the clearing firm will see to it that your old futures position is cancelled by your new, offsetting trade.

DELIVERY ISSUES

If you don't offset your futures position, you must make or take delivery of the item underlying the contract at expiration. The person with the short position is entitled to make delivery, and the person with the long position is required to take delivery. The contract specifies where, when, and how delivery may take place.

Physical delivery is the exception rather than the rule. The overwhelming majority—some experts estimate more than 98%—of futures contracts are terminated before expiration.

Some futures contracts, called cash-settled contracts, don't permit physical delivery. Rather, they are settled—if they're not offset—with a cash payment determined by the price change in the last two trading days before expiration.

PROTECTING THE PRICE

The exchanges have a mechanism, called **price limits**, to protect investors in a fast-moving market. If a contract price moves up or down to the pre-established price limit, the market locks up or locks down, and doesn't open for trading again until the price reaches an acceptable level.

In reality the lock-limit system often means that investors sustain huge losses or benefit from comparable gains because they are unable to sell a contract until the price has stabilized at the underlying commodity's new level. A suddenly devalued currency, for example, could send futures contracts on that currency into a tailspin. And when the dust clears, the value of the contract would probably be significantly lower than it had been when trading began.

REDUCING TRADING RISKS

The strategy called **spread trading** is one of the techniques used by futures traders to reduce the risk of losing large sums of money from a sudden shudder in the market, though it also limits returns.

Basically, it means buying one contract and selling another for the same commodity at the same time. One contract will usually make money, and the other one will lose. The key to ending up with a profit is getting the **spread**, or the difference between the two contracts' prices, to work in your favor.

For example, if you lose money on a contract to sell but make money on a contract to buy, the difference between those prices is the spread. If it's five cents in your favor, you might make $250 on the contract. If it's five cents against you, the $250 would be your loss.

When you go short, it's because you expect a contract's price to drop, or you're hedging a bet that it will rise. It's related to selling a stock short—which you do for similar reasons.

Hedgers and Speculators

Futures have the reputation of being a game for high-risk speculators. But they perform the important function of stabilizing prices.

There are two distinct classes of players in the futures markets.

Hedgers are interested in the commodities. They can be producers, like farmers, mining companies, foresters and oil drillers. Or they can be users, like bakers, paper mills, jewelers and oil distributors. In general, producers sell futures contracts while users buy them.

Speculators, on the other hand, trade futures strictly to make money. If you trade futures but never use the commodity itself, you are a speculator. Speculators may either buy or sell contracts, depending on which way they think the market is going in a particular commodity.

HOW HEDGERS USE THE MARKET

Hedgers are interested in protecting themselves against price changes that will undercut their profit. For example, a textile company may want to hedge against rising cotton prices as a result of boll weevil infestation. In August, the company buys 100 December cotton futures, representing five million pounds of cotton at 58 cents a pound.

During the fall, the cotton crop is infested and the prices shoot up. The December contract now trades at 68 cents. But the textile maker has hedged against exactly this situation. In December it can take delivery of cotton at 58 cents a pound, 10 cents less than the market price, and save $500,000 (10 cents x 5 million pounds).

Or the company can sell the futures contracts for 10 cents a pound more than it paid for them and use the profit to off-set the higher price it will have to pay for cotton in the cash market. In either case, there's no nasty surprise in added commodity costs because the cash price and the futures price cancel each other out.

HOW SPECULATORS USE THE MARKET

Speculators hope to make money in the futures market by betting on price moves. A speculator may load up on orange juice futures in November, for instance, betting that if a freeze sets in and damages the Florida orange crop, prices of orange juice and the futures contracts based on them will soar.

If the speculators are right, and the winter is tough, the contracts on orange juice will be worth more than they paid. The speculators can sell their contracts at a profit. If they're wrong, and there's a bumper crop, the bottom will fall out of the market, and the speculators will be squeezed dry by falling prices.

costs in the event of a freeze, and orange farmers couldn't earn enough money in a good year to pay their production costs.

Speculators also keep the market active. If only those who produced or used the commodities were trading, there would not be enough activity to keep the market going. Buy and sell orders would be paired slowly, erasing the protection that hedgers get when the market responds quickly to changes in the cash market.

INFLUENCES ON FUTURES CONTRACT PRICES

The price of a futures contract is influenced by natural and political events, but it's also affected by the economic news that the government releases, the length of time the contract has to run, and by what speculators are doing and saying.

Virtually every day of every month, the government releases economic data, sells Treasury bills, or creates new policies that influence the price of futures contracts for both natural and financial commodities. News on new home sales, for example, directly influences the price of lumber futures, as hedgers and speculators try to link the probable rise or fall of lumber sales to what the construction industry will be ordering.

If a producer agrees to hold a commodity for future delivery, the contract will reflect storage, insurance and other carrying costs to cover daily expenses until delivery. Generally, the further away the delivery date, the greater the carrying costs. Even so, prices rarely go up regularly in consecutive months. When the prices do increase this way, the relationship is called a **contango**.

Speculation also influences a commodity's price. Sudden demand for a contract—sparked by rumor, inside information or other factors—can drive its price sky-high. Or the reverse can happen when rumors or events make investors scramble to sell.

SPECULATORS ARE INDISPENSABLE

Speculators are crucial to the success of the futures market because they complete a symbiotic relationship between those wishing to avoid risk and those willing to take it.

Since hedgers, in planning ahead, want to avoid risk in what is undeniably a risky business, others have to be willing to accept it. Unless some speculators are willing to bet that orange juice prices will rise while others bet that prices will fall, an orange juice producer could not protect against dramatically increased

Investing in futures and options is different from investing from stocks, bonds and mutual funds because futures and options markets are **zero sum markets**. That means for every dollar somebody makes (before commissions), somebody else loses a dollar. Put bluntly, that means that any gain is at somebody else's expense.

How Futures Work

Though they have different goals, hedgers and speculators are in the market together. What happens to the price of a contract affects them all.

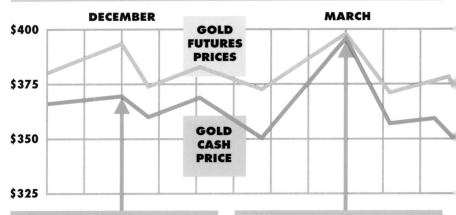

DECEMBER

GOLD IS $370 AN OUNCE IN THE CASH MARKET AND $385 FOR THE JUNE CONTRACT

In December, the price of gold in the cash market—what a buyer would pay for immediate delivery—is $15 less than the price of the June contract.

PRODUCERS (HEDGERS)

Gold producers hedge by selling futures contracts.

The gold producers sell June futures contracts because they won't have gold ready for delivery until then.

Earned in December sale $385

USERS (HEDGERS)

Gold users hedge by buying futures contracts.

The gold users buy June futures contracts because that's when they need the gold.

Cost of December buy   − $385

SPECULATORS

Speculators buy gold futures contracts if they think the price is going up.

Cost of December buy   − $385

MARCH

GOLD IS $395 AN OUNCE IN THE CASH MARKET. THE JUNE CONTRACT IS SELLING FOR $398

In March, the price of gold has gone up to $395 in the cash market. The June futures contract is selling for $398. The hedgers wait for the expiration date. Speculators sell offsetting contracts, thinking price has hit the top.

PRODUCERS (HEDGERS)

The producers can't sell their gold because it isn't ready yet.

BUYERS (HEDGERS)

This upswing in the cash price is exactly what the buyers were trying to protect themselves against.

SPECULATORS

The speculators sell, thinking gold has reached its peak. One clue is that the contract price is so close to the cash price. If speculators thought higher prices in the cash market were likely in the near future, they would be willing to pay higher prices for futures contracts.

This time the speculators made money in the market if they sold in March when the contract price reached its peak.

Price from March sell $398
Cost of December buy   −   385
Result of trade (profit) $ 13

> Note that this example doesn't include commissions or other costs that would result from trading futures contracts, and it assumes that everyone bought one option at the same price.

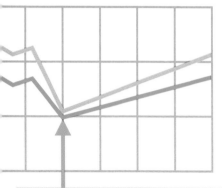

JUNE

The oldest futures contracts date back to 17th-century Japan, when **rice tickets** provided landlords who collected rents in rice with a steady secondary income source. They sold warehouse receipts for their stored rice, giving the holder the right to a specific quantity of rice, of a specific quality, on a specific date in the future.

The buyers who paid for the tickets could cash them in at the appointed time or sell them at a profit to someone else. Like futures contracts today, the tickets themselves had no real worth, but they represented a way to make money on the changing value of the underlying commodity—the rice.

JUNE

CONTRACTS EXPIRE WHEN GOLD IS $350 AN OUNCE IN THE CASH MARKET AND $352 IN THE FUTURES MARKET

In June, when the contract expires, both the producers and the users equalize their profit or loss in the futures market through offsetting trades in the cash market.

PRODUCERS (HEDGERS)

Because the price of the gold futures contract had dropped, the producers made money on the offsetting trade.

Earned in December sale	$385
Cost of June buy	– 352
Result of trade (profit)	$ 33

Even though producers had to sell their gold in the cash market for less than the anticipated price, the profit from their futures trades gave them the expected level of profit.

Earned in cash market	$350
Futures profit	+ 33
Gross profit	$383

USERS (HEDGERS)

THE GOLD USERS

The users lost money on the futures contracts because it cost more to sell the offsetting contracts than they had paid to buy.

Earned in June sell	$352
Cost of December buy	– $385
Result of trade (loss)	– $ 33

Since it cost the users less to buy gold in the cash market than they had expected, the total cost was what they anticipated.

Cost in cash market	$350
Cost of futures trade	+ 33
Actual cost of gold	$383

In any given futures contract, the profit or loss of the hedgers could be reversed, depending on the rise or fall of the futures price. In the end, however, their profit or loss in the futures trade would be offset by profit or loss in the cash market. The speculators could lose as frequently—maybe more frequently—than they gained, depending on changing prices and the timing with which they entered and left the market.

CORNERING THE MARKET

Some commodities traders aren't satisfied with the money they can make by betting on price fluctuations. They'd rather control prices by engineering a financial **corner**, or monopoly on the commodity itself. Frederick Phillipse has the dubious distinction of introducing the technique in North America. In 1666, he successfully cornered the market on wampum—Native American money—by burying several barrels of it. Fur traders had to pay his prices to carry on their business.

Reading Futures Tables

For futures traders, daily price reports chronicle the changing value of their accounts. For others, they're a hint of future prices.

The tables reporting on futures markets show opening and closing prices, price history and volume of sales for every trading day. Because the futures markets reflect current political and economic conditions, the charts also provide interesting commentary on the state of the economy and the way people feel it's headed.

Open is the opening price for sugar on the previous trading day. Depending on what's happened in the world overnight, the opening price may not be the same as the closing price the day before. Since prices are in cents per pound, the 22.37 means sugar opened for sale at 22.37 cents per pound. Multiplying this

amount by 112,000 pounds (the number of pounds in the contract) equals $25,054.40 per contract.

High, low and **settle** report the contract's highest, lowest and closing prices for the previous trading day. Taken together, they're a good indication of the commodity's market **volatility** during the trading day. Here the

FUTURES PRICES

Wednesday, February 17

Open Interest Reflects Previous Trading Day.

SEEDS

¼ 286	210¾	36,984	
½ 271½	217¾	54,414	
¼ 268½	225¼	102,846	
¼ 256¼	232¾	15,541	
¼ 260	238½	4,606	
½ 263¼	241	4,512	
¼ 251	240½	176	
¼ 255	238¾	2,892	
nt 221,971, −2,496.			
163½	128¼	2,759	
¼ 160½	129¾	3,527	
¼ 161	134	4,701	
11,135, −255.			
er bu.			
¼ 671	551	17,647	
¼ 655	551	29,442	
½ 638	554	14,451	
¼ 640	555½	77,674	
¼ 644	576½	7,526	
½ 648	589¾	2,570	
½ 648	592½	3,843	
650½	594½	3,985	
¼ 616½			

	Open	High	Low	Settle	Change	Lifetime High	Low	Open Interest
SUGAR-DOMESTIC (CSCE)-112,000 lbs.; cents per lb.								
May	22.37	22.38	22.31	22.31	− 06	22.73	22.00	4,058
July	22.50	22.75	22.73	22.74	+	22.90	22.10	2,963
Sept	22.80	22.80	22.80	22.80	....	22.95	22.28	2,790
Nov	22.50	22.50	22.50	22.50	....	22.51	21.99	1,684
Ja	22.25	22.25	22.25	22.26	−	22.27	21.75	547
Mar	22.28	22.28	22.28	22.28	+ .04	22.30	21.80	536
Est vol 64; vol Tu 8; open int 12,850, 2.								
COTTON (CTN) 50,000 lbs.; cents per lb.								
Mar	56.65	58.30	56.65	57.63	+ .89	77.25	56.00	14,855
May	57.25	.20	57.10	57.76	+ .57	77.65	57.05	27,399
July	57.90	58.70	57.80	58.25	+ .42	77.31	57.67	14,297
Oct	58.80	59.40	58.80	59.25	+ .50	77.05	58.75	1,610
Dec	59.40	60.15	59.40	59.73	+ .44	74.10	59.25	15,376
Mr	60.50	60.90	60.50	60.73	+ .45	74.00	60.50	1,743
May		....		61.23	+ .45	75.40	61.80	636
July	61.80	61.80	61.80	61.75	+ .35	73.25	61.80	263
Est vol 16,500; vol Tu 21,262; open int 76,199, −2,214.								
ORANGE JUICE (CTN)-15,000 lbs.; cents per lb.								
Mar	87.55	87.85	83.50	84.25	+ 3.20	127.75	83.10	14,930

The **product** is listed alphabetically within its particular grouping. Cotton may be listed under a heading such as Foods & Fibers. Generally, detailed information is given in these charts for the most actively traded futures contracts. Activity for additional contracts may be summarized at the end of the more detailed tables.

The **exchange** on which a particular contract is traded appears. Here CTN is The New York Cotton Exchange. Some commodities, like wheat and corn, trade on more than one exchange. The contract whose activity is watched most closely is the one that is shown.

The **size of each contract** reflects the bulk

trading unit used during the normal course of commercial business. One cotton contract covers the rights to 50,000 pounds of cotton. The **price per unit** is expressed in either dollars or cents per unit, depending on the commodity. Here, it's cents per pound. To find the total cost of the contract, multiply the price per unit by

opening price of a sugar contract was close to the high of 22.38. The contract settled at its closing price of 22.31 cents, down 0.06 cents from the closing price the previous day.

Change compares the closing price given here with the previous closing price. A plus (+) indicates prices ended higher and a minus (−) means that prices ended lower. In this case, sugar for March delivery settled 0.04 cents higher than the previous day.

The **month of the** **contract** is the month in which it expires. **Mr** indicates this contract will expire on the third Saturday of March. When the expiration date arrives, the contract is dropped from the table.

The expiration cycle for each commodity is different, based on demand. There are contracts expiring every month for some commodities, but as few as four times a year for others.

Lifetime highs and **lows** show volatility over the lifetime of a particular contract. Prices for heating oil no. 2 have been more volatile than sugar prices—meaning the investment risks are higher, but the chances of making a lot of money are also higher.

Open interest reports the total number of outstanding contracts—that is, those that have not been cancelled by offsetting trades. Generally, the further away the expiration date, the smaller the open interest because there's not much trading activity. In the case of grains and oilseed, however, there is increased activity in the months the new crop will be harvested.

HEATING OIL NO. 2 (NYM) 42,000 gal.; $ per gal.

	Open	High	Low	Settle	Change	Lifetime High	Low	Open Interest
Mar	.2950	.3010	.2920	.2984	+ .0032	.5830	.2920	37,713
Apr	.3020	.3065	.2990	.3047	+ .0036	.5900	.2965	29,223
May	.3075	.3130	.3060	.3112	+ .0036	.5330	.3040	15,102
June	.3140	.3195	.3130	.3177	+ .0036	.5300	.3115	14,029
July	.3245	.3290	.3230	.3262	+ .0036	.5290	.3220	12,047
Oct	.3515	.3580	.3515	.3542	+ .0031	.5200	.3510	5,089
Dec	.3690	.3750	.3690	.3712	+ .0031	.5275	.3680	12,279
Ja	.3750	.3780	.3745	.3772	+ .0031	.5170	.3700	11,855
Feb	.3765	.3795	.3760	.3777	+ .0031	.4960	.3750	1,908
Mar	.3765	.3775	.3760	.3772	+ .0031	.5060	.3760	665

Est vol na; vol Tue 44,727; open int 162,748, + 1,956.

GASOLINE-NY Unleaded (NYM)) 42,000 gal.; $ per gal.

	Open	High	Low	Settle	Change	Lifetime High	Low	Open Interest
Mar	.3280	.3375	.3255	.3307	+ .0015	.5230	.3240	29,906
Apr	.3620	.3675	.3580	.3610	− .0003	.5500	.3580	25,056
May	.3760	.3805	.3730	.3740	− .0006	.5500	.3710	18,475
June	.3850	.3885	.3830	.3840	− .0004	.5250	.3815	14,216
July	.3935	.3955	.3910	.3905	− .0009	.5260	.3900	14,921
Aug	.3970	.3970	.3950	.3945	− .0009	.5215	.3950	3,177
Sept	.3950	.4000	.3950	.3965	− .0014	.5065	.3950	3,065
Oct	.3925	.3930	.3890	.3890	− .0014	.4696	.3890	2,234

Est vol na; vol Tue 32,162; o...

SHORT STERLIN

	Open	High
Mar	94.66	94.70
June	94.93	94.98
Sept	95.05	95.07
Dec	94.85	94.87
Mr	95.03	95.06
June	95.03	95.06
Sept	94.97	95.00
Dec	94.85	94.88
Mr	94.86	94.89
June	94.88	94.89
Sept	94.86	94.88
Dec	94.86	94.86
Mr	94.77	94.79
June	....	....
Sept	94.73	94.76
Dec	....	....

Est vol 212,776; vol

LONG GILT (LIF

Mar	117.25	11...
June		

the number of units. The July cotton contract closed at $29,125 (50,000 x 58.25 cents).

There are also cumulative daily figures for all the contracts in each commodity combined. The volume for heating oil no. 2 was 44,727 trades, leaving an open interest of 162,748. The + 1,956 shows the increase in the open interest. Those contracts can be cancelled by offsetting trades.

COMMODITY INDEXES

Several commodity indexes track futures markets and reflect the performance of commodities as an asset class, parallel to the way stock indexes reflect what's happening on the stock markets. For example, when the indexes are significantly up or down in comparison to the previous year, it can indicate volatile commodity prices.

The Dow Jones-AIG Commodity Index is weighted by trading liquidity and includes 20 commodities from eight major sectors. The equally weighted Commodities Research Bureau (CRB) index includes 17 commodities, and the Goldman Sachs Commodity Index, which includes 22 commodities, is weighted by worldwide production values.

Financial Futures

Stocks, bonds and currencies are the commodities of the investment business.

Just as dramatic changes in the price of wheat affect farmers, bakers and ultimately the consumer, so changes in interest rates, the future value of currencies and the direction of the stock market send ripples—and sometimes waves—though the financial community.

With the creation of a market in financial futures, traders, like pension fund and mutual fund investment managers and securities firms that rely on financial commodities, can protect themselves against the unexpected. They're the **hedgers** of the financial futures market.

Financial Futures in Action

THE HEDGERS

Mutual fund with a portfolio of stocks similar to S&P 500 Index stocks when near-term price declines expected	**Hedges by taking a short position** to protect stock portfolio against falling stock prices	**If index rises**, gains on portfolio are matched by losses on short futures hedge **If index drops**, losses on portfolio are offset by profits on short futures hedge
Pension fund that plans to buy portfolio of stocks similar to S&P 500 Index stocks next month	**Hedges by taking a long position** to protect against rising prices until money is available to purchase stocks	**If index rises**, increased cost of buying stocks is offset by gains on long futures hedge **If index drops**, buying costs are less but fund has losses on the long futures hedge

THE SPECULATORS

Speculators who anticipate where S&P 500 Index will be in the future	**Buy S&P futures** when they think the index will rise **Sell S&P futures** when they think the index will fall	**If the index rises**, there's a gain on futures position, and **if it falls**, there's a loss **If the index falls**, there's a gain on futures position, and **if it rises**, there's a loss

KEEPING MARKETS LIQUID

As in other futures markets, **speculators** keep the markets active by constant trading. Speculators buy or sell futures contracts depending on which way they think the market is going. World politics, trading patterns and the economy are the unpredictable factors in these markets. Rumor, too, plays a major role.

Financial speculators are no more interested in taking delivery of $100,000 in Treasury bonds than grain speculators are in 5,000 bushels of wheat. What they're interested in is making money. So at what seems to be a good time, they sell a contract they own and take their profits. Or they may sell to cut their losses.

For example, the September contract on the **British pound** has been as low as $1.3980 and as high as $1.5800. If a speculator bought at the low and sold at the high, the gain (before commissions and other charges) would have been 18.2 cents per pound, or $11,375 on a contract worth $62,500.

CURRENCY

	Open	High	Low	Settle	Change	Lifetime High	Lifetime Low	Open Interest
BRITISH POUND (CME) —62,500 pds.; $ per pound								
Sept	1.4880	1.5070	1.4826	1.5056	+ .0190	1.5800	1.3980	32,026
Dec	1.4830	1.4980	1.4770	1.4968	+ .0188	1.5670	1.3930	444
Est vol 16,304; vol Mon 14,125; open int 32,507, −2,398.								
SWISS FRANC (CME) —125,000 francs; $ per franc								
Sept	.6625	.6670	.6603	.6654	+ .0042	.7100	.6380	
Dec	.6630	.6645	.6585		.0041	.7050		
Est vol 25,317								

WHAT'S BEING TRADED

The financial futures contracts in the marketplace are always in flux. Like other commodities, they trade on specific exchanges, where they're often among the most actively traded products.

Futures contracts divide into four categories:

- **Currencies**
- **Stock indexes**
- **Interest rates**
- **Individual stocks**

Currency trading has the longest history, dating back to 1972. Interest rate futures began trading in 1975, and stock index futures trading was added in 1982.

Single stock futures have been traded since 2001. Unlike other financial futures, these contracts are handled only electronically, through a joint venture of the Chicago Board Options Exchange (CBOE), the Chicago Mercantile Exchange (CME), and the Chicago Board of Trade (CBOT).

Because single stock futures have a dual identity, as securities and as futures, issues of oversight, trading, clearing, and settlement involve both the SEC and the CFTC.

ARBITRAGE: MANEUVERING THE MARKETS

Indexes and futures contracts on those indexes don't move in lockstep. When they are out of sync, the index futures contract price moves either higher or lower than the index itself. Traders can make a lot of money by simultaneously buying the one that's less expensive and selling the more expensive. This technique is known as **arbitrage**, and the tool they use is a very sophisticated computer program that follows the shifts in price.

Often, the price difference is only a fraction of a dollar. But arbitragers trade huge numbers of contracts at the same time, so the results are significant—if the timing is right. And since many arbitragers are making the same decisions at the same time, their buying and selling can produce changes in the markets in which they trade.

NO DELIVERY PLANNED Most financial futures contracts are offset before their expiration date, just as contracts on other commodities are. But if an investor takes delivery, it's the cash value of the contract.

INDEX

DJ INDUSTRIAL AVERAGE (CBOT)-$10 times average

	Open	High	Low	Settle	Chg	High	Low	Open Interest
Mar	9570	9630	9490	9575	— 1	9760	7220	17,416
June	9665	9705	9570	9655		9810	7670	1,406
Sept	9737	9780	9660	9738	+ 1	9891	7875	905
Dec	9820	9860	9745	9823	+ 3	9974	7987	864
Dc00			....					

Est vol 16,000; vol /
Idx prl: High 9611.3
S&P 500 INDEX (C

INTEREST RATE

TREASURY BONDS (CBT)-$100,000; pts. 32nds of 100%

	Open	High	Low	Settle	Change	Lifetime High	Low	Open Interest
Mar	123-21	123-31	121-23	122-26	— 29	134-26	103-04	515,524
June	123-07	123-10	122-03	122-11	— 29	134-02	110-07	286,223
Sept	122-23	122-24	121-24	121-29	— 29	131-06	115-11	8,620
Dec	121-11	121-18	121-09	121-09	— 29	128-28	118-07	3,299

Est vol 605,000; vol Mn 332,760; open int 813,666. −31,514.
TREASURY BONDS (MCE)-$50,000
Mar 123-20 123-25 122-17 122-24

READING THE FINANCIAL FUTURES CHARTS

The details of financial futures trading are reported daily.

The value of an index contract is calculated differently from other futures contracts. That's because an index is two steps removed from the commodity. Instead of dollars per yen or tons of soybeans per dollar, U.S. indexes are valued by multiplying a fixed dollar amount times the current value of the index. A DJIA contract, for example, is valued at $10 times its current value.

In other words, if you took delivery of a March DJIA contract at the value, or settle price, shown in this example, it would be worth $95,750, or $10 times 9575.

Interest rate futures contracts also differ somewhat from other contracts. Their value is figured as percentage points, or in the case of U.S. and U.K. bonds, in 32nds to correspond to the way changes in value are measured in the bonds themselves. For U.S. Treasury bills, and for Eurodollars, the tables report yield and changes in yield rather than lifetime highs and lows.

A World of Options

Options are opportunities to make buy and sell decisions—
if the market takes the right turns.

Holding an option gives you the right to buy or sell a specific financial product at a set price within a preset time period. But there's no obligation **to exercise the option**, and actually buy or sell, before it expires. The particular item that an option deals with—stock, index, Treasury bond, currency or futures contract—is called the **underlying instrument**.

Options are traded on stock or commodity exchanges at a specific **strike (or exercise) price**, which is the dollar amount you'll pay or receive if the trade takes place. The strike price is set by the exchange. The market price rises or falls depending on the performance of the underlying instrument on which the option is based.

BUYING OPTIONS

Buying options is a way to use leverage to take advantage of changes in the market price. If you buy **call** options, you are expecting that the price of the underlying instrument is going up. Conversely, if you buy **put** options, you think the price is going down.

With either type of buy option, your potential loss is limited to the **premium**, or dollar amount, you pay to buy the option. That's known in the securities industry as a limited, predetermined risk.

SELLING OPTIONS

One big difference between buying options and **writing**, or selling them, is the nature of your commitment. As a buyer, you have no obligation to do anything. You can simply let an option expire if you can't make a profit with it. Sellers, on the other hand, are required to go through with a trade if the purchaser of an option you sold—by writing a put or writing a call—wants to exercise the option and you are assigned. But you do collect a **premium**, or income, when you sell.

WRITING COVERED CALLS

The most basic form of options trading is **writing covered stock calls**, and it's the first type of options trading most people do. It means you sell the right to some other party to buy stocks that you already own for a specific price. The key is that you own them—that's what makes the call covered.

NAKED—BEARING IT ALL

The greatest risk in options trading is writing **naked calls** or **naked puts**. With a naked call, you sell the right to buy an underlying item from you even though you don't own it. If the price of the item exceeds the strike price and the call is exercised, you'll have to buy the item at market price in order to sell it at the strike price. Your cost could be substantial. With a naked put, you sell the buyer the right to sell you the underlying item at the strike price. That could mean paying much more than market price.

THREE WAYS TO BUY OPTIONS

Investor buys ten call options (1,000 shares) on stock X

Price: $55/share

Strike price: 60

Premium: $750

1 **HOLD TO MATURITY**

2 **TRADE BEFORE OPTION EXPIRES**

3 **LET THE OPTION EXPIRE**

TWO WAYS TO SELL OPTIONS

Investor owns 1,000 shares of stock X

Price: $55/share

Investor owns no shares of stock X

1 **WRITE TEN COVERED CALLS**
Strike price: 60
Collect premium $750

2 **WRITE TEN NAKED CALLS**
Strike price: 60
Collect premium $750

THE LANGUAGE OF OPTIONS

In the specialized language of options, all transactions are either puts or calls. A put is the right to sell and a call is the right to buy.

	CALL	PUT
BUY	The right to buy the underlying item at the strike price until the expiration date	The right to sell the underlying item at the strike price until the expiration date
SELL	Selling the right to buy the underlying item from you at the strike price until the expiration date. Known as **writing a call**	Selling the right to sell the underlying item to you until the expiration date. Known as **writing a put**

TRADE OR EXERCISE

Like futures contracts, options can be sold before the expiration date or neutralized with an offsetting order. Unlike most futures contracts, though, options are frequently exercised when the underlying item reaches the strike price. That's because part of the appeal of options, and stock options in particular, is that they can be converted into underlying investments even though the options themselves are derivatives.

THE OCC

The **Options Clearing Corporation (OCC)** is the actual buyer and seller of all listed options contracts. Investors can be confident that their trades will be matched and settled on the day following the trade. There is no risk that a buyer won't be found if you want to sell or that there won't be a seller if you want to buy. OCC also ensures that premiums will be collected and paid and the exercise notices will be handled equitably.

IF STOCK PRICE RISES TO 65
Exercise options at strike price of 60 and sell shares

$5,000 from trade
− $750 premium
$4,250 PROFIT

IF STOCK PRICE RISES TO 60
Let options expire

$0,000 from trade
− $750 premium
$750 LOSS

IF STOCK PRICE RISES TO 62
Trade options before expiration

$2,000 from trade
− $750 premium
$1,250 PROFIT

IF STOCK PRICE RISES TO 60
Trade options before expiration

$500 from trade
− $750 premium
$250 LOSS

IF STOCK PRICE DROPS TO 45
There are no takers for an option with a 60 strike price

less your premium only
$750 LOSS

IF STOCK PRICE RISES TO 57
No takers—options expire

keep the premium
$750 PROFIT

IF STOCK PRICE RISES TO 60
Buy 10 calls to cancel obligation and prevent losing stocks

$750 premium collected
− $750 premium on offsetting calls
BREAK EVEN

IF STOCK PRICE RISES TO 57
No takers—options expire

keep the premium
$750 PROFIT

IF STOCK PRICE RISES TO 65
Options are exercised. You must buy 1,000 shares at $65 to sell at $60

$750 premium
− $5,000 loss on transaction
$4,250 LOSS

Stock Options

Successful stock option trading requires lots of attention to detail—including information on what's happening in the marketplace.

If you're looking for options trading information, you can find tables reporting the previous day's trades in the financial press. And you can find options chains of all of the options currently available on a particular stock or other underlying instrument online. One place to begin is at www.888options.com, the site of the Options Industry Council (OIC).

TRADING OPTIONS

There is an active secondary market in stock options before their expiration date as investors trade to settle their positions.

The price of a stock option is closely tied to the current market price of the underlying stock. That's because the exchanges establish the **strike prices** to reflect analysts' evaluations of the stock and the market in general. In fact, the relationship between the two is so central to the way options trade that it's described using a special vocabulary.

An **at-the-money option** means that the market price and the strike price are the same. An **in-the-money option** means the market price is higher than the strike price of a call option and lower than the strike price of a put option.

With an **out-of-the-money option**, the opposite is true: The market price is lower than the exercise price of a call option and higher than the exercise price of a put option. That makes it unlikely that the option will be exercised, especially if it's due to expire shortly.

A **deep-out-of-the-money option**, or DOOM, has a strike price so far from the market price that there's little trading.

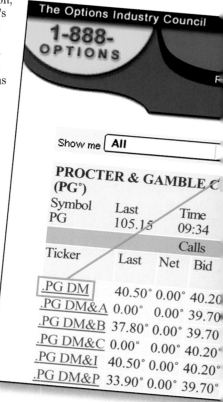

The Options Industry Council
1-888-OPTIONS

Show me [All]

PROCTER & GAMBLE C (PG°)

Symbol	Last	Time
PG	105.15	09:34

			Calls
Ticker	Last	Net	Bid
.PG DM	40.50°	0.00°	40.20
.PG DM&A	0.00°	0.00°	39.70
.PG DM&B	37.80°	0.00°	39.70
.PG DM&C	0.00°	0.00°	40.20°
.PG DM&I	40.50°	0.00°	40.20°
.PG DM&P	33.90°	0.00°	39.70°

Call options—options to buy—are reported separately from **put options**—options to sell. Sometimes calls and puts are traded on the same option, and sometimes only one or the other is traded.

GETTING WIRED

Options, like futures contracts, have historically been bought and sold on exchange trading floors, using a sometimes rough and tumble auction-style system known as **open outcry**. But the winds of electronic change, which have revolutionized stock trading, are stirring up options trading as well.

Order routing and execution on the U.S. options exchanges—the American Stock Exchange, the Chicago Board Options Exchange, the International Securities Exchange, the Pacific Exchange, and the Philadelphia Stock Exchange—is increasingly handled electronically. Traders on exchange floors are using hand-held computers to record transactions, replacing yesterday's paper order cards. And the ISE is entirely electronic.

What's more, options that once traded on only one exchange may now trade on several simultaneously, a move that supporters say provides a more efficient and liquid market for consumers.

Listed under **ticker** are the stock symbol, in this case Proctor & Gamble (PG), and two letters that indicate the type of option, the expiration and strike price. **D** indicates a call expiring in April. **M** indicates a 65 strike price.

Last is the most recent price for the option. It is typically updated regularly during the day if trading is active. The last price for the April 65 call was 40.50, or $4,050 per contract on 100 shares. The last price for the April put was 0.05, or 5 cents.

Bid reports what buyers are willing to pay for options and ask what sellers are willing to accept.

Net indicates how much the options price has changed, if it has. A positive number means an increase and a negative one, in red, a decrease.

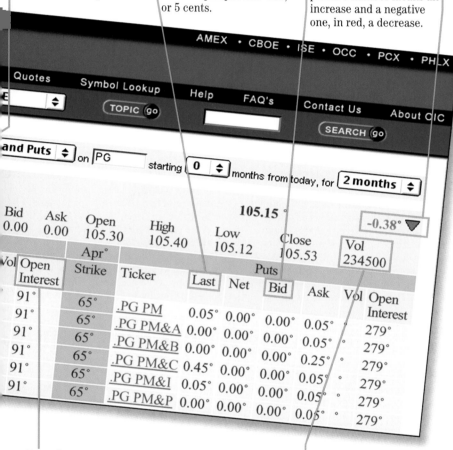

AMEX · CBOE · ISE · OCC · PCX · PHLX

Quotes   Symbol Lookup   Help   FAQ's   Contact Us   About CIC

TOPIC (go)   SEARCH (go)

and Puts ⇕ on PG   starting 0 ⇕ months from today, for 2 months ⇕

105.15

| Bid | Ask | Open | High | Low | Close | -0.38 ▼ |
| 0.00 | 0.00 | 105.30 | 105.40 | 105.12 | 105.53 | Vol 234500 |

Vol	Open Interest	Apr Strike	Ticker	Last	Net	Bid	Ask	Vol	Open Interest
91	91	65	.PG PM	0.05	0.00	0.00	0.05		279
	91	65	.PG PM&A	0.00	0.00	0.00	0.05		279
	91	65	.PG PM&B	0.00	0.00	0.00	0.25		279
	91	65	.PG PM&C	0.45	0.00	0.00	0.05		279
	91	65	.PG PM&I	0.05	0.00	0.00	0.05		279
	91	65	.PG PM&P	0.00	0.00	0.00	0.05		279

Puts

Open interest is the number of positions that have been opened and not yet offset.

You can set the limits of the searches you want to conduct, choosing to display all strike prices for both **calls** and **puts** on a particular underlying investment, or only those options that are in-the-money or close to being in-the-money.

In this example, all puts and calls with an April **expiration date** and a 65 **strike price** are being displayed. The calls are to the left and the puts to the right of the screen's center column.

The bold numbers to the right show the most recent **market price** for the underlying stock— $105.15—and the **net gain or loss** from the day's opening price—down 38 cents.

The reason there is much greater activity in calls than in puts, in this

example, is that the April 65 calls are deep-in-the-money and can be sold at a potentially large profit.

Volume reports the number of trades during the previous trading day. The number is unofficial but gives a sense of the activity in each option. Generally, trading increases as the expiration date gets closer if the strike price is in the money. But many factors contribute to trading volume and can be hard to isolate.

Using Options

Options can work for both conservative and speculative investors.

BULLS AND BEARS
Bullish traders, who think the market is going up, buy **calls**, or options to buy. Bearish traders, who think it is going down, buy **puts**, or options to sell.

Individual investors use options for a variety of reasons. Conservative investors, for example, might buy or sell options to help protect the value of their portfolios against falling prices, to lock in a favorable purchase price or to get some immediate income. Speculative traders like the **leverage**, or opportunity to have a potentially larger gain than they could achieve by owning the underlying investment. Of course, they could have larger losses, too, but that's the risk they're willing to take.

THE COST OF AN OPTION

Options are attractive because they cost less than actually buying the underlying stocks, Treasury notes or other investments they're based on, though commissions may add significantly to the price.

An option's **premium**, or nonrefundable price, depends on several factors, including the type of underlying investment,

its price, its volatility, the current interest rates and the time remaining before the option expires. Because premiums fluctuate, traders can make profits or have losses very quickly.

INVESTMENT STRATEGIES

You can use options conservatively to increase your income or to limit your risk.

The most popular income-producing strategy is selling **covered calls**. You write call options on a share-for-share basis against stocks you own. If someone exercises the calls, you meet your obligation to sell by handing over your stocks. The goals of covered calls are to provide some protection if the stock price falls, establish a selling price above the current market price or increase your income in a **sideways market**, when prices move up and down within a very small range.

Writing **cash-secured puts** is another income-oriented approach. You sell a put for each 100 shares of stock an investor is

The Following Rules of Thumb

For options expiring in the same month, the more in-the-money an option is, the higher its price is likely to be in the marketplace.

The closer the expiration date of an in-the-money option, the more *volume*, or trading activity, there tends to be.

OPTION/STRIKE		EXP.	-CALL- VOL.	LAST	-PUT- VOL.	LAST
3563	30	Nov	233	6¹⁰	1491	0⁵⁰
3563	35	Nov	1290	2⁵⁰	437	1⁸⁵
3563	40					
VerizonCm	50					
Vignette	7⁵⁰					
WalMart	45					
53⁸²	55					

OPTION/STRIKE		EXP.	-CALL- VOL.	LAST	-PUT- VOL.	LAS
28²⁹	25	Nov	3129	3⁵⁰	2206	0¹⁵
28²⁹	25	Jan	1516	4⁶⁰	818	1²⁵
28²⁹	27⁵⁰	Nov	3425	1⁴⁰	2724	0⁷⁰
28²⁹	30	Nov	6312	0³⁰	2999	2

When the stock price is $35.63, the price of the November 30 call, at $610 per contract, is much higher than the price of the November 35 call, at $250.

In this example, the November 25 call and put options were traded more actively in early November than January options with the same strike price.

willing to buy at a specific price. Then, as security, you invest an equivalent amount in U.S. Treasury bills or a money market account. If the put is exercised, you liquidate that investment and use the cash to buy the stock.

TRADING TECHNIQUES
You can trade options in more complex ways to hedge your investments. With a **straddle**, you buy a call and a put on the same underlying investment at the same strike price. A straddle costs more than an individual option but has the potential of making money whether the underlying price goes up or down.

If you use a **strangle**, you buy a call and a put on the same underlying invest-ment with different strike prices equally out of the money. A strangle costs less than a straddle, but the value of the under-lying investment has to change much more for the strangle to make a profit.

Spread trading means that you buy one option and sell another on the same underlying investment. The two options have either different expiration dates or different strike prices. If you are forced to buy or sell the underlying investment because someone exercises an option you sold, you can meet your obligation by exercising the option you bought.

TAKE THE LEAP
Long-term stock options, actually **Long-term Equity Anticipation Securities (LEAPS)** have expiration dates of up to three years. Because they last longer than other options, they are considered less risky. That's true in part because the price of the stock or stock index has much longer to perform as expected. It's also true that the money saved in buying an option instead of the stock itself can be invested elsewhere. Of course, options don't pay dividends.

The risk here, as with all options, is that the underlying stock or index must still perform as expected, and the decision to trade, exercise or let the option expire still has to be made within the option's lifespan.

Usually Apply to Options

The more time there is until expi-ration, the larger the option price because the chance of reaching the strike price is greater and the carrying costs are more.

Call and put options move in opposition. Call options rise in value as the underlying market prices go up. Put options rise in value as market prices go down.

OPTION/STRIKE		EXP.	-CALL-		-PUT-	
			VOL.	LAST	VOL.	LAST
1893	2250	Dec	1925	0.40	227	3.70
1893	2250	Jan	3508	0.70	191	4.20
1893	2250	Apr	1370	1.60	286	5
1893	25					
1893	25					
Citigrp	4750					
4810	4750					
4810	50					
CitrixSy	25					

OPTION/STRIKE		EXP.	-CALL-		-PUT-	
			VOL.	LAST	VOL.	LAST
11385	105	Nov	1695	10	553	0.30
11385	110	Nov	679	5	2090	1
11385	115	Nov	1376	185	550	

The put and call premiums are lower for options that expire in December than for those that expire in April.

When the market price is $113.85, the 105 call options have a premium of $1,000 per contract, while the premium on the out-of-the-money puts closed at $30.

Options Trading

Options are a growth industry: New ways to speculate on what the future holds crop up regularly.

You buy and sell options through a brokerage firm, as you do stocks and bonds. In addition to the premium you pay when you buy or collect when you sell, you pay a commission on the transaction. The charges will vary, and you may pay less for two transactions you handle at one time or if you trade frequently.

You owe capital gains taxes on any profits you make trading options, though the rules for figuring those gains and any offsetting losses depend on the type of option involved. Experts agree that this is one situation where getting professional advice is essential.

STOCK INDEX OPTIONS

Like stock options, stock index options are closely tied to the value of the underlying item. For each index option, it's a specific stock index, such as the Dow Jones Industrial Average (DJIA). One of the differences between stock options and stock index options is that stock options settle in shares of the underlying stock, while index options settle in cash. But there are also similarities.

For example, buying **put options** on stock indexes is a way for you to hedge your stock portfolio against sharp drops in the market. It gives you the right to sell your options at a profit if the market falls. The money realized on the sale will—hopefully—cover the losses in your portfolio resulting from the falling market.

For this technique to work, though, your options have to be on the index that most closely tracks the kind of stocks you own. And you have to own enough options

to offset the total value of your portfolio. Since options cost money and expire quickly, using this kind of insurance regularly can take a big bite out of any profits the portfolio itself produces.

Speculators use index options to capitalize on shifts in market direction. Like other methods of high-risk investing, this one offers the chance of making a big killing if you get it right. Otherwise there wouldn't be any takers. But the risks of getting the price and the timing right are magnified by the short lifespan of index options.

A complicating factor is that indexes don't always move in the same direction as the markets they track. When indexes are out of kilter, there are big profits to be made, too—often by the arbitrage traders with computer programs fine-tuned enough to take advantage of the differences.

PRICE CHECK

The **premium**, or price you pay for an option, whether that option is on an individual stock, stock index, or other product, is largely determined by two factors.

The option's **intrinsic value** is the difference between the strike price and the current value of the underlying product. The **time value** depends on how much time remains until the option expires.

TO MARKET, TO MARKET, TO BUY...
The hogs that end up as pork in the supermarkets also supply the futures and options markets—
at 40,000 pounds per contract. The hogs get sold, the futures contracts are traded and the options
on those contracts are exercised—or expire. The farmer makes money if the hogs are sold for
more than it cost to raise them. Futures contract traders make
money if the cash price for the hogs means they can trade their
contracts at a profit. But option buyers make money only if
they guess right on what price a futures contract will be on a
specific date. That's what a derivative market is all about.

paying products to earn the higher market rate. To protect itself, the company would buy the rate cap for the assurance that if rates went up, the seller would pay the amount specified in the agreement— ideally enough to offset the insurer's lending losses.

The rate cap seller, probably a bank, would be willing to take the chance on having to pay up because it would collect the **premium**, or fee, for selling the protection.

CURRENCY OPTIONS

Institutional investors with large overseas holdings sometimes hedge their portfolios by buying options on the currencies of countries where their money is invested. Since the investment's value depends on the relationship between the dollar and the other currency, using options can equalize sudden shifts in value.

For example, if the value of the British pound lost ground against the dollar, U.S. investments in British companies would be worth less than they were when the pound was strong. But an option to buy pounds at the lower price could be sold at a profit, making up for some of the loss in investment value.

WHAT THE OPTIONS ARE

While there are essential differences between options and futures contracts, in certain circumstances investors use them in somewhat similar ways.

If you're in the options markets to help protect your other investments from the effect of changing values, you're considered a **hedger**, in the same way that a rancher who buys a futures contract is a hedger. If you're in the market hoping to profit by changes in the financial markets that other investors don't seem to be expecting—a rapid rise in interest rates or the falling value of the dollar, for example—you're considered a **speculator**.

INTEREST RATES OPTIONS

Options on interest rates are actually options on bonds issued by the U.S. Treasury or by governments in other countries. Bondholders can hedge their investments by using interest rate options, just as stockholders can hedge by using index options. Interest rate options are intended to offset any loss in value between the purchase date of the option and the date the bond matures. If the money from the maturing bond has to be reinvested at a lower rate, the profit from trading the option can make up for some of the loss, provided that the cost of the option doesn't eat it up.

A related derivatives investment, known as **an interest rate cap**, can provide similar protection when interest rates increase.

An insurance company, for example, might anticipate that its policyholders would take the opportunity to borrow against their policies at below-market rates and invest the money in interest-

Tracking Other Options

There's a brisk business in a wide range of options on indexes and futures.

While the basic elements of all types of options trading are similar—there are puts and calls, exercise prices, expiration dates, and underlying investments—each type is also distinctive.

For example, the size and the substance of the underlying financial instrument can vary dramatically. Stock options are based on one round lot, or 100 shares. Options on futures contracts are based on the contract commodity: 44,000 pounds of feeder cattle, 12,500,000 yen, or 5,000 bushels of wheat. And index options are based on stock indexes.

INDEX AND FUTURES OPTIONS

Because the indexes on which they are based can be volatile, index options often have a broad range of exercise prices and a relatively short timeframe. In the example below, from early November, no option expires later than February.

In contrast, options on agricultural futures contracts often run longer. And while the prices aren't predictable, there are recognizable patterns linked to the growing, harvesting, and marketing cycle that routinely affect the prices of the underlying products and futures contracts.

INDEX OPTIONS TRADING

OPEN INT	STRIKE	VOL	LAST	NET CHG	OPEN INT	STRIKE	VOL	LAST	NET CHG	OPEN INT	STRI
1,909	**CHICAGO**					Mar 108 c	858	1.30	0.45	12,645	Feb
6,827	**DJ INDUS AVG(DJX)**					Mar 108 p	57	2.15	-0.95	625	Mar
7,526						Apr 108 c	228	2	0.45	3,575	Feb
9,649	Feb 99 p	40	0.05	...	2,373	Apr 108 p	5	3.60	-0.30	184	M
2,003	Mar 99 p	6	0.20	-0.20	617	Feb 109 c	18	0.10	...	1,212	N
2,610	Feb 100 p	20	0.10	...	7,136	Feb 109 p	162	2	-2.50	606	A
994	Mar 100 c	34	7.10	0.90	17,361	Mar 112 c	420	0.15	-0.15	370	
6,027	Mar 100 p	6	0.35	-0.10	21,616	Apr 112 c	6	0.60	0.15	1,745	
						116 c	220	0.15	0.05		

The **index** on which these specific options are based heads the list. You can buy options on a wide variety of indexes, from the Dow Jones Industrial Average (DJX) to the much broader Russell 2000, for the U.S. market. Or you can choose indexes that track specific industries or stock markets in other countries or around the world.

The **exchange** on which the index options are traded is shown first.

In this case, it's the Chicago Board Options Exchange (CBOE), where more than a dozen index options are traded.

The **strike** column shows the expiration date, followed by strike price and whether the option is a put (p) or a call (c). When puts predominate at one end of the scale, it suggests that traders think the market is headed down. And when there are more calls, it suggests that traders expect the market to go up.

Volume reports the number of trades during the previous trading day. In index options trading, the heaviest volume is usually in options closest to expiration and current market price.

Last is the closing price of the option at the end of the previous day's trading. As with stock options, prices are given in whole dollars and cents. (To get the actual price you multiply the number by 100, since each option is for 100 units.) For example, the February 109 call is trading at 0.10, which translates to $10.

Net change is the difference between the price reported here and the closing price two trading days ago. When there's no change, an ellipsis (...) appears.

FUTURES OPTIONS PRICES

Futures options trading includes agricultural products, other raw materials, and financial commodities like international currencies and interest rates.

The **futures contract** on which the option is based, the exchange on which it is traded, the number of units in the contract and the price unit by which the price of the commodity is figured are shown. In this example, the futures contract is on soybeans traded on the Chicago Board of Trade. Each contract is for 5,000 bushels and the price is quoted in cents per bushel, so that 575 means $5.75 a bushel.

Industry group

is a grouping of similar commodities traded on various exchanges. They include options on futures contracts in agricultural products, oil, livestock, currency, interest rates, and stock and bond indexes.

Puts gives the dates of the put options available in each commodity. Prices for puts and calls move in the opposite direction because they reflect the price movement of the underlying commodity. When calls are selling for more, puts are selling for less, as they are for feeder cattle here.

FUTURES OPTIONS PRICES

AGRICULTURAL

SOYBEANS (CBT)
5,000 bu.; cents per bu.

Strike Price	Calls–Settle Aug	Sep	Nov	Puts–Settle Aug	Sep	Nov
575	45½	51¾	57½	2¾	6¾	10½
600	28½	36	43	10½	16⅝	21⅝
625	18	27½	33¼	25	32	37
650	12⅜	22½	26½	44	51½	54
675	8⅛	17½	21¼	....	....	74
700	6	14⅝	18¼	....	....	96½

Est vol 15,000   Mon 14,310 calls 5,-945 puts
Op int Mon   109,516 calls 41,064 puts

SOYBEAN MEAL (CBT)
100 tons; $ per ton

Strike Price	Calls–Settle Aug	Sep	Oct	Puts–Settle Aug	Sep	Oct
185	10.50	12.45	13.25	1.25	3.25	3.70
190	7.50	9.75	10.50	3.25	5.25	5.95
195	5.50	8.00	9.00	6.00	....	9.50
200	4.00	6.60	7.50	....	....	12.90
210	2.20	4.75	5.50	....	19.75	20.80
220	1.40	3.60	4.50	....	....	....

Est vol 1,300   Mon 1,585 calls 951 puts
Op int Mon   16,262 calls 8,144 puts

SOYBEAN OIL (CBT)
60,000 lbs.; cents per lb.

Strike Price	Calls–Settle Aug	Sep	Oct	Puts–Settle Aug	Sep	Oct
2100	1.430	1.700	....	.250	.400	.460
2150	1.080	1.430	....	.400	.640	....
2200	.800	1.220	1.400	.650	.930	....
2250	.650	1.050	....	....	....	....
2300	.500	.920	1.08?	....	....	....
2350						

CATTLE-FEEDER (CME)
44,000 lbs.; cents per lb.

Strike Price	Calls–Settle Aug	Sep	Oct	Puts–Settle Aug	Sep	Oct
82	4.85	4.10	3.92	0.32	0.60	0.75
84	3.00	2.50	2.47	0.47	1.00	1.30
86	1.60	1.25	1.37	1.05	1.75	2.20
88	0.70	0.55	0.65	2.10	....	....
90	0.22	0.20	....	3.57	....	....
92	0.17	....	....	....	....	....

Est vol 278   Mon 40 calls 167 puts
Op int Mon   1,853 calls 7,340 puts

CATTLE-LIVE (CME)
40,000 lbs.; cents per lb.

Strike Price	Calls–Settle Jly	Aug	Oct	Puts–Settle Jly	Aug	Oct
70	....	3.57	....	....	0.17	0.47
72	....	1.97	2.70	0.07	0.55	0.95
74	....	0.75	1.52	0.75	1.32	1.75
76	0.05	0.20	0.72	....	2.75	2.92
78	....	0.05	0.32	....	....	4.50
80	....	....	0.12	....	....	....

Est vol 1,787   Mon 179 calls 5?
Op int Mon   12,90? ?

HOGS–LIVE (C?
40,000 lbs.?

Strike Price
44
46
48
50
52
54

Strike price is the price at which the option owner may buy or sell the corresponding futures contract by exercising the option. Each commodity has options covering a range of prices that increase in a regular sequence (200/210/220).

Calls gives the dates of the call options currently available on this commodity. In this example, options on soybean meal contracts are available for August, September and October.

Settle shows that the exchange has adjusted the price to reflect market values at the end of trading. Because futures contracts and the options on those contracts may not trade at the same pace, the exchange will adjust an option's price to coincide with its futures price at the end of the day.

So the settle price for the August 185 option is $10.50 per ton, or $1,050.

Estimated volume reports the number of trades on the previous trading day, separated into puts and calls.

Open interest shows the number of outstanding options contracts, broken out by puts and calls, that have not been offset by an opposite transaction.

Derivatives Over the Counter

Organizations turn to the private market for customized hedging tools.

Over-the-counter derivatives, which first appeared in the 1980s, are widely used by corporations, financial institutions and public agencies as tools to manage financial risk by hedging their long-term commitments to buy, sell or lend, particularly when foreign-exchange risks are involved.

OTC derivatives, including forwards, swaps and options, are often referred to as either **plain vanilla** or **exotic**. The plain vanilla contracts involve largely standardized products and practices, while the exotic varieties introduce highly tailored elements.

IN THE MARKET

In the OTC derivatives market, institutional investors or borrowers work directly with dealer banks to handle their transactions, typically negotiated by specialized traders. The dealer bank is generally known as the **counterparty**.

The deals usually don't require collateral to underpin a position, and there is no middleman to guarantee that the parties will make good on their commitments. However, dealer banks are working on developing more uniform standards to overcome problems that have cropped up and made some organizations hesitant to trade highly sophisticated derivatives.

DEFINING THE TOOLS

A **swap** is a customized financial tool an investor or borrower uses to exchange one cash flow for another. For example, an interest-rate swap exchanges a fixed interest rate for a floating interest rate.

In a typical currency swap, one party agrees to pay the equivalent of a stream of interest payments and final principal denominated in one currency in exchange for another stream of payments in a different currency at a preset exchange rate.

A **forward** contract covers the delivery and payment for a specific commodity at a specific date in the future at a specific price. That price may be higher or lower than the actual market price at the time of delivery, or what's known as the **spot price**. But the participants lock in a price early so they know what they will receive or pay for the product, eliminating market risk.

How a Currency Swap Works

BOND ISSUE
The bond issue raises money in Japanese yen.

Companies often go to a foreign bond market in order to attract investors and get favorable interest rates. Because the issue may be denominated in a currency in which the company doesn't generate revenue, the company will set up a currency swap.

FOREX DEAL
The forex deal converts the yen to Australian dollars so the company can make its investments.

CURRENCY SWAP
The currency swap converts some of the company's earnings in U.S. dollars to yen to pay the interest on the bond.

RISK POTENTIAL
Because of their complexity and the extent to which they may be leveraged, OTC derivatives can pose potentially large risks to the investors who use them.

MARKET BUSINESS

Foreign-exchange contracts and interest-rate contracts account for the bulk of OTC derivatives activity, trailed by equity and commodity contracts. A clear sign of the global nature of the OTC market is that more than half of all OTC derivatives deals are struck by parties from different nations.

Companies doing business in more than one country need to protect against sudden or dramatic changes in the relative value of currencies, so they hedge commitments to invest, sell or borrow with agreements that have predetermined **forex**, or foreign-exchange, **rates**.

For example, a Sydney-based mining company that wants to invest in an Australian gold mine decides to launch a three-year yen-denominated dual-currency issue in Japan, known as a Samurai bond. By raising yen in Japan, the company reduces its borrowing costs because Japanese interest rates are lower than Australian rates.

THE INVESTOR'S ROLE

For the investors, the issue is attractive because they will receive higher returns than with Japanese corporate bonds. The returns are higher because one of the currencies involved, the Australian dollar, is linked to higher interest rates than are available in Japan. But the risks are higher, too.

To get the higher interest rate, the investors have to take a greater risk on some part of the dual-currency bond. In this case, they are betting that the yen will at least be stable or perhaps will fall against other currencies over the next few years. The investor gets an instant reward for taking that currency risk, as the annual coupon on a dual-currency bond may be 5% for three years, compared with 0.7% for a three-year deposit in a Japanese bank.

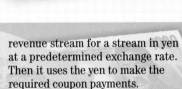

The first thing the mining company wants to do is reduce the risks involved in its exposure to the currency markets. Expecting to have yen from its bond issue on a specific date, the company can plan to sell yen for Australian dollars in the spot market after the bond issuance. Or it can enter a forward contract ahead of the issuance to buy Australian dollars at a certain rate at the time it expects to get the yen.

But the company will also pursue a separate agreement for a currency swap. It does this because it needs to make the interest payments on the bond in yen every six months. However, its revenue from the sales of gold produced in its mine is in U.S. dollars. So it sets up the deal, or currency swap, to exchange a portion of that dollar-denominated revenue stream for a stream in yen at a predetermined exchange rate. Then it uses the yen to make the required coupon payments.

Since the bond, or debt, must eventually be repaid in Australian dollars, the company also needs to ensure that it has sufficient capital set aside in that currency to cover the amount owed.

Risk of illiquidity
An investor could face difficulty finding a buyer for a highly tailored product.

Credit risk
The counterparty may prove unable or unwilling to make good on its obligations.

Systemic risk
A collapse at one firm or bank could trigger a chain reaction throughout the global financial network.

INDEX

A

American Depositary Receipts 79, 81
American Depositary Shares 79, 81
American Stock Exchange
   (AMEX) 62-63, 67-68, 70, 92, 100
Annual report 59
Annualized return 121
Arbitrage 141, 148
At the money 144
ATMs 15, 35
Auction 64, 101, 144

B

Back-end load 122
Barter 6
Basis..26
Benchmarks 70-71, 118-119
Bid and asked prices. 65, 96-97, 102
Blue chip stocks.......................37, 108, 111
Bond funds 100, 108-111,
               113, 117-120, 125
BONDS... 84-105
  Bonds, types of bonds
    Agency bonds 85, 102, 104
    Asset-backed bonds.....................98
    Baby bonds...............................87
    Bearer bonds...............................86
    Callable bonds 99
    Collateralized mortgage
      obligations (CMOs).................98
    Convertible bonds 98
    Debentures.................................98
    General obligation bonds.............95
    Junk bonds....................................91
    Mortgage-backed bonds.......98, 102
    Municipal 85, 90, 94-95, 104
    Prefunded bonds.......................98
    Revenue bonds............................95
    Self-amortizing bonds 98
    Senior bonds 98
    Subordinated bonds 98
  Bond offerings 84, 95, 101
  Book entry bonds..............................86
  Corporate bonds 85, 90-94, 100, 104
  Coupon rate 86, 94
  Credit rating 90-91
  Deep discount bonds 97, 99
  Discount 89, 97, 103
  Downgrading 91
  Floating a bond 84
  Floating-rate bonds..........................98
  International bonds..........................84

  Investment grade 91
  Make a market in 100
  Markup 100
  Maturity 84, 87, 89, 92-94,
           96-97, 99, 102-104
  Municipal bonds 85, 90, 94-95, 104
  Par value 84-85, 87-89
          93-94, 97, 100, 104
  Premium 89
  Sinking fund 98
  Tax-exempt bonds 94-95, 103-105
  Term, bond 84
  U.S. savings bonds 103
  U.S. Treasury bills, bonds
    and notes 85, 90, 96-97,
          100-102, 104-105
  Zero-coupon bonds 93, 97, 99
Book value..58
Brokerage firms 48-49, 53, 65, 100, 131
Brokers 48-50, 52, 64-65,
         89, 100, 115, 125, 130
  Buy and sell orders 48
  Deep discount brokers 49
  Discount brokers 49
  Floor brokers.............................. 64-65
  Full service brokers..........................49
  Online brokers 49
  Specialist 65
Broker-dealer......................................49
Bureau of Engraving and Printing 9
Bureau of the Mint 13

C

Call options 142-147, 151
Capital gain distributions 106
Capital gain 41, 80-81
Capitalization....................... 46-47, 63, 80
Cash market 128, 136
Closed-end funds 107, 125
Circuit breakers....................................46, 75
Collateralized mortgage
  obligations (CMOs)...........................98
Commercial paper 103
Commissions 34, 47-50, 53,
         100, 130, 137, 146
Commodities 128-132, 134-135,
         137-141, 151
Commodity Futures Trading
  Commission (CFTC) 130
Commodity indexes 139
Consumer confidence............................24
Consumer Price Index..................... 26-27
Contango 135

INDEX

Contigent deferred sales charge 122
Corporate bonds 85, 90,
  92-94, 100, 104
Correction 50
Country funds..125
Coupon equivalent yield 97
Coupon rate..................................86, 94
Covered stock calls.......................142, 146
Covering the short position 50-51
Credit cards................................ 14-15, 35
Creditors...86
Cumulative voting...................................39
Currency 6-7, 12, 30-33,
  35, 80-81, 125, 129,
  140-141, 149, 152-153
  Currency cross rates 30-31
  Currency options............................148
  Currency trading ... 32, 34-35, 152-153
  Hard currency 8
  Specie 8
  Tale 7
CUSIP 43
Cyclical stocks 41

D

Dartboard analysis 58
Day traders..47
Dealers 48
Debentures...98
Debit cards............................... 14-15
Debt securities.......................................98
Deep discount bonds.........................97, 99
Deep out of the money 144
Deferred sales charge 122
Deflation 29
Depression 28, 75
Derivative investments 126, 149
Discount rate 16, 19
Disinflation 29
Distributions 106, 109, 120
Diversification....................106, 113, 124
Dividends.....................41, 56, 58-61, 108
  Dividend yield 41
  Ex-dividend 61
Dividend reinvestment plan
  (DRIP) 48
Dow Jones-AIG Commodities
  Index 139
Dow Jones Industrial
  Average (DJIA) 49, 69, 70-75,
  108, 141, 148, 150
Downgrading...91

E

Economic cycle.......................................28
Efficient market.....................................112
Electronic trading 54, 62-67,
  76, 130-131, 144
Equity 36
Equity funds 108, 111, 125
Eurodollars...................................31, 132, 141
Exchange fees 122
Exchange traded funds (ETFs) 68-69
Expense ratio 117, 119, 122
Expiration 126-127, 133, 136,
  139, 143, 145-147, 150

F

Family of funds 109
Fannie Mae 102
Federal Deposit Insurance
  Corporation (FDIC) 17
Federal Reserve System............. 16-21, 53
Federal Reserve Banks 8-12, 85
Fees, mutual fund.........116, 119, 121-122
Financial commodities...........129, 140-141
Financial futures 140-141
Fixed-income securities.........................84
Foreign exchange 30-35, 152-153
Forex....................................32, 35, 152
Freddie Mac 102
Fund managers 106-107,
  111-112, 114-115
Fund performance 116-122
Fundamental analysis 59
Funds, types of
  (see mutual funds, types of)
FUTURES..................................... 126-151
  Dow Jones-AIG Commodities
    Index 139
  Expiration date 125-127,
    133, 136, 139
  Financial commodities 129,
    140-141
  Financial futures 140-141
  Hedgers 129, 134-137, 140, 148-149
  Open interest................................139
  Open outcry..................................131
  Speculators 129, 134-137, 140
  Trading pit 131
Futures contracts 128-129,
  132-137, 149, 151
  Go long..133
  Go short 133
  Initial margin 132

Marking to market 132
Meeting the margin 132
Offsetting trades 133, 137, 139
Price limits 133
Spread trading 133
Futures exchanges..............................130
Futures, options on 149, 151

G

General obligation bonds........................95
Ginnie Mae bonds..........................102, 110
Global funds 111, 124
Global markets.................. 76-81, 124-125,
152-153
GNMA (Government National Mortgage
Association) bonds 102, 110
Gold standard 7, 30
Good 'til cancelled (GTC)......................48
Greenbacks 10-11
Growth stocks 41

H

Hard currency 8
Hedgers........................111, 129, 134-137,
140, 148-149
High-yield funds 108-109

I

In-the-money.......................................144
Income distributions............................106
Income stocks 41
Index funds 111-112, 125
Index options 148, 150
Indexes and averages 70-71
*Dow Jones-AIG Commodities
Index* 139
*Dow Jones Industrial Average
(DJIA)* 49, 69, 70-75,
108, 141, 148, 150
*Index of Leading Economic
Indicators* 22-23
International indexes.................. 78-79
Lipper indexes 118
Mutual fund indexes.......................118
Municipal bond indexes 95
Russell 2000 index....................118, 150
*Standard & Poor's 500-stock
Index (S&P 500)* 70-71, 78,
112, 118-119, 140
Value Line indexes 70

Wilshire 5000 71
Inefficient markets..............................112
Inflation.................9, 28-30, 85, 88, 96, 103
Initial margin....................................127, 132
Initial public offering
(IPO) 44-45, 83, 85
Insider trading.....................................55
Institutional investors...............37, 39, 46,
54, 100, 125
Interest rate 21, 85-99, 102-103, 110
International funds .. 81, 110-111, 124-125
Investment bankers...............................44
Investment clubs 47
Investment companies..................85, 107
Investment grade....................................91
Investment objective...........107, 110, 113,
116, 122-123

J

Junk bonds 91, 109

L

Legal tender..11
Leverage 52-53, 122, 127, 146
Limit order 48
Lipper Inc. 116-118
Liquid assets 20
Load funds..............................117, 122-123
Long bond..87
Long-term Equity Anticipation
Securities (LEAPS)........................147

M

Make a market in................................100
Margin account 52
Margin call 53
Market crashes 74-75
Market cycles.......................................72
Market makers...............................63, 66
Market order 48
Marking to market...............................132
Markup 100
Maximum initial charge......................117
Meeting the margin......................53, 132
Minimun investments.....................53, 123
Monetary aggregates 20-21
Monetary policy 18-21
MONEY 6-35
Money market funds.........21, 108-110, 123
Money supply 20-21

Municipal bond funds............109-110, 113
Municipal bonds............85, 90, 94-95, 104
MUTUAL FUNDS........................ 106-125
  Annualized return 121
  Distributions 106, 109, 120
  Expense ratio 117, 119, 122
  Family of funds 109
  Fees 116, 119, 121-122
  12b-1 fees 116, 122
  Back-end load 116, 122
  Class A, B and C shares......117, 122
  Deferred sales charge 122
  Exchange fees...........................122
  Expense ratio 117, 119, 122
  Management fees 122
  Marketing fees 122
  Redemption charges 122
  Fund manager 106-107,
    111-112, 114-115
  Investment companies..............85, 107
  Investment objective 107, 113,
    116, 122-123
  Load funds 117, 122-123
  Minimum investments 123
  Mutual funds, types of
  Bond funds 100, 108-111,
    113, 117-120, 125
  Closed-end funds 107, 125
  Country funds 125
  Equity funds............108, 111, 125
  Global funds.......................111, 124
  High-yield funds.................. 108-109
  Index funds 111-112, 125
  International
    funds 81, 110-111, 124-125
  Market neutral funds 113
  Money market funds..................21,
    108-110, 123
  Municipal bond funds 109-110,
    113
  Open-end funds 107
  Precious metal funds 113
  Quant funds...............................112
  Regional funds 124
  Sector funds 108, 113
  Single country funds 125
  Socially conscious......................113
  Stock funds 108, 110-112,
    117, 119, 125
  Tax-free funds 109, 113
  Treasury and agency
    funds 109-110
  U.S. government funds 109-110
  Net asset value (NAV) 116, 120

  No-load funds 117
  Performance.....................116, 118-121
  Portfolio turnover rate 122
  Redemption options 123
  Reinvestment options 123
  Total return 117-121

N

Naked calls..............................142
Naked puts 142
NASD (National Association of
  Securities Dealers)....66, 115, 116, 122
Nasdaq Stock Market, The....................60,
  63, 66-67
National Futures Association (NFA)....130
Net asset value (NAV) 68-69, 71,
  116-117, 120
New York Stock Exchange
  (NYSE) 43, 46, 50-51,
  53, 56-57, 60, 62-65,
  67, 75, 92, 100, 149
No-load funds 117

O

Offsetting trades............133, 137, 139, 151
Online research 54
Online trading...............49, 54-55, 100, 115
Open interest 139, 151
Open outcry.................................131, 144
Open-end funds..................................107
OPTIONS 126-127, 142-153
  At-the-money 144
  Buying 142
  Call options 142-147, 151
  Deep-out-of-the-money 144
  Exercise price 142, 150-151
  Expiration date 143, 145-147, 150
  Futures, options on 151
  Hedgers 148-149
  In-the-money 144, 146-147
  Index options 148, 150
  Listed options 143
  Longterm Equity Anticipation
    Securities (LEAPS)....................147
  Open interest............................139, 151
  Options prices 142, 146-147
  Options on currencies....................149
  Options on interest rates.................149
  Out-of-the-money 144
  Premium 142-143, 146, 149
  Put options 142-148, 151

INDEX

Selling 142, 147
Speculators 146-149
Spread trading 147
Stock options 142-147
Straddle 147
Strangle 147
Strike price 142-143, 145,
147-148, 150-151
Underlying instrument 142
Writing puts and calls 142-143, 146
Out-of-the-money 144
Over-the-counter
(OTC) 35, 63, 100, 105,
129-130, 152-153

P

Paper money 8-13
Par value 43, 84-85, 87-89,
93-94, 97, 100, 104
Payout ratio 58
Percent yield 56, 89, 120
Precious metal funds 108, 113
Preferred stock 36
Premium 69, 88-89, 142-143, 146, 149
Price limits 132
Price/earnings ratio (P/E) 57, 67
Private equity market 44
Privatization 82-83
Program trading 46, 75
Prospectus 44, 122-123
Proxy 38-39, 122
Put options 142-148, 151

Q

Quant funds 112

R

Rating services........................... 90-91, 105
Real interest rates 21
Recession 28-29
Regional exchanges 62
Regional funds 124
Redemption charges............................122
Reinvestment options 113
Return 40, 58, 88, 117-121
Revenue bonds 95
Risk 50-51, 53, 69, 80-81, 91,
93, 98-99, 105, 110-111, 113,
125-126, 135, 142, 146-148, 152-153

S

S&P 500-stock Index 22, 38, 49, 70-71
78, 112, 118-119, 140
Sales charges 115, 117, 119, 122
Sallie Mae 102
Secondary market.................85, 87-88, 100
Secondary offering.................................45
Sector funds 108, 111, 113
Securities 42, 48
Securities and Exchange
Commission (SEC).......... 38, 42, 44-45,
48, 53-55, 69, 122, 130
Seigniorage...13
Selling options 142, 147
Selling short 50-51, 133
Shareholders 36, 38-39, 45, 68, 122
Sideways market...................................146
Silver certificates 8
Single country funds..............................125
Sinking fund 98
Smart cards 14
Socially conscious funds 113
Specie 8
Speculators 134-137,
140, 146-149
Spot market..............................35, 128, 152
Spread.........................57, 65, 133, 147
Spread trading 133, 147
Stock certificate 42-43
Stock exchange 48-49, 62-65,
67-69, 92, 100
Stock fund 108, 112, 117-119
Stock markets 62-81
Market crashes...................... 72, 74-75
Market listings...................................63
Overseas.................................... 76-81
Over the counter (OTC) 35, 63
Stock options 142-147
Stockbrokers 48-49, 53, 100
Stockholders 36, 38, 43, 45
STOCKS 36-83
Book value...58
Classes of stock 36
Common stock 36
Correction 50
Covering the short position........ 50-51
Decimal pricing 56
Dividends 41, 56
Dividend reinvestment plan
(DRIP)...48
Earnings per share 58
Initial public offering
(IPO) 44-45, 83, 85

CENGAGE
Learning®

RELG: World, 2nd Edition
Robert E. Van Voorst

Product Director: Suzanne Jeans

Product Manager: Debra Matteson

Senior Development Editor: Sue Gleason Wade

Content Coordinator: Joshua Duncan

4LTR Press Project Manager: Pierce Denny

Market Development Manager: Shanna Shelton

Content Project Manager: Alison Eigel Zade

Art Director: Kristina Mose-Libon, PMG

Manufacturing Planner: Sandee Milewski

Rights Acquisition Specialist: Stacey Dong

Production Service & Compositor: Integra

Text Designer: RHDG Design

Cover Designer: PremediaGlobal

Cover Image: Forest Woodward/Getty Images

> For product information and technology assistance, contact us at
> **Cengage Learning Customer & Sales Support, 1-800-354-9706**
>
> For permission to use material from this text or product,
> submit all requests online at **www.cengage.com/permissions**.
> Further permissions questions can be emailed to
> **permissionrequest@cengage.com**.

Library of Congress Control Number: 2013932744

ISBN-13: 978-1-285-43468-1

ISBN-10: 1-285-43468-4

Cengage Learning
200 First Stamford Place, 4th Floor
Stamford, CT 06902
USA

Cengage Learning is a leading provider of customized learning solutions with office locations around the globe, including Singapore, the United Kingdom, Australia, Mexico, Brazil and Japan. Locate your local office at **international.cengage.com/region**

Cengage Learning products are represented in Canada by Nelson Education, Ltd.

For your course and learning solutions, visit **www.cengage.com**.

Purchase any of our products at your local college store or at our preferred online store **www.cengagebrain.com**.

Instructors: Please visit **login.cengage.com** and log in to access instructor-specific resources.

Printed in the United States of America
1 2 3 4 5 6 7 17 16 15 14 13

Brief Contents

1 BEGINNING YOUR STUDY OF WORLD RELIGIONS 2

2 ENCOUNTERING INDIGENOUS RELIGIONS: WAYS TO TRIBAL LIFE 30

3 ENCOUNTERING HINDUISM: MANY PATHS TO LIBERATION 62

4 ENCOUNTERING JAINISM: THE AUSTERE WAY TO LIBERATION 94

5 ENCOUNTERING BUDDHISM: THE MIDDLE PATH TO LIBERATION 110

6 ENCOUNTERING SIKHISM: THE WAY OF GOD'S NAME 138

7 ENCOUNTERING DAOISM AND CONFUCIANISM: TWO VIEWS OF THE ETERNAL WAY 156

8 ENCOUNTERING SHINTO: THE WAY OF THE KAMI 188

9 ENCOUNTERING ZOROASTRIANISM: THE WAY OF THE ONE WISE LORD 206

10 ENCOUNTERING JUDAISM: THE WAY OF GOD'S PEOPLE 226

11 ENCOUNTERING CHRISTIANITY: THE WAY OF JESUS CHRIST 258

12 ENCOUNTERING ISLAM: THE STRAIGHT PATH OF THE ONE GOD 294

13 ENCOUNTERING NEW RELIGIOUS MOVEMENTS: MODERN WAYS TO ALTERNATIVE MEANINGS 332

A custom edition of *RELG2* can be created including readings from Van Voorst, *Anthology of World Scriptures*, 8/e. Contact your Cengage Learning representative for ordering information.

Contents

1 BEGINNING YOUR STUDY OF WORLD RELIGIONS   2

Your Visit to the Hsi Lai Temple in Southern California   3

1-1   Coming to Grips with Your Preunderstanding of Religion   4
    1-1a What Is Preunderstanding?   5
    1-1b Your Preunderstanding of Religion   5

1-2   What Is Religion?   5
    1-2a Defining *Religion*   5
    1-2b Notable Definitions of *Religion*   6
    1-2c The Definition Used in This Book   6
    A Closer Look: Is Religion *a Dirty Word?*   8

1-3   Why Study Religion?   8
    1-3a Studying the Persistence of Religion in the Modern World   8
    1-3b What the Academic Study of Religion Can Offer You   10

1-4   Dimensions of Religion   10
    1-4a The Cognitive Dimension   11
    1-4b The Ethical Dimension   11
    1-4c The Ritual Dimension   12
    1-4d The Institutional Dimension   12
    1-4e The Aesthetic Dimension   13
    1-4f The Emotional Dimension   13

1-5   Ways of Studying Religion   14
    1-5a Theology and Religious Studies   14
    1-5b History   15
    1-5c Psychology   17
    1-5d Sociology   18
    1-5e Cultural Anthropology   18
    1-5f Women's Studies   20
    1-5g Biology   20
    1-5h Conclusions about Methods of Studying Religion   21

1-6   Special Issues in the Study of Religion Today   21
    1-6a Tolerance and Intolerance   21
    1-6b Violence   23
    1-6c Pluralism   24
    A Closer Look: Statement on Pluralism by Harvard University's Pluralism Project   26
    1-6d Religion and Ecological Crisis   26
    1-6e New Religious Movements   27

VINZ 89/SHUTTERSTOCK.COM

© ISTOCKPHOTO/NINA SHANNON

Your Visit to the Petroglyph National Monument, New Mexico   31

2-1   Names for This Type of Religion   32
   2-1a Traditional Religion   32
   2-1b Primitive Religion   32
   2-1c Animism and Totemism   32
   2-1d Manaism   33
   2-1e Shamanism   33
   A Closer Look: Totemism in the Twilight Series   34
   2-1f Small-Scale Religions   34
   2-1g Nature Religion   35
   2-1h Indigenous Religions   35

2-2   Challenges to Study   36
   2-2a Lack of Written Sources   36
   2-2b Difficulty Discerning Continuity and Discontinuity   36
   2-2c Mainstream Guilt   37
   2-2d Misrepresentations in Popular Culture   37
   2-2e Misuse of Indigenous Rituals   37

2-3   Common Features of Indigenous Religions   38
   2-3a The Importance of Place   38
   A Closer Look: Movements toward Indigenous Unity   40
   2-3b Global Distribution   40
   2-3c Many Gods and Spirits   42
   2-3d Influenced by Other Cultures   43
   2-3e Based on Orality, Story, and Myth   43
   2-3f Oriented More to Practice Than to Belief   44
   2-3g In-Group Based   44
   2-3h The Goodness of the World   45
   2-3i The Role of Religious Specialists   45
   2-3j Continuing Vitality   45

2-4   A Native American Religion: Lakota   46
   2-4a Name and Location   46
   2-4b Basic Features of Lakota Religion   49
   2-4c Lakota Rituals   50
   2-4d Culture and Religion   51

2-5   An African Religion: Yoruba   53
   A Closer Look: Polynesian Religion in Hawaii   54
   2-5a High God and Other Gods   55
   2-5b Religious Specialists   57
   2-5c Spirits of the Ancestors   58

2-6   An Afro-Caribbean Religion: Vodou   58
   2-6a Location and Name   58
   2-6b Divinities   59
   2-6c Groups   59
   2-6d Worship   59
   2-6e Spell and Counter-Spell Rituals   60
   2-6f Political Influence in Haiti   61

Your Visit to Varanasi, India   **63**

3-1   **The Name** *Hinduism*   **65**

3-2   **The Hindu Present as Shaped by Its Past**   **65**
A Closer Look: The Symbols of Hinduism   66
3-2a   The Vedic Period (1500–600 B.C.E.)   66
3-2b   The Upanishadic Period (600–400 B.C.E.)   69
3-2c   The Classical Period (400 B.C.E.–600 C.E.)   70
3-2d   The Devotional Period (600 C.E.–Present)   71

3-3   **Essential Hindu Teachings**   **74**
3-3a   Main Deities in the Three Devotional
Movements   74
3-3b   Hindu Doctrinal Concepts   76
*A Closer Look: Popular Misunderstandings of Karma,
Mantra, Guru, and Avatar*   78

3-4   **Hindu Ethics and Ways of Life**   **78**
3-4a   The Caste System   79
3-4b   The Four Stages of a Man's Life   81
3-4c   The Four Goals of Life   83
3-4d   The Lives of Hindu Women   83
A Closer Look: Hindu Dress   84

3-5   **Hindu Rituals**   **85**
3-5a   Images   86
3-5b   Worship in the Temple and the Home   86
3-5c   Pilgrimage   87
3-5d   Festivals and Holidays   87
3-5e   Funerals   88
3-5f   Yoga   89

3-6   **Hinduism around the World Today**   **89**
3-6a   Hinduism in South Asia and Africa   90
3-6b   Hinduism in the West   90
3-6c   Hindu Migration and Life in North America   91
A Closer Look: Hindu Faith and Indian Food   92

WWW.CEPOLINA.COM

© DANSHUTTER/SHUTTERSTOCK.COM

© DINODIA PHOTOS/BRAND X PICTURES/JUPITER IMAGES

Your Visit with Jain Nuns   **95**

4-1   **The Name** *Jainism*   **96**

4-2   **The Jain Present as Shaped by Its Past**   **96**
A Closer Look: The Symbol of Jainism   97
4-2a   Founding and the First Thousand Years (600 B.C.E.–ca. 400 C.E.)   97
4-2b   The Next Thousand Years (600–1600)   99
4-2c   Early Modern Times through Today (1600–Present)   100

4-3   **Essential Jain Teachings**   **101**
4-3a   No Gods   101
4-3b   Time and the World   102

DINODIA PHOTOS/BRAND X PICTURES/JUPITERIMAGES

4-3c Jiva and Ajiva 102
4-3d Karma and Liberation 102
4-3e Theories of Knowledge 103

4-4 Ethics: The Five Cardinal Virtues 104
4-4a Do No Harm; Speak the Truth 104
4-4b Do Not Steal; Do Not Be Possessive 104
A Closer Look: Jainism and Food 105
4-4c Be Chaste 105

4-5 Jain Ritual and Worship 106
4-5a The Life of Monks and Nuns 106
4-5b Life of the Laity in Worship and Devotion 107
4-5c Two Jain Festivals 108

4-6 Jainism around the World Today 108
4-6a Jainism in the West 108
4-6b Jainism in North America 109

© STEVE ESTVANIK/SHUTTERSTOCK.COM

Your Visit to a Zen Retreat Center 111

5-1 The Name *Buddhism* 112
A Closer Look: The Symbol of Buddhism 113

5-2 Buddhism Today as Shaped by Its Past 113
5-2a Gautama's Road to Enlightenment 114
5-2b Achievement of Enlightenment 115
5-2c India, Sri Lanka, and Theravada 116
5-2d The Rise of Mahayana: China and Japan 118
A Closer Look: Koans 121
5-2e Tibet and the Diamond Vehicle 121

5-3 Essential Buddhist Teachings 123
5-3a The Four Noble Truths 123
A Closer Look: Popular Misunderstandings of Karma, Nirvana, and Zen 124
5-3b The Noble Eightfold Path 125
5-3c The Three Characteristics of Existence 125

5-4 Buddhist Ethics for Monastics and Laypeople 126
5-4a General Buddhist Morality 126
5-4b The Five Precepts 127
5-4c Other Precepts and Moral Rules 127

5-5 Buddhist Ritual and Meditation 128
5-5a Temples 128
5-5b Images of the Buddha 129
5-5c Prayer and Meditation 130
5-5d Protective Rituals 131
5-5e Funeral Rituals 131

5-6 Buddhism around the World Today 132
5-6a Buddhism in Modern Asia 132
5-6b Buddhism Comes to the Western World 134

SARAH M. GOLONKA/BRAND X PICTURES/JUPITER IMAGES

© SERG ZASTAVKIN/SHUTTERSTOCK.COM

© HENRY WILLIAM FU/SHUTTERSTOCK.COM

5-6c Early Buddhist Immigration to North America 134

5-6d The Next Wave of Buddhist Immigration 136

5-6e Conclusion 136

A Closer Look: Stealing Buddha's Dinner: A Memoir 137

6 ENCOUNTERING SIKHISM: THE WAY OF GOD'S NAME 138

Your Visit to a Sikh Temple 139

6-1 The Name *Sikhism* 140

6-2 Sikhism Today as Shaped by Its Past: Two Key Periods 140

A Closer Look: The Symbol of Sikhism 141

6-2a The Ten Gurus 141

6-2b Sikhism from British Rule until Today 144

6-3 Essential Sikh Teachings 145

A Closer Look: The Mul Mantar 145

6-3a The One God 146

6-3b Devotion to God 146

A Closer Look: Sikh Dress 147

6-4 Key Sikh Ethics 147

6-4a Rejection of Hindu Caste 147

6-4b Other Moral Rules 148

6-5 Sikh Ritual and Worship 149

6-5a The Gurdwara 149

6-5b The Langar 151

6-5c Sikh Life-Cycle Rituals 151

6-5d Other Festivals 152

6-6 Sikhism around the World Today 152

6-6a The Sikh Diaspora 152

6-6b The First Wave of Immigration to North America (1900–1940) 153

6-6c Second and Third Waves to North America (1965–Present) 154

6-6d Sikhism in Post-9/11 America 154

© SZEFEI/SHUTTERSTOCK.COM

© ERMESS/SHUTTERSTOCK.COM

7 ENCOUNTERING DAOISM AND CONFUCIANISM: TWO VIEWS OF THE ETERNAL WAY 156

Your Visit to the Forbidden City in Beijing, China 157

7-1 The Names *Daoism* and *Confucianism* 159

A Closer Look: The Symbols of Daoism and Confucianism 160

7-2 Daoism and Confucianism Today as Shaped by Their Past 161

7-2a China before the Birth of Confucianism and Daoism (ca. 3000–500 B.C.E.) 161

7-2b The Origins of Daoism (ca. 500 B.C.E.–200 C.E.) 163

A Closer Look: Religions or Philosophies? 165

7-2c Daoism from 200 C.E. to 1664 C.E 165

© LIJUAN GUO/SHUTTERSTOCK.COM

A Closer Look: The Four Editions of the Daoist Canon (Daozang) 166

7-2d The Near-Destruction of Daoism (1644–1980) 167

7-2e Confucius and the Origins of Confucianism (551–479 B.C.E.) 167

7-2f The Rise of Confucianism and Neo-Confucianism (ca. 350 B.C.E.–1200 C.E.) 169

A Closer Look: The Confucian Four Books 170

7-2g The Modern Period of Daoism and Confucianism (1912–Present) 170

7-3 Essential Daoist and Confucian Teachings 172

7-3a Ancient Teachings Common to Daoism and Confucianism 172

7-3b Daoist Teachings on the Dao 173

7-3c Chinese Traditional Deities 174

7-3d Daoist Teaching of Wu Wei 176

7-3e Daoist Views of Qi 176

7-3f The Daoist Quest for Immortality 177

7-3g Confucian Reformulations of Ancient Teachings 177

A Closer Look: A Famous Conversation between Confucius and Laozi 178

7-4 Daoist and Confucian Ethics 178

7-4a Daoist Ethics 179

7-4b Confucian Ethics 179

7-5 Ritual and Worship 181

7-5a Daoist Temples and Worship 181

7-5b Confucian Temples and Worship 182

7-5c The Traditional Chinese Funeral 182

7-5d A Final Comparison of Daoism and Confucianism 184

7-6 Daoism and Confucianism around the World Today 185

7-6a Daoism and Confucianism in the West 185

7-6b Confucianism in North America 185

7-6c Daoism in North America 186

© MICHAELJUNG/SHUTTERSTOCK.COM

8 ENCOUNTERING SHINTO: THE WAY OF THE KAMI 188

Your Visit to the Tsubaki Shinto Shrine in Granite Falls, Washington 189

8-1 Names 190

8-2 The Shinto Present as Shaped by Its Past 191

8-2a Before the Arrival of Buddhism (to 600 C.E.) 191

8-2b Shinto and Buddhism Together in Japan (600–1850) 192

A Closer Look: The Symbol of Shinto 193

A Closer Look: The Yasukuni Shrine Today 195

8-2c The Meiji Period (1850–1945) 195

8-2d Shinto in Recent Times (1945–Present) 197

8-3 Shinto Teachings 198

8-3a The Kami 198

8-3b Characteristics of Other Shinto Teachings 199

8-4 Shinto Ethics 199

8-4a General Characteristics 200

8-4b Purity 200

© SEAN PAVONE PHOTO/SHUTTERSTOCK.COM

8-5 **Shinto Ritual** **200**

    8-5a The Shinto Shrine 201

    A Closer Look: A Shinto Prayer for the Blessing of the Crops *201*

    8-5b The Shinto Priesthood 202

    8-5c Prayer Plaques and Fortunes 202

    8-5d The Wedding Ceremony 203

    8-5e The Home Shrine 203

    8-5f The Shinto Funeral 204

8-6 **Shinto around the World Today** **204**

9 ENCOUNTERING ZOROASTRIANISM: THE WAY OF THE ONE WISE LORD **206**

Your Visit to Yazd, Iran **207**

9-1 **Names for Zoroastrianism and Zoroastrians** **209**

    A Closer Look: The Symbol of Zoroastrianism *209*

9-2 **Zoroastrianism as Shaped by Its Past** **210**

    9-2a The Birth of Zoroastrianism (ca. 630–550 B.C.E.) 210

    9-2b The Spread of Zoroastrianism in the Persian and Sassanian Empires
        (550 B.C.E.–650 C.E.) 211

    9-2c The Coming of Islam and the Zoroastrian Dispersion
        (650 C.E.–Present) 214

9-3 **Essential Zoroastrian Teachings: Monotheism
and Moral Dualism** **216**

    9-3a The One God, Ahura Mazda 216

    9-3b The Spirit of Destruction, Angra Mainyu 216

    A Closer Look: The Zoroastrian Creed *217*

    9-3c Moral Dualism 217

    9-3d Supernatural Intermediaries 218

    9-3e Judgment and the Final Victory of
        Ahura Mazda 218

9-4 **Zoroastrian Ethics** **218**

    9-4a Zoroastrian General Morality 219

    9-4b A Current Ethical and Social Issue: Marriage
        and Children 219

9-5 **Zoroastrian Rituals** **220**

    9-5a Fires in the Fire Temple 220

    9-5b Interior Plan of the Fire Temple 221

    9-5c Worship 221

    9-5d Priesthood 221

    9-5e Other Rituals 222

    9-5f Funeral Rituals 223

9-6 **Zoroastrianism around the World Today** **224**

    A Closer Look: Thus Spoke Zarathustra *225*

© HOWARD SANDLER/SHUTTERSTOCK

Your Visit to the Western Wall in Jerusalem 227

10-1 The Name *Judaism* and Related Terms 228
A Closer Look: Symbols of Judaism 229

10-2 The Jewish Present as Shaped by Its Past 230
10-2a From the Creation to Abraham (ca. 2000 B.C.E.) 230
10-2b The Emergence of Ancient Israel (ca. 1200–950 B.C.E.) 231
10-2c The First Temple Period (950–586 B.C.E.) 231
10-2d The Second Temple Period (539 B.C.E.–70 C.E.) 233
10-2e Revolts and Rabbis (70 C.E.–ca. 650) 234
10-2f Jews under Islamic and Christian Rule (ca. 650–1800) 236
A Closer Look: Kabbalah 237
10-2g Emancipation and Diversity (1800–1932) 238
10-2h The Holocaust and Its Aftermath (1932–Present) 240

10-3 Essential Teachings of Judaism 242
10-3a Foundation of Jewish Teachings: The Tanak 242
10-3b One God 242
10-3c The Jews as God's Chosen People 244
10-3d Life after Death? 245

10-4 Essential Jewish Ethics 246
10-4a Ethics in the Image of God 247
10-4b The Torah 247
10-4c General Jewish Ethics 248
10-4d Modern Jewish Ethics 248

10-5 Jewish Worship and Ritual 249
10-5a Worship in the Synagogue 249
10-5b The Sabbath 250
10-5c Jewish Annual Festivals 250
10-5d Kosher Food 251
10-5e Circumcision, the Sign of the Covenant 252
10-5f Bar Mitzvah and Bat Mitzvah 252
10-5g Marriage 253
10-5h Funeral Rituals 253

10-6 Judaism around the World Today 254
10-6a Judaism in Israel 255
10-6b Judaism in North America 255

© NOAM ARMONN/SHUTTERSTOCK.COM

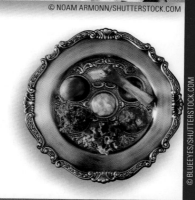
© BLUEEYES/SHUTTERSTOCK.COM

Your Visit to St. Peter's in Rome 259

11-1 Names 260
A Closer Look: Symbols of Christianity 261

11-2 The Christian Present as Shaped by Its Past 261
11-2a The Life, Death, and Resurrection of Jesus Christ (ca. 4 B.C.E.–30 C.E.) 262
11-2b The Earliest Church (30–100 C.E.) 263
11-2c The Ancient Period (100–500 C.E.) 265
11-2d Byzantine, Medieval, and Renaissance Christianity (500–1500) 268

11-2e Reformation in the Western Church (1500–1600) 270
11-2f The Early Modern Period (1600–1900) 274
11-2g Modern Christianity (1900–Present) 275

11-3 Christian Teachings as Reflected in the Nicene Creed 277
A Closer Look: The Nicene-Constantinopolitan Creed, 381 C.E. 278
11-3a God the Father 278
11-3b God the Son 279
11-3c God the Holy Spirit 280
A Closer Look: The Doctrine of the Virgin Mary 281
11-3d The Conclusion of the Nicene Creed: Church, Baptism, and Christian Hope 282

11-4 Christian Ethics: Following the Way of Jesus Christ 283
11-4a Foundations in the Ten Commandments, the Sermon on the Mount, and the Letters of Paul 283
11-4b The Enactment of Moral Life in the Church 284

11-5 Christian Worship and Ritual 286
11-5a Christian Worship before Constantine 286
A Closer Look: An Ancient Christian Service 286
11-5b Worship after Constantine 287
11-5c The Liturgical Year 289

11-6 Christianity around the World Today 290
11-6a Christianity in the Global South 290
11-6b Christianity in North America 291
11-6c The Different Churches: Roman Catholic and Protestant 291

© NANCY BAUER/SHUTTERSTOCK.COM

© CARLOS E. SANTA MARIA/SHUTTERSTOCK.COM

12 ENCOUNTERING ISLAM: THE STRAIGHT PATH OF THE ONE GOD 294

Your Visit to Mecca 295

12-1 The Name *Islam* 297

12-2 Islam Today as Shaped by Its Past 297
12-2a Arabia at the Time of Muhammad (500s C.E.) 297
A Closer Look: The Symbol of Islam? 298
12-2b The Life and Work of Muhammad (ca. 570–632) 299
12-2c Islam Immediately Following the Death of Muhammad (632–661) 302
12-2d Islam from the Umayyads until Today (661–Present) 302
12-2e Diverse Muslim Groups Today: Mainstream, Zealous, and Moderate 306
A Closer Look: "Islamic Fundamentalism"? 310

12-3 Essential Teachings 311
12-3a God Is One 311
12-3b Angels and Spirits 312
12-3c The Qur'an 312
12-3d Prophets 314
12-3e "People of the Book": Jews, Christians, and Zoroastrians 314
12-3f Final Judgment 315

12-4 Islamic Ethics 315
12-4a The Hadith 316
12-4b Shari'a 316

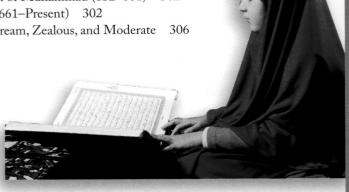
© ZURIJETA/SHUTTERSTOCK.COM

12-4c Diet and Other Regulations   317
12-4d Marriage and the Status of Women   317
A Closer Look: Muslim Dress for Women and Men   318
12-4e Jihad   319

12-5   Worship: The Five Pillars of Islam   320
12-5a Confession of Faith   321
12-5b Prayer   321
12-5c Fasting   323
12-5d Almsgiving   323
12-5e Pilgrimage   323

12-6   Islam around the World Today   325
12-6a Islam in Europe   325
12-6b Muslim Migration to North America   325
A Closer Look: Difficulties of the Hajj for Muslims in Western China   326
12-6c The Nation of Islam and the American Society of Muslims   327
12-6d Muslim Life in the United States after 9/11   329
A Closer Look: Muslim Views of Islamic-Western Conflict   330

© PETE NIESEN/SHUTTERSTOCK.COM

13   ENCOUNTERING NEW RELIGIOUS MOVEMENTS: MODERN WAYS TO ALTERNATIVE MEANINGS   332

Your Visit to Temple Square, Salt Lake City, Utah   333
13-1   Names for This Type of Religion   335
13-2   Common Features of New Religious Movements   336
13-3   New Religious Movements in the World Today: A Survey   337
13-3a NRMs founded in the Western World   337
13-3b Asian NRMs in the West   338
13-3c "Scientific" NRMs: Christian Science and UFO Groups   340
13-3d Nature NRMs: Neo-Paganism, Wicca, and Druidry   341
A Closer Look: Druidry Gains Official Status   342
13-3e NRMs in Asia   342

13-4   An NRM from Asia: Falun Gong   345
13-4a History   346
13-4b Teaching and Practice   346

13-5   A North American NRM: The Church of Jesus Christ of Latter-day Saints   347
13-5a History   347
13-5b Scripture   350
13-5c Teachings   351
13-5d Institutions, Practices, and Structure of the LDS Church   351

13-6   The Church of Scientology   353
13-6a L. Ron Hubbard's Life and Teachings   353
13-6b Organization of the Church   355
A Closer Look: Scientology and Celebrities   356
13-6c Controversy and Present Status   357

Index   359

© 2006 GETTY IMAGES

LONGTREKHOME

CHAPTER 1

Beginning Your Study of World Religions

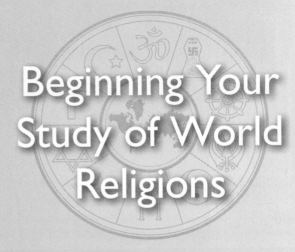

Learning Outcomes

After studying this chapter, you will be able to do the following:

1-1 State and explain your own "preunderstanding" of religion.

1-2 State and explain the definition of *religion* used in this book.

1-3 Give your own answer to the question "Why study religion?"

1-4 List and describe the six different dimensions of religion.

1-5 Discuss how the various academic disciplines contribute to the study of religion.

1-6 Explain the special issues in the study of religion today.

Study Tools

After you read this chapter, go to the Study Tools at the end of the chapter, page 28.

"Religion starts with the perception that something is wrong." —Karen Armstrong

Your Visit to the Hsi Lai Temple in Southern California

Imagine that you're walking up the broad flight of stone steps to the Hsi Lai (shee LAI) Buddhist temple in Hacienda Heights, California, just east of Los Angeles. Hsi Lai claims the distinction of being the largest Buddhist temple in North America, and it certainly looks like it from where you stand! When you get inside, you look around and realize that this is a religious building complex like none other you have ever seen. No large-group ceremonies are going on, at least not right now. Instead, small groups of worshipers and tourists come and go, doing their own thing. Some offer incense, a few are carrying flowers to leave in the temple, others are praying and meditating in front of statues, and out in the courtyard people are doing meditative exercise routines.

The neatly dressed families coming to this temple do not seem to reflect deeply here on their faith. You see nobody reading Buddhist religious texts, nor does any monk teach or preach to a group. Rather, people come here just to sense something of the sacred and be in its presence. Their minds are calmed by the familiar architecture, by the many statues of the Buddha, by the soft smell of incense. They engage in quiet, low-key activities.

You notice people who aren't doing traditional Buddhist worship. You wonder if this means that they might come from

Hsi Lai Buddhist Temple in Southern California

What Do YOU Think?

Most Americans with a religious faith don't know much about it.

Strongly Disagree				Strongly Agree		
1	2	3	4	5	6	7

other religious traditions. Some people you see are just tourists, a few of them interested in the tasty vegetarian buffet lunch served every day. But perhaps they too have come to absorb the beauty of this place, and at least a bit of its religious meaning. This temple was founded not only to bridge the differences between different groups of Buddhists, but also to be a bridge between Eastern and Western religions and ways of life.

Watch a video on the Hsi Lai temple ▶

As you are introduced to the academic study of religion, you may find yourself bewildered—by the varieties of religion, by distinguishing religions from other movements, by the different academic methods used to study religions, and by hot topics such as religion and gender, ecology, and violence. You may have questions about matters of fact and value: Is one religion true, are different religions true, or is none of them true? What might it all mean for *you*?

These issues may occur to you as well:

- Formal "separation of church and state" is strong in the United States and Canada, but religion and

 As sunlight moves over the Eastern Hemisphere, one can see the regions where most world religions were born. The new perspective of Earth from space has helped to stimulate global thinking in religions.

politics are mixed in powerful ways here and around the world. The government of China's continuous pressure on Buddhism in Tibet and on the Falun Gong movement is just one example.

Read about a law attempting to regulate reincarnation in China.

- Most people in North America affirm the importance of religion for their lives, but fewer actually practice it. For example, nearly 90 percent of all North Americans believe in the existence of God or gods, but only about half regularly participate in religious services or in other religious practices such as prayer, meditation, or giving to those in need.

See Stephen Prothero speak on religious illiteracy.

- Despite a high level of religious belief in the United States, the majority of Americans have surprisingly little knowledge of their faith. Stephen Prothero (PROTH-er-oh), a professor of religion at Boston University who has appeared on *The Colbert Report* and *The Daily Show*, has shown that Americans—even those who attend services regularly—are often "religious illiterates." As Laurie Goodstein of the *New York Times* wrote in summarizing a 2010 study of religious knowledge in the United States, "Americans are by all measures a deeply religious people, but they are also deeply ignorant about religion."[1] In Western Europe, most people don't hold formally to a religion, but they know a good deal about religion, because it is a required academic subject in the schools.

> "Americans are by all measures a deeply religious people, but they are also deeply ignorant about religion."
> —Laurie Goodstein

- Is religion in the world shrinking, or is it growing? Actually, both. Although Christianity is shrinking in Europe and North America, in other parts of the world this religion is growing; Islam and Buddhism are also growing. The number of people in North America who formally adhere to no religion at all is growing, but certain religious practices such as prayer are as strong as ever.

- Nearly all the major religions of the world come from ancient times. However, every decade of the past two hundred years has seen new religious movements born around the world, some of them now powerful, some controversial. You might wonder why we still get new religions—don't we have enough already?

- Religion has evoked the best and the worst among humans. Love, care for others, and social reforms have arisen from religion. It has inspired great music, art, and architecture and has lifted human life in countless ways. Ironically, it has also been the source of much destruction.

Take a "pre-quiz" on world religions.

Learning Outcome 1-1

State and explain your own "preunderstanding" of religion.

1-1 Coming to Grips with Your Preunderstanding of Religion

Imagine for a moment that a good friend tells you, "I've met and talked with an alien visitor from another planet." You might say to yourself, amid all the thoughts and emotions that you have when you hear something strange or upsetting, "I don't believe in space aliens!" But then you might think, "Are there alien visitors to Earth after all? Maybe they're real, and maybe my friend *has* been talking with them."

You might think this, but probably not. Instead, your mind automatically begins to sift through your knowledge for an explanation consistent with what you already "know" to be true. Only people who are already convinced, or seriously entertaining the idea, that a set of things is true—there is life somewhat similar to ours on other planets, beings from these places travel to Earth, and they talk with humans—will easily accept your friend's comment. Given your prior understanding that such things probably aren't factual, you won't likely entertain these theories as a serious possibility.

---

[1] Laurie Goodstein, "Basic Religion Test Stumps Many Americans," *New York Times*, September 28, 2010, A17, New York City edition.

1-1a What Is Preunderstanding?

We interpret all of our experience in just this way, because, as psychologists tell us, this is the way the human mind operates. Every understanding of our new experiences is made in light of an understanding that we already had going into the new experiences. **Preunderstanding** is the state of one's understanding of reality, in terms of which one makes sense of one's new experiences. It describes what we already know, whether that knowledge is correct or not. We assume that new experiences will be compatible with our prior understanding. Even if a new experience corrects our old knowledge—let's say that in this case you actually do meet a space alien with your friend—it is always understood on the basis of old knowledge. This new knowledge is then integrated into old understandings, and the preunderstanding grows. In other words, the term *preunderstanding* describes the existing state of our understanding before a new experience that calls for interpretation. Our preunderstanding is not static, but dynamic. It changes as we alter our beliefs and convictions over time.

1-1b Your Preunderstanding of Religion

All this raises the question, What elements of your preunderstanding of religion might influence your study of world religions? Each person must examine and answer individually. In all individual encounters with new people and new ideas, our knowledge of ourselves and our knowledge of others are connected and influence each other. You should first think through your own past encounters with religion and your experiences with it, pro and con. Here are several short but thought-provoking questions to consider as you think of your own preunderstanding of religion and religions:

1. Do I have an unprejudiced view of what "religion" in general is? Or am I biased for or against it?

2. Can I "suspend my disbelief" or "suspend my belief" in order to encounter religion as a whole, or specific religions, objectively?

3. If I hold a religious belief, can I study other religions without feeling threatened in my own?

4. Can I encounter practices that seem unusual to me without getting too upset?

5. Can I be humble and provisional in my conclusions?

6. Can I postpone any personal judgment on a religion until I've learned more about it?

Take a brief, entertaining quiz that will probe your preunderstanding of world religions.

You are now poised to begin your study of the world's leading religions, beginning with the question, "What is religion?" Your journey in understanding will encounter the lives and religions of other people. In this process, you will learn more about yourself as well.

Learning Outcome 1-2

State and explain the definition of *religion* used in this book.

1-2 What Is Religion?

Religion is found in all cultures today and throughout history. Evidence from early human remains shows signs of religion, including veneration of animal spirits in art and human burials that suggest belief in a life beyond death. Anthropologists today have concluded that Neanderthal humans who lived around 200,000 years ago may have had religious beliefs and practices but that Cro-Magnon humans (around 35,000 years ago) definitely had religion. From the dawn of human civilizations until modern times, religion has shaped the beliefs and values of all human cultures.

1-2a Defining *Religion*

But this talk of the prevalence of religion leads us to ask, What exactly is religion? Defining academic subjects can be a boring business, but many people have something interesting to say about what religion is. Grappling with this question involves both careful, objective academic thinking and personal engagement. University of Cambridge scholar John Bowker remarks, "We all know what [religion] is until someone asks us to tell them."[2] If pressed for an answer, people in the Western world would typically say first that religion is based on belief in and obedience to God. However, do

preunderstanding
State of one's understanding of reality, in terms of which one makes sense of one's new experiences

---

[2] John Bowker, ed., *Oxford Dictionary of World Religions* (New York: Oxford University Press, 1997), xv.

© ISTOCKPHOTO/NINA SHANNON

discussion. Here is a sampling of how *religion* has been defined in the Western world, by scholars and others. Religion is...

"The feeling of absolute dependence"
—Friedrich Schleiermacher, Christian theologian (1799)

"The opiate of the people"
—Karl Marx, nineteenth-century founder of communism (1843)

"A set of things which the average man thinks he believes and wishes he was certain of"
—Mark Twain, American writer (1879)

"The daughter of Hope and Fear, explaining to Ignorance the nature of the Unknowable"
—Ambrose Bierce, American social critic and humorist (1911)

"A unified system of beliefs and practices... which unite into one single moral community"
—Émile Durkheim, French sociologist of religion (1915)

"What grows out of, and gives expression to, experience of the holy in its various aspects"
—Rudolf Otto, German scholar of religion (1917)

"All bunk"
—Thomas Edison, American inventor (ca. 1925)

"An illusion deriving its strength from the fact that it falls in with our instinctual desires"
—Sigmund Freud, Austrian psychiatrist (1932)

"The state of being grasped by an ultimate concern... which itself contains the answer to the question of the meaning of our life"
—Paul Tillich, Christian theologian (1957)

"A set of symbolic forms and acts which relate man to the ultimate conditions of his existence"
—Robert Bellah, contemporary American sociologist

"Feeling warmer in our hearts, more connected to others, more connected to something greater, and having a sense of peace"
—Goldie Hawn, contemporary American film actress

religion Pattern of beliefs and practices that expresses and enacts what a community regards as sacred and/or ultimate about life

they mean the God followed in a particular religion or something more general, such as "gods"? A few major religions—certain branches of Hinduism and Buddhism, for example— have relatively little teaching about gods. A few religions such as Jainism have no gods at all.

Some people around the world would give a second answer to "What is religion?"—that it is a system of morality. On first reflection, this might seem to be a more all-encompassing definition than the previous one. Karen Armstrong, a former Roman Catholic nun and now a popular writer on world religions, wrote that "Religion starts with the perception that something is wrong," and that the value systems in religions deal with that wrong.[3] The three main Western religions— Judaism, Christianity, and Islam—have strong moral teachings. Confucianism is so centered on morality that the issue of whether it is a social philosophy or a religion is often debated. However, a few religions, such as Shinto, have little or no developed teaching about a way of life. All this shows how our prior perceptions color our answer to the question, "What is religion?" Despite the difficulties of this question, many scholars from various academic fields have attempted to answer it in as objective a manner as possible.

1-2b Notable Definitions of *Religion*

Another way of studying the issue of what *religion* means is by looking at definitions that have been offered in the past and have had an influence on the

1-2c The Definition Used in This Book

Each of you will have to wrestle personally with defining *religion*, because scholarship isn't settled on any one definition and because defining it involves some subjectivity. Here's the definition used in this book: **Religion** is a pattern of beliefs and practices that expresses and enacts what a community regards as sacred and/or ultimate about life.

Let's "unpack" this definition. First, religion is *a pattern of beliefs and practices*. All religions believe certain

---
[3] Karen Armstrong, *A History of God* (New York: Ballantine, 1994), 1.

things about ultimate reality in or beyond the world. They answer existential questions that humans have:

- Why am I here?
- What does it mean to be human?
- How can what is wrong in the world—and in me—be corrected?
- Where am I—and the world—going?

They answer these questions in different ways. The different religions believe in one God (**monotheism**) or many gods (**polytheism**). They believe, with or without belief in a god, in a world soul in Hinduism, in Nirvana in Buddhism, and in a cosmic Way in both Daoism (Taoism) and Confucianism. They practice these beliefs in certain ways: in worship, rituals of passage at various points of the individual life cycle, meditation, and ordinary actions in daily life. Each religion has its own way of arranging these beliefs and practices into a distinctive *pattern*. Second, this pattern *expresses and enacts* what is *sacred*. *Sacred* refers to what is considered most holy and important, whether in this world, in a supernatural world that transcends this one, or both. Religions draw on their experience of the sacred; express the sacred in all of its aspects; and enact it by continuing to make it real for believers.

> Some scholars doubt if "private religion" is a religion at all.

Because common Western notions of the "sacred" often entail belief in a holy God, we add this further phrase to our definition: *ultimate about life*. This "ultimate" may be a principle, an impersonal force, or a spiritual power, hidden in the world or beyond it. Sacredness or "the ultimate" in world religions is wider than a divine being. Third, note that it is a *community* of like-minded people that forms a religion. Religions sometimes begin with an individual (Buddha, Confucius, Jesus, Muhammad), but they soon become social communities of shared belief and practice. They persist through history as communities of religion. Not all religions try to grow throughout the world, but all of them are concerned with passing themselves from generation to generation, thus becoming "traditions."

The meaning of *religion* is typically traced to the ancient Latin word *religio* (ree-LIG-ee-oh), derived from the verb *religere*, "to bind/tie fast." This verb is itself built from the word *ligere*, "to bind" (compare our words *ligament* and *ligature*). Of course, the meaning of a word today can't be limited to what it meant thousands of years ago, but this ancient meaning of *religion* illustrates nicely the different parts of our definition. Ancient Romans used *religio* in several senses. First, it means a supernatural constraint on behavior, doing what is good, and especially avoiding evil. It "binds" people to what is right. Second, it entails a holy awe for the gods and sacred power in general. Third, *religio* means a system of life that binds people together in a group and orients them to the gods. Finally, it entails the practices of rites and ceremonies by which the Roman people expressed and enacted their religion.[4]

monotheism Belief in one God

polytheism Belief in many gods

private religion Pattern of belief held by only one person

Although the Romans and some other peoples used the term *religion* for their system of belief and practice, different religions of the world call themselves by different names, many of them not using the word *religion* at all. For example, Daoism is "the Way" to most Daoists; they don't refer to it as "the Daoist religion." Many Hindus call their religion "the Eternal Teaching"; Buddhists often call theirs a "school." Many Jews, Christians, and Muslims prefer the term *faith* instead of *religion*. But no matter what they call themselves, they are in fact *religions* as that term is used in scholarship and teaching.

A good definition will carefully identify the subject being defined, but it can also be used to exclude other things from the definition. How does the definition given above exclude things that *aren't* religion? Here are two examples. First, the definition speaks of religion as a system based on the sacred or on ultimate value; other systems that do not view themselves as religions do not usually speak about the "sacred" or "ultimate." This is true of political ideologies and parties such as Democrats and Republicans, academic philosophies, systems of popular psychology or "life coaching" such as that of Tony Robbins, and so on. (This isn't meant to demean these other groups; many people find a great deal of meaning and inspiration in them.) Therefore, people who belong to nonreligious groups can also practice a variety of religion or no religion at all. Second, a pattern of belief held by only one person can't be a religion as we define it here. Such do-it-yourself religion may be popular in Europe and North America, and it is usually sincere and important to the person who holds it, but it doesn't bring with it a social bond. Some scholars refer to this as **private religion**, but others question whether "private religion" is really religion at all.

Read an explanation of "Sheila-ism," a private religion.

----

[4] P. G. W. Glare, *Oxford Latin Dictionary* (New York: Oxford University Press, 1983), 1605–06.

Is *Religion* a Dirty Word?

To some religious people, *religion* is, if not a dirty word, at least a derogatory one. Some Christians, Jews, and Muslims think that "religion" is a bad thing. Many religious people want to have a strong connection with God/ultimate reality/cosmic power, but not a "religion." They call their own beliefs a "faith," "teaching," "school," "spirituality," or something similar, but they often call other people's belief systems, somewhat pejoratively, "religion." In his best-selling book *The Shack*, written for Christians, William Young even has Jesus say, "I'm not too big on religion."

People who don't like any religion at all also use *religion* in a negative way. A growing number of people in North America and Europe say, "I'm spiritual, but I'm not religious." A 2008 documentary film featuring comic and social critic Bill Maher was titled not *Religious*, but *Religulous*, Maher's unflattering combination of *religion* and *ridiculous*.

> *"I'm not too big on religion."*
> —Jesus, in The Shack

To study world religions well, you have to put aside prejudice you might have about the term *religion*, whether pro or con. All scholars of religion use *religion* as an academic, neutral, descriptive term, and you should too, regardless of your own personal stance on religious belief and practice. To use an analogy, many people today, including students, often use the word *politics* prejudicially. But to study well in the academic field called "political science," one must put aside prejudice about the term *politics*. The same is true with *religion* in the study of religion.

See a trailer for *Religulous*.

Learning Outcome 1-3

Give your own answer to the question "Why study religion?"

1-3 Why Study Religion?

At first, the question "Why study religion?" may seem pointless to you. You might say, "I'm taking the course, aren't I?" You may go on to give your reasons for taking this course: to get course credit, to fulfill a cultural studies requirement at your school and maybe pick up some knowledge and skills along the way, and ultimately to get an academic degree. But let's explore a bit further why students today should study religion.

1-3a Studying the Persistence of Religion in the Modern World

Religion should be studied—among other reasons—to understand its persistence in the modern world, which in many ways is not hospitable to religious belief and practice. The rise of **secularism**, or life without religion, particularly in the public sphere, has

secularism Life without religion

challenged most religions for the past two hundred years. Today, the secular approach to life rejects religion for the perceived evils of extremism ("Look what happened on 9/11!" is commonly heard); the inappropriateness of religious training for children ("Children should be allowed to decide for themselves when they are older"); and the better view on life offered by science ("Religion is false, because we know about evolution"). Secularism has led to a lessening of religious belief and practice, and in North America to widespread illiteracy about religion. Many people, including about half of all Europeans and a growing number of North Americans,

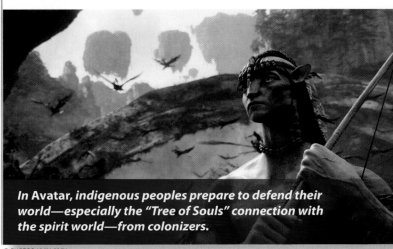

In Avatar, *indigenous peoples prepare to defend their world—especially the "Tree of Souls" connection with the spirit world—from colonizers.*

© PHOTOS 12/ALAMY

are neither especially religious nor completely irreligious; they are "in the middle" between them. They combine aspects of secular life with aspects of religious life.

This means that reports of the death of religion are mistaken. The **secularization hypothesis**, widely held in the twentieth century, said that science and education would diminish or end religion in the modern world. For instance, British philosopher Bertrand Russell said in 1952 that religion "will fade away as we adopt reason and science as our guidelines." But the secularization hypothesis has now been largely discredited. Religion is strong today even as science and secularism have become more widespread. More than three-quarters of the world's people identify with one or more religions. We still find religion everywhere: in high culture, in popular culture (for example, the 2009 film *Avatar* and the rock band U2), and in everyday life in North America and around the world. The religions of the world are now present in North America, and nearly every religion is as close as one's keyboard, on the Internet. In the Soviet Union and China—which tried with Communist fervor in the twentieth century to suppress and even extinguish all religion—it has come back vigorously. Only one in eight people in China now call themselves atheists, and the government of China is bringing back Confucian texts and teachings to counteract the "money-first" mentality among so many young people there. At the beginning of the twenty-first century, religion is at or near the center of global issues and cultural conflict. It has an increasingly visible role in national and even international politics. One simply can't understand many of the conflicts in our world without a basic knowledge of religion. What's more, new religious movements are arising every decade, so that the number of religions in the world is increasing, not decreasing. Religion is emerging as one of the main markers of human identity in the twenty-first century, along with gender, class, and ethnicity.[5]

Read about Confucius's reentry into China's schools.

THE RISE OF SECULARISM HAS CHALLENGED MOST RELIGIONS FOR THE PAST TWO HUNDRED YEARS.

Religion is powerful and persistent, and it shows no signs of disappearing.

Why does religion keep on thriving? First, despite the challenges to religion, it continues to be a powerful resource for everyday life all around the world. Religion still provides meaning, strength, and joy to many. Another reason is that religious traditions have proven themselves adaptable to the ever-changing situations of human

Read "Believers Can Be Reasonable" by psychologist David Myers.

life. They've changed over the thousands of years that many of them have existed, and the study of these changes forms a large part of the study of religion. (If religions can't or don't change, they usually die out.) Many religions even have some room for skepticism and for the secular, which gives them strength in our rapidly changing world. In many places, especially in central and southern Africa, indigenous religions tied to local cultures are fading, but universal religions such as Christianity and Islam have taken their place. If you want to understand the world today, understanding religion is an important part of it.

The study of religion is also a persistent part of the academic scene. Around 750,000 undergraduates each year in the United States take a religion course. Enrollment in world religion courses in the United States has grown rapidly since the religiously connected attacks on this country on September 11, 2001. A number of students decide to make the study of religion their major or minor. Religion is taught in the vast majority of liberal arts colleges, as well as in private and state universities. Leading universities that didn't have a religious studies program in the past because of a more secular orientation established one in the twentieth century—among them Harvard, Princeton, Cornell, and Stanford. In 2009 the American Historical

secularization hypothesis Idea that science and education would diminish or end religion in the modern world

---

[5] Stephen Prothero, *Religious Literacy* (San Francisco: HarperSanFrancisco, 2007), 5.

cultural intelligence
Ability to understand and deal with cultures other than one's own

Association reported that more historians in the United States now specialize in religious issues than in any others. Even the government of China, which is officially atheistic, is setting up undergraduate and graduate degree programs in religious studies in several of its selective universities. What's more, the study of religion in U.S. K–12 public schools is growing, with new guidelines from the American Academy of Religion, an association of religion professors.[6] In sum, the academic study of religion is alive and well.

1-3b What the Academic Study of Religion Can Offer You

The opportunity to shape one's knowledge and values is one of the advantages of being a student, but most students today are rightly concerned about how studying religion will help them earn a living in today's economy. A small proportion of students in religion courses choose to make a professional career in religion, either as the leader of a religious community (such as a rabbi, priest, or minister), an editor of religious publications, or a professor of religion. Some students take a world religions course to clarify or strengthen their own religious knowledge and values. They realize the truth in the proverb first uttered by Max Müller, "Those who know only one religion know none."

Students taking a world religion course learn more about an important aspect of the world today. This study offers students training in a unique combination of academic and everyday skills such as these:

- The ability to understand how religious thought and practice are related to everyday life, especially important today in careers such as teaching, health care, social work, and business
- The ability to understand the religious dimensions of conflicts within and between nations
- An appreciation of the complexities of religious language and values

- An ability to understand and explain important texts both critically and empathetically
- Cross-cultural understanding, or what is now becoming known academically as **cultural intelligence** or "cross-cultural competence"

Few academic fields bring together so many different forms of analysis as religion does. With this broad liberal arts background, many religion majors or minors go on to study law, business, education, and medicine in graduate school.[7] In short, the study of religion offers a foundation for a successful and fulfilling career, in addition to growth in personal knowledge and satisfaction.

Learning Outcome 1-4

List and describe the six different dimensions of religion.

1-4 Dimensions of Religion

As we examine the varieties of religious experience, all sorts of human beliefs and practices come into view. Religion seems to be as wide as human life itself. This was illustrated in one American publishing company's poster, which read: "Books about religion are also about love, sex, politics, AIDS, war, peace, justice, ecology, philosophy, addiction, recovery, ethics, race, gender, dissent, technology, old age, New Age, faith, heavy metal, morality, beauty, God, psychology, money, dogma, freedom, history, death, and life." To get a grip on this complexity, various scholars have organized the dimensions of religion in various ways. These dimensions are somewhat artificial, and they cannot fully describe the meaning and value that believers see in their religion. However, they're helpful in grasping the mass of information available about religions, for both beginning students and experienced scholars alike. Prominent scholar of comparative religion Ninian Smart first laid out five dimensions in the 1960s, but by the 1990s he had come to think there were nine.

"Those who know only one religion know none." —Max Müller

---

[6] "American Academy of Religion Guidelines for Teaching about Religion in K–12 Public Schools in the United States," http://www.aarweb.org/Publications/Online_Publications/Curriculum_Guidelines/AARK-12CurriculumGuidelines.pdf.

[7] This listing of skills is adapted from "The Religion Major and Liberal Education—A White Paper," http://www.aarweb.org/Programs/Religion_Major_and_Liberal_Education/default.asp.

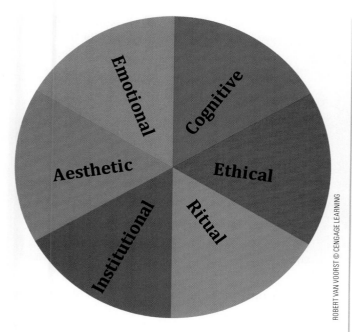

ROBERT VAN VOORST © CENGAGE LEARNING

Figure 1.1 Dimensions of Religion

Rodney Stark and Charles Glock have systematized the various interlocking aspects of religion in six dimensions (see Figure 1.1).[8]

1-4a The Cognitive Dimension

Religions have cognitive (thinking) dimensions that teach their followers what it is necessary to know. Most religions teach deep knowledge about their gods and founders, often in stories. They teach about the creation of the world, the meaning of life, and ways to overcome death. They teach about human identity, both individual and social: gender, class, ethnicity, and other aspects of human identity. They provide ways of understanding what the world is and what it should be. Often, the history of religion itself is explained so that followers can know that they stand in a great tradition. The cognitive dimension of religion entails analyzing and systematizing knowledge, as well as learning it and passing it on. Its teachings are framed in stories; in short statements that summarize beliefs (for example, the Four Noble Truths of Buddhism); and in songs, proverbs, laws, and many other forms. The cognitive dimensions of religion typically grow so comprehensive and important that religions contain an entire worldview. However, we must keep in mind that there is often a significant gap between official religious teachings and what is believed and practiced by ordinary members.

[8] Rodney Stark and Charles Glock, *Patterns of Religious Commitment* (Berkeley: University of California Press, 1968).

1-4b The Ethical Dimension

Ethics are important in almost all religions, because, as we saw above, religions seek to correct what they perceive to be wrong in the world. Personal ethics are found in religions, but the emphasis is on social ethics. All religions have moral expectations for marriage, families, religious societies or congregations, social classes, and even whole nations. We may think of religious ethics as "rules" more negative than positive, but most religions have a balance of both "do this" and "don't do that." These systems of social ethics can become the law of the nation where religion is not separated from the state, as is the case with Shari'a, religion-based law in some officially Muslim countries. Values, norms, and patterns of behavior in religions are internalized with the help of moral rules. Different people and activities serve to shape religious behavior: living models such as ordinary religious specialists who lead a religion (clergy, monks, gurus, and the like); celebrated models such as saviors, saints, and immortals; and behavior in the overall group. When social morality based on religion is constantly and carefully practiced, religion becomes a way of life.

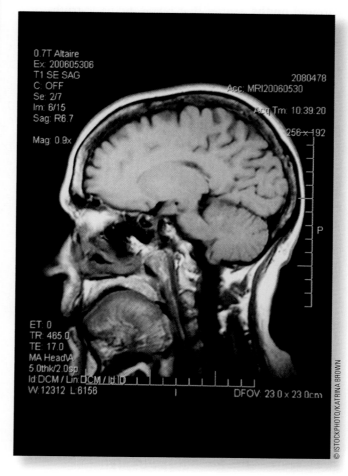

© ISTOCKPHOTO/KATRINA BROWN

1-4c The Ritual Dimension

Ritual is symbolic action in worship, meditation, or other religious ceremonies. It's symbolic and often abstract, but meant to achieve very practical goals. When most people in North America today think of religion, they think of the ritual ceremonies of worship. But ritual also includes formal and informal prayer, sacrifice, chanting of scriptures, public processions, and even travel. **Pilgrimage**—travel to a special destination to increase one's devotion or improve one's religious status—doesn't often come to the minds of modern North Americans as a religious ritual, but in 2009 millions of people worldwide went on a pilgrimage and spent the equivalent of $18 billion U.S. on it. Ritual can be long, elaborate ceremonies performed by religious specialists or simple daily acts such as a short prayer before eating a meal or going to sleep. Rituals are directed to one God, many gods, or to spirits or deceased ancestors. Ritual is not only symbolic, but also effective; it helps to reenact and reapply the deep truths of a religion to people in the present. Mircea Eliade (MUHR-chuh eh-lee-AH-deh, 1907–1986) advanced his influential theory of "eternal return" around **myths**, stories that relate the basic truths of a religion. (We often use *myth* today to mean an untrue story, but religions use it a completely opposite way.) This theory holds that rituals do not simply commemorate myths, but actually participate in them and bring believers to the gods. In a few religions, the sacrifice of food or drink is thought to "feed" the gods or deceased ancestors and make them happy with those who offer sacrifices to them.

Within religions there is often a mixed attachment to ritual. For example, in Christianity some Protestants minimize formal rituals, whereas most Roman Catholics and the Eastern Orthodox have many elaborate rituals. Sufi Muslims emphasize pilgrimage to God "in the heart," in part to contrast with other Muslims who view the pilgrimage to Mecca as the highlight of their life.

Ethical and ritual dimensions come together in a Hindu wedding in Ahmedabad, India.

Hindus at times have given up the rituals of the home and temple to seek salvation in solitary meditation. Although ritual may be downplayed in favor of other dimensions of religion, it never completely disappears.

1-4d The Institutional Dimension

Because religions are social more than personal, they give an organizational structure to their religious community and (usually) the wider society. Moreover, many religions are internally diverse, with different institutional structures for each internal group. Most religions come from ancient, traditional societies, so they aren't "democratic" organizations; power in religious institutions tends to flow from the top down. This is also true of **new religious movements (NRMs)**, religious groups that have arisen since the nineteenth century and now have sufficient size

Groom breaking a wineglass at a Jewish wedding, symbolic of mourning over the destruction of the Jerusalem temple in 70 C.E.

ritual Symbolic action in worship, meditation, or other religious ceremonies

pilgrimage Travel to a special destination to increase one's devotion or improve one's religious status

myth Story that relates basic truths of a religion

new religious movements (NRMs) Religious groups that have arisen since the nineteenth century and now have sufficient size and longevity to merit academic study

and longevity to merit academic study. Typically, one charismatic leader founds an NRM and wields great power; an example is L. Ron Hubbard of the Scientology movement. Religions make a valid distinction between specialists (religious healers, priests, monks) who lead the religions and the main body of people who practice a religion, typically called **laity**. This institutional dimension is so important that people often speak of "organized religion."

1-4e The Aesthetic Dimension

The aesthetic (beauty) dimension is the sensory element of religion. Beauty appeals to the rational mind but has a special appeal to human emotions. This dimension encompasses religion's sounds and smells, spaces, holy places, and landscapes. It also includes its main symbols (for instance, Judaism's six-pointed Star of David, Buddhism's wheel), devotional images and statuary, and all the religious items of material culture. Islamic religious art tends to be abstract, because of strong prohibitions of anything that could enable the worship of other gods. Most Hindu art, on the other hand, is fully representational, at times even sexual. The aesthetic dimension encompasses the architecture and decoration of religious buildings, as well

Sensual art put to spiritual use: a Hindu goddess

© MACIEJ MEDYNSKI/SHUTTERSTOCK.COM

Read about a book on religiously themed toys.

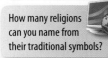

How many religions can you name from their traditional symbols?

as works of music, poetry, and hymns. It also includes ritual gestures: hand gestures in yoga, bodies kneeling in prayer, hands pressed together in Hindu greeting and Christian prayer, and many others.

1-4f The Emotional Dimension

This dimension includes the particular emotions and wider "moods" experienced in religion. They include senses of awe, fear, and love. They also include some religions' hope for life after death or other religions' hope for no more life after death. The emotional dimension includes confidence received to cope with death, suffering, and evil. The emotional self-confidence and sense of purpose that religion brings are so notable that "losing my religion" or "getting religion" about something are common expressions. The emotional dimension includes the emotions that come with belonging and personal identity, as well as with concern for others. It also includes extraordinary feelings and experiences such as isolation, union with an ultimate reality or divine being(s), and hallucinations. The emotional dimension of religion looms large today in the Western world, where belief for many is primarily a matter of emotion. In the words of the 1981 hit song by the rock group Journey, put to more recent use by such television shows as *Family Guy* and *Glee*, "Don't stop believing, hold on to that feeling."

Read a review of a book on "sacred terror" in horror films.

> The sense of purpose that religion brings is so notable that we speak informally of "losing my religion" or "getting religion" about something.

To conclude this section, let us consider that sometimes people reduce religion to one or two of these dimensions. For example, they may suppose that religion is primarily an ethical system, a system of teaching about the divine, an institution, or even a feel-good

laity Main body of people who practice a religion

Beauty adorns a wall and the dome of a mosque in Isfahan, Iraq, to the glory of Allah and inspiration of those who worship.

© SZEFEI/SHUTTERSTOCK.COM

theology Study of a religion, based on a religious commitment to that religion, in order to promote it

religious studies Academic study of religion that aims to understand all religious traditions objectively, in a religiously neutral way

emotion. This reduction is to be expected, but it's wrong. Almost all religions are multidimensional. That the many dimensions of religion are closely related to one another was suggested by British philosopher Alfred North Whitehead, who wrote that the power of religion lies in its grasp of this truth: "The order of the world, the depth of reality of the world, the value of the world in its whole and in its parts, the beauty of the world, the zest for life, the peace of life, and the mastery of evil, are all bound together."[9]

The Wabash Center Internet guide to religious studies underscores religion's many dimensions.

Learning Outcome 1-5

Discuss how the various academic disciplines contribute to the study of religion.

1-5 Ways of Studying Religion

The study of religion is pursued today with a wide variety of methods. These center largely on six different academic disciplines, some of which you may be studying. We'll consider these methods and the work of prominent scholars who have influenced the rise of religious studies as an academic discipline by contributing to these methods. Along the way, we'll encounter different theories of the origin and purpose of religion. Before we discuss these methods, however, we should deal with the important matter of the difference between theology and religious studies.

© AMR HASSANEIN/SHUTTERSTOCK.COM

Al-Azhar University in Cairo, founded in 972 C.E.

1-5a Theology and Religious Studies

The study of religion in America today is pursued in two main ways. **Theology** is the study of a religion, based on a religious commitment to that religion, in order to promote it. It is study from the "inside." Christian theology has been an important part of the Western university since the oldest universities were founded in thirteenth-century Europe. Theology is pursued today at many American schools, especially those with religious affiliations. As the eleventh-century Christian theologian Anselm (AHN-sehlm) said, theology is "faith seeking understanding." This statement is true of theological study in other religions as well, in both Eastern and Western religions. The university thought to be the oldest still existing today—at the Al-Azhar (al-ah-ZAHR) Mosque in Cairo, Egypt—was founded for theological study. Theology is older in Buddhism and Hinduism than it is in Christianity or Islam. Theology in these religions has typically relied closely on philosophy and textual studies to carry out its intellectual work.

The second branch is called **religious studies**, a relatively new field of academic study of religion that aims to understand all religious traditions objectively, in a religiously neutral way, from the "outside." Religious studies doesn't ask students to make religious commitments or even require students to reflect on those they have. In the Enlightenment (ca. 1650–1800), the independence and separation of human reason from religion had developed to the extent that a scholarly treatment of religion independent from theology could begin. Reason, not faith, was now seeking understanding of religion. A recent book by Guy Stroumsa, *A New Science: The Discovery of Religion in the Age of Reason*, describes how Roman

---

[9] Alfred North Whitehead, *Religion in the Making* (New York: World, 1960), 115.

Catholic and Protestant scholars in Europe forged this new area of study in early modern times. Stroumsa writes that three major events from 1500 to 1800 laid the foundation for the birth of the study of religion: the rise of European colonial empires, which gave birth to curiosity about other cultures; the Reformation, which permanently altered Christianity; and the new academic study of world languages and literature. By about 1875, religious studies was emerging as an academic field.[10] Now using academic methods from many disciplines in the humanities and sciences, religious studies has a broad intellectual interest in the different world religions. It offers a nonthreatening opportunity for students to encounter important issues about religion, different world religions, and life itself.

> After World War I, historians would become less naïve about their ability to be "scientifically" objective about their work.

1-5b History

History is the scholarly study of the past, whether that past is remote (the beginnings of human civilization, for example) or recent (the events of last year). It seeks to find out what really happened and why. This task is important because, as historian Philip Jenkins has written about religion, "Virtually everybody uses the past in everyday discourse, but the historical record on which they draw is littered with myths, half-truths, and folk-history."[11] When history is applied to religion, rich and important knowledge emerges, because religions come from the past, both remote and recent. The formal method scholars have developed is called the **historical-critical method**, the study of the past using careful scholarly methods such as archaeology and the study of texts in their original languages. History studies the process of a religion's beginnings, growth, diversity, decline, and so on. An example is a recent book entitled *Sacred Schisms: How Religions Divide*, which carefully

studies internal splits in a dozen religions and draws conclusions about the process of religious splits.[12] History has almost always been a main method in the study of religion.

Oxford historian of Indian culture Max Müller (1823–1900), whom we already met above, is one of the founders of religious studies—some would say *the* founder. He edited a fifty-volume collection of ancient sacred scriptures from the main Asian religions, translated for the first time into reliable English editions (the Sacred Books of the East series, 1879–1910), a foundational contribution to research and teaching in religious history. He promoted a scholarly discussion on developmental patterns in religious history and on the relation of myth, ritual, and magic to religion in the past. In his *Introduction to the Science of Religion* (1873), Müller argued that religious scholarship can be fully scientific in its methods and results. It can collect, classify, and compare religious texts just as scientifically as a botanist collects and studies plants. Müller's investigations led him and others to a supposed "oldest stage" of European and Asian culture and religion that extended from the Indians to the Germanic tribes—what he called the "Indo-Germanic" or "Aryan" stage beginning around 2000 B.C.E.

By the end of the 1800s, the notion of near-steady, almost evolutionary progress often assumed in these studies (and in much of European and North American higher learning and culture at that time) started to fade, and the surprising horrors of the First World War (1914–1918) ended assumptions of automatic progress in religion and culture. Müller's work in religious history was largely text based, especially in scriptures. This was a necessary first step, but the field of history would widen in the twentieth century to include popular history, the history of material culture, and additional areas. It would also become less naïve about the ability of historians to be "scientifically" objective about their work.

One particular approach taken by a number of historians of religions is the **history of religions school**.

> **historical-critical method** Study of the past using careful, scholarly methods
>
> **history of religions school** School of religious thought begun in nineteenth-century Germany; the first to study religion as a social and cultural phenomenon

---

[10] Guy Stroumsa, *A New Science: The Discovery of Religion in the Age of Reason* (Cambridge: Harvard University Press, 2010).

[11] Philip Jenkins, "Ancient and Modern: What the History of Religion Teaches Us about Contemporary Global Trends," ARDA Guiding Paper, http://www.thearda.com/rrh/papers/guidingpapers/jenkins.asp, accessed 7/17/10.

[12] James R. Lewis and Sarah M. Lewis, *Sacred Schisms: How Religions Divide* (Cambridge, UK: Cambridge University Press, 2009).

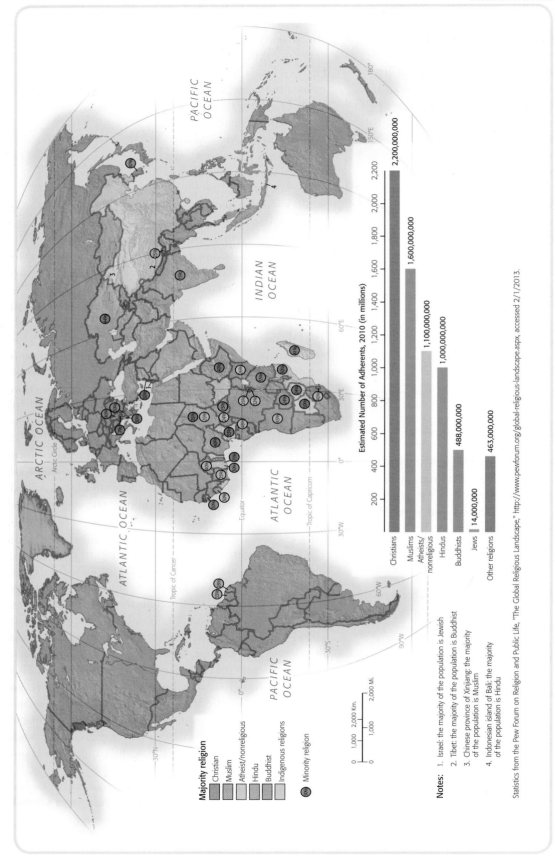

© CENGAGE LEARNING 2013

Majority religion

- Christian
- Muslim
- Atheist/nonreligious
- Hindu
- Buddhist
- Indigenous religions

🔵 Minority religion

Estimated Number of Adherents, 2010 (in millions)

Christians	2,200,000,000
Muslims	1,600,000,000
Atheists/nonreligious	1,100,000,000
Hindus	1,000,000,000
Buddhists	488,000,000
Jews	14,000,000
Other religions	463,000,000

0 200 400 600 800 1,000 1,200 1,400 1,600 1,800 2,000 2,200

Notes:
1. Israel: the majority of the population is Jewish
2. Tibet: the majority of the population is Buddhist
3. Chinese province of Xinjiang: the majority of the population is Muslim
4. Indonesian island of Bali: the majority of the population is Hindu

Statistics from the Pew Forum on Religion and Public Life, "The Global Religious Landscape," http://www.pewforum.org/global-religious-landscape.aspx, accessed 2/1/2013.

0 1,000 2,000 Km.
0 1,000 2,000 Mi.

Map 1.1
Distribution of World Religions Today

Christianity has the most believers in the world today and is the dominant faith in the Americas, Oceania, Europe, Russia, and central and southern Africa. Most people in the northern half of Africa, western Asia, and central Asia embrace Islam. Hindus are concentrated in India and Buddhists in East and Southeast Asia. Although China has been largely atheistic or nonreligious under Communist rule, its main religions—Daoism, Confucianism, Buddhism, Islam, and Christianity—are growing, now espoused by about 25 percent of the population.

This school of thought began in Germany in the nineteenth century, lasted with some strength into the middle of the twentieth century, and is still occasionally found today in Europe and North America. The history of religions school began the formal study of religion as a social and cultural phenomenon. It saw religion as evolving with human culture, from "primitive" polytheism to ethical monotheism. It divided world religions into steps of evolution from polytheistic to monotheistic and from informal to formal. Despite the obvious faults of such an approach, it contributed to a sharp increase in our knowledge about other religions. For the first time, an accurate "map" of the different religions of the world emerged (see Map 1.1).

View an animated map giving "5,000 Years of Religion in 90 Seconds."

Read about current global religious trends in historical perspective.

1-5c Psychology

Psychology deals with the structure and activity of the human mind. It is the scientific study of individual behavior, including emotions and other thoughts. Psychology has an interest in religion because of religion's role in shaping human behavior—for example in coping with life-cycle changes and death. Psychology also focuses on how religions understand the human self, including gender. It has been particularly concerned with research in conversion, mysticism, and meditation.

Psychology sought at first to explain the origins of religion in terms of the subconscious mind. Sigmund Freud (froid) and Carl Gustav Jung (yoong), the founders of psychoanalysis, sought in opposing ways to trace the origins from the strongest, most basic human needs and drives. Freud (1856–1939) and his school regarded religion as a neurotic condition that needed therapy when it persisted into adulthood. (See his definition of

Yoga is one popular form of meditation.

religion earlier in this chapter.) He held that religion, particularly a belief in God, derives from a need for a divine father figure when children gradually separate from their human fathers. These ideas can be found in his books *The Future of an Illusion*, in which the "illusion" is religion, and *Moses and Monotheism*. Freud finally admitted that a person could experience religion as an "oceanic feeling," but later Freudians would continue to be mostly negative toward religion until about the 1980s, when some change began.

Freud's pupil Jung (1875–1961), on the other hand, was appreciative of religion. In his books *Modern Man in Search of a Soul* and *Memories, Dreams, Reflections*, he held that conceptions of the divine, whether of god(s) or another form of ultimate reality, were related to an ancient archetypal pattern that resides in the subconscious of all human minds. Religion enables each developing person to bring out and employ this archetype as the individual personality grows and achieves what Jung called "individuation," or personal maturity and wholeness. The notion of individuation would become important in the human potential/humanistic branch of American psychology. This positive archetype is found in all societies, Jung argued, and his theory also became important for many researchers in the academic discipline of cultural anthropology.

William James (1842–1910), a professor at Harvard, was an American founder of the field of psychology. In his still-important book *The Varieties of Religious Experience*, James advanced a more pragmatic and positive view of religion than did either Freud or Jung. He maintained that the religious experience of individuals, not religious institutions, should be the primary focus of the psychology of religion and of religion itself. Intense types of religious experience in particular should be studied by psychologists, because they are the closest thing to a "microscope" into the mind. Individuals must develop certain "over-beliefs" that, while they cannot be proven, help humans live purposefully and in "harmony with the universe." After James, the psychological study of religion went

© PIOTR MARCINSKI/SHUTTERSTOCK.COM

into something of a decline, and scientific research into religious behavior faded.

> *Andrew Newberg has discovered that the benefits of meditation grow over years of practice, but even new practitioners get healthier brains.*

Since the 1980s, the psychological study of religion has been advanced by neuroscience, particularly with regard to research on the human brain. (Here the psychology of religion comes very close to biology, which we will discuss in section 1-5g.) A prominent researcher in this field is Andrew Newberg of the University of Pennsylvania. He has measured what happens in the brains of subjects while they meditate or pray—in a way, providing the "microscope into the mind" that William James sought. Newberg's research used brain imaging to study Tibetan Buddhists in meditation and Roman Catholic nuns in prayer. He found that during intense sessions of these activities, areas of the brain associated with concentration and emotion become more active and areas associ-

Watch Newberg explain his research.

ated with the sense of self become less active. Newberg hypothesizes that this may explain the sense of "otherness" and "oneness with God or ultimate reality" described by people who have had intense religious experiences. Much of this research is summarized in his fascinating book *Why God Won't Go Away: Brain Science and the Biology of Belief* (2001). More recently, Newberg argued that the physical and emotional benefits of meditation grow over years of practice, but even new practitioners get "healthier brains." After meditating twelve minutes a day for two months, most subjects who have just learned meditation gain significant improvement in memory, and their anxiety and anger decrease.

1-5d Sociology

Sociology, the scientific study of groups and group behavior, explains religion's role in society. Sociologists

studying religion are concerned with the mutual relationship between religion and society, how each shapes the other. They examine, by both qualitative and quantitative research, the practices of religions. Sociologists are interested in beliefs mainly as the backgrounds of social practices and behaviors. They also study the various groups within different religions.

Current debates in the sociology of religion have centered on issues such as the pace of secularization, **civil religion** (the popular, dominant religion of a nation or culture that typically involves a religious conviction about that nation or culture), and the cohesiveness of religions and religious practice in the challenges of globalization, multiculturalism, and pluralism. Sociology of religion based on empirical research is an influential tradition in the United States, and its flagship outlet for research is the *Journal for the Scientific Study of Religion*. Sociological studies have contributed greatly to our knowledge of religion, for example on current issues such as new religious movements and "fundamentalisms" in world religions.

Visit a leading website for the scientific study of religion.

Émile Durkheim (1858–1917), a founder of sociology, came from a long line of Jewish rabbis but studied religion from the "religious studies" approach. Many scholars today have concluded that the sociology of religion, and perhaps sociology itself, began with Durkheim's 1897 book *Suicide*, which studied among other things the rates of suicide occurrence among Catholic, Protestant, and Jewish populations in Western Europe. Durkheim theorized, especially in his essay "The Origin of Beliefs," that religion was necessary for a healthy society: Religion binds societies together. It creates group identity and reinforces common moral values. This is true even when society is secularizing, and Durkheim argued that secularization would continue in Europe. Like Karl Marx, Durkheim saw that religion helps to control the individual, but unlike Marx, he saw this as a good thing. Durkheim argued that the relationship between people and God mirrors the relationship between individuals and society. His memorable proverb in this regard is "God is society, writ large."

For a taste of sociology's take on religion, read the highlights of a sociological report on American religion.

1-5e Cultural Anthropology

Cultural anthropology is the scientific study of human life focused on various concrete human settings. It arose in the nineteenth century, and soon after its birth it

sociology Scientific study of groups and group behavior

civil religion Popular, dominant religion of a nation or culture that typically involves some religious conviction about that nation or culture

cultural anthropology Scientific study of human life focused on concrete human settings

was applied to religions of the world, especially the beliefs and practices of tribal cultures. Cultural anthropology uncovers the underlying values of cultures, their answer to the question "Why are we here?" It studies such broad cultural dynamics as honor and shame, the role of kinship, and so on. It explores the roles of symbols, culture, and the natural environment; the making of social boundaries; how sex is understood and gender roles are constructed; and rituals. A special focus of anthropology has been the **shaman**, a religious specialist traditionally belonging to an indigenous society who acts as a medium between this visible world and the spirit world, usually for healing and telling the future. Since the 1960s, the formal use of cultural anthropology has become more prominent in religious studies.

Aztec shaman

ISTOCKPHOTO.COM/RALF HETTLER

shaman [SHAH-muhn]
Religious specialist traditionally belonging to an indigenous society who acts as a medium between this visible world and the spirit world

life-cycle ritual
Ceremony to mark an important point in life such as birth, becoming an adult, weddings, and funerals; sometimes called "rite of passage"

"Anthropologists ... find in the little what eludes us in the large, stumble upon general truths while sorting through special cases." —Clifford Geertz

Cultural anthropology can study the past, especially texts, art, and other artifacts. Almost all world religions with sacred writings have had those writings subjected to some form of anthropological study. For example, in a study of early Christianity, Bruce Malina of Creighton University in Omaha, an anthropologist and New Testament scholar, has applied this method to several books of the New Testament, especially in his *The New Testament World: Insights from Cultural Anthropology.*[13] This is often called "historical

anthropology." However, cultural anthropology deals predominantly with living religions. It studies current practices including pilgrimages; **life-cycle rituals** (also called "rites of passage") such as weddings and funerals; belief in miracles; festivals; and the functions of guilt, confession, punishment, and forgiveness. History, sociology, and even psychology tend to make broad analyses and conclusions, but anthropology tends to study smaller-scale aspects of human life. As Clifford Geertz wrote in his book about Islam in Morocco and Indonesia, "The anthropologist is always inclined to turn toward the concrete, the particular, the microscopic.... We hope to find in the little

---

[13] Bruce Malina, *The New Testament World: Insights from Cultural Anthropology*, 3rd ed. (Louisville, KY: Westminster John Knox, 2001).

Cultural anthropology studies life through the generations, such as these young Masai women in east Africa.

© JEFF SCHULTES/SHUTTERSTOCK.COM

feminism Movement for women's equality

patriarchy Male-dominated societies

what eludes us in the large, to stumble upon general truths while sorting through special cases."[14]

For example, while historians made large studies about ancient Hindu sacred texts in the "dead language" of Sanskrit, anthropologists spent long periods of time in fieldwork in India to study the living use of contemporary oral traditions in other Indian languages.

Victor Turner (1920–1983), an influential cultural anthropologist of the past four decades, developed a powerful theory of ritual that drew the attention of scholars to religious behaviors. His conception of rituals was shaped during his fieldwork in the 1950s with the Ndembu tribe, in what today is Zambia. His personal background in Roman Catholic Christianity also forms a background for his work on ritual. He was interested in the "social drama" of ritual presentations, especially life-cycle rituals. Ritual creates the social breaks Turner called "marginality" and the thresholds of new kinds of life that he termed "liminality."

Watch as cultural anthropology looks at "black magic."

stem from—and most uphold today to some extent—**patriarchy** (male-dominated societies). In religions that have both male and female gods, the male gods nearly always predominate; this is true of both tribal and international religions. Women's identification with female gods—for example the new goddess Santoshi Ma in Hinduism—does provide religious strength, but this is qualified by male dominance among divine beings themselves. Predominantly masculine language is used to describe and address most gods, especially the one God of monotheistic religions.

Women's roles as professional religious specialists have been limited, even in those relatively few religious organizations that profess women's equality with men. (This limitation is sometimes called in the Western world the "stained-glass ceiling.") Their ambitions have often been constrained by the idea that their primary religious duty is to obey

Venus (or Woman) of Willendorf, Austria, the world's oldest religious statuette (24,000–22,000 B.C.E.)

their husbands and raise their children. A number of feminists have argued that a "Mother Goddess" religion centered on the Earth and on women is the earliest form of human religion, but this is contested. Women of many religions have made different responses to the pressure of patriarchy. For example, they press for wider roles as religious specialists, trying to break the stained-glass ceiling or at least push it higher. They look for wider opportunities in the world of work, often adapting this to their religious duties in the home. In general, they interpret and live their religions in ways more congenial to women.

Read about how the Buddha allowed an order of nuns.

1-5f Women's Studies

When **feminism**, the movement for women's equality, came to full bloom in the United States in the 1970s, the academic field of women's or gender studies quickly developed. It studies the social pressures, expectations, and opportunities of both genders but focuses on women, with the purpose of promoting their full equality and liberation. Feminism thus has both a descriptive and a prescriptive aspect. Gender studies is flourishing in North America but is not yet strong in Europe or other parts of the world.

Feminist scholars of religion have pointed to religion as one explanation of the nearly worldwide subordination of women to men. They argue, correctly, that all religions

1-5g Biology

Until recently, biology (the scientific study of all life) didn't contribute much to the study of religion, aside from religious studies scholars' uncritical application of evolutionary theory to religion. Now, with the ability to study the human genome, or gene system, new possibilities are opening for understanding complex human issues in the realm of religion. Many scientists are now

---

[14] Clifford Geertz, *Islam Observed* (New Haven: Yale University Press, 1968), 4.

seeking to explain religion in genetic terms, or at least to find the genetic connections of religion. Rapidly increasing knowledge of the human genome has made this possible. Some writers have suggested that the pervasiveness of religious beliefs is due to our genetic makeup.

The controversial theory advanced in Dean Hamer's *The God Gene: How Faith Is Hardwired into Our Genes* (2005) claims that religion is made possible by a genetic adaptation. Hamer even pointed to one gene, called *VMAT2* by the Human Genome Project, as the "God gene."[15] However, most scientists hypothesize that the genetic background of any complex human behavior such as religion probably flows from a combination of several genes. More generally accepted is the hypothesis by some biologists and anthropologists that the development of religious belief in prehistoric peoples may have been a key factor in the development of higher-order cognitive skills: A number of humans became capable of transcending themselves in thought and action, and this was passed on by natural selection.

> Some biologists and anthropologists hold that the development of religious belief in prehistoric peoples may have given humans their higher-order cognitive skills.

1-5h Conclusions about Methods of Studying Religion

We'll conclude our treatment of methods with two observations. First, it's obvious that the study of religion, like many other branches of scholarship, is multidisciplinary. It has no "religious method" all its own, but draws from many other methods. Second, religious studies is a human, not a divine, way of knowing. Religion itself can bring divine or sacred knowledge, but our academic study of it is method related and time bound. This means that religion scholars, just like other academic experts, are part of the "concrete epistemology" (ways of knowing) of current scholarly and cultural interests and current assumptions that different generations have about life. Religion scholars' (*and* beginning students') personal development, education, and

---

[15] Dean Hamer, *The God Gene: How Faith Is Hardwired into Our Genes* (New York: Doubleday, 2004).

individual religious experiences, as well as their generation-specific attitudes, all affect how they adopt and use a particular method of studying religion. Religious studies is conditioned in each generation by time, a fact that is often appreciated only by a later generation for whom temporal distance allows a better view. As we sometimes say with slight exaggeration, "Hindsight is twenty-twenty."

phenomenology of religion Study of religion through its observable practices ("phenomena")

This conditioning can be traced through time from the beginning of religious studies until today. Religious studies first went along with nineteenth-century optimism about the progressive evolution of human religion. Then, a Protestant bias crept into religious studies from the hidden values of scholars in the field, who were predominantly Protestant Christian: the privileging of sacred texts over oral traditions; the privileging of doctrine over ritual; and the belief in the primacy of private religious experience over received traditions—all crucial elements of the Protestant branch of Christianity. Next, the scholars in the **phenomenology of religion** movement of the 1920s, after the spiritual and intellectual crisis of the First World War, searched for the so-called essence of religion by studying its observable practices ("phenomena"). Then, the baby-boomer generation of scholars in the 1960s through 1990s was driven by the experience and values of an alternative culture to pose provocative questions that challenged traditional methods in religious studies. The realization that each generation of scholars has characteristic limitations, which it cannot see, need not diminish the value of religious studies. Indeed, knowing the limits and biases of knowledge makes our knowledge more certain.

Learning Outcome 1-6

Explain the special issues in the study of religion today.

1-6 Special Issues in the Study of Religion Today

1-6a Tolerance and Intolerance

In Cambridge, Massachusetts, a controversy breaks out in the blogosphere and then in the print media over Harvard College's decision to reserve six hours a week for women

atheism Conviction that there is no God

agnosticism Refers to those who "do not know" if a God or gods exist

tolerance Putting up with the views and actions of others that are opposed to your own, usually for the common good

only in the college's central gymnasium. The Harvard Islamic Society petitioned for the special hours, arguing that observant female Muslim students needed these special hours in order to observe Muslim rules about modesty and coverings for women. Although many Muslim women had exercised in the gymnasium during open hours, dressed in sweat suits and head scarves, the Harvard Islamic Society says that having hours restricted to women enables them to exercise better, in athletic shirts and shorts, without fear of male students "checking them out." Some argue that this is a reasonable toleration of another's faith; others say that this gives Harvard's approval to practices that reinforce intolerance toward women.

British scholar Christopher Hitchens (1949–2011) was one of a handful of current advocates of **atheism**— the conviction that there is no God and that religion is mostly mistaken—who are making sharp public attacks on religion. (**Agnosticism**, a related term, refers to those who "do not know" if a God or gods exist; agnosticism is not always antireligious, and rarely combative against religion.) Hitchens recently wrote that religion is "violent, irrational, intolerant, allied to racism and tribalism and bigotry, invested in ignorance and hostile to free inquiry, contemptuous of women and coercive toward children."[16] A few prominent atheists have recently pushed back against this extreme view. Edward O. Wilson argues in *The Social Conquest of Earth* that religion brought social order to early humans, giving

"Religion is violent, irrational, intolerant, allied to racism and tribalism and bigotry, invested in ignorance ... contemptuous of women and coercive toward children." —Christopher Hitchens

them an evolutionary advantage.[17] Alain de Botton, in *Religion for Atheists*, says that atheists can learn a great deal from religions about meaning and beauty in human life.[18] Nevertheless, Hitchens and other atheists articulate a strongly negative view of religion that many people share.

Tolerance means putting up with the views and actions of others that are opposed to your own, usually for the common good. We begin our discussion of tolerance and intolerance with the Western world. The modern Western idea of religious tolerance developed in Europe after brutal wars between Protestant and Roman Catholic Christians in the sixteenth and seventeenth centuries, and has gradually been extended to people of other religions. (The murderous violence between Protestants and Roman Catholics in Northern Ireland from about 1960 to 1998 serves to remind the modern world what was gained at the end of the seventeenth century.) The First Amendment to the U.S. Constitution guarantees tolerance in "freedom of religion." The state cannot interfere with basic religious rights and must actively protect them from restriction in law or policy. In the twentieth century, the Universal Declaration of Human Rights first advocated freedom of religion for all people. Since the Enlightenment, the fostering and maintenance of tolerance, religious or otherwise, has been regarded as a duty of government. Tolerance and intolerance are public, social things, but they are personal and individual as well. People of one religion can be intolerant toward people of other religions, and people outside religion can be intolerant of all or some religious people and groups.

The history of world religions reveals different ideas of tolerance. In ancient China, native religions were generally tolerated, but non-Chinese religions were admitted only by government consent; this is still true

> Read the Universal Declaration of Human Rights, especially articles 18–20 on religion.

> Read agnostic Gina Welch's reflections about her intolerance to evangelical Protestant Christians.

---

[16] Christopher Hitchens, *God Is Not Great: How Religion Poisons Everything* (Boston: Twelve Publishing Company, 2007), 56.

[17] Edward O. Wilson, *The Social Conquest of Earth* (New York: Liveright, 2012).

[18] Alain de Botton, *Religion for Atheists: A Non-Believer's Guide to the Uses of Religion* (New York: Pantheon, 2012).

of China today. Ancient Judaism was at times welcoming to other religions in its territory, at other times not. In the ancient Roman Empire, non-Roman religious groups were generally tolerated as long as they did not undermine the religious underpinnings of Roman imperial rule. Christianity, during the thousand years since it became the Roman state religion until at least the Protestant Reformation, tended toward religious intolerance. (Compare the maxim from Roman Catholic history that has parallels in other religions: "Error has no rights." The Roman Catholic Church did not formally accept religious tolerance until the Second Vatican Council in the 1960s.) Islam usually granted toleration of conquered peoples of certain other religions—as a rule, but not always in practice. This toleration did not extend to Arab polytheism, which was extinguished; and over time, even tolerated religions were dramatically reduced in Muslim lands.

Hinduism has been generally tolerant to other religions but has preferred to integrate them into its own system. Hindu relations with Muslims on the Indian subcontinent have been uneasy for centuries, and mass conversions of Hindus to Christianity and Buddhism can provoke a violent reaction. The regular, religiously motivated violence between Hindus and Muslims that has occurred since the division of India and Pakistan in 1947, and occasionally Hindu violence against Sikhs, means that the tolerance some see in Hinduism is not without qualification. Buddhism, which teaches tolerance, has seen intolerant periods in its history, recently in the civil war carried on by armed Buddhists in Sri Lanka, in the violently repressive Buddhist government in Myanmar (Burma), and on a much smaller scale in bitter struggles between different Tibetan monastic groups. In sum, achieving and maintaining tolerance is no easy matter for religions.

People today don't like to be called intolerant, but few people can be equally tolerant of all opposing ideas and actions.

Muslims and other religious minorities must sometimes protest for the freedom to practice their faith.

ISTOCKPHOTO.COM/STUDIO-ANNIKA

A difficult question involves the limits of tolerance. People in the world today don't like to be called "intolerant," but few people can be equally tolerant of all opposing ideas and actions. If they try, difficult questions arise. For example, can a religious group that is itself intolerant be tolerated in the public sector? In North America, with its legal tradition of granting a maximum of freedom to religious groups both tolerant and intolerant, this isn't so much of an issue. But can a religion be tolerated by another if it grows big enough to take over a society and perhaps impose its own intolerance? In general, private religious *views* are tolerated in Western nations, provided that they do not lead to *actions* that could challenge a majority consensus on public life. The line between private belief and public action isn't always easy to see, however. A good example is a continuing controversy in France involving Muslim women's attire in public. Legislation banns head scarves that cover the face and/or full-body veils, which the government views as an threat to the state and its secular nature. The Church of Scientology is under government pressure in Germany, in part because the post–World War II German constitution forbids "totalitarian movements," which the government suspects that Scientology is. And in China, the Falun Gong (FAH-luhn GONG) meditational movement is strongly repressed by the Chinese government as a "dangerous cult" that supposedly threatens public order and the health of its followers. These examples show that struggles over tolerance continue today all around the world.

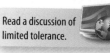
Read a discussion of limited tolerance.

Watch a presentation of the antiviolence "Charter for Compassion."

1-6b Violence

Faced in April 2010 with a spreading sexual abuse scandal in Europe, similar to one that took place in the 1990s in the United States, Pope Benedict XVI apologized in an official letter to almost 15,000 victims and their families in Ireland. He expressed "shame and remorse" for "sinful and criminal" behavior by some priests over the past fifty years. Most of these acts were sexual assaults against children. "You have suffered grievously and I am truly sorry," the pope said. "Your trust has been betrayed and your dignity has been violated."

But the pope didn't indicate in his letter that church leaders who looked the other way or actively covered up these crimes would be disciplined by the church or that the whole matter would be turned over to the police, as many victims and their families were hoping. The problem of sexual predators among religious leaders isn't unique to Roman Catholics, or even to Christianity.

Violence is a difficult topic to grapple with, both emotionally and intellectually. However, this grappling is necessary. Violence is the intentional use of physical force to injure or kill people, to damage or destroy their property, or both. Violence is motivated by a variety of factors—political, economic, national, and tribal. Religiously motivated violence includes all events in which a follower of a religion is either the perpetrator or the recipient of violent behavior or both. As with other kinds of violence, religious violence can be carried out by individuals or groups. It can be by direct attack, or by indirect means such as inducing famine. It includes violence of any kind by members of one religion against people of another religion (the Crusades by medieval Christians against Islam, Muslim holy war, and occasional violence between Sikhs and Hindus), between different groups in a religion (Sunni and Shi'a Muslims, occasional violence between different Hindu castes in India), and crimes by powerful people in a religion against those with less or no power. It includes persecution of one religion by another or by the state against its people, as in the Holocaust directed at Jews or in the current Chinese prosecution of the new Falun Gong religious movement. It also includes violence against explicitly religious objects, as in attacks on religious buildings or sites or burning of holy books. Because religions have cultural, political, and other aspects, different motivations often lie behind

> Watch former U.S. Secretary of State Madeleine Albright on religion and conflict.

In 2012, thousands of girls attend school in Afghanistan despite religiously motivated threats against them.

CAPT. JOHN SEVERN/UNITED STATES ARMY

what may appear to be purely religious violence. Sometimes violence can be inflicted on a public target in order to induce terror in a populace.

Religious violence committed by groups must be understood in its cultural context—not to excuse it, but to understand it. In particular, beginning students of religions should realize that not all religious violence is the same. Some religions tend to be non-violent, but others approve of violence in certain situations. A few religions began as explicitly non-violent movements—Christianity and Sikhism, for example—but changed over time. Religious violence often tends to place differing emphases on the symbolic aspects of violence. For example, sometimes violence is understood as a religiously significant act with ritual aspects. In the 1990s, Taliban Muslims dynamited ancient statues of the Buddha to remove "idolatry" from Afghanistan, and today they at times attack government schools for girls. Ritual violence may be directed against victims, as in human sacrifice, or it may be more or less voluntarily self-inflicted, as in self-flagellation with a whip. It may be a part of monastic practice, as for example when head monks in certain sects of Zen Buddhism beat their subordinates with sticks and rods to discipline them or try to induce sudden enlightenment. So-called "honor killings," in which family members kill another member of their family (usually female) in order to "preserve the family's honor," often have some religious motivation today, although other factors are at work there too.

> Read about a book on a notorious Swedish "honor killing," *In Honor of Fadime.*

1-6c Pluralism

Phil Jackson, the recently retired head coach of the Los Angeles Lakers, recognized today as one of the greatest NBA coaches, wasn't a typical professional basketball coach. He rarely stood on the sideline and shouted at his players. Instead, he sat so serenely that he was called "Buddha on the bench" and "Zen master," terms that apply as well to his religious approach to coaching. His teams didn't play seasons; they went on "sacred quests," as in Native American religion. Jackson taught his players short Buddhist meditations to use before they shot free throws. He called their main strategy on offense "five-man tai chi," and their locker room was filled with Native American religious objects. His 1995 autobiography is called *Sacred Hoops.* Raised by devout Christian parents who taught him to value both religious earnestness and compassion, he calls himself a "Zen Christian."

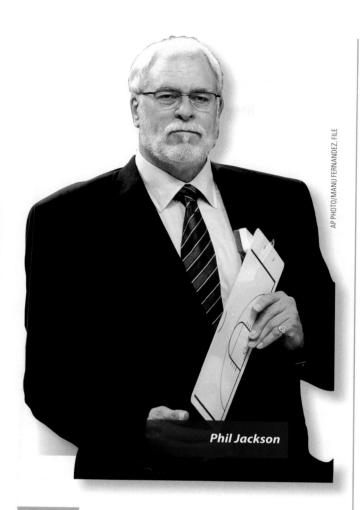

Phil Jackson

> *Different religions exist because religions are different. This makes dialogue between them both possible and necessary.*

Nonviolent relations between religions, and between cultures and nations with different religions, are based first on toleration. Religious **pluralism**, the recognition of religious differences and the effort to deal with them constructively, goes beyond toleration. Religious pluralism owes a great deal to the American and European experience of religious diversity. Chris Beneke, in his *Beyond Toleration: The Religious Origins of American Pluralism*, distinguishes carefully between tolerance and pluralism. By the 1730s, religious toleration toward minority religions was practiced in British colonies in North America. Toleration ended physical punishments and financial burdens on religious minorities, but it did not end prejudice and exclusion. Those "tolerated" were usually barred from

holding government and military positions and from universities. Religious persecution had ended, but religious discrimination had not. However, the colonies gradually expanded religious toleration, and religious liberty for all was achieved by 1790.[19] This was not primarily a compromise with rising Enlightenment secularism in America; it was an achievement of early American religious groups themselves. The different Protestant Christian groups—Episcopalians, Methodists, Quakers, Presbyterians, Baptists, Lutherans, and others—saw religious liberty for everyone as in their own best interests, and for the common good. The consensus for religious liberty was so strong that when a new national constitution was adopted at the end of the eighteenth century, the Bill of Rights was added almost immediately, with freedom of religion in the first amendment. The strength of religious freedom in the United States has greatly influenced the course of religious freedoms in the world.

Religious pluralism demands interfaith dialogue and significant cooperation. Interfaith dialogue is conversation between members of different religions to reduce conflicts between them and to achieve mutually desirable goals. Dialogue calls for care to be taken with the ideas of others, without necessarily agreeing with them or assuming (as many people think) that all religions are essentially the same or could be made the same. In the words of the subtitle of Stephen Prothero's thought-provoking book *The Eight Rival Religions That Run the World*, their *Differences Matter.*[20] To put it another way: Different religions exist because religions are different. These differences make dialogue between religions possible, and they make dialogue important if conflict between religions and between the cultures they shape is to be avoided. Dialogue is easier if a religion's members hold to inclusivism, a belief that other religions may lead to salvation or at least have a significant but partial knowledge of the truth. At the far extreme, believers with a completely exclusivist mindset—that only their religion leads to the truth—prefer

pluralism Recognition of religious differences and the effort to deal with them constructively

View the World Parliament of Religions 2009 intro video.

---

[19] Chris Beneke, *Beyond Toleration: The Religious Origins of American Pluralism* (New York: Oxford University Press, 2006).

[20] Stephen Prothero, *God Is Not One: The Eight Rival Religions That Run the World—And Why Their Differences Matter* (New York: HarperOne, 2010).

Statement on Pluralism by Harvard University's Pluralism Project

First, pluralism is not diversity alone, but *the energetic engagement with diversity*.... Today, religious diversity is a given, but pluralism... is an achievement. Mere diversity without real encounter and relationship will yield increasing tensions in our societies.

Second, pluralism is not just tolerance, but *the active seeking of understanding across lines of difference*. Tolerance is a necessary public virtue, but it does not require Christians and Muslims, Hindus, Jews, and ardent secularists to know anything about one another....

Third, pluralism is not relativism, but *the encounter of commitments*. Pluralism does not require us to leave our identities and our commitments behind, for pluralism is the encounter of commitments. It means holding our deepest differences... not in isolation, but in relationship to one another.

Fourth, pluralism is *based on dialogue*. Dialogue... reveals both common understandings and real differences. Dialogue does not mean everyone... will agree with one another.[21]

Visit the Pluralism Project at Harvard University.

[21] Diana Eck, at http://www.pluralism.org/pages/pluralism/what_is_pluralism, accessed 7/17/10.

---

to convert, not converse with, people of other religions. In between full inclusivism and full exclusivism is a wide range of attitudes, where most believers today live.

See Ziggy Marley perform "Love Is My Religion."

1-6d Religion and Ecological Crisis

At Windsor Castle, just outside London, representatives of nine of the world's largest religions gathered in November 2009 to discuss the ecological crisis. They'd been summoned by Prince Philip of the United Kingdom and United Nations Secretary-General Ban Ki-moon. The "Many Heavens, One Earth" conference sought commitments from religious organizations and the countries in which they predominate to reduce greenhouse gas emissions and curtail human damage to nature. In words addressed to the Christians in the delegation, but applicable to many (but not all) of the other delegates, Prince Philip remarked, "If you believe in God... then you should feel a responsibility to care for God's creation."

Read about the "Many Heavens, One Earth" conference.

Religion and environmentalism has emerged in the past generation as an important topic in religious studies. This isn't only because people everywhere realize that worsening pollution, especially of the air, is changing our Earth's climate rapidly and for the worse. It's also because, as the Muslim scholar Seyyed Nasr explains, "The environmental crisis is fundamentally a crisis of values."[22] Because they shape the values of cultures, religions are deeply involved in how humans treat their environment.

Historian Lynn White Jr. argued in 1967 that Western Christianity, with its view of nature as under human control and direction, bears a substantial responsibility for the modern environmental crisis.[23] White's essay provoked strong reactions ranging from complete denial of his argument to complete agreement with it. Some proposed that Asian religions and the religions of indigenous peoples such as Native Americans offer a more environmentally responsible worldview than does Christianity. By the 1990s, many scholars of religion began to analyze how nature is viewed in the world's religions. Conferences on religion and ecology were held at Harvard University from 1996 to 1998, resulting in a World Religions and Ecology series with one book for each of ten religions. An increasing number of courses on religion and the environment are offered in colleges and universities around the world. This topic needs careful study, because the world's religions sometimes have different views about the origin, nature, and value of the physical world. But it's probably safe to say that all religions

Read about pollution in Hindu India.

Visit the website of the Alliance of Religions and Conservation.

[22] Seyyed Hossein Nasr, *Man and Nature: The Spiritual Crisis in Modern Man*, rev. ed. (Chicago: Kazi Publishers, 1997).

[23] Lynn White Jr., "The Historical Roots of Our Ecologic Crisis," *Science* 155, no. 3767 (March 10, 1967).

Religion united to nature: the Eternal Spring Temple in Taroko National Park, Taiwan

© PATRICK LIN/SHUTTERSTOCK.COM

view the world around us as significant and would view as a tragedy the loss of a viable home for humanity.

1-6e New Religious Movements

Outside a movie premiere in Utah, crowds gather, waiting for the director, producers, and actors to arrive. Although the scene is similar to that of other premieres, the film is not. It is a feature-film adaptation of the main Mormon scripture, the Book of Mormon, and has been officially sanctioned by the Mormon Church, formally known as the Church of Jesus Christ of Latter-day Saints. Along with its general release to theaters and then to video rental outlets, the movie would be used in the missionary activities of the church. From the birth of the Latter-day Saint Church in the 1800s, its use of the Book of Mormon in missionary efforts has been a key factor in making this church probably the fastest-growing religious organization in the world.

New religious movements (NRMs), as we saw above, are a widely accepted area in the field of religious studies. NRMs are religious groups that have arisen since the start of the nineteenth century and now have sufficient size, longevity, and cultural impact to merit academic study. We will deal with NRMs more fully in Chapter 13, but we should consider them initially here.

New religious movements is preferable in some ways to other recent terms such as *alternative religious movements* and *marginal religious movements*. It's also clearly preferable to the older terms *sects* and *cults*. Although these terms still have some validity—especially in sociology, where scholars use them

objectively—they have become so loaded with value judgments that religion scholars no longer use them for new religious movements. To judge by the dimensions of religion discussed above, there is usually little difference between a religion and a sect or a cult. All of them have doctrines and ethics, rituals, social structures, and an aesthetic dimension, and their members typically describe powerful emotional religious experiences. The term *cult* has been used to describe many smaller, nontraditional religious groups. These groups often have new or innovative beliefs that set them apart from the prevailing religious worldviews, especially those of the religions from which they emerge. In recent times, *cult* has become rather derogatory, applied to groups that are deemed to be beyond commonly accepted bounds of social behavior. If they stay alive, sects go on to become recognized groups within the "parent" religion. The Protestant churches can be described as Christian sects that gained mainstream acceptance, as did the Hare Krishna (HAHR-ee KRISH-nah) movement (The International Society for Krishna Consciousness, or ISKCON) in Hinduism. Despite the intensity of its beliefs and actions that can make it look like a "cult" to some in the Western world, the latter is an authentically Hindu group.

Watch Tom Cruise speak on Scientology.

Visit the website of a journal devoted to new religions.

Thousands of groups around the world today are NRMs, for instance, Falun Gong, the Baha'i tradition, the Church of Jesus Christ of Latter-day Saints, the Christian Science Church, the Unification Church, and the Church of Scientology. Each year sees the birth of others. These and other movements called NRMs often don't see themselves as new religious movements at all, but instead as the true continuing body from an older religion now gone bad. Although scholars use the term "*new* religious movements," we must note that NRMs usually branch off from older religions. Falun Gong is an adaptation mostly of Mahayana Buddhism and a lesser amount of Daoism. Baha'i arose in the nineteenth century from Shi'a Islam and sees itself as the successor of Islam. The Church of Jesus Christ of Latter-day Saints, the Christian Science Church, and the Unification Church see themselves as Christian, and experts in comparative religions view this labeling as basically correct. That all three accept the Christian Bible is a good indication of their Christian roots. Moreover, outsiders to Christianity would almost certainly recognize them as belonging to the stream of Christian tradition. However, one shouldn't assume that all organizations that call themselves a church self-identify as Christian. For example, the Church of Scientology uses *church* to mean "religious organization"; so does the Buddhist Churches of America.

Some of these new religious movements are highly controversial. Many were persecuted or prosecuted in their early years by religious and civil authorities, and a few still are today. However, other faiths examined in this book were also controversial when they were new. New religious movements can and do change, sometimes dramatically, and often much more quickly than older religions do. This often occurs when their founder dies, but later change is possible as well. Careful students of religion will want to form judgments about new religious movements that take account of what believers say about themselves in their writings and in life. As always, our learning about a religion should precede any judgment concerning it.

Celebrity Scientology reaches **South Park:** *"I'm a failure in the eyes of the prophet," Tom Cruise said as he ran into Stan's closet. Cruise believed Stan was the reincarnation of Scientology founder L. Ron Hubbard, so Cruise was shocked to hear him say about his acting ability, "You're not, like, as good as Leonardo DiCaprio... but you're OK."*

© COMEDY CENTRAL/COURTESY EVERETT COLLECTION

Read an article about change in the Christian Science Church.

Study Tools 1

Ready to study? In the book you can:

- Review Learning Outcome answers and glossary terms with the tear-out Chapter Review card.

Or you can go online to CourseMate, at www.cengagebrain.com, for these resources:

- Chapter quizzes to prepare for tests
- Interactive flashcards of all glossary terms
- An eBook with introductions, interactive quizzes, and live links for all web resources in the chapter

ONE APPROACH.
70 UNIQUE SOLUTIONS.

CHAPTER 2

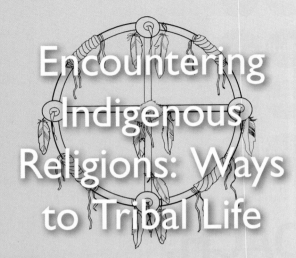

Encountering Indigenous Religions: Ways to Tribal Life

BONNIE VAN VOORST © CENGAGE LEARNING

Learning Outcomes

After studying this chapter, you will be able to do the following:

2-1 State and evaluate the different names for indigenous religions.

2-2 Explain in your own words the challenges to the study of indigenous religions.

2-3 Discuss the common features of indigenous religions.

2-4 State and explain the main features of Lakota religion.

2-5 State and explain the main features of Yoruba religion.

2-6 State and explain the main features of Vodou religion.

Study Tools

After you read this chapter, go to the Study Tools at the end of the chapter, page 61.

DANICA DELIMONT/ALAMY

Indigenous religions are striking in their plurality and their similarities.

Your Visit to the Petroglyph National Monument, New Mexico

O n a visit to Albuquerque, New Mexico, a friend suggests that you visit the Petroglyph National Monument. This area on a windswept rise just outside the city is famous for its rock carvings made by Pueblo Indian tribes. "Get an orientation at the Visitor Center before you begin, because there are several trails to choose from," she says. "And bring a bottle of drinking water."

The first trail, up a hill near the Visitor Center, takes fifteen minutes with continuous walking. Signs warning about rattlesnakes greet you; this gives you pause, but your walk will end without seeing or hearing one. This trail has more than a hundred glyphs (pictures) carved into hard, black rock created by volcanic lava flows. That these rocks are so hard means that carving on them is not a simple process, but it also means that the resulting pictures have lasted for hundreds of years—some for perhaps a thousand. (This of course makes modern vandalism more difficult.) A few pictures look to you like they were carved yesterday, but you know they are very old. Making stops to look at the petroglyphs—impossible not to do—makes this particular trail a half-hour walk.

The carvings are typically of some kind of animal. Birds, snakes, and other wild animals make up most of the pictures, but occasionally there are pictures of humans. All of them seem to you to exude life and energy. But you begin to wonder—why all these carvings (more than 20,000) in this one relatively small area? Native Americans still living near

Make a virtual visit to the Petroglyph National Monument.

What Do YOU Think?

Native American religions still have something significant to offer people of other religions or people of no religion.

Strongly Disagree   Strongly Agree
1   2   3   4   5   6   7

this area say that the petroglyphs are here to speak a message about human life to those whose spirits enable them to listen.

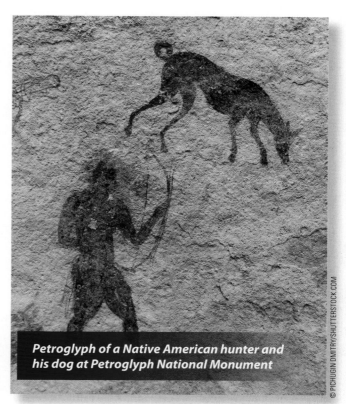

Petroglyph of a Native American hunter and his dog at Petroglyph National Monument

Mariana Aguinda, a shaman of the Cofán Indian tribe in Ecuador, lights a fire during a ritual.

As you begin formal study of indigenous religions, some questions about them will occur to you. Here are some things that students often wonder about:

- Why are there so many different names for this type of religion?
- Why are they so striking in both their similarities and their differences?
- Why are so many of their practices becoming popular among people of other religions?
- Why do they have relatively little emphasis on teaching when compared to other world religions, and focus so much on rituals?
- How much have they changed, and how much have they stayed the same, especially in the past two centuries or so?

Because of the large numbers of religions that are discussed here, this chapter has a special organization that differs from that of all other chapters (except the last, which is similarly organized). First, we will discuss the variety of names scholars have given to this overall type of religion and then explain why this book calls them *indigenous* religions. Second, we'll deal with the typical challenges to the academic study of these religions, especially the kinds of challenges that students face when they begin this study. Third, we'll draw out the common characteristics of these religions. In this section, we'll deal with history, teaching, ritual, and so on. Fourth, we'll take a closer look at just three indigenous religions: that of the Lakota (lah-KOH-tuh) tribes of North America, the religion of the Yoruba (YOHR-uh-buh) tribe of Africa, and the Vodou (VOH-doo, more widely known as *Voodoo*) of African-Caribbean peoples.

Learning Outcome 2-1

State and evaluate the different names for indigenous religions.

2-1 Names for This Type of Religion

Naming the overall type of religions with which we are dealing can be a challenge. But why is it necessary to name this group of religions at all, if such a comprehensive name may well distort or obscure their beliefs?

The answer is that religious studies itself has seen this as important despite its downside, so we must grapple with the issue here. This section will deal with generic names, suggesting what is strong and weak about each one, and then we'll discuss the term settled on in this book: *indigenous religions*.

2-1a Traditional Religion

Traditional religion correctly implies that religions were present in various societies around the world before European and American expansion. They are *traditional* in comparison to newer, imported religions. However, as we saw in Chapter 1, all religions are traditions, because they are comprehensive ways of life that come from the past and are passed on into the future. It has become common in scholarship to refer to Hinduism, Islam, and the rest as *traditions* as well as *religions*. Labeling only one type as *traditional* is misleading and potentially confusing.

> *Indigenous religions are often just as complex and comprehensive as other world religions.*

2-1b Primitive Religion

Primitive religion or **primal religion** were more popular in the past, especially among cultural anthropologists, who used them in a neutral, nonjudgmental way. These terms mostly describe religions that are not derived from other religions, and this is a helpful distinction. However, it's more difficult to use these terms in a neutral way in religious studies. They can imply that religions so described are undeveloped, unchanging, outmoded, or simple. Research into these religions has confirmed just the opposite: They are often just as complex and comprehensive as other world religions. Today, religion scholars generally avoid *primitive* but occasionally use *primal*.

 Read a short anthropological explanation of *primitive religion*.

2-1c Animism and Totemism

Animism and *totemism* are popular as labels for religions in some circles today. **Animism** (from the Latin *anima*, "soul, spirit") is the belief that individual spirits exist not only in people, but also in all individual things in nature, whether they appear to be alive or not: individual animals; plants, rocks, thunder, and lightning; and mountains, lakes, and rivers. In many religions, the spirits of deceased humans keep a close relationship with the living, so that they are part of myth and ritual. The appearance of the sacred in dreams and visions is a key element of animism. Edward B. Tylor, a founder of the field of anthropology, argued in 1891 that all religion began in animism. **Totemism** is a religion based on the idea that the spirit of one primary source in nature—the land itself, a particular species of animal, or the ancestors—provides the basis of life in one's tribe. (See "A Closer Look: Totemism in the *Twilight* Series.") Totemism is found in the Native American tribes of the Northwest coast (with their famous totem poles) and in the beliefs of the Aborigines of Australia. It fits these totemic religions well as a comprehensive name, but it doesn't fit other religions you are studying in this chapter.

2-1d Manaism

Some cultural anthropologists held that the first stage of all religion was **manaism**, a belief in an impersonal spiritual power and energy that permeates the world as a whole. Many religions, they argued, are still based on mana. Manaism is preanimistic, because it does not connect power to spirits in individual natural things (animism) or species/groups of things (totemism). It is drawn from the Polynesian term *mana*, "spiritual power." Some see the Yoruban idea of a general spiritual power that infuses the universe as an example of mana. At the beginning of the twentieth century, those who advocated manaism and those who advocated animism disagreed sharply with each other. Today this argument is largely a thing of the past.

animism Belief that individual spirits exist not only in people, but also in all individual things in nature

totemism [TOHT-em-iz-uhm] Religion based on the idea that the spirit of one primary source in nature provides the basis of human life in one's tribe

manaism [MAH-nah-iz-uhm] Belief in an impersonal spiritual power and energy that permeates the world as a whole

shamanism Religion based on the existence of shamans

2-1e Shamanism

A shaman is a tribal member with special abilities and the authority to act as an intermediary between the people and the world of gods and spirits (both good and evil). He, or rarely she, is known by different names in different tribes; the most common are *holy man*, *medicine man*, and *healer*. Shamans are so common in this type of religion that some scholars have called their beliefs **shamanism**. But this is controversial today, especially among cultural anthropologists. For example,

Watch a BBC video on shamanic trance among Kalahari Bushmen.

Totem poles

Close-up of a totem pole with an eagle face

A Closer Look:

Totemism in the *Twilight* Series

AP PHOTO/CHRISTOPHE ENA

Kristen Stewart, Taylor Lautner, and Robert Pattinson star in **The Twilight Saga.**

The leader of the Quileute (KWILL-yoot) Nation of Native Americans in northwest Washington first heard about the *Twilight Saga* novels from their readers, who wanted to know more about the place where the blockbuster vampires-and-werewolves tale of teenage love is set. When the novels were made into films, interest in Quileutes exploded. "Their interest in our tribe was a good surprise," tribal president Anna Rose Counsell-Geyer said to the press. "People are going to actually get to know the Quileute and we are going to be recognized as a people."

The Quileute's reservation on the Olympic Peninsula serves as the scenic backdrop to author Stephenie Meyer's fantasy novels, a place of thick woods, with rocks and cliffs rising along the Pacific Ocean. The reservation spans only one square mile. The wolf theme of *Twilight* draws on the Quileutes' own creation story, which features the transformation of an ancient wolf pack into people who became the Quileute tribe. Since that transformation, the wolf has been the tribe's totem.

In *Twilight*, the Quileute creation story is used to explain the Wolf Pack, a group of young Quileute men joined by Jacob Black (played in the film by Taylor Lautner), who shape-shift into large, powerful wolves to guard the reservation from marauding vampires. The present-day *Twilight Saga* marks a departure from Hollywood's long tradition of portraying the past, not the present, of Native Americans. It also departs from Quileute religion, which does not feature tribal members who can shape-shift into wolves. This particular element is not a part of totemism, but instead draws on European werewolf legends.

---

small-scale religion
Religions held by relatively small societies

Alice Kehoe, in her 2000 book *Shamans and Religion*, argues sharply that shamans are unique to each culture where they are found and cannot be generalized into a global type of religion called "shamanism."[1] Many indigenous peoples around the world, particularly in the Native American tribes, also reject this term as misleading when applied to themselves.

2-1f Small-Scale Religions

The term **small-scale religion**, from cultural anthropology, accurately implies that some of the religions to which it refers are held by relatively small societies. However, other so-called small-scale religions are actually practiced by more people than are some world religions such as Judaism, Sikhism, Jainism, and Shinto. Other than the relative size of *some* of them—and there were indigenous empires in the Americas and in Africa with

© ISTOCKPHOTO.COM/CLIFF PARNELL

A Zulu shaman in South Africa leans over a mat on which he has just thrown small bones; by reading their layout, he receives messages from dead ancestors.

---

[1] Alice Kehoe, *Shamans and Religion: An Exploration in Critical Thinking* (Long Grove, IL: Waveland Press, 2000).

empire-wide religions, we must remember—there is nothing small about these religions.

> Catherine Albanese argues that "nature religion" applies to different sorts of American beliefs, from those of precolonial times to the contemporary "New Age" movement.

2-1g Nature Religion

Some people informally use the term **nature religions**. This correctly suggests that indigenous religions can have a stronger connection to the natural environment than do other world religions. But there is much more to the religions in this chapter than a connection to the natural environment. Moreover, "nature" itself is a Western concept that many other societies, especially the societies we discuss here, do not share. These people groups usually have no strong distinction between the natural and supernatural that *nature religions* may imply to Westerners. Nor do they see human beings as so superior to the rest of the world that they almost stand above and apart from nature. A book by noted religion scholar Catherine Albanese, *Nature Religion in America*, argues that *nature religion* applies to a whole range of American beliefs, from precolonial Native American religions to the contemporary "New Age" movement.[2]

Read the first page of Catherine Albanese's *Nature Religion in America*.

2-1h Indigenous Religions

In this book, we'll use the term **indigenous religions**. *Indigenous* means "native, intrinsic to an area," especially in the sense of peoples who originate and belong to a specific area. (Students should avoid a common confusion with *indigent*, which means "poor.") As we'll see shortly, *indigenous* entails a strong sense of belonging religiously to a certain place, in a way that *native* alone might not. In current usage, *indigenous* implies religions and cultures that were present in a given place

for centuries, and usually millennia, before the arrival of other cultures with different religions. When used in this way, for example, it says more than the ambiguous term *Native American*. Strictly speaking, everyone born in North America is a "native American," but the vast majority of people born in North America don't belong to continuing indigenous groups of "Native Americans." *Indigenous* today often implies a lack of political power in the wider society, in a context where other groups of people have taken over the lands of indigenous peoples.

> **nature religion**
> Informal term for indigenous religions suggesting that they have a stronger connection to the natural environment than do other religions
>
> **indigenous religion**
> Term for religion of a people, usually a tribe, original to an area

When considering the names for individual indigenous groups, we should ask, What names do the individual groups use, and what names are given to them by others? The European colonizers of Africa and the Americas played a large role in giving them names that Westerners now know them by, so we will begin here. In general, European names for indigenous peoples and their religions have been inaccurate. Europeans did not often listen carefully to what other cultures called themselves, but instead adapted to European languages the sounds of indigenous peoples' names. This reflects a colonialist mentality. In later chapters, we will see that Westerners also had a key role in the rise of names such as "Hinduism" and "Confucianism." In recent times, there has been a movement to restore the original sound and spelling of Native American names: *Odawa* for "Ottawa" and *Algonkian* for "Algonquin," for example.

> Calling the earliest American peoples "Indians" was one of the biggest geography bloopers of all time.

The common European name for indigenous peoples is the historic Western term for peoples who inhabited the Western Hemisphere: *Indians*. In 1492, Christopher Columbus supposed that he had reached the islands off China called at the time the "Indies." However, he unknowingly had discovered a new continent between Europe and Asia, a continent that would become known as the *New World*. The name "Indians"

---

[2] Catherine L. Albanese, *Nature Religion in America: From the Algonkian Indians to the New Age* (Chicago: University of Chicago Press, 1991).

persisted even when it became obvious that it was wrong, and it was soon used by the English and French as well. To call the indigenous peoples of the Americas "Indians" was one of the biggest geography bloopers of all time, but it has endured for centuries. However, ideas about names do change, and sometimes in unpredictable ways. Today, many native peoples in the United States happily call themselves "Indians," not "Native Americans." The latest Census Bureau survey of terminology, done in 1995, showed that 49 percent of native peoples preferred being called "American Indian," 37 percent preferred "Native American," and only about 9 percent either preferred another term or had no preference. *Indians* grew in approval among Native Americans at the same time as it became incorrect in wider North American culture. For example, in his highly praised memoir *The Names*, Kiowa writer N. Scott Momaday speaks about how his mother embraced this name: "[S]he began to see herself as an 'Indian'. That dim native heritage became a fascination and a cause for her."[3] *American Indian* is still the main term used in the U.S. Census, although it is controversial there. Many scholars use it alongside *Native American*, and we will use it occasionally here as well. The safest policy is to use the names indigenous peoples themselves prefer.

In general, indigenous peoples of North America prefer their local group name as rendered in their language, not an English-language label or a traditional name recognized by whites. Sioux Nation Indians prefer to be known by the main name of "Lakota," "Dakota," or "Nakota" (each designating groupings within the same culture). They use "Sioux" as a name for themselves when speaking to outsiders, but inside their group they use "Lakota" or its variants. In the 2000 U.S. Census, fully 75 percent of people who identified their ethnic group as "Indian" also identified their main tribal or national group. Sometimes political differences within a tribe or nation lead to competing preferences for different names in the same group—for example, "Navajos" or *Diné* ("Earth People"). In Canada, the broad designation **First Nations** (note the plural) is widely accepted as a general term by native

groups and wider Canadian society, but the individual tribes still use their own names. In Australia and New Zealand, **Aboriginals** (people there "from the origin") is commonly accepted as an ethnic label, but this term is falling out of favor, and the specific names of the "Aboriginal" groups are preferred.

Learning Outcome 2-2

Explain in your own words the challenges to the study of indigenous religions.

2-2 Challenges to Study

In Chapter 1, we dealt with some challenges to the study of religion in general. When we encounter indigenous religions, some special challenges emerge that don't apply to most other religions we will deal with in this book. We can list and explain them briefly.

2-2a Lack of Written Sources

Because the cultures in which these religions are based are predominantly oral, their religions—with only a few exceptions—have not written down their stories, beliefs, or rituals. Where these features of religious life do exist in writing today, they have typically been recorded by anthropologists. Nor do we have as much archaeological evidence for indigenous peoples as we do for other world religions. Some tribes, along with their particular religions, disappeared long before the coming of Europeans—the victims of disease, famine, and intertribal warfare—and we know little about them. In the first chapter of this book, we noted the importance of history as a method of studying religion, but the use of history to study the first Americans is limited. This restricts the depth of study.

2-2b Difficulty Discerning Continuity and Discontinuity

By the time Western scholars began to study native groups in the Americas, Africa, and Australia, it was hundreds of years after the natives' first contact with European Americans. Sometimes this contact led to significant changes in indigenous belief and practices, and at other times it didn't. As a result, scholars of indigenous religions aren't certain about how far back

---

[3] N. Scott Momaday, *The Names* (Tucson: University of Arizona Press, 1976), p. 25.

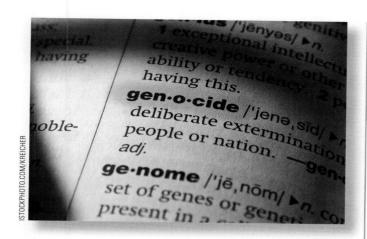

many beliefs and practices go: Are they precontact or postcontact? For example, some have argued that in Yoruba religion in west Africa, the high god developed as a reaction to Christian and Muslim missionaries who proclaimed a religion of one God. Other scholars dispute this, arguing that indigenous religions often have belief in one high deity without any Western religious influence.

2-2c Mainstream Guilt

Indigenous peoples have often been treated brutally during the whole sweep of human history and even prehistory, whenever one group came into the territory of another group and tried to take over. Treatment that was intended to reduce their numbers and their cultures is nothing short of **genocide**, the killing of an entire racial/ethnic/religious group of people. Today we think that this should have caused second thoughts among people of European origins who took over the lands of indigenous peoples, but in the ethos of the times it usually didn't. Many of their descendants today are ashamed of the actions of their ancestors and the continued bitter legacy of prejudice and discrimination. This is probably as it should be, but sometimes guilt, powerful emotion that it is, gets in the way of understanding; it can distort the careful study of indigenous cultures and their religions. People should regret the wrongs of the past, but a careful understanding of the past is a key part of knowing what to do in the present.

2-2d Misrepresentations in Popular Culture

Popular culture—and especially Hollywood film, which is so influential in shaping attitudes today—has distorted indigenous religions. On the one hand,

films such as *Dances with Wolves* and *Avatar* have portrayed indigenous tribes as habitually moral, master ecologists, or even **noble savages**. This last idea was an influential theme in the work of Jean-Jacques Rousseau (1712–1778), who held that indigenous peoples are naturally good but that so-called civilization corrupts them. Such an idealized view of indigenous peoples is based on superficial knowledge; if they were in fact so noble, they would not need practices to deal with misdeeds, social disorder, and outright crimes.

On the other hand, Hollywood has depicted some religions as dangerously exotic in order to amuse or frighten audiences, as in *Apocalypto* or the hundreds of films made about the white settlement of the American West. Negative portrayals have seeped down to the life of North American children, among whom playing games of "cowboys and Indians" has been popular for generations—if historically incorrect, because cowboys rarely fought Indians. Africa has frequently been depicted in film as a place of more savagery than nobility, with religions that are little more than superstitions. Popular culture's portrayal of Afro-Caribbean religions, Vodou in particular, is probably the worst of all. The 1973 James Bond film *Live and Let Die*, and the more frightening *Angel Heart*, portrayed Vodou as violent and dangerous. The popular *Night of the Living Dead*, originally from 1968 and remade in 1990, removed zombie lore from its Vodou context. Zombies have become increasingly popular ever since, as illustrated by the hit television show *The Walking Dead*. These misrepresentations of indigenous religions have affected how we understand them, and make it harder to study them today.

2-2e Misuse of Indigenous Rituals

In today's religious climate in North America and Europe, some people freely combine elements of indigenous religions with their own religions or other beliefs. It has become popular in some circles, for example, to use sacred objects of North American indigenous religions such as the stone pipe, medicine bundles, peyote, and sweat lodges in new religious ceremonies in non–Native American religions. This removes indigenous rituals from their deeply embedded cultural context and gives them a meaning that

genocide Killing of an entire racial/ethnic/religious group

noble savages Jean-Jacques Rousseau's term for indigenous peoples, who, he held, are naturally good

indigenous peoples wouldn't recognize. Some indigenous groups are offended by this and view it as detrimental to their long-term spiritual and cultural health. For instance, some Lakota leaders opposed this misuse in a controversial 1993 resolution, "Declaration of War against Exploiters of Lakota Spirituality." In 2012, Navajo authorities sued the Urban Outfitters clothing company for its use of the Navajo trademark and name in a new line of clothing.

Read the "Declaration of War against Exploiters of Lakota Spirituality."

As you conclude this section, you might be wondering, With all these problems in the study of indigenous religions, can they possibly be studied well? The answer is that they can indeed be studied well, and are. However, the first step in doing so is to recognize and deal with the obstacles to study that are in your way. Now that these are in plain view, we can turn to a discussion of these religions, beginning with their most important common features.

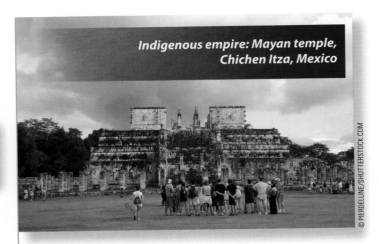
Indigenous empire: Mayan temple, Chichen Itza, Mexico

© PIERDELUNE/SHUTTERSTOCK.COM

Learning Outcome 2-3

Discuss the common features of indigenous religions.

2-3 Common Features of Indigenous Religions

Despite the terms Native American religion, African religion, *and* Aboriginal religion, *on the whole, no such things ever existed.*

In this section, we will discuss the common key characteristics of indigenous religions. (See also "A Closer Look: Movements toward Indigenous Unity," page 40.) But we must realize up front that there are many significant differences among them. They are as diverse as the cultures and times from which they come. Africa has over three thousand ethnic and language groups, with social organizations from small tribes to large empires. Africa today has more than forty nations (see

Map 2.1). In the Americas there have been more than two thousand tribes, some of them organized in large nations or even empires such as those of the Aztecs and Mayans. Each of the world religions that we'll consider in later chapters has some shared idea of sacred history—of the tradition's founders, sacred texts, rituals, and the like—that gives it unity. For indigenous religions around the world, diversity is the rule. Despite the terms *Native American religion*, *African religion*, and *Aboriginal religion*, no such specific things ever existed, and neither did *indigenous religion*. No single system of belief or ritual unites all African, American, or Aboriginal religions. We present here the basics of indigenous religions, but this doesn't imply that all indigenous religions are the same. Nor does it imply that indigenous peoples have ever thought of their religions as the same.

2-3a The Importance of Place

Anthropologists typically hold that the human race (*Homo sapiens*) gradually spread from one area of Africa across much of the globe beginning about 100,000 years ago (see Map 2.2). Many groups of humans have been on the move ever since, carrying their indigenous religions with them. This common origin and subsequent travel helps to explain how modern humans are similar genetically but have had some further genetic and cultural adaptations to their new environments. Despite all this movement, indigenous peoples are deeply rooted in a place. Moreover, they usually see themselves as created in or from that place, despite what modern anthropologists think about all humans originating in Africa. For them, *place* is much more than simply a location or even a type of geography such as forest, desert, plains, and so on. Instead, it is a matter of tribal and personal

Map 2.1

Contemporary Africa

Africa contains more than forty nations. Six sub-Saharan African nations and Algeria in North Africa experienced anti-colonial revolutions, and a dozen sub-Saharan nations have been racked by civil wars since independence. In 2011, Libya, Tunisia, and Egypt experienced popular revolts against oppressive regimes in a movement known as the "Arab Spring."

Legend on map:

⊛ Anticolonial revolution
✸ Civil war

© CENGAGE LEARNING 2013

identity. Place has great practical and symbolic significance for indigenous peoples and their religious beliefs and practices. What Vine Deloria Jr. says about Native American religion is true of all other indigenous religions: "The sacredness of lands on which previous generations have lived and died is the foundation of all other sentiments."[4]

---

[4] Vine Deloria Jr., *God Is Red: A Native View of Religion* (New York: Putnam, 1973), 278.

A Closer Look:

Movements toward Indigenous Unity

Native American drumming circle at an intertribal powwow

ISTOCKPHOTO.COM/WILLIAM PERRY

Smithsonian National Museum of the American Indian in Washington, D.C.

ISTOCKPHOTO.COM/MICHELLE LYLES

A recent development brings a surprising "twist" to diversity within indigenous religions. Indigenous peoples around the world are realizing that they are in a common situation with regard to their dominant cultures and are beginning to act on this in ways that draw the people and the culture together.

For example, a **Pan-Indian movement** began in the early 1900s and is now prominent in North America. This movement is based on indigenous American peoples' realization that they share many social and religious concerns today. One example of this is the American Indian Movement (AIM) organization. Cross-tribal memberships, powwow (intertribal gatherings, especially of leaders) networks among tribes, and national lobbying groups are found in contemporary Pan-Indianism. Increasingly, rituals

have been shared among the tribes. Their life has become more Pan-Indian, with wider use of ritual pipe smoking, sweat lodges, vision quests, sun dancing, and the use of peyote. Pan-Indianism is also found in universities, prisons, military forces, and urban settings where general Native American identity is more important than one's specific tribal identity. The Pan-Indian movement tries to respect local tribal identities and traditions, but some tribes object to the sharing of rituals.

Explore the AIM website.

Stories about the land deal with myths of tribal origins, rituals, and patterns of everyday life. Because indigenous religions are typically rich in traditions that deal with their particular places, they often speak of being created not just from Mother Earth, but from the earth "here in this valley." They communicate with spirits not just all around them, but "in a mountain cave over there" or reverence in particular a sacred animal "in that rain forest." Sacred place has a personal status in indigenous religions. For example, at their annual intertribal gatherings in the Sweet Grass Hills of Montana, the Chippewa-Cree people pray that owners of the mines in their sacred hills will see that "these hills are just as alive as anybody, and they want to live too." People and their places are

meant to live together in a harmonious balance. Many indigenous tribes displaced from their traditional lands in the Americas, Africa, and Australia have sought to reclaim them in some religiously meaningful way, even if they cannot live on their sacred ground. Other religions we will encounter in this book all have holy places, but they are typically not connected to specific places in the ways that indigenous religions are.

2-3b Global Distribution

Indigenous religions are found around the globe today, not just in North America and Africa. In Africa, indigenous religions are spread throughout the continent south of the Sahara Desert. In general, more-traditional forms of indigenous religions are found in central Africa; in the northern and southern thirds of Africa, indigenous religions have largely been blended into

Pan-Indian movement Movement begun in the early 1900s to bring more unity to North American tribes

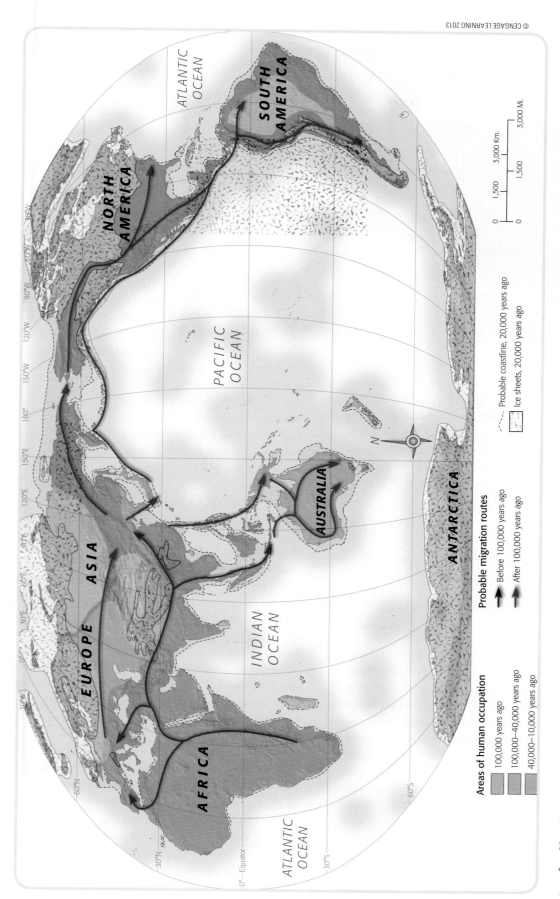

© CENGAGE LEARNING 2013

Map 2.2
Spread of Humans around the Globe

Areas of human occupation

100,000 years ago

100,000–40,000 years ago

40,000–10,000 years ago

Probable migration routes

Before 100,000 years ago

After 100,000 years ago

Probable coastline, 20,000 years ago

Ice sheets, 20,000 years ago

0   1,500   3,000 Km.

0   1,500   3,000 Mi.

View of the Black Hills, South Dakota, the holiest place for the Lakota tribe of Native Americans

© JIM PARKIN/SHUTTERSTOCK.COM

Islam and Christianity, respectively. In the Americas, indigenous religions are also widespread: Native peoples, with their distinctive religions, inhabit the hemisphere from the Arctic to the southern tip of Chile. Many indigenous peoples in the Americas today combine their indigenous religions with Christianity, in Central and South America particularly with Roman Catholic Christianity.

> *Indigenous religions are found around the world today, not just in North America and Africa.*

In Asia, the picture is complex. Indigenous religion persists almost undisturbed in some remote islands in south Asia, especially in Indonesia and Borneo. Polynesian and Micronesian cultures and religions have spread widely, so that today they are found from Hawaii to Taiwan and south. (In fact, native Hawaiian religion has begun to assert its continuing vitality, as we will see later in "A Closer Look: Polynesian Religion in Hawaii.") In Tibet, the ancient indigenous Bön religion persists inside, and occasionally outside, Tibetan Buddhism, despite persecution in the past by the Buddhist government of Tibet. Folk religions emphasizing local spirits and gods have been common for millennia in China; sometimes these divine beings have become Daoist divinities. Japan's indigenous religion of Shinto has played such a large role in modern world history that it is often treated separately, as this book will do in Chapter 8. The birth of Islam marked the end of pre-Islamic Arab indigenous religion, but other indigenous religions have been incorporated to a degree in some areas where Islam has spread. In Australia and New Zealand, original forms of Aboriginal religions exist alongside Christianity, although the great majority of Aboriginal people self-identify as Christians today. In Europe, Christianity gradually overwhelmed indigenous religions, but did so in part by absorbing some indigenous practices such as rituals to counteract evil elves and the tradition of bringing evergreens into homes at Christmas.

Watch a *New York Times* analysis of *Walkabout*, the critically praised film on Aboriginal life.

Visit a website introducing the variety of African indigenous religions.

Watch a National Geographic video on indigenous religion and other religions in Bali.

2-3c Many Gods and Spirits

A distinctive feature of indigenous religions, especially when compared to some other world religions, is that they aren't typically focused on one deity. Some African indigenous religions claim to tend toward monotheism, usually because they have one high god, but most believe in a number of gods. High deities seldom figure into everyday religious life. Instead, they are remote gods, as we'll see in our treatment of Lakota and Yoruba religion. Moreover, as we saw above, when high deities are regularly invoked, some scholars suspect influence from other world religions. For example, many Native American tribes believe in a high god such as the Great Spirit but don't talk about him on a regular basis or have rituals addressed to him. Where there is more frequent talk of the Great Spirit, and where this Spirit is seen as a single, personal Being, it may well be due to Native American accommodation to Christianity.

Deities or spirits are not worshiped in a detached way; they are ritually invoked and engaged as inhabitants and agents of the world itself. Some indigenous religions remember individuals from their past who were influential leaders, but none is seen as a founder of the religion. This emphasizes that native religions are less about human figures, or even gods and rituals, than they are about relationships. Relationships are shaped by prominent humans and deities and guided by morals, myth, and rituals, but they are ultimately about the people's connection to one another and the group's connection to the world around it.

2-3d Influenced by Other Cultures

Many world religions have had to deal with competition and conflict with other religions, but almost all indigenous religions have had to deal with being surrounded and suppressed by alien nation-states with alien religions. In Africa, for example, centuries of colonial rule by Europeans, and the Christian missionary efforts that went with it, changed some elements of many African indigenous religions. New gods came forth, and new rituals for worshiping them. Contemporary scholarship acknowledges that culture-contact changes are central to understanding indigenous cultures and their religions today. It studies their continuities and changes, and not simply their complete destruction. Indigenous religions *as they exist today* are worthy of study and appreciation. We should not use our knowledge of postcontact indigenous religions merely in order to strip away perceived influences by other religions and thereby to arrive at hypothetical precontact religions. Scholars have little data about the past of indigenous religions that are free from nonnative influence, so trying to get back to precontact religion is problematic. Indigenous religions themselves often erase any evidence that suggests that some of their beliefs and practices are products of a particular place and time.

2-3e Based on Orality, Story, and Myth

Indigenous religious traditions are oral, not written, because the cultures in which they are based are oral cultures. Orality can open up more room for adaptive change in religion because of not being bound in a book. Orality entails skilled, compelling storytelling. As all skilled storytellers know, audiences must be "brought into the story." In indigenous religions, this is done not just as entertainment. In the religion's stories, each person's life enters a larger group story, even a cosmic story that reaches backward and forward in time. Myths and their accompanying rituals have a critical

Aboriginal rock art, Kakadu National Park, Australia

role in maintaining good relationships between all sacred beings in the universe—human, divine, animal, and even plant.

Scholars have classified different myths according to their form and function. **Cosmogonic myths** about creation help to explain the origin of existence. They tell how the whole world was created, and especially how the particular tribe telling a myth was created. An **etiological myth** is one that explains how things have come to be as they are now, as large as why the sun travels in the sky or as small as why the beaver has no hair on its tail. The **semihistorical myth** is the elaboration of an original happening, usually involving a tribal hero such as the nineteenth-century Lakota leader Sitting Bull. Telling these myths and stories is a means of communication

cosmogonic myth
Story about creation that helps to explain the origin of existence

etiological myth Story that explains how things have come to be as they are now

semi-historical myth Elaboration of an original happening, usually involving a tribal hero

between humans and other beings. The religious specialist of the indigenous society is often the keeper of these stories and can perform them with power. Animals, ancestors, spirits, and gods all compose stories, and people understand the beings through the stories. Narrative is the mode that brings these indigenous traditions to life, through songs, chants, prayers, ritual dances, folktales, and genealogies. Oral tradition has not been erased by modernity and literacy, though it has taken new forms as storytellers have found modern means (including YouTube) for its expression.

Watch an explanation of African storytelling.

2-3f Oriented More to Practice Than to Belief

Indigenous traditions are not belief based, and they have few formal "teachings" on which one can do religious or theological reflection. Belief in gods and spirits is traditional and assumed, a part of the fabric of life, and children are rigorously socialized to know the moral codes of their society. These beliefs are "more caught than taught," and they are reinforced in initiation rituals as children become adults. The emphasis is on practices. Indigenous religions around the world are dedicated to maintaining personal, group, and cosmic balance through ritual actions. The purpose of this balance is that the group may thrive. The scope of rituals in indigenous religions is vast. Some mark life-cycle changes at birth, the beginning of adulthood, marriage, and death. Others are designed to bless people at trying times, heal them of diseases of the mind or body, attract rain, or produce a good hunt or good crops. Still others are for purposes of putting curses on people (sometimes called *witching*) and counteracting curses (*unwitching*). The purpose of most indigenous ritual is to control the power of the world—to attract good power when needed and to turn away dangerous power.

 Watch "Apache Girl's Rite of Passage."

2-3g In-Group Based

Indigenous traditions around the world are commonly in-group based. Few indigenous religions seek converts or even allow full entry by people not of their group. As we saw above, they often don't appreciate how others have recently adopted some of their beliefs and rituals or have come as "seekers" to explore their ways of life. This attitude can come as a surprise, even a shock, to well-intentioned outsiders who are on spiritual journeys that they believe lead to indigenous religions. (American popular culture sometimes portrays indigenous societies as open to be joined by outsiders, as for example in the film *Dances with Wolves*.) Unlike religions that seek converts, however, indigenous religions are ethnicity based. Either one is culturally a part of the group, or one is not. If a person is inside the group, then the religion of the group pertains to that person, for his or her place in the community and the world depends upon it.

In indigenous societies, extensive life-cycle rituals are employed to bring children to fully initiated membership in the group. Apart from this initiation, the group is closed to outsiders, and much of its religious knowledge is secret, sometimes even to members of the tribe. For instance, the Dogon (DOH-guhn) people of Mali, West Africa, have many rituals that are done in masks, but the meaning of the masks is known only to those initiated into a society of specialists. (For an example of a west African ritual mask, see Figure 2.1.) Tribal members may regard others outside the tribe as sincere, but they will not typically make them members of the community and give them access to religious secrets. The long oppression of indigenous peoples by others has made them even more wary of outsiders' actions and intentions.

> *Indigenous religion maintains the balance of life so that the group as a whole can thrive.*

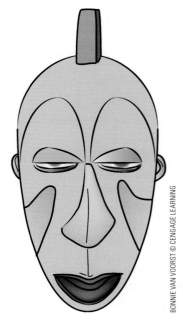

BONNIE VAN VOORST © CENGAGE LEARNING

Figure 2.1 West African ritual mask

2-3h The Goodness of the World

Indigenous peoples believe that each and every part of nature has a spiritual aspect that makes it live and gives direction to its life. All things in the world are related to humans in a cosmic natural balance. American and African indigenous cultures often see this balance as a circle. The Sioux lived in this balance by setting up their camps in circles, by gathering in circles for councils and rituals, and by erecting circular tepees. Therefore, these traditions do not deal with a concept such as "salvation," "enlightenment," or even "eternal life." Means of transcending or transforming this world aren't important here, because the world does not need escaping. Its natural harmony needs only to be preserved and lived in. Likewise, these traditions aren't typically future oriented—for example in believing that this world is heading toward some large goal. Rather, indigenous peoples value the past because it contains the model for identity and behavior in the present and the future. This desire to make the idealized past ever present makes these religions deeply "traditional." The point of indigenous religion is to maintain the balance of life so that the group as a whole can thrive in the world.

Read about the religious meaning of the painted tepee.

Painted tepee of Plains Indians

© MARFOT/SHUTTERSTOCK.COM

2-3i The Role of Religious Specialists

Indigenous societies have religious specialists of some sort—people selected or trained to do a variety of religious tasks at a higher level than do others. They are known by a variety of names: "holy men," "medicine men," "healers," "priests/priestesses," and others. **Tricksters** are gods, spirits, humans, or wily animals (often a coyote in North American lore) that play tricks on people or otherwise act contrary to conventional norms of behavior, often for the good of others. "Prophets" (a name, but not a phenomenon, drawn from contact with Christianity) arise from time to time to lead their tribes out of crisis. The most notable religious specialist is the shaman, an intermediary linking the human and spirit worlds. Many types of shamans exist throughout the world, although the main model for shamans comes from Siberian tribes.

They are the "spiritual leaders" of their tribes. Mircea Eliade identified their main features as follows:

trickster God, spirit, human, or wily animal that plays tricks on people or otherwise behaves against conventional norms of behavior, often for the good of others

- The shaman communicates with the spirit world, where good and evil spirits are found.
- The shaman can treat sickness or deal with other problems provoked by evil spirits.
- The shaman can leave his body and go to the spirit realm that surrounds this world, or his body can be possessed by the gods or spirits.
- The shaman evokes animal spirits as message bearers to other spirits.
- The shaman can tell the future by various forms of divination.[5]

Watch the story of "The Shaman and the Frost."

Watch "Dogon Dama," on the Dogon (African) ritual and shaman.

2-3j Continuing Vitality

In the past, politicians, missionaries, and even scholars predicted the imminent death of indigenous religions. If we consider the dire straits of many of these religions a century ago, we can understand why some observers have thought that native traditions were dying out. However, more than a few indigenous religions can now say, with the American humorist Mark Twain, when told that his death had been announced in a newspaper, "The reports of my death are greatly exaggerated." Not only have a number of native cultures

---

[5] Mircea Eliade, *Shamanism: Archaic Techniques of Ecstasy* (New York: Random House, 1964).

Shaman emerging from forest in a trance after an initiation ritual, 1914

also include the return of human remains and traditional cultural objects now in museums and in private collections. Various African-Caribbean religions that combine Christianity and native African religions are regaining their voice: Santería in Cuba, Candomblé in Brazil, Rastafarianism in Jamaica, and Vodou in Haiti. In Africa, a number of indigenous religions are more prominent today than in the past two hundred years, but many continue to be hard pressed by Christianity and Islam. Native African churches that combine Christianity with key aspects of indigenous religions are thriving, so parts of indigenous African religions survive within Christianity. The increased freedom of religion in China has led to the widespread rebirth and flourishing of suppressed folk religions that seem to have gone underground for more than fifty years. Indigenous religious traditions have persisted because they are, in a word—as Chippewa poet Gerald Vizenor has often said about his fellow indigenous Americans—"survivors."

Learning Outcome 2-4

State and explain the main features of Lakota religion.

2-4 A Native American Religion: Lakota

More than a hundred different Native American tribes are found in North America today. (See Map 2.3 for an overview of major Native American tribes in 1492.) The one offered here for study, the Lakota group, which figures large in the past and today, is meant to provide a more extensive look into the religious life of that tribe and also as a more definite description of what indigenous religion is.

> Explore Native American culture on Google Earth™.

survived against great pressures over the past five centuries, but some are now thriving in ways that would have been unthinkable until recently. Native peoples' numbers and cultural influence have risen dramatically in recent generations in many, but not all, parts of the world. Improved standards of living have helped, but more important is that being "indigenous" is shifting in many places from being a social liability in wider society to being a point of pride.

> Reports of the death of indigenous religions are, to adapt a quip by Mark Twain, greatly exaggerated.

We can point to ways in which indigenous religions have flourished over the past half-century. In North America, many native ceremonies that were banned in earlier times are now protected by law. Native peoples have fought hard for these protections and continue to do so, and the wider society has seen the wisdom in preserving them. These include the protection of peyote consumption, the use of eagle feathers in rituals, burial in traditional places, and rights to fish and hunt. They

2-4a Name and Location

The word *Sioux* (soo) applies today to seven tribal groups organized into three main political units. It dates back to the 1600s C.E., when the people were living in the western Great Lakes area (see Map 2.4). The Ojibwa (oh-JIHB-way) tribes called the neighboring Lakota *Nadouwesou*, meaning "poisonous snakes." This term, shortened by French traders to its last syllable, became *Sioux*. They

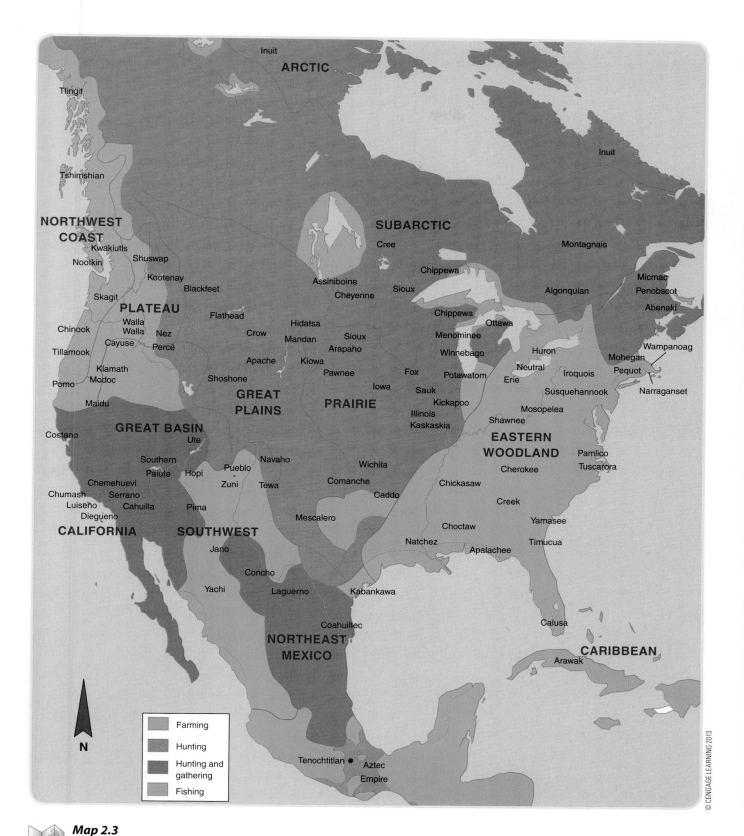

Map 2.3

North American Tribes in 1492

Native American tribes on the eve of European settlement were rich in regional variety. Regional geography (woodland, prairie, coastal) influenced their ways of life and religion.

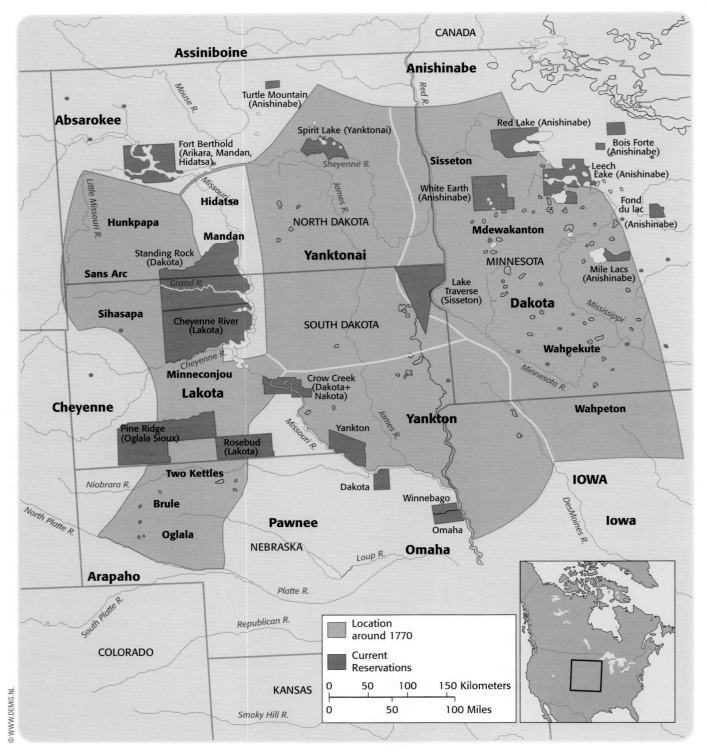

CANADA

Assiniboine

Anishinabe

Absarokee

Turtle Mountain
(Anishinabe)

Spirit Lake (Yanktonai)

Mouse R.

Fort Berthold
(Arikara, Mandan,
Hidatsa)

Red Lake (Anishinabe)

Bois Forte
(Anishinabe)

Leech
Lake (Anishinabe)

Sheyenne R.

Sisseton

White Earth
(Anishinabe)

Fond
du lac
(Anishinabe)

Little Missouri R.

Hidatsa

NORTH DAKOTA

Missouri R.

James R.

Hunkpapa

Mdewakanton

Mandan

Yanktonai

MINNESOTA

Mile Lacs
(Anishinabe)

Standing Rock
(Dakota)

Dakota

Mississippi

Sans Arc

Grand R.

Lake
Traverse
(Sisseton)

Sihasapa

SOUTH DAKOTA

Cheyenne River
(Lakota)

Wahpekute

Cheyenne R.

Minneconjou

Minnesota R.

Crow Creek
(Dakota+
Nakota)

Lakota

Cheyenne

Yankton

Wahpeton

Pine Ridge
(Oglala Sioux)

Yankton

Missouri R.

James R.

Rosebud
(Lakota)

IOWA

Two Kettles

Niobrara R.

Dakota

DesMoines R.

Brule

Winnebago

Iowa

Oglala

Omaha

Pawnee

Omaha

NEBRASKA

Loup R.

Arapaho

North Platte R.

Platte R.

South Platte R.

COLORADO

Republican R.

KANSAS

Smoky Hill R.

Location
around 1770

Current
Reservations

0   50   100   150 Kilometers

0   50   100 Miles

© WWW.DEMIS.NL

Map 2.4
Traditional Location of Sioux Tribes around 1770 and Reservations Today

called themselves the Seven Fire Places People. French Roman Catholic missionary Jean Nicolet first recorded the term *Sioux* in 1640. Wars with the Chippewas and the Crees resulted in the reduction of the eastern Sioux and gradual displacement of other Sioux. The western Lakota were the first Sioux to arrive on the plains. Horses transformed Lakota life, and the Oglala Sioux obtained them around 1750. They were not native to North America, but were introduced by the Spanish and later obtained by the Plains tribes.

Read a concise overview of current Native Americans, with blog comments.

2-4b Basic Features of Lakota Religion

The Black Hills is the Lakota's sacred place of creation and life. A story says that the hills are like a reclining woman whose breasts provided life-giving power. They are a mother to the Lakota, the "heart of everything that exists." The Sioux people were created in particular from the Bear Butte in the Black Hills of South Dakota, where the Creator first taught them his ways. Bear Butte is the most sacred of their holy places, and both Sioux and Cheyenne come there annually for ceremonies. The spirits of the Lakota dead are said to rest in the Black Hills.

The spirit world of the Lakota is called **Wakan Tanka**, which means "all that is mysterious, sacred." This is a generic, not a personal name. Wakan Tanka is eternal. It powerfully created the universe and, paradoxically, is the universe. The sun, the moon, the stars, and the earth and everything on it (including humans) are all within Wakan Tanka. This term has often been translated as "the Great Spirit" but must not be understood as the one God of monotheistic religions. Wakan Tanka is remote and unapproachable, and rituals are not often performed for it. Included in Wakan Tanka are individual gods and spirits called **Wakanpi** who exercise power and control over everything. Because the Wakanpi are incomprehensible to ordinary humans, they enable certain human beings to know them and deal with them. Shamans have the ability to interact with Wakanpi. They obtain their knowledge through direct contact with the gods and spirits in dreams and visions. They act as intermediaries through which the power of Wakan Tanka can flow. (For an example of a Lakota symbol for the spiritual power of Wakan Tanka, see the image of the medicine wheel in Figure 2.2.)

The Sioux pass down their religion to each new generation in story form. Tribal history is also passed along orally, but it has always been guided by myths of origin so that the recent past doesn't contradict

BONNIE VAN VOORST © CENGAGE LEARNING

Figure 2.2 Lakota medicine wheel

the deep past. Elders often gathered the young around the fire to impart important tales. Some of these tales, such as the stories of White Buffalo Calf Woman, can take up to seven evenings to tell and traditionally can only be told when the moon is shining.

The Sioux look on death and the afterlife in the spirit world as a natural part of life. Death is painful in close-knit indigenous societies, but funeral rituals help mourners cope with the pain of loss. Human souls are immortal; they come from Wakan Tanka at birth and return to Wakan

Wakan Tanka [WAHK-ahn THAHN-kuh] "All that is mysterious, sacred"; the spirit world of the Lakota that powerfully created the universe and, paradoxically, is the universe

Wakanpi [wah-KAHN-pee] Individual gods and spirits who exercise power and control over everything

Explore a collection of Sioux myths and other tales.

Tanka at death. Because these spirits are one with Wakan Tanka, they are everywhere and in everything, even at the grave for a period after death. Before battle, Sioux warriors embraced their possible death openly—thus their famous saying "Today is a good day to die." Death in warfare was preferable to that caused by old age. This heritage of bravery in battle has continued today, and Native Americans have been for nearly a century a highly decorated ethnic group in the U.S. Armed Forces.

Lakotas go on a vision quest to gain a personal religious vision.

2-4c Lakota Rituals

As with other religions, the Lakota believe that their rituals come to them from the gods. Lakota myths tell of spirits such as White Buffalo Calf Woman, who gave her people the sacred pipe and taught them its ritual use. Holy men received other rituals during trance-like states. We now discuss Lakota rituals that are still regularly held.

Indian ceremonial pipe
© ISTOCKPHOTO.COM/GILL ANDRÉ

Near the time of puberty, Sioux boys, and on occasion girls, go on a ritual of passage to adulthood called a **vision quest**, through which they undergo a symbolic death and rebirth and experience their personal guardian spirit. Through the vision quest, each male Lakota gains a personal religious vision that supplements the group-based religious understandings of the tribe. On returning from his vision quest, the vision seeker typically integrates his vision into the life of the community by performing it ritually in public. This integration of one's personal vision with the socially regimented roles passed down in tribal societies helps to make a good balance between individual and group life among the Lakota.

The modern healing ceremony is shortened from the traditional form. Prayer is still offered to the spirit of the stones, and spirit stones protect against danger or illness. This signifies a belief in a spiritual force in all forms of Creation. It isn't unusual to see a sacred stone at the bedside of sick or hospitalized Lakota even today.

The **sacred pipe** continues to be used to forge a ritual connection between Wakan Tanka and humankind, reinforcing the kinship ties of the people with all spirits in the world. It has become so important as a symbol that it now unofficially stands for the whole of Lakota life—indeed, it has become a Pan-Indian ritual implement. (Sometimes it is called a "peace pipe"; although it was used for peace ceremonies, its ritual use goes far beyond this.) Black Elk reported a common belief when he said that the red stone the pipe is made from symbolizes the earth; an animal carved in the stone represents all animals; the wood of the pipe stem symbolizes all growing things; and the feathers on it represents all birds, especially the eagle. All creatures in the natural world "send their voices" to Wakan Tanka when the pipe is smoked.

Cactus used in making peyote
© LOLLOJ/SHUTTERSTOCK.COM

The **sweat lodge** is a ritual sauna meant to cleanse participants in their spirits. (It isn't done, as our saunas today, for muscle relaxation or cleansing of the skin.) It can be a domed hut or a hole dug into the ground and covered with planks or tree trunks. Stones are heated in an outside fire and then placed in a pit inside the lodge. Ritual activities inside and around the sweat lodge include prayers, drumming and singing, and offerings to the spirits.

Watch a BBC video on the sweat lodge.

The use of **peyote**, a mildly hallucinogenic but not physically addictive drug made from a cactus bud, goes back for centuries among Native Americans in the Southwest. It was used as a medicine in healing ceremonies before its more modern and wider ceremonial use. It spread beyond the Southwest at the beginning of the twentieth century, when Native American culture was stressed, and some Lakota today continue the practice. Participants reported a cleansing of their spirits and occasionally some healing of their bodies. The peyote movement was one factor in the rise of the **Native American Church**, a blend of indigenous North American religions and Christianity that is still strong today. This group has successfully fought the U.S. legal system for permission to use the cactus-derived drug,

vision quest Ritual of passage to adulthood through which one undergoes a symbolic death and rebirth and gains experiences of one's personal guardian spirit

sacred pipe Pipe ritually used to forge a connection between Wakan Tanka and humankind

sweat lodge Ritual sauna meant to cleanse participants in their spirits

peyote [pay-YOHT-ee] Mildly hallucinogenic cactus bud used ritually in Indian ceremonies

Native American Church Church mainly composed of Native Americans, featuring a blend of indigenous North American religions and Christianity

which is generally illegal. Use of peyote began to decline in about 2009, because it has been poorly grown and over-harvested during recent years.

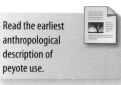

Read the earliest anthropological description of peyote use.

Finally, the **sun dance** ceremony is still practiced in almost twenty different North American tribes. It features dancing, singing and drumming, blowing on eagle-bone whistles, visions, and fasting. Some brave men known as *sun dance pledgers* come to the festival having already taken a vow to offer their bodies as a painful sacrifice to Wakan Tanka for the benefit of their tribe. The sacrifice usually takes the form of being attached to a pole by hide thongs (which pierce one's body above each nipple on the chest with a metal hook) and then tearing oneself away from the thongs. Each tribe holds the sun dance once a year, at the height of summer when the sun is the hottest, from four to eight days. It ritually enacts continuity between life and death, and offers a renewal of the life of the tribe as connected to the life of the earth. The sun dance continues to be an important ritual festival for the Plains tribes.

A Native American, probably a Lakota, blows an eagle-bone whistle while participating in the sun dance during the Inter-Tribal Indian Ceremonial in the late 1940s in New Mexico.

PHOTO BY MICHAEL OCHS ARCHIVES/GETTY IMAGES

2-4d Culture and Religion

sun dance Main festival ceremony of many Plains tribes, often featuring self-inflicted wounds

assimilation Entry of Indian peoples into mainstream white culture, either voluntary or forced

The buffalo holds a key place in Lakota life and history. From its hide they made clothing, ropes and snowshoes, and the round, moveable homes called *tipi* (also phonetically spelled *tepee*, the Lakota word for "dwelling"). The horns provided spoons, weapons, and ritual articles. The buffalo's sinew was used for bowstrings and sewing thread. The buffalo was the main friend of the Sun, and even controlled all affairs of love. Its spirit cares for the family, for the young of all beings, and for growing plants. Given the place of the buffalo in the life and thought of the Lakota, its extermination proved deadly for their traditional culture. Around 1800 there were possibly 60 million buffalo on the Plains; by 1884 the slaughter by hunters—encouraged by the federal government, in part to break the power of the Plains tribes—led to less than one hundred buffalo being left. The Lakota Sioux, along with other Plains tribes, were reduced to dependence on government rations on various reservations of small size and few resources.

View a U.S. Census Bureau map of current Native American populations.

> *Given the role of the buffalo for the Lakota, its extermination proved deadly for their traditional culture.*

The sad story of the gradual reduction of Native American life continued. Confinement to reservations was soon followed by a government policy to "civilize" Indian peoples by **assimilation** into mainstream white culture—by coercion if necessary. (Voluntary assimilation happened as well, but on a smaller scale.) Rapid white expansion into western North America meant that Indian conflicts had to end, and therefore much of their land granted by treaties was taken from them. Hiram Price, U.S. Commissioner of Indian Affairs in 1881, said history shows that "Savage and civilized life cannot prosper on the same ground." This was a conviction widely held among European Americans, and by the mid-nineteenth century it was allied to a

©ISTOCKPHOTO.COM/ERIC ISSELÉE

Little Big Horn Battle on June 25–26, 1876, in eastern Montana, in which Sioux and Cheyenne warriors defeated a U.S. Army regiment

ghost dance Movement inspired by the Paiute prophet Wovoka in the 1880s, looking for the restoration of Indian life and the departure of whites

racist theory of white superiority and the belief that it was America's "Manifest Destiny" to occupy all the lands from the Atlantic to the Pacific. Because European Americans as a group assumed that they were superior to indigenous Americans, they knew what was best for them. This portended the rapid destruction of Native American cultures, and their religions as well.

Much of the forced assimilation was targeted at children, because they were more changeable than their parents. In schools, Indian children were prohibited from speaking their own language, living out their own culture, or having a tribal identity. Children in both the United States and Canada were separated from their families and sent far off to boarding schools if their family's influence was viewed as "negative." Some government officials did have second thoughts about this. For example, in his Indian commissioner's report for 1934, John Collier urged an end to this assault on native culture. "The cultural history of Indians is in all respects to be considered equal to that of any non-Indian group." But this was not to become a widespread conviction until the 1960s. As late as the 1950s, it was U.S. government policy to promote assimilation toward the ultimate goal that Native American identity would disappear.

Violent conflict continued in the late 1800s. In the Sioux Wars of the 1870s, the Sioux and their allies did battle with the U.S. Army in the Black Hills. This culminated on

"The people were crying [in the ghost dance movement] for the old ways of living and that their religion would be with them again." —Black Elk

June 25–26, 1876, with a battle at **Little Big Horn** in eastern Montana. Hundreds of Sioux and Cheyenne warriors under the command of Sitting Bull, a Sioux chief and holy man, met the Seventh Cavalry Regiment of the U.S. Army, commanded by General George Custer. Sitting Bull quickly destroyed Custer's forces. Although Little Big Horn bolstered Native American morale, this did not last long. The federal military presence continued, as did increasing white settlement in the West, even on Native American reservations. In response to this worsening situation, the **ghost dance** movement arose in the late 1880s. It would be the last militant attempt to preserve the cultural life and independence of Native Americans.

The ghost dance movement was inspired by the vision of the Paiute prophet Wovoka (also known by his "white" name, Jack Wilson). Wovoka's vision spread, and reached the Sioux late in 1889. It spoke of dead native warriors ("ghosts") coming back to life; the restoration of youth to the living; the return of the buffalo, elk, and other game; and the departure of whites.

After the U.S. Army learned that the Sioux were armed, wearing their ghost shirts, and defying government agents, troops arrived at the Pine Ridge reservation on November 20, 1890, and at other Sioux areas as well. Sitting Bull was arrested on December 15 and killed in the process, and his followers fled. Alarmed at Sitting Bull's death and anxious at the troops' presence on their reservation, the Big Foot band of Lakota, numbering about 350, headed for Pine Ridge to confront the army. Intercepted by troops, they surrendered and were kept at Wounded Knee. On December 29, as

Ghost dance shirt

AP PHOTO/JILL KOKESH

troops tried to confiscate the weapons that some Lakota still possessed, a rifle discharged and shooting immediately broke out on both sides. Historians conclude that what began as an accident immediately turned into a battle and then quickly intensified into what has become known as the **Massacre at Wounded Knee**. Of the U.S. Army troops, twenty-five were killed; of the Lakota, eighty-four men and boys and sixty-two women and girls were killed—virtually half the prisoners. The ghost dance movement was now over. The ghost shirts worn by the Big Foot band had failed to protect them as it was believed they would. To use the words of Black Elk, "the dream died."

Ancient Pueblo city of Taos, New Mexico

© JOSEMARIA TOSCANO/SHUTTERSTOCK.COM

Native Americans then settled down to a long period of slow decline on the reservations

Make an online visit to the Wounded Knee Museum.

in the United States and Canada, but over time most left the reservations to assimilate with wider American culture. In the early 1970s, a social and political protest movement arose among Native Americans. At Wounded Knee, traditional Indians and members of the American Indian Movement (AIM) protested the appalling economic and social conditions on Pine Ridge reservation, which is today the poorest area in the United States. Wounded Knee was chosen for the protest because it symbolized a continuity of the suffering of those who died there in 1890.

To conclude this section, let's sum up our discussion. It is important in the Lakota culture to live in a healthy, life-giving relationship with the tribe and the land. As we have seen, this relationship has been seriously damaged by forced assimilation, relocations, and government policies under a U.S. Bureau of Indian Affairs that is widely recognized as incompetent. Also, high unemployment (up to an astounding 90 percent), poverty, domestic violence, and alcohol and drug abuse continue to take a toll on the reservations. Some signs of hope are appearing: Tribal identities are growing, religious rituals are practiced and taught to new generations, tribal casino gambling recognized by state and federal governments is bringing in financial resources for tribal use (although some consider casinos a mixed blessing), and social ills are being more seriously attended to. Indian tribes are realizing that if improvement in their condition is to come, they must bring it themselves. Many Lakota organizations are dedicated to the continuation of traditional ways. The Lakota continue the struggle to hold on to the Black Hills, even refusing in 1980 a $100 million offer in return for giving up their claim

to the Hills. This refusal is an indication of Sioux commitment to their traditional culture. The reestablishment of traditional Lakota ways of life requires no less than the rebuilding of the community from the family up, and much is being done to accomplish this.

This struggle to maintain indigenous identity in the face of opposition is shared by others. As an example, let's take "A Closer Look" at Hawaiian religion and its struggle to adapt to the coming of European Americans and the Christian religion.

Massacre at Wounded Knee Killing of about 150 Lakota prisoners of war by the U.S. Army on December 29, 1890

Visit the website of the White Buffalo Calf Woman Society.

Watch a news report on Native American casino gambling in Minnesota.

Learning Outcome 2-5

State and explain the main features of Yoruba religion.

2-5 An African Religion: Yoruba

To take a closer look at African indigenous religions, we will examine the Yoruba (YOHR-uh-buh) religion of west-central Africa. Not only is the Yoruba religion important in Africa today, but it is also important in the Western Hemisphere, because many Yoruba taken

A Closer Look:

Polynesian Religion in Hawaii

Hawaiian indigenous religion was brought by the first settlers to Hawaii from other South Pacific islands (Polynesia). As a variety of Polynesians came to Hawaii over time, its form of religion became a blended form of Polynesian religions, and also became more adapted to the particular life of the Hawaiian Islands. When Western colonialists came to Hawaii, Polynesian religion there faced another challenge to adapt, one that still continues.

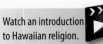
Watch an introduction to Hawaiian religion.

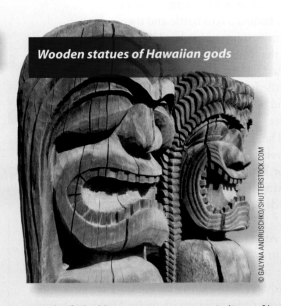
Wooden statues of Hawaiian gods

© GALYNA ANDRUSCHKO/SHUTTERSTOCK.COM

Hawaiian indigenous religion centers on the gods in and behind natural forces. For example, Lono is the god of rain and the fertility it brings, Kane (KAH-nay) the god of sky and creation, and Kanaloa (KAN-uh-LOH-ah) the ocean god. These and other deities are known by way of myth and ritual. The *Kumulipo* (KOO-muh-LEE-poh) song tells the creation myth in 1,200 lines of verse. In it, light overcame darkness, and the world was then created over several nights. The sea and life in it were created first; then land and its creatures; afterward the gods of earth, sky, and sea; and finally humans. The recital of these verses is traditionally led by the **kahuna**, a type of shaman who is both a cultural and religious leader, as a chant during a special festival to celebrate and renew the creation.

The main goal of Hawaiian indigenous religion is to maintain a balanced relationship with nature and society in which people can flourish. Gods, lesser spirits, and spirits of the ancestors all have a role in this relationship. Some kahunas have the power to communicate with the gods, using their abilities to treat the sick. Most illnesses are thought to be the result of evil forces and spirits that could invade the body. The ability to heal and the actual healing itself derive from the kahuna's connection to the deities and more often than not are simply a matter of speaking to the gods about the sick person.

Prayer is an integral part of Hawaiian traditional life. For example, one prays during the process of building a house or a boat. Prayer is offered to a specific god (usually not a high deity), depending on one's needs. Prayers are spoken before eating, drinking, traveling, and sleeping. Hawaiians typically sit for prayer and look up during it. Prayers can also be said in small temples, in front of shrines, and at other sacred places, and they accompany all sacrifices and offerings to the gods.

Specific cultural laws known as the **kapu**—a word related to the Polynesian term *taboo* or *tapu*—refer to strictly forbidden acts. These ensure ritual and moral purity by forbidding one to cross certain lines of behavior; even today, "kapu" is seen on doors in Hawaii to forbid entry. A priest from Tahiti introduced this system to the islands around 1200 C.E. It regulated one's actions regarding social status and gender. Breaking these laws was punishable by death, and on some rare occasions offenders against kapu would be used as human sacrifices in various rituals. Some examples: Women and children had to eat their meals in a separate place from men. Women could not enter religious shrines, temples, or the homes of their chief, and they were kept apart during menstruation. Members of a tribe could not touch their chiefs or even stand too close to them.

The kapu system was first dealt a blow by Hawaiians themselves, who chafed under its restrictions. They burned wooden statues of the gods and destroyed some of their stone temples. In 1831 the idols were banned, and inhabitants were forced to accept the one God of Christianity. The hula dance performances, chanting of songs with religious overtones, and other practices were outlawed and went underground. Some traditional aspects of Hawaiian religion outlasted the influence of the Christian missionaries, however. From around 1960, Hawaiian indigenous religion has come back into the light and experienced a rebirth of sorts. Hawaiian indigenous believers, some of whom combine native beliefs with Christianity or Buddhism, are now bringing back old rites and beliefs—without many of the restrictive kapus. In sum, like many indigenous religions around the world, Hawaiian religion has made an uneasy but creative adaption to new times and cultures.

in slavery to the Americas were instrumental in the founding of new Afro-Caribbean religions. Like indigenous religions that cover a wide area, the religions of the Yoruba peoples vary significantly in different parts of west-central Africa today, especially in Nigeria. For example, the name of a god often has variations, or the same deity may be female in one town and male in the next, and the rituals to worship them may vary as well. These differences inevitably arose as the myths were passed by word of mouth and as tribes among the Yoruba made changes in their religion over thousands of years. When we add the influence of Christianity and Islam into the Yoruba religion—with some of these "postcontact" changes disputed by scholars—the religion becomes even more diverse and challenging to understand.

Despite this internal variety, all Yoruba religion shares a similar structure and purpose. A supreme but remote god rules the world, along with hundreds of lower deities actively worshiped, each of whom has a specific area of rule. These gods guide believers to find their destiny in life, one that was determined at the moment of reincarnation of one's soul into a new life but then forgotten. The rituals of the Yoruba identify this destiny for the individual, and this blesses the life of the Yoruba people as a whole.

2-5a High God and Other Gods

The Yoruba all have a high god, usually called **Olorun** ("Ruler of the Sky") or *Olodumare* (oh-loh-DOOM-ah-reh, "All-powerful One"), but occasionally by a number of other names. They don't worship Olorun or make sacrifices to him, and he has no priests and no places of worship. He is a remote high god. Although the Yoruba believe that he is the creator and continual giver of life, almighty and all knowing, the Yoruba ignore him in their daily lives. He is invoked only at times of extreme need, and even then with difficulty. Some scholars argue that Olorun developed as a "postcontact" deity through the influence of Muslim and Christian missionaries—as an imitation of their God, but one that could not be integrated into other Yoruba beliefs or rituals. However, belief in Olorun is widespread among the Yoruba, both in those tribes that have not had much contact with Abrahamic religions as well as those that have. Moreover, we can find other African tribes and nations with remote high gods in their traditions.

The other main Yoruba deities controlling relations between the earth and the high god are known as **orisha**. They are the gods with whom humans have

contact through myth and rituals. The numbers, relationships, and names of Yoruba deities are exceedingly complex; they form a vast group of supernatural beings numbering between 401 and 601. Some Yoruba myths have a pair of gods, Orishala (also known as Obatala and Orisanla) and Odudua his wife, as the gods who created the world. This association with the creator and high god Olorun gives them a higher status than that of the other orisha. In one myth, Olorun creates most of the world and then has Obatala and Odudua finish it. Obatala is often portrayed as a divine sculptor, especially of individual human bodies. The Yoruba regard physically different humans to be either Obatala's special servants or the victims of his displeasure, leaving some room for interpretation.

The Yoruba see **Ogun** as the highest orisha. His status as the chief god of war, hunting, and ironworking makes him the patron of warriors, blacksmiths, and all others who use metals. Yoruba religion has a high regard for metal as a combination of earth, wind, and fire. Ogun also is the god of business deals and contracts. In Yoruba courts in Nigeria, Yoruba take their oath to tell the truth by kissing a knife. Ogun is fearsome in his revenge; if one breaks an agreement after invoking his name, swift punishment will follow. One myth that illustrates Ogun's importance tells of several orisha making a road through a dense jungle. Ogun was the only one with the right tools for the task and so won the right to rule the orisha. When he did not want the position, it went to Obatala. (For a geometric symbol of Ogun suggesting metalwork, one that is commonly used in his worship in both Yoruba and Vodou religion, see Figure 2.3.)

Shango the storm god occupies an important place among these orisha. Shango creates and controls storms by throwing "thunderstones" onto the earth. When lightning strikes, Shango's priests search for the stones, which are believed to have special powers because of

kahuna [kah-HOO-nuh] Cultural and religious leader in Hawaiian indigenous religion

kapu [KAH-poo] Specific cultural Hawaiian laws forbidding moral and ritual impurities

Olorun [OHL-oh-ruhn] "Ruler of the Sky," Yoruba high god

orisha [ohr-EE-shuh] Yoruban main gods who control relations between the earth and the high god Olorun, and with whom humans have contact through myth and rituals

Ogun [OH-guhn] Highest orisha, the chief god of war, hunting, and ironworking

Figure 2.3 Symbol of Ogun

their origin. As the stones are collected, they are put in Shango's shrines. A myth told about Shango provides a basis for his worship. When he was human and a king of an ancient Yoruba kingdom, he had power to create lightning, but he accidentally killed his entire family with it. He then killed himself in sorrow and became deified when he entered the spirit world. At that point he gained more power over lightning, as well as over thunder, wind, hail, and other aspects of storms. Scholars generally conclude that his popularity among the Yoruba peoples results from a need to avert the violent storms that often strike western Africa.

Shango came to the New World with newly enslaved Africans. In Annapolis, Maryland, a clay bundle about the size and shape of an American football was unearthed by University of Maryland and University of London archaeologists at an old crossroads. Dated to around 1700, it was filled with about three hundred pieces of metal and had a stone axe sticking out through the clay. Archaeologists quickly identified it as African in origin, and likely used as an object of spiritual power by African slaves recently brought to America. Although almost all slaves were baptized into Christianity, they continued to secretly observe some "spirit practices" in healing and in the worship of their ancestors. The archaeologist who discovered the bundle concluded that it was connected with rites of Shango.

A doll with bananas, both tied with red ribbon as offerings to Shango

Trickster gods can blur the line between good and evil in Yoruban religion. One myth dealing with the god Eshu (EH-shoo) illustrates his trickiness. Pretending to be a merchant, Eshu sold expensive items to a man's two wives, sparking a desire in each to outdo the other in purchasing. The battle for the husband's favor after this buying spree tore the family apart. This story is told as a cautionary tale against the evils of greed and ambition. Eshu is also, but not in his trickster role, the divine guardian of houses and villages. The relationship between Eshu and many Yorubans is so close that they call him *Baba* ("father") in worship. Because tricksters often blur the lines of good and evil, Islamic and then Christian missionaries among the Yorubans attacked Eshu as a demonic figure, even as a representation of the Devil. This of course betrays a misunderstanding of a trickster's overall role to promote morality, not undermine it.

The history of Shokpona (shock-POH-nuh), the god of smallpox, is an interesting story at the intersection of religion and medicine. Shokpona became important in the smallpox plagues that arose in intertribal wars in west Africa. The Yoruba also saw Shokpona's wrath in other diseases that have similar symptoms. Shokpona's wrath is so terrifying, and worshiping him is so challenging, that the Yoruba are often afraid to speak his name. Instead, they use expressions such as "Hot Earth," referring to high fever, and "One whose name must not be spoken in the dry season." Priests of Shokpona had great power; they could inflict smallpox on their enemies, especially by making a ritual potion from the powdered scabs and dry skin of those who had died from smallpox. They would then spread this potion in an enemy's area. Although this indirect contact with smallpox was less deadly than contact with living people infected by it, it worked well enough. However, because smallpox has been eradicated worldwide since about 1980, the worship of Shokpona has all but vanished, and his priests with it.

In the long history of the successful human battle against smallpox, African religious practice had a role at a key moment in American history. When a growing smallpox epidemic threatened the American revolutionary army encamped at Valley Forge, Pennsylvania, in 1777, George Washington ordered inoculations based on an account by a famous Christian minister in Massachusetts, Cotton Mather (1663–1728). Mather detailed how his African slave named Onesimus had been protected from smallpox by vaccination, probably in a religious ritual of body marking connected with the worship of Shokpona. A small bit of smallpox scab had been put on his cuts so that, as Mather later wrote, he "had smallpox and then did not have it." Mather himself had successfully inoculated his sons with this procedure, minus the Yoruban religious elements, of course. The method was a success at Valley Forge, and the American army was saved from smallpox.

2-5b Religious Specialists

With its many gods that must be attended to with rituals, Yoruba religion has a large place for religious specialists. These specialists don't teach or administer religious institutions; rather, they preside at the hundreds of rituals. Their skills are passed down from generation to generation.

Priests divine the future, offering advice for how to meet it. Male priests are known as a **babalawo**, "father of secrets" or "father of the priest," and females as an **iyalawo**, "mother of secrets/priest." They help people to understand the destinies they chose in the spirit world but lost when they were reincarnated on Earth. The priests also give people power and guidance to make their destinies come true. Seeking a priest to help with one's future is a common occurrence throughout life, but faithful Yorubas take their child to a diviner

soon after birth so that the child's destiny can be made clear from the very start.

The process of divination varies by priest and region, but following is perhaps the most common method. The believer, usually under some sort of duress, makes her or his way to a diviner. Contrary to many other systems of divination and fortune-telling, the believer doesn't tell the diviner what the problem is. Instead, the diviner summons the gods and then casts sixteen separate palm nuts or a chain of sixteen shells onto a divination board. Depending on the results, the diviner then chants a group of poems called **Ifa** verses, presided over by a god of the same name. The collection of Ifa verses is vast, and diviners often know several hundred of them by heart. These poems recount short stories about the gods and usually tell of some sacrifice, gift, or action the believer must take. It is then up to the believer to discern which of the poems and prescribed actions are correct in her or his situation. The Yoruba believer is very active in this process; it's not just a matter of telling one's problems to a priest and then getting some quick advice. This system of divination has worked for centuries, probably millennia, and even today many Yoruba consult an expert in the Ifa before making any important decisions.

A recent book by Velma Love, *Divining the Self*, shows how Ifa divination is practiced in African American communities in Oyotunji Village, South Carolina and in New York City.[6]

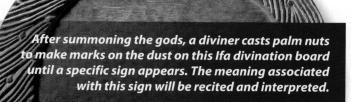

Ivory wand or tapper used for Ifa divination, Nigeria. The diviner repeatedly taps the Ifa board with the point of the tapper to summon the gods.

© WERNER FORMAN/HIP/THE IMAGE WORKS

After summoning the gods, a diviner casts palm nuts to make marks on the dust on this Ifa divination board until a specific sign appears. The meaning associated with this sign will be recited and interpreted.

WERNER FORMAN ARCHIVE/MUSEUM FÜR VÖLKERKUNDE, BERLIN/GLOW IMAGES

babalawo [BUB-uh-LAH-woh] "Father of secrets" or "father of the priest," the Yoruba male priest

iyalawo [EE-yah-LAH-woh] "Mother of secrets/priest," the Yoruba female priest

Ifa [EE-fuh] Poetic verses used in divination

6 Velma E. Love, *Divining the Self: A Study in Yoruba Myth and Human Consciousness* (University Park, PA: Penn State University Press, 2012).

Ifa poems are now being collected and published, but this takes them out of their living context in Yoruba divination.

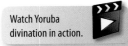
Watch Yoruba divination in action.

2-5c Spirits of the Ancestors

The Yoruba venerate their dead ancestors, which is typical of indigenous societies. Anthropologists disagree over whether the rituals for respecting the ancestors—prayers, sacrifices, and the like—are religious or cultural-traditional; but given the deeply enculturated nature of indigenous religion, we can safely conclude that a religious aspect is present. Some Yoruba groups believe that their dead ancestors become semidivine figures. This is related to another aspect of the Yoruba faith: possession of one's body by the gods. In these possessions, priests acting as mediums take on the individual characteristics of the deities. The behavioral patterns of how each god takes possession of a medium are so entrenched that mediums as far away as the Caribbean move their heads and legs just as mediums of Shango do in west Africa.

See a Brooklyn Museum collection of Yoruba art and religious objects.

Learning Outcome 2-6

State and explain the main features of Vodou religion.

2-6 An Afro-Caribbean Religion: Vodou

Those who follow the Afro-Caribbean religion of Vodou currently number an estimated 5 to 7 million people. Vodou is widely referred to in North America today, but with much misunderstanding, especially in American popular culture. In this section, we'll put this religion in its African and New World contexts and try to shed some light on its significance for today. An important part of our study of Vodou will be to rehabilitate the name of this religion, so that it doesn't always stir up negative emotions and misleading opinions. Although Vodou is not, strictly speaking, indigenous to Haiti, the centuries of its combination with Roman Catholicism in the setting of the New World qualifies it as an indigenous religion.

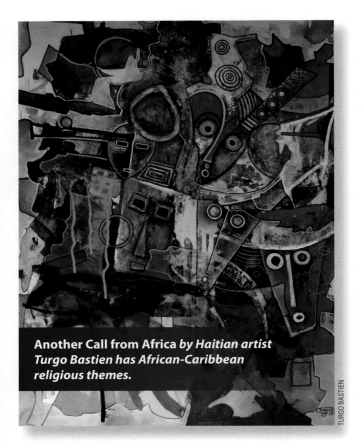
Another Call from Africa *by Haitian artist Turgo Bastien has African-Caribbean religious themes.*

TURGO BASTIEN

2-6a Location and Name

Like the Brazilian religions Candomblé and Umbanda, Cuban Santería, or Jamaican Rastafarianism, the Vodou religion is based on an African indigenous religion. An estimated 9 to 12 million slaves were brought to the New World between 1500 and 1850, most of them to Brazil and the Caribbean islands, and they brought their religions with them. Like other indigenous religions, Vodou is concerned mainly with bringing its followers into harmony with the gods that control the natural world, so that in this harmony their lives can be happy and blessed. These religions were brought to the New World by enslaved members of west African tribes, and there underwent an independent development to become Afro-Caribbean.

The word *Vodou* (or the lesser-used *Hoodoo*, which is often used on a popular level for the magical practices of Vodou) is from the Haitian Creole-French language. It is also spelled *Voudon* or *Vodun* in scholarship today. You probably know it as *Voodoo*. Until recently, this was the accepted spelling of the word, but many Haitians and modern scholars now acknowledge *Vodou* as the preferred spelling, because it is phonetically closer to the original

African word. It originated in the language of the Ewe Fon west African peoples brought to Haiti as slaves from present-day Benin and Togo. Specifically, it is from *vodú*, the Ewe Fon word for both "god" and "worship." Beginning in the seventeenth century, *Voodoo* was used in the missionary literature about the Ewe people in Africa, who called a newly initiated member of their religion a *vodúnsi* or *hunsi*, a "bride of the deity." But the use of *Voodoo* has prejudicial and exotic overtones in the Western world today. In general, Vodou in Africa is an African indigenous religion, not combined with Roman Catholic Christianity as it is in the Americas.

 Watch National Geographic's "Birth of Voodoo" in Africa.

In the Western Hemisphere, *Vodou* means various things. It often refers to an Afro-Catholic religion that is widespread on the island of Hispaniola, especially in Haiti. It can also be applied to persons—for example, spell-workers are often called "hoodoo doctors" in the southern United States. In Haiti, Vodou is applied as an umbrella term to a large number of Haitian religious groups with roots in African religion rather than Roman Catholic Christianity. In mainstream American usage, it has become a common pejorative for "deceptive nonsense," usually with no connection to religion. For instance, when George H. W. Bush and Ronald Reagan were competing in 1980 for the Republican nomination for president, Bush called Reagan's economic plan "Voodoo economics." Other uses of Vodou center on the current popularity of zombies, especially "zombie walks." Observers of American popular culture say that in 2009 zombies replaced vampires as the leading symbol of unnatural threats. To those who engage in careful academic study of Vodou, however, this interest in zombies distorts and demeans the religion.

Watch an introduction to Vodou in Haiti.

2-6b Divinities

Like other Afro-Caribbean religions, Haitian Vodou has authentic African traits. Vodou is a typical example of a religion centered on different groups of gods. These deities are called **loas**, meaning "divinities" or "mysteries." They are also commonly called "saints," in the sense of "holy ones." In Fon myth, there are three regions of the world, and various deities reign in each one: the sky, the earth, and, in between these, the clouds. The creator god (Yoruba, *Olorun*; Creole, *Bon Dieu Bon*—literally "good God good") lives in the remote sky. Because he isn't involved with everyday life, he isn't honored in everyday rituals. Through the influence of Roman Catholicism, Vodou believers also worship the

Christian God. It is not uncommon for them to worship in a Catholic church on Sunday morning and in a Vodou sanctuary on Sunday evening. They also venerate two other kinds of spiritual beings who live between the sky and the earth: souls of dead humans that have become spirits and spirits that have never been directly tied to matter. Vodou gods live on the earth—in the sea, in waterfalls, in springs, in forests, at intersections of roads, in cemeteries, and in piles of stones. Many earth gods of Vodou correspond to Catholic saints, on whose feast days the Vodou deities are also celebrated. The recognition and worship of these gods helps to bless the lives of people on earth, so that they can be happy, peaceful, and productive.

2-6c Groups

Gods and rites are divided into groups according to the geographical regions of their origin. The two main groups are the *Rada* and the *Petro*, who are found especially in urban areas. *Rada* derives from the old kingdom of Arada in Africa. *Petro*, more oriented to the indigenous Creoles, comes from the name of a Vodou priest, Don Pedro, who introduced a variant of the Vodou trance dance in the eighteenth century. (The Petro group is named after him, but he did not found it.) Petro gods and spirits are invoked especially for magical or counter-magical actions that we will consider below. Vodou priests may support both groups, and a believer is usually either Rada or Petro but may likewise take part in ceremonies of the other type.

2-6d Worship

As with Candomblé in Brazil and Santería in Cuba, Vodou is a fusion of African religions with Catholicism. Some traces of Caribbean Indian religion can also be found in it. The religion of Vodou refers not to a body of beliefs, creeds, sacred scriptures, or other elements of religion but to ritual practice. Vodou is often described as a **cult religion** (*cult* here refers to a *system of ritual worship*, not to a dangerous group). In particular, it is a **possession cult** in which the gods inhabit people and speak through them, usually for a short

loa [LOH-uh] "Divinity" or "mystery"; in west African and Vodou religions, a god or group of gods

cult religion Religion using a particular system of ritual worship

possession cult Religion in which the gods inhabit people and speak through them, usually for a short period of time during rituals

period of time during rituals. Rituals of animal sacrifice as well as trance dances forge and maintain a bond with the deities. The rites are practiced by initiated members called *hunsi*, "brides of the gods," presided over by priests and priestesses called *hugan* and *mambo*, respectively. Initiates are introduced into the group by a complicated and spectacular ritual. Worship is held in sacred cabins or city temples, all with an altar for the sacrifice of animals and other offerings. They have a central post that enables the loas to descend to believers and "ride" them like "horses" in a state of trance.

A few Vodou rituals tap into the power of the spirits of the dead, and cemeteries have become important places of Vodou gatherings for worship. The head loa in the cult of the dead is **Baron Samedi**, the "Lord of the Dead." His depiction and name vary, but he often wears a top hat, a black tuxedo, and cotton plugs in his nostrils, all of which are elements of a corpse prepared in a Haitian style for burial. Baron Samedi has a white, skull-like face and is regarded by all as a fearsome presence. Although dead, he is very much alive. He is charged with sexual energy and is frequently represented by phallic symbols. Baron Samedi is known for obscenity and debauchery, and he enjoys tobacco and rum. He is worshiped and celebrated in order to keep him at bay, so that he won't disturb the living.

Geoffrey Holder played Baron Samedi in Live and Let Die. *His face paint suggests that he is both alive and dead.*

PHOTO BY TERRY O'NEILL/HULTON ARCHIVE/GETTY IMAGES

Also connected to death—and the African experience of deadly slavery in Haiti—is the figure of the zombie. As we saw above, Yoruban religion has a large role for the spirits of the dead, and Vodou further blurs the distinction between the living and the dead. It believes that a human body can be revived by an especially powerful magician after the spirit of the dead has departed and used as a slave for the magician's purposes. These spirits are the ultimate slaves, the worst possible kind of "life" for Afro-Haitian people. Zombies remain under the control of the sorcerer because they have no will, mind, or soul of their own. This is why in popular culture zombies are usually depicted as mindless, almost robotic figures that shuffle around. However, the notion that zombies eat human flesh, thus making other people into zombies, is a mistaken view that taps into a revulsion against cannibalism.

2-6e Spell and Counter-Spell Rituals

Like some of the world's largest religions, Vodou has a place for "magical" practices, and, also like other religions, this is found more often on a popular, not an official, level. Magic is the preferred form of Vodou practice of the lowest social class in Haiti—the small farmers, the urban working poor, and the masses of unemployed—although today some members of the upper class are also drawn to it. People use magic to seek deliverance from all the difficulties of life, which for the lower classes in Haiti are many. Diseases, poverty, and other difficulties are seen as the effect of demonic spells, which need to be countered with magic. Probably the magical practice best known in the West is the one performed with a small doll, through which certain magical actions are seen as being able to harm someone's health or even cause death.

Also used are **gris-gris**, originally images of the gods in the shape of little dolls but now small cloth bags containing herbs, oils, pebbles, bits of bone, hair and finger- or toenails, and pieces of sweat-soaked cloth. These are gathered and bagged to protect the owner from harm. Legends of the most famous Vodou practitioner in the United States, New Orleans "Vodou Queen" Marie Laveau (1794–1881), say that her gris-gris contained bone, colored pebbles, cemetery soil, salt, and red pepper. In addition to protective uses, gris-gris are for gaining money and love, insuring good health, and for accomplishing other similar purposes. The ingredients are always an odd number of items, and are chosen to fit the purpose of the gris-gris.

Curse rituals, services of worship in cemeteries, the use of snakes in worship, and zombies have made the Vodou religion a favorite subject of **exoticism**—portraying something in another culture as strange or exciting, and distorting it in the process. Ever since Spenser

Baron Samedi [sah-MEHD-ee] "Lord of the Dead," head loa in the Vodou cult of the dead

gris-gris [gree-gree] In Vodou, small cloth bags containing items gathered and bagged under the direction of a god for the protection of the owner

exoticism [egg-ZOT-uh-siz-uhm] Portraying something in another culture as strange or exciting, and distorting it in the process

A shop selling Vodou supplies in the French Quarter of New Orleans

St. John's 1884 adventure account about Haiti, *Hayita or the Black Republic*, new sensations about Vodou have continually sprung up. The Vodou religion, by way of Hollywood, became an important part of the horror film genre. Filmmakers have found that exotic presentations of Vodou can easily frighten and entertain audiences.

Watch a History Channel video on Marie Laveau.

2-6f Political Influence in Haiti

Haitian Vodou has at times had an important political and social role. Its faithful were able to mobilize forces against the French colonialist rulers at the close of the 1700s; this led to the abolition of slavery and the country's independence from France in 1804. Through the years, Vodou believers opposed various Haitian regimes that were devoted to their own power even as the gap between the rich and the poor masses grew. The last instance of such resistance was to dictator "Papa Doc" Duvalier, who ruled from 1957 to 1971. After the devastation of Haiti in the earthquake of 2010, Vodou remains powerful on a popular level.

Socially, rural and urban forms of Vodou differ in Haiti. In rural areas, worship and belief are oriented to small farmers and are supported by extensive family alliances. Involvement with ancestors and ritual practices to bring about successful farming are the center of religious practice. Vodou believers in the cities have adapted their practice to urban relationships there. They find a "second family" in the temple communities. This urban adaptation of traditional rural Vodou has found its way to the urban centers of North America.

Widespread continuous poverty and political instability in Haiti have led to the need for a religion that can help the poor cope with their problems. Vodou offers this help; the other main religion of Haiti, Christianity, is tied in the minds of many Haitians to the social elites who oppress the common people. This dismal situation in Haiti has led to the emigration of Haitians to North America. They have taken the Vodou religion along with them to New York City, Miami, and Montreal, but especially to New Orleans, where today there is a museum of Vodou. (New Orleans Vodou tends to be more firmly attached to Roman Catholicism than other forms are.) Vodou is starting to get a foothold in some countries of Europe, but mainly as a magical practice adapted for those who are not initiates in the religion.

Visit the website of the Vodou Museum of New Orleans.

Study Tools 2

Ready to study? In the book you can:

- Review Learning Outcome answers and glossary terms with the tear-out Chapter Review card.

Or you can go online to CourseMate, at www.cengagebrain.com, for these resources:

- Chapter quizzes to prepare for tests
- Interactive flashcards of all glossary terms
- A timeline of events for this chapter
- An eBook with introductions, interactive quizzes, and live links for all web resources in the chapter

CHAPTER 3

Encountering Hinduism: Many Paths to Liberation

Learning Outcomes

After studying this chapter, you will be able to do the following:

3-1 Explain what *Hinduism* means and its strengths and weaknesses as a name.

3-2 Explain how the main periods of Hinduism's history have shaped its present, especially its unity and diversity.

3-3 Outline the essentials of Hindu teachings in your own words.

3-4 Relate Hindu ethics to the essential Hindu teachings.

3-5 Outline the ways Hindus worship, at home and in temples.

3-6 State the main aspects of Hindu life around the world today, especially in North America.

Study Tools

After you read this chapter, go to the Study Tools at the end of the chapter, page 93.

Encountering Hinduism is like a visit to an Indian buffet. You can't sample everything, but if you choose a good variety you'll have a good introduction.

Your Visit to Varanasi, India

Imagine that you're on a visit to the city of Varanasi (vuh-RAH-nuh-see) as a part of a tour of India. You know that Varanasi, located on the Ganges (GAN-jeez) River in north India, is unique among the cities of the world, but nothing can quite prepare you for its sights, sounds, and smells.

Your visit begins with a predawn boat ride on the Ganges. As your rowboat glides along the river, you see Hindu pilgrims on the western shore of the river descending the wide steps—two miles of them at Varanasi—leading down to the water. They wash themselves physically and spiritually, and pray toward the rising sun. A man dressed only in a loincloth and his sacred thread fills a small metal pail with river water and then pours it out on himself while saying a prayer in the ancient Sanskrit language. After the boat ride, you walk to the Golden Temple, the most sacred of the city's many shrines dedicated to Shiva (SHEE-vuh), the patron deity of Varanasi. There you see Hindus making offerings of flowers to the black stone emblem of Shiva. You also visit the newer Hindu temple inaugurated by Mohandas Gandhi, the father of modern Indian independence. You return to the hotel for breakfast before taking a guided tour of Varanasi.

 Take a virtual tour of Varanasi on Google Earth™.

As you walk with your group through the narrow, twisting streets down to the river, you pass several cows wandering freely, and even a bull sacred to Shiva. You notice many small temples and even smaller shrines that seem to be everywhere. You also notice many old, frail people, some in the doorways of ashrams and others living on the street, who have come to die in Varanasi in the hope of achieving liberation from the cycle of endless of rebirth and death. You see human bodies, wrapped

A Hindu pilgrim bathes ritually in the Ganges.

 The Hindu god Shiva is often portrayed as the Lord of the Dance.

and propped up on rickshaws, on their way to the water. As you get close to the Ganges, you notice three men with wild hair, squatting on a stone platform overlooking the river. You can't tell if they are wearing anything at all, and your tour guide explains that their bodies are smeared with ash and dried cow dung. On the right you see a large group of women bathing fully clothed in the water near the steps, and in a separate area close by a group of men in Indian loincloths. Both the men and the women have come to wash away their sins, and perhaps even the necessity of rebirth. The river seems polluted to you, but this means nothing to the thousands of Hindus who worship in it.

As you keep walking up the river, you notice a cluster of large fires and hundreds of large logs stacked up behind them, and you realize with a bit of a shock that you've reached Varanasi's open-air cremation area. In a scene that you'll remember for a long time, you see the steps of the Hindu funeral: members of the Dom group piling wood into a pyre and laying on it a body that has just been dipped into the Ganges, a son lighting a pyre, priests intoning ancient scriptures as a body begins to burn, Doms tending a body for three hours to burn it as fully as possible and then pushing the cremated remains into the river to float away. To die and be cremated in Varanasi is thought to bring automatic liberation from constant rebirth after death. Your group must stand respectfully at the top of the steps, where you have a better view.

In the evening, you join your guide at the shore of the Ganges to witness the happy Aarti ceremony that is part of the evening religious devotions to Shiva. The celebrative music and dancing, and small candles lit on miniature "boats" and put into the river to memorialize the dead, soothe your spirits and make for a good, inspiring end to a challenging day.

If this is your first encounter with the Hindu religion, you may become bewildered by all its varied beliefs and practices. Calling something a "religion" usually implies a unified system of belief and practice, but Hinduism has little obvious unity. It has no human founder, defined core beliefs, common scripture that guides all

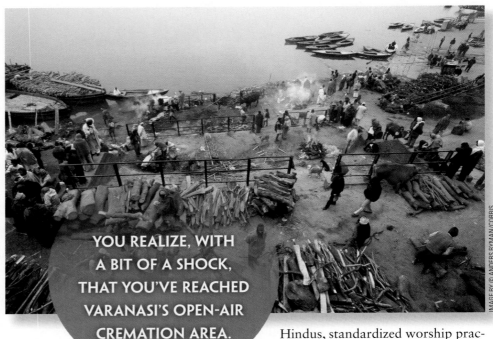

YOU REALIZE, WITH A BIT OF A SHOCK, THAT YOU'VE REACHED VARANASI'S OPEN-AIR CREMATION AREA.

IMAGE BY © ANDERS RYMAN/CORBIS

Hindus, standardized worship practice, or central authority. This diversity has led to what you may consider contradictions. For example:

- Hinduism has literally millions of gods, but many Hindus typically see one god behind them all, and some see only an impersonal Oneness in and beyond the universe.

- Hindus often control their bodies to pursue a hidden spiritual reality behind all physical things, seeking liberation from the endless cycle of rebirth of the soul after death and pursuing the peace that liberation brings here and now. At the same time, they joyously affirm bodily existence with a striking affirmation of sexuality, for example with erotic statues in a variety of temples.

- Many Hindus are strict vegetarians for religious reasons, but others eat meat on occasion, and some even sacrifice animals at Hindu temples.

- Hinduism teaches personal duties tied to one's place in a rather rigid social structure but allows some people to "drop out" of ordinary life completely to pursue individual religious goals.

- Hindus number around 900 million today in India, a number that includes some 220 million Indian "outcastes." The modern Indian state now considers them Hindus, but they are not considered as such by most other Hindus, nor do they often call themselves Hindus.

- Hinduism has a long history of three thousand years but constantly combines old traditions with new elements to produce a richer, more diverse faith and culture that bring ancient traditions into the twenty-first century.

In light of all this obvious diversity, what is the hidden unity of Hinduism that binds it together? Scholars have argued about this for more than one hundred years. The most common answer is this: Hinduism and its faithful have a reverence for the ancient Hindu scriptures called the *Vedas*, and they perform their caste duties. But this may seem a bit vague to you, and you should keep the question open as you study this chapter. In sum, encountering Hinduism is a bit like going to an Indian restaurant for the first time. When you see a wide variety of dishes on the menu, or even if you go to an Indian buffet, you realize that you can't taste them all. But at the end of the meal, you know that your experience in the restaurant gave you a good introduction to Indian cuisine.

 View a music video introduction to India.

> *Religion usually implies a unified system of belief and practice, but Hinduism has little obvious unity.*

Learning Outcome 3-1

Explain what *Hinduism* means and its strengths and weaknesses as a name.

3-1 The Name *Hinduism*

Like the names of some other world religions, the formal name of *Hinduism* came from outside the faith. *Hindu* first appears around 500 B.C.E. as the ancient Persian word for the Indus River and the inhabitants of its valley. From the 1300s C.E., invading Muslim rulers of northern India used "Hindu" for all non-Muslim Indians, whatever religion they practiced, to distinguish them from Indian converts to Islam. Beginning in the 1500s, European colonizers coming to India used it in its current sense—to mean the members of the supposedly single religion to which all Indians other than groups such as Muslims, Christians, and Zoroastrians belonged. From about 1800 on, *Hinduism* gradually became accepted by most Hindus in India as a valid name for their religion, especially to distinguish their religion from others. Thus, *Hinduism* is an umbrella term gradually imposed on Hindus and then accepted by them.

The approximately 2 million Hindus living in North America and the sizeable Hindu communities in other parts of south Asia (especially Bali, Indonesia), a few parts of Africa, and Great Britain also embrace this name. However, upper-class Hindus often refer to their religion as the "eternal teaching" or "eternal way of life." Some scholars of religion also question the adequacy of *Hinduism* as a name, preferring to speak of "Hinduisms." On the whole, it is fitting that a vague term such as *Hinduism* be used today for a religious tradition that has so much internal diversity. (This diversity is also reflected in the symbols of Hinduism; see the box "A Closer Look: Hindu Symbols.")

Learning Outcome 3-2

Explain how the main periods of Hinduism's history have shaped its present, especially its unity and diversity.

3-2 The Hindu Present as Shaped by Its Past

At dawn, four men in northern India sit around an outdoor fire pit and chant poetic hymns from memory. Nearby, outside a boundary rope that encloses the area of sacrifice, their teenage sons sit studying the ritual, quietly repeating the men's words and movements. Also outside the rope, women are pounding rice, cooking it, and shaping it into balls. The men occasionally pour a bit of liquefied butter from a wooden bowl onto the fire, which flares up for a moment. The men are singing ancient hymns to Agni, the Hindu god of fire, comparing him to the rising sun. After the sacrifice, the rice balls will first be offered to Agni, and then some will be eaten by the men (priests), then by their sons, the women, and the whole community. This ceremony from more than three thousand years ago is carried out with increasing frequency in India as interest in ancient Hindu practices grows. However, some Hindus are not happy about the re-creation of ancient sacrifices, preferring instead the adaptations of these rituals that have arisen in the course of Hindu history.

History is an important tool for those who study today's religions from a Western academic standpoint. We understand the present of religions by way of their

A Closer Look:

The Symbols of Hinduism

Although Hinduism has no official symbol, the common religious symbol sacred to Hindus is the mystical syllable **Om** (Figure 3.1). You will also find the spelling "Aum," and in fact the symbol is composed of the equivalent of our letters *a*, *u*, and *m*. Although as a syllable it has no literal meaning, Om symbolizes the fundamental hidden reality of the universe and is the basic spiritual sound the universe makes, particularly the sound of the world soul. Om is written daily in formal contexts and often pronounced at the beginning of religious reading or meditation. Many Hindus wear this symbol in jewelry, and it is found in family shrines and in temples. Pronounced in a deep, lengthy way, it can resonate throughout the body so that the sound of Brahman can penetrate to one's center of being.

Figure 3.1 Om

BONNIE VAN VOORST © CENGAGE LEARNING

Listen to Om.

You may be surprised, even shocked, to encounter the swastika (Figure 3.2) as a common, ancient symbol in Hinduism, Buddhism, and Jainism. *Swastika* is an ancient Indian word meaning "sign of good fortune." The swastika has "crooked" arms facing in a clockwise or counterclockwise direction (both directions are common in Asia). This feature of the arms extending in all directions suggests to Hindus the universal presence of the world soul. It is continually rotating like the wheel it resembles, symbolizing the eternal nature of ultimate truth. This symbol is often found on Hindu, Jain, and Buddhist temples, and it is worn on neck pendants as a good-luck charm.

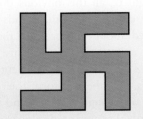

Figure 3.2 The swastika

BONNIE VAN VOORST © CENGAGE LEARNING

In 1935, the Nazi Party of Germany adopted the swastika as its symbol of the party and the nation—with no historical connection to the Indian swastika and, of course, with no intent to endorse Hindu teachings. It is still used today by some neo-Nazi groups. So we have an odd situation: For people of many Asian religions, the swastika is a much-loved symbol; for people in the Western world, the swastika is much despised.

---

past. Although Hinduism must be understood historically as well, history itself is not an important concept in Hinduism. Hindus don't usually think of their religion in historical terms, preferring to look to the spiritual truths beyond historical events. They often look to cycles of change for individuals (for example, death and rebirth of the soul) and for the universe itself (repeated creation and dissolution), not to the kind of linear developmental process that "history" implies to Westerners. Nevertheless, studying Hinduism's past is valid and helpful, particularly because in Hinduism new developments reinterpret and update past practices rather than end them. In Hinduism today, we can see important beliefs and practices throughout the entire sweep of Indian history.

> *Hindus don't often think of their religion in historical terms, but look to the spiritual truths beyond historical events.*

3-2a The Vedic Period (1500–600 B.C.E.)

Around 2500 B.C.E., an **Indus Valley civilization** thrived in northwest India, in what is now the nation of Pakistan (see Map 3.1). It centered in two city-states on the Indus River, Harappa (huh-RAHP-uh) and Mohenjo-Daro (moh-HEN-joh-DAHR-oh). The Indus Valley inhabitants were a dark-skinned people whom scholars connect with today's Indians called **Dravidians**. (About 25 percent of Indians today are Dravidians.) This civilization traded

Om (Aum) [OHM] Spoken syllable symbolizing the fundamental hidden reality of the universe

swastika [SWAHS-tee-kuh] Indian symbol widely used as a good-luck charm

Indus Valley civilization Culture of northwest India that thrived before the coming of the Aryans

Dravidians [druh-VID-ee-uhnz] Dark-skinned peoples of the Indus Valley civilization who now live mostly in south India

internationally and had a high material culture. Harappa and Mohenjo-Daro were carefully planned and even had a sewage system connected to private houses. Scholars have not yet been able to decipher their system of writing. The religion of the Indus Valley civilization is also largely unknown to us. Archaeologists have found many female deity figurines, so it is thought that the Indus Valley people probably worshiped goddesses of fertility in connection with their farming. The cows on their official seals, a variety of stone objects probably used in worship, and sculptures of people in seated meditation may suggest religious practices that influenced Hinduism. But until much more is known about these and other features of Indus Valley religion, its effect on Hinduism must remain uncertain.

The Indus Valley civilization was in decline around 1500 B.C.E., when nomadic tribes who called themselves **Aryans**, or "noble ones," migrated into northwest India from their home between the Black Sea and the Caspian Sea. These Aryans must be distinguished from the modern Nazi misuse of this term, which has been identified with a Nordic-Germanic people claimed to be of a superior race. Moreover, some Hindus dispute the Aryan migration/invasion, unattested as it is in Hindu scripture and lore, so Hindu scholars sometimes call it the "Aryan Invasion Theory." The Aryans were light-skinned cattle herders and warriors with horse-drawn chariots. They were a part of the migration from central Asia into both India and Europe; hence the term *Indo-Europeans* is much more common than *Aryans*. They soon took control of the Indus Valley peoples.

These Indo-Europeans spoke Sanskrit, a language related to European languages, including English. They had oral collections called the **Vedas**, which form the foundation of Hinduism. The *Vedas* represent a diversified and continuous oral tradition that extends from around 1200 to 800 B.C.E.; they were written down much later. The earliest *Vedas*, four in number, were "books of knowledge" consisting of hymns to various deities, instructions for sacrifice, songs for sacrifice, and spells to bring on blessings and keep away evil.

Listen to a *Rig Veda* hymn chanted in Sanskrit.

WWW.CEPOLINA.COM

The Indus Valley people's official seals featured the cows still venerated today in Hinduism.

The heart of Vedic religion was sacrifice by means of fire, accompanied by sung praises and requests to the gods. Vedic gods living in the skies or in heaven play a role in human life as forces of nature, forces that can be influenced by sacrifice. In general, Vedic sacrificial rituals aim at aiding and strengthening deities, who then strengthen the world, so that those who offer sacrifice may prosper. In this worldview the gods and humans are partners in a "circle of life" that maintains the ongoing creative processes of the world. Both need each other to thrive. The Vedic stage of Hinduism affirms the world, accepting the physical aspects of the world as good and proper. At the daily and domestic level, the simple **Agnihotra** ritual to the sun was performed by the heads of households three times each day and is still common in India. Even given its adaptations over time, the Agnihotra is arguably the oldest continually practiced ritual in the world. Agni (AHG-nee), the god of fire, carried the sacrificial offerings to Indra, the king of the gods and both a war god and a thunder god; to Varuna (vah-ROON-uh), the god guaranteeing moral order; and to Brahma (BRAH-muh), the god of creation. Many other deities, mostly male and some female, are also associated with the physical and spiritual forces of nature.

A key person of Vedic times was the **rishi**, or "seer" of the divine, a priest who was able to commune directly with the gods. The rishis achieved an altered state of consciousness in which they could see and hear the gods. To reach this state, they drank a hallucinogenic drug called soma, pressed out perhaps from a mushroom. When the rishi drank soma as a part of

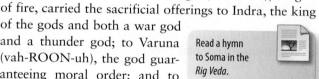

Read a hymn to Soma in the *Rig Veda*.

Aryans [AIR-ee-unzs] "Noble ones," Indo-European peoples who migrated into northwest India

Vedas [VAY-duhs] Hindu "books of knowledge" consisting of *Rig, Yajur, Sama,* and *Atharva Vedas*

Agnihotra [AHG-nee-HOH-trah] Ancient prayer to the sun recited by the head of the household

rishi [REE-shee] "Seer" of the divine and writer of the four *Vedas*

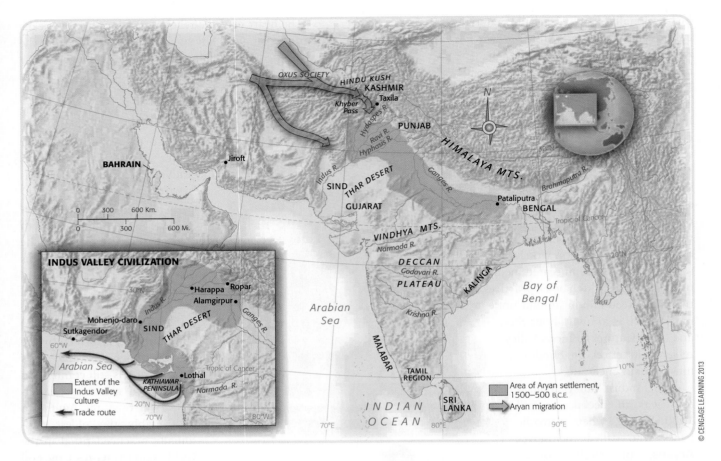

Map 3.1

Indus Valley Civilization and Aryan Migrations

The Indus Valley culture emerged in the city-states of the Indus River basin. It was in decline when the Aryan (Indo-European) peoples began migrating into India around 1500 B.C.E.

Vedic sacrifice, he took a trip to the realm of the deities and experienced their hidden truth. He then composed hymns in their praise, hymns that came into the *Rig Veda.* Soma even became a god, so powerful were its effects. This quest for a direct individual encounter with ultimate, hidden truth has persisted in the Hindu tradition to this day, although the encounter itself has changed. No longer is it an encounter with all the gods, but a discovery of an ultimate reality hidden in one's soul or an ecstatic devotion to one's chosen god. The means of achieving it have also changed (now with intense meditation rather than with a drug), as have those who can achieve it (no longer limited to soma drinkers, but now open to all).

Near the end of the Vedic period, for reasons not clear to us, the Vedic system of sacrifice grew into a dominant power in Aryan society. The power of

> *"The sun would not rise if the priests did not sacrifice." —Famous saying of Vedic times*

sacrifice ceased to be dependent on the gods' favor as influenced by the humble prayer and household sacrifices of ordinary Aryans; now what was important was the faultless priestly performance of increasingly more elaborate sacrificial rituals. At least sixteen priests, and many more assistants, were needed for the regular sacrifices. Sacrifice became a requirement for the maintenance of the world itself rather than just a means of attaining blessings such as children, long life, and prosperity. A famous saying of the time claimed that "the sun would not rise if the priest did not sacrifice" (*Satapatha Brahmana* 1.3.1). Religious and social power was consolidated in the hands of one type of priest among the many, those who called themselves Brahmins. The books detailing sacrifice and its power are called the *Brahmanas,* "Brahmin books." This concentration of power in the hands of the Brahmin priesthood, perhaps combined with other factors such as the influence of surviving indigenous Indus Valley religious practices, would spark change for Hinduism in its next period of history. Furthermore, this change would catalyze the birth of a new religion, Buddhism, which would transform religion in all of ancient Asia and, in modern times, the world.

3-2b The Upanishadic Period (600–400 B.C.E.)

In the first millennium B.C.E., Hindus added another dimension that has endured to this day. This is the quest for knowledge so deep and sacred that to know it is to bring eternal freedom from this world of appearances and constant change. The **Upanishads**, philosophical Hindu scriptures from this period, are primarily dialogues between teachers and young students who seek this sacred knowledge through a withdrawal from ordinary life. These teachers and students renounced the Vedic value put on ordinary life and pursued extraordinary truths. They criticized the Vedic rituals as unnecessary, and they rejected the rising social and economic power of the Brahmin priesthood. Their criticism of Vedic sacrifice was so effective that its only remnants surviving today are the relatively simple ones often incorporated into newer rites, especially weddings, funerals, other traditional rites of passage, and basic daily sacrifices. The *Upanishads* urge physical and mental rigors that become increasingly important for Hindu practice. Buddhism and Jainism, which will be considered in later chapters, arose at this time in India to teach a single way to enlightenment, but each one denied key Hindu teachings and practices. Hindus gradually rejected these new movements in favor of Hinduism's inclusive approach.

> For most Hindus, Brahman is spiritual but is not a spirit.

The *Upanishads* teach that underlying reality is a spiritual essence called **Brahman**, a single "world soul" that is the foundation of all physical matter, energy, time and space, and being itself—in short, of everything in and beyond this universe. (This term should not be confused with the Vedic creator god Brahma or the Brahmin priests.) Although it is cosmic, Brahman is present in all people in the form of the **atman**, a person's innermost self or soul. In other words, each person's innermost soul is a part of the one world soul. For most (but not all) Hindus, Brahman is not a personal being, as "world soul" might imply; it is spiritual, but it is not *a* spirit. The religious quest in the *Upanishads* involves understanding that Brahman and one's own atman are one and the same. The realization of this truth, which is the deepest form of self-understanding, brings freedom from ignorance and misery, and liberation from the endless cycle of **reincarnation** of one's atman. Unlike the Vedic hymns, the *Upanishads* do not affirm the physical world as real and good, but rather aim at transcending it.

This goal of liberating one's soul by perfect knowledge of it, and the use of physical and meditational techniques to achieve this knowledge, became important aspects of Hinduism. These techniques gradually coalesced into a system called **yoga**, Sanskrit for "yoke." Yoga is an ancient meditational practice that yokes the body and mind in the quest for religious deliverance. (You may know it as an exercise and meditation system, but it is much more than that for Hindus.) Yoga aims at removing humans from the overwhelming mental flow of the material world, if only momentarily, in order to recapture their original spiritual purity.

Upanishads [oo-PAHN-ih-shahds] Philosophical scriptures at the end of the Vedic period

Brahman [BRAH-muhn] "World soul," the foundation of all physical matter, energy, time and space, and being itself

atman [AHT-muhn] Person's innermost self or soul

reincarnation Cycle of rebirth of one's atman after death, in a different body

yoga [YOH-guh] Ancient meditational practice that yokes the body and mind in the quest for religious deliverance

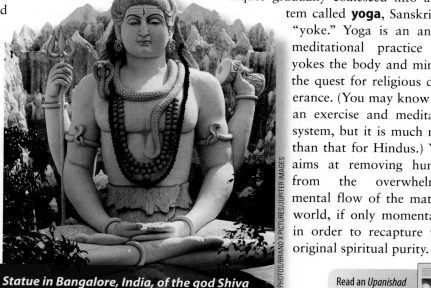

Statue in Bangalore, India, of the god Shiva meditating in the lotus yoga position

© DINODIA PHOTOS/BRAND X PICTURES/JUPITER IMAGES

Read an *Upanishad* praising meditation over sacrifice.

3-2c The Classical Period (400 B.C.E.–600 C.E.)

A growing number of conversions to Buddhism and Jainism was a threat to Hinduism. The Mauryan (MOHR-yuhn) dynasty that governed north India was pro-Buddhist, and its famous king, Ashoka (ah-SHOH-kuh), extended Aryan rule and Buddhist influence into all of India. Hindus dealt with this threat in a way that has become typical of Hinduism even today, by integrating foreign elements into the broader Hindu tradition. The new teachings of the *Upanishads* were seen as compatible with the earlier *Vedas* and accepted into the Vedic body of scripture.

In addition, Hindus incorporated a variety of religious practices of lower, non-Aryan populations that were converting to new religions such as Buddhism. To put it another way, the Sanskrit tradition of the *Vedas*—for the educated upper classes and the "high" gods—took in and controlled the tradition of the non-Aryan lower classes and the "low gods" of local village and tribal deities. As a result, local deities became a part of the village shrines and temples. The local deities were identified with the older gods, or regarded as their incarnations, or became one of their "family members." The non-Aryans were taken into this system, some into the lower castes and others into the "outcastes." This development solidified Brahmin power and religious teachings, and eventually stemmed the conversions of non-Aryans to other religions. However, conversions to Buddhism and Christianity in particular are still a difficult issue when they occur today among lower classes in India.

Goddess sculpture at a temple in Mathura, northern India

Around 400 B.C.E., as the wandering Aryans finally settled into towns and cities, they built permanent homes for themselves and temples for their gods. Before that, all sacrifice was done outdoors, with sacrifice as nomadic as the Aryan tribes themselves. During the Classical period the two great Hindu epics still popular today were written: the *Mahabharata* (MAH-huh-BAH-rah-tuh) and the *Ramayana* (rah-MAH-yah-nuh). Both relate royal rivalries, perhaps reflecting political turmoil during this period as different Aryan clans struggled for territorial power in the areas where they settled. They feature a tension between the aim of upholding the world found in the *Vedas* and that of isolating a person from society in order to achieve individual liberation found in the newer Upanishadic tradition. Both epics emphasize that social and moral obligation must be maintained, and that rulers acting in the Hindu tradition have a key role in maintaining it. However, many characters in these epics have renounced the world, live alone in forests or in small settlements, and are said to possess extraordinary powers to bless or to curse. The epics' heroes almost always treat these world renouncers, or **sadhus**—of whom we will speak more below—with great respect and learn much from them.

Another solution to this tension is found in the *Mahabharata*, particularly the part of it known by the separate title of **Bhagavad Gita**, "Song of Heaven" or "Song of the Lord." In the *Gita,* the god Krishna appears to the warrior-class leader Arjuna (ar-JOON-ah), to convince him to do his caste duty of fighting, but in a way in which he understands and controls its effect on him. The *Gita*'s solution is a masterful blend of world-affirming action and world-denying detachment from the results of one's actions. True renunciation does not involve renouncing socially responsible actions. Rather, it involves cutting off a desire for the results of actions even as one fulfills one's social duty. For example, this means for Arjuna that he must fight well but not care about whether he wins or loses. Selfless action without desire for reward is true renunciation for the *Gita*, and no tension should exist between one's dual obligation to support the world and to seek individual liberation.

sadhus [SAH-doos]
Renunciants, also known as "holy men"

Bhagavad Gita
[BAH-guh-vahd GEE-tuh]
"Song of the Lord"; a long poem on religious duty in the *Mahabharata*

True renunciation does not mean renouncing socially responsible actions.

The *Gita* recognizes that this is difficult and that people must use yoga and other disciplines to accomplish it. This ingenious approach has con-tributed to the *Bhagavad Gita*'s status as the best-loved of Hindu scriptures today.

 View a Kathakali performance.

A different genre of literature also concerned with society arose at this time, the law codes—particularly the single most important code, the **Laws of Manu**. What epics do in a liter-ary way, the law codes do in a formally legal way. They carefully restrict renunci-ation of the world to older males. One must earn the right to renounce the world by first being in the world as a good student, then as a husband and father. Opting out of ordinary life can only be done after one has success-fully engaged in it. Underlying all the law books is the strong Hindu affirmation that doing one's duty for an orderly, stable society is necessary for this world and after one's death leads to better reincarnation. This social order involves the proper functioning of the main social-religious classes that arose in Vedic times, as well as the proper observance of interaction within and among these classes. Women belong to the various classes even though their social roles are not as determined by their class as their hus-bands' roles are. We will consider these classes more fully below.

3-2d The Devotional Period (600 C.E.–Present)

The next period in Hinduism is characterized by three developments: the rise of devotional movements, espe-cially those devoted to Shiva (SHEE-vuh), Vishnu (VISH-new), and the Goddess; Tantrism; and the rise of Hindu reform movements. Of these developments, the first is so influential that it has given its name to the entire period.

Devotion to one's chosen god is a main way of being Hindu. Devotion, or **bhakti**, enters the Hindu tradition as early as the *Bhagavad Gita*, where devotion to Krishna brings a cognitive mental discipline to guide action in the world. Around the sixth century C.E. in southern India, advocates of bhakti praised Shiva and Vishnu in emotional poetry and song. This devotional experience involves often-uncontrollable joy in one's

WWW.CEPOLINA.COM

An actor in traditional clothing and makeup performs part of an Indian epic.

god, sometimes with fainting, frenzy, weeping, and ecstatic speech. By the seventeenth century, bhakti had spread into most Hindu traditions, where it remains. The devotional movement gradually coalesced into three movements, one each for Shiva, Vishnu, and Shakti (SHAHK-tee), the Goddess.

Devotion is typically described in its poetry and song as deep love for one's god. Devotees will sacrifice anything to revel with their god in divine happiness. A well-known example is the followers of the cowherd Krishna, women who abandon their husbands to frolic in the forest with Krishna. Women have played an important role in the rise of devotional movements. Two famous women devotees, Mahadeviyakka (MAH-huh-DEH-vee-YAHK-uh) and Mirabai (MEER-uh-bigh), were both unhappy in traditional marriages and eventually left their hus-bands to devote themselves entirely to a god. Despite this practice, Hinduism finds a way to balance devotion to a god and renunciation of the world. The language of love that breaks Hindu social rules is made a sym-bol of deep love within these rules. Even holy men who have renounced everyday life typically wear devotional marks to Vishnu or Shiva.

> *Hinduism finds a way to balance devotion to a god and renunciation of the world.*

The **Tantras**, the basis of the second major devel-opment of this period, are hundreds of writings based on practices that arose outside the elite Brahmin tradi-tion. Many Westerners today associate Tantrism with exotic sexual practices, but it is much broader than

Laws of Manu [MAH-new] Main Hindu law code

bhakti [BAHK-tee] Devotion, particularly in a devotional movement or group

Tantras [TAHN-truhs] Writings in the Tantric movement of Hinduism

that. The *Tantras* often criticize the religious "establishment," especially the Brahmins. However, the *Tantras* can also affirm traditional Hindu teachings. For example, an individual is a microcosm of the universe, and by knowing the sacred "geography" and life forces of one's body one may, using yoga, reach liberation from reincarnation. The *Tantras* speak of a right-handed path that all Hindus can take, one that employs **mantras** (short sacred words or sounds used widely in prayer or meditation, not just in Tantrism), sacred diagrams called *mandalas,* and ritual techniques based on body geography. The left-handed path, appropriate for those with an especially adventurous, fearless temperament, centers on ritual actions strictly forbidden in Hinduism, gaining liberation by transcending the tension between good and evil. For instance, by expressing lust in sexual intercourse with a forbidden woman, a man may seek to overcome lust. Left-handed Tantrism is highly controversial among many Hindus, but right-handed Tantrism is commonly approved.

We turn now to the next topic in the Devotional period: Hindu reform or revisionism. Hinduism was not, on the whole, so affected by Islam during Muslim rule in India that it had to make adaptive changes. However, with the arrival of European colonizers and Christian missionaries in the nineteenth century, their interaction with Hindus led to Hindu movements for change. Attempts were made to change Hinduism spiritually and socially, ending practices that the majority of Hindu reformers found objectionable: the harshest features of the caste system, "superstitions" such as Vedic astrology, popular blessings and curses, the worship of images, and the like.

- Rammohan (RAHM-moh-hahn) Roy (1774–1833), perhaps the world's first scholar of comparative religion, had watched in shock as his sister burned to death on the funeral pyre of her husband (a practice we will discuss in section 3-4d). He was dismayed at what he saw as the harmful effects of caste divisions. He founded the Society of Brahmanism in 1828. Roy claimed that the *Upanishads* reveal the one God of all people. The One was to be worshiped through meditation, quiet worship, and a moral life, not by the emotions of devotional Hinduism.

- Dayananda Sarasvati (DAH-yuh-NAN-duh SAH-rahs-VAH-tee) founded the "Noble Society" (Arya Samaj) in 1875. Dayananda found the pure, original essence of Hinduism in the *Vedas* as centering on monotheism and a reasoned morality. He opposed much of devotional Hinduism and also rejected Islam and Christianity. His movement, along with Ram Roy's, gained little steady acceptance from Hindus.

- Ramakrishna (RAH-muh-KRISH-nah), who lived from 1836 to 1886, taught traditional Hindu beliefs and spiritual techniques. He was a devoted temple priest of the goddess Kali, but he worshiped other Hindu deities as well—even the God of Christians and Muslims. He incorporated selected Western ideas and religions into a Hindu context and did not attempt to change Hinduism by making it conform to Western ideas of religion or rationalism. This program was widely effective and led to Ramakrishna's lasting fame in Hinduism.

The twentieth-century Indian movement for religious reform and independence from the British Empire—particularly its religious and political leader, Mohandas K. Gandhi (moh-HAHN-dahs GAHN-dee; 1869–1948)—shows once again the persistence and adaptability of Hinduism. Gandhi is widely known by his honorific name, Mahatma ("great soul"), and he certainly was one of the great figures of the twentieth century. The civil rights movement in the United States and South Africa is heavily indebted to him for nonviolent resistance as a religious-political program. Although Gandhi drew on different religious traditions, especially nonviolence in Jainism (*ahimsa,* found to a lesser extent in Hinduism) and Christianity (the teaching of Jesus on forgiving one's enemies while refusing to cooperate with them in evil), he was thoroughly Hindu. He emphasized Hindu teachings and practices that the masses could appreciate—such as devotion, prayer, and trust in divine grace—and combined this with strong moral reasoning and action. His favorite book was the *Bhagavad Gita,* which provided the religious foundation for his system of "persisting in the truth." This approach involves expressing the truth in every action, no matter what the result and regardless of possible rewards. Acting for social good without any regard for personal reward is a main point of the *Gita,* but Gandhi read the *Gita* as a text urging nonviolence, not war. He forbade violence as a tool in his political campaigns; instead, he urged self-control, negotiation and tactical compromises, and even self-sacrifice.

Gandhi's lifestyle drew on the renouncer tradition in Hinduism. At middle age he practiced strict poverty and later in life took a vow of celibacy. He wore little clothing and lived on a bare minimum of food, becoming very

mantra [MAHN-truh]
Short sacred formula used in prayer or meditation

thin. This austere lifestyle built spiritual strength for the liberation of Hindus from caste hatred, colonialism, and widespread poverty. The nonviolent movement Gandhi led secured independence from Great Britain in 1947, but to his sorrow this independence resulted in not one nation but two: India and the officially Muslim nation of Pakistan, to which many Indian Muslims migrated. He was assassinated by a Hindu in 1948, after rising complaints that he was too much of a pluralist and too accommodating to Muslims—some Hindus had even mocked him as "Mohammed Gandhi." Unfortunately, his murder increased the tension between Hindus and Muslims—something that challenges the whole Indian subcontinent even today—but his positive legacy continues in India and throughout the world.

The government of modern India has tolerated all religions and has brought some significant improvement to the lives of the lower classes and the outcastes. This has provoked a religious-political reaction widely but controversially referred to as "Hindu fundamentalism." For the members of Hindu fundamentalist groups, Hinduism is just as much a symbol of national political identity as a religion. The main group of this type is the Indian People's Party, often known by its Hindi-language initials, BJP. The principal concern of members is the perceived danger to the Hindu majority by conversions among untouchables and other Hindus, which they see as a threat to what they call the "Hindu-ness," **Hindutva**, of India. They have enacted laws restricting efforts at conversion by Muslims and Christians. In 1992, a Muslim mosque in the city of Ayodhya was destroyed by a mob of militant Hindus, and then rioting by Muslims and Hindus killed more than a thousand people.

ISTOCKPHOTO.COM/NILESH BHANGE

Gandhi's image is known to most Indians today through their currency—ironic in view of Gandhi's self-imposed poverty.

SOME HINDUS MOCKINGLY NICKNAMED MOHANDAS GANDHI "MOHAMMED GANDHI" BECAUSE THEY THOUGHT HE WAS TOO ACCOMMODATING TO MUSLIMS.

Read about Gandhi's views on the *Bhagavad Gita*.

Hindutva [hihn-DOOT-vah] "Hindu-ness" of India as promoted by modern right-wing political parties

From 1998 to 2004, the BJP was in control of the Indian government, with a leader of the BJP as prime minister. It was during this time that India openly deployed nuclear weapons, prompting Pakistan to do the same. Although they now are out of power in the national government, the BJP and its supporters still control a few Indian states and have a strong influence on the nation. They continue to promote Hindutva. For example, in 2007 they got the Indian government to give up a plan to build a shipping canal between India and Sri Lanka, claiming that this canal would destroy an ancient, holy "bridge" to Sri Lanka that Hindus believe was built by the gods. Hindus typically see Hindu fundamentalism as contrary to the generally inclusive, tolerant spirit of Hinduism. This feeling will probably dampen the group's long-term growth potential.

Read an article about Narendra Modi, current leader of the BJP.

The Taj Mahal, built in the 1600s as a Muslim tomb, has become the architectural symbol of India and is widely considered one of the most beautiful buildings in the world.

© AND INC./SHUTTERSTOCK.COM

3-3 Essential Hindu Teachings

In central India, a woman offers prayer and a sacrifice of food in a temple dedicated to Santoshi Ma (san-TOH-shee mah), or "Mother of Satisfaction." Santoshi Ma is a goddess of prosperity—especially the wife's prosperity, including modern appliances in her home—and the woman in the temple is asking for a more bearable load of housework. Santoshi Ma was unknown until a few devout Hindus discerned her existence in the 1960s. A few temples were then built in her honor, and in 1975 she was featured in a blockbuster Hindi-language film, *Hail Santoshi Ma*. The film presented a mythology for Santoshi Ma's divine birth and growth as the daughter of Ganesha, and featured a simple devotional ritual to gain her blessing. Santoshi Ma became an important, much-loved goddess practically overnight, the first time that modern mass media have influenced the rise of a deity. Because the establishment of new deities has a strong precedent in Hinduism, Santoshi Ma is now well integrated into the pantheon of Hindu deities, and her many devotees see her as one with all the other goddesses.

Watch the preview of *Hail Santoshi Ma*.

In this section, we will discuss the main beliefs of Hindus about the world, human society, and the individual. We begin with a treatment of the main deities in the three devotional movements we encountered in the previous section.

3-3a Main Deities in the Three Devotional Movements

Shiva. Shiva is the god who meditates in his home in the Himalayas. He is a fearsome deity with tangled hair and an ash-covered body. Animal skins are his clothing, and he carries snakes and human skulls. He repeatedly burns the god of love to ashes when the god tries to distract him. In the cosmic cycle of creation, destruction, and re-creation, Shiva guides and empowers destruction.

lingam [LING-gahm] Symbol in Shiva's shrines probably of erect phallus

However, Shiva devotees today view this destruction positively, as a symbol of the removal of obstacles to salvation; destruction is a necessary part of re-creation. The destructive side of Shiva is depicted in the popular bronze statues called Shiva Nataraja (NAH-tuh-RAHJ-uh), "Shiva the Lord of the Dance" (see the photo on page 62). Shiva is surrounded by fire, which destroys in order to purify. He embodies the world-renouncing side of Hinduism and provides a model for this aspect of the tradition.

The sons and consorts of Shiva are particularly appealing. Much of Shiva's mythology tells of his marriage to the goddess Parvati (PAHR-vah-tee), stories in which a feminine, life-affirming side of Shiva emerges. His other consorts are Durga, the goddess of death, and Kali, the frightening destroyer of evil. His son Ganesha (or simply Ganesh), the elephant-headed god who clears away obstacles to success, is one of the best-loved Hindu divinities. Ganesha's image is found in nearly every Hindu shop, restaurant, and office around the world. Shiva's special image in his temples is the **lingam** ("sign"). The meaning of this is disputed; it may depict the erect phallus, which celebrates Shiva's power, but for Hindus this meaning is not important. Shaivites often worship Shiva by pouring milk over the lingam. Another main symbol of Shiva is the bull Nandi, whose statue is often found, and venerated, outside his temples. Shiva is also represented by the trident, and his followers often wear horizontal stripes painted on their forehead and display a trident.

Watch a video on Shiva and Vishnu.

Vishnu. Vishnu is a cosmic king who lives in blissful splendor in his heavenly palace. He supervises universal order and prosperity, protecting and preserving the world. When needed, he descends to the world in various incarnations to defeat enemies—both humans and deities. Vishnu is a gracious god, revered by his devotees with loving loyalty. His female counterpart is Lakshmi (LAHK-shmee), the much-loved goddess of fortune and wealth. Vishnu is often depicted with blue skin, because he once killed a five-headed snake; the snake's venom that he took into himself turned his skin blue. To his followers, this blue color is a symbol of his power.

Vishnu's familiar incarnations are Rama, hero of the *Ramayana*, and Krishna, hero of the *Bhagavad Gita*. Both Rama and Krishna are today among the best-loved Hindu gods. This has ironically led to Vishnu himself being seen as too remote to intervene directly on behalf of an individual in trouble. Devotees of Vishnu who

The deceptively lovely Durga, goddess of death

yoni [YOH-nee]
Symbol probably of the human female genitalia representing the feminine power of the cosmos

focused devotional movements, how do Hindus put it all together in a way that makes everyday sense for them? Whether a Hindu honors Vishnu, Shiva, or Shakti, that particular deity is for her or him the sole and the highest god, whereas other Hindu gods are lower forms. Thus, one god is thought to appear at various levels. At the "top" is a nonpersonal absolute, Brahman, the world soul that cannot be described. Brahman is so comprehensive

have renounced the world typically wear two vertical markings on the forehead that come together on the bridge of the nose.

Shakti and the Goddess. The worship of Shakti and the feminine side of the divine originates in the *Vedas*. The *Rig Veda* portrays Shakti as the powerful upholder of the universe. She is the sister of Krishna and is also Shiva's wife. Shakti is worshiped as Devi (DEH-vee), "the Goddess," who is one with Brahman. The literature of Shaktism is found in the *Tantras*; they have a high view of women and oppose ways in which the caste system holds down women. In some regions of India, the Great Goddess (*Mahadevi*) is revered as the supreme divinity. Female power in the Goddess alone is seen as the ultimate cause of the creation, preservation, and end of the world.

Like Shiva, the Goddess is venerated both in her gentle, motherly aspects and in her cruel, dangerous, and erotic aspects. Accordingly, she is honored under a wide variety of divine forms. The best known are Lakshmi, the goddess of wealth and consort of Vishnu; the black goddess Kali ("dark one"), riding on a lion; and the demon-slaying goddess Durga. The **yoni**, probably a stone representation of the human female genitalia, is a symbol of the feminine power of the cosmos. The lingam is often set within the yoni to suggest that the universe is powered by a combination of the male and the female.

With Hinduism's millions of deities—traditionally put at 330 million!—and even with these three more

Ganesha with Om on his forehead

that some Hindu scriptures describe it as encompassing everything that exists. Brahman manifests itself in various personal high divinities that create the world (Brahma), maintain it (Vishnu), and destroy it again (Shiva). In practice, however, followers of one deity will attribute all three functions to him or her, as our treatment above suggests. They see all other gods as standing under their god or as further manifestations of that deity. Although the teaching of the ultimate world soul plays little or no role in the religious everyday—it's hard to pray, sacrifice, express emotion to something that is unknowable—it leads to most Hindus seeing no problem in acknowledging other Hindu traditions, and sometimes even other religions, as authentic paths to the divine.

Lingam set in a yoni, receiving worship to Shiva

© GRIGORY KUBATYAN/SHUTTERSTOCK.COM

View a gallery of the visual traits of Hindu gods.

the *Bhagavad Gita*. Following the social and religious rules of one's caste leads to better reincarnation; neglecting it leads to a lesser reincarnation. For a man to leave his caste for a higher one is unthinkable. Opposing the caste system itself leads to a bad reincarnation. One could find oneself an outcaste, a lower animal, or an insect in one's next life. This has led to a remarkably conservative social structure and explains why, even today, traditional Hindu values often frustrate attempts at social change for women, the lower castes, and Dalits.

3-3b Hindu Doctrinal Concepts

Dharma is the foundational concept in Hinduism, a wide-ranging term for righteousness, law, duty, moral teachings, religion itself, or the order in the universe. Dharma is also the god who embodies and promotes right order and living. The ancient *Vedas* emphasize the order of the cosmos, and dharma builds on it by emphasizing the correct ordering of human life. Dharma is more than a set of cosmic-order ideas applying in the same way to all Hindus. It's specific to one's place in the world: one's social position, caste membership, stage of life, and gender. The dharma of a member of the warrior class is distinct from that of a laborer; the dharma of a youth differs from that of the father of a family, and a husband's dharma differs from his wife's.

A Hindu must conform primarily to his or her class and caste dharma. Hindu scripture teaches this, and it is a particular theme in

dharma [DAHR-muh]
Righteousness, law, duty, moral teaching, order in the universe; also, the first goal of life in Hinduism

A soul, symbolized by a ray of light, travels to enlightenment through seven different lives.

© THEIMAGEWORKS.COM

Hinduism divides life into four stages, each with its own particular dharma—what is seen as right for each stage. Some classes, and most women, do not need to observe such dharma, but the stages are an important aspect of what a Hindu would consider dharma to be. These four stages will be dealt with in more detail in section 3-4b.

Samsara is the cycle of reincarnation, endured as a hardship by the spiritual essence of all living things. The **jiva** (individual soul) is subject to reincarnation, because it is only the jiva that earns reward or punishment in the next reincarnation (see the upcoming discussion of karma). One's atman, the deeper soul identical with Brahman, is not subject to karma, but it goes along with the jiva. It travels with the jiva in reincarnation but is beyond it. Because actions in life involve choices, at every moment an individual is capable of making the choices to ensure a good situation in the next life. The *Brihadaranyaka* (BREE-hahd-uh-RUN-yah-kuh) *Upanishad* describes this well: "An individual creates for himself his next life as a result of his desires, hopes, aspirations, failures, disappointments, achievements and actions performed during this life of his. Just as a caterpillar gets its front feet firmly on the next leaf before it leaves the one it is on, a soul creates its next life before it departs the present one." This leads us to a fuller consideration of karma.

Karma is derived from the Sanskrit for "deeds" and is related to one's behavior in preceding lives. After a person's death, her or his spiritual essence is reborn in another life if any karma is attached to it. Whether one is rich or poor, healthy or sick, male or female, intelligent or not, talented or untalented, a member of a high or low caste, a Hindu or not, and endowed with many other life-defining traits depends on the karma inherited from the lives that have gone before. Karma explains all human inequalities. Although the conditions of an individual's current life are determined in advance by her or his deeds in previous lives, individuals must assume personal responsibility for their present actions and the associated consequences. (See "A Closer Look: Popular Misunderstandings of *Karma, Mantra, Guru,* and *Avatar.*")

Moksha means the "liberation" from rebirth that comes with the entry of the individual soul (atman) into the highest reality (Brahman). The idea of reincarnating endlessly, or even attaining eternal life as an individual, is abhorrent to Hindus. The ultimate goal is to merge one's atman with Brahman, like a drop of water enters the Indian Ocean. To be liberated from samsara, one must be rid not only of bad karma, but also of good karma; any karma at all causes rebirth after death. Although actions take place, if the self that does them is not egoistic, karmic results cannot attach to them. Paradoxically, one must even give up the desire to achieve liberation in order to reach it. (To illustrate this from everyday life, if you've ever had trouble falling asleep at night, you may have found that to fall asleep you must give

> *"Just as a caterpillar gets its front feet firmly on the next leaf before it leaves the one it is on, a soul creates its next life before it departs the present one."*
> —Brihadaranyaka Upanishad

samsara [sahm-SAH-ruh] Cycle of reincarnation

jiva [JEE-vuh] Individual, personal soul that collects karma and is subject to reincarnation

karma [KAHR-muh] Deeds or acts as they influence reincarnation

moksha [MOHK-shuh] Liberation from rebirth and samsara

Garlands for the gods for sale outside a Hindu temple

© DINODIA PHOTOS/BRAND X PICTURES/JUPITER IMAGES

Popular Misunderstandings of *Karma, Mantra, Guru,* and *Avatar*

Karma is not "fate," as we often hear today in North America and Europe. Fate is a random, uncontrollable power that determines human actions and events. Karma is the *opposite* of what "fate" means in the Western world. In karma, each person generates her or his own reward or punishment, which comes in one's condition after reincarnation. Also, one hears muddled talk about "group" karma—for example, Hollywood actress Sharon Stone's suggestion that the 2008 earthquake in China that killed seventy thousand ordinary people was some sort of karmic retribution for the Chinese government's violent crackdown on dissent in Tibet. Stone said, "And then all this earthquake and all this stuff happened, and I thought, is that karma—when you're not nice that bad things happen to you?"

A mantra is not a slogan or proverb of "words to live by," such as "Her mantra is to enjoy life to the fullest" or "The candidate's mantra of change was very powerful." Rather, a mantra is a short mystical utterance of great sacred power, as illustrated by the greatest of all mantras, Om.

A guru is not anyone who acquires followers in any sort of movement, or a person who has wide authority because of his or her secular knowledge or skills. On the contrary, a guru is a private teacher of transcendent religious truth; a guru leads the student to full knowledge and release.

An avatar is not only a computer user's self-representation in a three-dimensional model for computer games or a two-dimensional icon for Internet communities. In Hinduism, an avatar is an incarnation (different, human form) of a god, as for example Krishna is an avatar of Vishnu. This understanding of avatar was adapted by film director James Cameron in his 2009 blockbuster film by that name, in which a human mind is projected into the body of a human-like being.

---

up trying to fall asleep or must even try to stay awake.) Many Hindus, however, find that moksha is difficult to achieve, especially in a time when many Hindus believe that their religion is in decline. They are content to collect good karma and be reincarnated to a better life.

Three main paths lead to moksha, whether one finds it or not. There is a tendency among Hindus to see one chosen path as the best, but the paths are often combined as well. The way of active, obedient life—called the *path of deeds* (karma)—is doing ritual actions of worship and meditation, as well as carrying out daily conduct according to one's own dharma, but without a selfish intent that causes bad karma. Second, those on the *path of knowledge* see the central problem with human beings as their inability to realize that they are living in an unreal world and that the only thing real is the spirit. The path of knowledge brings personal merging with the ultimate unity behind the visible things of the world, particularly knowledge of the unity of the individual soul and the world soul through yoga and meditation. Third, the *path of devotion* is a loving surrender and service to one's main deity. Some who follow this path see their deity as a manifestation of the impersonal Brahman, but others see their god or goddess as the Supreme Being, with no Brahman above him or her.

Relate Hindu ethics to the essential Hindu teachings.

3-4 Hindu Ethics and Ways of Life

Krishnan, a thirty-year-old computer engineer in Illinois, logs onto shaadi.com to begin the process of finding a wife. This Indian website bills itself as the "world's largest matrimonial service." Some of Krishnan's friends have used it and have urged him to try it, because his parents' efforts at matchmaking haven't succeeded. He enters the search terms "Hindu" for his religion, "Brahmin" for his social-religious class, and also his birthday (for a "Vedic astrology horoscope" used in traditional Hindu matchmaking). In his personal statement for the website, he writes that he is looking for a traditional Hindu young woman who can grow to love him after they are married. His parents will always come first in his life, he says, then his wife, and then his brothers and other relatives.

Explore the Indian marriage website shaadi.com.

Hindus often say that Hinduism is more a way of life than a religion. For observant Hindus today, everyday life and religious life are not separated, because Hindu ethics traditionally plays a leading role in everyday life: caste and class, marriage and children, career and retirement.

> *Hindus often say that Hinduism is more a way of life than a religion.*

3-4a The Caste System

You've probably heard about the Hindu **caste** system (Figure 3.3), which divides people in society into economic and social groups, giving all people their occupations, level of income, and particular pattern of religious duties. The foundation of the caste system was laid in Vedic times, but it grew into its present form in classical times, especially with the writing of the *Laws of Manu*. India today has more than six thousand castes and subcastes, and scholars have long debated the roles of color, economics, and power in the caste system. Hinduism has produced some opposition to the caste system—and there are many activists working to reform it today—but for the most part it has endured as one of the main features of Hinduism. Two words are used in Hindu society to refer to this social system: *varna* and *jati*.

Varna means "color" (it is related to our word *varnish*). Varna is a system dating back to Vedic times that groups Hindu society into four classes. (See Figure 3.3, "The Hindu Caste System.") Some scholars have theorized that social classes are based on varna, with the lightest at the top and the darkest on the bottom. This is probably an oversimplification, and it is controversial in Hinduism, but even today in India there is a general cultural preference (in films, for example) for the lighter skin tones found in the upper varnas. Also, class is generally related to economic standing: The lower one's class, the lower one's income. But there are many exceptions to this; some upper-caste Brahmins are of modest means, and one can find members of the common-people Vaishya class who are wealthy merchants. As a rule, **outcastes** are desperately poor, existing on the equivalent of a few dollars a day.

A well-known hymn in the *Rig Veda* (10.90) tells of how the four main classes arose from the sacrifice of Purusha (POOR-oo-shuh), a man as large as the universe. "The Brahmin was made from his mouth; his arms were made into the Prince; his thighs became the common people; and from his feet the servants were born." The **Brahmin** priests spring from Purusha's mouth so that they can chant the songs for sacrifice. When the Aryans came into India, their ritual lore was controlled by the priests, who claimed to be the only class able to learn and enact them with ritual correctness. This correctness was needed to perform effective

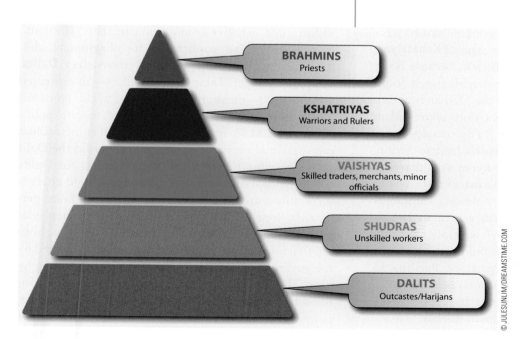

Figure 3.3 The Hindu Caste System

BRAHMINS
Priests

KSHATRIYAS
Warriors and Rulers

VAISHYAS
Skilled traders, merchants, minor officials

SHUDRAS
Unskilled workers

DALITS
Outcastes/Harijans

© JULESUNLIM/DREAMSTIME.COM

caste [kast] System of social organization

varna [VAHR-nuh] "Color," a system of classification of people in Hinduism into four main classes

outcastes Members of the lowest social class, outside the caste system; also called "Dalits"

Brahmins [BRAH-munz] The top priestly class in the varna system

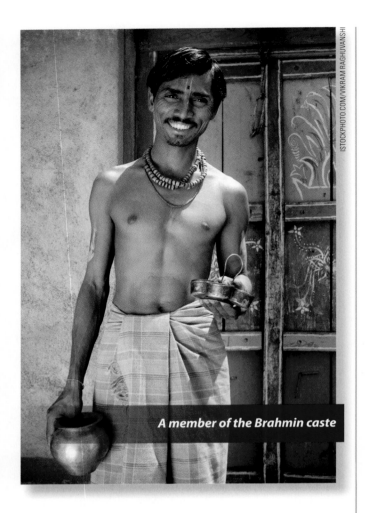

A member of the Brahmin caste

common people, the **Vaishyas**, who provide the necessary semiskilled labor for society. They are merchants, small farmers, and artisans. Finally, the **Shudras** are servants or peasants born from the feet of Purusha. The task of the Shudras, people in the fourth caste, is to support the higher castes by lowly service. Only men in the top three castes are "twice-born," receiving the sacred thread to wear on their body when they are ritually initiated into the formal stages of Hindu life. Shudra men and women, and women of the top three varnas, are thought not to have the personal qualities to be twice-born Hindus. But Shudras can do well economically, and women (not men) are allowed to marry a person one social step above them. If Shudras follow their dharma well, they can be reincarnated into a higher social class.

> "Outcastes" are those outside the caste system, not those "cast out" of it.

Below the class system are the *outcastes*, a term not legally accepted in India today. (Note that this term means "those outside of the caste system," not "those cast out.") The Indian government calls them "scheduled classes," but others call them Harijans (HAHR-ee-jahns), "Children of God," a positive term with an unfortunate negative connotation in that "Harijans" is also an Indian euphemism for illegitimate children. They prefer today to call themselves **Dalits**, "oppressed ones." Their sheer numbers—an estimated 160,000,000—mean that they can wield considerable political power in elections. Some rise to political fame, and there have been a number of cabinet ministers and even one prime minister from the Dalit class. Despite affirmative action programs for Dalits that provide a higher education and well-paid government jobs, strong discrimination against Dalits persists. In June of 2007, a group of Shudra shepherds petitioned to be downgraded into the Dalit class, hoping to gain access to preferential treatment afforded by the government; their attempt was met with rioting by other Hindus. The vast majority of Dalits are still confined to menial, ritually polluting jobs such as street cleaning, manual scavenging, and handling bodies of dead animals or humans. They cannot drink from the same water pumps as the twice-born castes or eat in

Read about the four castes.

ceremonies that mediated between humans and the gods, bringing blessing to both.

This hymn also relates that the arms of Purusha were made into the "Prince." This is the caste of **Kshatriyas**, who are kings and government officials. Because being a ruler entails defending and enlarging one's kingdom, the Kshatriyas are also warriors who lead in battle. The strong arms of Purusha lead to action, so the hymn says that it is the dharma of this caste to defend others. Brahmins or Vaishyas cannot be rulers or warriors, because they would not have the right parts of Purusha to be Kshatriyas. (However, Brahmins have often been advisors to rulers.)

The thighs of Purusha form the large caste of the

Kshatriyas [kshuh-TREE-yuhz] The warrior and princely varna class

Vaishyas [VIGH-shuhs] Third varna class, the "common people"

Shudras [SHOO-druhs] Fourth varna class, "servants"

Dalits [DAHL-its] "Oppressed ones," the outcastes below the four Hindu castes

Dalits in northern India protesting the caste system, 2009

REUTERS/MUNISH SHARMA

this does not preclude a member of one caste working at the occupation of another, for example in agriculture—an added complexity. The Brahmin class is subdivided into many castes, just as there are many castes in the Kshatriya, Vaisya, and Shudra classes, and even among Dalits. Just as the four varnas are hierarchically organized, so also are the various castes within a particular varna. A male is obligated to marry within his jati. Expulsion from the family and caste as a whole is likely to result should this obligation be broken, but if this and other caste obligations are kept, the individual is provided a strong network of support and protection.

3-4b The Four Stages of a Man's Life

The life of a Hindu male is traditionally divided into four stages of time. In modern India, fewer people than in previous centuries observe the system completely and formally, but even today it is an influential pattern for a man's life. However, Shudras, Dalits, and women of all four classes rarely follow these stages. Most Hindu males do not go through the four stages; many never advance beyond the second. Hindus who do complete all four stages sustain this world and pursue ultimate liberation from it.

The first period of life is the **student stage**. A male is taught by his family's elders from childhood, sometimes by a guru as well. His education will not only fit him for a future profession appropriate to his caste, but will equip him also for family, social, and religious life in a way appropriate to his varna and jati. In older times, this period

restaurants with them. In some villages, occasional violence is used to keep Dalits "in their place." Hindus of the four main classes do not consider them to be Hindus, and their rights and political status have been problematic in modern India. They are today the poorest of Indians.

Jati means "birth," and this birth caste is more important than varna for Hindus because it affects so many aspects of daily life. (Modern scholars disagree about how to translate *varna* and *jati*. Here we render *varna* as "class" and *jati* as "caste." Together, they comprise the caste system.) Although there are only four varnas in Hinduism, there are thousands of jatis. Caste is not a religious institution as the varna system is, but is economic and geographical in origin, now combined with varna into an overall religious system. Hindus today refer to jati when they talk of caste, and it is one's jati that really dictates the life of the average Hindu. Each jati has its own rules about food, jobs, marriage, contact with other jatis, and the like. From each caste come a number of subcastes, making the whole system even more complicated. Castes may often be occupational, but

Watch a BBC report on defections from Hinduism.

Read a *National Geographic* article on the Dalits.

Indian wedding ceremonial plate with a variety of foods and spices

© DINODIA PHOTOS/ BRAND X PICTURES/JUPITER IMAGES

jati [JAH-tee] Caste into which one is born

student stage First period of life, in which a Hindu male gains knowledge for caste duties

could last for twenty years or more, but today the first stage has shrunk to between twelve and fifteen years, except for those few who obtain higher education in a university.

> A Hindu man today averages age twenty-three at marriage; a woman, eighteen.

The second period is the **householder stage**, in which the Hindu male must marry and raise a family. Marriages are often arranged by parents while their children are still young—marriage is much too important to family and society to leave it up to young people! In villages "child marriages" often occur, but after the marriage the child bride and child groom are separated until puberty sets in. On average, a young man is around twenty-three at the time of marriage, a young woman around eighteen. Hindus have always placed a high value on raising a family, and poor Hindu couples will keep having children until a boy or two are born. During the householder stage a man works at a trade or profession appropriate to his caste, primarily for his family, but also for his community. He also engages in public and private religious duties derived from his caste.

Watch a video of a Hindu wedding.

The third stage of life is that of *retirement*, traditionally called the **forest-dweller stage**. When a man's children have grown up, when he sees signs of aging such as gray hair and wrinkles, his duty as a householder can end. In this third stage—if he lives to see it, which in much of Hindu history isn't a given—the man is expected to retire not only from his job, but also from family and social life and much (but not all) of his wealth and possessions. Sometimes a man in this stage retreats to the forest to live a more spiritual life, either alone or in a small group of retirees, but this is

A renouncer in northern India

ISTOCKPHOTO.COM/TIR83

rarer today than in the past. He gives up pleasures and comforts. His life is that of a celibate recluse. In view of the hardships that this partial renunciation brings, it's easy to see why this stage has become obsolete for all but a few.

The fourth stage is that of the "renouncer" or **sannyasin**, when a Hindu renounces the world and his previous life completely. This stage traditionally does not necessarily follow retirement; a man can enter it directly from the householder stage. All cares and pleasures of life are abandoned, and his concentration is devoted to achieving moksha before he dies. The sannyasin engages in intense study and meditation, typically with yoga and rigors such as solitude and a sparse diet. He is treated with greatest respect in Hindu lands. But this respect is mingled with a certain degree of fear and skepticism, because some holy men can be hostile, even ferocious, in their words, and a few can be frauds. On taking up the life of the sannyasin, he will often burn an effigy of his body to show that he has died to the world. When a renouncer who

householder stage
Second period of life, in which a Hindu man marries and raises a family

forest-dweller stage Third period of life, in which a Hindu man retires

sannyasin [sahn-YAH-sin] **stage** Fourth period of life, in which a Hindu man becomes a renunciant

has achieved moksha dies, his fellow renouncers tie stones onto his body and throw it in a river. He needs no funeral with cremation, for the soul has already been released from the dreaded cycle of reincarnation.

Watch a report on renouncers at the 2013 Kumbha Mela festival.

3-4c The Four Goals of Life

Hindus hold to four main goals in life and connect them roughly with the stages of life. The first goal of life, dharma, a term we have seen above, is a comprehensive concept that governs all stages of life. A good Hindu must know the dharma of Hinduism, particularly the truth that relates to his or her caste status, and practice it. This practice includes both social morality and ritual duties. Without this first goal, the others cannot be met, and spiritual practices such as yoga will fail.

The second goal of life is **artha**, material success and prosperity. This is pursued for the sake of one's family and the wider good of society. A householder is expected to become as prosperous as possible, while observing the bounds of proper dharma. This ties into the world-affirming side of Hindu tradition, and it makes Hinduism one of the few religions in the world to make financial prosperity an important religious goal. It also helps to explain the entrepreneurial drive and economic success of many Indians in modern times. One's dress reflects, among other things, the level of prosperity one has achieved (see "A Closer Look: Hindu Dress").

> *The Kama Sutra is often seen as a sex manual, but kama is much more than that.*

The third goal of life is **kama**, aesthetic pleasure both of the mind and the body, obviously also world-affirming. This goal is restricted to the householder stage. *Kama* is a comprehensive term for all types of pleasures: spiritual, intellectual, artistic, and physical. The *Kama Sutra* (SOO-trah), or *Scripture on Pleasure,* is often seen as a sex manual, but both kama and the *Kama Sutra* are much more than that. Hinduism is unique in teaching that the pursuit of pleasure is a valid and important religious goal. Though this may seem either strange or appealing to you, remember that in Hinduism the pursuit of pleasure is always subject to the retributive laws of karma.

The fourth goal of life is moksha, which we defined above. It means "release" from life, particularly from the continuous cycle of death and rebirth. This goal is best practiced in the retirement and renouncer stages of life, although it can be sought in all the stages, particularly in the two paths of deeds and devotion that are thought to lead to release.

artha [AHR-thuh] Material success and prosperity, the second goal of life in Hinduism

kama [KAH-muh] Spiritual, mental, and physical pleasure, the third goal of Hindu life

3-4d The Lives of Hindu Women

The vast majority of Hindu young women get married. The Hindu wife bears children, raises them, and runs the home. Motherhood is so important that a woman is considered a failure if she is without children, especially a son; this is true even of modern Hindu women who may work outside the home. On the other hand, being a mother of sons brings great pride and auspiciousness. The wife performs worship in the home at the household shrine, often leading worship there. However, no woman who is menstruating is traditionally allowed at the shrine or in the kitchen. She is considered ritually unclean, and her husband will not touch her during this time. After ritual bathing at the end of her menstrual period, a woman resumes normal life in the home.

Read about the traditional life of Hindu women.

Despite the value placed on motherhood, abortion is legal and very frequent in India, even among Hindus. Prenatal testing by ultrasound is now used widely to ascertain the sex of a fetus in the womb, even though this has been outlawed in India since 1994; if it is a female, it is often aborted. Some parents think it better to abort a female than to support a second or third daughter and pay for her expensive dowry. The Indian government encourages contraception, but having sons is necessary for economic support in one's old age because India has no national pension system. One also needs a son to perform one's funeral rites. The use of selective abortion to obtain sons has led in some parts of India to an ominous imbalance between the proportion of males and females. As a result, in 2007 the

A Closer Look:

Hindu Dress

Hinduism requires no particular type of clothing, as you might expect, and regional styles in India vary considerably. The traditional dress for most Indian women (Figure 3.4) is the sari, a piece of cloth five or six meters long that is wrapped and pleated around the waist and then drawn around over the shoulder so that the free end is loose. Underneath the sari are a short blouse and a long skirt, often leaving the midriff bare. In northern India, women prefer light, baggy trousers called "pyjamas" (from which we get our term) and a long, loose-fitting shirt. In mixed company outside the home or when offering puja in the home or temple, women usually cover their hair with the free end of their saris. This is a sign of respect to the gods and to other people, women as well as men.

Indian women of all classes typically love jewelry. Long earlobes are an ancient Indian sign of nobility, so women use heavy earrings to stretch their earlobes. The distinctive decorative mark of a married woman is the **bindi** ("little drop") on her forehead. The bindi may be a circle of colored paste, or of felt with an adhesive backing, which can more easily be put on and decorated with sequins. Unmarried women and young girls often have a small black spot on their forehead; it is not a bindi, but rather a protection against the "evil eye."

Figure 3.4 Woman in sari, with bindi on her forehead

BONNIE VAN VOORST © CENGAGE LEARNING

Although Hindu women often dress in traditional Indian ways, Hindu men very often wear Western clothing, especially in cities. Men in Indian villages traditionally dress in the *dhoti* (Figure 3.5). This single, large piece of fabric is wrapped around the waist and tucked up around the thighs. The *kurta* (called a "panjabi" in the U.K. and Canada) is a long, loose shirt coat falling to the knees and is worn by both men and women. It can be worn with a dhoti or with pants, and is both casual and formal. Turbans are usually connected with observant Sikh men (see Chapter 6), but in India some Hindu men also wear one. The most important item worn is the sacred thread, a thin cotton cord worn on the body by men of the upper three classes, symbolizing full Hindu status. It is given in a special ceremony near the age of ten. The traditional garb of Hindu men, long disdained by the Indian upper classes in favor of more-Western-style clothing, is now making a strong comeback in some social circles and in fashion design.

Holy men have a distinctive but not uniform look. Their hair is often wildly matted, and they sometimes cover their body in light-colored dust or powdered cow dung, giving them the look of death. Some go around only in a thong or at times nude, to symbolize their full control of the senses and bodily desire. They can sometimes be seen with their sacred thread, but not wearing one shows that they have left the distinctions of once-born and twice-born behind.

Figure 3.5 Man in dhoti and sacred thread

BONNIE VAN VOORST © CENGAGE LEARNING

Indian government and private agencies launched a "Save the Girl Child" campaign.

Read about "Save the Girl Child" on its website.

Divorce is difficult for a woman to obtain, especially for women of the higher classes, despite the Hindu Marriage Act of 1955 that ostensibly made it possible for any woman to get a divorce. Although divorce and remarriage are quite common among the lower castes, there is still a general feeling in villages that a wife is to blame if divorce occurs or even if the husband dies before she does. Family and friends are liable to regard a divorced or widowed woman as "unlucky," so life can be difficult for her. Widows rarely remarry and are often socially ostracized. The suicide rate for widows is high, even if the ancient (if irregularly practiced) **suttee**, "widow burning," is now almost unheard of. Widows would climb onto their dead husband's funeral pyre to go to heaven with him, an act of great merit; the British colonial government outlawed this practice in the 1800s. In urban areas women do have more status today; for example, they can now own property, keep their own salary, and open bank accounts in their own name. Many young Hindu women go to college, get a job, and delay marriage. Yet marriage is important, and a woman's self-esteem and social standing still have much to do with her husband. By serving him faithfully, just as she serves a god, good karma will come to her.

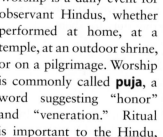

ISTOCKPHOTO.COM/ANANTHA VARDHAN

IN 2007 THE INDIAN GOVERNMENT AND PRIVATE AGENCIES LAUNCHED A "SAVE THE GIRL CHILD" CAMPAIGN.

with altars, each with a statue of a different deity. All Hindu immigrants, no matter what god they worship, can feel comfortable in the Omaha temple.

You are struck at once by the many colorful sights, unusual sounds, and fragrant smells of the temple. Women are dressed in traditional Indian saris; men are in Western clothing, except for the two priests, whose upper bodies are half bare and who have a sacred thread visible over the shoulder. You see different sorts of worship activities: people bowing and prostrating themselves in front of the statues and people sitting quietly in meditation, some in a yoga position. In a side room, men and women are practicing sacred songs to be sung at a service later in the week. You also notice that in some areas of the temple men tend to be separated from women and children.

Your tour guide is a University of Nebraska professor, a member of the temple's leadership. As he skillfully leads you around, he tells you that the temple was built as a center of worship, teaching, and Indian cultural life for people from India who live in Nebraska and Iowa. The temple is open for Hindu festivals, for a main weekly service on Sunday morning—an adaptation to American religion, he says—and for traditional ceremonies marking the life stages of Hindus, from birth to death. He adds that a part of the temple's purpose is to educate people of other religions about Hinduism.

Learning Outcome 3-5

Outline the ways Hindus worship, at home and in temples.

3-5 Hindu Rituals

As you drive up to the new Hindu temple in Omaha, Nebraska, you notice its traditional Indian architectural design. Inside, the diversity of Hinduism is reflected in the many deities there. Large temples in India are dedicated to one god, but this temple has twelve separate holy areas

As you might expect, worship and meditation in Hinduism are diverse. Worship is a daily event for observant Hindus, whether performed at home, at a temple, at an outdoor shrine, or on a pilgrimage. Worship is commonly called **puja**, a word suggesting "honor" and "veneration." Ritual is important to the Hindu, and much of it is ancient, although with regional and devotional-group variations.

bindi [BIHN-dee] Forehead mark of a married Hindu woman

suttee [suh-TEE] Burning of a widow on the funeral pyre of her husband, thought to be an act of great merit

puja [POO-juh] Devotional actions of worshiping a god or venerating a human person

3-5a Images

Hinduism has many gods, all of them represented by images. Westerners, especially Protestant Christians who look upon images as objects that encourage false worship, often use the term *idol*, but *image* is more appropriate. *Idol* suggests that it is the statue or picture alone that is worshiped, and it is generally a pejorative term, although one will hear Hindus using it happily. *Image* suggests something beyond the visible form that receives the worship offered to the visible form. Hindus use the term **murti** for the image of a deity, whether three-dimensional (as in a statue) or two-dimensional (as in a picture or poster). A murti is a representation of the deity, rather like a photograph represents a person. It draws the mind of the devotee to the gods themselves. However, an image can be more than just a symbol. The power or essence of the deity is believed to be in the murti, either temporarily, as for some festivals, or permanently, as in the case of some temple images that are treated as the deities themselves, with the god thought to reside inside the statue.

Shiva has both an anthropomorphic form in an image and the powerful symbols of the lingam and the trident. The female side of the divine, the Goddess, is represented by the yoni, the symbol of creative female power that is the counterpart to the lingam. Hindus of the lower castes and those Hindus outside caste do not worship the "high" gods of Hinduism, but rather the "low gods," especially village and city deities. The high gods such as Vishnu and Shiva are generally considered to be uninterested in the daily events of the ordinary man or woman; their avatars and related lower deities do that duty for them.

3-5b Worship in the Temple and the Home

Temples large and small are found all over India, from great pilgrimage centers to humble side streets. At some of these temples more than one god is venerated in words and deeds. Usually the deity and the temple belong to one of three strands within the Hindu pantheon—Shaivite, Vaishnavite, and Shakta, including all their avatars and family members.

An image draws the mind to the greater essence of the god.

© DINODIA PHOTOS/BRAND X PICTURES/JUPITER IMAGES

The deity, represented by a statue, picture, or other symbol, is the central part of the temple. The god is considered to be an honored guest and is treated with adoration, attention, and even amusements. Purification is essential before doing puja, and one usually bathes in running water and sips a little water three times. Washing the murti is essential but often symbolic—a flower or a small piece of cotton is used to touch the deity. Dressing the deity is also important, and the clothes chosen are bright, beautiful, and often embroidered with gold-colored threads. Ornaments are placed on the murti, as well as flower garlands, perfumes, and oils. Because the deity remains at a temple, it is both woken up in the morning and put to rest at night. At many temples, sculptures help to teach about the gods and their stories, and they both shape and direct devotion. Larger temples will have priests who act as teachers.

The offering of food is also important—usually cooked rice, fruit and vegetables, liquefied butter, and sugar. The deity receives the essence of the food, and the "leftovers," called *prasad* (PRAH-sahd), are given back to those who brought them. Whatever the edible offering, both the gods and the worshipers eat the food and benefit from its richness. Fragrance and light are also offered the deity—fragrance in the form of incense sticks and light in the form of a burning lamp usually made from a burning wick placed in clarified butter, which is waved before the deity. By applying a *tilak* (TEE-lahk)—a mark made with crushed flowers sometimes mixed with another substance—to the forehead between the eyebrows of the deity, the worshiper indicates awareness of the spiritual purity and power of the god. This in turn is passed to the worshiper. The worshiper may also entertain the deity with hymns that offer praise and of course increase the devotion of the worshipers. Groups of people—usually males, but sometimes with women, who sit separately—can be seen singing hymns informally on the temple verandas in the evening.

murti [MUHR-tee]
Image of a deity

Bowing is the traditional way of showing respect to someone in India. The more respect one wishes to show, the lower one bows. In the case of a god or a royal person, lying flat on one's face is in order. Bringing the palms together and raising them to the forehead are actions normally used in greeting in India, and they are used to greet the gods as well. The Hindi word *namaste* (NAHM-ahs-tay) or its equivalent in other Indian languages, "I bow to you," is spoken as this is done. Because famous gurus are also honored with puja, people might touch the guru's feet in respect or remove by hand the dust from his feet before touching their own head, indicating that the dusty feet of the guru are holier than the head of the one paying respect.

Worship in the home has long been an important part of Hinduism. Nearly every Hindu household has a home shrine, frequently in a special devotional room or in the kitchen, which is considered ritually pure. In this shrine, the family god—as well as the gods and goddesses honored by individual family members—have center stage, in the form of images done in brass; often, photographs of a guru or saint and the family ancestors are also in the shrine. To begin daily worship in the home, the believer purifies himself or herself by bathing. Then, with the help of mantras, the place of ritual is purified, and any evil spirits lurking to interfere with the puja are driven away. A small bell is rung to honor the deities and get their attention as the ritual begins. On occasion the gods are washed, clothed, fed, and given gifts, but worshipers always stand reverently with palms joined. At the climax of the ritual, a small lamp is swung before the shrine; the divinity resides in the fire, and the faithful receive it within themselves by holding the palms of their hands over the flames for an instant and then touching their eyes.

South Indian bride making namaste

© DINODIA PHOTOS/BRAND X PICTURES/JUPITER IMAGES

Worship at a home shrine

© DINODIA PHOTOS/BRAND X PICTURES/JUPITER IMAGES

3-5c Pilgrimage

Pilgrimage is an aspect of ritual life important for many Hindus, although few of them have the time or money to engage in it. The destination of a pilgrimage is often a river, the ocean, or a spring. But temples built on sacred mountains or in sacred cities are also places of pilgrimage. Doing puja in a place with a strong connection to the divine brings purification from sin and ritual impurity, gains merit, fulfills vows, leads to the betterment of one's next lives in this world, and even brings deliverance from the cycle of rebirth. Millions of pilgrims go to Varanasi on the Ganges River every year to wash their sins away in the water. The largest pilgrimage event in the world is the **Kumbha Mela**, a festival held once every twelve years in Allahabad (the most recent held in 2003), when tens of millions of pilgrims gather where the two sacred rivers—the Ganges and the Yamuna—merge. As it is with all religions of the world, pilgrimage in Hinduism is "big business" in the cities that host it.

Watch a BBC report on the Kumbha Mela festival.

3-5d Festivals and Holidays

With the size and diversity of Hinduism, you would expect that its festivals and holidays would be diverse as well—and you would be correct. Estimates range from roughly one holiday per day to thousands per year, especially when regional festivals are considered. Hindu holidays tend to be based on the cycle of nature. They indicate the change of

Kumbha Mela [KOOM-buh MEHL-uh] Festival held every twelve years in Allahabad, India

seasons, celebrate harvests, and promote fertility of animals and crops. Others are dedicated to a god or goddess and celebrate their deeds. Still other popular holidays mark events in the Indian epics, such as the *Bhagavad Gita.*

Festivals observed by most Hindus, and sometimes by other Indians, include the following, in chronological order:

- *Holi* Festival of colors applied to the body, marking the coming of spring (February or March)

- *Shiva Ratri* Festival for Shiva (February or March)

- *Rama Navami* Birthday of the god Rama (April)

- *Krishna Jayanti* Birthday of Krishna (July or August)

- *Raksabandhana* Festival to renew family bonds (July or August)

- *Ganesha Chaturthi* Festival for Ganesh (August or September)

- *Diwali* Festival of lights; this holiday is celebrated by almost all Indians, whatever their religion (September or October)

- *Dassera* Rama's victory over Ravana, the king of evil (September or October)

3-5e Funerals

Despite all the emphasis in Hinduism on karma and reincarnation, its death rites still emphasize the deceased happily joining dead ancestors rather than achieving a good reincarnation or release from all moksha. (A period of refreshment in heaven is often thought of as a prelude to being reincarnated.) Death is considered so ritually polluting and inauspicious that the images of deities in the home shrine are removed while the body is in the house. Unlike Western funerals, no one partakes of food or drink in any part of a Hindu funeral ritual.

The body of the deceased is washed soon after death, wrapped in a new cloth—white for men and red for women—and carried on a stretcher from the home to the cremation ground in a procession led by the eldest son. (Of course, funerals are held all over India, not just at the cities on the Ganges River, such

An Indian boy with the colors of Holi splashed on him.

ISTOCKPHOTO.COM/ABHISKEK AGGARWAL

as Varanasi.) Cremation on a wood fire is the traditional Indian method of disposing of human remains. Cremation is thought to separate the immortal soul from the body in a good way, resembling a fire sacrifice. At the funeral ground, Dalits of the Dom caste handle the body and incur the ritual pollution of burning it. Fresh, flowing water is usually near the cremation grounds, and the body is dipped in it for ritual purification. The body is then placed on the wood, with the feet facing south toward the home of the god who rules the dead. It is covered with a layer of wood and then clarified butter, and scriptures are chanted over the body by a priest as the family circles the deceased. The eldest son then lights the funeral pyre, which will burn for two to three hours. After cremation begins, the youngest son leads the procession home.

The Doms tend the fire for several hours to keep it burning hot, occasionally turning the body with long poles to ensure that it is consumed more fully. The ashes and remaining bones (the larger and denser bones of the human body cannot be disposed of by a natural cremation alone) are finally put by the Doms into flowing water and left there, for a cooling and purifying effect. When the period of death rites is over, a Dalit is given all the household linen to wash. On the twelfth day, four balls of rice are offered to symbolize the happy union of the deceased with his or her forebears, the point of the funeral rites. Only when the house has been thoroughly cleaned can the household deities be returned.

Although cremation is the desired method of disposal of the dead, burial is not uncommon. The poorer classes usually practice burial because it is cheaper. Young children of most castes who die are buried, or sometimes put into a flowing river, rather than cremated. In the cities of India, cremation in modern crematoriums is now the norm, with ashes scattered later in sacred rivers.

Watch a video of funeral rites at Varanasi.

Visit the website of a company that scatters ashes in the Ganges.

3-5f Yoga

Yoga, with its emphasis on fitness for the body and mind, has become a main tool for achieving liberation, or at least the mental discipline that can lead to liberation. Buddhists, Christians, and people of no formal faith have adapted yogic methods to help them on their own paths to peace and freedom, or just to physical fitness. As explained above, *yoga* means "yoke," which its spelling resembles. This refers to the path of union with, or yoking to, a god or Brahman. The most popular type of yoga in India and the West is *hatha yoga,* which emphasizes breathing and physical posture as a way to ultimate knowledge of Brahman in one's atman; *karma yoga* is the path of active service that breathing and postures assist; *jnana yoga* is reflective, philosophical yoga; and *bhakti yoga* is the path of devotion to a god. Bhakti yoga is the simplest form, using repeated chanting of a mantra in a fixed posture to focus on a deity and offer one's life to a god.

Yoga classes in North America emphasize the physical benefits of yoga.

Watch an explanation of the "Take Back Yoga" campaign to emphasize its Hindu roots.

Read about a controversy over yoga in a California public school.

> The most popular form of yoga in the West is hatha yoga, with its emphasis on breathing and physical posture.

Yogic practices draw, at least in significant measure, on these eight steps.

1. Following five guidelines on behavior toward others: avoiding violence, untruthfulness, stealing, lust, and covetousness
2. Following guidelines on behavior toward oneself: cleanliness of body and mind, contentment, sustained practice, self-knowledge, study, and surrender to God
3. Learning and using formal yoga postures
4. Performing breathing exercises, coordinated with physical postures

5. Withdrawal of the senses, so that the exterior world is no longer a distraction from discovering the world within oneself, particularly the atman within
6. Concentration, so that one can focus on a single thing without distractions
7. Meditation that moves beyond concentration, so that one's awareness is all-encompassing
8. Finally, achieving *samadhi,* or "bliss." The self transcends itself through meditation and discovery of the atman, which brings one to Brahman.

Read about the practice of yoga.

Watch a video about the yoga controversy in Muslim Malaysia.

Learning Outcome 3-6

State the main aspects of Hindu life around the world today, especially in North America.

3-6 Hinduism around the World Today

Shortly before the 2008 release of the Hollywood film *The Love Guru,* written by and starring Mike Myers, self-styled North American Hindu leader Rajan Zed complains about it to mass-media outlets. Zed charges that its portrayal of Hinduism is inaccurate and insulting. The potential for damage to Hindus is great, Zed argues, because Hinduism is not widely understood outside of India. Despite Zed's efforts, the consensus among Hindus in the West seems to be that they feel comfortable laughing at themselves and even laugh at well-meaning stereotypes such as Apu the convenience-store merchant on television's *The Simpsons*. However, some portrayals of Hinduism in the mass media—such as in the 1984 film *Indiana Jones and the Temple of Doom*, with its false, brutal depiction of worship of the Hindu goddess Kali—have caused concern to many Hindus. Any disquiet over *The Love Guru,* however, fades rapidly as it is harshly reviewed in the press and then fails miserably at the box office.

In this final section, we will consider briefly the current spread of Hinduism in the world, with a particular focus on North America.

3-6a Hinduism in South Asia and Africa

Sometimes Indian military conquests brought along with them the main aspects of Hindu culture and belief. This is how Hinduism came to Nepal and Sri Lanka. Although Hinduism moved beyond its own borders before the modern period, this was primarily a result of Indian emigration to other countries and the resulting expansion of Hindu culture in such places as Nepal, Sri Lanka, and Bali. In the 1800s, the heyday of the British Empire, Indians moved freely to many parts of the world controlled by Great Britain, especially to south Asia and Africa. Hindus in these areas engaged in trade and other businesses, and practiced their religion; they were predominantly of the Vaishya caste. In the main, Hinduism has been the religion of only the Indian people, and converting other peoples has not been undertaken. This is true both in India and in the Hindu dispersion. However, in the past two centuries various Hindus have indeed sought to spread Hinduism outside of India, particularly in North America.

Distinctive practices developed in Hinduism as it spread through Asia. Although Hinduism in the diaspora did not take on different gods, some rituals changed. For example, the Hindu women of Bali, Indonesia, make elaborate pyramids of food that they carry to the temple on their head as a sacrificial offering to the deity. The wealthier the family is, the higher the pyramids. A cooked chicken may be put in the pyramid, surrounded by rice dishes and many kinds of fruit. (See also "A Closer Look: Hindu Faith and Indian Food.")

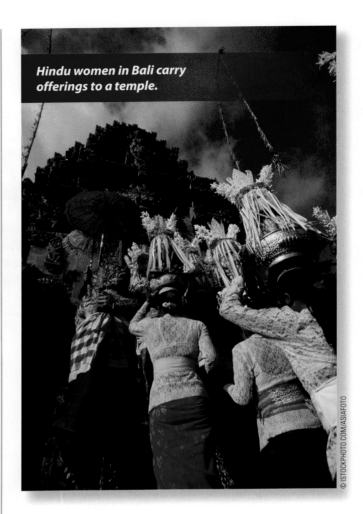

Hindu women in Bali carry offerings to a temple.

© ISTOCKPHOTO.COM/ASIAFOTO

3-6b Hinduism in the West

Hinduism has been viewed in widely differing ways in the West during the past two centuries. Customs such as widow burning (rarely done these days) and a caste system that resists reform have made many North Americans resistant to Hinduism until more recently. However, some Westerners were attracted by Hindu ideas of physical and spiritual life in harmony with nature. Vegetarianism and Hindu philosophy, particularly Vedanta, have also attracted Westerners to Hinduism, especially in the more intellectual echelons of North America. Hinduism came to Great Britain in the 1800s with Indian migration there. Around 560,000 people in the United Kingdom called themselves Hindus in the 2001 census, but other estimates have put the figure as high as 1.5 million. Most Hindus in the U.K. live in England, with half living in London alone. However, Hindus in Great Britain did not have a traditional, stand-alone temple until 1981.

Hindu customs are slightly different in the West. In funeral practice, for example, the body will be washed and dressed in new clothes, placed in a coffin, and surrounded by flowers. Cremation cannot be immediate as in India, but has to take place a day or two after death because of the necessary legal arrangements. At the crematorium the priest will talk about the life of the person, and upon returning to the house after cremation has begun, prayers are said for the departed soul in front of the sacred fire or household shrine. The ashes of the deceased would preferably be sent to a relative in India to be scattered in the Ganges, or sent to one of the businesses recently set up for that purpose, or, if that is not possible, cast into a fast-flowing river nearby.

In the past century or so, varied expressions of Hinduism have found their way to the West in movements led by Hindu gurus. Ramakrishna's favorite disciple, Vivekananda (VIH-veh-kah-NAHN-duh; 1863–1902), was the first successful Hindu missionary to the West. In 1893 he addressed the first World Parliament of Religions at Chicago; he was enthusiastically received there and in his other travels throughout the United States. Vivekananda established the first Hindu temple in North America, in San Francisco. He returned to India as a national hero. The Hinduism of Vivekananda was much less devotional than Ramakrishna's own piety and stressed the philosophical teachings of the *Upanishads*. Vivekananda believed that the Vedanta was the sum of all world religions, and he was one of the world's first advocates of religious pluralism. After Vivekananda came the Self-Realization Fellowship of North America, founded by Paramahansa Yogananda (PAR-uh-mah-HAN-suh YO-guh-NAN-duh) in 1920 and based in Los Angeles, where it still has its headquarters. It teaches a form of yoga to enable members to realize "the god within." The Self-Realization Fellowship has more than one hundred local meeting places in the United States and Canada today, and one hundred more in Europe.

Two recent gurus who have gained wide popularity in North America are Maharishi Mahesh Yogi (MAH-ha-REE-shee MAH-hesh YOH-gee; 1911–2008), founder of the Spiritual Regeneration Movement better known as **Transcendental Meditation (TM)**, and Swami A. C. Bhaktivedanta (BAHK-tee-veh-DAHN-tuh; 1896–1977), founder of the International Society for Krishna Consciousness, or ISKCON. Both movements have emphasized how their teachings align with Western science and the mental or emotional benefits obtained from them. TM is based on Vedanta, emphasizing each person's inner divine essence and the liberating powers that may be harnessed when one knows one's true identity. Yogic meditation practiced in the morning and evening is the way to tap into the transcendent and its calming, directing power. When the English musical group the Beatles took continued instruction in Great Britain and in India from the Maharishi in the late 1960s, Transcendental Meditation became even more popular. The popularity of yogic meditation today in North America, severed from its deep religious connections, is due in large part to the TM movement. (For more on TM as a New Religious Movement, see Chapter 13.)

ISKCON is more commonly known as the Hare (HAHR-ee, "divine lord") Krishna movement, after its main mantra. A part of the devotional movement, it emphasizes enthusiastic devotion to Lord Krishna. Many academics regard it as an authentic (true to Indian roots) form of Hinduism practiced in the West, but at times it has been dogged with charges that it is a dangerous "cult."

> *Some Hindu parents in North America send their children to a Hindu summer camp.*

3-6c Hindu Migration and Life in North America

In the past few decades, especially since a liberalization of immigration laws in the 1960s, an increasing number of Indians who practice Hinduism have moved to the United States and Canada. This Hindu **diaspora**, a "spreading" from its native land, has brought hundreds of thousands of Hindus to North American cities, especially on the East and West Coasts. Some of these more recent immigrants are merchants, but many of them are highly skilled professionals who are eager to integrate into North American civic life. They also want to preserve basic Hindu beliefs and behaviors in an environment not

Transcendental Meditation (TM)
Meditational system, popularized by the Maharishi Mahesh Yogi, emphasizing the power of knowing one's divine identity

diaspora [dee-ASS-pohr-uh] "Spreading" of Hinduism outside of India

conducive to them. Every home of observant Hindus has a shrine to the god(s) the family serves, and worship is conducted at the shrine a few times a day. In 2001, the American Museum of Natural History in New York City opened an exhibit, "Meeting God," that documented the home and business shrines of several Hindus in the New York area.

Many Hindus join cultural organizations to keep traditions such as music and cuisine alive. Some Hindu parents have started to send their children to summer camp—but camp that provides teaching and experience in Hindu life. They also build Hindu temples in which to practice Hindu worship, and at times workers come from India to build them in an authentic way. Finding Brahmin priests from India to staff these temples is difficult, so activities such as singing devotional songs that can be practiced by all Hindus become even more important than in India. Having many different Hindu

Watch an examination of second-generation Hinduism in America.

groups worshiping under one roof, something not done in India, can be a challenge.

Hindus typically view marriage within one's caste as a necessity, and because marriages are often still arranged to some extent, Hindu parents may network for suitable spouses living in North America or even in India. As with other immigrant groups in North America, intergenerational tension often springs up as second- and third-generation Hindu young people take on the values and practices of their non-Hindu peers. Dating and mating are often difficult for Hindu young people with Western ways; this is the theme of several films, such as Mira Nair's excellent *Monsoon Wedding* and *The Namesake*. Over time, Hindus, like other religious groups, will probably reach a workable, if uneasy, compromise between their religion and life in North America.

Watch "Understanding Hinduism," produced for cross-cultural training of law enforcement officers by the Chicago Police Department.

A Closer Look:

Hindu Faith and Indian Food

India has considerable regional variations in food, many of which have gone into the wide Hindu diaspora, but the important aspect is a preference for vegetarianism. Because all animals are sacred to Hindus due to a general reverence for life, and particularly for the souls incarnated in animals, it is considered wrong to kill animals for food. Vegetarianism is believed to benefit the body, the mind, and the soul. Even so, many Hindus are not strict vegetarians, and those who can afford it will eat meat occasionally. The sacrifice and subsequent eating of animals, the goat in particular, is common enough in India and Nepal. Brahmin priests are rarely involved in such sacrifices, which are performed by lower-caste priests and mainly in the smaller village temples.

The cow is the most sacred of all animals to Hindus, and no observant Hindu would ever eat beef. (You should never look for a beef dish at any self-respecting Indian restaurant!) Although meat from a cow is forbidden, cow's milk and the products made from it are considered very healthy. To put it in modern Western terms, vegetarianism is common, but a vegan diet that excludes all animal products would be unthinkable to observant Hindus.

Foods high in protein are important in a basically vegetarian diet, and *dal*, a lentil dish, is popular throughout the world wherever Indian cuisine is found. Vegetables cooked in spices are common, as are foods that are quickly fried in butter. The *Bhagavad Gita* (17:8–10) teaches that healthy foods are "tasty, soothing and nourishing." It describes unhealthy food as things that are "acidic, sour, and excessively hot." (The strong curries of Indian food often make Westerners' eyes water, but of course what makes food "excessively" hot is a matter of acculturation. The *Gita* notes foods that will give an Indian indigestion.) The particular balance of having both hot and cool foods in a meal is also important for bodily and spiritual health.

The males of the family traditionally eat first and separately from the women, and then the females eat what remains. Because all food in Hindu sacrifice is first offered to the deities and then received back by the worshiper, the practice of eating the males' leftovers as a sort of sacrificial food enables the wife to pay honor to her husband. This custom is still maintained in traditional India today, though it is not so common among Hindus living in the Western world.

Study Tools 3

Ready to study? In the book you can:

- Review Learning Outcome answers and glossary terms with the tear-out Chapter Review card.

Or you can go online to CourseMate, at www.cengagebrain.com, for these resources:

- Chapter quizzes to prepare for tests
- Interactive flashcards of all glossary terms
- A timeline of events for this chapter
- An eBook with introductions, interactive quizzes, and live links for all web resources in the chapter

CHAPTER 4

Encountering Jainism: The Austere Way to Liberation

BONNIE VAN VOORST © CENGAGE LEARNING

Learning Outcomes

After studying this chapter, you will be able to do the following:

4-1 Explain the meaning of *Jainism* and related terms.

4-2 Summarize how the main periods of Jainism's history have shaped its present.

4-3 Outline the essential Jain teachings in your own words.

4-4 State the main ethical precepts of Jainism for monks/nuns and laity, and relate them to Jain teachings.

4-5 Outline the way Jains worship and practice other rituals.

4-6 Explain the main aspects of Jain life around the world today, especially in North America.

Study Tools

After you read this chapter, go to the Study Tools at the end of the chapter, page 109.

ISTOCKPHOTO.COM/DAVID KERKHOFF

"Do no harm; let all creatures help each other." —*From the modern symbol of Jainism.*

Your Visit with Jain Nuns

Imagine that you're traveling through northern India and come across a group of three Jain nuns. Like you, they're walking on the outskirts of a small town, but they walk much more slowly and deliberately than you. You notice that they're dressed all in white and have a whisk slung across the shoulder that they occasionally take down and use gently on the road in front of them.

After you greet them respectfully, they invite you to the ashram where they're currently living. You hesitate, thinking to yourself, "Should I visit with nuns in their house? Is that proper?" You try to hide your expression, but they're so perceptive that it makes you feel like they can read your mind. They assure you that it's okay, that they are able to receive visitors and know how to conduct themselves properly with them. So you accompany them, keeping a respectful distance behind them as they walk.

At their house, you meet five other nuns. Led by their teacher, who is clearly in charge, they are walking around to different towns and villages in the area. You learn that a man next door is fixing their evening meal in a way that is approved by Jains, which is to do as little harm as possible to insects and other small beings, all of which have a soul. Soon women of the town start to gather in the ashram. They greet the teacher, and she conducts a short service of prayer and meditation for them. It ends with blessings on all who have come, especially with the saying "May you attain spiritual prosperity."

After sleeping in another building, you rejoin the nuns very early the next day. They stop at a Jain temple for prayer and meditation, and you wait for them there. Then you all leave to walk to the next town, about twenty kilometers away. The progress is slow, because the nuns must watch where they walk and because some of them

What Do YOU Think?

The most important Jain teaching in the world today is nonviolence as a way of life.

Strongly Disagree   Strongly Agree

1   2   3   4   5   6   7

have been fasting and have diminished physical strength. When you arrive in the town at the end of the day, you bid a fond farewell to them all. As you're about to leave, one of them startles you with the question "Why don't you become a monastic?"

See photos of an actual visit with Jain nuns.

Jainism is an ancient religion of India that follows a path of doing no harm to any living being. Your introduction to Jainism will soon encounter these unique features:

- Jainism is similar in many ways to Buddhism but has been a distinct Indian religion for more than two thousand years.

- Jainism shares much vocabulary (*karma*, *nirvana*, and other terms) with Hinduism and Buddhism, but usually with a wrinkle: The Jain nuance of these words is different.

- Jainism teaches self-effort to bring one's soul to release from constant reincarnation. However, this goal can be accomplished only by those who become a monk or a nun; other Jains keep a lesser version of Jain practice, and have lesser goals.

- Jains have a challenging and restrictive diet, but in general they are remarkably healthy and prosperous.

 Offerings rest at the feet of the colossal statue of Gommateshvara, a Jain hero, in Shravanabelagola, India.

- With an estimated 5 million followers, Jainism is among the smallest of the faiths called "world religions." However, the contribution of Jainism, both directly and indirectly through other religions, is much more significant than what might be expected from its small numbers.

Learning Outcome 4-1

Explain the meaning of *Jainism* and related terms.

4-1 The Name *Jainism*

Jainism (JINE-ism) is commonly traced to the Sanskrit word for "conquer." This conquering refers to the battle Jains wage within themselves to gain the full knowledge that leads to enlightenment. The person who has achieved Jain enlightenment is called a **Jina**, "Conqueror," and all who follow this religion are called **Jains**, "Followers of the Conquerors." In particular, Jains are followers of the Jina who founded Jainism, **Mahavira**, but the religion was never named after him. Mahavira is the main model of how to achieve enlightenment, but he himself does not enlighten people or rescue them from error.

> *The name* Jain *is so important to Jains that many have done something unique in the religions of the world— taken* Jain *as their family name.*

Jina [JEE-nuh] "Conqueror," a person who has achieved Jain enlightenment

Jains [jines] "Followers of the Conquerors," all who follow Jain religion

Mahavira [MAH-hah-VEER-uh] "Great Hero," whose given name was Vardhamana, the twenty-fourth and last Tirthankara of this age and the founder of Jainism

Jain or *Jaina Dharma* ("Teaching of the Conquerors") probably replaced a more generic name from the earliest Jain scriptures, *Nirgrantha* (neer-GRAHN-thuh) *Dharma*, "Teaching of the Bondless Ones." The name *Jain* is so important to its followers that they have done something unique in the religions of the world—many of them have proudly taken the name of their religion as their family name. For more on how Jainism understands itself, see "A Closer Look: The Symbol of Jainism."

Learning Outcome 4-2

Summarize how the main periods of Jainism's history have shaped its present.

4-2 The Jain Present as Shaped by Its Past

For thirty years, the Jain monk Gurudev Shree Chitrabhanu (CHIT-ruh-BAHN-oo) was a spiritual leader for Jains in India. He walked more than 30,000 miles there, barefoot. Deciding to give up his monastic vows, he left India in 1970 to attend conferences in Switzerland and in Boston. He did so at first to raise funds and recruit volunteers to help Indians impacted by famines and floods. Then Chitrabhanu wrote educational materials from Jain scriptures that he said could apply to Jains and non-Jains alike, and he interacted with people of other religions in ways that were unusual for a Jain. Eventually, he settled in New York City, where he married, took up the life of a householder, and founded the Jain Meditation Center. In several ways, Chitrabhanu embodies the tension between the historic values of an ancient religion and the challenges of modern life, especially in the West.

Jains believe that their religion has no founder and no early history. For them, Jainism has always existed and will always exist in the future, even though it goes through long cycles of decline and reform just as the world does. Historians of what Jains consider their present cycle can trace out the main lines of Jain history and point to moments of its founding, growth, and change. These benchmarks help us to explain how Jainism got to be the way it is today.

> *Jains believe that their religion has always existed and will exist forever.*

A Closer Look:

The Symbol of Jainism

Until recently, the common symbol of Jainism has been the *swastika*, an ancient and widespread Asian religious symbol with none of the racist overtones that the swastika has for Westerners today. The Jain swastika is often seen with four dots in it. (See page 66 for more on the swastika.)

Figure 4.1 Symbol of Jainism

BONNIE VAN VOORST © CENGAGE LEARNING

In 1975, Jain representatives, at a meeting to commemorate the 2,500th anniversary of Mahavira's death, drew up an image as an official symbol for the Jain religion. (Jainism is one of the few world religions to have an officially adopted symbol.) Since then, its symbol has become widely accepted and used. One sees it in almost all Jain official publications, religious magazines, and even in religious greeting cards and wedding announcements.

The overall shape of the image is modeled on the human torso, a shape Jains believe the universe shares. The small arc at the top symbolizes a realm above heaven. All liberated souls reside there as individual beings, forever in a blessed state, freed from the recycling of souls through life and death. The three dots just below the zone of liberation stand for the "three jewels": right belief, right knowledge, and right conduct. By gaining these three jewels, one can achieve the liberated zone.

In the next portion, there is a swastika, which is said to have several different meanings. As a wheel, it suggests the eternal nature of the material world. It represents the four parts of the Jain community: monks, nuns, male laity, and female laity. It also represents the four infinite characteristics of the soul: knowledge, perception, happiness, and energy. (Some North American and European Jains substitute a different symbol for the swastika.) The symbol of the human right hand in the lower portion shows openness and fearlessness. The circle in the middle of the hand is a wheel with twenty-four spokes of light, symbolic of the twenty-four ancient teachers of the religion. The word in the center of the circle is *ahimsa*, "doing no harm" toward all the living things in this world. Ahimsa is the key to liberating oneself from the cycle of reincarnation, and the spokes emanate as light from this key word. A phrase at the bottom does not always appear with the use of this symbol. Sometimes it is translated as "Live and let live," but this is a cliché in contemporary English. It's better to translate it as "Let all creatures help one another."

4-2a Founding and the First Thousand Years (600 B.C.E.–ca. 400 C.E.)

Jainism arose during the sixth century B.C.E. in the Ganges River valley of northeastern India, a time and place of intense religious activity and reform. Jains opposed the dominant Hindu priestly groups who emphasized salvation by the sacrifices that their priests performed and interpreted. The new religious perspectives promoted **asceticism**, physical denial and mental self-discipline as a necessary part of liberation. Jains also promoted the abandonment of sacrificial rituals and the pursuit of enlightenment that brings freedom from **reincarnation**, the unhappy passage of the soul at death from one body to another. Jainism began as a reform movement within Hinduism, but over time it grew into a distinct religion.

Jains believe that the present era has had a series of twenty-four religious leaders. The first Jain leader of whom we know something historically reliable is the twenty-third, **Parshvanatha**, a religious reformer who lived in the 600s B.C.E. He rejected Hindu sacrifices and taught the abandonment of worldly attachments. Jains regard Parshvanatha as the twenty-third of the twenty-four **Tirthankaras**, "Ford Finders" who lead the way across fords in the rivers of constant reincarnation. Tirthankaras are not gods, but rather enlightened humans whose stories and teachings point the way for others. Connected with this line of ford finders are some Hindus, especially Krishna, whom Jains consider a cousin of the twenty-second

asceticism [ah-SET-uh-SIHZ-uhm] Physical denial and mental self-discipline, a necessary part of liberation in Jainism

reincarnation Unhappy passage of the soul at death from one body to another

Parshvanatha [parsh-VAHN-ah-thuh] Religious reformer who lived in the 600s B.C.E, regarded by Jains as the twenty-third Tirthankara

Tirthankaras [tuhr-TAHN-kah-ruhz] "Ford finders" who lead the way across fords in the rivers of constant reincarnation

Shvetambar [shveht-AHM-bahr] Jain group with "white-clothed" monks and nuns

Digambar [die-GAM-bahr] "Sky-clothed" Jain group with naked monks

Tirthankara. By incorporating and redefining key Hindu figures in their religion, Jains kept some contact with the surrounding Hindu world—important for Jain survival and growth—and yet distinguish themselves from it.

Vardhamana (VAHR-duh-MAHN-uh), also known as Mahavira, "Great Hero," was the twenty-fourth and last Tirthankara of this age. He is seen as the last and perfect teacher of true knowledge and practice, but Jains do not call him the "founder" of their religion, because it has always existed. Mahavira is commonly said to have lived from 599 to 527 B.C.E., although some put him a century later. Mahavira's life is written down in the Jain scripture, but these accounts are filled with later, legendary material. They also vary in content, depending on which of the two main Jain groups is writing his story. Despite these historical challenges, the scriptures provide an adequate basis for our historical understanding of his life and the early Jain movement.

Like the Buddha, Mahavira was born in northeast India into the Kshatriya class of rulers and warriors. When he was around thirty years old, he renounced his privileged status and took up an ascetic life. Mahavira spent the next twelve years in strict asceticism, punishing his body in order to free his soul. After pushing himself to the point of death several times, he experienced a sudden flash of enlightenment that gave him omniscience, or full knowledge of everything in the universe. He then converted eleven male disciples as the nucleus of his movement and formed a monastic community with them. They had no permanent home, but instead wandered as monks from place to place. Mahavira taught his followers extensively, but many Jains believe that after his enlightenment he communicated through a divine sound that emanated from his body, which his followers could interpret into human words. He was no longer hungry, thirsty, or tired, nor did he age. Unlike the Buddha, who found a "middle way" between intense self-denial and ordinary life, Mahavira and his followers kept to the path of radical asceticism. After more than thirty years of activity, and after starving himself at the end of his life, Mahavira's body died and his soul reached full eternal blessing, never to be reincarnated

again. Two of his original eleven disciples, Indrabhuti and Sudharman, survived Mahavira and led his movement into its second generation.

Read about Mahavira's enlightenment in Jain scripture.

Jains believe that Mahavira attracted 14,000 monks and 36,000 nuns to Jainism before he died. These numbers are probably exaggerated, but they accurately suggest that the movement grew rapidly at first, especially among women. Mahavira rejected the Hindu caste system, drawing his followers from any social and economic class. Under his leadership, Jainism also went from being a movement of only monastics to a movement that had many more lay members than nuns and monks. Early Jainism saw some disagreements over monastic doctrine and practice, as we might expect in a religion that prizes individual accomplishment. The main disagreement to arise early (lasting until today) was over the degree of renunciation that monks and nuns should practice. Just how much self-denial is necessary for liberation? For example, some argued that they should wear white robes and have only minimal possessions, and others claimed that a true monk should be naked and have no possessions. (This nakedness never extended to nuns; Indian cultural attitudes could permit male nudity in public, but never female.) Another dispute is also a gender issue: whether a soul can attain deliverance from a woman's body, with some arguing that a soul must be reborn in a man's body to achieve release from reincarnation.

The results of these differences took time to assume the formal shape we know today, with Jainism split into two main groups. The **Shvetambar** ("white-clothed" monks and nuns) group wears clothing as allowed by their scriptures. The **Digambar** ("sky-clothed," a euphemism for naked) group advocates nakedness for monks as a symbol of complete denial of the world. Shvetambar monastics own only a few possessions, such as scripture books and a whisk for clearing away small beings as they walk, but Digambar monks typically own nothing. (The sight of naked monks out in public, sometimes carrying a colorful whisk of peacock feathers, is a striking reminder of this total renunciation.) Digambars believe that a soul in a female body cannot reach liberation, but Shvetambars affirm that it can. The details of this split remain unclear, because the later accounts of it were written to defend each sect and attack the other. So today, Shvetambar texts and images

Seated Tirthankara in the Jain temple, Mumbai

© 0STILL/SHUTTERSTOCK.COM

Jain monks "clothed with the sky"

REUTERS/JAGADESH N.V

4-2b The Next Thousand Years (600–1600)

The early part of this next period saw the flourishing of Digambar Jainism. Achieving success in the region of modern-day Karnataka, the Digambars gained the support of three Indian kingdoms. As Jain monks did earlier, Digambar monks probably influenced the succession of some kings in these dynasties, thus guaranteeing royal patronage of the new religion. Jain monks acted as spiritual teachers and counselors to many rulers and their advisors. (It might seem strange to us that those who have completely renounced the world would advise rulers, but this is a long Indian tradition.) For centuries kings, queens, state ministers, and generals gave tax revenues to the Jain community, providing richly for their temples and monasteries and for the support of Jain writers and artists. Most prominently, in 981 a general paid for a colossal statue of the Jain hero Gommateshvara (go-MAHT-esh-VAR-uh) at Shravanabelagola (SHRAH-vahn-BEL-uh-GOHL-ah). This statue is today one of the holiest and often-visited sites in Jainism.

Take a virtual tour of Shravanabelagola on Google Earth™.

Visit an exhibit of Jain art.

In the time of their greatest political influence from about 500 to 1200 C.E., Jain monks of both main groups gave up wandering asceticism and lived permanently in Jain temples or monasteries. The causes of this are disputed, but many historians point to the influence of money, power, and prestige that came from the patronage of monks by rulers. One contemporary legacy of this change is the Digambar practice of ordaining a monk to lead a Jain institution such as a temple, school, or foundation. In this practice, a new Digambar monk doesn't wander in a naked, ascetic state, but rather is a settled, clothed administrator. Some Jains saw these changes as a defection from Jainism's original ideals of ending attachments to the world, but the practices persist today.

The Shvetambars in the north were not as involved in politics as the Digambars to the south, but they held their own there. On the whole, however, this period of Jainism's second millennium belonged to the Digambars. The Shvetambar community suffered under the conquest of India by Muslims in the 1100s, and the continuing Islamic power of the Mughal (MOO-guhl) Empire there. Jains in the north were persecuted and their important shrines were destroyed.

of Mahavira have him clothed, and Digambar texts and images have him naked.

The Shvetambar-Digambar division was probably made permanent by a series of Jain councils that formalized the new Jain scriptures, which from earliest times were only oral collections of teaching and monastic practice. A council held around 455 C.E. formally adopted the Shvetambar canon that is still in use today. Digambar monks refused to attend this meeting. They denounced the Shvetambar canon, and the split between the two groups was formalized.

During these early centuries, Jainism spread westward from the Ganges River valley, settling in areas where it could enjoy royal protection in the different Hindu kingdoms of northern India. Jain tradition claims that in the first century B.C.E. a monk even led a movement to overthrow a king, replacing him with a ruler more sympathetic to the Jains. During the Gupta (GOOP-tuh) dynasty in north India (320–600 C.E.), a time of Hindu revival there, many Jains left the Ganges valley area and migrated to southern, central, and western India. Jainism became stronger in these areas than it had been in its original home, and even though Jains are still concentrated in the north and west of India, Jainism gained a more national base throughout India, which it enjoys today.

It might seem strange that those who have renounced the world would advise rulers, but this is a long Indian tradition.

Doing puja at Shravanabelagola, using flowers while reading Jain scripture

worshipers" and those who are not continues today. Both Shvetambar and Digambar movements have "idol worshipers" and "non–idol worshipers" among them.

4-2c Early Modern Times through Today (1600–Present)

These unhappy divisions provoked a variety of reform movements among the Shvetambar and Digambar laity. An important Digambar reform came in the early 1600s, sparked by the lay poet Banarsidas (bah-NAHR-sih-dahs). This reform stressed the traditional mystical, austere steps on the Jain path. It also attacked the Digambar temple ritual and what it saw as the corruption and worldly comforts of leading monks.

By 1850, idol-venerating Shvetambar monks had been severely reduced in numbers, and lay leaders controlled Jain temples. Shvetambar monasticism then experienced a revival led by monks such as Atmaramji (1837–1896), and the numbers of image-worshiping monks and nuns

Although some Jains advised Muslim rulers, they could not use this to regain their former position. Islam was not as tolerant toward Jainism as Hinduism was. The Shvetambar community was gradually reduced and marginalized, but its successful adaptation to this new status probably contributed to the long-term survival of Jainism.

During this period, sects called **gacchas** arose in the Shvetambar movement. Some of these sects still exist today, for example the Kharataras founded in the eleventh century and the Tapas in the thirteenth century. Both monks and male laity belonged to these gacchas, with the monks playing the leading role. The gacchas disagreed with other Jains about monastic authority, veneration of images/idols, the sacred calendar, and scripture canons. Their leaders worked for generations to end monastic practices they saw as harmful.

The work of the gacchas was not all internal to Jainism, however; they converted Hindus, who became Shvetambar Jains. A more radical group, the Lonka Gaccha, did not accept the newer Jain practices of image veneration and worship in temples. Around 1653 they emerged as the **Sthanakvasi** ("meeting-house dweller") sect of Shvetambars. This division between Jains who are "idol

gacchas [GOTCH-uhs] Sects that arose in the Shvetambar movement from 800–1300 C.E., some of which still exist today

Sthanakvasi [STHAHN-ahk-VAH-see] "Meeting-house dweller" sect that does not accept the newer Jain practices of image veneration and worship in temples

Pilgrims anoint the statue of Gommateshvara during a festival held every twelve years in Shravanabelagola, India.

grew to around 1,500 and 4,000, respectively, by about 2000. The image-venerating Tapa sect is now the largest group of Shvetambars; the non-image-venerating Shvetambar sects, the Sthanakavasis and Terapanthis, are much smaller. At present, all the Shvetambar groups together have about 2,500 monks and 10,000 nuns, and Digambar groups have about 550 monks and 500 nuns, according to a Jain accounting in 2006. As we saw above, the total number of Jains in the world today is about 5 million, so the proportion of monastics is low indeed.

Today both Shvetambars and Digambars maintain their temples in India and distribute their scriptures. Modern Jains also participate in social and economic relief for the general public, such as drought relief in India. They assist Jain widows. They maintain rescue shelters to save animals from slaughter, as a part of their strict teachings on nonviolence and vegetarianism. A unifying movement within Jainism grew in the twentieth century. For example, in 1974 a committee with representatives from every sect compiled a new common text recognized by all Jain groups, called the **Saman Suttam**. Given the divisions in Jainism, this common scripture was a significant accomplishment and has served to unify contemporary Jains.

Read the new *Saman Suttam* scripture.

4-3 Essential Jain Teachings

A Jain monk, after a long and fruitful life, decides to begin the process of "holy death." He has already gained the permission of his monastic order, and he has the required physical strength and soundness of mind to carry it out. He travels to a place of Jain pilgrimage and ritually "leaves his body" there. After taking vows to fulfill this ritual, he begins to eat nothing and to drink only milk and water. Then, after a week, he drinks only water on every third day. About a month after beginning this process, the monk is so physically weakened that he dies, surrounded by a large crowd of reverent witnesses. This "holy death" isn't as common among Jains today as it was centuries ago, but it ritually affirms many key teachings of Jainism. The soul of one who dies this way will find a blessed reincarnation.

Sculpture of the Jain wheel adorns the roofline of a Jain temple in Rajasthan, India.

DINODIA PHOTOS/BRAND X PICTURES/JUPITERIMAGES

Our survey of Jain history has introduced many of the key teachings of Jainism. In this section, we'll look more closely at these important teachings.

4-3a No Gods

Strictly speaking, Jainism has no gods, and some have called it an atheistic (or at least a nontheistic) religion. Because the world is eternal, there is no need for a divine being to create it. Also, the process of karma and reincarnation works on its own, because it is a part of the universe itself and does not need a deity to preside over it. The way to salvation is shown by human "ford finders" and must be accomplished by one's own effort, not given by any divine being. Thus, Jainism not only *has* no gods, it *needs* no gods. Sometimes one will hear Jains in the West say that all liberated souls together are the God of Jainism, but this is not a traditional Jain understanding.

> *Jainism is sometimes called an atheistic religion.*

Although most Jains do believe in good and evil spirits and other heavenly beings, these are not considered gods. Jain lay followers worship some spirits of earth and heaven for daily protection and

Saman Suttam
[SAH-muhn SOOT-ahm]
Common scripture recognized by all Jain groups, compiled in 1974

kalpa [CALL-puh] Sanskrit for "eon," one whole rotation of the wheel of time

jiva [JEE-vuh] Soul, a living substance

ajiva [AH-jee-vuh] Not a soul, an inanimate substance

guidance, but not for eternal release. Ritual veneration of Tirthankaras is done mainly to dedicate oneself more fully to finding one's own release by moral and mental practice, just as they found release on their own.

4-3b Time and the World

Time is real to Jains, who compare it to a turning wheel with twelve spokes; six spokes go up and six go down. The spokes going up signify a time of improvement. In this time, human progress in knowledge and goodness, and liberation from reincarnation is possible. In the descending direction, all human life—including religion—deteriorates, and deliverance is not possible. The two directions make one whole rotation of the wheel of time, a **kalpa** (Sanskrit for "eon"). Hindus think that a kalpa is 4.3 billion years; Jains haven't usually been that precise, but they do think that a kalpa is a very long time. Because Jains hold the universe to be eternal, without beginning or end, these kalpas repeat themselves forever, turning like an eternal wheel.

Unlike some forms of Hinduism and Buddhism, Jainism views the visible, physical world as real, not illusory. The world is eternal and uncreated. It did not come into existence, and it will not pass out of existence. The world is made up of five building blocks of reality: soul, matter, space, motion, and rest. These building blocks are eternal, and they interact constantly; this makes the cosmos and everything in it "run."

Jains see the universe as having four parts. Hell is the lowest part; it has seven vertical levels, with the worst level at the bottom. Jain depictions of hell are meant to teach about the nature of evil and warn people away from it. The middle world has many concentric continents, all with life on them, and separated by seas. At the center are the two continents where humans live, the only area where souls can achieve liberation. The heavenly world consists of twelve levels in two layers: one for the souls of those who are far from their deliverance and another just above it for those who are close to it. Souls become reincarnated from this heaven after a period of rest. At the top of the cosmos is the eternal home of souls that have permanently escaped the material world.

 Read "The World Is Uncreated" from Jain scripture.

Three stories of the Jain cosmos

COURTESY OF MR. SANJAY SURANA OF SHREE DIWAKAR PRAKASHAN

4-3c Jiva and Ajiva

According to Jains, the cosmos is made up of **jiva**, a soul made of a living substance, and **ajiva**, something not a soul, made of a substance that is not alive. Jiva is conscious of itself and the world, happy, and energetic. Jivas, which are infinite in number, are either immobile or mobile. Immobile souls have only one sense: touch. They inhabit tiny particles of earth, water, fire, and air, and are also found in plants of all sorts. Mobile souls inhabit bodies with between two and five sense organs.

As Jains say, just as a lamp can light up a large or small room, a jiva can fill any body it occupies. When the soul fills a body and takes on its shape, it causes the body to live. At death it keeps this shape until it is reincarnated again. Jainism is unique among many south Asian faiths in its teaching about souls: Individual souls are not parts of one cosmic soul to which they will return, but rather each soul (jiva) is eternally individual.

4-3d Karma and Liberation

Each soul in itself is pure. However, the soul is made impure through time by its contact with matter, or ajiva. When this ajiva influences the chain of birth and death, it is called **karma**, "deeds" and the negative result of deeds. Karma is a form of matter so small that some modern Jains call it "fine," or even "atomic," dust. If the body that a soul inhabits dies, that soul may be reborn in any of four types of living beings: humans, animals, or plants on the earth; humans or other beings in heaven; or humans or other beings in hell.

Because of karma, a soul is confined in a series of bodies and must advance in spiritual development before becoming free from this confinement. To be free from karma and reincarnation, a Jain must stop collecting new karma and remove all previous karma. (Some Jains speak informally of "bad karma," but that is redundant—all karma is bad.) Acquired karma can be "worn away" by many different activities: fasting, restricting one's diet to approved Jain foods, controlling taste and other senses, retreating to lonely places, strict discipline of the body, modesty, service, reading Jain scriptures, meditation, and controlling one's ego.

> Most Jains don't believe that anyone can reach liberation in the present period of cosmic decline.

Release from reincarnation, called—as in Hinduism—**moksha**, is the central teaching of Jainism. Moksha is prevented by karma that attaches to the soul, making it too heavy to ascend after the death of the body to the abode of the Jinas. Because it hasn't reached this permanent home, the soul must be reincarnated. This process also prevents self-realization, happiness, and freedom of the soul—all elements of Jain **nirvana**. People are called "victors" (*Jinas*) when they achieve spiritual freedom. This is accompanied by a great inner peace. Becoming liberated is difficult, because it demands a near-perfect mental, moral, and physical observance of Jainism. Most Jains don't believe that anyone can reach liberation in the present period of cosmic decline. Thus, Jain nuns and monks do not seek immediate enlightenment. Instead, they practice Jainism as well as they can to pursue a reincarnation that will bring them closer to deliverance. In other words, they take one step at a time, in one life at a time, to liberation.

4-3e Theories of Knowledge

In religions that have a large role for meditation in the quest for deliverance, theories of knowledge can get complex, especially for nuns and monks. Jainism has theories of arising, change, and decay in a world of space

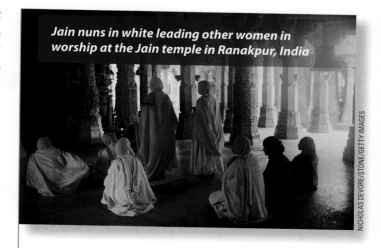

Jain nuns in white leading other women in worship at the Jain temple in Ranakpur, India

and time that is real, as opposed to permanence based on a hidden spiritual reality (for many Hindus) or impermanence of all things (for Buddhists). The Jains developed a complex theory of knowledge with four stages.

1. *Subjective knowledge* is ordinary observation, recognition, determination, and impression.

2. *Scripture knowledge* is based on one's reading and meditation on scriptures and general religious truths. Both subjective knowledge and scripture knowledge arise from sense perception and thinking.

3. *Unmediated knowledge* involves supersensory perception (what we might call "extrasensory perception," or "ESP" for short), reading the thoughts of others (clairvoyance), and knowing everything there is to be known about other beings and things (omniscience).

4. *Direct, immediate knowledge* is knowledge of one's soul in its pure form; this brings freedom from reincarnation. A person with this knowledge is a **kevalin**, "possessor of omniscience."

Yoga—yoking of soul and body—is the best way to full knowledge and liberation. Yoga cultivates true knowledge and leads to faith in Jain teachings and a proper Jain lifestyle. It helps one reach the goal of Jainism, to free one's soul to have its true nature.

karma [KAR-muh] "Deeds" and the negative result of deeds; small matter that attaches to the soul and causes it to be reborn after death

moksha [MOHK-shah] Release from reincarnation

nirvana [near-VAH-nuh] In Jainism, the self-realization, happiness, and freedom of the soul

kevalin [keh-VAHL-in] "Possessor of omniscience," a person who has attained liberation from reincarnation

4-4 Ethics: The Five Cardinal Virtues

A Jain blogger in Great Britain raises a question: Why do some people have extramarital affairs, sometimes one after the other? After discussing how common it might be among her friends and acquaintances, she goes deeper to analyze the possible causes. She invites comments on this observation from her Jain belief: Marital infidelity is caused by the attraction of evil masquerading as something positive. It leads to the loss of self-control and self-esteem, and ultimately it results in the accumulation of much karma.

Liberation from the cycle of reincarnation is the ultimate goal of Jains, but this isn't accomplished only by meditation and knowledge. Jains believe that one must first practice the following five moral principles in thought, speech, and action. They aren't "rules" as such, but ways to live according to the true nature of the soul. The principles are directed against practices that harm one's *jiva*, and harm others as well, by increasing its attachment to *ajiva*. Jain scriptures call them "vows," particularly "greater vows" for monks and nuns and "lesser vows" for layfolk. As these terms imply, the degree to which the principles are practiced is usually stricter for monastics than it is for the laity. Lay Jains are encouraged to practice them in a way that is appropriate to their life in the world, but nuns and monks must observe them rigorously.

Watch a video about the guiding principles of Jain life.

4-4a Do No Harm; Speak the Truth

The first and fundamental moral command in Jainism is **ahimsa**: "Do no harm" to any other living being, whether human, animal, plant, or microscopic organism. Compassion for all life, both human and nonhuman, is central to Jainism. Ahimsa is sometimes interpreted as

ahimsa [ah-HIM-zuh] "Doing no harm" to any other living being in this world

not physically harming another human, but it is much larger than that. One must not injure others physically or spiritually in thought, word, or deed. Jains have a strict diet (see "A Closer Look: Jainism and Food"), because all animals and many plants have souls, and to kill them causes their souls to undergo reincarnation. Mohandas Gandhi, the twentieth-century Hindu who led the struggle for Indian independence from Great Britain with nonviolent opposition, was deeply influenced by the Jain practice of ahimsa. Through Gandhi, nonviolent resistance to social evils spread to South Africa and the United States in their civil rights movements, and ahimsa found a wide, deep role in the world.

Ahimsa also caused all Jains long ago to give up farming, which does harm to many souls in the soil. Jains went into commerce and finance instead, where they prospered, and today many Jains are also in the medical and engineering professions. Monks and nuns practice a strict form of ahimsa. They often wear a cloth over the mouth to avoid harming small insects near them, and they gently whisk away these insects as they walk along, and especially before they sit down. In sum, for monastics ahimsa entails taking no life at all. For laity, it prohibits taking life needlessly.

The second Jain virtue says that one must always speak the truth and never deceive others. This is an essential part of "doing no harm." Saying and hearing the truth often depends on one's perspective, and Jains promote "not one-sidedness," the ability to see and explain all sides of an issue. So one must see that what one says is correctly understood and that true communication takes place. One must speak the truth as long as it does no harm. If speaking truth will lead to another person's harm, one should be silent. But lying to avoid harm is not an option.

4-4b Do Not Steal; Do Not Be Possessive

The third and fourth commands, not to steal or be possessive, apply especially to Jain laity. Monks and nuns have only a few possessions (Shvetambars) or no possessions at all (Digambars). Jains must not take any object that is not willingly and fairly given. One must be satisfied with one's possessions, and then one will not steal. Also, one must labor, buy, and sell honestly. Any attempt to get the better of others financially is considered theft. Some particulars of "do not steal" are:

- Always give people a fair price for their labor or products. To use one's business power to force an unfair, harmful price is forbidden.

A Closer Look:

Jainism and Food

Jain vegetarianism is based on the principle of "doing no harm" to other living beings rather than on any principles of health and nutrition, and is more radical than Hindu vegetarianism. Monks and nuns follow these dietary practices strictly, and the laity in a basic (but still careful) way.

Jains practice a unique concept of extended vegetarianism. Not only do they eat no meat, but they also abstain from root vegetables such as potatoes, garlic, onions, mushrooms, and radishes. However, they consume rhizomes such as dried turmeric and dried ginger and eat plantains. Root vegetables, which are grown underground, are believed to contain far more bacteria than other vegetables, and all these bacteria are living beings with souls. (Buddhists often refrain from onions, garlic, and the like, not because small beings live in them, but because the heat they cause in the body is thought to increase sexual desire.)

Jains refuse any food, whether from animals or plants, obtained with what they consider to be unnecessary cruelty. Many have a diet similar to veganism (no dairy products), in order to avoid harm to souls in processed dairy products such as cheese, although unpasteurized milk is a common drink. Observant Jains do not eat or drink between sunset and sunrise, when more harm is done to small living things because the cooking fire attracts insects that cannot be seen. Jains drink water that is gradually boiled for purification and then cooled to room temperature, to allow tiny beings to escape in the process.

- Do not take things not explicitly given to you.
- Do not take things that other people leave, drop, or forget. Return these things if you can, or leave them where they are.
- Do not purchase things if they are made in a way that does harm to others.

Because Jains have such strict norms for truth and honesty, they have a reputation in India for being scrupulously honest businesspeople. This in turn has contributed to their prosperity.

> Jains have a reputation in India for being scrupulously honest businesspeople.

Possessiveness does not always result from owning things, but often results from emotional attachment to a possession. When that happens, one is owned by one's possessions, and a temptation to steal may arise. Nuns and monks must be nonpossessive when they enter the celibate state, having no lingering feelings for the possessions they left behind. By detaching oneself from possessions, including home and family, one takes a first step to liberation. Householders are nonpossessive when they are not emotionally tied to the things they own. Householders are to relate to people and objects as their manager or steward, not as their owner. True nonpossessiveness also means that one can lose one's possessions without having it affect one's inner self.

4-4c Be Chaste

All sexual intercourse binds one to karma, so it is best to avoid it as much as possible. This includes thinking about it as well as doing it. For monastics, being chaste entails complete abstinence from all sexual intercourse and any other type of sexual activity. For them, chastity means celibacy. Lay Jains must be faithful within marriage to uphold chastity in a way appropriate for them. Sex outside of marriage is seen as particularly powerful in attracting karma.

In addition to keeping their version of these five principles, lay Jains who want a better reincarnation are urged to do a variety of things. Among them are to limit their travel, limit the number and value of their possessions, guard against avoidable evils, devote specific times to meditation, and observe periods of self-denial. Bringing oneself into close contact with monks and nuns is also urged, such as spending occasional days as a nun or a monk, or giving alms in support of monastics.

Read a modern Jain's reflection on root vegetables.

Learning Outcome 4-5

Outline the way Jains worship and practice other rituals.

4-5 Jain Ritual and Worship

Near Shravanabelagola, India, at the statue of Jain hero Gommateshvara, a variety of religious activities are taking place. At the foot of the massive statue, carved from a single piece of rock in 981 C.E., dozens of well-dressed Jains reverently place fruit and flowers as offerings to the hero. Coconuts are especially common. Devotees are sitting on mats, reading Jain scriptures, saying prayers and mantras, and meditating. At times they break out in song and dance, both celebratory and reverent. At the top of the statue, accessible by a flight of stairs, a group of Jain men prepare to pour buckets of colorful, fragrant liquids on Gommateshvara's head, to venerate the statue and pay honor to the Jain ideal of finding release from reincarnation. When standing at the figure's feet, the worshipers must look up to see the inspiring vision of the Jina against the vastness of the sky. His face is designed to inspire serenity and peace in those who look on it in faith.

> Read a British Jain woman's blog on the importance of inner attitudes in worship and morality.

4-5a The Life of Monks and Nuns

Monastics live lives of strong self-denial and self-control in order to liberate their souls at some point in their future lives. They have permanently left their families and spend days in ritual activities: study of scripture, recitation of scripture, meditation, going on "begging rounds" for their main daily meal, and occasionally teaching laity. The entire life of nuns and monks is directed toward the eternal welfare and liberation of their souls. We should now look at some of the details.

Monastics always walk, and always have bare feet, no matter the weather. They don't use any vehicle—such as an automobile, ship, plane, or even a cart—for traveling, because this harms more tiny beings than walking does.

(No Jain monk traveled to Europe or North America until the 1890s, and when one did, his trip by ship was controversial among Jains.) By not wearing shoes, they can more easily avoid killing or injuring insects living on or in the soil. As they wander, they teach Jainism and give spiritual help to those they meet. Monks and nuns typically go around in groups of at least two. They stay only a few days in one location, except in the three months of the Indian rainy season. This constant movement is intended to inhibit personal attraction to material things and the people they meet.

Jain monastics neither cook their food nor have others cook it for them. They go once every day to Jain households and receive from each house a little uncooked food suitable for raw consumption (so householders don't have to prepare more food after the monks have departed). Unless a cook is very careful, the heat of the cooking process does violence to small creatures, as does vegetable chopping and water drinking; nuns and monks don't want to be a part of any violence. They don't accept any food or drink outside a house, but instead go inside where the food is cooked or kept, out of concern for small creatures more numerous outside than inside. When they return to their religious quarters, or to their temporary home if they are wandering, they eat their food in one main meal for each day, sometimes leaving a little for a smaller, unheated meal or a snack.

Jain monks and nuns don't shave their heads or even cut their hair, nor do they go to a barber. They regularly pluck out the hair on their head, or they have others do it. This plucking is a form of self-discipline and self-denial in which one bears pain calmly.

As stated above, Digambar monks are traditionally naked at all times, but there are exceptions. Digambar nuns and all Shvetambar monastics wear unstitched white clothes. For a monk, a loincloth covers his midsection and reaches below the knee, another cloth covers the upper part of his body, and another cloth goes over his left shoulder and almost reaches his ankles. Monks

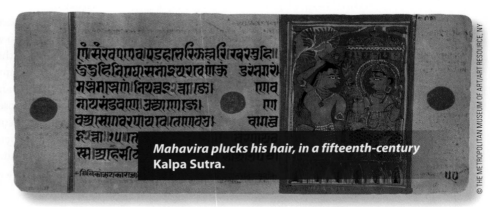

Mahavira plucks his hair, in a fifteenth-century Kalpa Sutra.

also carry a bedsheet and a mat, both made of wool, to sit on. They have a piece of cloth either in their hand or tied on their head, to cover their mouth. They use a small broom of soft woolen threads to clean away bugs before they sit or as they walk, especially outdoors. Digambar monks often have a broom and mouth cloth, but do not wear them or hang them from their bodies, because this could be considered a body covering that compromises their nakedness.

Monks and nuns give a blessing on all Jains they meet, especially the saying "May you attain spiritual prosperity." They make no distinctions between class or caste, or gender or age. Some put a little sandalwood dust on the heads of Jains as a sign of blessing. In sum, monastics teach the path of a righteous and self-controlled life to all Jains. At the end of their lives, as we saw above, monastics traditionally have the option to practice self-starvation, called "holy death," but this is no longer a common practice.

4-5b Life of the Laity in Worship and Devotion

Observant Jain laity have a number of daily rituals. Because Jainism arose in Hindu India and has existed mainly in India for more than two thousand years, many of these are adapted from Hinduism or formed in opposition to Hinduism. Ritual acts of compassion and ahimsa include spreading grain as food for birds and filtering or boiling water for one's drinking and cooking. (Boiling water gives small creatures a chance to leave the water.) Worship before Jain images kept in one's home—bowing to them and lighting a lamp in front of them—is the best way for Jains to start their day. Some Jains oppose these rituals as no better than Hindu worship, or even as superstition. Others recognize that, while the Jain idols have no spiritual power in themselves, the practice of venerating them daily promotes a reverent state of mind. Meditation is done early in the morning and often at noon and night. It typically takes forty-eight minutes (twice the number of the twenty-four Tirthankaras) and has periods of quiet recollection and spoken prayer. It involves the letting go of all passions and negative attitudes and gaining a sense of purity and peace.

The main prayer of Jainism is the **Namokar Mantra**. The term *mantra* correctly suggests that this prayer is brief. It is always repeated in its original language of Sanskrit, in which *namokar* means "I bow." In English translation, it reads: "I bow to the Prophets. I bow to the Liberated Souls. I bow to the Spiritual Leaders. I bow to the Teachers. I bow to all the Holy Ones." This prayer, if spoken in true

Woman with devotional flowers at the Jain temple, Ranakpur, India

© STEVE ESTVANIK/SHUTTERSTOCK.COM

faith, is thought to destroy sins and obstacles and help the one who prays it to move down the road to liberation.

Listen to the Namokar Mantra.

More-elaborate worship is usually done in the temple. Jain temples in India are typically for individual worship and meditation, which can be carried out on any day at any time. In Europe and North America, the Jain community gathers for group activities. One enters a temple saying, "I bow to the Jina" and then banishes distracting thoughts about everyday affairs. Puja, veneration, involves several different activities:

- Ritual washing of the idol/image. Those present at this washing touch their heads with the fluid applied to the image.

- A series of prayers over three days in a temple to help remove karma that obstructs the rising of the soul to a release from reincarnation.

- Paying respect to the images of the Tirthankaras. This can take the form of bowing before them, sitting reverently in prayer or meditation in their presence, or making small offerings of approved fruit and flowers.

Namokar Mantra
[NAHM-oh-cahr MAHN-truh] Main prayer of Jainism, repeated in its original language of Sanskrit

Paryusana [PAR-yoo-SAHN-uh] Most important festival for Jains, an eight-day period of repentance and fasting

Diwali [dee-WALL-ee] Indian festival of lights; for Jains, marks the anniversary of Mahavira's death

- A ritual of prayer focused on a lotus-shaped image that has the "five praiseworthy beings": a Tirthankara, a liberated soul, a religious teacher, a religious leader, and a monk. This image also depicts the "four qualities" that benefit one's soul: perception, knowledge, conduct, and austerity.

As we saw above, the members of some sects of Jainism do not worship or venerate the images found in temples. They will be found there at times, but not participating in any of these rites. Instead, they engage only in meditation and silent prayer in the temple.

4-5c Two Jain Festivals

Like other religions in India, Jainism has many festivals; and like other religious festivals, cultural and religious elements are mixed together in the celebrations. In what follows, we will deal briefly with the two main festivals, Paryusana and Diwali.

Paryusana (also spelled *Paryushan*) is the most important festival for Jains, an eight-day period that falls in August or September. Paryusana is a time to make amends for bad acts of the prior year; one engages in austerities to shed accumulated karma. It also helps to control the desire for sensual pleasures, preventing new karma. During this period, some people abstain from eating and drinking for all eight days, and some for three days, but it is obligatory to fast at least on the last day. Regular ceremonies are held in the temple, with readings of the *Kalpa Sutra*, the principal scripture for Shvetambars, to the congregation. On the final day of Paryusana, Jains seek forgiveness from family, friends, and foes for any wrong acts against them in the previous year. Shortly after Paryusana a dinner is often held, when all Jains gather and eat together, regardless of their socio-economic status.

Read a Jain blog on reading the *Kalpa Sutra* during Paryusana.

For Jains, **Diwali**, the Indian festival of lights, remembers Mahavira's death. The festival falls at the end of the Indian calendar year, in October or November. The eighteen kings of northern India who, according to legend, were with Mahavira when he died, decided that the light of their master's knowledge would be best remembered by the lighting of lamps.

Learning Outcome 4-6

Explain the main aspects of Jain life around the world today, particularly in North America.

4-6 Jainism around the World Today

In Chicago, a thirtyish computer engineer named Churinder worships weekly at the Jain temple. Like other Jains around the world, he offers prayers for his blessing in this world, and especially for eventual release from endless reincarnation. He also makes small offerings to statues of Tirthankaras who have found this release. But there is another reason he comes to the temple, one not so spiritual: to talk to married Jain women who serve as unofficial matchmakers in his search for a suitable Jain wife. He is looking for a young woman who is educated and cultured, one who can live with him in Chicago. Even more, he wants a wife who is a faithful Jain, meditates every day, says her prayers, and observes a Jain diet. With their connections in India, the women are able to put him in touch with a suitable partner there, to whom he soon becomes engaged.

4-6a Jainism in the West

For more than two thousand years, Jains stayed in India, faithful to their duty to minimize travel and the damage it does to other beings. It wasn't until the 1800s that Jainism became a more worldwide faith. As a result of age-old trading links, many Jains from western India settled in eastern African countries that were, like India, in the British Empire—especially Kenya, where

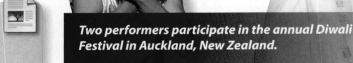

Two performers participate in the annual Diwali Festival in Auckland, New Zealand.

© GREG WARD NZ/SHUTTERSTOCK.COM

the first Jain temple outside India was built, and Uganda. They pursued commerce and international trade. Political unrest in the 1960s forced many of them to relocate to the United Kingdom, where today they number about 30,000. Many Jain students came to the West for higher education, and most of them stayed in the West. They often distinguished themselves in their fields, as for example Anshu Jain, who in 2012 became the co-CEO of one of the largest banks in the world, Deutsche Bank.

Jainism has tried to make as few accommodations as possible to life in the Western world. It has not sought conversions, nor has it been interested in spreading its meditative methods among non-Jains. For instance, although Hindu forms of yoga have become widespread in the Western world as exercise systems (generally detached from Hindu religion), Jain forms of yoga have not.

4-6b Jainism in North America

In North America, Jains have continued their traditional business and professional occupations, the same proportion of professions as in the U.K.: About 30 percent are engineers and 15 percent are in medicine, with others in banking, real estate, computers, and teaching. The high point of Jain immigration to the West was in the late 1970s and 1980s. In the United States, Jains number approximately 30,000, and in Canada about 10,000. Because of their prosperity and because Jains in North America are concentrated in ten states in the United States and one province in Canada, the Jain community has been able to build and operate over sixty social centers, temples, and other organizations. These uses are often combined in one building.

Jain temples sponsor worship (often held on Sunday mornings to fit a Western weekly calendar), education, and social fellowship. Although they have strong lay leadership, Jain temples in North America typically have no monks attached to them, so they function with little of the contact between monastics and laity common in India. Another distinctive feature of North American temples and social centers is that they generally accommodate all the different Jain groups to which their members belong. In this way, they further Jain unity and survival in a North American context that makes sectarian differences less important than in India.

JAINA Federation of Jain Associations in North America, founded in 1981, the leading Jain organization in North America

Visit the Jain Center of America in New York.

A desire to preserve their religious identity in North America, and the increasing challenges of passing on their faith to their second and third generations, has led Jains to form organizations such the Federation of Jain Associations in North America, **JAINA**, founded in 1981. Like most local Jain temples and cultural associations, JAINA crosses the lines of regional Indian customs and the different Jaina sects. English-language publications such as the *eJain Digest* (available online) and *Jain Spirit* have presented Jain ideals such as nonviolence and vegetarianism to the faithful and to the wider world. Recently, Jains have been addressing issues of environmentalism. Their religious convictions that the world is eternal and that one must do no harm to all its living beings strengthen their interest in a sustainable planet.

Study Tools 4

Ready to study? In the book you can:

● Review Learning Outcome answers and glossary terms with the tear-out Chapter Review card.

Or you can go online to CourseMate, at www.cengagebrain.com, for these resources:

● Chapter quizzes to prepare for tests

● Interactive flashcards of all glossary terms

● A timeline of events for this chapter

● An eBook with introductions, interactive quizzes, and live links for all web resources in the chapter

CHAPTER 5

Encountering Buddhism: The Middle Path to Liberation

Learning Outcomes

After studying this chapter, you will be able to do the following:

5-1 Explain the meaning of *Buddhism* and related terms.

5-2 Summarize how Buddhism was founded and developed into what it is today.

5-3 Outline the essential Buddhist teachings.

5-4 State the main ethical precepts of Buddhism for both monastics and laypeople.

5-5 Discuss the way Buddhists worship and meditate.

5-6 State the main features of Buddhist life around the world today, especially in North America.

Study Tools

After you read this chapter, go to the Study Tools at the end of the chapter, page 137.

"I take refuge in the Buddha; I take refuge in the Dharma; I take refuge in the Sangha." —Basic Buddhist affirmation

Your Visit to a Zen Retreat Center

Imagine that you're going on a weekend retreat to a Zen Buddhist temple and retreat center. You've read some popular books on Zen and can recite a few Zen riddles. The retreat will take you to Singapore in south Asia, but Zen centers in North America from Woodstock, New York, to San Diego, California, hold similar retreats.

As you walk into the temple, you notice a comfortable area where visitors can relax at a café near the entrance. You'll return there regularly during "rest time" during the retreat. It gives an impression of simplicity that is reflected in the whole retreat center. You then sign in and are required to surrender your cell phone—it will be given back when you leave, you are told. You are shown to your dormitory, where you notice about thirty woven straw mats in one large room, much like the sleeping arrangements in a Buddhist monastery. You claim one by placing on it the sleeping bag and pillow that you've brought with you.

Then you go to the main meditation hall. Meditation cushions have been neatly laid out throughout the hall, which has a white statue of the Buddha with small arrangements of flowers and small votive candles (but no incense) at one end. You also see a drum and handbell at the front. You begin each day with yoga and stretching exercises, so that the physical process of sitting in meditation won't distract your mind. Then come Buddhist prayers, both spoken and meditated, for thirty minutes each. The main part of each day is dedicated to several meditation sittings. They are only thirty minutes long and go quickly, with exercises such as yoga between them. The monks leading the retreat give regular lectures as well as informal talks. You learn three different ways to meditate: breath meditation, self-questioning meditation, and

What Do YOU Think?

The most important aspect of Buddhism today is meditation to bring inner peace.

Strongly Disagree				Strongly Agree		
1	2	3	4	5	6	7

"silent observation of the mind" meditation. The time at the retreat center also teaches you eight sitting positions and two sleeping positions.

The monks awaken you at 5 AM, and lights-out is at 9:30 PM. Three meals a day, all freshly prepared according to Buddhist dietary customs, are served buffet style. You are thankful that you don't have to go out begging for your food every morning as Buddhist monks do. You are surprised how hungry you get, and how good the food tastes, but then you remember with a little guilty feeling not to develop an attachment to the food—that's not Buddhist at all! So you quietly resolve not to go up for seconds any longer.

At the end of the retreat, you have your first and only small-group session to share experiences from the past three days. When you finally leave the retreat center with a friend, you notice that your "silent observation of the mind" meditation is continuing. You take in all the sights and sounds of the city, but your mind isn't affected by it. Your friend remarks, referring to the film, "It's like living in the Matrix!"

Encountering Buddhism can be a "mind-bending" experience. As you are introduced to Buddhism in this chapter, you will notice these features:

● Buddhism has many numbered lists of teachings and practices that must be learned, but Buddhism can't be known, much less lived, "by the numbers."

 The lotus, a symbol of Buddhism, is a beautiful flower that grows in the muddy waters of this world.

Zen temple, Japan

© DARIUS M/SHUTTERSTOCK.COM

- Because all Buddhist teaching is said to flow from the Buddha and his carefully conceived system, we might expect it to be unified. However, Buddhism is one of the world's most diverse religions, befitting a religion that teaches that all things are impermanent.

- Buddhists follow the teachings of the Buddha carefully, as the best model of the way to find liberation from suffering, the main problem with the world. But they also frequently quote the Buddha's saying, "Don't believe because of what your teacher says—follow your own wisdom."

- Many Buddhists have no concept of an all-powerful god, but some Buddhists view the Buddha as a supreme heavenly being.

- Buddhism is unique among the major religions of the world in its combination of deep meditation and earnest morality, but Buddhists who aren't monks or nuns don't meditate regularly. Instead, they worship various buddhas and other divinities in ways that are similar to Hindu worship.

- It is common for people who call themselves Buddhists—especially in China, Japan, and the West—to also practice other religions. Moreover, they often say, "People of other religions can practice Buddhism too."

Buddhism [BUHD-ihz-um] Religion of enlightenment

Buddha [BUH-dah] "Enlightened One"; although Gautama is "the Buddha," the term applies to all individuals who attain this state

---

Buddhism is unique in its combination of deep meditation and earnest morality.

Learning Outcome 5-1

Explain the meaning of *Buddhism* and related terms.

5-1 The Name *Buddhism*

Buddhism is the religion founded by Siddhartha Gautama (sih-DAHR-tuh GOW-tah-muh), who became the Buddha. Despite the similarity of the words *Buddhism* and *Buddha*, the religion isn't named after him. **Buddhism** means the religion of enlightenment, not the religion of the Buddha. The English word *Buddhism* didn't appear until the 1830s, but it expresses accurately enough designations used by Buddhists, such as *Buddha Law*, *Buddha School*, or the *Teachings of the Buddha*. Today, *Buddhism* is used as the name for their religion by Buddhists in Europe and North America, and it is widely accepted in Asia as well. (For more on Buddhism as the religion of enlightenment, see the "Symbols of Buddhism" box.) The related term the **Buddha**, or Enlightened One, usually refers to Siddhartha Gautama after his enlightenment. Both words derive from the ancient Sanskrit word *buddha*, "enlightened, awakened." *Buddhism* and *Buddha* are best pronounced BUHD-ihz-um and BUHD-ah, respectively, with first syllables rhyming with *could*, but you will often hear BOOD-ihz-um and BOO-dah.

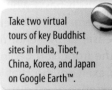

Watch the introduction to a PBS-TV program on Buddhism.

Take two virtual tours of key Buddhist sites in India, Tibet, China, Korea, and Japan on Google Earth™.

Buddhism teaches that anyone can become enlightened, even a buddha. Gautama is the model Buddha, but many Buddhists believe that he taught his followers to think for themselves and carefully examine the teachings of the religion to determine what is right for them. When anyone becomes fully enlightened, that person is a buddha too. So the word *Buddha* is a term, not a personal name, as mentioned above. We'll stay true to this by referring in this chapter to *the Buddha*, with *the* and a capital *B*, when Gautama is meant. When another

A Closer Look:

The Symbol of Buddhism

Buddhism is a diverse religion, and it is difficult to express in art the state of nirvana that the Buddha achieved, so Buddhism has a number of symbols. The swastika is one, seen often in temples and jewelry; the beautiful lotus blossom that grows out of the muck of the world is another; the deer is a third, especially used to symbolize Buddhist teaching; and the image of the Buddha in seated meditation is a fourth.

By far the most common Buddhist symbol, and perhaps the earliest, is the wheel. This is called the **dharmachakra**, "wheel of the teaching." It may look to you like the steering wheel of a ship,

BONNIE VAN VOORST © CENGAGE LEARNING

Figure 5.1 "Wheel of the teaching," symbol of Buddhism

but it's really the wheel of a cart or chariot. Like other ancient religious symbols, it has multiple layers of meaning. First, the Buddha "turned the wheel of the teaching" to get his movement going. Second, the dharmachakra's implied motion is a symbol of the spiritual change created by Buddhism. Third, the different parts of the wheel summarize Buddhism. The rim represents the endless cycle of rebirth, escaped only by following Buddhist teachings to enlightenment. The eight spokes stand for the Noble Eightfold Path taught by the Buddha. Finally, the wheel's hub symbolizes moral self-discipline, the first step toward enlightenment.

The dharmachakra was a familiar symbol in early Buddhism. It stood for the Buddha's teachings and for the Buddha himself. Today, the dharmachakra is used in every Buddhist land. In statues of the Buddha, a wheel is sometimes seen in his palms and on the soles of his feet. It also appears when he holds his hands in the circular dharmachakra position.

Buddhist wheel with deer on the roof of Jokhang Temple, Lhasa, Tibet

STEVE ALLEN/BRAND X PICTURES/JUPITER IMAGES

---

person who achieves the buddha nature is meant, we will omit *the* and use a lowercase *b*.

Learning Outcome 5-2

Summarize how Buddhism was founded and developed into what it is today.

5-2 Buddhism Today as Shaped by Its Past

A layman sits in the lotus position in a temple in Busan, South Korea. He is meditating in turn on eight murals dealing with different events in the life of the Buddha. They deal with his birth through his death, but they center on the story of how he discovered the Middle Path to enlightenment and then shared it with others. As the man finishes his contemplation of one picture, he shifts slightly and turns to the next until he finishes all of them. Many Buddhist temples have these series of pictures depicting the life of the Buddha. Both monks and layfolk find

instruction and inspiration in them, showing how the life of the Buddha continues to have a profound effect on Buddhists.

Today's Buddhism has a long and significant history behind it. Buddhists believe that Siddhartha Gautama discovered the **Middle Path** out of suffering, a new way between the extreme self-denial characteristic of Hindu asceticism and the ordinary life of the Hindu householder. Gautama reached the full enlightenment that rescued him from constant reincarnation into this world. This Middle Path is built on Hindu ideas of the time and uses some similar vocabulary, but by and large Buddhism from the first was an alternative to Hinduism. The Buddha then taught his discovery to a monastic community that he founded. After his death, his teachings spread throughout the Indian subcontinent, and then over the next thousand years to the largest part of Asia. In

dharmachakra
[DAHR-muh-CHAHK-ruh] "Wheel of the teaching," a symbol of Buddhism

Middle Path Style of life between extreme self-denial and ordinary life, which can lead to enlightenment

The Buddha teaching monks, sculpture in Wat Charkyai, Thailand

discern in them a reliable outline of his life. This life is not what we would consider a modern biography, because Buddhist scriptures speak of only four key events in the Buddha's life: birth, enlightenment, first sermon, and death.

Siddhartha Gautama was born into a royal family in the northern Ganges River valley, in what is today southern Nepal, and lived for eighty years. Scholars disagree on the dates of his life. The traditional dating of his lifespan is about 566 to 486 B.C.E., but more-recent research tends toward 490 to 410 B.C.E. His family name was Gautama and his personal name was Siddhartha, but in the custom of the times, his family name is used more than his first name. In Buddhist scriptures, his followers do not call him "Buddha," but "Lord." Another common name for the Buddha is **Shakyamuni**, "the sage of the Shakyas," referring to the clan to which Gautama belonged.

Watch a BBC report on the life of Buddha shorn of its legends.

Gautama's parents were Hindus in the Kshatriya caste of warriors and rulers. An astrologer told his father, King Suddhodana, that his son would either become a powerful emperor or renounce this to become a powerful religious leader. Queen Maya dreamed one night that a baby elephant came into her womb through her side. Ten lunar months later, her son was born from her right side. The whole earth reacted to his birth, and when Baby Gautama alighted by his own power on the ground, he proclaimed, "I am born for the salvation of the world; this is my last rebirth." These are probably legendary touches, of course. Gautama's early life as a prince was affluent and comfortable, protected from the ills of the world. At age sixteen he married the Princess Yashodhara, with whom he had a son. Until he was twenty-nine Gautama had a privileged, luxurious life as he waited to become king. However, this would soon change.

The story of the Buddha's enlightenment begins with a profound experience he had in the **Four Passing Sights**. On chariot rides outside the palace, Gautama

Shakyamuni [SHAK-yah-MOO-nee] "The sage of the Shakyas," the clan to which Gautama belonged; another name for the Buddha

Four Passing Sights Gautama's encounter with old age, sickness, death, and an ascetic—the first step in his enlightenment

modern times, Buddhism has come to the West and has become probably the most influential religion from Asia. With between 400 and 450 million adherents throughout the world, Buddhism is the fourth-largest religion today. This section will recount Buddhism's story and introduce its diverse groups and teachings along the way.

5-2a Gautama's Road to Enlightenment

Buddhism is founded on the life of Siddhartha Gautama (in the Pali language in which many Buddhist scriptures are written, *Siddhatha Gotama*). His life is known through scriptures written hundreds of years after his death. As Damien Keown has said, by the time the scriptures were written, the story of the Buddha's life "had become embellished with fanciful details, which makes it difficult to separate fact from legend."[1] Nevertheless, scholars have managed to

The story of the Buddha's life "had become embellished with fanciful details, which makes it difficult to separate fact from legend." —Damien Keown

[1] Damien Keown, *Buddhism* (Oxford, UK: Oxford University Press, 1996), 17.

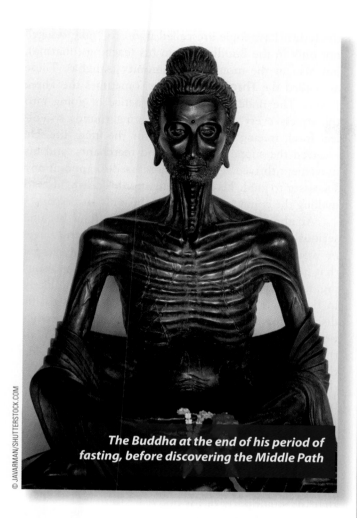

The Buddha at the end of his period of fasting, before discovering the Middle Path

two states, but the Buddha forged a new path between them.

5-2b Achievement of Enlightenment

Living in this Middle Path, the prince sat in long meditation under a tree in the city of Bodh Gaya (bohd GUY-uh) and achieved his own enlightenment. He reached an understanding of life that he would soon teach to his followers. Under the tree, called in Buddhist tradition the **Bodhi Tree**, or "Bo Tree" for short, he became *the Buddha*. Not only did he gain perfect knowledge of himself and the release this brought, but he also attained full knowledge of all his past lives. He could have passed immediately from life into full release, but he postponed this in order to help others find the way to liberation. From this point on, Buddhist scriptures call him the **Tathagata**, "one who has gone" to enlightenment, and the Buddha insisted that his followers call him by this name. The Bodhi Tree that stands in Bodh Gaya today has become one of the holiest sites in all Buddhism.

Bodhi Tree [BOH-dee] Tree in Bodh Gaya under which Gautama Buddha gained enlightenment, now a holy site

Tathagata [tah-THAH-gah-tuh] "One who has gone" to enlightenment; honorific term for the Buddha

"Decay is inherent in all things; work out your salvation with diligence!"
—last words of the Buddha

saw for the first time (1) an old person, (2) a gravely ill person, (3) a human body on the way to cremation, and (4) a holy man who had renounced ordinary life. He was so shaken by the first three sights and attracted by the last one that he renounced his wealth, his throne, and his family in order to become a holy man and answer his religious questions. During the next seven years, he received instruction from several Hindu teachers and practiced meditation with them. With five companions who were also holy men, he practiced extreme mental and physical self-denial that reduced him to "skin and bones." Eventually he passed out from weakness, and when he regained consciousness, he knew that this extreme self-denial wouldn't lead to his goal. Instead, it weakened his mind and even threatened his life. He then devised the Middle Path that could lead to enlightenment. Hindus taught that liberation could be found in these

In a scene from the film **Little Buddha**, *Siddhartha (played by Keanu Reeves) reaches enlightenment by the Bo Tree, accompanied by modern friends.*

The Buddha then taught publicly in a deer park in Sarnath, India, announcing his discovery of the Four Noble Truths and the Noble Eightfold Path, teachings that we'll consider below. For the next forty-five years, the Buddha taught throughout northeastern India and established an order of monks called the **sangha**, or "community." In fact, Buddhism became the first of the world's religions to develop monasticism (muh-NAS-tuh-sɪz-uhm), a life of meditation, prayer, and self-control in a tightly regulated community of monks or nuns. (Sometimes lay Buddhists call their organizations a "sangha," but this is not the original or historic use of

the term.) Laypeople are called upon to "take refuge" not only in the Buddha and in his teaching (dharma), but also in the monastic community (sangha). These are called the **Three Refuges**, or sometimes the Three Jewels. The Buddha began the practice of going into the streets every morning on begging rounds to collect food, freeing up more time for the inner life. He received the support of kings and merchants, and his movement thrived. The Buddha refused to appoint any successor to guide his movement after his death, instead making the community of monks his only successor.

At about the age of eighty, the Buddha became seriously ill in Kusinara (koo-sin-AHR-uh) and knew he would soon die. Some older scholarship suggested that he ate a bad piece of pork and got food poisoning, but many scholars now think that this is unlikely in light of his strict vegetarianism. He met with his disciples for the last time to impart his final instructions, ending with the words, "Decay is inherent in all things; work out your salvation with diligence!" He then lay down on his right side and went into meditation. He passed through several levels of meditative trance until, when he died, he passed into full nirvana, an event called his **parinirvana**. His body was cremated on an open pyre according to Indian custom. His followers decided that the small parts of his body that remained—wood-fire cremation doesn't reduce stronger bones and teeth to ash—would be distributed as relics and enshrined in monuments.

Read a short explanation of "The Buddha in the Context of Buddhism."

Tour the Asia Society's exhibit on "Buddhist Art and Pilgrimage."

After the Buddha's funeral, hundreds of monks met in Rajagrha (rahj-AHG-ruh), India. The monastic rules and the teachings of the Buddha were finalized and formally recited. These rules, called the *Vinaya* (vihn-IGH-uh), were an oral collection for more than two centuries. The rules and teachings were recited and memorized at the council, and would soon be used in spreading the religion to the many peoples and languages of India. Over time they would be written down and come to form the most important part of Buddhist scripture.

5-2c India, Sri Lanka, and Theravada

Buddhism became more diverse as it spread. A significant point of diversity arose at the second Buddhist council, around 375 B.C.E. After debates between

Monks praying and meditating at the Bodhi Tree, Mahabodhi Temple, Bodhgaya, India

those who advocated keeping strictly to what they considered the earliest practices of Buddhism and those advocating change, the second group left and called itself the "Great Sangha." This group belittled the traditionalists as **Hinayana**, or "small vehicle" Buddhists, but the traditionalists' self-designation of **Theravada** eventually stuck. This name is usually translated as "tradition of the elders," but more accurately means "original/abiding teaching." The Theravadins themselves experienced disagreements that led to a number of splinters. Over time, eighteen different Theravadin groups developed, each with its own distinctive teachings, and spread throughout India and Southeast Asia. Today, only one of these groups survives, in Sri Lankan Theravada.

Palm-leaf Buddhist sutra, with prayer beads

> Buddhism has been a "missionary religion" in ways that other Indian religions haven't.

The next momentous event in the development of Buddhism was the meeting of a Buddhist monk and the third-century B.C.E. Indian ruler named Ashoka (ah-SHOHK-uh). A ruler of the large Mauryan (MOHR-yuhn) Empire in India, Ashoka had expanded it until it covered modern-day India. But he had become deeply troubled by the bloodshed he caused in his conquests. Listening to the monk convinced Ashoka to devote himself to the peaceful message of Buddhism. Ashoka erected thousands of rock pillars all over his kingdom with the teachings of the Buddha carved into them, the first written evidence we have of Buddhism. He didn't make Buddhism the official religion of the Mauryan Empire, but he did support it in various ways, including building Buddhist monasteries and schools of higher learning. More importantly, Ashoka sent monks as missionaries all over India and to several foreign lands in south Asia, from which Buddhism would eventually travel to the rest of Asia and the world. Ashoka sent his son and daughter, both of them now Buddhist monastics, to Sri Lanka (Ceylon)—an island nation just off the southern Indian coast—around the year 240 B.C.E. Its king was converted, and his kingdom

went with him into Buddhism. One of the gifts for the king that Ashoka's children took with them was a cutting from the original Bodhi Tree. Trees said to have descended from this cutting can still be found in Sri Lanka. Buddhism has been a "missionary religion" in ways that other Indian religions haven't, a fact that is directly traceable to Ashoka.

Sri Lanka was the site of the fourth Buddhist council, in the first century B.C.E. For the first time, all **sutras** (scriptures) were recorded in writing, on palm leaves and in the Pali language. Much of our knowledge of Buddhism stems from this early sutra collection. It is formally known as the *Tipitaka*, or "Three Baskets." The three "baskets" are the *Vinaya Pitaka* (basket of rules for monastics), the *Sutta Pitaka* (basket of the Buddha's teachings), and the *Abhidamma* (AH-bih-DAHM-uh) *Pitaka* (the higher-teaching basket, for monks).

Historians today agree that Sri Lankan monks saved the Theravada branch of Buddhism from extinction. It had spread in early years to Sri Lanka and other parts of Southeast

Hinayana [HIN-ah-YAHN-uh] "Small vehicle" of southern Buddhism, an insult used by Mahayanists for Theravada

Theravada [THAIR-uh-VAHD-uh] Usually translated as "tradition of the elders," but more accurately means "original/abiding teaching"

sutra [SOO-truh; Pali: *Sutta*] Canonical scripture text

Tipitaka [TIH-pee-TAH-kuh] "Three Baskets," the main internal divisions of the canon (Sanskrit: *Tripitaka*)

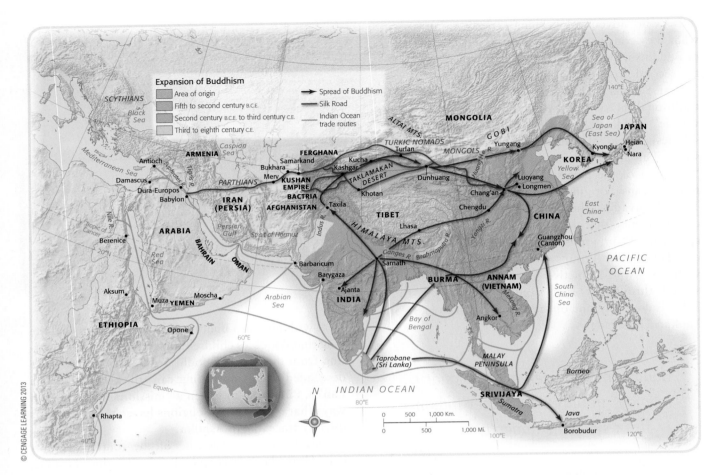

Map 5.1

Spread of Buddhism in Asia, 400 B.C.E.–800 C.E.

Buddhism originated in what is today Nepal and soon became a major religion in India. From India it spread to what is today Sri Lanka, then to central and Southeast Asia, China, Korea, Japan, and finally Tibet.

Asia, while it declined in India. In fact, it nearly died out in its homeland in the northern parts of the Indian subcontinent when a revived Hinduism reduced its numbers and again when India was largely taken over by Muslims in the 1500s C.E. Only Sri Lankan Buddhism survived, becoming the oldest form of Buddhism in the world. Theravada monks from Sri Lanka brought Buddhism to Myanmar (MEE-ahn-mahr, formerly called Burma), Thailand, Malaysia, Cambodia, Vietnam, and Laos (lous) (see Map 5.1).

> Explore Buddhist sites in China and Korea after 1279.

Mahayana [MAH-hah-YAHN-uh] "Large vehicle" branch of Buddhism in northern and eastern Asia

Trikaya [trih-KIGH-yuh] "Three bodies," of the Buddha: the historical Gautama Buddha, many heavenly buddhas, and the Buddhist teaching

5-2d The Rise of Mahayana: China and Japan

Mahayana—the "large vehicle" branch of Buddhism found today in China, Japan, and Tibet—was a development of the split at the first Buddhist council. The monks of the Great Sangha held that Buddhism should be a large community, not just a vehicle for monks. They wanted to allow Buddhist layfolk to have a much greater participation in Buddhism than before. This meant that adaptation to indigenous religions was easier for Mahayanists, although Theravadins made accommodations as well. People would convert to Mahayana Buddhism more easily if some of their gods and religious practices were a part of it. So the doctrine of **Trikaya**, the "three bodies," of the Buddha, was developed. The historical Gautama Buddha was his first body, his second body was that of many heavenly buddhas adapted from other religions, and his abstract third body was the Buddhist teaching itself.

More significant in Mahayana was the increased importance of the **bodhisattva**, or "buddha-to-be," someone who has attained enlightenment but compassionately remains in this suffering world to bring others to enlightenment. Local divinities, spirits, and heroes of other religions were often reinterpreted as bodhisattvas, and they became the object of Buddhist worship in order to bring adherents closer to nirvana. New scriptures soon arose to explain these new teachings and practices. Mahayana Buddhists believe that they come from the Buddha himself, even though their ideas are mostly new to Buddhism. One of the scriptures, the *Diamond Sutra*, defends its new teaching by having the Buddha say, "I preach with ever the same voice." However, the differences between Theravada and Mahayana teachings are unmistakable. At the root of these differences is the belief in Theravada Buddhism that individuals must find the way to nirvana on their own. Mahayana Buddhists believe that others—especially the Buddha and bodhisattvas—must help the individual find nirvana, or in some Mahayana groups simply give it to them.

> "I preach with ever the same voice." —The Buddha

See a "zoomable" photo of the Chinese *Diamond Sutra*, the world's earliest printed book (868 C.E.).

China already had two main religions, Confucianism and Daoism (Taoism). Both religions, but especially Daoism, had elements of folk religions reaching back to the dawn of human life in China. Folk religion consisted of local gods and spirits, mythologies, astrology, divination, magic, folk medicine, and so on. Over time, the Mahayana beliefs that began in India became a truly "large vehicle," spreading to China and later to Korea, Japan, Nepal, and

A **Buddhist nature-spirit statue**

SARAH M. GOLONKA/BRAND X PICTURES/JUPITER IMAGES

Vietnam. Many historians also consider Buddhism in Tibet to be a part of Mahayana, but it is also commonly considered a third "vehicle." So what began as a small protest by monks soon after the death of the Buddha would become—after a long period of adaptation—the dominant form of Buddhism in northern and central Asia as well as the third main religion of China and the principal faith of Japan. Ultimately it would become the branch of Buddhism best known in the Western world.

The different Buddhist groups in China and Japan illustrate the diversity within Mahayana. The Pure Land Schools of Buddhism soon became a leading Mahayana group. In the *Pure Land Sutra*, the Buddha reveals Amitabha (AH-mee-TAB-uh; in Japanese, Amida) Buddha and his "Pure Land," or heaven. If one can be reborn there, one can easily achieve nirvana. The people of China had for millennia sacrificed to gods and goddesses; venerated their ancestors; prayed for the health of their families, animals, and crops; hoped for heaven and feared hell; and so on. The Chinese found that Mahayana Buddhism met these needs and habits. The growing conviction that this period of time was one of religious decline helped along the idea that people could not reach enlightenment by themselves but could rely on the power of higher beings to bring them to enlightenment. Amitabha Buddha and his heavenly Western Paradise (the "Pure Land") fit this idea. All one has to do, Pure Land Buddhism says, is faithfully chant the name of Amida Buddha, and when that worshiper dies, he or she goes to the "Pure Land." This is not nirvana itself, but rather a place in which the obtaining of nirvana is easy.

Read about early Confucian opposition to Buddhism.

Another Buddhist group that arose in China was Ch'an (chahn), better known by its Japanese name, **Zen**. The Indian monk Bodhidharma came to China around 520 C.E., bringing the "silent transmission" of secret teaching about enlightenment that supposedly reached back to the Buddha. He became the founder of Zen. Zen meditation aims for the immediate acquiring of a "Buddha mind." Zen Buddhism focuses on developing the immediate

bodhisattva [BOHD-hee-SAHT-vuh] "Buddha-to-be," someone who comes very close to achieving full buddha nature but postpones it to help others reach it

Zen Buddhist group that aims for the immediate acquiring of a "buddha mind"; its Chinese name is "Ch'an"

Buddhism's accommodation to ancestor worship: offering a paper lotus to ancestors at a Buddhist temple in Vietnam

© BRAND X PICTURES/JUPITER IMAGES

koan [KOH-an]
Zen riddle meant to induce nonrational enlightenment

zazen [ZAH-zehn]
Seated meditation, often for long periods, in Zen Buddhism

patriarch, around 700 C.E.; the *Blue Cliff Record*, from around 1000 C.E.; and *The Gateless Gate*, from around 1200 C.E.

Buddhist legend says that a group of Korean monks came to Japan with gifts for its emperor in 538 C.E. Among these gifts were a bronze Buddha and several sutras. After rejecting Buddhism and even throwing the gifts into the sea, the imperial court of the 600s was then drawn to the religion. Although Buddhism began in the Japanese aristocracy, in the 900s the Pure Land group became popular among the lower classes. In the 1200s, Ch'an came to Japan, where it was met with an enthusiastic response by the Samurai warrior class, among others, and renamed *Zen*. Two Japanese Buddhist monks took Zen back to Japan after having studied it in China. One introduced the Rinzai branch of Ch'an/Zen, with its koans to punish the mind and physical blows to punish the body. The other brought in the more sedate Soto (SOH-toh). Both forms of Zen have always had an artistic side, and Japanese Zen monks developed an elegant but simple style of writing, drawing, and painting. The tea ceremony, known for its sophisticated simplicity, also became expressive of Zen, as did the seventeen-syllable poems known as *haiku* (HIGH-koo). (Perhaps the best-known haiku is "Old Pond": Old pond / a frog leaps in / water's sound.)

awareness of a "Buddha mind" through meditation on emptiness. One of the methods for inducing this sudden awareness has been the **koan**, a Zen riddle meant to help reach nonrational enlightenment (see "A Closer Look: Koans"). Because Zen riddles and the process of administering them could be intellectually brutal, they were especially used in the Rinzai (RIHN-zigh) school of Zen that we will discuss below. Zen is known for rejecting the written word and for its sometimes-rough physical tactics. Rinzai abbots can and do strike monks with a stick or baton if they do not like their answers, or if the monks get sleepy during the prolonged sitting meditation called **zazen**. Although a common picture from Zen history is of Bodhidharma ripping up a Buddhist scripture book, Zen Buddhists do have an appreciation for the Buddhist tradition even when they are seemingly ignoring or belittling it. Zen has contributed key books to the Mahayana canon, especially the *Platform Sutra*, written by Hui Neng, the sixth Zen

"What did your face look like before you were born?" —Zen koan (riddle)

Japanese daruma doll depicting Bodhidharma

© HENRY WILLIAM FU/SHUTTERSTOCK.COM

Zen became more important in Japanese Buddhism than it had been in Chinese Buddhism, and from Japan, Zen would spread in the twentieth century to Europe and North America.

Watch a video on Zen and the Japanese tea ceremony.

A final Japanese innovation to be considered here was led by Nichiren (NEE-shee-rehn), a monk who lived from 1222 to 1282. He came to believe that the *Lotus Sutra* contained everything Buddhists needed. So Nichiren encouraged his students to chant the saying "I devote myself to the wonderful Law of the *Lotus Sutra*." This alone

A Closer Look:

Koans

In the West, koans are known as short, independent riddles employed in Rinzai Zen. Some of the more famous are these:

- What did your face look like before you were born?
- What is the sound of one hand clapping?
- Why did Bodhidharma come from the West?
- If you meet the Buddha, should you not kill him?

However, in Zen, koans typically come in the context of a short story. This story does not make gaining sudden insight from the koan any easier, but it does provide a context and an opportunity for sudden insight.

Here is one of these stories, centered on the koan "How many virtues does a cup have?"

Zen master Ummon inquired of a teaching monk, "What sutra are you talking about?"
"The *Nirvana Sutra*," the monk answered.
"The *Nirvana Sutra* speaks of the Four Virtues, doesn't it?"
"Yes, it does."
Then Ummon picked up a cup and asked, "How many virtues does this have?"

"None at all," the monk replied.
"But ancient people said it has virtues, didn't they?" Ummon asked. "What do you think about that?"
Then he struck the cup and asked the monk, "Do you understand?"
"No," the monk replied.
Finally Ummon said, "You had better go on with your lectures on the sutra."

After a Zen master poses a koan to a monk, he carefully studies the monk's reaction and his answer. He then judges how much intuitive direct insight it shows. Answers that are rational are forbidden and will sometimes result in blows from the teacher. (For example, one could answer the first koan in the list above with "Like the face of my grandmother" if one resembles her. But this answer would be rational and incorrect, and might bring punishment.) Or the teacher may say nothing, respond in words, or simply walk away.

Read a story from *The Gateless Gate*, illustrating the successful answer to a koan.

---

ensured enlightenment in this life. He argued that other groups of Buddhists had little value, reflecting a rare type of Buddhist intolerance that earned him opposition from other Buddhists. The Nichiren School nevertheless proved to be a highly popular form of Buddhism in Japan.

5-2e Tibet and the Diamond Vehicle

Buddhism arrived in Tibet in the 700s C.E. when an Indian monk skilled in Buddhist Tantrism, named Rinpoché (RIHN-poh-shay), is said in Buddhist legend to have battled Tibetan demons for control of that land. Rinpoché defeated the demons and then made them protectors of Buddhism in Tibet. This story indicates well the syncretistic nature of Tibetan Buddhism—the combination of more-exotic forms of Buddhism with elements of the native animistic Bön religion. Buddhism had a difficult time getting established in Tibet; during the 800s and 900s C.E., it suffered a setback there, but it eventually won over the country in the 1000s. It then developed into four main schools. In 1578, the rulers of Tibet named the head of the Gelug ("Yellow Hat") School of Tibetan Buddhism the **Dalai Lama**, a title that means "ocean of wisdom" or "oceanic teacher." The fifth Dalai Lama brought virtually all of Tibetan life under his control, and the dalai lamas were from that point on the absolute rulers of Tibet. This made the country's government a true theocracy (rule by clergy). Tibetan Buddhism also spread to Bhutan, Nepal, and Mongolia, but the direct political rule of the Dalai Lama did not extend to these areas.

Tibetan Buddhism, also known as the Diamond Vehicle or **Vajrayana**, is the most complete blend of Buddhism and an indigenous religion. (The Diamond Vehicle is also referred to as *Lamaism* for its leaders, who are called **lamas**, meaning "gurus,

Dalai Lama [DAHL-eye (not "dolly") LAH-muh] "Ocean of wisdom," head of the Gelug School of Tibetan Buddhism and ruler of Tibet

Vajrayana [VAHJ-ruh-YAH-nuh] "Diamond Vehicle," formal name for Tibetan Buddhism

lama [LAH-muh] "Guru, teacher," leader of Tibetan Buddhism

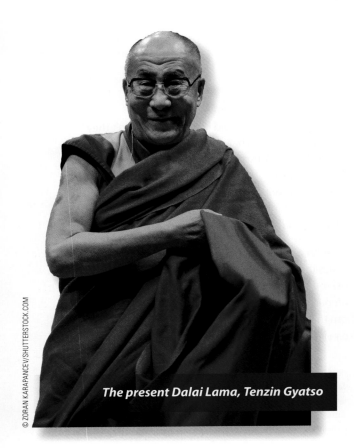

© ZORAN KARAPANCEV/SHUTTERSTOCK.COM

The present Dalai Lama, Tenzin Gyatso

Lama by Tibetans and others when he made public appearances in 2009 and 2010.

> *The boy was said to have correctly claimed the possessions of the previous Dalai Lama, even exclaiming, "That's mine!" about particular items.*

Tenzin Gyatso (TEHN-zihn gee-YAHT-soh), who was born Lhamo Dondrub in 1935, was identified when a young boy as the reincarnation of the thirteenth Dalai Lama, a bodhisattva named Avalokitesvara (AV-uh-loh-KIT-esh-VAHR-uh), the famous "Bodhisattva of Compassion." As the Dalai Lama himself tells it, he was presented with various objects, including toys, some of which had belonged to the thirteenth Dalai Lama and others not. He correctly claimed the possessions of the previous Dalai Lama, even exclaiming about some, "That's mine!" He became the fourteenth Dalai Lama in 1950. In 1951 the Communist Chinese invaded Tibet and permanently annexed it. More than 1 million Tibetans were killed in the aftermath, including the majority of its monks, many of them in mass executions. Six thousand monasteries were destroyed or shuttered.

Watch a BBC report on the Dalai Lama in exile.

Read an essay on a possible female Dalai Lama.

The Dalai Lama fled in 1959 to exile in north India, where he leads a Tibetan government in exile. In 1989 he won the Nobel Peace Prize for spreading a message of tolerance and world peace. He has traveled around the world for speaking engagements and Tibetan Buddhist rituals. Tibetan leaders in exile charge that human rights abuses continue in Tibet, including

teachers"; *Esoteric Buddhism* for passing its teachings secretly from guru to student; and also *Tantric Buddhism* for developing some of its doctrines from the *Tantra*.) This blending helps to explain why Tibetans have various important features unknown in the rest of Buddhism: doctrines such as many divinities and demons, as well as the incarnation of a single buddha in the whole line of Dalai Lamas; organizational practices, for example the theocratic and near-absolute rule of the Dalai Lama; ritual practices such as prayer wheels, prayer flags, religious pictures made of colored sand, and oracles for telling the future; and unusual (for Buddhism) scriptures, including the *Tibetan Book of the Dead*. This combination of Mahayana and indigenous religion has sometimes caused problems. In 2009, the current Dalai Lama said that a group of Tibetan Buddhists with whom he disagrees do not represent a true form of Buddhist religion, but rather are "spirit worshipers" who should give up their practices. This ruling sparked large street protests against the Dalai

Read about the *Tibetan Book of the Dead* as explained by Donald Lopez.

Tibetan Buddhist prayer flags, Nepal

© ALEXNIKA/SHUTTERSTOCK.COM

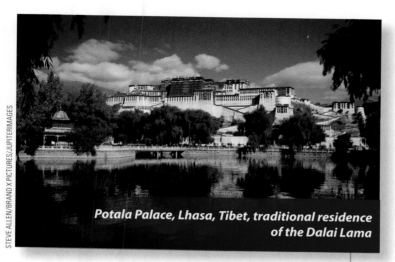

Potala Palace, Lhasa, Tibet, traditional residence of the Dalai Lama

STEVE ALLEN/BRAND X PICTURES/JUPITERIMAGES

the recent immigration into Tibet of tens of thousands of Chinese. (We will examine the current situation of Buddhism more in the last section of this chapter.)

Learning Outcome 5-3

Outline the essential Buddhist teachings.

5-3 Essential Buddhist Teachings

A leading Buddhist authority in Thailand urges the country's 300,000 monks to join in the fight against AIDS. Chatsumarn Kabilsingh (CHAT-soo-mahrn KAHB-ihl-sing), the first woman to receive full ordination as a nun in Thailand, urges that monks acquire a better understanding of Buddhist teachings, to be more effective in teaching the scriptural command against adultery. She says that sex outside of marriage is a primary form of suffering caused by desire, as addressed in the Four Noble Truths. Without getting into the touchy question of whether AIDS is a retribution for sexual sins, she stresses the positive: "Sex springs from the love and care shown by two individuals, and they need to be responsible to each other. With true love, there is no need to change partners, and that is the best prevention against AIDS."

> *Some people in the West regard reincarnation as a happy form of eternal life, but this is not what Buddhists think.*

Many Indian religions in the fifth century C.E. had several basic beliefs about an unseen spiritual reality that formed a common worldview. Buddhists call their version of this worldview the **dharma**, "law, teaching" about the universe and release from it. The universe operates by **karma** ("actions"), the law of the cause and effect of actions done by sentient (with senses) beings. These beings have been reborn from eternity in different realms of the cosmos: in heaven, earth, and hell. This endless cycle of **samsara** ("wandering") is the cause of all suffering, and the goal of Buddhism is to end that suffering. Some in the West regard reincarnation as a happy or at least neutral form of eternal life, but this is not at all what Buddhists or traditional adherents to other Asian religions think—it is a source of never-ending suffering. (See "A Closer Look: Popular Misunderstandings.")

The means of escape from samsara usually comes over millions of lifetimes, as one gains perfection and ultimately finds the way out of constant rebirth. Those who are fully enlightened are not reborn again as humans after they die, nor do they become absorbed into the world-soul Brahman, as many Hindus have taught. Rather, they go beyond suffering into **nirvana** (literally "blowing out, extinction"). Buddhists have been unwilling to discuss what nirvana actually is, because it is indescribable, but those who come close to nirvana in this life have a deep sense of peace and calm. In short, the goal of Buddhism is a complete and definitive liberation from the painful transience of life. This can be attained through the recognition and elimination of the factors leading to endless death and rebirth.

5-3a The Four Noble Truths

A brief summary of Buddhist teaching is the **Four Noble Truths** that the Buddha taught in his first sermons. The Four Noble

dharma [DAHR-muh] "Law, teaching" of Buddhism

karma [KAR-muh] Law of the cause and effect of actions done by sentient beings

samsara [sam-SAR-uh] "Wandering" through endless reincarnations, a main cause of human suffering

nirvana [neer-VAH-nuh] "Blowing out, extinction" of desire, attachment, and suffering

Four Noble Truths Basic teaching of Buddhism that (1) all life is suffering, (2) suffering is caused by desire, (3) to end desire is to end suffering, and (4) to end desire one must follow the Noble Eightfold Path

A Closer Look:

Popular Misunderstandings of *Karma, Nirvana,* and *Zen*

Just as key Hindu terms are often misunderstood in the West, as we saw in Chapter 3, so too are some key Buddhist terms.

Karma in Buddhism isn't "fate" as we often hear today in North America and Europe. Neither is karma a system of reward and punishment worked out primarily in this present life. In fact, karma in Buddhism is the *opposite* of these ideas. In karma, each person generates her or his own reward or punishment, which comes with one's condition after reincarnation.

Nirvana is for many Western people today a state of personal bliss where an individual has complete peace, fulfillment, and joy. This understanding aligns with some Mahayana groups, such as Socially Engaged Buddhism, but not with Theravada or Tibetan Buddhism. In these latter beliefs, it means "to become extinct," and for Buddhists it often connotes "to cool," as a flame of desire cools when it is snuffed out. As long as individual existence continues, samsara continues. Because Mahayana traditions of Buddhism are much more prevalent in the Western world than are Theravadin traditions, Westerners tend to read all of Buddhist teaching on nirvana according to Mahayana views. This leads to distortion about the variety of Buddhist thought on this topic. Buddhists are usually unwilling to say much about nirvana, because it is indescribable, even unknowable.

Zen is the most misused in the West. It is often used to describe any ironic or profound statement, whether or not it's meant to lead to enlightenment. *Zen* is also linked in the popular imagination to martial arts. Popular fiction, film, and television have long drawn on the image of the otherwise peaceful Zen monk who is a master of hand-to-hand fighting. A few Ch'an/Zen groups, especially the Chinese Shaolin (shaw-LIHN) school—of *Crouching Tiger, Hidden Dragon* film fame—use martial arts to build energy and focus the mind. But Zen groups don't typically use martial arts, and martial arts practitioners aren't usually Zen Buddhists.

Watch a BBC report on martial arts at the Shaolin Monastery.

Truths diagnose the human problem, describe its cause, propose a cure, and prescribe a treatment.

1. *All life is suffering.* The First Noble Truth states that all thinking beings experience suffering. Suffering ranges from great physical and mental pain to mild emotional unhappiness. People suffer because they are born, get sick, age, and die. Suffering also arises from negative emotions such as anger and sadness. Even happiness is an occasion for suffering, because our happiness comes and goes. Regardless of its surface quality—long or short, happy or sad, poor or rich—this life is actually one of suffering.

> To paraphrase the Second Noble Truth, we are addicted to life, and, like any other addiction, this one causes suffering.

2. *The cause of suffering is desire.* Humans always want what they do not have and should not have. Insatiable desire, a craving for physical gratification, personal happiness, and even life itself is the cause of suffering. To put it another way, we are addicted to life, and, like any other addiction, this one causes suffering. Due to the impermanence of the world and the fickleness of our own minds, our sensual and emotional gratifications pass, and we find ourselves once again in the grip of desire. Craving also takes the form of pursuing wealth, power, reputation, and so on, while avoiding unpleasant and undesirable things. We want to be something other than what we are. This constant craving, which is grounded in an erroneous view of the self, is the cause of suffering.

3. *To end desire is to end suffering.* The Third Noble Truth puts together the first and the second. The means of ending our suffering is ending the craving that causes it. This cessation of craving, which is an ending of the ignorance at its root, breaks the working of negative karma, causing one not to be reborn again. This is easier to understand than to do, and this difficulty leads to the Fourth Noble Truth.

4. *To end desire, one must follow the Noble Eightfold Path.* Buddhism requires this as the path toward nirvana. Following the Eightfold Path does not *cause* nirvana, but it is a required aid in finding it. Nirvana is the state that is free from all

suffering, because in it one is free from delusions and cravings about the nature of the self and reality.

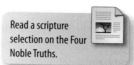 Read a scripture selection on the Four Noble Truths.

5-3b The Noble Eightfold Path

The **Noble Eightfold Path** consists of eight aspects of thought and behavior that need to be cultivated on the path to nirvana. These steps on the path form the basis of Buddhist ethical teaching. Each step begins with *right*, which can be understood as "full," "skillful," or "correct." These are:

1. *Right understanding:* gaining a perspective that ends one's delusions and brings knowledge of reality.

2. *Right intention:* developing a sincere commitment to embark upon the path to liberation with determination and diligence; people must *want* to change before they *can* change.

3. *Right speech:* speaking the truth and refraining from lying, deceptive speech that adds to the suffering of the world.

4. *Right conduct:* following the "Five Precepts" of not killing, stealing, lying, drinking intoxicants, and being sexually immoral; conduct should be without ego and self-centeredness.

5. *Right livelihood:* doing work and living one's life in a way that does not injure others and is conducive to the attainment of liberation.

6. *Right effort:* the development a consciousness that is free from craving; this requires a sustained effort to release consciousness from its unwholesome mental states and cultivate wholesome ones.

7. *Right mindfulness:* the practice of meditative awareness; by mindfulness, harmful thoughts and feelings as well as their attendant cravings and ego-boosting activities may be discerned and dealt with.

8. *Right contemplation:* the deepening of mindfulness that leads to focused states of consciousness, akin to deep concentration, in which tranquility and penetrating insight may be obtained.

5-3c The Three Characteristics of Existence

Soon after his enlightenment, the Buddha taught that all life is marked by the **Three Characteristics of Existence** (or Reality): impermanence, suffering, and no soul. These characteristics are echoed in many aspects of Buddhism, especially in its philosophical teachings.

- Impermanence, **anicca** in Sanskrit, means that the outer appearance of all things is constantly changing, but the inner essence does not. For example, when an animal dies and decomposes, the appearance of the animal ends, but the components that formed it go on to be a part of something new. The most dramatic illustration of the impermanence of all things is when Buddhist monks make a **mandala** out of colored sand and soon after the completion of this highly symbolic picture sweep it up and throw the sand into moving water.

Noble Eightfold Path Right understanding, intention, speech, conduct, livelihood, effort, mindfulness, and contemplation

Three Characteristics of Existence Impermanence, suffering, and no soul

anicca [uh-NEEK-uh] Impermanence, the first characteristic of existence, which leads to suffering

mandala [MAHN-dah-luh] Symbolic Buddhist picture

Impermanence performed: Monks create an intricate sand mandala, only to destroy it.

© BESTWEB/SHUTTERSTOCK.COM

dukkha [DUHK-uh]
Suffering, the Second
Characteristic of Existence,
caused by desire

anatta [ah-NAHT-uh] No soul, the Third
Characteristic of Existence

precept Buddhist
moral command for
monastics and laypeople

• Suffering, **dukkha**, is the Second Characteristic of Existence, in addition to being the first of the Four Noble Truths. Nothing in the physical world or even in one's mind can bring true satisfaction. Because humans are never satisfied, they form an unhealthy attachment to things, and even to life itself. This produces dukkha, of which the First Noble Truth speaks.

• "No soul/self," **anatta**, is third. In contrast to Hinduism, the Buddha taught that there is no permanent "soul" or "self" (*atman*). Impermanence thus extends even to the deepest parts of human nature, and this too produces suffering. Various elements of the human mind work together to create an illusion of a permanent soul, but these elements dissolve at death. (So the self is not a "figment of our imagination"; it is a figment of the whole mind.) The task of the Buddhist is to find enlightenment before death, because enlightenment (gaining a Buddha nature) will end the cycle of reincarnation. This teaching of anatta is still carried out in much of Theravada Buddhism, but many Mahayana schools teach that there is in fact an essential, permanent self/soul that transmigrates in this world and lives forever when it is liberated from reincarnation.

Watch Tibetan Buddhist monks in lively debate.

Learning Outcome 5-4

State the main ethical precepts of Buddhism for both monastics and laypeople.

5-4 Buddhist Ethics for Monastics and Laypeople

As they visit a new Buddhist theme park in southern Vietnam, a family goes through an exhibit not found in other theme parks—a tour through hell. In paintings, surround sound, and animatronics, eight rooms depict the various tortures inflicted on sinners before they are sent back to the earth for their next life. The mother and father occasionally chuckle nervously at the exhibits, but the children cling tightly to their parents. Like other depictions of punishment in the next life—and a number of religions have such teachings—this "Hell Pavilion" is meant to impress on people the dangers of doing wrong. Buddhist literary or even painted depictions of hell are not often as scary as this, and some doubt whether it is wise or even possible to "scare people out of hell" by "scaring the hell out of them" in an amusement park.

The Buddhist religious life is grounded on morality. The Eightfold Path indicates that the cultivation of meditation and wisdom is dependent on morality. Meditation and reaching release cannot be done without it. Moreover, Buddhist layfolk, in their worship of the Buddha or other buddhas, must build their worship on a foundation of solid moral goodness.

5-4a General Buddhist Morality

As in most religions, morality in Buddhism is well developed. If you asked any Buddhist what the heart of the Buddhist moral system is, he or she would probably say, "Show compassion to all beings." In the face of the suffering in the world, all sentient beings need compassion if they are to cope with their bad situation and finally gain liberation from it.

Aside from this general, comprehensive command, the more detailed heart of Buddhist ethical thought is *sila* (SEE-luh). This term means "virtuous behavior," "morality," "ethics," or **precept** (moral command). A precept is an action committed in a deed, a word, or in the mind. It involves a strong, intentional effort, because no precept "comes naturally." Following the precepts leads to purity in thought, word, and deed, as well as to a proper foundation for meditative cultivation of the mind. Keeping the precepts is meritorious and brings peace of mind to the person who obeys them, and peace with others as well—for monks, nuns, and layfolk. It also prevents rebirth in hell or as an animal on the earth. Breaking the precepts will certainly mean that one will not be in a position to reach release in one's next life.

> *Keeping the Buddhist precepts involves a strong, intentional effort, because none of them comes naturally.*

Besides the general command to all Buddhists to be nonviolent, moderate, and compassionate to all beings, Buddhists are urged to live moral, generous lives. The social outworking of Buddhist morality helped to differentiate it from Hinduism and aid in its spread through Asia. Two examples must suffice here. First, the Buddha didn't oppose wealth, but he also didn't make it a main goal of life as Hinduism had, and he said that wealth doesn't end suffering, but only masks it. One should develop a detachment from one's wealth and use it for the good of others. The Buddha also opposed Hinduism's caste system and the power of its priests, arguing for equality among all people. Therefore, he allowed men from all Indian castes to be monks. Today when Indian "untouchables" (Dalits) have mass conversions to other religions in order to improve their social and religious conditions, they typically turn to Buddhism or to Christianity.

5-4b The Five Precepts

The Five Precepts are ethical guidelines for a life in which one is happy, is moderately self-confident without being self-absorbed in one's ego, and can meditate well. They are necessary for morality in this life and a better rebirth in the next. The precepts are considered not only commands, but also training for life in the dharma (teaching, law). This dharma is built into the universe, governing nonsentient things just as much as it governs living beings. Following the dharma brings happiness in this life and good karma for the next; not living according to the dharma brings endless suffering in continuous rebirths. The Five Precepts call for Buddhists to keep themselves from five different errors. They are virtually universal among Buddhists, both monastic and lay. The Buddhist must not:

1. Kill sentient beings

2. Steal

3. Commit sexual immorality

4. Lie

5. Drink any intoxicants

Different Buddhist branches and groups have added to these precepts in different ways. In the Theravada branch, layfolk wishing to practice Buddhism more fully but not able or willing to enter a monastery may adopt three precepts in addition to the Five. Some adopt them permanently, but most who take them on

do so temporarily, particularly on holy days. The third of the Five Precepts is made stricter, adding the requirement of celibacy—no sexual activity at all, even within marriage. The three additional precepts command that the Buddhist must not:

6. Eat between noon and the following sunrise, as monks do

7. Dance; enjoy music, jewelry, or cosmetics; or attend artistic performances

8. Use luxurious seats and beds

As is typical of Buddhism, lay practice is based on and adapted from monastic practice. The precepts have several levels of achievement: basic morality in keeping the Five Precepts, basic morality with self-denial in keeping the Eight Precepts, novice monasticism in keeping the Ten Precepts, full-monk status with hundreds of precepts, and even more for nuns. Laypeople typically follow the Five Precepts only. They can, at their discretion, follow eight or even ten for a short time, practicing more rigorous self-control and self-denial. Although the precepts are typically worded in the negative, Buddhists realize that much positive meaning lies behind them.

5-4c Other Precepts and Moral Rules

The complete list of the Ten Precepts is a requirement for novice monks before they have taken their final vows, especially in Theravada. The seventh precept given above is made into two precepts, and a tenth added. To keep these added precepts, the Buddhist monk must not:

7. Dance, listen to, or engage in music, singing, or shows

8. Use garlands, perfumes, lotions, or other things that beautify the body

9. Use luxurious seats and beds

10. Accept money

For fully initiated monastics, more than two hundred additional precepts apply. These now take on the character of hard-and-fast rules. If they are broken, disciplinary actions are specified in the precepts. For example, in the command of celibacy, Buddhist monks and nuns are forbidden to even think about sex. Although this may strike you as extreme, for someone who is strictly celibate, to think about sex when one never carries out one's thoughts will only increase the suffering that Buddhists see as the root of all evil. Nuns have extra rules added to the rules for monks, designed in part to keep them under the supervision of nearby monks. These precepts seek to order monastic life for the purpose of promoting good morality and achievement in meditation. They are listed in the "Monastic Disciplinary Code" in the Pali canon and are broken into several groups. In the Mahayana canon, they are found in a three-volume book called the *Vinaya*. Monks must memorize these rules and follow them carefully.

Learning Outcome 5-5

Discuss the way Buddhists worship and meditate.

5-5 Buddhist Ritual and Meditation

Buddhist monks gather daily in a Chinese monastery to read sutras. A low hum fills the reading room as the head monk leads them in reciting in unison. Like Buddhists everywhere, they are "making merit" by carefully reciting their key scriptures, thereby doing a deed that will wear away the effects of negative karma. This merit will enable them to be reborn after death into a better existence, perhaps eventually to achieve nirvana and be reborn no more. If layfolk are present in the temple for this recitation, they listen reverently to the chanting, believing that the ritual will accrue to their benefit as well.

Like other aspects of Buddhism, ritual and meditation must be related to the monks and the laypeople. In some countries, it is common for male Buddhists to enter a monastic order for a temporary period at least once in their lifetime—as in Myanmar, Cambodia, Laos, and Thailand today. This temporary monasticism causes men to rise in social standing. In nearly all the Buddhist world, monks and laypeople live in a reciprocal relationship. Each group provides the other with an opportunity to gain merit, and thereby to make a contribution to their "karma account." For ordinary Buddhists today—monk or layperson—nirvana is far too remote and intangible a goal to be striven for immediately, so religious practice focuses on the gaining of merit. Monks recite and explain the sacred texts to laypeople, conduct protective ceremonies for them, and lead other religious rituals for them, especially funerals. The laypeople give the monks material support: food in their morning rounds outside the monastery, new garments at an annual ceremony, and money for the maintenance and adornment of the monastery. Layfolk do engage in one ritual practice that monks generally do not: going on pilgrimage to sacred Buddhist sites.

Watch a video of Buddhist meditation.

Watch recitation of the scripture "Reverence to the Bodhi Tree."

5-5a Temples

Inside a typical Theravada temple, you will see the following. At the front of the temple will be a statue of the Buddha, most often seated and in meditation. Sometimes additional statues of the Buddha will also be present at the front. An altar on which worshipers place offerings of flowers and oil stands right in front

Buddhist monks on the king's birthday, 2010, Bangkok, Thailand. Collecting their daily food from others enables monks to spend more time in meditation and study.

© CHARLIE EDWARD/SHUTTERSTOCK.COM

Monk studying using a laptop, Bangkok, Thailand

of the statue. A place to set up burning incense sticks is on or near the altar, and larger temples will have places to burn incense in an open-air courtyard. Many temples contain pictures on the walls, showing the stages of the Buddha's life. As a rule, Mahayana and Tibetan temples are more elaborately decorated than Theravadin temples. The main hall of the temple is open space in which worshipers sit or stand in meditation. One may see mats

there, but not (in a traditional Buddhist temple) chairs or pews. Buddhist temples built in the West sometimes have a different arrangement, which we will discuss in the section on Buddhism in North America on page 134.

> **mudra** [MOOD-ruh]
> Position in which the hands, and often arms, are held during meditation

5-5b Images of the Buddha

The spiritual center of any Buddhist temple, and one also found in Buddhist home altars, is a statue of the Buddha. (Paintings and printed pictures of the Buddha are also displayed, but not as prominently as the statue. Buddhists typically do not consider them as inspiring as statues of the Buddha.) The Buddha is usually depicted as seated in the lotus meditational position. His eyes are closed or mostly closed, symbolizing that he has shut out the distractions of the world to find release within himself. He often has a circular mark on his forehead, called an *urna*, showing that he has achieved enlightenment. His large earlobes are a traditional Indian symbol of nobility. He is dressed modestly and is physically strong and healthy, but not overfed. He holds his hands, and often his arms, in one of a variety of formal positions called **mudras**, some of which are as follows:

- Left hand resting on thigh, right hand pointing downward or touching the ground, symbolizing the attainment of enlightenment
- Right hand held up with the palm facing forward, symbolizing a blessing of those venerating the statue
- Right hand upward with thumb and forefinger closed (our "okay" sign), symbolizing teaching the Buddhist way
- Forming both hands into a circle, symbolizing the wheel of dharma

One will also see statues of the Buddha reclining on his right side, symbolizing his entry into full nirvana at death. Less often, one will see statues of a standing Buddha.

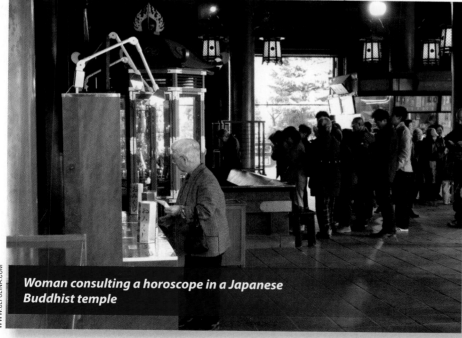

Woman consulting a horoscope in a Japanese Buddhist temple

5-5c Prayer and Meditation

For monks, prayer has a highly meditational dimension. For layfolk, however, Buddhist prayer means expressing praise and requests to a supernatural power or being. As mentioned at the beginning of this chapter, lay Buddhists don't meditate regularly. Buddhism doesn't have a main deity on whom the religion centers and to whom worship and prayer are offered. But Buddhists do pray, which raises—at least for us—this question: To whom do Buddhists pray, and for what do they pray? Mostly, Buddhists pray for blessings from the Buddha, other buddhas, and bodhisattvas, and ask especially for help toward enlightenment. Some Tibetan Buddhists have "minor" gods, both male and female, to whom prayer is made for blessing and protection. They also pray for the same things people pray for in other religions: for health and healing, safety, spiritual strength, and for understanding.

Buddha in deep meditation, Kamakura, Japan

Buddha with right hand downward, symbolizing enlightenment

Much more important than prayer for Buddhist monastics is meditation, an altered state of consciousness induced in a controlled manner. You are used to trances that come in the form of daydreams, and we even do things such as drive a car for several minutes and suddenly realize that we haven't been paying attention to driving at all. Buddhist meditation, however, is controlled and purposeful—there is no inattentive driving in a Buddhist

trance meditation
Comprehensive form of meditation that goes all the way to nirvana

Buddha in "blessing" pose

life! Two basic forms of meditation have been widely practiced in the Theravada tradition and have also come by way of Mahayana practice to North America.

Buddhists do pray, but to whom and for what?

The first form of meditation is called **trance meditation** and has several steps. First, meditators detach themselves from impure and erroneous thoughts, becoming mildly satisfied and happy. In the second stage, thinking leads to a complete inner serenity; the mind is concentrated, and the happiness from the first stage lessens. In the third stage, all feelings disappear, and the meditator becomes uninterested

Reclining Buddha, symbolizing reaching nirvana at death

in everything. In the fourth stage, any tendency toward serenity is left behind, and the meditator becomes completely indifferent to self. One then begins the pursuit of higher attainments in trance meditation, reaching beyond the perception of physical and mental forms, and resting in infinite time and space. There follows a state of unlimited consciousness. Next, by fixing the mind on how everything is impermanent to the point of nonexistence, the meditator reaches the nothingness suggested by nirvana. Finally, one reaches the state in which there is neither perception nor nonperception. He or she has thought the way out of thinking!

The meditator has thought the way out of thinking!

The second type of meditation is **insight meditation**. This practice also requires intense concentration, which in insight meditation leads to a complete concentration of the mind called awareness or mindfulness. The mindfulness is not an end in itself, but enables the meditator to see that all reality is impermanent, filled with suffering, and has no self. This insight propels the meditator toward nirvana. Theravada texts recommend both trance and insight meditation. Since 1900, an emphasis on insight-meditation practices has grown, and insight movements became widespread in Mahayana and among Buddhist groups in the West. Of course, some Buddhist groups, such as Zen, have different patterns and practices of meditation. Other groups, for example Nichiren, have meditation that focuses on their main chants.

© ISTOCKPHOTO.COM/ BARTOSZ HADYNIAK

Tibetan woman using a prayer wheel to earn good karma

5-5d Protective Rituals

Buddhism has rituals designed to protect the faithful and the whole world against danger and evil. In Theravada these involve the recitation of scripture texts as **parittas**, "protections." The texts are chanted in public, often with drumming

Scroll through a recent collection of parittas.

and ringing of handbells, to avert collective danger. Parittas are used privately to protect a person who pays for monks to recite scripture against illness and other difficulties. Most of such rituals do not speak explicitly of protections from danger; they usually comprise regular scripture texts, recited with the intent of using their truth and power to keep away evil.

In Mahayana and in Tibet, protective rituals are used more widely than elsewhere in Buddhism, as we might expect from the branches of Buddhism that give more attention to supernatural beings and forces, including evil ones. **Dharanis**, brief statements of basic Buddhist teachings that are thought to share their power, are frequently used for protection, as are even shorter one- or two-word **mantras**. Protective rituals were important in the conversion of Tibet and East Asia to Buddhism; people there wanted to be assured that the new religion could deal with the spiritual forces that threatened them. Such observances are still important in these areas. Even today, the Buddhist Tibetan government in exile holds protective rituals for itself and will also consult traditional religious oracles to discern the best choices when making decisions. In Japan, worshipers in Buddhist temples can get a printed horoscope-based prediction for their life. If they tie it to a special board or a designated tree in the temple area, a good fortune will come true, but a bad fortune will be thwarted. More will be said about these in Chapter 8, on Shinto.

5-5e Funeral Rituals

Monks do not normally perform life-cycle rituals for laypeople. They do not lead ceremonies for newborn babies, mark passage to adulthood, or conduct weddings. These are primarily family events and more cultural than religious, although monks may bestow blessings on newborns and newlyweds in the monasteries.

insight meditation Meditation leading to awareness or mindfulness, from which nirvana can be achieved

paritta [puh-REET-uh] Protective ritual carried out for an individual or community

dharani [duh-RAHN-ee] Brief statement of basic Buddhist teaching thought to share its power, frequently used for protection

mantra [MAHN-truh] Short formula or single word that focuses the mind and expresses great religious meaning

© ZZVET/SHUTTERSTOCK.COM

Buddhist monk deep in contented thought

Monks do participate in funerals, however. In fact, Buddhism has a leading role in funeral rituals in almost every country in which it has a presence. Because Buddhism has a strong interest in death, karma, and reincarnation, monks often lead services for the dead. Even before that, monks will visit the dying, because one's state of mind while dying impacts one's rebirth. Monks read sacred texts to a dying person to prepare the spirit before death. The elaborate procedures spelled out in *The Tibetan Book of the Dead* are the apex of this guidance for the dying and recently deceased. The soul, or consciousness (where Buddhists are strict on the no-soul teaching), stays in or around the body for three days after death. In general, Buddhist funeral observances originated in India and are illustrated in the story of the Buddha's funeral. After cremation ceremonies simpler than that for the Buddha, the ashes and bones of leading monks were collected and **stupas**, burial mounds or monuments, built over them. The large number of stupas found near monasteries indicates that these funeral rites for leading monks were widely held.

Watch a BBC video on the "Temple of the Tooth."

> *Buddhists commonly agree that the thoughts held by a person at the moment of death are significant for his or her future.*

The dead bodies of ordinary monks and laypeople in Asia and the West undergo cremation. After cremation, typically carried out today in a modern crematorium, the ashes are usually buried in a cemetery. Many Buddhists will ritually honor their ancestors at their gravesites, especially in China, where the rituals are similar to those we will discuss in Chapter 7 (on Daoism and Confucianism). Some regional differences should be noted here. In Sri Lanka, whole-body burial is also common. Because wood is scarce in Tibet, cremation there is unusual. The bodies of great Tibetan lamas are reverently put in stupas in a posture of meditation. A striking Tibetan practice is one where monks cut apart the bodies of pious Tibetan Buddhists, both monastics and layfolk, and distribute them, piece by piece, to

stupa [STOO-pah] Burial mound or monument, often with relics of the Buddha or famous Buddhists

the waiting birds. Although this may seem revolting to Westerners—and is not easy for mourners in Tibet to watch—this feeding of birds with the bodies of the dead is seen as an act of compassion.

Learning Outcome 5-6

State the main features of Buddhist life around the world today, especially in North America.

5-6 Buddhism around the World Today

As U.S. president Barack Obama toured Southeast Asia in November of 2012, a monk in a famous Buddhist temple approached him to have a brief word. We can imagine that the president may have anticipated a profound spiritual comment, but what the monk said to him, with reporters standing by, became international news: "Mr. President, good luck with the fiscal cliff." He was referring, of course, to a difficult situation with the U.S. national budget, one that was causing a good deal of suffering in the United States. People were surprised, and the press also, that a monk should make such a comment, but they shouldn't have been. Many monks are well informed about current world events. They are particularly aware of suffering, even financial suffering, in order to act against it.

5-6a Buddhism in Modern Asia

During the nineteenth and twentieth centuries, Buddhism faced a variety of new issues. Several countries with significant Buddhist populations came under colonial Western rule, and many other Buddhists felt the pressure of Western religions and culture. In South Korea, Christianity has converted nearly half the population from Buddhism. Even more damaging to the size and influence of Buddhism were the rise of communism in China, Mongolia, North Korea, Vietnam, Cambodia, and Tibet, as well as the rise of secularism in Japan. Around 1800, one in every four people in the world was a Buddhist, but by 2000 it was down to one in seven.

Buddhists have responded in a variety of ways to these challenges. First, Buddhism has adapted traditions it liked in Christianity. Peaceful competition between Buddhists and Christian missionaries from the

West often led to Buddhist adoption of Christian practices such as Sunday schools, mission societies, and the distribution of religious literature. Some Buddhists also promoted missionary activity modeled after Christian missions in non-Buddhist parts of Asia and the West, with voluntary conversion of individuals. That differed from the historic Buddhist missionary approach of sending monks to convert kings, with the kingdoms following the ruler into Buddhism.

A second way in which Buddhism has responded to the Western Christian challenge is to seek greater Buddhist unity. Three main societies were established to promote ecumenical cooperation between Buddhists: the Maha Bodhi Society (1891), which regained a Buddhist presence at the pilgrimage site at Bodh Gaya, India; the World Fellowship of Buddhists (1950); and the World Buddhist Sangha Council for monks and nuns (1966). These societies are still at work today to promote Buddhist unity and cooperation.

 Watch "Buddhism Rebounds in Mongolia."

A third response to modernity is the development of social and political activism by monks, including a formal movement usually called Socially Engaged Buddhism, founded by the South Vietnamese Zen monk Thich Nhat Hanh (tick naught hahn) in the 1960s. He may be the most prominent leader of Buddhism today next to the Dalai Lama. Some Asian and Western Buddhists have advocated progressive political and economic changes, including ones in the areas of ecology and feminism. Although they are not a part of Socially Engaged Buddhism, Buddhist monks in Myanmar (Burma) have helped to organize protests against long-term dictatorships in that nation. At times they have been brutally suppressed and have paid a high price for their political activism.

 Read the *Newsletter for Western Socially Engaged Buddhism.*

A fourth Buddhist response to modernity involves giving laypeople more of a role in the religion. In Theravada, traditionally directed by monks alone, lay-oriented meditation movements have been successful. In East Asia, especially in Japan, this trend has led to a founding and rapid expansion of Buddhist groups run by lay Buddhists, a novelty in the history of Buddhism. A sadder current form of lay action has been the public self-immolation of dozens of Tibetan Buddhists living in China in protest over Chinese government actions against their religion in Tibet.

A final pattern of Buddhist adaptation to modern life is a response to a problem too common in world

Lay-oriented meditation societies in the West have spread meditation widely; here an American Buddhist sits in meditation.

religions—that of illicit behavior by some religious specialists. In Southeast Asia, some monks break their vows by playing violent video games in arcades, drinking alcohol, and even having sexual relations with lay women and men. At the same time, monastic authorities in Theravadin lands typically keep women from any leadership role in the religion—something that could potentially bring reform. Until recently in Sri Lanka, monks even participated in warfare against the Tamil rebels. The number of men who enter the monastery is declining, and it may also be true (although it's hard to prove) that the quality of monks is declining. The majority of monks are not behaving badly, but problems with those who are have increased. Scholars have even argued that rising illicit behavior by monks has caused life in general in Southeast Asia to deteriorate. But Buddhism has spiritual resources to deal with these problems, and it is in the process of doing so.

 Watch a report on Thai "body collecting."

 Watch a video on Buddhism and science.

5-6b Buddhism Comes to the Western World

European contact with China and Japan brought knowledge of Buddhism to the West in the 1800s, and Buddhism soon became popular here, even though the number of Buddhists was small. In England, societies were organized for the promotion of Buddhism, prominently the Pali Text Society that translated and published Buddhist scriptures for wide dissemination. The Buddhist Society of Great Britain explained Buddhism in the expectation that this would bring converts. Books appeared recommending Buddhism—for example Edwin Arnold's *The Light of Asia* (1879), a long poem telling of the life of the Buddha that was a best seller in England and America. In Germany and France as well, Buddhism captured serious attention and soon became the best known of Asian religions.

Some of this interest in Buddhism bordered on exoticism. This resulted in a one-sided view of Buddhism that emphasizes its philosophy and meditation to the exclusion of its religious practices, unfortunately still typical today of the Western approach to Buddhism. The first European conversions to Buddhism took place around 1880. In the twentieth century, the Buddhist Society of Great Britain won thousands of converts to Theravada. But the main story of Buddhism in the West begins with emigration from China, Japan, and Southeast Asia, to which we now turn.

5-6c Early Buddhist Immigration to North America

Tens of thousands of Chinese immigrants with Buddhist backgrounds—usually combined with lay Daoist practices and basic Confucian social values—came to the west coasts of the United States and Canada in the late 1800s. Like the vast majority of immigrants to North America, they came seeking a better life, not for religious reasons. They provided labor for mining, fishing, and farming, and especially for building the railroads. The only religious objects they had were small images of the Buddha and Chinese traditional gods for their own personal use. When the railroads were finished and these immigrants settled down in "Chinatowns" in the coastal cities, Americans began noticing their forms of Buddhism, especially when temples were built.

The size of the Chinese immigrant population grew rapidly; by 1870 one-tenth of the population of California and Montana was Chinese. Their numbers provoked a backlash in the form of discriminatory laws and practices against Chinese people, some of which were aimed at cultural customs (festivals, music, public funerals) that were grounded in Chinese religions. In 1882 the national Chinese Exclusion Act suspended further immigration, and in 1924 new quotas were set for all Asians. Many immigrants continued to practice their faiths, however. By 1900 there were hundreds of Chinese Buddhist temples and smaller shrines along the West Coast and in the Rocky Mountains. Almost all of them were founded and led by laypeople, because Chinese monks did not emigrate with them. But as discrimination persisted, and with a continued absence of monks (who for thousands of years had guided lay Buddhism), many second- and third-generation Chinese began to leave Buddhist practices behind in an effort to assimilate more fully to their new culture.

Japanese immigration to North America began in the 1880s. It was much smaller in scale than Chinese immigration, and was controlled and financially supported by the Japanese government. Japanese immigrants tended to be merchants and businesspeople. Also, entire families immigrated, unlike the case with the Chinese, who were predominantly males who had to leave their families behind in China. The immigrants quickly built cultural associations and temples. By 1898, the Young Men's Buddhist Association (modeled, as its name implies, on the Young Men's Christian Association, the Y.M.C.A.) had been established. By 1910 more than twenty Japanese Buddhist temples had been established on the West Coast, led by ordained Buddhist monks from Japan who had been sent by the Japanese government.

Meanwhile, on the East Coast, contact with Buddhism came from books, not immigrants. Leading intellectuals were reading about Buddhism, especially transcendentalists such as Henry Thoreau and Ralph Waldo Emerson. In 1878, the eccentric mystic Helena Blavatsky and the more conventional Henry Steel Olcott, founders of the so-called Theosophical Society, went to Sri Lanka and formally received the Five Precepts for layfolk. Olcott was committed to Buddhism. When he became aware of how little Asian Buddhist groups knew about or cooperated with each other, he worked for better relations among these groups, even publishing a *Buddhist Catechism* (CAT-uh-KIHZ-um) to state what he considered the main, common ideas of Buddhism.[2] (A catechism is a basic statement of faith in question-and-answer form.) He was widely known as "the White Buddhist," a term not acceptable today but at the time considered correct and complimentary.

---

[2] Henry Steel Olcott, *Buddhist Catechism* (London: Truebner, 1882).

Main worship hall as well as bell and drum towers at the Chuang Yen Monastery complex just north of New York City

the Christian term *church* a Buddhist application.

A surge of interest in Zen came after the World War II, when many Asian Buddhists—such as Zen expert D. T. Suzuki (1870–1966)—came to the United States to live permanently. Zen became particularly popular in the United States, even contributing to what was called at the time a "Zen boom." A number of Americans went to Japan and began a more serious, committed study of Zen. It was not uncommon for American troops based in Japan after the war to gain an appreciation for Japanese ways of life in general

During World War II, the internment of all Japanese in camps set back the religious life of the Japanese in the United States. After the war, membership in Buddhist temples declined as numerous Japanese Buddhists sought to assimilate by becoming Protestant Christians at a time when Protestantism was at the height of its cultural influence in America. Many Buddhist religious institutions adapted by "Protestantizing" themselves, adding pews, pulpits, hymnbooks, and organs to their temples. The largest Buddhist group in the States, the Jodo Shinshu sect of Sokka Gakkai, formally changed its name to the Buddhist Churches of America, giving

and Buddhism in particular. In the 1950s, Zen became a part of the countercultural "Beatnik" movement, a precursor to the more diffuse "hippie" movements of the 1960s and 1970s. It was known as *Beat Zen* and marked the first time that an Asian religion became a part of American popular culture. In 1974 Zen would again appear in American pop culture, in the form of Robert Pirsig's perennially best-selling *Zen and the Art of Motorcycle Maintenance: An Inquiry into Values.*[3] Zen Buddhism had come to be seen in North America as a way of spiritual liberation that was suited to people of Western cultures.

Some institutional dimensions of Buddhism did continue in the United States. Since the 1950s, Europeans and Americans who studied Buddhism in Asia returned home to found monasteries and societies. Also, Asian Buddhist monks came to Europe and America to found meditation centers. But Buddhist influence from the 1800s until about 1970 remained largely intellectual, cultural, and meditational. The full spectrum of

Seattle Buddhist Church with "Protestantizing" influences

---

[3] Robert Pirsig, *Zen and the Art of Motorcycle Maintenance* (New York: Harper, 2008; originally published in 1974).

Buddhism as a religion was yet to appear. Two main events in the rise of Buddhism in North America would soon occur: the arrival of Tibetan Buddhism as well as Vietnamese immigration into the United States after the end of the Vietnam War.

5-6d The Next Wave of Buddhist Immigration

The Tibetan Buddhist presence in North America began in the 1970s, when Tibetan meditation centers were first established by monks who had eventually settled here after fleeing Tibet. By 1990 almost every main Tibetan group had a center, especially on the East and West Coasts. These meditation centers serve Americans of non-Tibetan backgrounds, because relatively few Tibetan laypeople live in North America.

The 1990s also saw the rise of what some have called "Hollywood" or "celebrity" Buddhism. Various films about Tibet and its form of Buddhism gained much attention, especially *Seven Years in Tibet* and *Kundun*. Film stars such as Naomi Watts, Tina Turner, Steven Segal, Uma Thurman, and Richard Gere have publicly espoused Buddhism, especially Tibetan Buddhism. Gere has become a well-known spokesman for Buddhism in the world. Although golfer Tiger Woods has not openly championed his Buddhist beliefs, the disclosure of his multiple extramarital affairs in 2009 led to a public discussion of his adherence to Buddhism. In sum, "celebrity Buddhism" has played a role in the past twenty years in shaping the North American perception of Buddhism—in mainly positive, but sometimes superficial, ways.

Is Tiger Woods the creator of his own suffering?

Richard Gere is honored by the Dalai Lama after the latter received the Congressional Gold Medal in 2007.

PHOTO BY STEPHANIE KUYKENDAL/GETTY IMAGES

> "Celebrity Buddhism" has shaped the North American perception of Buddhism in mainly positive, but sometimes superficial, ways.

In 1965, another U.S. Immigration Act resulted in a surge in emigration from Asia. Buddhists from Korea, Taiwan, Thailand, and Hong Kong filled old temples in the United States and established new ones. The major growth of Buddhism in the United States came in 1975 (see "A Closer Look: *Stealing Buddha's Dinner*"), when the Vietnam War ended as Communist forces defeated the South Vietnamese army after U.S. withdrawal. The fall of South Vietnam occasioned another large wave of Buddhist immigration to the United States. When the mass-murderous Pol Pot regime in Cambodia fell in 1979, a wave of Cambodians came. By 1990 there were approximately 1 million Vietnamese and Cambodians living in the United States. At first, these traumatized immigrants could only gather in their own homes to conduct basic forms of Buddhist worship and meditation, but by around 2000 they had made enough social and economic progress to found hundreds of temples and community centers to carry on their culture and faith for the second generation.

5-6e Conclusion

As befits a religion that teaches that all things are impermanent, Buddhism has been constantly growing and changing. The Buddhist experience here—as for other religions in North America—has been one of adaptation and assimilation. A form of "American Buddhism" is growing, in which different people of different branches, countries, and sects of Asian Buddhism increasingly mix and cooperate with each other. In Asia, these different groups from Japan, Korea, Vietnam, Tibet, Thailand, and Taiwan seldom needed to work together—and indeed rarely wanted to meet. The situation that Henry Olcott found there more than a century ago is still too prevalent. In North America, however, Buddhists find themselves in a new context, where Buddhists are not numerous or socially powerful. The partly self-imposed pressure on Buddhists to secularize, convert to Christianity, or adapt elements of their worship to Christianity has

A Closer Look:

Stealing Buddha's Dinner: A Memoir

In this critically praised novel, the author tells the story of her childhood as a Vietnamese Buddhist child in America. Bich Minh Nguyen (bit mihn nwin) was just eight months old when her father took her, her sister, and her grandmother out of Vietnam in 1975. They settled in Grand Rapids, Michigan, under the sponsorship of a Protestant church. Nguyen tells her story in terms of American and Vietnamese foods as she wrestled with conflicting desires for her grandmother's native cooking and American food, much of the latter the "junk food" her American friends ate. She also refers often to the pop songs she heard on the radio and sang along with, as well as the TV shows she watched, in the 1980s and early 1990s. More significantly, she traces out her complex family relationships, showing that the lives of displaced persons are often difficult for a variety of reasons.

Nguyen's short, engaging novel, published by Penguin in 2007, is a sometimes-humorous coming-of-age tale that develops themes of loss, displacement, and new identity. The *San Francisco Chronicle* recommended it as "resonating with anyone who's ever felt like an outsider," but it makes a particular appeal to those who want to know what it's like to live as a young Buddhist immigrant in the United States. Although the author does not deal explicitly with her Buddhist background very often, the book itself is named from one short chapter that does deal with food offered to the Buddha in a home sacrifice: "Stealing Buddha's Dinner."

often been strong. The North American context fosters a level of internal Buddhist dialogue and cooperation that has never before been seen in Buddhism. At the same time, a few groups

Watch a news report on the growth of Buddhism in North America.

such as Zen and Tibetan monastic orders have become strong enough in North America to carry out their life on their own, without much interaction with other Buddhists.

Read a short article about Buddhist nuns in the Theravada tradition, ordained for the first time in North America.

Study Tools 5

Ready to study? In the book you can:

- Review Learning Outcome answers and glossary terms with the tear-out Chapter Review card.

Or you can go online to CourseMate, at www.cengagebrain.com, for these resources:

- Chapter quizzes to prepare for tests

- Interactive flashcards of all glossary terms

- A timeline of events for this chapter

- An eBook with introductions, interactive quizzes, and live links for all web resources in the chapter

CHAPTER 6

Encountering Sikhism: The Way of God's Name

BONNIE VAN VOORST © CENGAGE LEARNING

Learning Outcomes

After studying this chapter, you will be able to do the following:

6-1 Explain the meaning of *Sikhism* and related terms.

6-2 Summarize how Sikhism developed over time, especially its founding by the ten gurus and its life from the British Empire through the present.

6-3 Explain the essential Sikh teachings.

6-4 State and discuss the main ethical precepts of Sikhism.

6-5 Outline the way Sikhs worship and practice other rituals, especially life-cycle rituals.

6-6 Summarize the main features of Sikh life around the world today, especially in North America.

Study Tools

After you read this chapter, go to the Study Tools at the end of the chapter, page 155.

"There is only one God, whose name is true. Repeat his name!"—*Sikh scripture*

Your Visit to a Sikh Temple

Visitors are welcome in any Sikh house of worship. Because all Sikh temples are run basically the same way, your experience will be mostly the same whether you visit one in India, Great Britain, Canada, or the United States. The Sikh temple you'll visit today is the spacious new house of worship in Houston, Texas, which was established by Sikh immigrants to the Houston area from northern India.

As you go in the front door of the temple at about ten o'clock on Sunday morning, you notice that the main hall is right in front of you. Like Sikh worshipers do, you must remove your shoes; they belong in a special little "shoe room" just before the main hall. Also like Sikhs, you must cover your head before entering the main hall. Because you didn't bring a head covering with you, a simple cloth is provided for you; you don't feel out of place, because many Sikhs in the main hall wear the same type of cloth. Smoking or even taking tobacco into the temple is forbidden, and if you have any alcohol on your breath you won't be admitted, even if you're completely sober.

Sikhs will bow to the big book under the canopy at the front of the main hall. This is the focal point of the temple. You also can give a slight but noticeable bow as a sign of respect, even if you don't share this religion. Sikhs go further with their bow, and they touch the floor with their forehead after kneeling down. This shows their respect for the book, to the truths contained in it, and to God. People then walk closer to the book and put an offering in front of it. These offerings are used to support the temple and the kitchen attached to it. If a

person is too poor to offer money or food, he or she may offer a flower or a few words expressing thanks to God. You too can put a little money in front of the book.

About two hundred people are attending the Sunday service. You notice that everyone sits on the floor during the service; there are no cushions or seats. This is designed to make you humble in the presence of God, and it suggests that all are equal as they worship God. However, men and women must sit on separate sides. No one sits with their feet pointing at the book at the front; this is a sign

Sikhs at a service in the Gurdwara Sahib (Sikh temple) of Southwest Houston, Texas

A Sikh guard at the golden-roofed temple in Amritsar, India, the holiest site in Sikhism of disrespect, so be careful where your toes point. If you walk around the book itself, you must do so in a clockwise direction, the way it's done in various Sikh ceremonies.

The service consists of a few readings from the scripture book under the canopy and several songs led by musicians to the side of the canopy. The event ends with the serving of a handful of a sweet vegetarian food. You should take this in cupped hands as a gift from God. It's not really an "appetizer," but there is more food to come in about an hour; a free meal of vegetarian Indian food is offered in the adjoining hall, something Sikhs consider an important part of the service.

Sikhism is much smaller than Hinduism and Islam, but it is nonetheless important on the world stage. Today Sikhs number around 25 million. Most Sikhs are ethnic Punjabis (poon-JAHB-ees) living in northwest India. Sikhism is a tenacious faith that has been able to endure under much pressure from Hinduism and Islam, and now also from the national government of India. Your study of Sikhism will soon encounter these unique features:

- Founded from 1500 to 1700 C.E., Sikhism is one of the newest major world religions, but it isn't considered one of the "new religious movements."

- Some religion scholars conclude that Sikhism was influenced by mystical, devotional movements in Hinduism and Islam, but Sikhs view it as a direct revelation of a new religion from God.

- Sikhism began as a more-or-less pacifist religion but shifted to militancy for reasons of self-defense early in its history.

- Sikhism is one of the smaller faiths treated as a "world religion," although Sikhs often say that their religion is the fifth largest in the world and rightly point out that it is widely spread in the world today.

Sikh [seek] "Disciple" or "student," follower of the Sikh religion

Panth [pahnth] "Path," an early name for the Sikh religion

Gurmat [GOOR-maht] "Guru's Way," Sikhs' formal name for their faith

Guru Granth [GOO-roo GRAHNTH] "Guru Book"; the main scripture of Sikhism, also known as the *Adi Granth*, the "First Book"

Watch a music video introduction to Sikhism by Manak-E, an Indian singer based in the United Kingdom.

Watch a BBC introduction to Sikhism.

Learning Outcome 6-1

Explain the meaning of *Sikhism* and related terms.

6-1 The Name *Sikhism*

Sikh means "disciple" or "student." Because the religion was founded by a line of gurus, or "teachers," it's appropriate that those who follow it are called "students." *Sikh* is usually pronounced "seek," but occasionally like "sick." *Sikhism* is the common, everyday name for the religion of the Sikhs. The early Sikh community called it the **Panth**, meaning "path." This name is found in their scripture but was too generic a name to last—all religions are paths, after all. The Sikhs themselves more formally call their faith **Gurmat**, "the Guru's Way."

Sikhism was established by Guru Nanak (NAHN-ahk) around 1499 C.E. and then led by nine other gurus. Sikhs believe that all ten gurus had the same soul, that of Guru Nanak. The tenth guru, Gobind Singh (GOH-bind sing), led a change in Sikhism from pacifism to militarism (see "A Closer Look: The Symbol of Sikhism" box). When he died in 1708, the soul of these gurus was believed to have gone into the scripture of Sikhism, the **Guru Granth** (literally, "Guru Book"). Now this soul is believed to reside in each and every true copy of this scripture—the soul of the guru became the soul of the *Granth*.

Learning Outcome 6-2

Summarize how Sikhism developed over time, especially its founding by the ten gurus and its life from the British Empire through the present.

6-2 Sikhism Today as Shaped by Its Past: Two Key Periods

Regional Sikh officials in British Columbia, Canada, gathered to address the 2006 arson of the Sikh temple in Williams Lake, BC. The main hall was damaged in the fire, and much repair work would need to be done before the building could be used again. In addition to calling on

A Closer Look:

The Symbol of Sikhism

Sikhism has several unofficial symbols: the turban; the Ek Onkar (ehk ON-kahr), or "God is One" phrase from the opening of the Sikh scriptures; and the Five Ks (all of which will be discussed below). They are dwarfed, however, by the use of the **khanda** (literally, "double-edged sword") as the main Sikh symbol. You'll see it on the Sikh flag that flies in front of and inside many gurdwaras (Sikh houses of worship). Four items, all traditional Sikh weapons, form the khanda. The Sikh symbol is unique among all the symbols of world religions for its military features.

The center is a vertical double-edged sword with a broad blade. On the outside are two curved single-edged swords; many Sikh men carry a small one at all times, and we'll talk more about this further on. The two swords are often said to represent both the spiritual and the political

Figure 6.1 Symbol of Sikhism

power of Sikhism. At the top center is a metal ring called a *chakkar* (CHAHK-uhr). As a weapon thrown at the enemy, it's similar to a discus, and effective up to about 150 feet. You may have seen a chakkar in popular film and television.

> The Sikh symbol is unique among all the symbols of world religions for its military features.

Like most religious symbols, the khanda has also been interpreted symbolically. The circle is often said to represent the unity and eternity of God. The vertical two-edged sword symbolizes God's concern for both truth and justice, and two crossed kirpans curved around the outside (the fourth type of traditional weapon) signify God's all-encompassing spiritual power.

---

police to solve this case, the gathering announced plans for the ritual cremation of the "body" of the main Sikh scripture book, the *Guru Granth*, which was damaged in the arson. They called the damage done to this book "attempted murder of the living leader and teacher of the Sikhs." This startling statement reflects the long-standing Sikh devotion to their scripture as the literal embodiment of the soul of the ten founding gurus. It reflects as well the long, sad history of Sikhs having to endure persecution.

Browse a website popular among Sikhs.

6-2a The Ten Gurus

When we think of India, we tend to focus on Hinduism, but for more than a thousand years Muslims have been influential there. Sikhism arose in predominantly Hindu northern India while it was under Muslim control (see Map 6.1). During the time of the first few gurus, Muslim rulers tended to be tolerant of this new group; at the time of the later gurus, however, the rulers grew intolerant, and at times used violence.

Around 1499 C.E., Guru Nanak (1469–1539) began teachings that many saw as a new sect within Hinduism. Nanak was a Hindu and came to accept some features of the mystical **Sant** (meaning "saint")

tradition of northern India, a devotional movement of both Hindus and Muslims. The Sants composed songs about the divine presence and power that they saw in all things. Several of these hymns were even incorporated later into the Sikh scriptures. The Sants promoted devotion to God as essential to obeying God (important for Muslims) and liberation from the endless cycle of reincarnation (important for Hindus). However, Nanak also had differences with the Sant poets; for example, he started his own religious community and passed his teachings and leadership of this community to successors. Nanak preached a message of universal love and tolerance, downplaying the differences between religions and highlighting their similarities. Because of the religious situation in northern India, he particularly related his movement to Hinduism and Islam. One story tells that when a Muslim awakened him from sleep and complained that his feet were pointing disrespectfully to Mecca, Nanak replied, "Show me where God is not, and I will point my feet in that direction."

Nanak collected a small number of students, and it was from this first

khanda [KAHN-duh] Double-edged sword, the main symbol of Sikhism

Sant [sahnt] Devotional movement of Hindus and Muslims in northern India

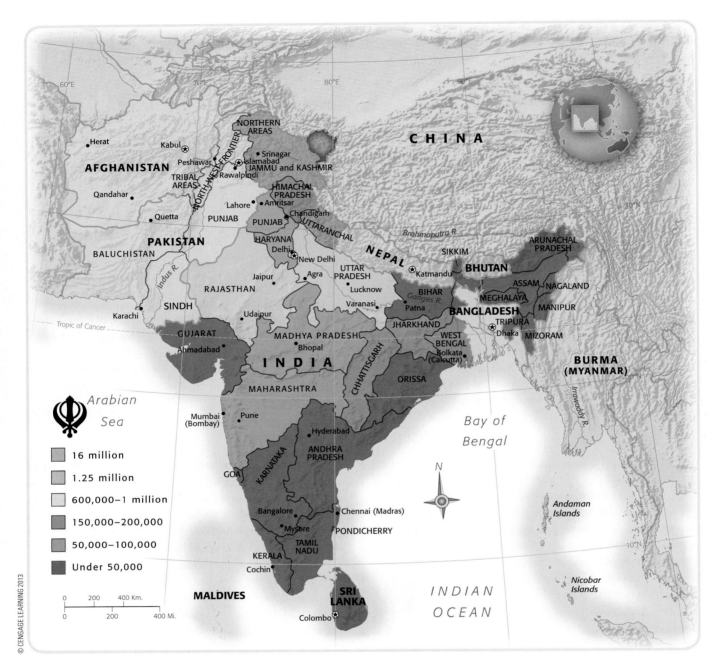

Map 6.1
Sikh Population in India and Sri Lanka, 2005

Arabian
Sea

16 million

1.25 million

600,000–1 million

150,000–200,000

50,000–100,000

Under 50,000

guru-students relationship that the name *Sikhism* came. He composed many mystical hymns that were eventually collected in the Sikh scripture. Nanak visited pilgrimage sites throughout India to spread his message of "remembering the name" of the one and only God by meditating on God constantly and devoting oneself to him. This devotion was to be carried out not by withdrawing from the world, but by worship and meditation in everyday life. Moreover, like most devotional

mystical movements, Nanak's had a peaceful, even pacifistic message: God's purposes could not be advanced by coercion or violence. This message, except for pacifism, became the foundation of Sikhism through today. Beyond this very little is known for certain about Nanak. The story of his life has been expanded at length in the *janam-sakhis* (JAH-nahm SAHK-ees; "life stories"), composed in the century after his death. Today scholars (but not pious Sikhs) see them as legendary.

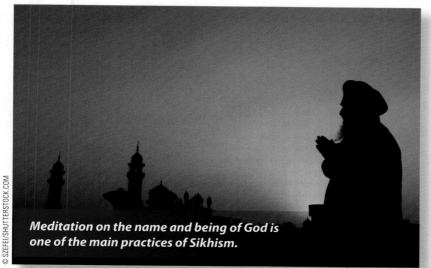

Meditation on the name and being of God is one of the main practices of Sikhism.

By the time of Arjan, the fifth guru, Sikhism was well established as a separate religious movement. Arjan made Amritsar the capital of the Sikh world, made it the religious center of Sikhism with the Harmandir Sahib, and began to compile the main Sikh scripture, called the *Adi Granth*, or "First Book" (now known more commonly as the *Guru Granth*). However, the Mughal rulers felt threatened by Arjan, and he was executed in 1606 after days of continuous torture. First the emperor's agents sat him in a tank of boiling water, the next day on a plate of red-hot iron. On the third day they poured hot sand over his blisters. Arjan remained calm and peaceful throughout this ordeal, to show that people should accept the will of God; he became the first Sikh martyr upon his execution. The significance of Arjan's death was not lost on the Sikhs. The sixth guru, Har Gobind, began to arm the Sikh community to resist the rising persecution they encountered. Like his predecessors, Har Gobind exercised spiritual leadership, but he added governmental leadership as well, making the Sikhs a political community. All Sikhs gradually accepted this new dual authority of the gurus.

Read a *Guru Granth* passage by Arjan on "Remembering God."

Darbar Sahib (Harmandir Sahib)
[HAR-mahn-dear SAH-ihb]
"House of God" temple in Amritsar, also known as the Sacred Court and (more popularly) the Golden Temple

Nine gurus followed Nanak. They led the Sikh community and developed its religious beliefs and practices over the next two centuries: Angad Dev (guru from 1539 to 1552), Amar Das (1552–1574), Ram Das (1574–1581), Arjan (1581–1606), Har Gobind (1606–1644), Har Rai (1644–1661), Har Krishan (1661–1664), Tegh Bahadur (1664–1675), and Gobind Singh (1675–1708). These ten gurus are greatly revered in Sikhism today, particularly because the single soul that inhabited all of them when they were gurus has now entered the Sikh scripture.

Ram Das, the fourth guru, married a daughter of the third guru, Amar Das, thus keeping leadership of the religion "in the family." Ram Das is famous in India for founding the city of Amritsar (uhm-RIT-suhr), which would soon become the center of Sikhism. In Amritsar Sikhs built the **Darbar Sahib**, the "Sacred Court," also called the **Harmandir Sahib**, the "House of God." The most common of its names, the Golden Temple, came after it was overlaid with gold in the early 1800s, but Sikhs do not typically use this name. The Mughal (MOO-gull) emperor Akbar respected the new faith, and he granted Ram Das the land for the new temple and permission to build it. Another lasting legacy of Ram Das is hymn singing during worship. He designated his son Arjan (AHR-juhn) to succeed him, and all the gurus after Arjan were Ram's descendants as well.

Watch a BBC report on the *Guru Granth*.

The short knife carried by many Sikh men symbolizes resistance to oppression.

> To cremate the body of guru Tegh Bahadur without raising Muslim suspicions, a Sikh brought it to his own house and then burned down the house.

The Sikhs then lived in relative peace with their Muslim overlords until a less tolerant Mughal emperor tried to force his subjects to accept Islam. In the course of this persecution, he arrested and executed the ninth guru, Tegh Bahadur (tehg BAH-hah-duhr), in 1675. A Sikh stole Bahadur's body and hid it in his own house. To cremate the guru's body

Guru Nanak and Gobind Singh, with the other eight gurus and the *Guru Granth* at the center

while avoiding detection and certain death, he burned down his house.

> *"The temple and the mosque are one. . . . All men are one though they seem to be many."* —Gobind Singh

The tenth guru, Gobind Singh, who died in 1708, was the most important guru since Nanak. His portrait and that of Guru Nanak are prominently displayed in Sikh homes. The son of the ninth guru, he brought Sikhism to the basic form it has today. Gobind Singh finished the compilation of the *Adi Granth*, and it was renamed the *Guru Granth*. (Sikhs usually refer to it more honorifically as the "Guru Granth Sahib," the "revered" *Guru Granth*.) He formed the **Khalsa** ("the pure ones") as a select society within Sikhism in 1699, so that Sikhs would be soldier-saints, able and willing to defend their religion. Current Sikh scholarship debates whether Gobind Singh intended the Khalsa

Khalsa [KALL-suh] "The pure ones," Sikh society dedicated to strict observance

Dasam Granth [DAH-sum grahnth] "Book of the Tenth Guru," Gobind Singh

to continue as a select formal group within Sikhism or to elevate gradually the whole of Sikhism to the ideals of the Khalsa. At any rate, the Khalsa has been a select and influential society within the main body of Sikhs since its inception, but not all Sikhs have belonged to it or even desired to belong. Gobind Singh established the current Sikh rite of initiation and the distinctive dress of the Sikhs. A number of his sayings have been collected into a book called the ***Dasam Granth***, commonly called the "Tenth Book" but better understood as the "Book of the Tenth Guru." Often quoted from this book is his statement, "The temple and the mosque are one; so too are puja [Hindu worship] and prostration [Muslim worship]. All men are one though they seem to be many."

6-2b Sikhism from British Rule until Today

Sikhs lived and on the whole prospered in the Punjab in the 1700s. However, by 1757 Great Britain had begun its century-long conquest of India to make it the "jewel in the crown" of its empire. In 1845 to 1846, British troops defeated the Sikh armies and took over a great deal of Sikh territory in the Punjab, a prosperous region of India. The Sikhs, who under Ranjit Singh had founded the first and only independent Sikh nation in northern India in 1819, rebelled in an effort to regain their independence. The British quickly crushed this revolt. The Sikhs and the British then managed to build a working relationship. Soon the Sikhs were serving with honor in the British army in India and in police forces in the worldwide empire. The British also got a good public relations spin among Sikhs when they were able to put pro-British Sikhs in charge of the gurdwaras. After about 1860, Sikh migration to Africa and the West began, especially to Britain and parts of the British Empire such as Canada.

The situation of Sikhs in the world today has largely been shaped by the partition of British India. When India became independent in 1947, its territory was divided between India and the new Muslim nation of Pakistan. This partition disadvantaged the Sikhs; the new border ran right through their home in the Punjab. Most Sikhs preferred to live in a secular state dominated by Hindus rather than in an officially Islamic state. Sikhs who suddenly found themselves in the new Pakistani areas of the Punjab fled to the Indian side, often displacing Muslims who fled to Pakistan. Considerable violence ensued, with loss of life on both sides. When the dust settled, the Sikhs found that they had lost much of their homeland, and were understandably embittered over this loss.

The Sikhs' continued desire for their own nation, which had persisted since the 1700s, was something that the new state of India refused to grant. However, in 1966, India did respond to Sikh demands by dividing its Punjab state into three parts. A new, smaller Punjab comprised one of these parts, this time with a Sikh majority and limited powers of self-rule. Many Sikhs were not satisfied with this, however. As Sikh discontent grew, the political conflict suddenly became violent. Jarnail Singh Bhindranwale (JAHR-nail sing BIN-drahn-wail), a Khalsa member known for his zeal for Sikhism, began around 1980 to lead the most radicalized Sikhs. In 1983, Bhindranwale and hundreds of his followers, heavily armed, captured the entire Sacred Court complex in Amritsar. They demanded that the Indian government set up an independent Sikh homeland, which they would call *Khalistan* (KALL-ih-stahn), "land of the Khalsa." In 1984, the Indian army launched an assault to crush this rebellion. The fighting to retake the Sacred Court complex was fierce. Tanks had to be brought in to finally overwhelm the resistance. Over one thousand Sikh militants and Indian soldiers were killed, and the Sikh buildings were heavily damaged.

Watch BBC News anchor Sonia Deol, a Sikh, tell the story of the taking and retaking of the Sacred Court complex.

The assault shocked most Sikhs, even those who opposed Bhindranwale. They saw Prime Minister Indira Gandhi, who had ordered it, as another in the long line of Indian rulers who persecuted the Sikhs. In October 1984 Gandhi's Sikh bodyguards assassinated her in reprisal. Four days of anti-Sikh rioting followed, with mobs roaming the Indian capital of Delhi and other cities, burning Sikh shops and even setting Sikhs on fire with gasoline. Thousands of Sikhs, perhaps as many as ten thousand, were killed.

These events are a sore point for Sikhs today, but are only a part of the story of Sikhism since 1947. On the whole, Sikhs in India have enjoyed prosperity and educational opportunities for women and men. As the twenty-first century began, the Sikh demand for their own nation still had not been met, but the Punjab has been mostly peaceful despite some continuing tensions. The appointment of Manmohan (muhn-MOH-huhn) Singh, an Oxford-educated Sikh economist, as prime minister of India in 2004 created great pride and confidence for Sikhs around the world. It has given Sikhs a calming assurance that their concerns are heard—and spoken of—at the highest levels in India.

Learning Outcome 6-3

Explain the essential Sikh teachings.

6-3 Essential Sikh Teachings

Manmohan Singh, first Sikh prime minister of India

© ANDIA/ALAMY

Sikhs appeal to the city council of Cardiff, U.K., for permission to scatter the ashes of their deceased loved ones at a fixed site in a park along the Taff River. The scattering ceremony takes about fifteen minutes and includes prayers (see "A Closer Look: The Mul Mantar") and recitation of Sikh scripture passages as well as the actual scattering of the ashes. Sikhs had previously obtained

A Closer Look:

The Mul Mantar

The first chapter of the *Adi Granth* is the *Japji* (JAHP-jee). Pious Sikhs repeat this entire lengthy poem from memory every morning during prayers. They consider it the essence of their faith. The *Japji* moves back and forth among several topics: (1) God's name, greatness, and power; (2) God's creation of the world; (3) the way of salvation by meditating on God's name; (4) good and evil; and (5) relations with Hinduism and Islam. The rich sonority of the *Japji* comes through in the translation below. It begins with the Mul Mantar (mool MAHN-tahr], the "root saying" that is a confession of faith. It's the capstone and summary of the whole composition, not just its introduction. The Mul Mantar runs thus:

There is only one God, whose name is true, the Creator who has no fear or hatred. He is immortal, unborn, self-existent; [He is known] by the favor of the guru. Repeat His Name!

Waheguru [VAH-heh-GUHR-oo] Name for God used especially in worship

Ek Onkar [ehk ON-kahr] "One God"; its written form is a prominent symbol of Sikhism

Nam [nahm] Name of God

the permission of the regional agency in charge of environmental affairs and conducted a few scatterings. But the city council found out about it, took exception, and a follow-up request to the council ran into some opposition. The issue is a sensitive one: Not only is the scattering of ashes a matter of a funeral rite, but it touches on basic Sikh teachings on reincarnation and release from it.

As we saw previously, Sikhism is often compared with Islam and Hinduism, the main religions among which it was born and grew. Sikhism does share several key beliefs with parts of Hinduism and Islam, especially with devotional Hinduism and Sufi Islam. However, it has its own beliefs and practices that make it a distinct religion. We shouldn't discount the originality of Sikh teachings and the practices built on them.

6-3a The One God

Sikhs worship one universal God and hold that only one God actually exists, so they are rightly considered monotheists. God is one, holy, loving, and gracious. God does not have a body, nor does he become incarnated in human form, so God cannot and should not be pictured. This belief makes Sikhism a strongly aniconic (against images) religion. Neither do Sikhs have a specific name for God; the way that Guru Nanak spoke of God, as "The True Name," has become the most common. Sikhs use the phrase **Waheguru**, meaning "praise to the Guru," for God, especially in the context of worship.

"Guru" in this usage refers of course to God as teacher, not any human guru. The second important symbol of Sikhism, the **Ek Onkar**, means "One God." It is found in the Mul Mantar, the opening lines of the *Guru Granth*, and is repeated every day by observant Sikhs.

6-3b Devotion to God

Devotion to the one God in knowledge, emotion, and behavior is central to Sikhism. As in Hindu devotional movements, music has been a key way to cultivate and express this devotion. Sikh worship features extensive singing of passages from the *Guru Granth*, to cultivate emotional and intellectual devotion to God. Salvation from the endless cycle of reincarnation comes from remembering God constantly and devoting one's life to God. Although Sikhism began as a pacifist movement, persecution by some Mughal emperors induced it to become almost militaristic in the defense of its faith, so devotion to God now means a willingness to put one's life on the line for God. Devotion to God causes traditionally observant Sikhs, especially members of the Khalsa, to dress in a way that is distinctive, both in India and in the wider world (see "A Closer Look: Sikh Dress").

Let's look more closely now at some of these key teachings. As do other religions native to India, Sikhism teaches that all people undergo the transmigration of their soul. This cycle of reincarnation causes pain, suffering, and ignorance of God, because the world in which souls transmigrate is filled with illusion. The only way of release from this cycle is meditation on the divine **Nam** ("Name"). Nanak taught that the Nam is centered on God and encompasses the whole of God's creation. Having heard the divine word through divine grace and knowing that there is only one true God, the Sikh believer undertakes the main practice of this religion, "meditation on the Name" or "remembering the Name." Many Sikhs use forms of yoga adapted for their religion to help in meditation. Devoting oneself more and more to God, the believer is blessed with increasing inner peace and joy. Finally, the believer reaches the "abode of truth" and enters perfect union with God. At this point, there is no more reincarnation.

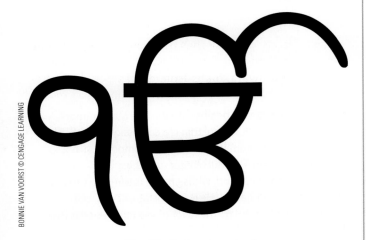

The Ek Onkar symbol

BONNIE VAN VOORST © CENGAGE LEARNING

> *The main practice of Sikhism is "meditation on the Name" or "remembering the Name."*

146 CHAPTER 6 ENCOUNTERING SIKHISM: THE WAY OF GOD'S NAME

A Closer Look:

Sikh Dress

A Sikh who is a member of the Khalsa wears the **Five Ks**. Other Sikhs *may* wear it, but members of the Khalsa *must*. Both men and women observe the Five Ks, the men more fully. They are as follows:

- *Kesh* (kehsh), uncut hair. Sikh men and women never cut or trim hair anywhere on their bodies. Hair on one's head is covered with a scarf for women and a turban (a single long cloth wound around the head) for men. (The turban was a common head covering for Muslim men in earlier times and is still used in Muslim areas such as Afghanistan.)
- *Kanga* (KAHN-guh), small comb. This is used to keep one's long hair neat.
- *Kirpan* (KEER-pahn), sword. This steel sword symbolizes one's defense of the faith and of oppressed people. It's worn at all times on the outside of the body, usually in a small form similar to a knife.

- *Kara* (KAH-ruh), bracelet. This stainless steel item is worn on the right wrist, a reminder of unity with God and the Sikh community.
- *Kachha* (KAHCH-uh), underpants. These are a reminder of the duty of purity and also a prompt to Sikhs to act for the faith.

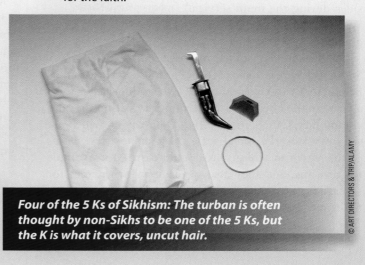

Four of the 5 Ks of Sikhism: The turban is often thought by non-Sikhs to be one of the 5 Ks, but the K is what it covers, uncut hair.

© ART DIRECTORS & TRIP/ALAMY

Learning Outcome 6-4

State and discuss the main ethical precepts of Sikhism.

6-4 Key Sikh Ethics

During the fall elections of 2010, Nikki Haley became governor of South Carolina, its first governor who is not a white male. Born Nimrata Nikki Randhawa to devout Sikh parents in Bamberg, South Carolina, she has attended with her husband and children both the local Sikh temple and a United Methodist church. She has served in the South Carolina House of Representatives and run a fashion business. Haley is known for her personal charm and political poise, and she is a rising star in the Republican Party; she was featured in a 2010 cover story in a national magazine. But in the sometimes-nasty arena of South Carolina politics, Haley was accused in the primary campaign of having two extramarital affairs. She sharply attacked these claims of infidelity, conduct that both Christianity and Sikhism

strongly forbid. She won the primary and general elections handily, becoming a prominent face of Sikhism in the United States.

Sikhs have a strong sense of ethics that is closely related to their view of one God. We'll examine in particular the Sikh social ethic that rejects traditional caste distinctions, and then we'll treat personal ethics.

6-4a Rejection of Hindu Caste

Sikhism from the first has strongly rejected Hindu caste distinctions, so there is usually no toleration of caste in a gurdwara. Sikhs from all caste backgrounds sit together, but with women on one side, men on the other. The gurus denounced caste as irrelevant for access to God, to God's name, and to liberation from sin, ignorance, and transmigration. Another sign of the Sikhs' belief in social equality is the food for the service, which people of all social

> **Five Ks** Five items of appearance and dress for Khalsa members: kesh (uncut hair), kanga (comb), kirpan (sword), kara (bracelet), and kachha (underpants)

langar [LAHN-gar]
Communal meal that follows every main Sikh service

backgrounds donate, prepare, and eat together. In the **langar**, the communal meal that follows every main Sikh service, everyone sits in a straight line where no one can claim a higher status. (Men and women are usually in different lines, however, just as they sit on different sides during the main service.) We'll discuss the langar at greater length below.

See a *New York Times* article and short video on the langar in the Sacred Court, Amritsar.

Although Sikhism has opposed Hindu castes, many Sikhs still have a caste. More than 60 percent of Sikhs belong to an agricultural caste. Two trading castes form a very small, albeit influential, minority within the Sikh community. Others include two Dalit castes, which are the lowest on the social scale. Sikhs have a few castes of their own in addition to Hindu castes, for example the artisans, and they also have distinctive names for several castes shared with Hinduism. This use of caste has some bearing on how Sikhs live and worship. Sikhs

Serving the langar in a Sikh temple in New Delhi, India

PHILIPPE LISSAC/GODONGPHOTONONSTOP/GLOW IMAGES

typically marry within their caste. Moreover, despite what was said above about caste in gurdwaras, Sikhs have occasionally established gurdwaras intended for particular castes, especially in the United Kingdom.

6-4b Other Moral Rules

In Sikh personal ethics, the use of alcohol, drugs, or any addictive substance is forbidden. Tobacco is forbidden as well. Sikhs believe in hard work and generous charity. Members of the Khalsa are required to wear the Five Ks and to avoid four particular sins: cutting their hair, eating meat not butchered according to Sikh rules, adultery, and using tobacco and intoxicants. Sikhs who commit these sins must confess them openly and be reinitiated into the religion. If they are known to commit these sins and don't confess, they are excluded from the faith.

Read a report on Sikh efforts to promote the Indian government's "Save the Girl Child" campaign.

Sikhs have drawn up several "codes of conduct" that enumerate the moral principles and behaviors by which they are to live. Here is a popular code:

- Only one God exists; remember and worship only the one God.
- Work hard and honestly and share your gains with others.
- Be truthful in all of life.
- Women are equal to men in God's sight and must be treated as equals.
- All humans are the same and members of one human family, so distinctions based on caste or color are to be avoided.
- Do not trust in superstitions or follow empty rituals; do not use idols, magic, omens, fasts, religious body markings, sacred threads, etc.
- Dress simply and modestly; showy or revealing clothes reflect poorly on those who wear them.
- Sikh women must not wear a veil, nor should they or Sikh men have body piercings.
- All persons should marry and have children, and stay in the married state; asceticism and renunciation of marriage are pointless.
- Have faith in the *Guru Granth*, not in any other book or person.
- Control the Five Evils—lust, anger, greed, attachment to material things, and arrogance.
- Practice the Five Virtues—truth, contentment, compassion, humility, and love.

Outline the way Sikhs worship and practice other rituals, especially life-cycle rituals.

6-5 Sikh Ritual and Worship

Worshipers at a Sikh temple on a weekday afternoon see three life-cycle ceremonies. First, a baby is brought in for a naming ceremony. The official reader opens the *Guru Granth* at random, and the first letter on the left-hand page becomes the first letter in the child's first name. Second, a young couple comes to be married. During the ceremony, the couple circles the *Granth* several times as musicians sing verses from its marriage hymns. Third, the relatives of a recently deceased Sikh come for the conclusion of his funeral rites. A prominent feature of the funeral is the continuous reading of the entire *Granth*, a process that takes two days, and the relatives are present for the solemn end of the reading.

> *Like most mystics who value thought and emotion, Guru Nanak and his successors were deeply suspicious of formal ritual practices.*

Like most mystics who place the primary value of religion on individual thought and emotion, Guru Nanak and his successors were deeply suspicious of formal ritual practices. He rejected the Hindu priesthood and all its ritual activities, and not just because it was connected to caste. In his new religion, he discarded priesthood, sacrifices, the use of incense, religious images, pilgrimage, Muslim and Hindu dietary rules, and the like. Instead, Nanak taught that only with strong devotion shown in faith and love can one reach God. Nevertheless, like any other religion, Sikhism has a significant ritual component. We'll begin by discussing the center of Sikh life—the Sikh temples—and what happens there.

Read the *Guru Granth*'s critique of Hindu ritual.

6-5a The Gurdwara

The Punjabi word **gurdwara** means "the Guru's door," which implies that the gurdwara is the residence of the Guru. The Guru is the living Sikh book, the *Guru Granth*. The gurdwara is the place of everyday worship, in the morning. It's where children learn Sikh history, morals, and sacred writings. Especially in the Western world, the gurdwara is also a community and social-welfare center for Sikhs. Gurdwaras are supervised by a committee drawn from the membership.

There are four doors into a gurdwara, modeled after the four doors of the main temple in Amritsar. They are the doors of peace, livelihood, learning, and grace. These doors symbolize the conviction that people from all locations and castes are welcome. Gurdwaras often fly the Sikh flag outside. Small rooms for coats and shoes can be found near the entry; shoes must be removed before worship. No statues or even religious pictures are in the gurdwara, because Sikhs regard God as having no physical form and having no incarnation that can be pictured. Nor are there any candles, incense, or bells—used prominently in Hindu and Buddhist worship. Flowers are often present, however, especially in front of the scripture book.

The focus of attention in the gurdwara, both architecturally and in worship, is the *Guru Granth*. Sikhs give the "Guru Book" as much respect as a human guru—perhaps even more. It is kept in a special room at night ("put to bed") and carried ceremonially to the main hall before worship begins in the morning. Then it is placed on a platform called a "throne," and covered with a richly woven cloth when not being read. When Sikhs enter the main hall, they bow deeply to the book, sometimes touching their head to the floor. A man with a ceremonial fan, the **chaur**, waves it over the *Guru Granth* while it is being read. Although Sikhs revere their scripture book, this reverence is paid directly to its spiritual content and the living soul of the gurus in it, not to the book itself.

Sikh worship in a gurdwara does not follow an official form, although there is an informal order of service. Worship usually commences with the singing of "Asa Di Var" (AH-sah dee vahr), written by Guru Nanak. Instruments then accompany the singing of other hymns from the *Guru Granth*. Hymn singing, called **kirtan**, is

gurdwara [guhr-DWAHR-uh] "The Guru's door," Sikh house of worship

chaur [chowr] Fan used to venerate the *Guru Granth* in the gurdwara

kirtan [KEER-tahn] Devotional singing of hymns from the *Guru Granth*

A reader moves a chaur over the **Guru Granth** to venerate it.

called the *hukamnama*, to be read out, and the passage is published on the Internet for all Sikhs around the world to read.

In India many Sikhs go to their gurdwara before work or during the day for private prayer and meditation. Sikhs do not observe a fixed day of the week as a holy day, but in the West they usually go to a gurdwara on Sunday morning, when services are regularly held. Services are also held there on important Sikh holy days.

As stated above, Sikhs do not have ordained priests, although sometimes high officials at Sikh gurdwaras are mistaken for priests. Any male Sikh can (if he can read the language of the *Guru Granth*) lead the congregation in prayer and read the scriptures. Every gurdwara has at least one **granthi**, who cares for the *Guru Granth*, reads from it during the service, and in general organizes the daily services. A granthi must be fluent in the Gurmukhi dialect in which the *Granth* is written, and must be able to care for the *Granth*. Granthis can be male or female, although women granthis are still rare and typically found only in the West. Granthis are most often Khalsa members.

Near the end of the service, food is offered to the congregation. This is **parshad**, a warm dessert-like treat made from flour, sugar, and liquefied butter. (Visitors sometimes don't appreciate its sweet, oily taste, but it should be graciously accepted, to avoid giving unintended offense. Sikhs who don't like its taste ask for a small portion.) The first five portions of parshad are offered to Khalsa members present. Then it is served to everyone else without further social or religious distinctions.

Try an easy recipe for parshad.

vak lao [vahk low] "Taking [God's] word" by opening the *Guru Granth* at random

granthi [GRAHN-thee] Official who cares for the *Guru Granth* and reads from it

parshad [PAHR-shahd] Simple food served at the end of a Sikh service

a major element of Sikh worship. Many gurdwaras have a small group of musicians who lead the kirtan from the front. A short talk comes next, usually drawing on a teaching from Sikh tradition. Then comes the singing of "Anand Sahib," written by Guru Amar Das. After the singing, the congregation stands for prayer, keeping their eyes closed and their bodies still. Next, the *Guru Granth* is opened at random, and a passage beginning on the left-hand page is read as the lesson of the day.

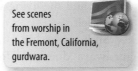

See scenes from worship in the Fremont, California, gurdwara.

This latter, memorable feature of Sikh scripture usage is called **vak lao**, "taking [God's] word." In the home or in the temple, the scripture is always opened at random, and the reading begins from the top of the left-hand page. This reading is thought to hold special significance for the occasion, and Sikhs believe that God guides which page falls open. This is God's word for the moment, a word that must be "taken" into the believer's life. Every day in the main temple in Amritsar, the *Guru Granth* is opened at random for the "passage of the day,"

Read the hukam-nama for today.

> *Most people in the service stay for the communal meal; observant Sikhs in the Western world don't go out for Sunday brunch.*

6-5b The Langar

Every gurdwara has a langar, a dining hall, attached to it. As we saw previously, this term is also used for the communal meal itself. An extension of the service, this meal helps to build social and spiritual solidarity in the gurdwara. Most people in the service stay for the communal meal; observant Sikhs in the Western world don't go out for Sunday brunch. The food in the langar must be uniform and plain, to discourage wealthy Sikhs from using it to display their prosperity. Many Sikhs are vegetarian, so only vegetarian dishes are served

Hands of a Sikh bride and groom in India

© JOSHKO/DREAMSTIME

in a langar. This allows any Sikh or visitor to eat there, and it keeps the meals simple and low cost. The meal typically includes dal, a variety of vegetables, and rice pudding; water and tea are served as beverages. In Europe and North America, members of a gurdwara sign up to buy and prepare the food for the Sunday-noon langar, which is considered both a duty and an honor.

6-5c Sikh Life-Cycle Rituals

Sikh rituals, like rituals of all religions, have evolved over time. For example, although Gobind required that Khalsa members carry arms and have uncut hair, the wearing of the Five Ks wasn't an obligation of all Khalsa members until the late 1800s. Other ritual reforms were also carried out then, many of them in an effort to distinguish more sharply between Sikhism and Hinduism.

Even though Sikhism is mainly nonritualistic, it does not downplay or ignore the meaning of life-cycle changes. Sikhism recognizes four major life-cycle events with formal rites of passage. The first ritual is a naming ceremony for newborns, held in a gurdwara when the mother has recovered from childbirth. A hymn is selected at random from the *Guru Granth* by an official reader, and, as mentioned above, parents choose a traditional Sikh name for newborn children that begins with the first letter on the left-hand page. (This means that well-prepared Sikh parents have to think through possible names for all the letters of the Gurmuki alphabet.) *Singh* ("Lion") is given as a second personal name (as we say, a middle name) to all males, and *Kaur* ("Princess") to all females.

A second life-cycle ritual is marriage, called by Sikhs "blissful union." As a part of the ceremony, always held in a gurdwara, the bride and groom walk four times around the *Guru Granth* as one of its hymns is sung. It's likely that this circling of the holy book was introduced around 1900 to distinguish Sikh marriage from the Hindu wedding ritual of walking around a sacred fire. Whatever its time of origin, this makes a dignified recognition of the central importance of the Sikh scripture in one's marriage.

View highlights of an upscale Sikh wedding in Vancouver, British Columbia.

The third rite is initiation into the Khalsa, called Amrit (UHM-rith). Outsiders often call this "baptism," even though that term is of Christian origin. Five initiated Sikhs officiate at the ritual, while a sixth is positioned reverently at the *Guru Granth*. Amrit includes pouring water into an iron bowl and then dissolving sweet powder in the water. One of the officiants then stirs this with a double-edged sword. The Sikh sitting at the *Guru Granth* then recites certain portions of the Sikh scriptures, and the initiates drink five handfuls of the water, now called amrit ("nectar" of immortality). Each time this is done, the Sikh giving the water cries the main slogan of Sikhism, "Praise to the Guru's Khalsa! Praise to the Guru's victory!" Amrit is then sprinkled on the initiates' head, and they drink the rest of it. They recite the lines that begin the *Guru Granth*, and the obligations of being a Sikh are taught to them briefly. Finally, parshad is distributed, each person taking it from the same dish.

The fourth rite is the funeral ceremony. Cremation and scattering of ashes into fresh, flowing water is done soon after death. These are not done at the gurdwara, of course, but an important part of a funeral service is the continuous reading of the entire *Guru Granth*. This is for the consolation and support of the grieving family. Relatives and friends of the deceased are expected to be in the gurdwara for the completion of the reading, at which time the funeral is considered finished. Musicians sing appropriate hymns, and short parts of the *Guru Granth* are read again. After the final prayer, parshad is given to the congregation.

6-5d Other Festivals

Sikhism probably seems like a serious religion to you, and Sikhs are indeed serious about their religion, but it does have its festive side. In fact, Sikhism probably has more festivals than any other world religion. There are three holidays every year for each of the ten gurus—to mark their birth, their becoming a guru, and their death. In addition to these holidays for the gurus, Sikhism has eight major festivals. Four of them mark the more important events in the lives of the gurus—those besides their birth, becoming a guru, and death. The other four are the festival of the installation of the *Guru Granth*, the New Year festival of Baisakhi (buy-SAHK-ee), the all-Indian winter festival of lights known as Diwali (dee-WALL-ee), and Hola Mahalla (HOH-luh ma-HALL-uh). Festivals often have processions in the streets and visits to gurdwaras, particularly to those associated with one of the gurus or with some historical event. Speeches are commonly made to crowds of worshipers.

Hindus, Sikhs, and Jains alike observe the festival of Diwali. The Sikh celebration centers on the Sacred Court, which is illuminated for the occasion. For Sikhs, Diwali has a historical connection with the happy release of Guru Hargobind from imprisonment by the Mughal emperor. Gobind Singh established Hola Mahalla, which is held the day after the Hindu festival of Holi, as an alternative to the Hindu holiday. It's celebrated with parades and displays of Sikh martial arts.

Buildings in the Sacred Court complex in Amritsar, lit up for Guru Nanak's birthday

© ISTOCKPHOTO.COM/JATTISM

6-6 Sikhism around the World Today

A leading Sikh organization in the United States, United Sikhs, gathered signatures on a petition. It asked that the U.S. Census Bureau designate *Sikh* as a separate term for race in the 2010 national census. In the past, those who wrote *Sikh* in the "other race" space have been automatically labeled by the more general term *Asian Indian* when the forms are processed by computer. Arguing that this is incorrect, and noting that social and political power comes from census results, the organization urged American Sikhs, "Sign the petition to have Sikhs assigned a code to be counted correctly." When the Census Bureau responded to the petition, however, it said that a change could not be made for 2010, but it would be considered for the 2020 census.

6-6a The Sikh Diaspora

Until well into the 1800s, Sikhs who left the Punjab, in relatively small numbers, were traders who settled in other parts of India or in closely neighboring countries. When India came under British control, Sikhs spread more widely in the unified nation. In the late 1800s, the posting of Sikh soldiers in the British army to stations in Malaya and Hong Kong prompted other Sikhs to migrate to those territories. This migration eventually spread to Australia, New Zealand, Fiji, and China as Sikhs discovered that their skills in commerce and trade—and not just those of soldiers and police—were widely valued in Asia. Many Sikhs migrated to the United Kingdom and established a strong presence there that lasts through today.

A recent book, *Sikhism in Global Context* by Pashaura

Singh of the University of Michigan, carefully examines the current Sikh diaspora. Singh writes that the Sikh community has made its presence felt worldwide because of this dispersion. Although he does not specifically make this claim, his analysis shows that Sikhism has become a "world religion" in ways it was not earlier, when it was largely confined to India. Singh describes a significant variety of caste and gender within world Sikhism, and an ability of diaspora Sikhs to use modern media to promote understanding of their faith. An appreciation of the Sikh experience in various countries serves to help in understanding Sikhs from a global point of view, particularly how Sikhism is changing in the world. The author finds that the *Guru Granth* has been a constant source of shaping the Sikhs wherever they have gone—even for nonviolence, which challenges traditional Sikh ideas about militant self-defense.[1]

6-6b The First Wave of Immigration to North America (1900–1940)

The first Sikhs—usually single young men, because of immigration rules that prevented families from entering the country—arrived around 1900. Many of them sought opportunities on the West Coast of North America. Some worked in factories, in sawmills, and building railroad lines. Others worked on farms in California, Washington, and British Columbia, because they had been farmers in the Punjab, India's richest farmland. These started as migrant farmworkers, but soon many of them were so successful that they could buy their own farms and settle down. As with other immigrants from Asia, it was difficult to practice their faith here. They had left their religious institutions behind, and assimilation to North American ways of life (dress, diet, schooling, and so on) posed a direct challenge to Sikh identity.

The story of Sikh life in Canada is told well by Kamala Elizabeth Nayar in her book *The Sikh Diaspora in Vancouver: Three Generations amid Tradition, Modernity, and Multiculturalism*.[2] Most Sikh immigration to North America was to Canada, especially to British Columbia, because Indian immigration within the British Empire and the British Commonwealth was usually easier than it was into the United States. However, many Sikhs did head for the United States.

> By 1910, Sikhs were called "ragheads," a term of abuse that has persisted until today.

The first generation of Sikh migration to the United States saw the rise of a permanent feature of Sikh life here: mistreatment by other Americans, which included ignorance, intolerance, discrimination, and sometimes mob violence. Immigrant Asians were often seen as unwelcome competitors by labor unions and their (all-white) members, because they worked for low wages. By around 1910, Sikhs were called "ragheads" on the streets and in newspapers, a term of abuse that sadly has persisted in slang until today. In 1913 the California "Alien Land Act" prohibited noncitizens from owning property, which severely disadvantaged Sikh farmers, and in 1917 the U.S. Congress choked off all immigration from India and other Asian regions. The U.S. Department of Justice even went so far as to revoke the citizenship of Sikhs who had been granted it, and the Supreme Court ruled that Sikhs did not qualify for citizenship. The Court said that though they are from Indo-European stock, they are not "white" in the same way that non-Sikh "white" Americans were.

For Sikhs, the most grievous effect of this racial bias was that they were now unable to bring their wives and families to America. (Then, as now, family issues in immigration are difficult matters.) Against these forces, Sikhs persisted in the process of assimilation, all the while trying to maintain the strong Sikh identity that marked their religion from its earliest years. The first gurdwara was established in the United States in 1912, in the farming town of Stockton, California; for two generations it was the center of the Sikh religion in the United States. From around 1910 to the 1960s, Sikhs in the United States tried to keep moving forward against occasional opposition.

All this played out against the backdrop of a rising Indian movement for independence from the British Empire. Sikhs had their troubles in North America, but they still cared deeply about events in their Punjabi homeland. In 1913, Hindus, Muslims, and Sikhs in California—all from a Punjabi background—founded the Ghadar (GAHD-uhr, meaning "revolt") Movement in order to raise money for resistance to British colonial rule in India, especially in the Punjab. Sikhs

---

[1] Pashaura Singh, *Sikhism in Global Context* (Oxford, UK: Oxford University Press, 2012).

[2] Kamala Elizabeth Nayar, *Sikh Diaspora in Vancouver: Three Generations amid Tradition, Modernity, and Multiculturalism* (Toronto: Toronto University Press, 2004).

© ISTOCKPHOTO.COM/CATHERINE JONES

Young Sikhs line up for a Sikh Day parade in New York City.

main hall so people could sit on the floor before the *Guru Granth Sahib.* Shoes were again taken off for worship, music in the service became more traditional, and the langar meal was reemphasized.

A third, smaller wave of Sikh immigrants arrived from India after the violent events of 1984 in Amritsar. They were much more politicized than the second wave and brought an urgent sense of Sikh identity. Talk about "Khalistan," at times unhappy and divisive for Sikhs, began to be heard in American gurdwaras. This continuous reworking of Sikh identity in the United States complicated the challenging task of raising Sikh children to willingly affirm their religiously Sikh and culturally Punjabi heritage. Despite these challenges, Sikhs are thriving in North America, and not just economically. Moreover, Sikhism in North America is doing something that Sikhs in the Punjab have not tried to do—they are attracting converts to the faith and healthy lifestyle of Sikhism. This movement of young American converts is now headed by an organization called the Sikh Dharma.

Learn about converts to Sikhism in North America.

predominated in the Ghadar organization and gave it a militant flavor. Some Sikhs even returned to the Punjab to lead ill-fated attacks on British authorities there. Although Ghadar fortunes were set back around 1917 to 1918 during World War I, by negative publicity from court trials and the killing of one of its leaders, it reorganized in the 1920s and played a role in the resistance to British rule until Indian independence was established in 1947.

6-6c Second and Third Waves to North America (1965–Present)

In 1965, the Sikh situation in the United States changed significantly for the better, with new federal legislation that lifted old prohibitions and quotas. A large number of Sikh immigrants—many of them educated professionals such as physicians, scientists, and educators—came to the United States looking for economic opportunity. Their numbers in the United States tripled in a few short years. Sikhs settled not only throughout California, but also in New York and Texas, and also near major Midwestern cities such as Detroit and Chicago. The first wave of Sikh migration had settled in the countryside, but this second wave settled directly into the suburbs.

These Sikhs also brought tensions to established gurdwaras. The newcomers were more traditionally Sikh than the more assimilated Sikhs who had been in the United States for more than three generations; some of the old-timers had married non-Sikhs and given up on distinctive Sikh dress and diet. As newcomers gradually took over, the Punjabi language was heard much more frequently in worship. Chairs were removed from the

6-6d Sikhism in Post-9/11 America

Some events in the aftermath of the attacks on the United States on September 11, 2001, have done "collateral damage" to Sikhs in the Western world. Al-Qaeda, the Afghanistan-based group that launched these attacks, was aligned in Afghanistan with the Taliban movement of Sunni Islam. The Taliban has a "dress code" for men quite similar to the way members of the Khalsa dress. For almost entirely coincidental reasons, both Taliban Afghanis and observant Sikhs do not cut their hair or beards, and they both wear turbans. (Taliban members do not wear the kirpan knife, however.) Although people in south Asia have the "cultural intelligence" to tell them apart, many residents of the United States do not. A number of Sikhs in the United States have now been under suspicion and have sometimes experienced outright opposition and occasional violence, as "Muslim terrorists." Gurdwaras have been threatened with arson. Sikh children in public schools are under particular pressure by some students who don't know the difference between Sikhs and Muslims, and think all Muslims must be terrorists. For Sikhs to be identified with Muslims at all—let alone with a separatist Muslim group that carries out mass terror attacks—is a grievous thing for them. Sikhs have responded with a patient effort to educate other Americans about the differences between themselves and the Taliban.

By far the worst incidence of violence against Sikhs in the United States occurred on Sunday, August 5, 2012, when a single gunman killed six people and wounded four others at a gurdwara in Oak Creek, Wisconsin. The members were preparing the langar for that morning. The gunman, Wade Michael Page (who took his own life at the scene), was a white supremacist who had spoken to his friends about a "racial holy war." No particular reason was ever found for why he targeted Sikhs.

View "Mistaken Identity": Sikh Americans deal with the aftermath of 9/11.

Examine the "Hatred in the Hallways" report about anti-Sikh bias in the New York City school system.

Despite the challenges of living in the Western world, Sikhs continue to live faithful lives in North America. They do struggle with issues of assimilation and discrimination, and regularly must go to court for the right to keep their distinctive appearance at their jobs. But these North American problems are much smaller than the challenges Sikhism has faced in India for the past five hundred years. The Sikh community in the Western world is facing its problems resolutely and decisively. By 2000 the Sikh population of the United Kingdom was more than 300,000, and there are an estimated 150,000 to 200,000 Sikhs in both Canada and the United States. They continue to follow the Guru, who proclaims, "There is only one God, whose name is true. Repeat his name!"

Watch an introduction to Sikhism produced by the Chicago Police Department for its officers and the general public.

Listen to a rap song by young Sikhs on the possible demolition of their gurdwara in Austin, Texas.

Study Tools 6

Ready to study? In the book you can:

- Review Learning Outcome answers and glossary terms with the tear-out Chapter Review card.

Or you can go online to CourseMate, at www.cengagebrain.com, for these resources:

- Chapter quizzes to prepare for tests

- Interactive flashcards of all glossary terms

- A timeline of events for this chapter

- An eBook with introductions, interactive quizzes, and live links for all web resources in the chapter

CHAPTER 7

Encountering Daoism and Confucianism: Two Views of the Eternal Way

BONNIE VAN VOORST © CENGAGE LEARNING

Learning Outcomes

After studying this chapter, you will be able to do the following:

7-1 Explain the names *Daoism* and *Confucianism* and related terms.

7-2 Outline how Daoism and Confucianism developed over time into what they are today, especially in relationship to each other.

7-3 Explain the essential teachings of Daoism and Confucianism, especially their similarities and differences.

7-4 Paraphrase in your own words the main ethical principles of Daoism and Confucianism.

7-5 Outline the way Daoists and Confucianists worship and practice other rituals.

7-6 Summarize the main features of Daoism and Confucianism around the world today, especially in North America.

Study Tools

After you read this chapter, go to the Study Tools at the end of the chapter, page 187.

Like the yin and yang, Confucianists and Daoists both agreed with each other and worked against each other. Chinese culture was shaped and empowered by this dynamism.

Your Visit to the Forbidden City in Beijing, China

A highlight of your tour of China is the Forbidden City, located in Beijing (bay-JING), a city formerly known as Peking. Most tourists to Beijing see at least a bit of it, but because of your interest in world religions and cultures, you are looking forward to a more in-depth view. The traditional name "Forbidden City" comes from the fact that it was formerly closed to all but the emperor, who was considered the "Son of Heaven," and his court officials. It was sacred to both Daoists and Confucianists. Now it doesn't seem at all forbidding to you, but inviting. The current official name for this complex, the Palace Museum, also seems more inviting.

The complex consists of an astounding 980 surviving buildings spread out over an area one mile long and one-half mile wide. It covers 183 acres, which your guide puts in terms you can understand—it's the size of 166 football fields. It has two parts, both of which you can enter: the outer court, where the emperor ruled the nation, and the inner court, where he and his closest courtiers lived with their families. A wide moat as well as a wall thirty feet high surround the complex. As you cross into the Forbidden City through its only entrance at the Tiananmen (tee-YEN-ahn-MEN) or "Heavenly Peace" Gate, your guide says that it's helpful for you to understand more about the history of the area.

She relates the following: The Forbidden City was built in the early part of the 1400s and was home to two dynasties of China's emperors until 1912.

The Ming dynasty, which ruled from 1368 to 1644, built the palace and courtyard. The Qing (ching) dynasty then governed the area until the last emperor of China left his position in 1912. Religious ceremonies in the Forbidden City ceased in that year. It was designated a World Heritage Site in 1987 by the United Nations.

Many halls in this complex have names with religious significance, because the emperor was the intermediary between Heaven and the Chinese people. Today, these buildings are the most ancient collection of wooden buildings

The Chinese see dragons as powerful, good-natured creatures from whom people could seek favors.

© MARY416/SHUTTERSTOCK.COM

< People gather at dawn at the Hall of Prayer for Good Harvests in the Temple of Heaven complex, Beijing. From 1420 to 1911 C.E., emperors of China came to this temple to pray for good crops.

157

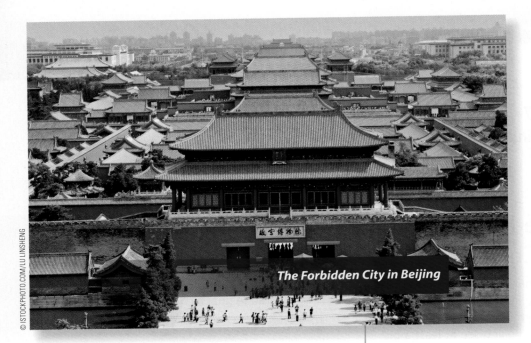

The Forbidden City in Beijing

these faiths, the "three traditions" of China, there are today. The worldwide population of those who follow mostly Daoism is estimated by the authoritative World Religion Database at around 8 million, and the Confucianist population at around 6 million. But if we take into account those who practice major *features* of Daoism and Confucianism, their numbers rise to around 300 million each.[1]

in the world. The Forbidden City was made fit for tourism in the 1950s, and Tiananmen Square in front of the Gate of Heavenly Peace was developed into a huge public square. For five hundred years imperial China had the largest palace complex in the world, and now Communist China proudly has the largest public square. You notice, however, that the guide doesn't mention how, in the spring of 1989—the year that several Communist governments in Europe fell— a prodemocracy demonstration with thousands of people took place over several weeks in this square, complete with a small replica of the Statue of Liberty, called a "goddess." In early June, Chinese army units brought in by the government opened fire on the protestors when they refused to disperse. Estimates of the dead range from five hundred to three thousand, and hundreds were imprisoned. Your knowledge of what happened here in Tiananmen Square makes your attitude about it more somber.

In your study of Daoism and Confucianism, you'll be introduced to these unique, sometimes puzzling features:

- Some scholars hold that Chinese people in the world today are Confucianist in a significant sense just by virtue of being culturally Chinese, whether they self-identify as Confucianist or not. This is true, these academics say, even if they don't think of themselves as "religious."

- Many Chinese who see themselves as either Daoists or Confucianists practice elements of the other religion, and a great number are Buddhists as well, in some aspects of their lives. This makes it difficult to estimate how many followers of

- Confucianism is traceable with certainty to a historical founder; Daoism is not. Daoism grew out of various religious and philosophical traditions in ancient China, including shamanism and belief in the ancient gods and spirits. This difference in beginnings has proven to be one important factor in making Confucianism a more coherent system than Daoism.

Watch an introduction to the three main traditions of China.

- Confucianism is a thoroughly Chinese tradition, but its influence has spread widely in East Asia beyond China, especially to Taiwan, Korea, Vietnam, and Japan. It has some influence in south Asian countries such as Malaysia and Indonesia. The reach of formal, organized Daoism hasn't been as extensive; it is mostly contained in China and Taiwan.

"If you google 'Confucius,' you [get] page after page of 'Confucius says' jokes ... before you arrive at any actual quotations." —Stephen Prothero

- Both Daoism and Confucianism have been widely misunderstood in nonacademic popular settings in the Western world, perhaps more than any other world religions. Daoism has been misrepresented

_____

[1] http://www.worldreligiondatabase.org/wrd_default.asp

as "just doing what comes naturally." The wisdom teaching of Confucius is often trivialized in popular culture, from fortune cookies to the Internet. For example, as Stephen Prothero remarks, "If you google 'Confucius,' you have to wade through page after page of 'Confucius says' jokes … before you arrive at any actual quotations from the man himself."[2]

In this chapter we'll make a slight change in our treatment of world religions. Since Chapter 3, we've examined one religion per chapter. Here, we'll consider together the two main religions of China: Daoism and Confucianism. The benefits of discussing them together outweigh the downsides, especially if one is careful to keep them separate. Confucianism and Daoism are similar in that they have affected, and been affected by, Chinese culture; they differ in that they have been competing formal traditions in China, with two views of the Way and how to live in it.

Learning Outcome 7-1

Explain the names *Daoism, Confucianism,* and related terms.

7-1 The Names *Daoism* and *Confucianism*

Before we discuss the names of these religions, we must explain the two common systems used for rendering Chinese into English—the older Wade-Giles and the newer Pinyin (PIN-yin). Some key Chinese words in religion are spelled the same in each system, but other words are spelled differently. For instance, the Wade-Giles system spells the *d* sound in Chinese as *t*; the newer Pinyin system spells it as *d*. So the more traditional spelling is "Taoism," rather than the Pinyin system's "Daoism"; both are pronounced DOW-ihz-um. Wade-Giles spells the Chinese word for *classic book* as "ching," but Pinyin

For help on pronouncing Pinyin, check out a guide from Carnegie Mellon University.

has "jing." As a result, Wade-Giles spells the name of the main Daoist scripture "Tao Te Ching," and Pinyin spells it "Daode Jing."

Popular usage in the West stays mostly with Wade-Giles. For example, on March 24, 2012, a Google search for "Tao" returned 283 million hits, whereas a search for "Dao" returned 182 million. Nevertheless, the Pinyin system is increasingly used in scholarship. It's usually closer to the way Chinese is pronounced, which makes it easier for beginning students of Chinese religions to pronounce Chinese terms correctly. This book uses the Pinyin spelling but occasionally refers to a significant Wade-Giles spelling the first time a word appears.

Daoism, the religion of the natural Way, refers to diverse but related Chinese traditions that have shaped Asia for more than two thousand years and have had an influence on the Western world since the nineteenth century. The word *Dao* roughly translates as "way," "path," or "road," and by extension "way of life." Scholars often divide Daoism into "religious" and "philosophical" branches. A leading scholar of Daoism, Livia Kohn, has more carefully divided it into three categories: (1) philosophical Daoism, the oldest branch, based on the texts *Daode Jing* and *Zhuangzi* (JWAHNG-zee; in Wade-Giles, *Chuang Tzu*); (2) religious Daoism, a collection of formal, organized religious movements originating from the Celestial Masters movement around 200 C.E.; and (3) folk Daoism, the widely diverse Chinese indigenous local religions taken up into Daoism after 200 C.E.[3]

Confucianism originated as a Western term, not a Chinese term. Its first use was in the 1500s C.E. by Roman Catholic

Daoism [DOW-ihz-um] Religion of the natural Way

Confucianism [kun-FYOO-shuhn-IHZ-um] Religion based on reforms by Confucius; originated as a Western alternative to the common Chinese term "the Scholarly Tradition"

Confucius in a traditional pose

LIESKA/DREAMSTIME

---

[2] Stephen Prothero, *God Is Not One: The Eight Rival Religions That Run the World—And Why Their Differences Matter* (New York: HarperOne, 2010), 101.

[3] Livia Kohn, ed., *Daoism Handbook* (Leiden: Brill, 2000), xi, xxix.

A Closer Look:

The Symbols of Daoism and Confucianism

Daoism and Confucianism don't have official symbols of their faith. The Chinese character for *Dao*, "Way," is sometimes used as a symbol of both Daoism and Confucianism. (Each of these two religions follows its concept of the Way.) However, for people who can't read Chinese, this symbol doesn't hold a lot of meaning, so it is not widely used as a symbol of either Daoism or Confucianism.

Figure 7.1 Dao

The most common symbol of Chinese religion is the **yin-yang**, also called the **Taiji** or "Great Ultimate." It is used often by Daoists and sometimes by Confucianists to represent their faiths, but it is also found to such an extent

Figure 7.2 Yin-yang

outside these two formal religions that it has become one of the most often-seen symbols in the world. The circle formed by the yin and yang represents the universe, both matter and spirit, that encircles all things and holds them together. The light and dark areas inside it represent the balance of the two opposite powers in the universe. If the line between them were straight, it would suggest motionless stability between the two areas of the circle. In fact, the line is deeply curved to show that they move and that their motion and change are constants in the cosmos. When they move with each other, not against each other, life is peaceful and productive. When there is conflict between them, confusion and disharmony result. The ideal harmony between these two is suggested in many depictions of the symbol by a small circle of light in the dark area, and vice versa. The task of life is to live according to this balance in the symbol.

What do the two parts of the yin-yang symbolize?

- Yin represents what is feminine, soft, yielding, underneath, nurturing, cool, calm, passive, and dark.
- Yang represents what is masculine, hard, powerful, above, guiding, warm, energetic, active, and bright.

Although a purely gender-oriented understanding of yin-yang is possible—that all aspects of yang are masculine and yin feminine—this isn't necessary, nor was it the only view in Chinese history. Another view has the yin primarily representing aspects of the night and yang aspects of the day, which may arise from its likely original meaning of the sunny side of a hill (yang) and shadowed side (yin). Almost all interpretations of the yin-yang do hold that it is hierarchical, agreeing with the general Chinese cultural preference for hierarchy: The yang side and its aspects are superior to yin. One meaning it *doesn't* have is a moral dualism—it should not be understood in terms of good and evil. In the traditional Chinese view shared by both Daoism and Confucianism, life is good. Only when the balance of natural and supernatural forces symbolized by the Taiji goes into decline does evil result.

yin-yang [yihn yahng] Cosmic forces such as passivity and activity, darkness and light, and other opposing pairs

Taiji [TIGH-jee] The "Great Ultimate," another name for the yin-yang symbol

missionaries in China. They bypassed the common Chinese term for this tradition, "the Scholarly Tradition," a name that stresses the role of official scholars in Confucianism. The missionaries added *ism* to the Latinized form of founder Kong Fuzi, *Confucius* (kon-FYOO-shuhs), to make *Confucianism*. Some scholars, Lionel Jensen among them, have argued that Kong Fuzi and Confucius as formal names are Western inventions and that we should keep to what Chinese tradition calls him, *Kongzi* (KONG-zhee) or *Fuzi*.[4]

European scholars of religion in the 1800s widely spread the new name *Confucianism*. Although Confucius would probably have objected to naming his movement after himself, it has now "stuck" in usage. Moreover, the name *Confucianism* is accurate enough. Both Confucian and non-Confucian scholars of religion use it. More importantly, many people who follow the religion use this name. So, as in most scholarship, we will use it here.

---

[4] Lionel Jensen, *Manufacturing Confucianism: Chinese Traditions and Universal Civilization* (Durham: Duke University Press, 1998).

Learning Outcome 7-2

Outline how Daoism and Confucianism developed over time into what they are today, especially in relationship to each other.

7-2 Daoism and Confucianism Today as Shaped by Their Past

In China, the annual celebration of Confucius' birthday has become one of the biggest holidays in the relatively short history of the Communist People's Republic of China. The festivities are televised nationwide, and thousands of socially prominent people, including many high-ranking Communist Party members, make their way to Confucius' birthplace in Shandong Province. The leaders of the party are seeking to use Confucian values to counteract social problems such as rising social unrest, lack of traditional respect for aging parents, and the growing "money first" mentality. Ironically, these were some of the same problems that prompted Confucius to begin his social and religious reforms more than 2,500 years ago. The government of China has also begun to promote the Daoist religion by reopening and even renovating temples and monasteries.

In this section we'll briefly trace the history of Daoism and Confucianism together, from their earliest times until today. They competed with each other on an official level, especially when emperors favored one and tried to put down the other; more often they cooperated on a popular level. These two religions went with and against each other for more than two thousand years—almost like the yin and yang—and Chinese culture was deeply affected by this fluctuation. Before we discuss the founding of the two religions, we should look at their common background in Chinese culture.

> *Chinese civilization is so old that the foundations of Confucianism and Daoism are as close to our time as they are to the beginnings of China.*

7-2a China before the Birth of Confucianism and Daoism (ca. 3000–500 B.C.E.)

Daoism and Confucianism arose in a civilization that was already ancient. In fact, Chinese civilization is so old that the foundations of Confucianism and Daoism are just as close in time to us today as they are to the beginnings of civilization in China. Civilization probably began there before 3000 B.C.E., with scattered settlements along the Yellow River basin in northeast China, the "cradle of Chinese civilization." This society seems to have been highly militarized, probably because of the necessity to defend its open northern borders. Religion at this time included the worship of many gods, poetry inscribed on pottery, use of animal bones and shells in divination, and use of clay phallic statues in rituals for the fertility of crops, animals, and perhaps humans. Some of these surviving artifacts testify to religious beliefs and practices that would endure in both Confucianism and Daoism.

The earliest period in Chinese history for which there is good evidence is the Shang (shahng) dynasty period, from about 1500 to 1122 B.C.E. This society was also based in the Yellow River valley and, like other early human civilizations, centered on raising crops and animals. Powerful landowning aristocrats controlled Shang society, enjoying luxurious homes and outfitting lavish tombs for their happiness in the next life. Almost everyone else in Shang society was a peasant or a slave; there were relatively few artisans. A system of writing using pictograms or ideograms as characters was developed at this time, the forerunner of the system that exists in China today. The demands of memorizing thousands of characters and acquiring the skills to draw them well limited literacy to the upper classes and professional scribes. This would help to shape the literary aspects of Chinese religions, especially

A golden burial mask from the Shang dynasty

© ISTOCKPHOTO.COM/GERMAN

Oracle bone on tortoise shell from the Shang dynasty

MUDONG/DREAMSTIME

The rulers of the Shang dynasty led the worship of the gods, as emperors of China would continue to do. The Shang practiced human sacrifice, usually of slaves, in some of their rituals. This practice was discontinued in later periods; terracotta figures took the place of slaves in burials of kings and nobles. The final contribution of the Shang period was the writing of religious books that would become scriptures—or as the Chinese call them, **jing**, or "classics." A collection of traditional poems began to take shape; it would greatly influence later Chinese culture and religion when it became known as the *Book of Poetry*. Another classic book to influence Chinese culture and religion was the **Yi Jing** (Wade-Giles, *I Ching*), the *Classic of Changes*, a collection of sixty-four mystical symbols and their descriptions used to foretell the future. The main theme of this book is that the main forces of life are in a state of constant flux, an idea symbolized in the yin-yang. To be able to predict how flux will affect one's life is the kind of religious knowledge that this book offers its users. Flux is not a negative thing, but it makes life "run." The *Yi Jing* testifies clearly to a deep Chinese cultural and religious attitude that shaped Daoism and Confucianism. The universe and the natural world in which humans live are good; human life is (or can be) basically good as well, but needs guidance and correction in order for it to reach its full potential in the Way.

their scriptures. Animal **oracle bones** inscribed with this writing were used to foretell the future and maintain good connections with ancestral *spirits* and nature spirits. Other methods of divination later took the place of oracle bones, but divination, especially fortune-telling, is still popular in Chinese religion today.

Visit a website on Chinese history sponsored by the University of Maryland.

Another practice that began during the Shang dynasty has grown widely in China and is popular in the Western world today—**feng shui**, or the positioning of objects to maximize the good effects of the flow of energy. Feng shui was used at first in selecting the location of graves. When the dead are buried according to feng shui principles, the flow of energy in the earth brings yin power to their bones. This strengthens the spirits of the dead, and then blessing comes to their living families. Feng shui practices spread to altars and buildings, for the strengthening of the living. Especially in the Western world, feng shui has now been applied to furniture and decorative items. As often happens when an ancient practice is popularized commercially in the modern world, its original meaning has been altered.

Watch an explanation of feng shui today.

Great Wall of China, built on China's northern borders beginning around 200 B.C.E. to keep out nomadic invaders. That it can be seen with the naked eye from the moon is a popular but mistaken notion.

© LUKAS HLAVAC/SHUTTERSTOCK.COM

Terracotta army in the 210 B.C.E. tomb of Emperor Qin Shi Huang in Xian

brought. Two of these new movements were Daoism and Confucianism.

Distinctive religious beliefs arose in Zhou times, especially about **Heaven**. Heaven was not usually considered a god or set of gods, as it probably was before the Zhou, but an impersonal cosmic force working for the continuation and enrichment of life. The Zhou dynasty ended when the king of the Qin (chin; Wade-Giles, ch'in) state conquered the others and declared himself the first emperor of China, naming the whole nation after his state. The Qin was followed by the Han (hahn) dynasty, a four-hundred-year period of relatively stable rule (206 B.C.E.–220 C.E.) in which Confucianism was officially established in China.

7-2b The Origins of Daoism (ca. 500 B.C.E.–200 C.E.)

Daoism's origins have been traced to different periods: Chinese folk religions at the beginning of the first millennium B.C.E.; the composition of the *Daode Jing* around 350–250 B.C.E.; or the founding by Zhang Daoling (jahng dow-LING) of a movement around 150 C.E. from which would come the first main Daoist group, the Celestial Masters school. Some argue that Daoism as a religious identity only arose later, by way of contrast with the newly arrived religion of Buddhism, or with the first Daoist scripture canon in the fifth century C.E. Early religious Daoism was rooted in the religious ideas of Daoist thinkers, to which were added already-ancient local rituals and beliefs. This helped to integrate Daoism into the worldviews and religious life of Chinese society, but it resulted in a religion that was not as internally consistent as Confucianism or even Buddhism.

Laozi (low [rhymes with "how"] DZUH) in Wade-Giles, Lao Tzu), whose name means "Old Master," is the traditional founder of Daoism. However, many historians conclude that we have no direct, dependable evidence that he ever existed. (Some modern Daoists counter by saying that Laozi deliberately remained a shadowy figure so that others would later wonder about him.) Laozi is said to be an older contemporary of Confucius and, like Confucius, a disappointed

The Zhou (joh) dynasty that came next was the longest in Chinese history, from 1122 to 221 B.C.E. The king's duty was to lead the worship of the gods in order to insure a good harvest, and his power and even right to rule often depended on how those prayers were answered. The end of the Zhou dynasty is also known as the Warring States Period (481–221 B.C.E.), when the seven states of ancient China renounced their allegiance to the Zhou emperors and battled among themselves for supremacy (see Map 7.1). This prolonged period of war and social turbulence was not all destructive. By its end, China was the most populous society in the world, with between 20 and 40 million people. Many peasants had moved south to better farmland in the Yangzi (YAHNG-tsee) River area, and the merchant class grew in size and influence. This period was also a fertile time for Chinese thought and belief, producing a number of new movements seeking to restore order to a society deeply torn by continued wars and the social troubles they

Heaven Impersonal cosmic force working for the continuation and enrichment of life

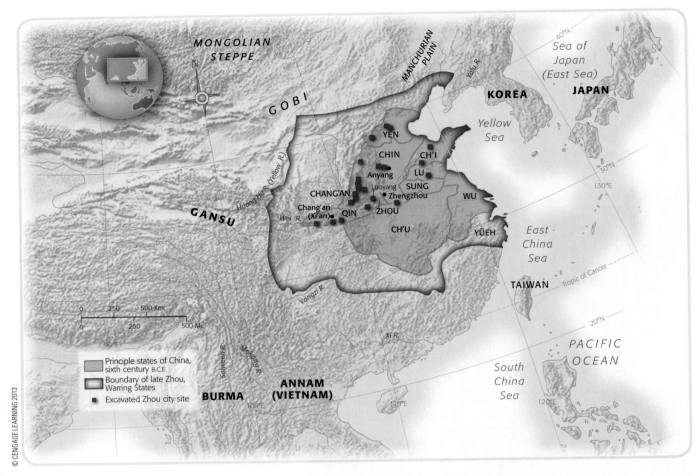

Map 7.1
China in the Sixth Century B.C.E.
During the late Zhou era, China was divided into competing, often warring states ruled only loosely by the Zhou kings. Some, such as Chiu and Wu, were large. In the third century B.C.E., the westernmost state of Qin conquered the others and formed a unified empire.

Laozi riding an ox, in a traditional portrait

government official who became a wandering teacher. He is also said to be the author of the *Daode Jing* and the *Zhuangzi* (in Wade-Giles, *Chuang-Tzu*), but no good literary or historical evidence supports this. It's more likely that these books were written anonymously between 300 and 200 B.C.E., and later came to be associated with Laozi.

However and whenever it originated, Daoism was widely recognized as a religious system by 300 B.C.E. (See "A Closer Look: Religions or Philosophies?") The publication of the *Daode Jing*, and other Daoist works following it, provided a focus for Daoist thinking. Daoism became a semiofficial Chinese religion during the Tang dynasty and continued during the Song dynasty. As Confucianism gained in strength, Daoism gradually returned to its roots as a popular religious tradition.

A Closer Look:

Religions or Philosophies?

At this point, a common question in the study of Chinese religions should be asked: Are Confucianism and Daoism philosophies or religions? For Confucianism, the debate is livelier, because Confucius himself—and most of his followers for the past two thousand years—had much more to say about the "natural" world than the "supernatural," and his religion seems to Westerners to center on social ethics. The current Chinese government does not list Confucianism among its five officially permitted religions, even though it is reviving Confucian moral values, temples, and rituals. For Daoism, the question appears in the distinction scholars often make between "religious Daoism" and "philosophical Daoism." Beginning students of world religions often encounter this issue, but it's not just a debate for beginners. For example, the eminent scholar Wing-tsit Chan (1901–1994) argued that Daoist religion is a "degeneration" of Daoist philosophy and that Daoist philosophy and Daoist religion are entirely different things.

Many religion scholars—even some of those who hold Chan's ideas—realize that our interest in trying to separate philosophy and religion shows a Western mindset, where philosophy and religion are separate academic disciplines. The Western inclination to separate these subject areas dates to the classical Greek period of philosophy and has been reinforced in early-modern and modern times. An artificial partition is often imposed between Chinese religion and philosophy, but Daoists themselves have been uninterested in such distinctions, today even finding them unhelpful. Also, it doesn't fit China. There, the closeness of what we call "philosophy" and "religion" is suggested by the commonly used words for them, *jia* and *jiao*, respectively.

A closer study of Confucianism and Daoism shows clearly that they are religions as commonly defined in academic study, although with strong strands of what we call "philosophy." Even "philosophical Daoism" has had distinctly religious aspects throughout its history. Philosophical Daoists have sought to increase their span of life, sometimes to the point of gaining immorality; they have interaction in various ways with supernatural forces and beings; and they order life morally according to the cosmic Dao. They practice meditation in conjunction with physical exercises, study nature for diet and health, and form monastic orders. These are all "religious" aspects of life, as Western academics define *religion*. Confucianists believe that human fulfillment comes from proper engagement in this-worldly affairs, but they also deal with matters of ultimate concern. Confucianists, as did Confucius, make room for the gods and other supernatural things but do not make them the center of their religion. As a result, Confucianism is a "humanistic" religion, but it *is* a religion as scholars generally define it.

To return to our main question, Are Daoism and Confucianism philosophies or religions? If we must answer, perhaps the best answer is that they are *both*. Of course, this book focuses on their religious aspects.

7-2c Daoism from 200 C.E. to 1664 C.E

Daoism was a broad-based movement. In its religious aspects, it developed many different monastic orders, each with its own monasteries. Because Daoists looked to nature to show the way humans should live, they built a number of monasteries on mountain peaks and in the countryside. But they could also build monasteries near cities, the White Cloud Monastery in Beijing being the most famous of these. Each monastic order tended to write its own religious literature, eventually giving rise to thousands of books in the Daoist canon, the **Daozang**. (See "A Closer Look: The Four Editions of the Daoist Canon (*Daozang*).")

Another product of the monasteries was martial arts. This was at first a meditational technique coupled with exercise, but it developed into a sophisticated form of fighting, usually hand to

Two martial arts masters

© ISTOCKPHOTO.COM/C-VINO

Daozang [DOW-zhahng] Daoist canon

A Closer Look:

The Four Editions of the Daoist Canon (*Daozang*)

A main indicator of the fortunes of a Chinese religion is the state of its sacred books. The first *Daozang* was assembled around 440 C.E. This was the first time that scriptures from across China were brought together, and it signaled the rising strength of Daoism. It totaled around 1,200 scrolls. The second *Daozang* arose in 748 C.E., when the Tang emperor Xuan Zong, who claimed descent from Laozi, collected even more Daoist scrolls, and the *Daozang* grew to about 2,000. The third *Daozang* was made around 1000 C.E.; it was revised, many texts were added, and some scrolls collected earlier were removed. This third *Daozang* totaled about 4,500 scrolls. The fourth *Daozang* was made in 1444 C.E. in the Ming Dynasty, when the canon used today emerged, consisting of approximately 1,130 different titles in 5,300 scrolls.

hand but sometimes with weapons. Over time, the Daoist or Buddhist meditational aspects of martial arts were downplayed or lost completely. The martial arts sought to use an enemy's force against him. As this method spread beyond Daoism through Asia, it assumed many different forms: judo, karate, ju-jitsu, taekwondo, and others. It was not widely known in the West until after World War II, when Western armed forces that had encountered it in hand-to-hand combat with Japanese troops began teaching it regularly as a part of basic military training. (The author's father learned it at that time in the U.S. Marine Corps; because he was short and slim, he was often used to demonstrate its effectiveness against other Marines who were beginning to learn it—who thought they could "take him" easily.) Daoism developed other meditational techniques and a fuller evolution of its philosophical teachings. Hundreds of commentaries were written on basic Daoist scriptures such as the *Daode Jing* and *Zhuangzi*. Daoism's popular religious aspects served to integrate thousands of local gods and cults into a Daoist pantheon.

 View a report on the White Cloud Monastery.

The return of Daoism after it was suppressed in the Han dynasty is known as **Neo-Daoism**. Wang Bi and Guo Xiang wrote commentaries on the *Daode Jing* and the *Zhuangzi*, and they became important figures in this movement. The "Seven Sages of the Bamboo Grove" forged a new Daoist way of life that influenced wider culture, not just that of mountain monasteries. This broader cultural influence of Neo-Daoism was felt in calligraphy, painting,

Neo-Daoism Rebirth and reform of Daoism after the Han dynasty, with strong cultural influence on calligraphy, painting, music, and poetry

Practicing calligraphy with a brush pen

music, and poetry. Daoist ideas on landscape painting contributed to a style that would last until modern times—the placement of human activities against a very large, imposing natural setting. The most well-known Daoist philosopher of this period was Ge Hong

(283–343 C.E.). He pursued not only philosophical reflection, but alchemy as well, in the search for longevity (long life) and immortality. His main book, the *Inner Chapters of the Master Embracing Simplicity*, or *Baopuzi* (BOW-poo-tsee) for short, became an influential Daoist scripture whose authority continues today. It has been the leading scripture for those seeking longevity by meditation, alchemy, and traditional Chinese medicines.

Read a short extract on longevity from the *Baopuzi*.

Take a brief tour of the Man Mo Daoist temple in Hong Kong.

Watch an explanation of calligraphy.

7-2d The Near-Destruction of Daoism (1644–1980)

The Manchurians, who became rulers of China in 1644, were in the Confucian camp, and they trimmed the political and cultural power of Daoism. They removed the politically powerful Daoist head of Dragon Tiger Mountain Monastery from his position at the imperial court. Later events would prove even more detrimental to Daoism. In the 1780s, Christian missionaries arrived in China and converted large numbers of Daoists. In 1849, the Hakka people of southern China—one of China's poorest ethnic groups—followed Hong Xiuquan (hoong shee-OH-chwahn), who claimed to be Jesus Christ's younger brother, in open rebellion against the emperor. Hong's movement was built on a combination of Daoism and Christianity, and sought to establish the "Heavenly Kingdom of Peace" (*taiping*). As the so-called Taiping Rebellion conquered southeast China, its faithful systematically destroyed Buddhist and Daoist temples and scriptures until it was finally crushed by the emperor's troops.

In the 1900s, pressure against Daoism increased. In the 1920s, the reformist "New Life" movement induced students to destroy Daoist sites and scriptures. By 1926, only two copies of the Daoist canon *Daozang* were left, and the Daoist heritage was in great jeopardy. But the copy of the canon kept at the White Cloud Monastery was eventually copied, and thus this important work was saved for posterity. There are 1,120 books in the collection, in a total of 5,305 volumes. Scholars have yet to study much of it.

Recent times have seen an even stronger pendulum swing in the fortunes of Daoism. After the Communist takeover of China in 1949, Daoism was banned and its leaders "reeducated" and forced into other occupations. All but a few temples and monasteries were closed. The number of practicing Daoists fell drastically, probably 90 percent in ten years. At this time Daoism began to flourish in the greater freedom of Taiwan and also Hong Kong, a British colony then separate from China. During the "Great Proletarian Cultural Revolution" (1966–1976) instigated by the Chinese leader Mao Zedong (mow [rhymes with "how"] zuh-DOONG), strong attacks were made on the remaining vestiges of religion. Fengyang Yang writes in his recent book, *Religion in China: Survival and Revival under Communist Rule,* that the Cultural Revolution brought the most radical suppression of religion in history.[5] Daoist monks were killed or sent to labor camps. Before 1900 there were three hundred Daoist sites in Beijing alone; in the Cultural Revolution, they were all shuttered or destroyed, and Daoism, along with all other religions in China, went underground. After the Cultural Revolution, the Chinese government began to allow a small measure of religious freedom again. Daoism began to revive in China; some temples and some monasteries were gradually reopened. Today, observant Daoists can be found throughout the country, and what only thirty years ago was called a dying religion is now growing again.

Read a *New York Times Magazine* article on the current revival of Daoism.

7-2e Confucius and the Origins of Confucianism (551–479 B.C.E.)

We now return to the sixth century B.C.E., to discuss the origins of Confucianism. The details of Confucius's life are sketchy, but we know its main outline. Confucius was born in or around 551 B.C.E. in Qufu (CHOO-foo), the capital of the small state of Lu. His real name was Kong Qiu (kong choh), but his students called him Kong Fuzi (kong foo-ZEE), "Master Kong." His ancestors may have been aristocrats but perhaps brought low during a period of social instability. This would explain how someone of a relatively low social class had such a feeling for high culture from an early age. His father, who never married Confucius's

See a slide show of images of Confucius.

See a World Heritage Tour video of the Qufu Temple.

---

[5] Fengyang Yang, *Religion in China: Survival and Revival under Communist Rule* (New York: Oxford University Press, 2012).

mother, died when Confucius was very young, so he was taught by his mother. Confucius distinguished himself as a passionate learner in his teens. He gained a mastery of the six traditional basic arts of the time: ritual, music, archery, charioteering, calligraphy, and arithmetic. He also developed a strong attachment to Chinese history and traditional poetry that would be reflected in Confucianism and then deeply affect Chinese culture.

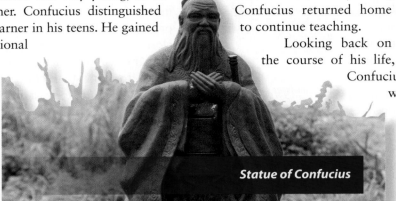

Statue of Confucius

JACK HOLLINGSWORTH/JUPITER IMAGES

> Confucius was a reformer, not a revolutionary.

As a young adult, Confucius began serving in minor posts in the government's ministry of agriculture, managing stables and granaries. He married a woman of similar social standing when he was nineteen and had children. He started his teaching career in his thirties. Confucius developed concepts about society and government that he hoped to put into practice in a political career. His loyalty to the king provoked opposition from the powerful landowning families, and his teaching that a ruler must set a moral example for his people did not sit well with the king's advisors, who were influencing the ruler by procuring sensuous pleasures for him. At the age of fifty-six, when he realized that his superiors in Lu had no interest in him, Confucius left to find another ruler who might listen to his ideas and make him an official. He gathered a growing number of students during the next twelve years, perhaps as many as three thousand. His reputation as a man of vision spread, and he was an occasional advisor to rulers. However, he was never able to get his teachings adopted in any Chinese state, or even find a steady position as a royal advisor. Confucius's own times were not right for implementing his ideas.

Mandate of Heaven
Right to rule as king or emperor, given by Heaven by means of order and prosperity in the land

When he was sixty-seven, Confucius returned home to continue teaching.

Looking back on the course of his life, Confucius summarized it this way: "At the age of fifteen, I set my heart on learning; at thirty, I firmly took my stand [for what was right]; at forty, I had no delusions [about life]; at fifty, I knew the **Mandate of Heaven**; at sixty, my ear was attuned [an obscure phrase of uncertain meaning]; at seventy, I followed my heart's desire without doing wrong" (*Analects* 2:4). Despite this remarkably positive view of himself, Confucius could be a humble man. He admitted that he had not become the kind of person that he taught others to be, and at the end of his life he thought that all his teachings would perish with him. He died in 479 B.C.E. at the age of seventy-three. The fame that he brought his family is illustrated by the more than 100,000 of his descendants buried in the same cemetery as he was, making it the largest family cemetery in the world and the oldest still in operation.

The story of Confucianism does not really begin with Confucius, nor was Confucius the founder of Confucianism in the way that others have been the

Watch a preview of the 2010 film *Confucius*.

Read more about the character of Confucius in the *Analects*.

Take a video tour of Confucius's home and temple in Qufu.

The Apricot Platform, where Confucius taught disciples at his home in Qufu

© STRINGER SHANGHAI/REUTERS//CORBIS

University students in Seoul, South Korea, perform during an annual ritual to honor Confucius and Confucian sages.

in China until Dong Zhongshu (dawng ZHAWNG-shoo) effectively promoted them in the second century B.C.E. Confucianism was recognized as the official state religion in the Han dynasty (206 B.C.E.–220 C.E.). New religious elements, including sacrifices to Confucius, were introduced. More importantly, the four main Confucian books (see "A Closer Look: The Confucian *Four Books*") were canonized and became the core of education and culture in China.

Despite the strong influence of Daoism and Buddhism, Confucian ethics have had the strongest influence on the moral fabric of China. A revival of Confucian thought in the Song dynasty of the twelfth century produced **Neo-Confucianism**, which incorporated many Daoist and Buddhist ideas, forging a sort of compromise that enabled Confucianism to continue its role as the leading influence on Chinese culture. The philosopher Zhu Xi (JOO shee, 1130–1200) believed that the ideas of Confucius had been misrepresented over the centuries. He advocated what he called a return to Confucius's original teachings, which Zhu saw as moral self-improvement largely directed by reason. Despite this emphasis on a return to Confucius, he was influenced by both Daoism and Buddhism, leading to a new and closer balance between their systems. Xi wrote commentaries on the classics that became "required reading" for the civil service exams. This exam system, which had been established in the 200s B.C.E., then grew in importance, and until 1905 it was the only way to get an official appointment in the vast imperial government. It was also the leading way for men of the lower classes to rise in rank. In time, Neo-Confucianism replaced traditional Confucianism in the higher levels of Chinese society, especially in the universities and the government.

In 1530 C.E, a Ming emperor reformed the Confucian cult to focus more on Confucius's teachings than on the sage himself. For example, images of Confucius in Confucian temples were replaced with

founders of religions. Rather, Confucius was a transmitter of the best of the past, a reformer rather than a revolutionary. He retrieved the meaning of the past by breathing new life into it. Confucius's love of antiquity drove him to ask why certain rituals such as funeral ceremonies and reverence for Heaven had survived for centuries. He had faith in the power of culture to stabilize human life. Confucius's sense of history was so strong that he saw himself as a conservationist responsible for the continuity of the cultural values and social norms that had worked so well for the civilization of China, especially in the earlier years of the Zhou dynasty. In his system of teaching, he successfully formed a coherent system of thought and life that would shape the future of China and several other lands.

7-2f The Rise of Confucianism and Neo-Confucianism (ca. 350 B.C.E.–1200 C.E.)

Others kept Confucianism alive until it finally was recognized as a state religion. Mengzi (MUHNG-dzuh), who lived from about 372 to 289 B.C.E., is traditionally known in the West as Mencius (MEN-see-us) and, like Confucius, was a wandering advisor to rulers. His main work, the *Book of Mencius* (or *Mencius* for short), shows his positive view of the basic goodness of human nature. Heaven (*tian*) is found in the human heart; the ruler need only set a good example for his people and they will follow it. Historians generally hold that Mencius is second only to Confucius in influence on Confucianism. Confucius's beliefs were not significant

Neo-Confucianism
Revival of Confucian thought in the twelfth century, incorporating Daoist and Buddhist ideas

A Closer Look:

The Confucian *Four Books*

The *Four Books* of the Confucian canon are built on what Confucius and his followers saw as the main teachings of the earlier Chinese *Five Classics*. The *Analects* (*Lun yu*) of Confucius is by far the most important text in the history of Confucianism, and it gives us insight into Confucius himself. It contains sayings of Confucius, whom it calls "the Master," and occasional stories about him as remembered by his disciples and recorded after his death. The *Analects* has 12,700 characters (ideograms) in twenty short books. Like other collections of wise sayings, the *Analects* is loosely organized. It treats, and repeatedly returns to, all the important concepts of the Confucian tradition: the virtues of humanity, propriety, and respect for parents; becoming a superior man; and proper government. Some people think that the proverbs in this book are no more helpful than proverbs that occasionally appear in fortune cookies, but they should not be atomized. In the context of the whole *Analects*, and in the living tradition of Confucianism, they are both profound and powerful.

The second of the *Four Books* is the *Mencius* (*Mengzi*), named for its author. Mencius (ca. 371–289 B.C.E.) was the most significant figure in Confucian tradition after Confucius. His disciples compiled the book of Mencius's teachings after his death. More than twice as long as the *Analects*, the *Mencius* has well-developed treatments of several important topics, especially proper government. Mencius saw filiality as the greatest of the virtues and held strongly to the teaching of innate human goodness.

Third is the *Great Learning* (*Ta xuei*), a short book that is an excerpt on virtuous government from the *Li Jing*. Its first, short chapter is held to be the work of Confucius. The next ten chapters are a commentary on the first by one of Confucius's disciples. The *Great Learning* teaches that rulers govern by example. If the ruler is morally good, so will be his government and his subjects. If the ruler is not good, his subjects will incline to evil, and his rule, along with the Mandate of Heaven to govern, will collapse.

Fourth is the *Doctrine of the Mean* (*Chung yung*). Like the *Great Learning*, it was originally a chapter in the *Li Jing*. *Mean* here is better translated today as "moderation" because of the negative connotations of *mean*. "The mean" is a broad concept, embracing many aspects of virtue: moderation, right conduct, decorum, and sincerity. The good Confucianist is expected to "keep to the middle" between emotional and intellectual extremes. The superior person is formed in the middle and comes into harmony with the Dao, the cosmic "Way" of life. This book was important in the Neo-Confucian movement that arose in the twelfth century. Harvard Confucian scholar Tu Wei-Ming has argued that the *Doctrine of the Mean* is the most explicitly "religious" of the *Four Books*.

---

tablets inscribed with his name and honorific titles. The ritual, worshipful veneration of Confucius declined after the founding of the Chinese Republic in 1912, but the social influence of Confucianism has continued. Neo-Confucianism was a major influence in Korea from 1392 to 1910, and it remains an important foundation of culture in South Korea. Some Confucian scholars blamed Daoism for the fall of the Ming dynasty and the subsequent establishment of the Qing dynasty (1644–1912) by the foreign Manchus. The Manchus then led a movement called "National Studies" that urged a return to traditional Confucianism. The Confucian classics came back into imperial favor, and Daoism was almost completely suppressed. For example, during the 1700s an imperial library was established, but excluded virtually all Daoist books. By the 1920s, as we saw above, Daoism had fallen from favor, so much so that only two copies of the *Daozang* still remained.

7-2g The Modern Period of Daoism and Confucianism (1912–Present)

In 1911 to 1912, the Chinese Revolution ended the three-thousand-year-old imperial system and put a republic in its place. The Nationalist Party leaders who struggled to rule China from 1912 to 1949 embraced science, modernity, and Western culture, including aspects of Christianity. They tended to view traditional Chinese religions as reactionary and parasitic. Many progressive Chinese intellectuals also rejected much of the three Chinese religions. The Nationalists confiscated some temples and monasteries for public buildings and, like the emperors of China before them, controlled traditional religious activity.

©ISTOCKPHOTO.COM/GIRGIO FOCHESATO

A portrait of Mao still hangs at the Gate of Heavenly Peace in Beijing. The sign reads "Long live the People's Republic of China."

The Communist Party of China led by Mao Zedong took power in 1949. As a Communist regime, it is officially atheistic, and initially suppressed Daoism and Confucianism with even more zeal than the Nationalist Party had. ("Religion is poison," states an old Communist propaganda slogan that Mao repeated to the Dalai Lama.) Despite this suppression, most religions were still able to operate, but at a severely reduced level. Persecution of religion, along with the Cultural Revolution as a whole, stopped when Mao died in 1976, and soon many Daoists and Confucianists began reviving their traditions. Since then, some of the more scenic temples and monasteries have been repaired and reopened.

The government of China now permits Daoism and Buddhism (along with Islam, Roman Catholic Christianity, and Protestant Christianity) and supervises their activities. The government considers some other religions, such as Falun Gong (which we'll discuss in Chapter 13), to be dangerous to public order, and has fiercely cracked down on them. Sensitive areas with Chinese religions include the government's relationship to the influential Zhengyi Daoist group and their leader—who lives in Taiwan, as does the current leader of the extensive descendants of Confucius. The government occasionally suppresses various traditional temple activities such as astrology and shamanism, which it calls "superstitions." It also censors films that depict popular Daoist ideas such as child vampires, ghosts, and martial-arts cults with supernatural abilities. But it has become more accommodating to religious beliefs and practices, no longer automatically seeing them as dangerous to Communist rule or the good of the people. Daoist temples and monasteries are operating more freely, and local gods have come out of hiding.

Two recent events in Confucianism point to more Chinese openness to it. First, the education ministry is setting up programs of religious study in several selective Chinese universities, at the undergraduate and graduate levels. Students will soon be able to major in Christian, Islamic, or Chinese religion. Second, the government has taken to promoting traditional Confucian values in primary and secondary schools, where students now read the *Analects* and other Confucian texts. Statues of Confucius are now seen in public places, especially in front of schools. This is being done to fill a spiritual vacuum in Chinese society. The values of communism are waning as China moves to a modified form of a free-enterprise system; social friction, crime, and corruption have arisen that China's rulers see as inimical to China's well-being.

> **Watch a BBC report on the revival of Confucianism in China.**

PHOTO COURTESY OF THE U.S. ARMY/TIM HIPPS

Performers portraying disciples of Confucius recite passages from the Analects at the opening ceremonies of the 2008 Olympics in Beijing, China.

DAOISM AND CONFUCIANISM TODAY AS SHAPED BY THEIR PAST **171**

Explain the essential teachings of Daoism and Confucianism, especially their similarities and differences.

7-3 Essential Daoist and Confucian Teachings

At the giant Expo 2010 in Shanghai, China, people form lines to enter the dozens of new pavilions showcasing the theme of the Expo—how the Chinese past is shaping its desired future. Although the lines are long and a bit slow, people wait in a patient, orderly way. As an American couple just arriving at the Expo gets in the back of a line, a security agent asks to see identification. With foreboding, they produce their drivers' licenses. To their surprise, they are shown to the front of the line and let into the exhibit immediately, because anyone who is at least seventy-five years of age doesn't have to wait in line. The woman remarks to her husband that this policy is even better than a "senior citizen" discount, because it means that they can see much more of the Expo than they could otherwise. This preferential treatment is based on the Chinese respect for advanced age, a leading aspect of ethics in both Confucianism and Daoism. Such practices are not monoliths and can change over time, but Daoism, with its emphasis on attaining old age, and Confucianism, with its emphasis on respect for one's parents, have contributed to a cultural heritage of honoring the elderly.

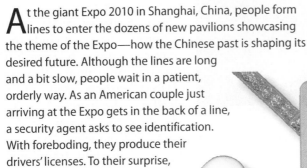

Ancestor tablets with names of the dead are thought to be the dwelling places of the ancestors when they visit earth.

In this section we'll consider first the religious teachings that predate both Confucianism and Daoism and are important for each; then we'll examine the main Daoist and Confucian teachings that build on them.

Dao [dow] Cosmic "Way" of life

de [duh] "Power" or "working" that enables a person to follow the Dao

qi [chee] Cosmic energy that enables beings to live and links them to the universe

7-3a Ancient Teachings Common to Daoism and Confucianism

Many of the key teachings of both Daoism and Confucianism did not originate with them around 500 B.C.E. Rather, they go back hundreds, sometimes thousands, of years in China before these religions were recognized as separate movements. Most of the gods worshiped by Daoists and by Confucianists also predate these religions. We have already considered ancient religious ideas such as yin-yang, teachings of texts such as the important *Yi Jing*, and the religious ideas behind rituals such as feng shui and divination. The other ancient teachings common to both Confucianism and Daoism are as follows:

- **Dao** is the cosmic "Way" of life, the Way of nature that became a Way for people to walk in. This Way brings value to human culture, it shapes better relationships, and it advances health and long life. Both Daoism and Confucianism speak about the Dao, but in different ways and to different degrees. But they share a positive view of the world and Dao within it: The world is a good place, and humans must find the fullness of life within the Dao that guides the world.

- The "One" is the essence of the Dao, the energy of life. Living in this One enables things and human beings to be truly themselves. The One is often seen as operating in dualistic form, as in the yin-yang: The circle that contains the yin and yang is the One.

> *"The Dao that can be spoken is not the eternal Dao; the name that can be named is not the eternal name."* —Daode Jing

- **De** is typically translated "virtue," but this implies later Confucian teaching about morality and can be confusing. Another way of looking at de is "power" or "working" that enables a person to follow the Dao. The scripture text *Daode Jing* suggests the relationship of de to the Dao, and not just for Daoists: "The Book of the Way (Dao) and its Power/Working (De)." The Dao is not a static thing with only being; it has a working power by which it reaches out to shape every living thing.

- **Qi** is the cosmic energy that enables beings to live and links them to the universe as a whole, and it is also the basic material of all that exists. Qi gives life to the human body; its quality and movement determine human health.

> *In the Abrahamic monotheisms, Heaven is often synonymous with God, but in China it means a cosmic order and principle.*

- **Tian** (Wade-Giles, *T'ien*) is "Heaven," an impersonal cosmic force that guides events on earth and a cosmic principle that distinguishes right from wrong. In earliest times Tian was a personal god, probably the highest deity among many, but in the Zhou dynasty it became an impersonal force guided by its own principle of what is right. In the Abrahamic monotheisms (Judaism, Christianity, and Islam), *Heaven* is closely tied to God; even for nonreligious people in the Western world today, it suggests a Being who lives there. In China, *Tian* does not suggest a god, but rather an order and principle that both transcends the world and is deeply embedded in it.

- *Ancestor veneration* or *worship* became a common practice in ancient China. Each family was expected to remember the names of its male ancestors and pay regular homage to them. Over time, their names were written on small rectangular tablets. This veneration made ancestors in the world of spirits happy, and they would bless—not haunt—their living descendants.

These ancient religious teachings and the ritual practices associated with them were established by about 750 B.C.E. They would endure throughout Chinese history, and all Chinese religions to come had to incorporate them in some way. Even foreign religions such as Buddhism, Christianity, and Islam had to make adjustments to this religiously shaped Chinese worldview in order to grow in China. Because Daoism and Confucianism drink deeply at this common well of ancient Chinese thought and practice, they share similar ideas that make it easy for Chinese people to combine them in daily life.

Despite all the differences between these two religions at a high, official level—and despite the conflicts with each other that they have had in the past—Daoism and Confucianism can "fit" together for most Chinese.

Tian [tee-AHN] "Heaven," impersonal cosmic force that guides events on earth and distinguishes right from wrong

7-3b Daoist Teachings on the Dao

How do Daoists understand the Dao? The first thing that Daoists say is that it cannot be described exactly in words. Human language can only sketch an outline of the Dao, not give a full picture. The important thing to be said about the Dao is that it works to empower, structure, and guide the world; a close second in importance is how human beings choose to relate to it. So the Dao is, broadly speaking, the way of the universe and the way of human life that ideally ties into it. The Dao is not a thing, a substance, or a being. The Dao is not a god or even a spirit, and Daoists do not worship it. Daoism does have many deities, but they are as dependent on the Dao as everything else in the universe. Paradoxically, the Dao gives rise to all being, but it does not have a being of its own. It is not an object of human thought or activity, but it is the hidden subject of all things. It cannot be perceived in itself, but it can be observed in the workings of the natural world.

The Dao is a Way of cosmic reality and human fulfillment. All animals and plants in the world live fully and naturally in the Dao. To some extent humans also live naturally in the Dao, but in certain aspects humans have become distant from it. To live fully in the Dao takes knowledge and intention. Despite the Dao's deep connection to the world of nature, living in the Dao isn't "naturally" easy. Moreover, living in the Dao isn't a

Daoist deities arrayed in a heavenly court in the Dongyue Temple in Beijing

© CLAUDIO ZACCHERINI/SHUTTERSTOCK.COM

ESSENTIAL DAOIST AND CONFUCIAN TEACHINGS **173**

matter of "achieving union with the Dao," as some people might put it, but rather being in complete conformity with the Dao. The Dao includes several concepts in its one word: the source, the ultimate, the inexpressible and indefinable, the unnamable. It is the natural universe as a whole, as well as the principle and power within it.

Read a *Daode Jing* passage on the Dao.

7-3c Chinese Traditional Deities

Confucianists generally recognize the main Chinese deities, and Daoists recognize them all. The relationships among the vast number of gods and goddesses in China is often said to parallel, even mimic, the government bureaucracy of imperial China. Although there may be truth to this idea, some writers argue that the reverse is true: The imperial government patterned itself after the structure of the heavenly beings. Whether this argument can ever be settled is unlikely. At any rate, it is safe to say that the imperial administration and the religious culture of the time were closely intertwined.

Westerners who know only the philosophical side of Daoism are sometimes surprised to discover that most Daoists worship gods. To Westerners, there doesn't seem to be a need for deities in Daoism. Daoism does not have a God in the way that the Abrahamic religions do, or even as Mahayana Buddhists in China have deities. In Daoism, the universe constantly springs from the Dao, and the Dao impersonally guides things on their way. But the Dao itself is not God, nor is it a god, nor is it worshiped by Daoists. The Dao is much more important than that. Moreover, deities are within this universe and are themselves subject to the Dao just as much as humans are. This may seem surprising, as Daoists occasionally use what Westerners think of as language for God—for example when the Dao is called the "Venerable Lord." Some Daoists even go so far as to occasionally revere Laozi both as the first god of Daoism and as the personification of the Dao, just as some Confucianists declared Confucius a god in the early 1900s as a last-ditch effort to prop up their place in Chinese society.

In sum, China has many gods, more than a few borrowed from other cultures. A great number of the deities are known and worshiped by their particular role rather than as personal divine beings; they have titles rather than names.

The Jade Emperor

The supreme ruler of Heaven in Chinese tradition is popularly called the Jade Emperor, or Yu Huang. (Note how the supreme god is called an "emperor.") The Jade Emperor lives in a luxurious palace in the highest Heaven, where he rules and directs all other gods. He can grant titles to the spirits of outstanding individuals and even elevate them to deities. His image, and that of the gods and goddesses under his direction, can be found in various Daoist temples. Many historians of Chinese religion conclude that *Jade Emperor* was an early Daoist title for the more ancient Chinese deity called, by various names, the "Lord of Heaven."

The Earth God

We will follow the Chinese tendency in religion to think of "Heaven and earth" together; after discussing the supreme god of Heaven, we deal now with the main god of earth. In the countryside of Chinese lands, one can see small temples and shrines, some only a foot high, that feature a picture of a smiling, bearded old man. This is the Earth God, commonly called Tudi Gong or "Land Elder," and more formally known as Fu De Zheng Shen, "Righteous God of Good Fortune and Virtue." Tudi Gong has thousands of incarnated spirit forms who look after plots of land and the people residing on them. This guardian spirit is a popular divinity in Daoism, and his image is often found on family altars.

Mazu

Mazu (MAHT-soo; Wade-Giles *Ma-tsu* is also common), or "Mother Ancestor," is the spirit of Lin Moniang. Lin was a young woman who lived on an island off the coast of China sometime during the Song dynasty (960–1279). Her legend says that she was a strong swimmer and employed her supernatural powers to cure the ill and save people on the sea from imminent danger. For this, she was deified after her death and is also known as

The Jade Emperor on his throne

the Sea Goddess. Mazu became the most highly venerated of all female deities in Daoism—especially after an emperor of China named her the "Queen of Heaven"—and she is known to Buddhists as well.

The popularity of Mazu in Taiwan is seen by the more than four hundred temples dedicated to her and also by the processions in communities all over the island, during which her statue is carried on a chair so she can spread her blessings. Tens of thousands of worshipers join in a week-long pilgrimage in her honor, and many now make a pilgrimage across the Taiwan Strait to venerate her at her grave. Mazu is widely worshiped in the provinces of China that are on the sea, and in the Chinese diaspora as well. The oldest Daoist temple in the United States, the Tin How ("Heaven's Queen") Temple—built in 1852 in the Chinatown district of San Francisco—is dedicated to Mazu.

Mazu, goddess of the sea, the most popular goddess in Daoism

of Shanghai during the First Opium War. He vowed to defend China to the death, and was killed in battle against the British.

Wang Ye

Wang Ye is a generic term denoting some 360 "Lords of Pestilence" whose lives before becoming deities are recounted in different tales. These lords are people of great merit and exemplary lives, who after death were charged by the gods with the task of protecting humans from evil spirits and epidemics. (They become "Lords of Pestilence" in the sense of *controlling* pestilence.) Rituals for worship of these protectors differ widely. A popular ritual for driving away disease, held twice every

City Gods

When we think about the gods of a religion, the first thing that comes to mind are the principal deities that everyone in a religion knows and worships, such as the three we have just discussed. However, in China there are many gods who are known and worshiped only in select locales, as are the **city gods**. The Jade Emperor has commanded them to guard particular cities against attack by enemies and protect their inhabitants from various evils. City gods were originally humans who served the people righteously during their lifetimes, had compassion for those in danger, and protected people and good spirits from being dragged into the underworld by evil ghosts. For their demonstration of classic virtues, the righteous spirits of these people were made divine at some point after their deaths.

The City God Temple in Shanghai is dedicated to three city gods, all of whom were human beings who were deified after their deaths. Huo Guang (died 68 B.C.E.) was a famous Han dynasty chancellor. He is venerated for his role in deposing one young emperor and replacing him with another, more worthy ruler. Qin Yubo (1295–1373) was a prominent citizen of Shanghai and served in the late Yuan dynasty. When the Ming dynasty was founded, he refused two commands to serve at the court. He finally relented and served in several offices, including that of chief imperial examiner. Chen Huacheng (1776–1842) was a Qing-dynasty general who led the defense

Temple of the City God, Shanghai, China

A "techno-neon" type of Daoist god dances at a 2010 festival in Taiwan.

act, even are active, but their action is carefully attuned to their perception of the Dao—therefore, easier, happier, and "natural." To use a modern analogy, North Americans typically make a distinction between *work* and *pleasure*: If an activity is pleasurable, we don't think of it as work, which is supposed to be at least a little difficult. As a result, Westerners can think of the expression "act naturally" as a nonsensical contradiction similar to "found missing" or "minor catastrophe." But in the Daoist view, when work is done naturally—if a carpenter cuts wood with the grain, not against it, for example—it as a pleasure, and we do in fact "act naturally." This is wu wei in action. Wu wei doesn't forbid action in one's life, but it does command that one's activities fit into the natural pattern of the universe. After Buddhism entered China and made an impression on Daoism, wu wei was also understood as action that is not ego driven, but rather detached from individual desires. In sum, Daoism requires individuals to live and "work" the same way as nature naturally follows the Dao.

year, is "Burning Wang Ye's Boat." A full-sized boat made of paper and wood is burned along with its spirit-money cargo. This offering is designed to make the Lords of Pestilence more inclined to do their protective work.

Like most religions with many deities, Daoism can "lose" gods, add new ones, or update the portrayal of older gods. A variety of "techno-neon" portrayals of Daoist gods are popular in Chinese lands today.

7-3d Daoist Teaching of Wu Wei

The only method of following the Dao is by **wu wei**. This term is difficult to translate and has been rendered as "nonaction," "passive action," "uncontrived action," or "natural nonintervention." *Nonaction* wrongly implies that one does nothing at all, that one is completely passive. The *Daode Jing* might be read to support this interpretation, as in its "When nothing is done, nothing is left undone" (Chapter 48). However, wu wei is best understood as going along with nature, letting things in life take their natural, Dao-determined course.

> Read a passage from the *Zhuangzi* that explains the key points of wu wei.

Daoists try to live balanced and harmonious lives that are attuned to the Dao as it is seen in nature—they "act naturally." They find their way through life in the same way as breezes blow in the air, as rain falls from the sky, or as a river flows through the countryside by finding its natural course. They

wu wei [woo way]
Literally, "not asserting"; going along with the true nature of the world

7-3e Daoist Views of Qi

Daoists understand the human body to be a miniature of the universe. Like the universe, each human body has many parts, but it is filled with the Dao. The human body, as much as the larger universe, is also inhabited and ruled by a large number of deities.

The body also has spiritual energy that is cosmic, but not a part of the gods. Daoists believe that every living person has a normal, healthy amount of qi and that personal health results from the balance, harmony, and smooth flow of qi. This flow is seen in several texts as a complex system analogous to the movement of water, with a sea of qi in the abdomen, its main location; rivers of qi flowing through the torso and through the limbs; streams of qi flowing to the wrists and ankles; and small springs of qi in the fingers and toes. Any disruption in this system can influence the whole and require readjustment. Balance and natural smoothness in the working of qi is the general goal. Daoists want to empower their qi and be empowered by it.

KYLET/DREAMSTIME

American man practices tai qi

© MICHAELJUNG/SHUTTERSTOCK.COM

7-3f The Daoist Quest for Immortality

Immortality doesn't mean escaping death by living forever in the present physical body. This is the stuff of Western and Chinese horror stories. Daoists believe that all spirits are immortal in some sense—they survive the death of the body and go into the next world. The world of spirits is connected to the world of the gods. Spiritual immortality, a special goal of some Daoists, raises to a whole new level the practice of pursuing immortality in this life. To attain spiritual immortality, one must change all one's qi into primordial qi and then refine it. This finer qi will gradually turn into pure spirit, enabling one to become a "spirit-person" already in this life. This process requires intense training in meditation and trances, radical forms of diet, and esoteric sexual practices. The result is a bypassing of the effects of death on the spirit; the end of the body has no impact on the continuation of the spirit-person. After death, the spirit lives forever in a wonderful paradise, and the person is said to be an "immortal."

7-3g Confucian Reformulations of Ancient Teachings

The Confucian reworking of ancient Chinese teachings centered on ethics—what the Western tradition calls "personal ethics" and "social ethics." Confucianism is often called a system of social ethics, and from the Western perspective that is true enough, but we should remember that this distinction between "personal" and "social" is not often made in China. It doesn't make a great deal of sense in a culture where the personal and the social are so fully blended, and where Western-style individualism is rejected. We'll consider Confucian ethics later in this chapter; here, however, we should state the Confucian "take" on ancient Chinese religious teachings and practices.

As stated above, Confucius and his followers were highly appreciative of Chinese tradition. His teaching reaffirms many aspects of Chinese religion that predated him: the role of Heaven, particularly in government; the importance of the Way (Dao); the assumption, made explicit in Confucianism, that humans are basically good and will follow the truth when they know it; and respect for the gods and traditional rituals. On respect for ritual, Confucius once defended the sacrifice

> *Tai qi is mostly known in the West as an exercise system, but this is not its significance for Daoism.*

All individuals receive a core of primordial qi at birth and need to sustain it during their lifetimes. They do so by drawing qi into the body from air and food, as well as from other people through social and sexual interactions. But they also lose qi by breathing bad air, eating and drinking too much, having negative emotions, and engaging in excessive sexual or social interactions. Traditional Chinese medicines drawn from nature can be used to restore the flow of qi, and acupuncture is also commonly used to unblock qi flow. Tai qi and other movement-and-meditation systems arose to maximize the flow and presence of qi in the body. Breathing properly is key to tai qi. Although it is known in the West as an exercise system especially good for older people, this is not its significance for Daoism. Nevertheless, the medical benefits of tai qi are well established. For example, a study done by Emory University's medical school concluded that training in tai qi was highly effective in improving the balance, strength, and even self-confidence of those 70 years and older.[6]

---

[6] S. L. Wolf, M. O'Grady, K. A. Easley, Y. Guo, R. W. Kressig, and M. Kutner, "The Influence of Intense Tai Chi Training on Physical Performance and Hemodynamic Outcomes in Transitionally Frail, Older Adults," *Journal of Gerontology* 61, no. 2 (2006): 184–89. A summary can be found at http://www.ncbi.nlm.nih.gov/pubmed/16510864.

A Famous Conversation between Confucius and Laozi

The meeting of Confucius and Laozi probably never happened, and it appears to have been invented in later times to illustrate the differences between their systems, at least on an official level. Confucius, committed as he was to bringing proper order to social and political life, promotes to Laozi the value of ancient religious rituals and ideas of justice. He speaks positively about the way ancient kings ruled, especially Zhou rulers. Laozi is interested in acquiring peace and inner equilibrium. He urges Confucius in sharp words to seek wu wei, which leads to unity with the Dao.

> *"Today I have seen Laozi, and I can only compare him to the dragon."*
> —Confucius

Confucius asked Laozi about his opinion regarding the ancient rites and rulers. Laozi is said to have answered:

> The men about whom you talk are dead, and their bones are moldered to dust; only their words are left. When your "superior man" gets his opportunity, he succeeds; but when the time is against him, he is carried along by circumstances. I have heard that a good merchant, even if he is rich, appears as if he were poor. Likewise, the truly superior man appears outwardly unintelligent. So put away your proud airs and your many desires to change things. They are of no advantage to you; this is all I have to tell you.

In this conversation, it became clear that neither would convince the other. After their meeting, Confucius said to his disciples,

> I know how birds can fly, how fish can swim, and how animals can run.... But there is the dragon: I cannot tell how he mounts on the wind through the clouds and rises to Heaven. Today I have seen Laozi, and I can only compare him to the dragon.

of sheep by saying to someone who objected to it, "You love the sheep, but I love the ceremony" (*Analects* 3.17). Confucius's system sought to reform traditional Chinese religious and ethical ideas, not so much by changing them as by showing people their inner meaning. Confucius believed that if people knew *why* these things are important, they would follow them more fully and carefully, and life would become what it should be. (See "A Closer Look: A Famous Conversation.")

Learning Outcome 7-4

Paraphrase in your own words the main ethical principles of Daoism and Confucianism.

7-4 Daoist and Confucian Ethics

Throughout North America, Amy Chua's book *Battle Hymn of the Tiger Mother* (2011) raised a storm of controversy on television, on the web, and in print. In it Chua (CHEW-ah), a law professor at Yale, details how she raised two daughters with traditional "tough love" and "Chinese mother" parenting, as opposed to what she calls the "lax" current models of American parenting. She demanded straight As from her daughters and pushed them to excel in everything they did, often using methods that seem harsh and unloving to her readers. Many Chinese American parents do take the time to guide their children in doing homework and often give them some academic work besides what is assigned; children usually respond by taking their studies seriously. This is in line with traditional Confucian values, especially the importance of self-cultivation for one's family. Chua's approach struck a nerve, as it was designed to do (notice its provocative title), but many experts on Chinese culture wonder if she hasn't misrepresented Confucian values and thereby done these values a disservice.

Confucian ethics are more fully developed, and more central to Confucianism's religious system, than are Daoist ethics. For example, it is often said about Confucianism that it is a system of ethics, but this is not said about Daoism. Before we discuss Confucianism, we will consider some main moral principles from the *Daode Jing* and other early texts that have become important in Daoism.

Watch an NBC-TV news report on the "Tiger Mother."

7-4a Daoist Ethics

The basis of Daoist ethics is the *Daode Jing*. Although it is elusive in style and meaning, challenging the reader to figure out what it means, the main lines of Daoist moral teaching are clear. The *Daode Jing* teaches that one must follow the way of the Dao in order to live a good life. Other living beings in nature—plants and animals, as well as the system of nature as a whole—follow the Dao automatically; they can't do otherwise.

But human beings do not follow the Dao naturally. The *Daode Jing* suggests that human distinctions such as good and evil, beauty and ugliness generate the troubles and problems of existence (Chapter 3). Humans impose such things on the Dao; they aren't really there. Persons following the Dao must not live according to human-made distinctions (Chapter 19). Indeed, these distinctions emerge only when people aren't following the Dao (Chapters 18, 38); they are a form of disease (Chapter 74). Daoists believe that the Dao unties the knots of life, blunts the sharp edges of relationships and problems, and soothes painful occurrences (Chapter 4). So it is best to practice wu wei in all endeavors, to act naturally, and not to oppose or tamper with how life is flowing.

This passage from Chapter 7 of the *Zhuangzi* explains the key points and the promise of wu wei:

> Wu wei makes the person who practices it the lord of all fame. It serves him as the treasury of all plans. It fits him for the burden of all offices. It makes him the lord of all wisdom. The range of his action is inexhaustible, but there is nowhere any trace of his presence. He fulfills all that he has received from Heaven, but he does not see that he was the recipient of anything.... When the perfect man employs his mind, it is a mirror. It does nothing and anticipates nothing. It responds to what is before it, but does not retain it. Thus he is able to deal successfully with all things and injures nothing.

All this can seem very abstract, but Daoism carries out these ideas in everyday practice. For example, Daoists often have a preference for vegetarianism, which they see as more "natural" than meat eating. This Daoist moral practice, along with the Buddhist promotion of vegetarianism, explains why Chinese restaurants have so many vegetarian dishes on their menus.

7-4b Confucian Ethics

Filial Piety

Although Confucianism has not often ranked its moral virtues, filial piety, **xiao**, is traditionally considered among the most important and has had a powerful

Daoist priest in Taiwan addresses an audience about Daoist morality.

© YANFEI SUN/SHUTTERSTOCK.COM

effect on Chinese culture. As a phrase, "filial piety" is a bit unwieldy and old-fashioned, but no other term has taken its place. *Filial* means "of a child" (*filius* is the Latin word for "son"), and *piety* means "inner devotion" and "outward obedience." Both evoke meanings bordering on religious reverence. So *filial piety* is first of all the honor and obedience that children owe their parents.

The *Book of Filial Piety* is our main source for this topic, attributed traditionally to Confucius and one of his sons but almost certainly written anonymously in the 200s B.C.E. Filial piety must be shown towards both living parents and dead ancestors, and this leads to ancestor worship. It binds families into an eternal bond. This relationship was extended by analogy to the Five Relationships: (1) ruler and subject; (2) father and son; (3) husband and wife; (4) elder brother and younger brother; (5) older friend and younger friend. Each person in these sets

xiao [show; rhymes with *now*] Filial piety; honor and obedience to one's parents and deceased ancestors

ren Humaneness, reciprocity, virtue; also spelled "jen"

of relationships had specific duties; the first person in the relationship must lead with honor and kindness, and the second person must faithfully obey. Duties extended to the dead, who were expected to bless descendants that honored them and lived well, and withhold blessing from descendants who didn't. The only relationship where respect for elders did not apply was that of friend to friend. In all other relationships, high reverence was held for the older person of the two.

All this was traditional in Chinese culture by the time Confucius came onto the scene. He stressed not only the duty to perform the actions of filial piety, but much more the inner attitude of these acts. Only when inner attitude empowers and guides the outer acts will filial piety "work" to improve society. One must have the genuine reverence that xiao, piety toward parents, implies. Confucius taught, "Filial piety nowadays means the support of one's parents. But dogs and horses are also able to do something in the way of support [for the dogs and horses that gave them birth]. Without reverence, what is there to distinguish the one support from the other?" (*Analects* 2.7).

Read a short explanation of the Five Relationships from the *Classic of Rites (Li Jing)*.

Even for those outside the Chinese cultural and religious system, Confucius's teaching on relationships has a great deal of wisdom. For example, he said that filial piety can be illustrated by "not making your parents anxious about anything else than your being sick." To those with aging parents he said, "The [advanced] age of one's parents should always be remembered, as a reason for joy and for fear" (*Analects* 2.6, 21).

> *One's family name is traditionally put first, then one's personal name—family is more important than any individual member.*

Note how family relationships are the center and key to the five relationships. When people in the West speak of "family values" in wider society, their ideas

Caption: **Family relationships are key to Confucian ethics.**

pale in comparison with China's emphasis on these values. The importance of one's family is shown by traditional Chinese names. The family name is put first, then the personal name—family is more important than its individual members. In general, the individual lives for the family, not vice versa. (When Chinese people in the West put their personal name first, it can get a little confusing for non-Chinese to tell the personal name from the family name. The family name typically has one syllable and the personal name has two. In the traditionally ordered name of the scholar Tu Weiming, *Tu* is the family name, *Weiming* the personal name. For a scholar who Westernized his name, Wing-tsit Chan, his two-syllable personal name is first.) Filial piety has continued to play a central role in Confucian thinking, and in Chinese culture, to the present day.

Reciprocity

Ren—variously translated "humaneness, reciprocity, virtue"—is a basic Confucian value, second only to filial piety in its importance. Despite the hierarchical and authoritarian structure of life that Confucianism encourages, the more powerful people in every relationship must act with humane, gentle reciprocity toward the less powerful in the relationship. Confucius himself once said that *ren* is the key moral teaching, and summarized it by saying, "What you don't want done to yourself, don't do to others."

Loyalty

Loyalty (**zhong**) is closely related to filial piety. Loyalty is an extension of one's duties to friends and family, and is carried out in the Five Relationships. Loyalty to one's father is first, then to one's spouse, one's ruler, and one's friends. Confucius's teaching on loyalty was undermined by the authoritarian social structure of China. More emphasis was put on the ruler's power over his subjects and much less on the ruler's obligations to his subjects, whether that ruler was an emperor, a father, or a husband. Nevertheless, loyalty was always considered one of the greater human virtues.

The "Perfect Man"

The term **junzi** (Wade-Giles, *chun-tzu*), literally "a prince's or lord's child," is crucial to Confucianism. More than any other Confucian concept, it expresses the process of self-cultivation and self-improvement. A succinct description of the junzi is one who, in the Anglo-American expression, is a "scholar and a gentleman." In ancient times, the masculine gender of the phrase was intentional—only males could become a junzi. In modern times, the masculine translation in English is still frequently used, although women are also urged (in parts of the Confucian world) toward self-cultivation.

In addition to sexism, this term has been linked with elitism. The junzi is seen as a better person than others, and he is expected to act as a moral guide to the rest of society. Indeed, *junzi* has often been translated "exemplary person." However, becoming a junzi by education and then experience was open to every class. Confucius would take on as a student anyone who could pay him even the smallest amount, and later Confucianism was in many respects a meritocracy of learning and virtue, not an aristocracy of automatic privilege for the highborn.

For Confucianists, the great example of the "perfect man" is Confucius himself. Perhaps the biggest disappointment of his life was that he was never awarded the high official position that he desired, where he would demonstrate the social blessings that would ensue if humane, wise persons ruled and administered the state. Despite this disappointment, he continued to teach his system, even when he thought that it would die out when he did. His students carried on his teachings for hundreds of years before his system took root in Chinese life.

Watch a student-made instructional video on business manners in China.

7-5 Ritual and Worship

A solitary sage studies ancient Chinese poems in Hong Kong. He pauses to reflect on their meaning, especially on how they relate to his Confucian beliefs. After reflecting, he writes out the passage calligraphically; his artistic brush-strokes as he draws the Chinese word-characters show the inner meaning of the text and the results of his meditation. This simple ritual helps him improve his character toward becoming a "perfect man," the highest goal of the Confucian tradition, and his study of the ancient classics is a key ingredient in this self-cultivation. Daoists also use the drawing of key words and passages to promote living more deeply in the Dao.

As you study ritual and worship in Daoism and Confucianism, you will notice some important commonalities. Both religions center their worship in temples, where many of the same activities can be found: burning incense, bowing to images, sitting meditation, meditative walking, and others. Both religions have a notable lack of emphasis on life-cycle rituals, with the exception of funerals. Funeral rites also tend to be similar for Daoists and Confucianists, for two remarkable reasons: Both religions draw on ancient Chinese funeral ideas and practices, and Buddhism has strongly influenced the way the Chinese look at death. We will now look more fully at both similarities and differences in Confucian and Daoist ritual.

7-5a Daoist Temples and Worship

Daoist temples are more colorful and elaborate than those of other religions in China. They are ornately decorated both on the exterior and in the interior. Those who visit and worship there often add brightly colored flowers and streamers to decorate the temple. Color, particularly red, is seen as bringing blessing and good luck. Vendors outside most temples sell small statues for

zhong Loyalty, an extension of one's filial duties to friends and family

junzi [JUHN-tzoo] Literally, "a prince's or lord's child"; in the teaching of Confucius, a "superior man" made so by the study and practice of virtue

taking home, as well as incense and flowers to use in the temple. Inside is an altar at the front, on which flowers can be placed and incense burned. Worshipers may kneel in reverence in front of this altar. Behind the altar, the focal point of the temple, are statues of the gods honored in that temple.

Sometimes there are group ceremonies in the temple, such as continuous reading of a scripture text to earn merit or for monastic worship on holy days, and people in the temple are welcome to look on. But people generally come to the temples for individual experiences, to seek the favor and blessing of the god(s) for a particular need. One of their most pressing needs is to gain direction for their future. In ancient times, various divination rituals were used, going all the way back to oracle bones inscribed with writings; the bones would be put into the fire, and how they cracked would indicate the future. Other methods arose over time, and what is common today (in or just outside Daoist temples) is selecting yarrow sticks to obtain a passage from the *Yi Jing*, which a diviner will then interpret.

Offering incense to Daoist gods

7-5b Confucian Temples and Worship

In China before the twentieth century C.E., every county had one official temple to Confucius. These temples were usually next to Confucian schools. The front portal of the temple was an ornamental gate. Inside, there were usually three courtyards, two in smaller temple complexes. The main building on the inner courtyard was the "Hall of Great Achievement"

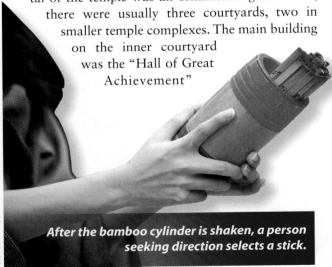

After the bamboo cylinder is shaken, a person seeking direction selects a stick.

or "Hall of Great Perfection." This housed the ancestral tablet of Confucius and the tablets of other important masters and sages, usually the first main disciples of Confucius. A second significant temple building was the "Shrine of the Great Wise Men," which honored the ancestors of Confucius.

Unlike Daoist or Buddhist temples, Confucian temples do not normally have images. In early years, Confucius and his disciples were probably represented with wall paintings and statues. However, there was rising opposition to this practice, which over time was seen as Buddhist. In the 1500s C.E., all existing images of Confucius were replaced with memorial tablets in imperial temples in the capital and other bureaucratic locations. However, statues are still found in temples controlled by Confucius's family descendants, such as that in Qufu. The point of almost all Confucian temples is to honor and promote Confucius's teachings, not Confucius himself. Confucius is a human example, not a god.

The state-mandated worship of Confucius centered upon offering sacrifices to Confucius's spirit in the Confucian temple. A dance known as the "Eight-Row Dance," consisting of eight columns of eight dancers each, sometimes carrying feathers or a weapon, was also performed. Today this is performed on Confucius's birthday and is accompanied by musical performances and prayers. Animal sacrifices (the animals are killed before the service, not as a part of it) and incense are offered to the spirit of Confucius.

In addition to honoring Confucius, Confucian temples also honored other disciples and Confucian scholars through history. The composition and number of figures venerated changed and grew through time. Because temples were a statement of official Confucian teaching, the issue of which Confucians to enshrine was often difficult. Today, a total of 162 figures are venerated in Confucian temples.

7-5c The Traditional Chinese Funeral

Life-cycle rituals are not as plentiful or as important in China as they are in some other cultures and religions. Marriage is more a social arrangement than

The temple of Confucius in Tainan, Taiwan—the oldest on that island—shows the simplicity of Confucian temples.

a religious one, for example. But the traditional Chinese funeral is well developed and has great religious and cultural significance. It still reflects some of the most ancient Chinese beliefs about life, death, and life after death.

> *Cremation is rare for Daoists and Confucianists, because it destroys the qi in the bones of the dead.*

Cremation is rare, even unthinkable, for Daoists and Confucianists, because it destroys the qi that remains in the bones of the dead. This qi is important for the spirit of the deceased in the next world. In-ground burial of the whole body is the rule. (For Chinese Buddhists, however, cremation is common.) Male heads of the family receive elaborate funerals, infants or children very simple ones, and people in between get rites on a sliding scale.

Funerals take place in the home and the cemetery, not in a temple or mortuary business. An undertaker is hired to oversee all funeral rites, especially actions involving physical contact with the corpse, because this contact is defiling to the family. When the family prepares to receive visitors who come to pay their respects, all statues of gods in the house are covered so that they will not be exposed to the body or coffin.

All mirrors are removed or covered, because seeing a body in a mirror is thought to be inauspicious. When the body of the deceased is cleaned and dressed in the deceased's best clothing, it is put in the open coffin and placed inside the house or in its courtyard. Flowers, gifts, food, and a portrait of the deceased are placed near the coffin as an offering to the deceased and as a comfort to the bereaved family. The immediate family is now ready to receive visitors from among their wider family, neighbors, and friends.

Various activities take place in the home during the period of visitation. Relatives typically cry or even wail during mourning, both out of genuine emotion and as a sign of respect and loyalty to the deceased. The spirit of the dead will see this grief and be pleased by it. A small altar with burning incense and a candle is put at the foot of the coffin. This honors the dead, and helps to keep the smell of death at bay. Symbolic paper money is burned continuously outside to provide the deceased with income in the afterlife. Visitors light incense for the deceased and bow to the family out of respect. A monk reads aloud verses from Buddhist or Daoist scriptures. (Confucianists generally rely on Buddhism and Daoism for funeral rites.) Before they can enter the happier afterlife, the souls of the dead face many troubles and even torment, for the sins they have committed in life. Chanting by the monks eases the passage of the deceased's soul into a happy afterlife. These prayers are accompanied by music, and the family arranges for as much scripture and music performance as it can afford.

A solemn procession then goes from the home to the cemetery. Chinese cemeteries are traditionally located on hillsides, where feng shui is best. (As we saw earlier in this chapter, feng shui began with burials, and its influence on burial is still strong.) When the coffin is removed from the hearse and lowered into the ground, the mourners look away. Then family members throw a handful of earth into the grave before it is filled. As they depart, the keeper of the cemetery offers other prayers for the deceased.

After the burial, the ritual continues. All clothes worn by the mourners are burned, to avoid bad fortune associated with death. Special prayers to the deceased will be offered by the family at home, especially directed at the ancestral tablet that now has the deceased's name on it. The family's mourning period continues for one hundred days, signified by a piece of colored cloth worn on their sleeves. From this time on, for as long as the family endures, the dead will be venerated in the home (and in a family temple if the family is wealthy), and imitation paper money will be sent to the deceased by burning it at their graves.

Watch the burning of possessions being sent to the deceased's spirit.

Watch a National Geographic report on "second burial."

7-5d A Final Comparison of Daoism and Confucianism

Before we turn to the topic of Daoism and Confucianism in the Western world, it may be helpful to sketch a final comparison of Daoism and Confucianism. Daoism shared some emphases with classical Confucianism, such as the necessity of self-cultivation and a concern for the practicalities of life, but not abstractions (the latter seen, for example, in Buddhism). Both Daoism and Confucianism are world-affirming religions, and religions that also affirm the ancient cultural and spiritual life of China. Despite these similarities, Daoism and Confucianism have been competing alternative religions—in main teachings, ethics, and ritual.

As we saw previously, Daoism teaches that human distinctions such as morality and beauty generate the troubles and problems of existence. They are imposed on the world by the human mind; they do not exist in the world itself. The person following the Dao must cease living by human distinctions. Daoists believe that the Dao naturally makes human life full and right. So it is best to practice wu wei, to act naturally, and not to oppose or tamper with how nature or even human reality is moving. Daoism teaches that it is better to be passive rather than active, yielding rather than assertive, quiet rather than vocal. In terms of the yin-yang, Daoism is the yin of China.

> *"Daoists take their hands off life, but Confucianists put their hands on everything."*
> *—Chinese saying*

Confucius and his followers, on the other hand, have viewed themselves as the yang, the active and assertive side of life. They have been "proactive," to use a current term, in setting human life straight. They study current life in the light of Confucian thought, plan changes, educate people to be active, and develop solutions to China's problems. A familiar Chinese saying is that Daoists "take their hands off life" and let it go its own way; Confucianists "put their hands on everything" in an effort to guide and shape people. To use another illustration, Daoists let life shape them like natural forces shape a piece of rock or wood; Confucianists carve themselves into a sculpture.

Burning money for deceased ancestors

Learning Outcome 7-6

Summarize the main features of Daoism and Confucianism around the world today, especially in North America.

7-6 Daoism and Confucianism around the World Today

For thousands of years China was an insular nation that kept to itself, and Chinese religion did the same. Daoism and Confucianism spread into the wider world first when its scriptures were translated, and then when Chinese people migrated to the West.

7-6a Daoism and Confucianism in the West

Daoism first entered the world beyond China when scholars translated its main works into European languages, beginning in the 1700s. The *Daode Jing* has been consistently popular for more than two centuries and is today one of the most translated books in the world. From 1927 to 1944, the chief advocate of Daoism for the Western world was Professor Henri Maspero in Paris. More recently, Michael Saso (born 1930), an academic expert in Daoism and author of several leading books on it, has advanced Daoism in the West. He was the first Westerner to become a Daoist priest. He also served as coeditor of *Taoist Resources*, a major academic journal devoted entirely to Daoism; it ceased publication in 1997. Today, many Daoist organizations have been established throughout the West.

Confucianism also came to the West by means of its writings. The *Analects* and the *Mencius* were among the first books translated in Max Müller's *Sacred Books of the East* project in the 1800s, and dozens of translations have been made since that time, into every major European language. The practice of Chinese religions spread to the West not primarily from China itself, but from neighboring lands in which these religions have long been present: Taiwan and Korea in particular, and to a lesser degree Japan, Vietnam, and Indonesia. In Taiwan, despite the modernizations that have made it a thriving democracy and economic powerhouse, traditional Chinese religions remain stronger than on the mainland. Nine out of ten residents of Taiwan call themselves Buddhists, Daoists, Confucianists, or a mix of the three. In South Korea, almost half the population is Christian, but the other half is devoted to Buddhism, Confucianism, and/or the service of local gods.

> *Confucianism is probably the only world religion to come to North America that doesn't have formal temples here.*

7-6b Confucianism in North America

Confucianists and Daoists came to North America from the lands mentioned above as well as from China. We will deal with Confucianism first. Because Confucianism is a moral system that is built on elements of traditional Chinese religion found in much of Daoism, and because Confucian temples in Chinese lands were state sponsored, Confucian temples couldn't be transplanted in North America as Daoist or Buddhist temples could. The temples to Confucius, with their associated schools—from primary schools in every county to the imperial university in Beijing—that anchored Confucianism in Asia could not be built in North America. Indeed, they wouldn't make sense here, in a society that isn't Confucian and doesn't establish any religion as the national faith. Chinese people did eventually build social and educational associations that had an appreciation for Confucianism, sometimes even with a room or two dedicated to the veneration of Confucius and his main disciples. But they couldn't, and didn't, build temples such as one finds in China as well as in lands in the Chinese cultural orbit. Confucianism is probably the only world religion to come to North America that doesn't have formal temples here. Chinese cultural centers often must host Confucian ceremonies.

A much more recent feature is the establishment of **Confucius Centers** or "Confucius Institutes" in major North American cities, usually connected with

Watch a Confucian ceremony in Maryland.

Confucius Centers
Educational and public relations institutes set up by the government of China in Western cities, usually connected with universities

Daoist temple built in 1874, now preserved in a state park in Weaverville, California

© CAITLIN MIRRA/SHUTTERSTOCK.COM

7-6c Daoism in North America

Daoism came to North America with the first Chinese, who arrived to participate in California's gold rush. The new settlers established several temples in San Francisco. One of these, the Tin How Temple, was built in 1852 and still stands today. It was built out of gratitude to Mazu, as the Queen of Heaven, for protecting the settlers on their long sea voyage. In the next decades, statues and name tablets of other gods were installed in the temple. By 1890, dozens of Chinese temples were found along the West Coast of the United States and Canada. Together they served a multitude of deities, just as their temples in China had. A trusted caretaker who acted as a janitor for the building would usually supervise the worship and sacrifices as well as organize festivals. Daoist priests were not yet to be found in the New World, and neither were monks. Despite the hard pressure on Daoism in China during the 1800s, priests and monks did not make the perilous trek to a non-Chinese culture in the West. Most of these temples disappeared over time, but some of them—such as the Tin How Temple—continue today.

Should these be considered *Daoist* temples? This depends on how one understands Daoism. To use the threefold understanding of Daoism advanced by Livia Kohn, they certainly were not temples of "philosophical Daoism." They can make a good claim for "religious Daoism," and certainly they were "folk Daoist" temples. But the majority of the gods worshiped in these temples were not the main Daoist deities, with the exception of the Jade Emperor. Rather, they were local gods that Chinese Americans could still look to for help, ones that had long ago been taken up into the vast Daoist collection of gods.

The ups and downs of Daoism in the United States varied with immigration policies, just as did all other religions of immigrants. The federal Chinese Exclusion Act of 1882 effectively stopped all new Chinese immigration, and Daoist temples suffered. When the Immigration Act of 1965 was passed, a good level of

universities, by the government of the People's Republic of China. Dozens of these centers have been set up since about 1990; in Chicago alone, there are several. These centers and institutes are an effort at "public diplomacy" by the Chinese government, an outreach especially to secondary schools and higher education. The main Chicago Confucius Center describes itself this way:

> The Confucius Center is a nonprofit institute aiming to enhance intercultural understanding in the world by sponsoring courses of Chinese language and culture, so as to promote a better understanding of the Chinese language and culture among the people of the world; develop friendly relationships between China and other countries; accelerate the development of multiculturalism at the international level; and help bring about global peace and harmony.

So it's clear that, despite the name "Confucius Centers," the spread of Confucianism itself isn't what they are primarily about. But there is something traditionally Chinese about this arrangement: Chinese culture and Confucian values are so deeply intertwined that to deal with the first is necessarily to deal with the second. As a result, Confucianism is found at these centers and institutes not only in the plentiful Confucian scriptures that are there, but even more in the promotion of Confucian values in Chinese life and learning.

Watch an explanation of the Confucius Institute at Purdue University.

Chinese immigration resumed. Temples revived, and many Daoist organizations were founded that still exist today. The largest of these is the network of "Healing Tao" centers in the United States and Canada, a movement that combines Western and Daoist healing arts. These new associations and temples typically have well-educated members from the middle and upper classes of Chinese immigrants. They have also drawn a strong following of non-Chinese and non-Daoists who are attracted to various aspects of Daoist thought and practice. Probably the greatest "draw" is the practice of tai qi, which is promoted as a system of physical, mental, and spiritual exercise and health, not as a system that depends deeply (as we saw previously) on Daoist beliefs about the cosmos and its relationship to the human body and soul.

Take a tour of the Daoist Temple of Original Simplicity in Boston.

The greatest influence of Daoism on the Western world continues to be its foundational teachings. The *Daode Jing* influences life and thought far beyond the lives of Daoists in the West. It continues to be the most translated book from Asia, and its elusive style and challenging wisdom have never ceased to fascinate North Americans. The appeal of this book is echoed in the titles of more than fifty recent books, such as *The Tao of [Winnie the] Pooh*, *The Tao of Parenting*, *The Tao of Love and Sex*, *The Tao of Spycraft*, *The Tao of Coaching*, *The Tao of Sales*, and even *The Tao of Jesus* and *The Tao of Islam*. Of course, many of these books include Westernized adaptations of vaguely Daoist ideas—*The Tao of Golf* doesn't have a great many authentic Daoist teachings to help the author's game—and bear little resemblance to the rich Daoist understandings of the Dao. In a different category is the use of Daoism in psychology and psychotherapy, in which Wayne Dyer is the leading figure. All this adaptation of Daoism may raise questions in some minds, but it is probably exactly what we should expect—a wide-ranging but wu-wei attempt to tap into the elusive, all-encompassing Dao.

Watch American psychologist Wayne Dyer explain the use of the *Daode Jing* in his work.

Study Tools 7

Ready to study? In the book you can:

- Review Learning Outcome answers and glossary terms with the tear-out Chapter Review card.

Or you can go online to CourseMate, at www.cengagebrain.com, for these resources:

- Chapter quizzes to prepare for tests

- Interactive flashcards of all glossary terms

- A timeline of events for this chapter

- An eBook with introductions, interactive quizzes, and live links for all web resources in the chapter

CHAPTER 8

Encountering Shinto: The Way of the Kami

BONNIE VAN VOORST © CENGAGE LEARNING

Learning Outcomes

After studying this chapter, you will be able to do the following:

8-1 Explain the meaning of *Shinto* and *Kami no michi*.

8-2 Summarize how the four main periods of Shinto's history have shaped its present.

8-3 Outline essential Shinto teachings in your own words.

8-4 Describe the main features of Shinto ethics.

8-5 Outline Shinto worship and other rituals, and explain why they play a leading role in Shinto.

8-6 Explain why Shinto religious practice has such a small role in North America.

Study Tools

After you read this chapter, go to the Study Tools at the end of the chapter, page 205.

© SEAN PAVONE PHOTO/SHUTTERSTOCK.COM

Shinto connects the people of Japan to their land, and Japan's present to its past.

Your Visit to the Tsubaki Shinto Shrine in Granite Falls, Washington

When you meet your guide to the Tsubaki (tsoo-BAH-kee) Shrine just outside the gate, he says, "Please remember that the shrine grounds are a sacred place, so correct behavior is very important. No food, drink, or smoking is allowed. Keep a quiet, hushed voice. You may make a formal prayer and personal prayer at any time. If you wish to talk to the priest or have him do a ceremony for you, you must not be barefoot or wearing shorts or a sleeveless shirt. And no cell phone use, please."

First you visit the hand water station to purify yourself, because purity is important in Shinto. You follow the actions of your Shinto guide, using a wooden dipper to pour water on your left hand. You lean back slightly from the basin as you pour, so water from your hands doesn't mix with the pure water. You pour water on your right hand and then into your left palm to rinse your mouth. Then you pour water again on your left hand. Last, you let the small amount of water still in the dipper run back down its handle, and you place it back in the basin.

Next, you approach the shrine building. Continuing to follow your guide's actions, you bow slightly at the inner shrine gate and then walk on. The centerline is reserved for the kami, whom you know to be the gods and spirits of Shinto, to walk on, so you carefully avoid walking on it. As you get farther in, you offer a prayer to the gods and spirits of the shrine with two bows, then two claps, then one bow. Inside the shrine, you move to the offertory box, where you drop in a few coins. Standing next to the centerline, you grip the bell rope tightly and pull it to ring the bell. You fix your gaze toward the mirror in the inner shrine and then

What Do YOU Think?

The Shinto religion explains the Japanese "love affair" with robots and robotics.

Strongly Disagree				Strongly Agree		
1	2	3	4	5	6	7

bow deeply twice. You clap twice and pray while keeping your hands together at the center of your chest. When your short, quiet prayers are done, you bow once again.

A follower of Shinto ceremonially washes her hands outside a Shinto shrine.

 Famous "floating gate" of the Itsukushima Shrine, Miyajima Island, Japan, showing that the sea around Japan is considered sacred

Your guide says, "If you have a question for shrine staff, please ring the buzzer." You don't, so you look around and see little shops where you can buy small prayer plaques and slips of paper for fortune-telling. You buy a plaque, write your wish/prayer on it, and hang it up with similar ones nearby for the gods to read.

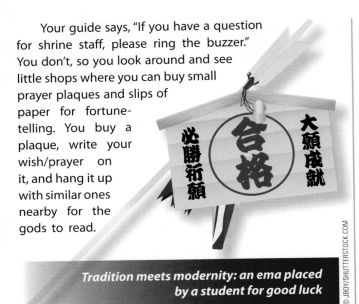

Tradition meets modernity: an ema placed by a student for good luck

© JBOY/SHUTTERSTOCK.COM

Then you draw at random a fortune-telling slip; these slips of paper contain several predictions ranging from "great good luck" to "great bad luck." By tying your slip to a rope where others have tied theirs, good fortune will come true or bad fortune can be averted. As it happens, you drew a good fortune, making for a happy conclusion of your visit to the shrine.

 Visit the Tsubaki shrine by way of its website.

> *Shinto is an indigenous religion with origins in ancient times, but it has succeeded in a starkly modern nation.*

Shinto is a religion of formal rituals and inner feelings more than of doctrines, ethics, and organization. Its sentiments and rituals are directed especially to the natural world of the Japanese islands and secondarily to the history of the Japanese state. Shinto connects the people of Japan and their land, as well as Japan's present and its past. In your study of Shinto, you'll encounter these unique features:

Shinto [SHIN-toh] "The way of the gods"

- Some scholars hold that all Japanese are Shinto just by virtue of being culturally Japanese, whether they practice Shinto or not. Many Japanese who see themselves as Shintoists also practice elements of other religions, especially Buddhism. This makes it difficult to know how many Japanese practice Shinto, and estimates vary widely—between 2 million and 127 million, the latter being the current estimated population of Japan.

- Shinto has no founder, no creed, and (for most of its history) no central authority. It didn't even have a name until the sixth century C.E., when it was necessary to distinguish it from Buddhism once that religion reached Japan from China.

- Shinto has no scripture. In fact, Shinto is the only religion based in a literate culture that hasn't developed a scripture. It does have books of ancient Japanese mythology and history written in the eighth century, but these don't function in an authoritative way in the religion.

- Shinto has been a major part of Japanese life and culture throughout the country's history, but for more than a thousand years it has shared its spiritual, social, and political roles with Buddhism and Confucianism. This mirrors the religious situation in China, where most believers combine Daoism, Buddhism, and Confucianism in various ways.

Shinto is an indigenous religion with origins in ancient times, but it has succeeded (at least until now—some scholars think its future is bleak) in a starkly modern nation. Although it could be treated with other indigenous religions, Shinto's unique dual role as an indigenous religion and a faith of the modern world makes separate treatment worthwhile.

 Watch a BBC introduction to Shinto.

Learning Outcome 8-1

Explain the meaning of *Shinto* and *Kami no michi*.

8-1 Names

Shinto means "the way of the gods." It derives from the Chinese *shen dao*, combining two words: *shin*, "gods," particularly the higher gods, and *tao/dao*, the "way" of thought and life. After the arrival of Buddhism in Japan in the sixth century C.E., *Shinto* was invented to counter the Japanese term *butsudo*, "the way of the Buddha." A more Japanese way to express this name, but not more prevalent in scholarship, is **Kami no michi**, "the way of the kami." This name is more accurate than *Shinto*, because the typical notions of "gods" in the religions treated in this book don't fit this religion very well. **Kami** are spirits, deities, or essences of something notable. They can be humanlike, animistic, or natural features or forces in the world (for example, mountains, rivers, trees, rocks, lightning, and wind). Most kami are morally good, but a few are unpredictable or downright dangerous. Kami and people exist within the same world and are interrelated in it.

YURIKO NAKAO/REUTERS

Official shrine maidens perform a Shinto ritual dance for purification at the Meiji Shrine, Tokyo.

The ritual reinforced the pre–World War II belief that the emperor was a living god. No one but the emperor has ever witnessed the ceremony or knows its details, and Akihito's continued participation in it was controversial among some Japanese.

Explore Japanese culture and religion on Google Earth™.

Shinto history can be presented in four major periods: before the arrival of Buddhism in Japan in the 600s; Shinto and Buddhism together in Japan from 600 until about 1850; the Meiji (MAY-jee) reinterpretation of Shinto from 1850 to the end of the World War II in 1945; and Shinto from 1945 until today.

8-2a Before the Arrival of Buddhism (to 600 C.E.)

Before Buddhism came to Japan in the sixth century C.E., there probably was no religion that we would recognize as Shinto, but rather many local gods and shrines that are now grouped under Shinto. The first, aboriginal inhabitants of Japan were animists, devoted to powers of nature that they saw around them. These powers were the kami that were found in all significant natural things: plants and animals, mountains and fertile plains, rivers and seas, earthquakes, storms in the air and the seas, and even powerful human beings. Shrines began to be built in places where the kami were thought to be particularly present. At these shrines, simple worship would be offered to the spirits of the place, and the blessings offered to the kami would result in the kami's blessings on the people. Some of these shrines had women called **miko** who acted as shamans. With the passing of time and the coming of more-patriarchal Chinese religions and culture, the miko became the "shrine maidens" of today—unmarried

Learning Outcome 8-2

Summarize how the four main periods of Shinto's history have shaped its present.

8-2 The Shinto Present as Shaped by Its Past

When the present emperor, Akihito (AH-kih-HEE-toh), became the 125th emperor of Japan in 1989, he spent a night with the Sun Goddess as a dinner guest, something every emperor is required to do shortly after ascending to the throne. First recorded in 712 C.E., the ritual takes place at night because the Sun Goddess is in the sky during the day; she comes down on this special occasion to be present with the new emperor. After a bath for purification, the emperor carries out the ritual called the Great Food Offering. It takes place in two specially constructed log huts at the Imperial Palace in Tokyo. During the rite, the emperor receives an essence of the Sun Goddess's spirit and thus becomes with her a kind of living ancestor of the entire Japanese family.

Kami no michi [KAH-mee noh MEE-chee] "The way of the kami," another term for Shinto

kami [KAH-mee] Spirits, deities, or essences found in both animate and inanimate objects

miko [MEE-koh] "Shrine maidens" who assist male priests

young women who assist the male priests in rituals but who no longer act as shamans.

Like other indigenous peoples, the early Japanese developed myths that enabled them to make sense of life in their place, as well as rituals to bless it. For example, the myth relating the creation of the Japanese islands probably arose at this time, telling how the husband-and-wife gods **Izanagi** and **Izanami** made Japan. Other religious groups arrived from Korea to settle in Japan in late prehistoric times; they were absorbed into Shinto. The realms of earth and the supernatural, as well as those of the common and the sacred, were closely related in the worldview of the early Japanese. Things that modern people regard as "supernatural" were just another part of the natural world, although with great power. The oldest Shinto ceremonies were dedicated to agriculture and emphasized obtaining ritual purity that would lead to the blessing of fields and flocks. Worship took place outdoors, at sites thought to be sacred to the kami of the place. In time, the ancient Japanese built permanent structures to honor their gods. Shrines were usually built on or near mountains, at the edge of forests, or in rural areas.

8-2b Shinto and Buddhism Together in Japan (600–1850)

The second stage in Shinto history is the long sweep of time from about 600 to 1850, when Shinto coexisted with Buddhism and Confucianism, religions that arrived at the beginning of this period from China. The introduction of the Buddhist religion and Confucian social values from China and Korea brought a different way of life for the Japanese, including changes to their religion. (Daoism, the third main religion of China, made little effort to enter Japan, perhaps because Shinto already had a full complement of gods and spirits.) Japan established close connections with the Chinese and Korean courts that would last for four hundred years, and adopted a more sophisticated culture. This new

The "Wedded Rocks" of Futami, Japan, tied together by a one-ton rope of rice straw, represent the union of Izanagi and Izanami and celebrate the marriage of male and female.

© ISTOCKPHOTO.COM/KEVIN FREEMAN

culture was essentially Chinese and included, in addition to Confucianism and Buddhism, literature, philosophy, art, architecture, science, medicine, and government. Most important was the Chinese writing system that transformed Japan, which had no system of its own. The *Kojiki* (*Records of Ancient Matters*) and *Nihongi* (*Chronicles of Japan*), Japan's earliest histories, were written in the early 700s, soon after the introduction of Chinese writing. Ever since that time, the relationship of Shinto with Chinese religions in Japan has been complicated—sometimes peaceful, at times conflicted. Indeed, the name *Shinto* arose then to distinguish indigenous Japanese religion from the new Buddhist beliefs coming from China. Many Shinto shrines were completely changed into Buddhist temples, made a part of Buddhist temples, or kept as Shinto shrines and led by Buddhist priests. Separate new Buddhist temples were built as well. From this time comes the distinction in names still used today: Buddhist houses of worship are called "temples," but Shinto houses of worship are called "shrines." (See "A Closer Look: The Symbol of Shinto.")

Izanagi [EE-zah-NAH-gee (hard g)] "Male who invites"; the male deity who created the Japanese islands, according to Shinto mythology

Izanami [EE-zah-NAH-mee] "Female who invites"; the female deity who assisted her husband, Izanagi, in creating Japan, according to Shinto mythology

Kojiki [koh-JEE-kee] *Records of Ancient Matters*, one of Japan's earliest histories

Nihongi [nee-HAWN-gee (hard g)] *Chronicles of Japan*, one of Japan's earliest histories

A Closer Look:

The Symbol of Shinto

A **torii** is a traditional Japanese gate or portal at the entrance of, and often within, a Shinto shrine. (Its original meaning is "bird perch.") It consists of two upright wooden posts connected at the top by two horizontal crosspieces, the top one often curved up slightly at the ends. The outer gate is sometimes said to separate the "ordinary" area from a sacred area, but in view of the strong Shinto belief that *all* Japan is sacred, it's probably more accurate to say that the outer gate marks ordinary sacred space from extraordinarily sacred space. Seeing a torii at the entrance is usually the easiest way to determine that this is a Shinto shrine. Smaller torii are also found occasionally inside the grounds of Japanese Buddhist temples.

The first mention of torii is in 922. Torii were commonly made from wood or stone, but today they can also be made of metal, stainless steel, or other modern materials. They are usually either unpainted or painted a striking vermilion, with black tops. A person who has been successful in business often donates a torii to the shrine in gratitude. The Fushimi Inari (foo-SHEE-mee in-AHR-ee) shrine near Kyoto has some ten thousand torii, each bearing its donor's name, along paths that lead three miles up a mountainside.

BONNIE VAN VOORST
© CENGAGE LEARNING

Torii frame a sacred walkway at the Fushimi Inari shrine.

© HINOCHIKA/SHUTTERSTOCK.COM

> *The emerging combination of Shinto, Buddhism, and Confucianism made for religious and cultural unity, important in a land undergoing rapid change.*

In general, the emperors and ruling aristocracy approved this rising combination of Shinto, Buddhism, and Confucianism. It made for religious and cultural unity—important in a relatively small land undergoing rapid change, and still true in Japan today. The rulers took a role in religions by establishing a government office to oversee them, something that persisted until 1946. Shinto was the native religion of Japan and had a richer feeling for the natural environment than did Buddhism and Confucianism. Shinto had a disadvantage compared to Buddhism and Confucianism in its lack of complex teachings. Unlike the other religions, Shinto had no sacred scriptures in which doctrine was formulated

and by which it could be passed along. This meant that the doctrinal development of Japanese religion and philosophy inevitably drew on the comparative intellectual richness of Buddhism and Confucianism. But Shinto had found its niche in Japanese life, one that continues today.

As the Japanese nation was formed, the idea grew that humans should follow the will of the gods in political and social life. The emperor and the court had clear religious obligations, particularly the meticulous rituals that ensured that the powerful kami looked favorably on Japan and its people. These annual ceremonies for purification and blessing, which soon included many Buddhist and Confucian elements, became a regular part of the Japanese government. As time went on, the Japanese became more accustomed to integrating Shinto and Buddhism. For example, they accepted the Buddhist idea that the kami were incarnations of the Buddha, manifested in Japan to save all sentient beings. During the seventh and eighth centuries, the spiritual status of the

> **torii** [TOH-ree-ee]
> Traditional Japanese gate or portal at the entrance of, and often within, a Shinto shrine

The Seven Lucky Gods are a mixed group of Shinto and other deities popular in Japan, all thought to bring good luck.

emperor as the descendant of Sun Goddess **Amaterasu**, the chief deity worshiped in Shinto, became official doctrine when it was written up in the *Kojiki* and *Nihongi*. This was buttressed by rituals and the establishment of the important **Ise Shrine** of the imperial household.

From 800 to about 1800, Buddhist influence in government grew steadily stronger. Japan was in the hands of three power blocs: the emperor, the aristocracy, and the leaders of Buddhism and Shinto. Throughout Japanese history up until the end of World War II, the aristocracy had more power than the emperor, despite what the creation myths implied about him. Religion became more controversial when Roman Catholic Christian missionaries arrived in Japan in the 1500s and started making converts from Shinto and Buddhism. Over time, Christianity came to be seen as a political threat; it was a foreign religion, didn't allow converts to blend Christianity formally with other religions, and was beginning to convert the aristocracy. Various rulers ruthlessly tried to stamp it out from the 1500s until 1640. Most notably, in 1597 dozens of Japanese Christians were crucified in a macabre imitation of the death of Jesus Christ—and more than forty thousand died in other persecutions. Surviving

Amaterasu [ah-MAH-tehr-AH-soo] Sun Goddess, the chief deity worshiped in Shinto

Ise Shrine [EE-say] Leading Shinto holy place, established by the imperial family

"From the divine descent of the Japanese people proceeds their immeasurable superiority to the natives of other countries in courage and intelligence." —Hirata, nationalistic Shinto scholar, 1836

Christians were driven underground for hundreds of years. Buddhism dominated the seventeenth century, partly because an anti-Christian measure forced every Japanese citizen to register as a Buddhist at a Buddhist temple and pay a tax.

Japan included many elements of Confucianism in its ideas about government, but popular Japanese religion was a pragmatic fusion of Shinto and Buddhism. Confucianism provided social ethics to the nation; Shinto provided everyday rituals that helped to unify the nation; Buddhism provided philosophy and (because it was Mahayana Buddhism) a hope for life after death. Just as China had "Three Traditions" in Daoism, Confucianism, and Buddhism, so too Japan had its three traditions of Shinto, Buddhism, and Confucianism.

After this long period of powerful influence of Buddhism on Shinto, Shinto pushed back. Around 1700 there was a movement toward what was considered a purer form of Shinto, with particular emphasis on the Japanese people as the descendants of the gods and therefore superior to other races. (This, of course, is something that Japanese Buddhists denied.) Buddhist and other influences were filtered out of institutions and rituals. Historians generally hold that this wasn't so much a return to something that had once existed as it was the creation of a more unified religion from a group of many different Shinto rituals and beliefs. During this period Shinto acquired a stronger intellectual tradition than it had previously enjoyed. A part of the Shinto revival entailed the renewed study of archaic Japanese texts. Just as Shinto myths were written down in the eighth century for national political reasons, so now they were reinterpreted for nationalistic purposes.

As Japan encountered East Asia in ways that it had avoided for a thousand years, it drew on its indigenous religion to buttress its national claims. A leading Shinto scholar during this period, Hirata (hih-RAH-tah), wrote in 1836, "The two foundational doctrines of Shinto are that Japan is the country of the gods, and her inhabitants are the descendants of the gods. Between the Japanese people and other peoples… there is a difference of kind, rather than of degree. The Emperor is the true Son of

A Closer Look:

The Yasukuni Shrine Today

The **Yasukuni** Shrine was founded in 1869 under the orders of Emperor Meiji and is dedicated to the souls of all Japanese military personnel who have fallen in battle since that time. Most controversially to some (to Japan's enemies in World War II, at least), it does not distinguish between honored dead and dishonorable dead. For example, it honors fourteen men, such as Prime Minister Hideki Tojo (hee-DECK-ee TOH-joh), who were convicted of war crimes—crimes that included the killing of prisoners of war and civilians—and hanged for them after the war. Within the shrine the dead are venerated rather than just remembered. They willingly sacrificed their lives for Japan, and this has made them kami. Surrounded by war banners and military regalia, they are venerated by the hundreds of thousands of visitors who attend the shrine each year. Some

come as tourists to this site and are not interested in venerating the dead, but others come to worship them, some even believing that the souls of the war dead live in the shrine.

Junichiro Koizumi (joo-NEE-chee-roh KOH-ee-ZOO-mee), who was the prime minister of Japan from 2001 to 2006, sparked international protest when he visited the Yasukuni Shrine in person every year. He refused to explain his reason for these visits, which caused tension with China and South Korea. Tensions have lifted a bit as subsequent prime ministers haven't gone in person to the shrine, but public controversy continues in East Asia over this. When Shinto appears in the international news, it is frequently in connection with visits to the Yasukuni Shrine.

Visit the Yasukuni Shrine website.

Heaven, who is entitled to reign over the four seas and the ten thousand countries. From the divine descent of the Japanese people proceeds their immeasurable superiority to the natives of other countries in courage and intelligence."[1] This growing, religiously oriented nationalism contributed to the rapid "modernization" of Japan in the 1800s (see Map 8.1). It would prove damaging to East Asia as Japan began to build an empire around 1900, and it would prove near-disastrous to many Pacific Rim nations from China to the United States in World War II.

8-2c The Meiji Period (1850–1945)

The third major period of Shinto began with the Meiji Restoration in 1868, so called because Emperor Meiji was restored to his powers after a rebellion by warlords. (The emperor was still dominated by the aristocracy, however.) The Meiji Restoration accelerated the revival of Shinto that had been going on for two centuries and launched Japan on a path that would change its history and the history of the world. Japan had been modernizing rapidly; the Industrial Revolution that took almost two hundred years in Europe and North America was accomplished in Japan in less than a century. The aim of the new religious climate was to provide a sacred foundation and a religious rationale for the new Japan and its national ethos. Emperor worship became a leading mark of "state Shinto" during this period.

In the Meiji period, Shinto was reorganized and brought under state control. The state distinguished between the new "state Shinto," "shrine Shinto" of the traditional past, and "sect Shinto" comprising new movements in popular religion. Many historians of religion consider these new Shinto sects a result of the "culture shock" that Japan experienced after opening to the West. Between 1882 and 1908, the government recognized thirteen Shinto sects, and their number constantly increased. They are forerunners of a number of Japan's new religious movements today. A new shrine was set up at Yasukuni to honor Japanese war dead. (See "A Closer Look: The Yasukuni Shrine Today.")

> **Yasukuni** [YAS-soo-KOO-nee] Shrine set up in 1869 to memorialize war dead, now controversial

---

[1] *Transactions of the Asiatic Society of Japan*, vol. 3 (Yokohama, Japan: Asiatic Society Press, 1873), 36.

The main hall of the Yasukuni Shrine

© FOTORIN/SHUTTERSTOCK.COM

Amaterasu, who until then had not been a major divinity, was brought to center stage and used to validate the role of the emperor, not only as ruler, but also as the high priest of Shinto.

Another result of Meiji rule was the separation of Buddhism from Shinto. The kami could no longer be explained as incarnations of the Buddha or various bodhisattvas. Ritual was also affected. All Shinto shrines were purged of every trace of Buddhist imagery (for example, statues of the Buddha) and ritual (chanting scriptures). Buddhist priests were stripped of their status, and new Shinto priests were appointed to shrines. Japan's militaristic aristocracy supported Shinto, stressing that the emperor was a divine being directly descended from the gods who had given birth to the Japanese islands. Japanese children were taught

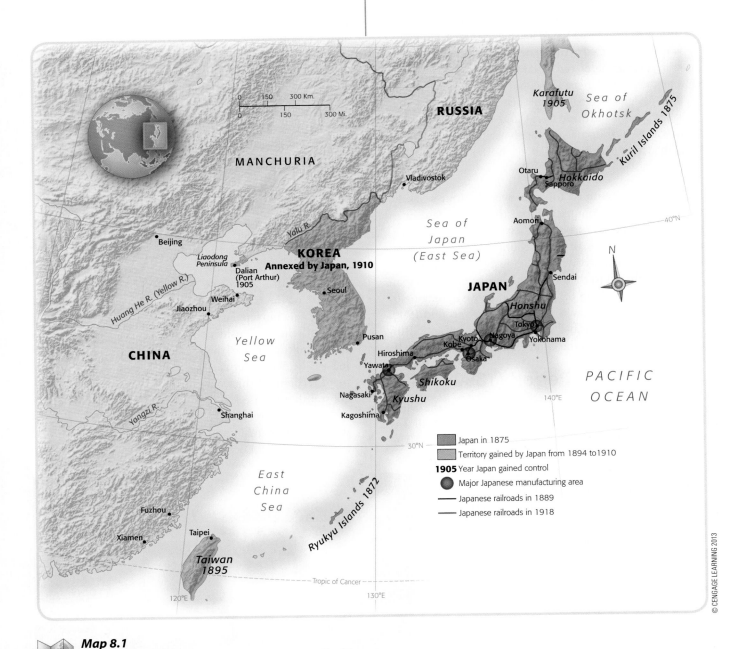

Map 8.1

Japanese Modernization and Expansion, 1868–1918

Japan undertook a crash modernization in the later 1800s. This modernization coincided with the rise of state Shinto. By 1910 its military power had increased and it had won a war with Russia and colonized Korea, Taiwan, and Sakhalin (then known as Karafutu).

at school that the emperors were descendants of Sun Goddess Amaterasu, and every classroom had a small shrine to the emperor on the wall. Shinto bound the Japanese people together with a powerful mix of devotion to kami, ancestor worship, and group loyalty to family and nation; Buddhism, with its more pacifist and international tendencies, was demoted. This separation of Buddhism and Shinto continues today, with both religions having different shrines, priests, and rites.

> *Despite the religious devotion of Japanese warriors in World War II, the Divine Wind did not come, and the emperor's rule as a god would soon end.*

Shinto played a significant role in World War II, which started in Asia with the Japanese invasion of northern China in 1937. Since the 1870s, it had been fueling a strong nationalism among the Japanese, a force that would inevitably lead to war. Service in the military was a religious as well as a civic obligation, and the spirits of those who died were honored as kami. **Kamikaze** pilots intentionally crashed their planes into American warships at the end of the war in a last-ditch effort to stave off an invasion of Japan. *Kamikaze* is often used popularly today as meaning "reckless to the point of suicide," but it really means "Divine (*kami*) Wind (*kaze*)." The Divine Wind was a typhoon that destroyed a Chinese fleet threatening Japan in the 1200s, and the modern Divine Wind was meant to reproduce that deliverance. Another well-known feature of that war was the Japanese shout "Banzai!" (bahn-ZIGH)—"ten thousand years!"—and was understood to mean "May the emperor live ten thousand years!" This was frequently used as a cry of attack by Japanese forces. Despite the religiously motivated self-sacrifice of Japanese warriors, the Divine Wind did not come, and the emperor's rule as a god would soon end, falling far short of ten thousand years.

> *Banzai literally means "ten thousand years" and was understood to mean "May the emperor live ten thousand years!"*

8-2d Shinto in Recent Times (1945–Present)

The last and current stage of Shinto history begins when the victorious Allied powers ended the status of Shinto as the state religion in 1946. Japan was allowed to keep Hirohito (HEER-oh-HEE-toh, who lived from 1901 to 1989) as emperor, but he lost his claim to divine status as part of the Allied reforms in Japan. He went on the radio to tell his people that Japan was surrendering (although such direct language was not used)—the first time that ordinary Japanese had heard an emperor's voice. He later wrote in a message to the nation,

> The ties between Us and Our people have always stood on mutual trust and affection. They do not depend upon legends and myths. They are not predicated on the false conception that the Tenno [emperor] is divine, and that the Japanese people are superior to other races and destined to rule the world.

Then he affirmed that the Japanese people still had an important role to play in the world: "By [the Japanese people's] supreme efforts... they will be able to make a substantial contribution to the welfare and advancement of mankind." This contribution did indeed come in the postwar revival of Japan, when Japan became a model of economic development, democracy, and peace in Asia. Since about 1990, however, Japan has been in a prolonged economic slump that has dispirited its people and lessened the appeal of Japanese ways of business to other nations. The dwindling attendance at many Shinto shrines is probably related to this economic downturn.

Japan's postwar constitution separates religion and state.

A Japanese commander prepares a young pilot for battle in World War II, tying on a white cloth featuring the image of the sun used to honor kamikaze pilots.

HULTON ARCHIVE/GETTY IMAGES

kamikaze [KAHM-ih-KAHZ-ee] "Divine Wind" that saved Japan

Although the constitution of modern Japan had guaranteed freedom of religion since 1873, it finally came true. No religion receives support from the Japanese state. No citizen has to take part in any religious act, celebration, rite, or practice. Many (but not all) governmental ceremonies were stripped of their explicitly religious aspects. Despite the loss of its official status, Shinto retains a significant influence in Japanese spirituality and culture. Considerable Shinto religious meaning still surrounds some regular imperial ceremonies, and a few well-attended Shinto shrines honor those who died in World War II.

In sum, Japan is today both a secular and a religious society. Industrialization and urbanization have led to the declining influence of Shinto, which has accelerated since the end of World War II. Continuing controversy over the Japanese role in that war has diminished Shinto influence among the younger generation, many of whom see Shinto myths as outmoded. Most young people go to a Shinto shrine only as tourists or to pray for success in school exams. Some Japanese, especially the older generation, still frequent Shinto shrines regularly, and all generations have a strong, even spiritual feeling for the physical beauty of Japan that is a heritage of Shinto. New religious movements have combined Buddhism, Shinto, and other religions to address contemporary Japanese issues such as family finances, environmental pollution, and family solidarity. The widespread destruction visited on northeastern Japan in the 2011 earthquake and tsunami caused many Japanese, even the younger generations, to draw upon both traditional and newer religions for comfort and strength.

> Read a CNN report on how the Japanese drew on their religions to cope with the 2011 disasters.

However, on the whole, the Japanese people are becoming more secular. In a 2000 census, although a strong majority of Japanese called themselves Buddhists or Shintoists or both, not even 15 percent reported a formal religious membership or regular religious practice. Remarkably, this rising secularization hasn't had significant negative social effects, and Japan continues to be the most peaceful, law-abiding society in the developed world. (Even after the 2011 tsunami, there was virtually no increase in crime.) Sociologists say that this is due to a desire to honor one's living relatives or other social group and an even stronger reluctance to shame them, rather than from a connection to the spirits of one's ancestors or other aspects of Shinto or Buddhist religion. To students of Japan, the strongest religious influence today may be that of Confucianism. It has virtually no formal presence in Japan, but the system of Confucian social values that arrived in Japan 1,400 years ago still influences the lives of the majority of Japanese today.

> Read the Allied powers' "Directive for the Disestablishment of State Shinto."

Learning Outcome 8-3

Outline essential Shinto teachings in your own words.

8-3 Shinto Teachings

A September 13, 2010, blog in the *New York Times* has a discussion about a writer's remarkable claim that Shinto religion explains the Japanese "love affair" with robots and robotics. He claims that Shinto's blurring of the boundaries between the animate and the inanimate has shaped the positive Japanese view of robots as "helpers" and not as the rebellious, violent machines sometimes portrayed in Western stories and films. These helpers even include the recent invention of a "female" robotic companion for men. As one writer said of Japan, "A humanoid and sentient robot may simply not feel as creepy or threatening as it does in other cultures."[2]

The *Kojiki* and *Nihongi*, Japan's earliest histories, were compiled on the orders of the imperial family in the early 700s C.E. Although they show a political aim to unite all the regional and clan deities under the authority of Sun Goddess Amaterasu, who was the clan deity of the emperor's family, these legends provide an explanation for the basic ideas in Shinto teachings—ideas that endure even today. We begin with three basic concepts that emerge in Shinto teachings about the kami.

8-3a The Kami

First, the kami are not "gods" as Westerners understand them or even as Mahayana Buddhists see them, but should be understood as powerful natural forces with a spiritual dimension. No clear distinction exists between

---

[2] Hiroko Tabuchi, "Robot Invasion Welcomed in Japan," *New York Times*, accessed September 23, 2010, http://lens.blogs.nytimes.com/2010/09/13/robot-invasion-welcomed-in-japan/?scp=3&sq=shinto&st=cse.

what is alive and not living, natural and what is socially constructed, or human and divine. The kami are identified with natural features but are spirits in and beyond those features. One well-placed rock can have a kami just as much as Mount Fuji can. The whole world, including human life, is an expression of spiritual powers. Spiritual power is not found distributed evenly throughout the world, but is especially powerful in particular things, including humans.

Second, the kami are virtually countless. Shinto focuses on the kami that are important to people and influence human life directly. Kami are identified with places—especially forests, mountains, or waterfalls—that seem especially spiritual to the Japanese. They are also identified with awe-inspiring things in nature, such as wind, thunder, and lightning, and with destructive phenomena, such as the earthquakes that regularly shake Japan and tsunamis that sometimes follow them. Additionally, particular kami are identified with ordinary places and activities in human life, such as the kitchen, safety on the roads, education, and other things. Living individuals who have a special charisma or are very successful in business, politics, or life might be called kami. Other spiritual forces are recognized as kami—for example, mischievous elements such as fox spirits or tree spirits. On special occasions, a kami may possess a human medium to send a message.

Third, individuals should know and venerate the kami important to them. Not only is the kami's goodwill required, but the spirits are said to respond to an individual's concern. They are not all-knowing, because their identity and activity are typically restricted to special objects in nature. They want to be informed about significant events that involve their activities, so prayer to the kami will sometimes contain reports about these.

Watch a National Geographic video about Mount Fuji.

8-3b Characteristics of Other Shinto Teachings

The main thing to be said about Shinto teachings is that Shinto has no developed teachings about either this world or the next. It doesn't speak about the original creation of the whole universe, only of Japan. Nor is there anything about a future end of the world.

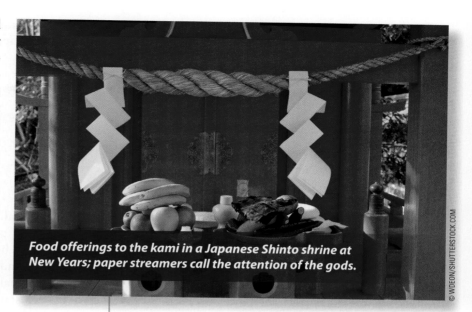

Food offerings to the kami in a Japanese Shinto shrine at New Years; paper streamers call the attention of the gods.

Likewise, there is no clear description of any afterlife. Some Shintoists believe that after people die, they become deeply related to their ancestral kami and have no individual soul in the afterlife, as in much of Mahayana Buddhism. Others believe that their souls go to a shadowy, gloomy underworld; this was probably the original Shinto thought. The living honor the dead as individuals, but they are not individuals as they were in this life.

> *The main thing to be said about Shinto teachings is that Shinto has no developed teachings.*

Learning Outcome 8-4

Describe the main features of Shinto ethics.

8-4 Shinto Ethics

A follower of Shinto goes to a shrine in Kyoto. She has committed a bad act; it's weighing on her mind, and she wants to deal with it. So she goes to her local shrine and there undergoes a simple ritual of purification. She washes at the cleansing station before entering and then contacts one of the shrine priests to pray with her in front of the shrine gods. She leaves, at peace with herself and determined that she will do better. Shinto teaches that humans are born pure. Evil actions and impurity are things that come later in life and can usually be dealt with by simple cleansing or purifying rituals.

8-4a General Characteristics

To identify the distinctly Shinto elements in Japanese ethics isn't easy. Confucian values have inspired much of Japanese social ethics, supplemented by more-individual ethics derived from Buddhist monastic rules. In general, Shinto ethics are based not on a set of commands or of virtues that tells one how to behave, but on following the general will of the kami, understood through myth and ritual. The "way" implied in the word *Shinto* is primarily a ritual way, to keep the relationship with the kami on a proper footing. Good moral practice flows from this relationship.

However, the kami aren't always perfect, so they don't serve as moral examples. Shinto texts tell many stories of kami behaving badly. As we saw above, some of them are mischief makers and therefore wouldn't serve well as role models in such an orderly, proper populace as that of Japan. This clear difference with religions whose gods are morally perfect and can serve as moral examples is probably a main reason why Shinto ethics avoids absolute moral rules.

8-4b Purity

Purity is essential to pleasing the kami, providing a happy life, and turning back disappointment or disease. A number of rituals feature the exorcism of sins in order to restore purity. Cleanliness in particular signifies a good character and freedom from bad external influences. In Western societies one hears the proverb "Cleanliness is next to godliness." In traditional Japanese society, cleanliness—of body, mind, and spirit, both ritual and practical—*is* godliness. To be in harmony with the kami, one must keep one's person, home, and business clean. The Japanese emphasis on freshness and purity in food and drink brings a high quality to the diet, and practically it means that shopping for food is often done every day. Purity in relationships entails being honest, sincere, and thoughtful about how other people feel; therefore, apologies for unintended affronts are very common. The kami particularly dislike blood and death. Therefore, women traditionally were excluded from shrine events during menstruation, as were people who worked with the bodies of dead animals, such as leather makers. Soldiers require special purification after battle, and people helping at funerals need to purify themselves as well.

> *In Western societies one sometimes hears the proverb "Cleanliness is next to godliness." In traditional Japanese society, cleanliness IS godliness.*

The overall aims of Shinto ethics are to promote harmony and purity in all spheres of life. Purity isn't just spiritual, but also moral—having a pure and sincere heart, leading to good conduct. It has a connection with ritual purity: doing things in a certain way, in a certain state, with a certain attitude. Shinto views both human beings and the world as morally good. Evil enters from outside the world of nature and human society, usually by the agency of evil spirits. This affects humans in a manner similar to that of a physical disease. When people do wrong, they bring ritual pollution and moral fault upon themselves. This blocks the blessings of life as they flow from the kami, and must be dealt with in ceremonies of cleansing.

 Read a Shinto statement on ecology.

Learning Outcome 8-5

Outline Shinto worship and other rituals, and explain why they play a leading role in Shinto.

8-5 Shinto Ritual

Most Shinto rituals are tied to the life cycle of humans and the seasonal cycles of nature. Life-cycle rituals include naming ceremonies for children and ceremonies for blessing children as they grow. The time surrounding university entrance exams is particularly trying for Japanese young people, and going to the shrine to pray for success is important for them and their parents. We'll consider the Shinto wedding ritual below. Although Shinto does have a funeral ritual and although the emperor always receives a Shinto service, for more than a thousand years Japanese have preferred Buddhist funerals. Funeral rites will be treated below as well.

Visit a photo and video blog on a 2010 festival honoring the dead.

Incense sticks burn down in a Shinto shrine.

© ISTOCKPHOTO.COM/MATTHEW RAGEN

8-5a The Shinto Shrine

Rituals at Shinto shrines mark one's entry into a different world, the world of the kami. Even in a bustling city, shrines offer a quiet atmosphere removed from the busy noise of modern Japanese life. Surrounded by evergreen trees and approached on a gravel path, everyday conversation is hushed before one enters; the silence is broken only by ritual hand claps or the sounds of nature. Shinto ritual, including music and dance, is remarkably simple and brief, much like the Japanese tea ceremony and quite unlike complex Buddhist ritual. It has a slow, measured pace thought to be pleasing to the kami and contrasting with normal daily life outside. However, at special festivals in and around the shrine this changes dramatically. A mass of local people will be crowded together in noisy festivity, "letting themselves go" in front of the kami in ways they would never dream of doing outside the shrine. Sometimes this includes enough consumption of alcohol to get worshipers slightly drunk. This religious carousing serves as a temporary release from a society that prizes almost-constant orderliness and properness.

Take an interactive tour of a Shinto shrine.

Shrines are built to blend in with the environment chosen by the kami of the place. (See "A Closer Look: A Shinto Prayer for the Blessing of the Crops.") The main sanctuary building of each shrine is the **honden**, in which symbolic sacred objects such as a mirror or a sword are kept at the center front, where they receive worship. Traditionally built from wood and usually left unpainted, the buildings need regular repair or rebuilding by the local community. This is still the tradition of one of Japan's famous shrines, the Ise Shrine, which is reconstructed in time-honored style every twenty years.

See the activities surrounding the ritual rebuilding of the Ise Shrine.

The kami dwell near, not in, the shrines and must be invited politely. As we saw above, at least one torii marks the entrance to a shrine, and a basin is just inside to rinse one's hands and mouth. A shrine is usually dedicated to one particular kami but may host any number of smaller shrines

honden [HAHN-den] Main sanctuary building of a Shinto shrine

A Closer Look:

A Shinto Prayer for the Blessing of the Crops

This Shinto prayer found in the *Yengishiki* prayer book clearly demonstrates the Shinto feeling for kami and the natural world.

I declare in the great presence of Amaterasu who sits in Ise:

Because the sovereign great goddess bestows on him [the emperor] the countries of the four quarters over which her glance extends—

As far as the limit where Heaven stands up like a wall,
As far as the bounds where the country stands up distant,
As far as the limit where the blue clouds spread flat,
As far as the bounds where the white clouds lie away fallen—
The blue sea plain as far as the limit, where come the prows of the ships,

The ships which continuously crowd on the great sea plain,
And the roads which men travel by land,
as far as the limit whither come the horses' hoofs,
with the baggage cords tied tightly,
treading the uneven rocks and tree roots,
and lining up continuously in a long path without a break.

Making the narrow countries wide and the hilly countries plain,
And drawing together the distant countries by throwing, so to speak, many ropes over them,
He will pile up his crops like a range of hills in the great presence of the sovereign great goddess, and will peacefully enjoy the remainder.

representing other kami that local people should also venerate. Sacred places, such as particular trees and rocks, will be marked off by ropes of elaborately plaited straw or by streamers of plain paper. The kami are summoned by a series of brief actions: ringing a bell outside the shrine, making a money offering, clapping hands twice, saying a short silent prayer, and bowing twice.

8-5b The Shinto Priesthood

The work of Shinto priests is located largely in the shrine. New Shinto priests, like their Japanese Buddhist monk counterparts, must now be university graduates. Women priests are to be found, but they aren't nearly as numerous as men, because traditional Japanese society is still strongly patriarchal. Most priests are "volunteers" who have their main jobs outside the shrines. They are typically married and have families.

> "The contemporary miko is typically a university student collecting a modest wage in this part-time position."
> —Lisa Kuly

The Shinto priesthood exists mainly to carry out Shinto rituals and run the shrines, and duties such as teaching, religious counseling, etc., are minor activities for the priests. Traditionally, the priesthood was limited to the great shrines, and it rotated among the able men of the community. But now this has been opened up to many shrines and has also grown to about twenty thousand monastics, including two thousand women. All but the smallest shrines are staffed by a team of priests of various ranks, assisted by a team of shrine maidens (the miko discussed above). These miko assist with shrine functions, assist priests in ceremonies, perform ceremonial dances, sell souvenirs, and distribute omikuji (see below). Lisa Kuly writes that today's miko is typically "a university student collecting a modest wage in this part-time position."[3] A miko is traditionally dressed in red trousers, a white kimono

ema [AY-muh] Wooden plaque inscribed with prayers and wishes

omikuji [OH-mee-KOO-jee] Fortunes on preprinted slips of paper

jacket, and white or red hair ribbons. Shinto has no overall leader in Japan, and each shrine is self-governed and self-supporting through offerings and donations by worshipers. Most shrines are associated through a national shrine organization.

8-5c Prayer Plaques and Fortunes

In Shinto shrines, it's common to see **emas**, small wooden plaques hung in prominent places. Worshipers buy an ema, write personal wishes and hopes on the reverse, and then hang it near a sacred tree together with emas made by others. The kami then read them and help make them come true. This ritual is understood today more as "asking for wishes" or "making hopes" than as praying, although prayers can also be written on an ema.

Next, we should discuss the **omikuji**, literally "sacred drawing/lottery." They are fortunes on preprinted slips of paper. For an offering of about 100 yen (approximately one dollar), worshipers can obtain an omikuji from a person at a shrine desk, or even from

A Japanese woman ties an omikuji at Sensoji Shrine in Tokyo.

---

[3] Lisa Kuly, "Locating Transcendence in Japanese Minzoku Geino," *Ethnologies* 25 (2003): 201.

a vending machine. Opening the paper allows one to see a fortune that has several items on it. The first deals with the general category of "blessing" and ranges from "great blessing" to "great curse." Then it gives fortunes for various aspects of life—for example, business, schooling, the stock market, falling in love, and others. (No matter the general category of blessing, in the area of schooling every omikuji advises one to study more, study harder, and the like!) If the prediction is bad, the paper is folded up and attached to a tree, to ropes, or to wires. If the prediction is favorable, one can either take it home or tie it up in the shrine; the latter is more common.

Love is in your future.

We connect the fortune cookie with China, but some think that it comes from the Japanese omikuji.

KEITH BEL/SHUTTERSTOCK.COM

> *The Shinto priesthood exists mainly to carry out Shinto rituals and run the shrines, and duties such as teaching and religious counseling are minor activities for the priests.*

8-5d The Wedding Ceremony

The Shinto priest (or priests) and the mikos conduct the wedding ceremony at the front of a shrine, after a formal procession. The families are present in the room. The groom and bride typically wear formal Japanese clothes. After the couple is ritually purified, the priest offers prayers for their good fortune and happiness, as well as for protection and guidance by the kami. Then the miko serves three sips of purified rice wine to the wedding couple. Brief words are spoken to the kami and rings are exchanged, followed by the offering of a small sacred evergreen branch. One more sip of rice wine is shared, and the ritual is complete.

8-5e The Home Shrine

Traditional Japanese show respect for the kami by having a small shrine or worship space in their house or outdoors. They also have a **kamidana**, a "kami shelf" on which small statues of the kami are placed, sometimes along with small memorial tablets containing the names of ancestors. The kamidana is typically placed so high on a wall that it is near the ceiling. It holds several different items, at the center of which is a small circular mirror, a stone, or a jewel. Worship at the kamidana includes placing flowers; offering food such as rice, fruit, and water; and saying short prayers. Family members carefully cleanse their hands with water before they perform these daily rituals.

>>> See a video of a kamidana for sale.

kamidana [KAH-mee-DAH-nuh] "Kami shelf" found in most private homes

A wedding procession at the Meiji Shrine, Tokyo: main priest, assistant priest, temple maidens, bride (with white hood), groom, and family members

© IAIN MASTERSON/ALAMY

8-5f The Shinto Funeral

As we saw above, Japan is a land of multiple religions, which affects how the Japanese deal with death and how they believe in an afterlife. Keeping memorial tablets with the names of one's ancestors in household shrines and offering food and drink to them is Confucian in origin. In ritual matters of entering the afterlife, such as funerals and memorial services for deceased relatives, a Buddhist priest officiates with basically Buddhist rites.

The general lines of the historic funeral rite are still discernible in villages. It particularly applies to men who are heads of households; in what follows, we will describe this sort of funeral. In towns and cities today, the rite has been adapted or lost, especially as the burial of cremated remains has replaced full-body burial for reasons of space and cost. The immediate family members of the deceased keep themselves in their houses. The men of the neighborhood gather near the family home to make the items required for the funeral, including paper flags containing prayers, paper processional lanterns, and a wooden candlestick. The women prepare the food required for the feast, given before the burial. One woman of the neighborhood has the special honor of sewing a white pilgrim's cloak that will shroud the body for its journey to the land of the dead. Meanwhile, the men who will be pallbearers dig a grave in the cemetery.

The spirit of the dead is thought to still be present and listening, so as the relatives shroud the body, they politely describe out loud the tasks they are performing. To mask the odor of death, burning incense is kept nearby. So that the spirit may pay the ferryman for passage into eternity, a bag with a few coins is put near the body; also, meditation beads are entwined in the dead man's hand. A fan is laid in the coffin, together with a small favorite object belonging to the deceased. The Buddhist priest tells the spirit of the dead to begin its journey to the land of the dead, and other ancient formulas are recited. On completing their tasks, the family members wash their hands in saltwater.

The funeral procession reaches the cemetery with a lot of noise. For the grave, a round hole has been made, just big enough to pass the body through. The hole widens continuously as it goes deeper, until it is much wider at the usual depth of six feet. (This requires some skill at digging the grave from the top.) At the bottom, to one side, a large compartment, approximately six feet long and four feet wide, has been excavated. The body is taken out of the coffin and laid into the grave on straw floor mats along with the objects put earlier into the coffin. The oldest son praises his father for his honorable life as his mother continues to pray for the soul of her husband.

A few days after the burial, the family holds a "feast of consecration," at which time they feed and entertain numerous guests. This feast ends with a procession in which relatives, friends, and neighbors wear sackcloth. The property of the deceased is then divided, with the oldest son receiving most of it. In older times a small "memorial house" was built over the grave; more commonly today, a tombstone is erected. At each of these events a Buddhist priest recites prayers before the deceased's portrait. Although the number of commemorative meals varies, they are still common in Japan today as the conclusion of the funeral ritual. Life is then expected to return to normal.

Learning Outcome 8-6

Explain why the practice of Shinto in North America is so small.

8-6 Shinto around the World Today

Shinto has a very small presence outside of Japan. Shintoists do not seek or even encourage converts, so almost all followers of Shinto are Japanese. Because the kami are tied so closely to the land of Japan, Japanese people living in the wider world often have a lessened connection with Shinto. Although the people of and in Japan combine Shinto with Buddhism, people of Japanese descent living outside Japan typically see themselves only as Buddhists if they keep to one of the traditional Japanese religions. One estimate of Shintoists in North America has them at only two thousand people. In the recent Canadian census, fewer than 1 percent of the approximately one hundred thousand Japanese Canadians called themselves Shintoists. In the United States, most of those who practice Shinto are found on the West Coast. They are served by a small number of Shinto shrines, including the Tsubaki Shinto Shrine in Granite Falls, Washington. Of course, Shintoists in North America can and do have kamidanas in their

SHIGTHENEWT

Entrance to the Tsubaki Shinto Shrine in Granite Falls, Washington

homes, at which the simple, regular home rituals can take place.

Even though the formal presence of Shinto in the West is remarkably small, it has a certain appeal to some Westerners today. Its reverence for nature, feeling for ritual, and open acknowledgment of pluralism (at least in a Buddhist and Confucian context) have attracted independent-minded religious seekers. Small movements to practice Shinto have arisen here and there in North America. Whether or not Shinto will have a larger role in North America, it will probably continue for the foreseeable future to be a significant feature of life in Japan.

Study Tools 8

Ready to study? In the book you can:

- Review Learning Outcome answers and glossary terms with the tear-out Chapter Review card.

Or you can go online to CourseMate, at www.cengagebrain.com, for these resources:

- Chapter quizzes to prepare for tests
- Interactive flashcards of all glossary terms
- A timeline of events for this chapter
- An eBook with introductions, interactive quizzes, and live links for all web resources in the chapter

CHAPTER 9

Encountering Zoroastrianism: The Way of the One Wise Lord

BONNIE VAN VOORST © CENGAGE LEARNING

Learning Outcomes

After studying this chapter, you will be able to do the following:

9-1 Explain the meaning of *Zoroastrianism* and related terms.

9-2 Outline how Zoroastrianism developed over time into what it is today.

9-3 Explain the essential Zoroastrian teachings of monotheism and moral dualism.

9-4 State the main ethical precepts of Zoroastrianism.

9-5 Outline the way Zoroastrians worship and observe rituals.

9-6 State the main features of Zoroastrian life around the world today, especially in North America.

Study Tools

After you read this chapter, go to the Study Tools section at the end of the chapter, page 225.

© RELIGIOUS IMAGES/UIG/GETTY

"I acknowledge my faith in Good Thoughts, Good Words, and Good Deeds, the Good Religion of Ahura Mazda." —*Zoroastrian declaration of faith*

Your Visit to Yazd, Iran

For more than a year you've planned and prepared for a hiking trip through Iran. You've been careful to get the correct visa and learn about cultural ways. Now that you're hiking there, you come across fascinating remains of the past as you approach the ancient city of Yazd (yahzd) on the ancient Silk Road. You already know about the importance of Silk Road caravan trade routes that ran from China to the Mediterranean Sea. Now you see the remains of a stone way station on the Silk Road, one of hundreds that are spaced every thirty kilometers. They had lodging and food for humans and animals—even running water. It occurs to you that they were like full-service rest stops along this ancient highway.

Yazd is the historic center of Zoroastrianism (ZOHR-oh-ASS-tree-uh-NIHZ-uhm) in present-day Iran, although many Iranian Zoroastrians now live in the capital city, Tehran. Yazd has an active Zoroastrian temple, one of the most beautiful in the world, housing a fire that the faithful believe has burned for more than a thousand years. Zoroastrians are not "fire worshipers," as you may have heard some Iranians say, but use fire as a symbol of the spiritual essence of God.

You hoped to hike out into the desert to Chak-Chak, an important pilgrimage site for Zoroastrians about 110 kilometers north of Yazd, to see a four-day festival that was about to start. But then you hear that only the faithful can attend the festival and that the temple will be closed at that time to non-Zoroastrians, so you travel out there right away before the festival starts. Chak-Chak, literally "drip-drip" in Persian, is a small group of buildings constructed on the side of a mountain cliff. According to legend, a Zoroastrian princess who was fleeing the invading Muslim Arab armies escaped from Yazd into the desert. She arrived at this cliff and was cornered, with the army closing in on her. She prayed to God to be spared, and the cliff opened and she disappeared inside forever. From that time on, dripping water from a spring has marked the place of her rescue. Legends such as this one have helped Zoroastrians cope with the predominantly Muslim nation in which they find themselves.

Back in Yazd the next day, you hike out of town to the round stone "towers of silence" built on the hills, used as the funeral buildings for Zoroastrians until recent times. After climbing to the top of a tower, you think about the somber scene. For more than two thousand years, Zoroastrians didn't bury or cremate their dead, believing that this would contaminate the earth. Instead, they left dead bodies in these towers, to be eaten there by vultures until only clean bones remained to be bleached white by the sun. The bones were then swept into a central depository within the tower, but you can't see them any longer. On the plains of Yazd below, you see partially ruined temples and buildings used for funeral rites. Beyond the ruins, you can see the well-maintained, modern Zoroastrian cemetery where the faithful now bury their dead inside concrete-lined graves. You take in the whole scene from the tower, amazed by how this site is so peaceful now. The towers are indeed silent.

What Do YOU Think?

The belief that the world is locked in a cosmic struggle between good and evil, as Zoroastrians hold, makes for a powerful faith.

Strongly Disagree						Strongly Agree
1	2	3	4	5	6	7

Visit Chak-Chak and Yazd in an ABC Australia video.

Explore Zoroastrianism in Yazd, Iran, on Google Earth™.

Zoroastrian priests officiate at a fire sacrifice.

Zoroastrian pilgrimage shrine in Chak-Chak

© ARAZU/SHUTTERSTOCK.COM

from so long ago that is still present today deserves to be studied carefully. But scholars also study Zoroastrianism today for a wider reason: to discern the possible influence of this religion on other Western religions. Scholars generally conclude that Zoroastrianism had a direct influence on ancient Judaism and then some indirect influence (mainly through Judaism) on Christianity and Islam. The exact extent of this influence is sharply debated. On the one hand, a leading scholar of Zoroastrianism, Mary Boyce, argues for a maximum influence: "Zoroastrianism has probably had more influence on human life, directly and indirectly, than any other single faith." She also argues that Zoroastrianism's teachings on judgment, heaven and hell, the resurrection of the body, and eternal life were borrowed by Judaism, Christianity, and Islam.[1] This position is frequently seen on the Web. On the other hand, Hebrew Bible scholar James Barr and others have argued that significant borrowing of Zoroastrian ideas, directly or indirectly, cannot be demonstrated in early Judaism, aside from a few small points of contact. Barr argues as well that later Christian and Islamic beliefs cannot be shown to have drawn from Zoroastrianism.[2] In any case, Christians and many people who aren't Christians know about the Bible's story of the "wise men from the east" visiting the newborn Jesus to honor him and bring him gifts. Two of these gifts, frankincense and myrrh, have been offered in Zoroastrian worship for more than 2,500 years now. The term the Bible uses for the wise men (which we will consider below) is a special Zoroastrian word for their priests.

In your study of Zoroastrianism, these unique, initially puzzling features may appear:

- Zoroastrians place a strong emphasis on morality in thought, word, and deed. But unlike many other religions that stress moral purity, Zoroastrianism deals with hundreds of ritual impurities, because these are thought to ruin the effect of moral deeds.

- Zoroastrianism is a monotheistic religion, teaching that only one God exists. But it also features dozens of other spirits—good and bad, most of them named—who have large roles in human life. Sometimes they are even called "divinities," as for example on the opening page of a matchmaking website for Zoroastrians, which invokes the power of Ava Ardvisur, the "Divinity of fertility and childbirth."

Begun thousands of years ago by Zarathustra, the prophet known to the Greeks as Zoroaster, Zoroastrianism became the state religion of the ancient Persian and Sassanid empires. Some historians estimate that it had as many as 40 million followers, making it one of the largest religions in the ancient world. Today its numbers are severely reduced, for reasons we will explore in this chapter. At most 150,000 adherents, the overwhelming majority of them ethnic Persians, are clustered in eastern Iran and Mumbai (Bombay), India, and about another 50,000 are scattered in twenty-three nations of the world, including 20,000 in North America. These numbers are estimates, because exact numbers are hard to come by.

> "Zoroastrianism has probably had more influence on human life, directly and indirectly, than any other single faith." —Mary Boyce

Despite the reduced number of followers, the study of Zoroastrianism has an appeal all its own. Any religion

---

[1] Mary Boyce, *Zoroastrians: Their Religious Beliefs and Practices* (London: Routledge and Kegan Paul, 1979), 1, 29.

[2] James Barr, "The Question of Religious Influence: The Case of Zoroastrianism, Judaism, and Christianity," *Journal of the American Academy of Religion* 53 (1985): 201–35.

Zoroastrianism has a proud past, but many of its followers fear for its future. It was once perhaps the world's largest religion, but now it has been reduced to around 200,000 members. Many observers think that it may die out, at least in its traditional form, by the end of the twenty-first century.

View a BBC introduction to Zoroastrianism.

Learning Outcome 9-1

Explain the meaning of *Zoroastrianism* and related terms.

9-1 Names for Zoroastrianism and Zoroastrians

Zoroastrianism is the common designation of the ancient Persian monotheistic religion. This name is built from the Greek form of the name of its founder, Zoroaster (ZOHR-oh-ASS-ter). The founder is known as **Zarathustra** in the religion's most ancient writings. *Zoroastrianism* was originally a European name for the faith and reflects the European tendency to name religions after their founders whether the religions themselves do so or not. Zarathustra would probably not have been pleased with this name. But *Zoroastrianism* "stuck," and followers of the faith use it today.

Zarathustra [ZAHR-uh-THOOS-truh] Original name of the founder of Zoroastrianism, now widely called "Zoroaster"

faravahar [FAHR-uh-VAH-har] "Divine glory," winged symbol of Zoroastrianism stressing morality

> *Zoroastrianism was originally a European name and reflects a tendency to name religions after their founders.*

Ancient Zoroastrian sources called it the "Good Religion," not in a generic sense (after all, what religion doesn't think of itself as good?) but as pointing especially to the key role of struggle for good in Zoroastrianism. This moral dimension of the faith is richly reflected in its symbol, the **faravahar** (or farohar), which means "Divine glory" (see "A Closer Look: The Symbol of Zoroastrianism"). More specifically, Zoroastrians have

A Closer Look:

The Symbol of Zoroastrianism

BONNIE VAN VOORST
© CENGAGE LEARNING

Zoroastrianism has had a few different symbols throughout its history. One ancient symbol still seen today is a sacrificial fire burning in a ritual urn. But the symbol closely associated with Zoroastrianism for more than 2,500 years is the faravahar, the figure of a human being with eagle's wings. Its origins are debated. Some think that it originally represented Ahura Mazda, because it seems to draw some elements from the symbols of gods in Assyrian religion. However, Zoroastrians have always considered God to be a spirit that cannot be depicted.

The central human figure represents the individual Zoroastrian believer. The figure is obviously a male, with the long beard that Persian men wore, but this hasn't prevented Zoroastrian women from identifying with the symbol. He is aged in appearance, so the soul is wise. He wears a traditional Persian hat, suggesting respect for culture. One hand is open and lifted upward, symbolic of faith in and obedience to Ahura Mazda. The other hand holds a ring, which may represent loyalty and faithfulness. The circle around the center of the human figure stands for the immortality of the soul or the eternal significance of human actions in the here and now.

The two wings have three main rows of feathers, representing good thoughts, good words, and good deeds. Doing these things lifts up one's soul as on powerful wings. The tail below also has three rows of feathers, said to signify bad thoughts, bad words, and bad deeds. The two streamers below the human figure represent the spirits of good and evil. Every person must constantly choose between the two, so the figure is facing the good and turning his back on evil.

Mazdayasnian religion [MAHZ-duh-YAHZ-nee-uhn] Name of Zoroastrianism used in the past by most Zoroastrians

Ahura Mazda [ah-HOOR-uh MAHZ-duh] "Wise Lord," the single, all-powerful god worshiped by Zoroastrians

Parsis [PAR-seez] Name for Zoroastrians in India, also spelled "Parsees"

Axial Age Name given by philosopher Karl Jaspers to the period from 600 to 400 B.C.E. when many religions and value (axial) systems were founded

called their faith the "Mazda-worshiping" or **Mazdayasnian religion**. The latter name refers to **Ahura Mazda**, the "Wise Lord," who is the only God. He created the universe as a place in which good will eventually prevail. This book will follow the current scholarly convention of referring to the name of the religion as Zoroastrianism and the name of its founder as Zarathustra.

One other name for Zoroastrians has become important. Zoroastrians who moved to India from Iran in the 900s C.E. are called **Parsis** (sometimes spelled "Parsees"), a name derived from *Persians*. The Zoroastrian communities in east Africa, Great Britain, and North America descend largely from this group, so the term has spread beyond India. *Parsis* is often used as a synonym of *Zoroastrians*.

Learning Outcome 9-2

Outline how Zoroastrianism developed over time into what it is today.

9-2 Zoroastrianism as Shaped by Its Past

Freddie Mercury (1946–1991), the lead singer in the British band Queen, was one of the most prominent Zoroastrians in the twentieth century. Born as Farrokh Bulsara to a Zoroastrian family in present-day Tanzania, he was raised as a devout Zoroastrian and was initiated into the faith as a teenager. Mercury sang many hit songs, including "Bohemian Rhapsody," "We Are the Champions," and "Crazy Little Thing Called Love." Although he hadn't formally observed his ancestral religion as an adult, his funeral in London was led (at Mercury's wishes) by Zoroastrian priests. It was conducted entirely in the Avestan language and included prayers and hymns from the Zoroastrian scriptures. After the service, his body was cremated. The debate over Mercury's legacy indicates a divide in modern Zoroastrianism:

Can it be followed by keeping just its main moral commands, as some argue Mercury tried to do, or is it necessary to keep the full, traditional way of life of Zoroastrianism, as he did not?

The early history of Zoroastrianism is still shrouded in the mists of antiquity. We aren't certain of many key details about its beginnings, because most of its earliest writings were destroyed in persecutions. But closer to our time, Zoroastrianism emerged from the mists of time and became a key religion in the world. It can be divided into three main periods: birth and formation (ca. 630–550 B.C.E.); growth into the official religion of the Persian Empire, decline under Greek and Parthian rule, and revival and renewed official status in the Sassanian Empire (550 B.C.E.–650 C.E.); and slow, steady decline under Islamic rulers and in the modern world (650 C.E.–today).

> *Zoroastrianism emerged from the mists of time and became a key religion in the world.*

9-2a The Birth of Zoroastrianism (ca. 630–550 B.C.E.)

The question of when Zarathustra lived isn't easy to answer. A few scholars and many traditional Zoroastrians date it all the way back to 7500 B.C.E., at what they consider the dawn of human civilization; others hold to a time between 1400 and 900 B.C.E. Commonly today, historians put his birth around 630 B.C.E., at the beginning of the **Axial Age** in Europe and Asia. Modern philosopher Karl Jaspers gave this term to the period from 600 to 400 B.C.E. when many religions and value (*axial*) systems were founded. This wide chronological range, so unusual for dating the founder of a major religion, shows that firm evidence for the life of Zarathustra is lacking. The Zoroastrian scriptures that he is thought to have authored, the central chapters of the *Gathas*, do not locate him chronologically. No historical sources outside the religion give reliable information that can be used in dating his life. Moreover, Zoroastrian scriptures weren't typically written down until about 400 C.E., at least a thousand years after the events they relate.

The birth of Zarathustra is said by some sacred writings to have been foretold by prophecies and accompanied by miraculous signs. For example, the glory of Ahura Mazda descended on Zarathustra's mother, resulting in a virginal conception, and the baby was said to have laughed when he was born. The main outline of Zarathustra's teaching, which he gave to disciples and at the court of the Persian kings, can be reliably traced, although the details are sketchy. The ancient Persians were polytheistic, as were all other Indo-European peoples. The basic structure of Persian polytheism was probably the same as that of Vedic Hinduism. For example, both religions worshiped many gods in nature, sacrificed animals whose souls were thought to join the gods, and used a hallucinogenic drug in occasional sacrifices.

Zarathustra saw this religion as mistaken. He had a revolutionary monotheistic vision that only one god existed, Ahura Mazda. He also had a vision of an evil figure (supernatural but not divine), named Angra Mainyu, who opposed God. Zarathustra taught that all people had to choose which of these two moral forces they would follow, a choice that would either improve the world or make it worse. This choice determined the judgment by God of a disposition to heaven or hell when they died, but Zarathustra taught that a final restoration would come when Ahura Mazda completely defeated the forces of evil. In this restoration, even hell would come to an end, and all people would then be resurrected with a re-created body to an eternal, blessed life. Despite the up-and-down fortunes of this faith, Zarathustra's powerful teaching has endured through today.

9-2b The Spread of Zoroastrianism in the Persian and Sassanian Empires (550 B.C.E.–650 C.E.)

The first certain date in Zoroastrian history is its establishment in Persia during the reign of the Persian kings, beginning in 550 B.C.E. These kings created and ruled over the largest empire the world had yet seen, and Zoroastrianism spread with it (see Map 9.1). Some Persian kings drew explicitly on the religion for the legitimacy of their empire, claiming that Ahura Mazda wanted his fame and goodness spread throughout the world. However, the Persians never attempted to impose Zoroastrianism on subject peoples with other religions. Given the religion's monotheism and moral rigor based on individual choice—religious ideas not widely shared in the ancient Middle East—this was a wise policy. Persian rule was autocratic, but it respected and even embraced cultural and religious differences in its subjects. As the ancient Greek historian Herodotus wrote, "No nation so readily adopts foreign customs as the Persians do."[3]

Cyrus (SY-rus) II, later called Cyrus the Great, ruled the small Persia homeland from 550 to 530 B.C.E. He began the expansion of Persia by overthrowing the king of Media to the north, and he kept on marching. Within ten years he had conquered much of the Middle East. He was a faithful Zoroastrian, as were the emperors of Persia who came after him, but tolerant toward other religions in his empire. When he captured Babylon, he rebuilt the temple of its main god, Marduk (MAHR-dook). The **Cyrus Cylinder**, an archaeological treasure from Cyrus's time, tells how he released many captive peoples held in Babylonia, allowing them to return to their homes and pursue their religions. For example, Cyrus allowed the thousands of Jews taken to Babylon in 586 B.C.E. to return to Jerusalem in 539, to rebuild their temple and land as a loyal part of the Persian Empire. Historians who argue for a large influence of Zoroastrianism on Judaism typically point to this "Persian period" in Jewish history as the time when it occurred.

> "No nation so readily adopts foreign customs as the Persians do."
> —Herodotus, ancient Greek historian

Cyrus Cylinder Artifact recording Cyrus's rule, including his release of captive peoples

Read Herodotus' short essay on the Persians.

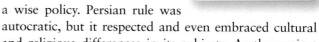

Watch a presentation on "2600 Years of History in One Object," the Cyrus Cylinder.

Miniature relief carving of Cyrus the Great

© ISTOCKPHOTO.COM/GRAEME GILMOUR

---

[3] William Stearns Davis, "Readings in Ancient History: Illustrative Extracts from the Sources", vol. 2, *Greece and the East* (Boston: Allyn and Bacon, 1912), 60.

Darius (dah-RY-us) I, called "Darius the Great," ruled from 521 to 486 B.C.E. He is known mainly for his great building projects, such as a spectacular new capital at Persepolis. He was adept at managing his empire and expanded Persian rule to its greatest extent. Darius referred to Ahura Mazda in his royal inscriptions as the source of his successes, and he had monumental faravahars carved on many walls in Persepolis and in older cities. He attempted to conquer Greece, but wasn't successful.

Darius's son Xerxes (ZUHRK-seez), who ruled from 486 to 465 B.C.E., also tried to conquer Greece, this time with a massive effort. Like his father, he failed. Several relatively small Greek city-states turned back the mighty Persian Empire, marking a turning point in Persian fortunes. (This story is told in historical-fantasy form by the much-mocked 2006 film *300*, with its false depiction of the Persians and of Xerxes.) Xerxes and his successors changed the policy of tolerating different religions and ethnic groups as their predecessors had, betraying Zoroastrian values. Local and regional imperial officials were now drawn only from Persian ranks, not as before from local national and ethnic groups. Over the next hundred years, the empire suffered from various revolts and struggles over the throne. It was greatly reduced in size and splendor by the time Alexander the Great of Macedon, a nation that had once been a part of the Persian Empire, easily toppled it in 334 B.C.E.

Zoroastrians today see much to be proud of in this period, including the birth and early growth of their faith. But they view the accomplishments as short-lived due to the onslaught of Alexander. They blame him for many of the troubles of later Zoroastrianism. In fact, Zoroastrians have so hated Alexander that they have called him not "Alexander the Great" but "Alexander the Accursed." They cursed him for murdering priests and scholars, extinguishing ritual fires, destroying temples, and carrying off sacred writings and having them burned or (worse) translated for non-Zoroastrians. Some of these charges are no doubt exaggerated; Alexander, like the Persians, tended to be basically tolerant of other religions. But the fact remains that Alexander overthrew the empire to which Zoroastrianism had become closely connected, and the faith was greatly damaged in the process. In particular, the loss of much of the sacred literature at this time and in later book burnings means that we are no longer able to reconstruct the history of Zoroastrian teachings.

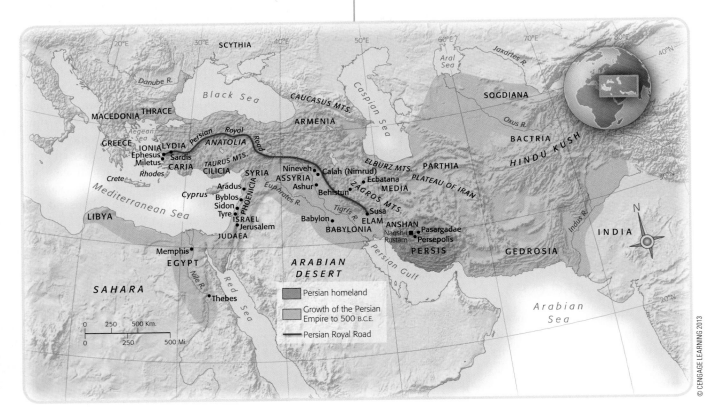

Map 9.1
The Zoroastrian Persian Empire, ca. 500 B.C.E.
At its height around 500 B.C.E., the Persian Empire controlled a huge territory that included northern Greece, Egypt, and most of western Asia, from the Mediterranean coast to the Indus River in India.

Zoroastrianism struggled under Hellenistic, Roman, and Parthian rule, which controlled parts of its homeland from 334 B.C.E. until 224 C.E. But Zoroastrian religious leaders praised the kings of the Sassanian Empire (224–651 C.E.; also known as "Sassanid") for powerfully reestablishing the religion. For the second time, Zoroastrianism was the official religion of a large empire (see Map 9.2). This was the "golden age" of Zoroastrianism. Several Sassanian rulers featured Zoroastrian symbols in official inscriptions and coins. Their patronage enabled the establishment of many Zoroastrian temples and the rise of a professional priesthood to staff them. The **Avesta**, the first and basic Zoroastrian scripture, was collected. **Towers of silence**, stone funeral structures for the Zoroastrian dead, were built throughout the land. In the Sassanian period, Zoroastrianism reached the basic form that it would keep through today.

The Sassanians presented themselves as pious Zoroastrians, putting religious images on their coins and buildings.

Later sources celebrated some Sassanian kings as a blessing to Zoroastrianism. Zoroastrians still use the date of the coronation of the last Sassanian king, Yazdgird, in 631 C.E. as the first year of their calendar (for example, 2013 C.E. = 1382 Y). However, modern Iranian Zoroastrians blame the Sassanians for beginning the decline of their religion, saying that its misuse for political purposes led to the downfall of the empire. Zoroastrian religion had been too closely tied to imperial rule, they say, and the strong moral essence of the religion was compromised. Arabic Muslim forces conquered the Sassanian Empire around 650 C.E. As happened earlier with Alexander's conquest of the Persian Empire, the brutal Muslim conquest of the Sassanian Empire caused

Avesta [ah-VEHS-tuh] First and basic Zoroastrian scripture

tower of silence Stone funeral structure where the Zoroastrian dead were placed and bones stored; no longer used in most locations

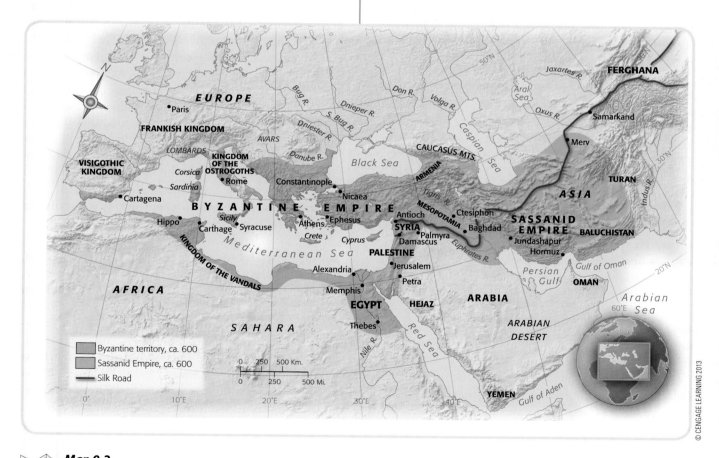

© CENGAGE LEARNING 2013

Map 9.2
The Sassanian and Byzantine Empires, 600 C.E.
By 600 C.E., the Christian Byzantine Empire controlled the eastern Mediterranean. The neighboring Zoroastrian Sassanian Empire dominated most of inland western Asia. It was centered in the older Persian homeland, which today is in southern Iran.

great damage to the state-sponsored Zoroastrian religion. Zoroastrians found themselves in a Muslim empire that would, over time, further reduce their numbers and influence.

9-2c The Coming of Islam and the Zoroastrian Dispersion (650 C.E.–Present)

The Arabic conquest of the Sassanian Empire began a process of Islamic growth and Zoroastrian decline that would last for centuries. Muslim rulers considered Zoroastrians to be "People of the Book" and did not forcibly convert them, but most converted to Islam nonetheless, probably drawn by its rigorous monotheism and strict morality. Those who remained Zoroastrians had their religious liberty restricted, and they were often persecuted. Up to three-quarters of their sacred literature was destroyed. A few times, various Zoroastrian communities openly revolted against their Muslim overlords, only to be crushed and decimated. By 900 C.E. the Zoroastrians were reduced to such a small minority that they were concentrated in a few areas of Iran.

These pressures on the Iranian Zoroastrians led many to flee to the western coast of India, in the Gujarat area, in 936 C.E. In the course of time, they developed a specific ethnic identity with a strong sense of shared history, and even a language they named Parsi-Gujarati. The Hindu authorities tolerated Zoroastrianism, but did not allow conversions of Hindus to Zoroastrianism (which Zoroastrians prohibited as well) or even Hindu visits to Zoroastrian temples. For centuries, Zoroastrians in India had their own dress and diet codes. These have now largely disappeared in everyday life but are carefully observed on important occasions such as holidays, weddings, and funerals. Thus began the development of two different communities of Zoroastrians, Iranians and Parsis, a split that continues. An effort in the early twenty-first century to found an organization for all Zoroastrians failed to overcome the old differences.

The Parsi communities blossomed during Mughal (Islamic) and British rule in India. These latter groups were more tolerant of Zoroastrianism than were the rulers of Iran. Many Parsis today regard these times as a high point of their community's history—in material wealth, social prestige, cultural achievements, and political influence. Zoroastrians in India prospered economically in commerce and the professions. An unprecedented number of temples were built, most of them in urban Mumbai, still the modern stronghold of Zoroastrianism.

> *The Arabic conquest of the Sassanian Empire began a process of Islamic growth and Zoroastrian decline that would last for centuries.*

At the same time, Zoroastrianism underwent considerable change beginning around 1800. The fear of demons and of unwitting ritual pollution that characterized earlier Zoroastrianism ended. The socioreligious position of the clergy declined, and lay participation in leadership was firmly established, along with certain rights for women. Social and religious reform movements representing a minority of Parsis started to fight against what they regarded as Zoroastrian "superstitions" and advocated a return to what their members considered the original teachings of Zarathustra. Since the late nineteenth century, the question of the permissibility of conversion to Zoroastrianism and mixed marriages has fueled an ongoing debate about Zoroastrian identity. Parsis did not permit conversion to their religion, and although intermarriage with people of other faiths happens in many Zoroastrian families, it is still regarded as taboo. The religious status of persons of other religions who marry Zoroastrians, and the children born of such marriages, is still a matter of controversy today almost everywhere Zoroastrians are found.

Indian independence in 1949 was a mixed blessing for the Parsis. It brought a greater measure of freedom, but it also brought the challenge of numerical decline. Parsis now number fewer than seventy thousand, down from more than one hundred thousand a century ago. Part of this decline is due to a reluctance to procreate—typical of modern groups with upper-class social standing such as that of the Parsis—but this is clearly at odds with the exhortations to bear children that can be found throughout Zoroastrian religious literature. Migration has also contributed to dwindling numbers in India. Starting with the late 1700s, Parsis settled in distant parts of the British Empire—including Chinese port cities, Burma, Ceylon, and parts of Africa—but mainly in Britain itself. Since the 1960s, new waves of immigration

Read a 2004 interview with the leader of India's Zoroastrians.

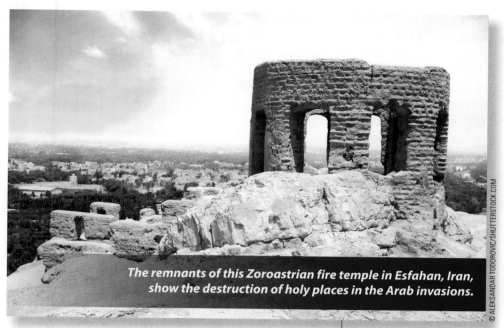

The remnants of this Zoroastrian fire temple in Esfahan, Iran, show the destruction of holy places in the Arab invasions.

The *Yasna* (YAHZ-nuh) ceremony, for example, which the Parsis regard as an important liturgy (it takes a pair of trained priests several hours to perform it), is celebrated only rarely nowadays, and in a drastically reduced format; only a few Iranian priests can perform it. Purification rituals have largely been discarded. The professional priesthood has seen a sharp decline, and the leading priests have joined the social and intellectual elite in a crusade to uproot ancient "superstition" in the faith, including some rituals for women, devotion to "lesser" divinities such as Mithra, and animal sacrifice. The fear of being called "fire worshipers" led the Iranian community to emphasize the symbolic role of fire in their worship; new temples occasionally even have gas fires. Consecrated wood fires are still kept burning but aren't tended according to past ritual.

took Parsis to North America, Australia, New Zealand, and the Persian Gulf nations.

In Iran, Zoroastrianism had been reduced to a tiny minority of fewer than ten thousand by 1900. These believers had to bear a wide range of harsh discriminatory practices from the dominant Muslim population. Help from Zoroastrians in India and substantial political and legal changes improved the lot of the Iranian Zoroastrians and led to a tripling of their numbers. Many of them left agriculture, migrated to the modern capital of Tehran (which is now the main stronghold of the Iranian Zoroastrians), and went into the new middle-class professions. As the Parsis did in India, some Iranian Zoroastrians found great success in commerce.

Modern Iranian Zoroastrianism has undergone fundamental changes. When Zoroastrians were freed during secular Iranian rule from many restrictions in much of the twentieth century until 1979, the religion was reconceived as a message of moral freedom. Iranian Zoroastrians have claimed that this was the essence of Zarathustra's message. The ceremonial ritual system has been deliberately neglected, and many rules and rituals that are still carefully upheld by Indian priests have been all but abandoned in Iran.

Zoroastrianism in Iran gradually transformed itself into a religion of freedom and morality claiming to represent the splendor of ancient Iran. For most of the 1800s and 1900s, Zoroastrianism became an appealing alternative to Shi'a Islam for many Iranians, where pride in Iran's Persian heritage is widely felt. Some even converted to Zoroastrianism. This more liberal form of Zoroastrianism is also represented today by an international organization

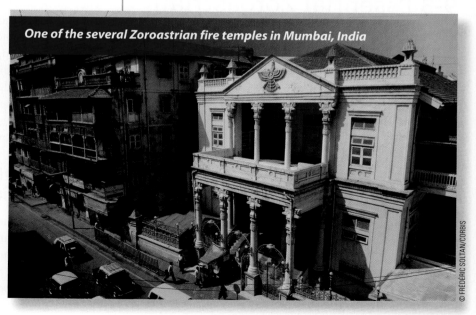

One of the several Zoroastrian fire temples in Mumbai, India

based in California called the **Zarathushtrian Assembly**. This group advocates the modernized form of their religion and accepts people willing to convert. However, it is strongly opposed by other Zoroastrian organizations, including a traditionalist organization based in Mumbai called the **Zoroastrian Studies Association**. When the Islamic Republic of Iran was established in 1979, conversion to Zoroastrianism or any other religion became nearly impossible, and Zoroastrian life in Iran became more difficult. The New Year festival, which is widely shared by Iranians who are Muslims, is among the few accepted occasions for celebration that include both Zoroastrians and Muslims.

> *"Ahura Mazda is the creator, radiant, glorious and best; the most beautiful, firm, wise, perfect and bounteous Spirit!"—The Avesta*

Learning Outcome 9-3

Explain the essential Zoroastrian teachings of monotheism and moral dualism.

9-3 Essential Zoroastrian Teachings: Monotheism and Moral Dualism

On the crowded streets of Mumbai, India, a young Zoroastrian woman sees an automobile with a familiar name: Mazda. The auto company's logo she sees on this car looks like the wings of a bird, suggesting to her the main symbol of her faith, the faravahar. This causes her both wonder and consternation: Is it really connected to Zoroastrianism? Why should a car company abuse the name of God? So she goes on the Internet and finds the website of the Mazda automotive company. It says that the company name is indeed from Ahura Mazda, whom it calls "a god of the earliest civilizations in West Asia, the god of wisdom, intelligence and harmony." The website states further, in something of a contradiction, that "Mazda" also comes from a shortening of *Matsuda*, the last name of its Japanese founder.

The teachings of Zoroastrianism stress belief in one God and moral dualism. Zoroastrianism was probably the first faith to put these two features together, and Zoroastrian teachings are deeply connected to them.

9-3a The One God, Ahura Mazda

Zoroastrianism's foundational teaching is that there is only one supreme God, Ahura Mazda, a name that means "Wise Lord" or "Lord of Wisdom." Ahura Mazda is the source of all light, truth, goodness, and life. He is infinite, and infinitely good. Zarathustra emphasized the central importance of Ahura Mazda by portraying him as the one God, accompanied by many spirit-lords—all the other older, Indo-Aryan gods who were "demoted" in the new religion. In later Zoroastrianism, the name Ahura Mazda was compacted into a single-word form, Ormazd. As the first verse in the ancient *Avesta* scripture proclaims, "Ahura Mazda is the creator, radiant, glorious and best; the most beautiful, firm, wise, perfect and bounteous Spirit!" Zoroastrians look to Ahura Mazda as the source of all created things that are good, the one who sustains goodness and life in the present, and the one who at the end of time will defeat all evil and give eternal life to all people (see "A Closer Look: The Zoroastrian Creed").

For Zoroastrians, only Ahura Mazda is a true God; only he is to be worshiped. All the other "lords," ahuras, and demons are beneath him and are not gods. They form an entourage of spirits that accompany the forces of either good or evil. In sum, Zoroastrianism is properly called monotheistic because it teaches the existence of one God. However, it was never as assertively monotheistic against other faiths as Judaism, Islam, or Christianity tended to be. It lacks a clear denial of the existence of other gods, characteristic of these more radical monotheisms. This may be connected to its historic tolerance toward other creeds.

9-3b The Spirit of Destruction, Angra Mainyu

Opposition to the evil and impurities in the world was also a fundamental feature of Zoroastrianism from its beginning. Because Ahura Mazda is good and made the world to be a good place, he desires the people in his creation to be morally good as well. This entails a positive effort to do what is right and a negative effort

A Closer Look:

The Zoroastrian Creed

At key moments in a Zoroastrian's life, the Fravarane is recited. This declaration of faith is a shortened version of the full creed from the Zoroastrian scriptures.

"Come to my help, Ahura Mazda. I am a Mazdayasnian according to [the way of] Zarathustra. I firmly declare my faith. I acknowledge my faith in Good Thoughts well conceived. I acknowledge my faith in Good Words well spoken. I acknowledge my faith in Good Deeds well done. I acknowledge my acceptance of the Good Religion of Mazda, which ends strife and disarms violence, which makes us righteous and self-reliant. It is the religion of those who have been, and shall be, the noblest, the best, and most sublime. The religion of Ahura Mazda was brought to us by Zarathustra. All good derives from Ahura Mazda. This is the declaration of the Mazdayasnian religion."

to engage in a real fight with evils of all sorts. People who think, say, and do evil on earth are deceivers and liars who turn others against the one true, good God by promoting a variety of wickedness. Evil doesn't always look like evil, nor is it always easily recognized. Instead, it disguises itself as good; hence one of the main figures of wickedness is known as the Druj (drooj), the "Spirit of Deceit" or the "Spirit of the Lie." The supreme evil spirit, Zarathustra taught, is **Angra Mainyu**, the "Spirit of Destruction." Zarathustra seems to have used this as only a title, to judge from the oldest parts of Zoroastrian scriptures, but later it became a proper name and was shortened to Ahriman (AH-rih-mun).

9-3c Moral Dualism

Another foundational feature of Zoroastrianism is **dualism**, the notion that the cosmos is composed of two competing forces. This opposition between good and evil is also found in early Vedic Hindu sources, so it probably was a part of pre-Zoroastrian Persian religion, but Zarathustra developed it significantly. From the beginning of the world, the Zoroastrian scriptures say, there have been two incompatible, antagonistic spirits in the world. One is the good God, Ahura Mazda; the other is a devil-like figure, Angra Mainyu. The **Twin Spirits** under Ahura Mazda made an ominous choice: The Bounteous Spirit chose to be truthful in thoughts, words, and deeds, but the Deceitful Spirit chose to be a follower of evil. When the Zoroastrian scriptures teach this dualism, it is always with a command to follow the good; for example, "Let those who act wisely choose correctly between these two, not as evil-doers choose" (*Yasna* 30:3).

After the Twin Spirits, it was the turn of the old gods of pre-Zoroastrian Persian religion to choose between good and evil. These gods, called **daevas**, all chose badly. Ever since, the daevas have tried to corrupt people's choices also. The two powers of good and evil are roughly equal to each other in this world, so the fight between good and evil is real. The powers draw all people into their service as they fight this cosmic moral battle, as people decide which spirit to follow. The two forces will continue to limit and challenge each other until the end of time, when evil will finally be defeated.

Zoroastrianism's form of moral dualism never claimed that good and evil are exactly equal, because its dualism was qualified by monotheism. If there is only one God, and if this God is both good and has supreme power, evil at the end of the day doesn't have much of a chance to win. The forces of good are assured of eventual triumph. Ahura Mazda limits the exercise of his supreme power as this struggle plays out. Humans can join the struggle because they possess free choice.

The dualism is moral, but it isn't physical—the idea that matter is evil and spirit is good. Humans serve either good or evil with both their souls and bodies, because both the human soul and the human body participate in the divine nature. For example, fasting and celibacy—important practices in many religions to control the body and its supposed impulses to do or think wrong—are almost unknown in Zoroastrianism. The fight does, however, have a ritual aspect: Humans must

Angra Mainyu
[AHN-gruh MIGHN-yoo] "Spirit of Destruction," supernatural head of all evil in the cosmos, opponent of Ahura Mazda

dualism Notion that the cosmos is composed of two competing forces

Twin Spirits The Bounteous Spirit and the Deceitful Spirit, two supernatural beings under Ahura Mazda

daevas [DIGH-vuhs] Pre-Zoroastrian gods who chose to serve evil instead of good, and who still tempt humans to do wrong

keep themselves pure in body and soul by treating fire with great respect and avoiding demons in their dreams. And keeping pure also means that dead human bodies must not come into contact with the earth, which led to the practice of exposing them to birds of prey. There are short but necessary rituals for cleansing oneself after cutting hair or nails, sneezing, eliminating bodily wastes, and using toothpicks. Thus, traditional Zoroastrianism has ritual aspects that are just as all-pervading as its ethical aspects.

9-3d Supernatural Intermediaries

Zoroastrianism's strong moral dualism is buttressed by supernatural intermediaries that personify and promote what is morally good. Between Ahura Mazda and human beings there are six intermediary beings called **Amesha Spentas**, or benevolent immortals. They are Good Thoughts, Perfect Truth, Desirable Lordship, Beneficial Devotion, Plenty, and Immortality. These immortals are the entourage of personified virtues that constantly surround Ahura Mazda. They are individual divine beings and at the same time cosmic moral virtues. Humans who choose to follow Ahura Mazda take on, one by one, the moral characteristics of these immortals, progressing from Good Thoughts to Immortality.

9-3e Judgment and the Final Victory of Ahura Mazda

In Zoroastrian belief, the soul hovers above the body for three days after death. On the fourth day, it takes a rapid journey to the next world and faces judgment on the **Chinvat Bridge**. The Requiter (Chinvat) weighs the soul's deeds during all of life. If its good deeds outweigh evil ones, the soul ascends to the stars (representing good thoughts) then to the moon (good words), to the sun (good deeds), and finally to paradise, where eternal lights shine. There the Good Mind leads the soul to the

Political and cosmic power of fire: coin of Sassanian King Shahpur II (309–379 C.E.), with a fire altar and priests

CLASSICAL NUMISMATIC GROUP INC. WWW.CNGCOINS.COM

golden throne of Ahura Mazda. However, if evil outweighs good, the soul is dragged off to hell, to be punished there until the end of time.

Read a description of judgment on the Chinvat Bridge.

In a great struggle near the end of time, the armies of good and evil will battle to the death, and Ahura Mazda's soldiers will defeat their evil enemies. Then a final judgment comes at the end of the world, after all the bodies of the dead are resurrected and reunited with their souls, whether they have been in heaven or hell. A final cleansing of fire purifies the souls and bodies of evil human beings, so that all people are fit to live in paradise. This will restore the goodness of the world that existed at the time of creation. The personified Spirit of Fire and Angra Mainyu will melt the metals of the mountains and flow down as rivers of molten fire. All resurrected humans must walk through this valley of trial. The fire will burn off the sins of the wicked for three painful days, but to the righteous it will be as delicious and restorative as warm milk. Then all people will enjoy happiness and divine blessing forever. On the renewed Earth, men and women will have no shadow because they are sinless. Hell will be emptied of souls and sealed forever, and Angra Mainyu and all his forces will be annihilated.

Learning Outcome 9-4

State the main ethical precepts of Zoroastrianism.

9-4 Zoroastrian Ethics

A young Zoroastrian man in California logs onto a Zoroastrian matchmaking website. Because his religion is important to him and because it commands marriage within the faith, he is now looking for a suitable Zoroastrian who could possibly become his wife. He has tried to find a possible mate in San Francisco, but the Zoroastrian community there is too small. The website gives him worldwide possibilities, especially in India, where his family came from generations ago. Some of his friends, both male and female, have married non-Zoroastrians, and his religious community has refused to welcome them or recognize their children as Zoroastrians. The young man would like to avoid these difficult problems.

As we have seen previously, the two main doctrinal teachings of Zoroastrianism are monotheism and morality. These are deeply intertwined. In a culture that rarely thought of its gods as morally good, Zarathustra proclaimed that the one God, Ahura Mazda, was infinitely good and was attended by six spirits who personify his righteousness and mediate it to humankind. Ahura Mazda fights a cosmic battle against evil, a force that is strong and real (*Gathas*, *Yasna* 44:10; 53:1).

Because Ahura Mazda does what is good, he expects all people to follow him in doing what is right and putting away evil. In this way, they join the ongoing cosmic spiritual and physical battle for righteousness, a battle that Ahura Mazda will certainly win. Zoroastrians do not simply fight against evil in themselves or in society around them, but by their good actions they fight against demons and Angra Mainyu himself. People have the freedom to know right from wrong and choose what is right, and Ahura Mazda holds them responsible for these choices. Most Zoroastrians have a lively sense of the heavenly reward for doing right and the hellish punishment for doing wrong.

9-4a Zoroastrian General Morality

Zoroastrian moral teachings focus generally on the preservation of good and the destruction of evil, but this abstract ideal is carried out in very concrete ways. The oldest scriptures of Zoroastrianism relate that one must make an honest living in cattle herding and farming. This wasn't just a cultural given—it was a religious norm. Zoroastrians went into commerce and prospered in it, in part because they had a reputation for being honest with all people, not just those of their faith or ethnic group. At one time, Zoroastrians in Mumbai owned more businesses than did Hindus, who vastly outnumbered them.

Zoroastrians hold to values of speaking and acting truthfully, being faithful to Ahura Mazda, and doing what is good in the world. Goodness in one's individual life can be attained only by living a balanced, morally healthy life of good thoughts, good words, and good deeds. In the Avestan language, these three have the same beginning sound, suggesting they go together: Humata (hoo-MAHT-uh), Hukhta (HOOK-tuh), and Huvereshta (HOO-vuh-RESH-tuh). This threefold statement of morality is so important in the faith that it is a key part of the Zoroastrian confession of faith, as we saw previously. It is inscribed over many a door to Zoroastrian temples and community centers. In the past few centuries, generous giving to Zoroastrian philanthropies has become a hallmark of the faith's moral effort. The steady work of the faithful to spread good in the world has improved the education of girls and the social status of women in India, Iran, and other countries.

> At one time, Zoroastrians in Mumbai owned more businesses than did Hindus, who vastly outnumbered them.

Traditional Zoroastrians live their lives in this world with a view of their individual judgment after death. Their reward or punishment in the next world, at least from the time of their death to the end of the world, is decided by the total balance of their deeds, words, and thoughts. If good predominated in their life, they go to heaven; if evil predominated, they go to hell. This principle, however, is flexible enough to accommodate human failings. Zoroastrians don't believe that all their sins must be weighed on the scales. Two ways exist of erasing negative effects at one's personal judgment. The first of these is confession of one's sins, which brings forgiveness and lightens the weight of sin at the judgment. The second means is the transfer of merits from the Zoroastrian saints, whose good thoughts, words, and deeds are far more than what the saints need to pass judgment and enter heaven. This is the rationale for Zoroastrian funeral prayers and rituals asking Ahura Mazda for mercy on and forgiveness of the souls of the dead.

9-4b A Current Ethical and Social Issue: Marriage and Children

Another key moral command in Zoroastrianism is the duty to marry and have children. To Zoroastrians, the world is a good place even though evil has marred it. Marriage and children are good things for every Zoroastrian; in contrast with some other religions among whom Zoroastrians have lived (for instance,

Hinduism and Jainism), one won't see any form of celibacy at any stage in Zoroastrian life. Moreover, marriage must be to another within the faith, preferably a member in a clan relationship, although avoiding incest. In other words, marriage must be close, but not too close. Zoroastrians have even called their religion the **faith of kindred marriage**.

Watch a BBC video of a traditional Zoroastrian wedding.

The fact that many Zoroastrians in India and the Western world have only one or at most two children, and others marry outside the faith, means that these ancient values are threatened. Unless more Zoroastrians marry within the faith, and unless Zoroastrian couples have more than one or two children on average, the faithful may all but disappear in a few centuries. Many Zoroastrians are apprehensive about the future of their faith. Other groups within the religion that call themselves "reformist" accept children of mixed marriages into the faith, but this is strongly rejected by the main body of Zoroastrians.

Learning Outcome 9-5

Outline the way Zoroastrians worship and observe rituals.

9-5 Zoroastrian Rituals

As he sits on the floor in a Zoroastrian temple in a Chicago suburb, a priest offers sacrifice for the souls of the dead. In his secular occupation, Kersey Antia is a clinical psychologist specializing in panic disorders. As a Zoroastrian priest, he officiates at fire ceremonies, feeding sandalwood and frankincense into a blazing fire in a large urn. He recites prayers that he learned to pronounce by special training in the Avestan language at a school in India. Although the faithful today understand only a few Avestan words, the Zoroastrian god Ahura Mazda does speak Avestan, so the words are still effective.

faith of kindred marriage Zoroastrians' informal name for their religion, stressing the requirement to marry only Zoroastrians

fire temple Zoroastrian house of worship centering on sacred fire burning in it

Read a brief introduction to Kersey Antia, and listen to his recitation of scriptures and prayers.

9-5a Fires in the Fire Temple

The Zoroastrian house of worship, in which all worship takes place, is the **fire temple**. In the Western world an "eternal flame" is a symbol of honored memory; in Zoroastrianism every temple has an eternal flame for the worship of Ahura Mazda. Fire temples and their activities center on the fire within them, and they are named with reference to three types of fires.

> In the Western world an "eternal flame" is in memory of an honored person; in Zoroastrianism every temple has an eternal flame for the worship of Ahura Mazda.

The Appointed Place Fire is the first classification of sacred fire. Two priests can consecrate it in two hours, with one reading scriptures out loud as the other lights and tends the fire. After it is consecrated, an approved layperson may tend the fire when no ritual is being performed with it. The smallest Zoroastrian temples have only this sort of fire. It is also found along with the two greater fires in more impressive temples, where priests celebrate the main rituals of the faith and believers invoke blessings in front of the fire.

The next level is the Fire of Fires. It requires a gathering and mingling in one sacrificial urn of fires from representatives of the four main social groups: priests, soldiers and civil servants, farmers and herders, and craftsmen and laborers. These are the traditional classes in Zoroastrian society from ancient times. Eight priests must consecrate this fire in a ritual that takes up to three weeks.

The highest level is the Fire of Victory. Its consecration involves the gathering of sixteen different fires from sixteen different sources, including from lightning and a metal-molding furnace. Each of the sixteen fires goes through a rite of purification before its flames are put into a common fire. Thirty-two priests are needed for the consecration, which takes almost a year. When Zoroastrians venerate the completed and dedicated Fire of Victory and the Fire of Fires, they address only the fire itself, using the songs of praise in the Zoroastrian scriptures. Priests and believers don't ordinarily make requests of Ahura Mazda before these two higher fires.

9-5b Interior Plan of the Fire Temple

When they enter a fire temple, both men and women must wear a head covering. First, one goes through a large hall where ceremonies take place. The faithful then enter an anteroom smaller than the main hall. Connected to this anteroom—but not visible from the hall, to ensure a sense of holiness and quiet—is the "place of the fire" in which the actual fire altars stand. These fire altars are usually large urns that sit on the floor; priests sit or stand in front of them as they offer sacrifices of spices and incense into the constantly burning flame. Lay Zoroastrians stand before the fire to offer their prayers to God.

Only priests enter the inner, most sacred room, which has a double-domed roof. Each dome in this roof has vents where the smoke of the fires escapes. The outer dome's vents are offset from those of the inner dome, preventing anything but air from entering the room below and potentially desecrating the holy flame. The walls of the inner room are made of tile or marble, but there is no other decoration. The only light in the inner room is that of the fire itself, an arrangement that is powerfully symbolic to Zoroastrians.

Priests ring a bell, installed in the main room, five times every day to mark each new "watch" period. The fire is usually fed at this time with dried sandalwood. Tools for maintaining the wood fire are hung on the wall or stored in an adjoining room. Non-Zoroastrians may not enter any space from which they can even glimpse the fires. This typically means no entry into a temple at all, and many Parsi temples in India have "Parsis Only" signs at their front door. If non-Zoroastrians are permitted to enter during ordinary times, the temples are closed during feasts and holy days. Traditionalists say that these restrictions aren't meant to offend non-Zoroastrians. Iranian and "reformist" Zoroastrians more often open their temples to non-Zoroastrians.

9-5c Worship

When a Zoroastrian enters the room where the fire burns, he or she offers wood for the fire. The person making an offering doesn't put the wood directly into the fire, but gives it to the priest. At the proper time, the priest places the offering in the fire, using silver tongs. He wears a white cloth mask over nose and mouth so his breath doesn't pollute the flame. The priest uses a special ladle to give some ashes to worshipers, who then dab the ashes on their forehead and eyelids.

The Zoroastrian priest doesn't preach or teach, but offers prayer and sacrifice at the fire, which he tends. Temple attendance is especially high during festivals, particularly the New Year's festival. There is no instrumental music or group singing in Zoroastrian worship, only the musical chanting of the scriptures and prayers by the priests. Social events may occur in the main hall, especially at festivals and initiations, but rarely as a part of regular worship.

> *A Zoroastrian priest doesn't often preach or even teach, but rather tends the sacrificial fires.*

9-5d Priesthood

The **magi**, an order of non-Zoroastrian priests, learned about the prophet Zarathustra's teachings before 400 B.C.E.

Fire temple in Yazd, Iran, one of the oldest in Zoroastrianism

© M. KHEBRA/SHUTTERSTOCK.COM

haoma [HO-mah] Sacred liquid offered in the fire sacrifice to Ahura Mazda

navjote [nahv-JOH-tee] Initiation ceremony when young Zoroastrians reach the age of seven or ten

kusti [KOOS-tee] Sacred thread tied around a Zoroastrian's body at initiation

patet [PAH-teht] Formula expressing resolve not to sin again

Nowruz or Noruz [NOH-rooz] Iranian New Year festival celebrated by both Zoroastrians and Muslims

and converted to the faith. The priests rose to power quickly and had a monopoly on priestly power at the Persian court. Under the Sassanians, a three-level hierarchy of priests developed among the magi. Admission to the priesthood is hereditary, but all priests must go through one or more ceremonies of ordination. In 2010, a violent confrontation broke out in India when a group of more liberal Zoroastrians unsuccessfully tried to ordain to the priesthood a Russian convert to Zoroastrianism. Training for the priesthood has always centered on performing the ceremonies, especially the ritual words and actions.

The main ceremony conducted by priests, the Yasna, is a sacrifice of **haoma**, the sacred liquid, to Ahura Mazda. The sacrifice is held in the presence of the sacred fire and features recitation of long portions of the *Avesta*. Bread and milk are also offered, substances that replace the former offerings of meat or animal fat. The sacred fire is fed with sweet-smelling wood at least five times a day, at the beginning of each watch. Prayers are also offered five times a day in the presence of the fire.

9-5e Other Rituals

All young Zoroastrians must be initiated in the **navjote** ceremony when they turn seven (in India, Africa, Europe, and North America) or ten (in Iran). A priest leads the ceremony, and the young people must receive instruction before the navjote. They receive a shirt and the sacred cord called a **kusti**, items to be worn for the rest of their

life. The kusti is tied around the waist and symbolizes a lifelong commitment to keeping the tenets of the religion.

In a religion that stresses ritual purity, Zoroastrian rituals of purification are particularly important. Three types of purification come in order of increasing importance: the ablution, ordinary washing for the smallest compromises of one's purity; the full-body bath, for medium-sized impurities; and the fullest purification ritual, the *bareshnum* (ba-RESH-num), a complicated ritual performed at special places and lasting several days. It includes a dog, whose left ear is touched by the person seeking cleansing. Evil spirits are believed to flee from the dog's threatening looks.

 Read a contemporary explanation and defense of the patet.

Penance for sins is necessary for keeping the accumulation of one's sins from resulting in condemnation after death. It entails reciting the **patet**, the firm resolve not to sin again. The patet also calls for one to confess one's sins to a priest.

Festivals are an important aspect of Zoroastrianism, and full of happy celebration. There are six seasonal festivals throughout the year, and at year's end a few days are dedicated to the memory of the dead. The New Year feast, **Nowruz** (also spelled **Noruz**) is the most joyous of all Zoroastrian festivals. Iranian Muslims have a similar celebration of Nowruz.

Watch a PBS video on Nowruz.

A Parsi woman weaves a kusti, the sacred thread given in the navjote.

© SAM PANTHAKY/AFP/GETTY IMAGES

9-5f Funeral Rituals

The funeral ritual varies in the Zoroastrian world today, but here is the traditional format. After death, the body is washed and clothed in a simple white garment. A "four-eyed" dog with a spot above each eye is then brought in. The dog's appearance frightens evil spirits into fleeing but does not threaten the soul of the dead person, which hovers above the body for three days. The ritual is repeated five times a day. On the second day after death, mourners bring fire into the room and keep it burning there for three full days after the funeral. Placement of the body in a tower of silence must be done in the daylight.

Tower of silence in Yazd, Iran

The inside of the tower had three concentric circles, one each for men, women, and children, and a large central well in the center of the tower. The body was then unclothed, and after it was exposed, the mourners left the tower. The vultures descended from their circling flight and took only about an hour to eat the flesh from the bones. Dried by the sun for a few days, the bones were swept into a large stone box in the central well, to preserve them reverently until the resurrection. The fourth day after death is the most solemn in the funeral; the soul goes into the presence of Ahura Mazda and is judged. Special prayers are offered on this day for souls of the dead.

Zoroastrian funeral practice has changed in Iran and India. In its role as a religion in a modernizing country, Zoroastrianism replaced the towers of silence with cemeteries during the twentieth century. By the 1960s, the towers in Iran had fallen into complete disuse. In the new cemeteries, care was taken to protect the earth from direct contact with bodies of the dead, a key Zoroastrian value. The towers of silence are still used at times in Mumbai, India, despite the fact that there are no more vultures there to devour the corpses. Bodies are put in the towers to decay in the sun and open air, a practice that has led to some inner Zoroastrian controversy as well as conflict with local officials over health issues.

Vultures consumed dead bodies, maintaining the purity of the earth.

Watch a BBC report on Zoroastrian burial.

Learning Outcome 9-6

State the main features of Zoroastrian life around the world today, especially in North America.

9-6 Zoroastrianism around the World Today

Residents of a rural area outside Washington, D.C., are upset about the construction of a Zoroastrian temple in their community. One man who lives next to the temple property worries that the temple, which will include a parking lot for fifty cars and its own water and septic system, will limit the already-declining water supply for residents. Others say the worship center will bring an unwanted influx of traffic. The complaints, government officials say, have nothing to do with the religious nature of the project, but are about allowing the temple in a residentially zoned area. But the Zoroastrian community has all its permits for construction in order. The leader of the community has said, "We are a very small religion," adding that only three hundred Zoroastrians live in the Washington, D.C., area. "Our finances aren't good. We have no home for gathering together for worship."

"Marry inside our community, and SAVE our religion." —From a Zoroastrian website

Watch an audio slide show, "A Religion in Decline," featuring Chicago-area Zoroastrians.

Most Zoroastrians in North America are from India; they speak English and their own dialect of Gujarati. More-recent Zoroastrian immigrants are from Iran; they speak Farsi. Because these two communities were separated in Asia for more than a thousand years, they developed some differences in their rituals and festivals that are still reflected in North America today.

Zoroastrians began to arrive in North America in the 1860s, in very small numbers, settling on the East and West coasts. They engaged in a variety of professions, from gold prospecting to farming and commerce. The first Zoroastrian "congregation," formed by seven believers in New York City in 1929, met in private homes. As with other people of Asian origin, Zoroastrians were largely prohibited by U.S. immigration laws from entering the country from about 1900 until the 1960s. Then, when the laws were liberalized, many Zoroastrians came to North America seeking a more prosperous life, and additional Zoroastrian organizations were founded. The main goal of these organizations, like those of almost all other Asian religions that came to North America, was to establish the faith in the New World so that it would be successfully passed down to the Zoroastrians' children. Maintaining the religious culture—language, dress, food, and festivals—through the generations is also important in North America. Many Zoroastrian temples have cultural centers attached to them where these cultural values are emphasized. One of the more unusual Zoroastrian "public-relations" tasks in North America today is to counter a false impression that North Americans get when they read the book *Thus Spoke Zarathustra* (see "A Closer Look: *Thus Spoke Zarathustra*").

After the 1979 Islamic Revolution in Iran toppled the more religiously tolerant regime of the Shah, many Iranian Zoroastrians no longer felt safe there. Thousands fled their ancient ancestral homeland, and a majority went to North America. The number of Zoroastrians there

A young girl dances at a Zoroastrian cultural center.

© BEHROUZ MEHRI/AFP/GETTY IMAGES

A Closer Look:

Thus Spoke Zarathustra

The most influential work on Zarathustra in North America today—*Thus Spoke Zarathustra* by the German philosopher Friedrich Nietzsche (FREED-rik NEE-cheh)—is not about Zoroastrianism at all. This book is widely regarded as a literary masterpiece and has had a wide cultural impact in the arts and in philosophy. It uses Zarathustra to express Nietzsche's views, including the introduction of the controversial doctrine of the "Superman," a term later twisted by Nazi propagandists to connote racial supremacy. (The comic-book and film hero known today by the same name isn't drawn from Nietzsche's book; that Superman is traditional in moral matters.) A passionate, semibiblical style is employed to inspire readers to transcend conventional morality. This work remains a standard on college reading lists.

However, *Thus Spoke Zarathustra* has been disavowed by almost all Zoroastrians from the time of its publication, because its theme of an individual getting beyond conventional morality, and then even beyond morality itself, contradicts one of the main beliefs of Zoroastrianism. The universe is deeply moral, because it is based on Ahura Mazda's goodness, and people must follow the way of Zarathustra to live out Ahura Mazda's morality, not invent their own.

---

quickly doubled, and tensions arose between Indian and Iranian Zoroastrians. For the most part, they manage to coexist, if only because their small numbers force them to get along. In a few larger Zoroastrian communities, worship services are held separately for each group, with only some important festivals celebrated by Iranians and Indians together. In 2010 it was estimated that the entire population of Zoroastrians in North America was around twenty thousand. Zoroastrians have taken to cyberspace with many websites, to promote the common faith of all Zoroastrians and also some of the distinct groups such as the "reformist" Zarathushtrian Assembly and the traditionalist Mazdayasni Zoroastrian Anjuman. Many observers of North American Zoroastrianism expect the differences between the groups to soften over time—especially when the second and third generations take over—and an "American Zoroastrianism" to be established. The websites often have matchmaking areas to encourage the faithful to marry each other; as one pleads, "Marry inside our community, and SAVE our religion." This will help to keep alive into a new millennium one of the world's most ancient faiths.

Visit the website of the Zarathushtrian Assembly in the United States.

Study Tools 9

Ready to study? In the book you can:

- Review Learning Outcome answers and glossary terms with the tear-out Chapter Review card.

Or you can go online to CourseMate, at www.cengagebrain.com, for these resources:

- Chapter quizzes to prepare for tests

- Interactive flashcards of all glossary terms

- A timeline of events for this chapter

- An eBook with introductions, interactive quizzes, and live links for all web resources in the chapter

CHAPTER 10

Encountering Judaism: The Way of God's People

Learning Outcomes

After studying this chapter, you will be able to do the following:

10-1 Explain the meaning of *Judaism* and related terms.

10-2 Summarize how the main periods of Judaism's history have shaped its present.

10-3 Outline the essential teachings of Judaism in your own words.

10-4 Describe the main features of Jewish ethics.

10-5 Summarize Jewish worship, the Sabbath and major festivals, and life-cycle rituals.

10-6 Outline the main features of Judaism around the world today, especially in Israel and North America.

Study Tools

After you read this chapter, go to the Study Tools at the end of the chapter, page 256.

"Hear, O Israel: The Lord our God is One."—Jewish statement of faith

Your Visit to the Western Wall in Jerusalem

In your hotel the evening before you visit the Western Wall, your tour guide gives you instructions for the next day's events. "Everyone is welcome at the Wall," she says. "But you must wear modest clothing—no one in shorts, sleeveless tops, or jeans is allowed. Men must wear a hat or other head covering. Women must wear clothing that covers their shoulders and knees; they can borrow shawls at the entrance. Proper behavior is a must; be respectful of others." All this is pretty standard stuff, you think, and applies to important religious sites around the world. But there's one item that's unique to a visit to the Western Wall: People are allowed to put a paper note with a prayer written on it into a seam between the stones, where (many Jews believe) God will pay special attention to one's prayer.

Nearly everyone in Israel calls this place simply "the Wall." But your guide gives you a warning: Don't call it "the Wailing Wall." This term is often used today, but many residents of Jerusalem find it offensive. "Wailing" is supposed to refer to mourning for the destruction of the temple in 70 C.E. There is typically no wailing here, so the term is indeed misleading.

Despite the preparation you've done for visiting the Wall, some things still surprise you during your visit. First, long-established Jewish rules apply here, so women must go to their own section and not stand with the men. Even in the women's section, they may not read aloud from Jewish scriptures or wear men's prayer shawls. (In 2013 a group of Jewish women defied this ban and were arrested at the wall.) There's some murmuring in your tour group over this, but the women do have access to the wall itself and can place prayer notes in it. Second, when you ask an official about what happens to your prayer, you learn something surprising. More than a million notes are left in the Wall each year,

A Jewish man wearing ritual clothing and accessories prays at the Western Wall in Jerusalem, into which papers with prayers have been inserted.

© ISTOCKPHOTO.COM/ELDAD CARIN

 A Jewish man wearing a prayer shawl blows a ram's horn to herald the Jewish New Year holy day.

and you see that the cracks between the stones are jammed with papers. Twice a year the notes are collected and buried on Jerusalem's Mount of Olives. Third, most surprising of all is how emotionally moved you are. The closer you get to the Wall, the more it towers over you. The prayerful piety of others at the site impresses you and helps to explain why this is for Jews the holiest place in the world.

Watch a video about the Western Wall. ▶▶▶

Judaism is a monotheistic religion that believes that the world was created by an all-knowing, all-powerful God and that all things in the world were designed to have meaning and purpose as part of a divine order. God called the Israelites to be a chosen, special people and follow God's law, thus becoming the means by which divine blessing would flow to the world. God's law guides humans in every area of life; it is a gift from God so that people might live according to God's will.

The main influence of Judaism stems directly from its strong devotion to God over more than 2,500 years. Some of the impact of Judaism has been lost in the modern world, and Judaism itself is more fragmented in recent times than ever before. Its deep influence on everyday life and on patterns of Western culture is still clearly visible, however. The belief that there is only one God, now self-evident for believers in all Western religions, is the main gift of Judaism. The idea that the world is a real and mostly good (or at least redeemable) place has shaped Western religion and thought. Our seven-day week with its rest on the weekend originates in Judaism as well. The convictions that all people are equally human before God, each other, and the law; that the human race is one family; and that each individual can fully realize the meaning of life regardless of social or economic class have also come to the Western world from Judaism.

> *Key teachings and values of Judaism have spread in Christianity and Islam to over half the people of the world.*

In your study of Judaism, you'll encounter and study in some depth these unique features:

- For a relatively small religion, around 13.5 million adherents today, Judaism has had a big impact.

The teachings and values of Judaism have spread in Christianity and Islam, which are closely related to Judaism, to over half the people of the world. However, Islam and Christianity have often been rivals of Judaism as well.

- The world has had a mixed attitude to Judaism for more than two thousand years. The Jews' strong, clear monotheism and morality have been influential, but Jews have drawn near-constant opposition as well. Prejudice against them, often leading to violent persecution, has sadly been a recurrent feature in Jewish life.

- Judaism is both geographically scattered and centered. Since about 300 B.C.E., the majority of Jewish people haven't lived in the traditional Jewish area now in modern Israel. Instead, they've lived in the wider Middle East, Europe, and North America. In fact, as many Jews now live in the United States as live in Israel. Still, Israel is an essential part of Judaism today.

Learning Outcome 10-1

Explain the meaning of *Judaism* and related terms.

10-1 The Name *Judaism* and Related Terms

Judaism is commonly and correctly defined as the historic religion of the Jewish people. This name comes from the ancient tribe of Judah, one of the original twelve tribes of Israel. When the leaders of the southern kingdom of Israel came back from exile in Babylon in the 530s B.C.E., the name of their larger tribe became the name of the political area (Judah) and the people who lived there became the *Judahites* (JOO-duh-ights), or *Jews* for short. In time their religion became known as *Judaism*, a term derived from the ancient Greek language. For most of the history of the Jewish people, to be Jewish was to practice Judaism in some way. But around 1800 C.E., it became possible in Europe to give up Judaism and still call oneself Jewish. Jewishness then became for many Jews a matter of ethnic status and cultural identity, not of religion. Other Jews replied that only by keeping Judaism do Jews stay Jewish. Although

© ISTOCKPHOTO.COM/
FIREBRANDPHOTOGRAPHY

these two positions cannot be completely separated, this chapter will focus on Judaism as a religion.

Before 500 B.C.E., the ancestors of the Jews went by other names. The first was **Hebrews**, the name of the people during patriarchal times through the Exodus (1800–1200 B.C.E.). This name is from *Habiru* (ha-BEE-roo; also spelled "Hapiru"), a word for nomads that is found in many languages in the ancient Fertile Crescent and seems to have been attached to the descendants of Abraham while they lived in Egypt. When they settled in Palestine after the Exodus and became a nation there, they became known as **Israelites**, a name derived from the ancient patriarch Israel (whose original name was Jacob). Historians speak generically of their religions during this period as "Hebrew religion" and "Israelite religion," not as "Judaism." A more recent twist adds some confusion to these names. The modern nation of Israel, founded in 1948, calls itself by the same name as that of ancient Israel, but the people of modern Israel (whether Jewish by religion or not) are called **Israelis**, not "Israelites."

Hebrews [HEE-brewz] Name of God's people during patriarchal times through the Exodus

Israelites [IHZ-ray-EHL-ights] Name for God's people during the period of the Judges and during the First Temple Period

Israelis [ihz-RAIL-eez] Name of people who live in the modern nation of Israel

menorah [men-OHR-uh] Large candelabra in the Jerusalem temple, today a common symbol of Judaism

Star of David Six-pointed figure that is the most common symbol of Judaism today

A Closer Look:

Symbols of Judaism

Several symbols have served Judaism over time, and we will begin with the lesser-used one.

Chai

Chai (chigh, with a throat-clearing initial sound; Figure 10.1), a symbol of modern origin popular and fashionable in jewelry today, is the Hebrew word for "living." Some say that it refers to God, who alone is perfectly alive; others think it comes from the common Jewish toast "Le chaim" (leh CHIGH-ihm), "To life!" More likely, it reflects Judaism's stress on the significance of life. For many people who wear it, it is a symbol of their Jewish faith.

BONNIE VAN VOORST
© CENGAGE LEARNING

Figure 10.1 Chai

Menorah

The oldest symbol of Judaism is the **menorah** (Figure 10.2), a large, usually seven-branched candelabrum. It was a prominent accessory in the Jerusalem temple, and one sees it today in many Jewish homes and houses of worship. It's especially

BONNIE VAN VOORST
© CENGAGE LEARNING

Figure 10.2 Menorah

prominent during the celebration of Hanukkah, when a nine-branched menorah is used for the nine days of the festival. For many Jews, the menorah symbolizes Israel's mission to be "a light to the nations" (Isaiah 42:6). It is featured on the coat of arms of the modern nation of Israel.

Star of David

The six-pointed **Star of David** (Fig. 10.3) is the common symbol of Judaism today, but it isn't nearly as old as the menorah. A symbol of two overlaid equilateral triangles was a common symbol of good fortune in the ancient Near East and in North Africa. It is found in early Jewish artwork as far back as the first century C.E.—in the stones of the ancient synagogue of Capernaum, Israel, for example—but not as a symbol of Judaism. In the 1600s it began to be used to mark the exteriors of some Jewish houses of worship in Europe, to identify them, and then began to be associated with the ancient King David. The Star of David reached its current status when it became the symbol of the Zionist movement to resettle Palestine in 1897 (see page 239). Today it appears on the flag of the modern nation of Israel.

BONNIE VAN VOORST © CENGAGE LEARNING

Figure 10.3 Star of David

Summarize how the main periods of Judaism's history have shaped its present.

10-2 The Jewish Present as Shaped by Its Past

An American college professor leads his class on European religious history through the Dachau (DAHK-ow) concentration camp outside Munich, Germany. They walk through the gate, and the professor explains the macabre meaning of its inscription, *Arbeit macht frei* ("Work makes [you] free"). He explains, as they walk by, the barracks for prisoners and the other buildings around the site. They see the gas chamber disguised as a shower room and then inspect the crematorium. This is all a somber experience, but the full horror of this site doesn't really register on the students until they go into its museum, with exhibits of what went on here. A suspicion and hatred of "alien" groups, especially the long history of hatred of the Jewish people, reached a horrific outcome in dozens of camps such as this one. Everyone in the class is in tears as they leave, including the professor, who has been here before and isn't an emotional person. He brings his students here for this searing experience so that they'll never forget the evil humans can do and the courage it takes for persecuted groups to continue on in life.

The Jewish people have a long, storied history that includes both tragedy and triumph. In Judaism today we can see important beliefs and practices from the entire four-thousand-year sweep of Jewish experience. The periods of the history that we will consider here are these: from the creation of the world to Abraham (ca. 2000 B.C.E.); the emergence of Israel (ca. 1200–950 B.C.E.); the First Temple Period (950–586 B.C.E.); the Second Temple Period (539 B.C.E.–70 C.E.); revolts and rabbis (70 C.E.–ca. 650); Jews under Islamic and Christian rule (ca. 650–1800 C.E.); emancipation and change (1800–1932); and the Holocaust and its aftermath (1932–Present).

patriarchs [PAY-tree-arks] Hebrew founding fathers: Abraham, Isaac, and Jacob

covenant [CUH-veh-nent] Agreement in which God promised to be with Abraham and his many descendants and Abraham promised to follow God

circumcision Ritual of the covenant, removing the foreskin of the penis

10-2a From the Creation to Abraham (ca. 2000 B.C.E.)

Chapters 1 through 11 of the first book of the Bible, Genesis, span the creation of the universe to the time of Abraham, father of the Jewish people (ca. 2000 B.C.E.). It narrates and provides a religious perspective on the creation of the world, the rebellion of the first humans against God and their expulsion from the Garden of Eden, the wide dispersal of people, Noah and the flood, and other topics. These stories echo the earlier mythology of Mesopotamia and provide an Israelite alternative to them. The rest of Genesis (chapters 12–50) covers just four generations of one family of the **patriarchs** and their wives: Abraham and Sarah, their son Isaac and his wife Rebekah, their son Jacob (Israel) and his wives Rachel and Leah, and Jacob's twelve sons who founded the twelve tribes of the nation of ancient Israel. The Israelite and then the Jewish people emerged from these tribes. Scholars debate the meaning and historical accuracy of the early biblical story, but they don't doubt the role that it played in shaping Judaism.

> *Scholars debate the early biblical story, but not the role that it played in shaping Judaism.*

Genesis 12 begins by narrating the migration of Abraham from Ur in Mesopotamia to the land of Canaan, a journey commanded by God. God makes a **covenant** with Abraham in which God promises to be with Abraham, be the God of his many descendants, and bless the world through these descendants. In return, God demands that Abraham follow him faithfully. Abraham then carries out on himself and all the males in his clan the ritual of **circumcision**, cutting off the foreskin of the penis, which is the perpetual sign of the covenant. Abraham's son Isaac marries Rebekah; she secures the line of succession for her younger son, Jacob. Jacob's simultaneous marriages to Leah and Rachel produce twelve sons, who are the origins of the twelve tribes. Genesis 37 to 50 tells the story of Joseph, the youngest of Jacob's twelve sons. Joseph is betrayed by his jealous brothers, who sell him to slave traders on their way to Egypt, but Joseph rises to great power under a sympathetic pharaoh. All Abraham's descendants then move to Egypt and prosper there until a later pharaoh enslaves the Israelites.

Explore Judaism in Google Earth™.

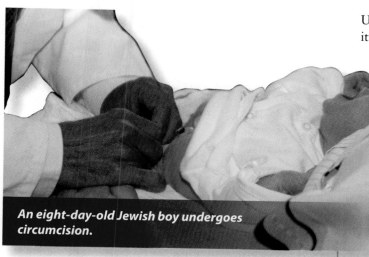

An eight-day-old Jewish boy undergoes circumcision.

10-2b The Emergence of Ancient Israel (ca. 1200–950 B.C.E.)

The book of Exodus contains the story of Israel's enslavement in Egypt, God's call to Moses to lead his people out of Egypt, Pharaoh's stubborn resistance, and the Israelites' escape through the parted waters of the Red Sea. Moses leads the Israelites to Sinai, a mountain in the wilderness where they enter into a covenant relationship with God. The Israelites agree to live by all the teachings and commandments, the **Torah**, conveyed to them by Moses. In keeping the Torah, they will live out their calling to be God's chosen people. After a forty-year journey through the wilderness, a new generation of Israelites arrives at the Jordan River, where they prepare to cross over and occupy the land promised to them. The books of Joshua and Judges relate the story of the Israelites' conquest of Palestine, its division among the tribes, and the first hundred years of settlement.

The focal center of early Israelite religion during this period was the movable tent-shrine housing the **Ark of the Covenant**, a sacred box with angels on the top containing two tablets inscribed with the Ten Commandments, Moses' staff, and a pot of manna. This tent, called the *tabernacle*, is where the first formal worship of ancient Israel took place, with sacrifice, prayer, and praise to God.

Modern replica of the Ark of the Covenant, the holiest object in ancient Israel

Unlike the nations around it, Israel had no national government; the twelve tribes were bound together in a tribal confederacy under their covenant with God. When Israel's enemies threatened, the tribes would act together under charismatic leaders, some of them women. Israel changed its form of government from a tribal confederacy to a monarchy. Saul was anointed king around 1025 B.C.E. Israel's second monarch, David, consolidated the monarchy over all Israel. The Bible celebrates the reigns of David and his son Solomon as a golden age, but it doesn't gloss over their considerable failings.

10-2c The First Temple Period (950–586 B.C.E.)

Solomon's construction of a temple to God in Jerusalem (ca. 950) inaugurated the **First Temple Period**, which lasted until the temple was destroyed in 586. The royal court became increasingly lavish as the power and size of the state increased. So did the tax burden on the lower classes. Many viewed the increasing social and economic divisions, with "the rich getting richer and the poor getting poorer," as a violation of God's will. Over the next centuries, a line of **prophets**, mostly men and some women who spoke for God, denounced the leaders of Israel for their greed, exploitation

Torah [TOHR-uh] Teachings and commandments conveyed by Moses, particularly in the first five books of the Bible

Ark of the Covenant Sacred box in the tabernacle and then the Temple

First Temple Period Era of Israelite history from ca. 950 B.C.E. until the destruction of Jerusalem in 586 B.C.E.

prophets Mostly men and some women who spoke for God to ancient Israel to call them to greater obedience

Watch a trailer for Steven Spielberg's animated film on Moses and the Exodus, *The Prince of Egypt.*

Read another, revisionist explanation of the origins of ancient Israel.

of the poor, and other social injustices and immoralities. They also criticized the leaders' faith in alliances with other nations and lack of faith in God's power to protect the nation. Today, prophets are those who can see the future, but prophets in Israel were much more forth-tellers of God's will than foretellers of the future. The importance of prophets to Israelite and Jewish religion is indicated by the fact that the books of the prophets make up the largest section of the Bible. (We'll consider the formation and use of the Bible below, at the beginning of "Essential Teachings of Judaism.") As contemporary Jewish scholar Abraham Heschel wrote, the prophets portray the righteousness of God and God's anguish over Israel's disobedience.[1] The prophetic tradition that demands justice in God's name for the poor and oppressed is one of the great gifts of Judaism to the world.

This statue of the prophet Ezekiel by Carlo Chelli captures Ezekiel's power and intensity as he speaks God's word.

© ONLY FABRIZIO/SHUTTERSTOCK.COM

[1] Abraham Heschel, *The Prophets*, study edition (Peabody, MA: Hendricksen, 2007).

> *Today's prophets are said to see the future, but prophets in Israel were much more forthtellers of God's will than foretellers of the future.*

When Solomon died in 922 B.C.E., the people of God divided into two different nations, each with its own king: Israel, comprised of ten tribes in the north, and Judah, comprised of only the two tribes of Judah and Benjamin in the south (see Map 10.1). Each nation claimed to be the true successor of the united kingdom of Saul, David, and Solomon. Sometimes the two kingdoms warred with each other, and at other times they cooperated against common enemies. But two centuries later, in 722, the Assyrian Empire wiped out the northern kingdom of Israel. Its ten tribes would never appear again, becoming in Jewish lore the "ten lost tribes." The southern kingdom of Judah was crippled at the same time by the Assyrians, who conquered several Judean cities and deported their citizens. Judah was finally conquered in 586 by the Babylonian Empire. The temple in Jerusalem was destroyed and the population decimated by death and exile. The First Temple Period had ended with a disaster, and Israelite religion was poised to disappear into the mists of time like the religions of so many other conquered peoples.

Exile and return provides "the structure of all Judaism."
—Jacob Neusner

Those carried off to Babylon in the exile were members of the Judean ruling class and skilled craftsmen. Although some exiles probably assimilated into Babylonian religion, others viewed recent events as confirmation rather than disproof of the sovereignty of Israel's God. The warnings of the prophets, remembered in the exile, helped Israel interpret what had happened to them as God's punishment for repeated violations of the covenant. In the ancient world, military defeat and exile usually spelled the end of a particular ethnic group, as it already had for the northern kingdom of Israel. Despite the disaster of 586 B.C.E. and even larger disasters to come, Israelite religion survived and emerged from the ancient world into the medieval and modern periods with a continuing religious identity

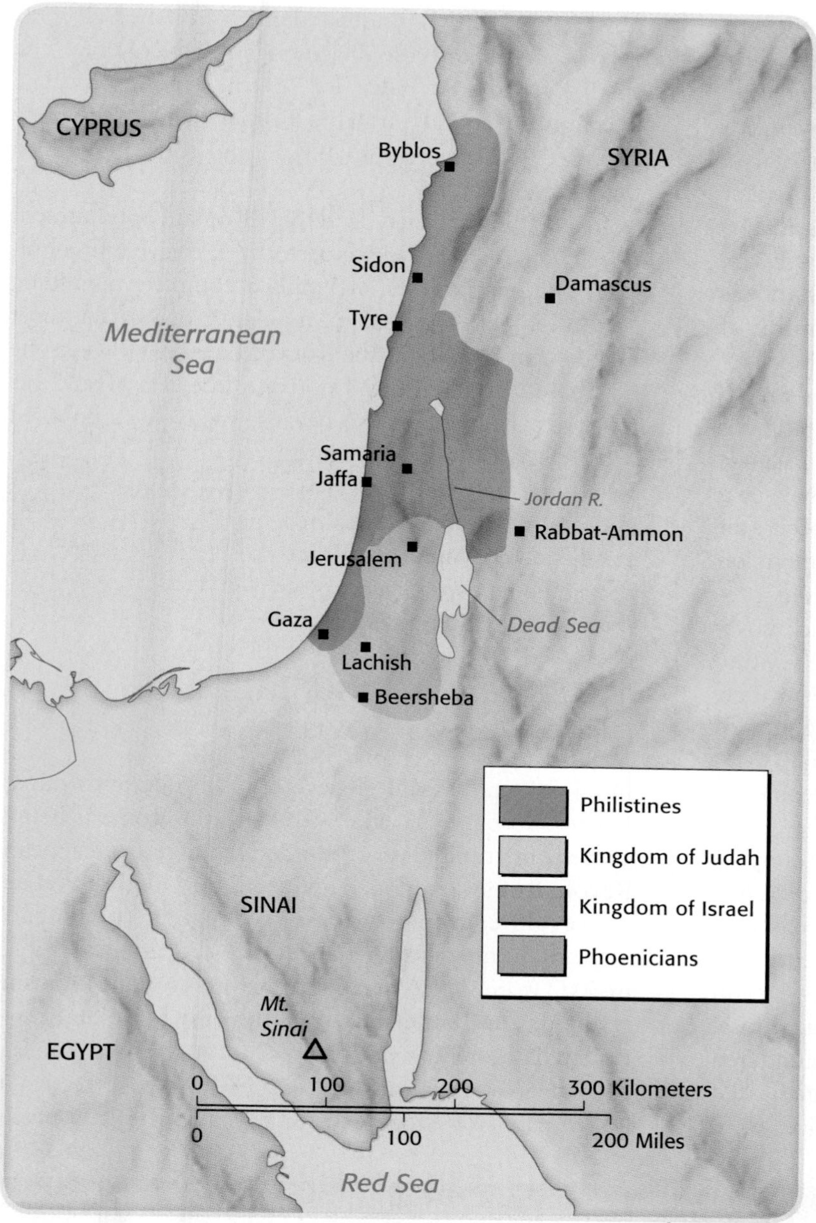
CYPRUS
Byblos
SYRIA
Sidon
Damascus
Tyre
Mediterranean Sea
Samaria
Jaffa
Jordan R.
Rabbat-Ammon
Jerusalem
Gaza
Dead Sea
Lachish
Beersheba
Philistines
Kingdom of Judah
Kingdom of Israel
Phoenicians
SINAI
Mt. Sinai
EGYPT
0
100
200
300 Kilometers
0
100
200 Miles
Red Sea

© CENGAGE LEARNING 2013

Map 10.1
The Monarchies of Israel and Judah, 924–722 B.C.E.
The northern kingdom of Israel and the southern kingdom of Judah had expanded beyond the traditional areas of the twelve tribes, especially at times when neighboring kingdoms and empires were relatively weak. The kingdom of Israel fell to the Assyrian Empire in 722 to 721 B.C.E.

now called *Judaism*. The pattern of exile and return would provide a historical and religious pattern that a leading scholar of Judaism, Jacob Neusner, calls "the structure of all Judaism."[2]

[2] Jacob Neusner, "Judaism," in Arvind Sharma, ed., *Our Religions* (New York: HarperOne, 1994), 314.

10-2d The Second Temple Period (539 B.C.E.–70 C.E.)

In 539 B.C.E. the Babylonians were defeated by Cyrus (SIGH-rus) of Persia, a Zoroastrian whose empire covered virtually the whole Near East (see Chapter 9). Cyrus authorized the rebuilding of the Jewish temple of Jerusalem. The exiles would be allowed to return to Judea and live as a subject state within the Persian Empire. In Judea, the new leaders Ezra and Nehemiah zealously promoted a renewed commitment to the covenant made at Mount Sinai. Increasingly, community life was organized around the Torah, which was now in written form as the first five books of the Bible. The Second Temple was completed between 521 and 515, and the **Second Temple Period** would extend until 70 C.E., when the Romans destroyed the Second Temple. During this time, another abiding feature of Jewish life arose: the **Diaspora**, or "dispersion," of Jews outside the ancient territory of Israel. Many, perhaps most, of the Jews in Babylon stayed there when others returned to Jerusalem in the 530s. Within a hundred years or so, there would be more Jews living outside the territory of Israel than inside it. Large Jewish communities could be found in Alexandria, Egypt, and in Antioch, Syria, and smaller ones in hundreds of cities that would come into the Roman Empire. This Diaspora situation became permanent in Judaism and endures even today.

Take a 3-D tour of the Second Temple.

In the 330s B.C.E., Alexander of Macedon (in northern Greece) began conquering and amassing the largest empire yet seen, taking Israel in his conquest. In Alexander's time, tens of thousands of Greeks migrated to all parts of his vast empire. Greek culture in Palestine extended until the rise of Islam in the 600s C.E., because many Jews in Palestine were significantly Hellenized in culture while keeping to Judaism. The two centuries after Alexander's conquests

Second Temple Period Era of Jewish history from ca. 539 B.C.E. to 70 C.E., when the Romans destroyed the Second Temple

Diaspora [dee-ASS-pohr-uh] Dispersion of Jews outside the ancient territory of Israel

saw the formation of Jewish movements with diverse understandings of Judaism. The Sadducees were a priestly movement who accepted only the earliest books of the Bible as authoritative and cooperated with the Romans. The **Pharisees** were a lay movement of Torah teachers who later became religious leaders and developed the oral traditions of the Torah. The **Essenes** probably began the separatist ultra-Torah-observant community at Qumran on the Dead Sea. Various prophetic or messianic movements also arose within Judaism from time to time, including one led by Jesus of Nazareth (4 B.C.E.–30 C.E.) that would later become the Christian religion.

Alexander's successors had a significant impact on Judea and Judaism. After gaining control of Judea in 198 B.C.E., the Seleucid (sell-YOO-sid) dynasty of Greek rulers that controlled the Middle East rewarded the pro-Seleucid faction of Jews. But a struggle soon arose over the office of high priest. The Seleucid king suspected a revolt, captured Jerusalem, and plundered the Temple in 168 B.C.E. The Temple was rededicated to the Greek high god Zeus, and pagan sacrifices were made there. Many Jews were outraged, and when foundational Jewish observances such as circumcision and Sabbath observance were forbidden on pain of death, the **Maccabean Revolt** broke out. The revolt was led by Judas Maccabeus, of the Hasmonean clan, and his sons. The Seleucid armies were defeated, and the Temple was liberated and rededicated to God in December, 164 B.C.E., an event commemorated by Jews to this day in the winter festival of **Hanukkah**. Before and during the revolt, many devout Jews were tortured and killed, leading to the first written accounts of Jewish martyrs. Their example has echoed strongly through Jewish history until

now. In 142 B.C.E., independence from the Seleucids was secured, and the Hasmonean family ruled the small kingdom of Judea for several generations. The Hasmoneans ruled until the Roman general Pompey captured Jerusalem in 63 B.C.E. and took Judea into the Roman Empire.

King Herod ruled Israel by Roman appointment from 37 to 4 B.C.E. He undertook extensive and ambitious building projects, including a complete rebuilding of the Temple in Jerusalem, making it one of the most magnificent temples in the Roman Empire. However, he was hated by many Jews not only for cruelty and his loyalty to Rome, but also because many Jews doubted if he really was Jewish by birth. Relations between the Jews and their Roman overlords steadily deteriorated, and Rome appointed its own governors to the area after Herod died.

Take an interactive tour of Jerusalem at the end of the Second Temple Period.

10-2e Revolts and Rabbis (70 C.E.–ca. 650)

In 66 C.E., a full-scale Jewish revolt broke out against Rome. Although it began well, with the Romans being chased out, it ended very differently than the Maccabean Revolt. Rome summoned all its military might to crush the revolt, engaging in massive slaughter of combatants and noncombatants alike. It destroyed the Temple in 70 C.E., and a permanent transformation of Judaism resulted. The Temple had been the only place that represented the whole nation to God and was the location of great religious events such as Jewish festivals and the Day of Atonement. It was also the only place

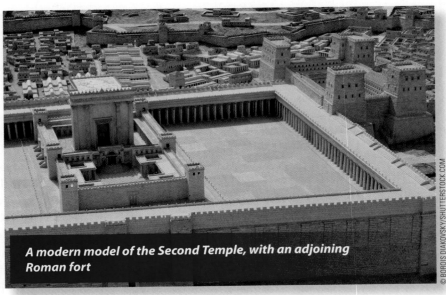

A modern model of the Second Temple, with an adjoining Roman fort

© BOROJS DIAKOVSKY/SHUTTERSTOCK.COM

Arch of Titus in the Roman Forum, showing trophies from the Jewish temple

where sacrifices could be offered to God. In addition, the Temple was a forum for Jewish teachers and the location of the high council of religious leaders that governed Judaism. The destruction of the Temple was a disaster for Judaism, and the end of the revolt against Rome brought the end of every group in Judaism except the Pharisees, who would eventually take over the religion's leadership.

Take a panoramic tour of the Arch of Titus.

Jewish hopes for independence and Roman heavy-handed tactics continued in the ensuing decades, climaxing in a revolt in 130 led by messianic claimant Simon Bar Kochba. This rebellion was also crushed by Rome. The Jewish population had now been hit hard by two wars of their own making in only sixty years. However, during this period a small and peripheral group connected to pre-70 C.E. scribes and Pharisees preserved a Torah-centered, lay-led Judaism. It would be at least two centuries before these teachers, or **rabbis**, would begin to win broader influence and judicial authority over Judaism. In the 300s and 400s, the rabbis gradually became spiritual leaders in local Jewish communities, the **synagogues**.

When Christianity became the official faith of the Roman Empire around 400 C.E., Jews were allowed to survive but not thrive. From about 100 to 400 C.E., Christianity and Judaism had been in the process of separation, and mutual hostility was often strong. The Code of Justinian in 527 C.E. contained discriminatory legislation against the Jews and Judaism that was to influence European legal systems for centuries and contribute to **anti-Semitism**, prejudice and discrimination against the Jewish people. Anti-Semitism isn't Christian or even European in origin or expression. Its oldest

forms can be traced to 500 B.C.E. in Egypt, and today the strongest forms of it are found in the Muslim Middle East. Despite these hardships, or perhaps because of them, many Jews chose to form their communities around synagogues. The local synagogue became the chief organization of Jewish life in late antiquity and remained so until the modern period.

The single most important Jewish community from about 600 to 1500 C.E. was in Babylonia, outside the sphere of Greek, Roman, and then Christian power. As we've seen, Israelites arrived in Babylonia during the time of their exile in 586 B.C.E. In later periods there was some immigration from Palestine, but scholars didn't make their way to Babylonia and establish a home there until the persecutions after the Bar Kochba revolt in the 130s C.E. Over the next centuries the status of the Babylonian Jewish community grew in prestige, and immigration increased. Although the Babylonian Jewish community confronted problems and occasional persecution, its freedom from Christian government and from the hardships that prevailed in Palestine enabled it to develop into a vibrant center of Jewish intellectual and cultural life. By 600, it had surpassed the Palestinian community in its leadership of world Judaism.

> All modern forms of Judaism are built on, or react to, the foundation of the Babylonian Talmud.

The work of the rabbinic academy in Babylon centered first on the Mishnah, a collection of primarily legal traditions based on all aspects of the Torah—what we today would call civil, criminal, and religious law—produced in Palestine and brought to Babylonia in the early third century C.E. Generations of Babylonian rabbis discussed the Mishnah and related teachings, adding to them and ultimately producing a huge legal work known as

rabbis [RAB-ighs] Teachers of the law and successors of the Pharisees who eventually gained authority over Judaism

synagogue [SIN-uh-gawg] "Gathering" of local Jews in a congregation for worship and community life; later applied to a building

anti-Semitism [SEHM-ih-TIHZ-um] Prejudice and discrimination against the Jewish people

the **Babylonian Talmud**. Rabbinic Judaism is the Torah-centered way of life that finds expression in the vast sea of materials produced by Palestinian and Babylonian rabbis from 70 to 630 C.E., particularly the Babylonian Talmud. The Talmud achieved a remarkable degree of power in Jewish communities worldwide, a power that withstood serious challenges well into the early modern period. All forms of Judaism in the medieval and modern ages are built on, or react to, this foundation of the Talmud as interpreted by the rabbis.

Examine an interactive sample page of the Babylonian Talmud.

10-2f Jews under Islamic and Christian Rule (ca. 650–1800)

Jews in the medieval period lived under either Muslim or Christian rule. Muslims guaranteed religious toleration as long as the Jews recognized the supremacy of the Islamic rule. They had a second-class but protected status. On the whole, Jews adapted well to the Islamic regime and the political, economic, and social changes that it brought. They lived predominantly in major Arab cities; worked in commerce, banking, and the learned professions; and participated in cultural life, even adopting Arabic as their everyday language.

Some rabbis from these **Sephardic** Jewish communities—which were centered in the Middle East, North Africa, and Spain—were interested in the philosophical clarification of religious beliefs and the systematic presentation of their faith, just as Muslim and Christian theologians were doing. The most prominent medieval Jewish philosopher was Rabbi Moses ben Maimon (1135–1204), known as Maimonides. He addressed his *Guide for the Perplexed* to a student whose education in philosophy left him confused about his religious faith—a common situation for many students from a religious background!

Babylonian Talmud [TALL-mood] Jewish law code, a compilation of the "oral Torah"

Sephardic [seh-FAR-dik] Jews in medieval and modern times living in the Middle East, North Africa, and Spain

Kabbalah [KAHB-uh-luh] System of Jewish mysticism emphasizing the immediate, personal, and emotional experience of God

Ashkenazi [ASH-kuh-NAHZ-ee] Jews in medieval and modern times living in Western, Central, and Eastern Europe

ghetto Town or city neighborhood to which Jews were restricted

Maimonides was a brilliant legal scholar whose fourteen-volume work on Jewish law immediately became authoritative. In modern editions of the Talmud, his views are often cited.

The intense rationalism of medieval Jewish philosophy was undergirded by a rational system of Talmud interpretation. This emphasis on rational thought and action was countered by the rise of Jewish mysticism, emphasizing the immediate, personal, and nonrational experience of God. In twelfth-century France and thirteenth-century Spain, mystical forms of Judaism would combine with mainstream Judaism to produce **Kabbalah** (see "A Closer Look: Kabbalah"). The rabbis strongly condemned such practices, but they grew nonetheless. They remain popular among Jews and non-Jews today.

Jews were outsiders in medieval Christian society in Western, Central, and Eastern Europe, where they called themselves **Ashkenazi**, as distinguished from Sephardic. Rulers granted them permission to live in specified neighborhoods. In these neighborhoods, Jews ran their own affairs and maintained their own institutions, such as social-relief funds, schools, a synagogue led by a rabbi, a council and court for religious affairs, a bathhouse for ritual cleansing, kosher meat shops, and so on. They developed their own language, Yiddish, a combination of Hebrew and German that originated in Germany but spread widely to European Jews. Jews in Western and Central Europe typically lived in cities. Many of those in Eastern Europe (Poland and Russia) lived in small villages centered on farming, the kind of society depicted in an 1894 collection of short stories by Sholem Aleichem (SHOH-luhm uh-LIGHK-uhm), which became the basis of the Broadway musical and 1971 film *Fiddler on the Roof*.

Watch Jonathan Ginsburg's explanation of Yiddish.

In the 1200s, decrees by the Roman Catholic Church after the Fourth Lateran Council altered the life of European Jews. Christians were now forbidden to lend money at interest, so Jews were free to move into banking, which they did with great success. Direct restrictions on Jews arose at this time: wearing distinctive clothing (especially hats) or a yellow badge alerting others to their presence; exclusion from the crafts and trades by guilds that controlled access to training and jobs; exclusion from the new universities being founded in Europe; restriction to Jewish neighborhoods called **ghettos**; and special permission required to work outside the ghetto. The rising view of Jews as dangerous

A Closer Look:

Kabbalah

Kabbalah pictured God not as a simple unity, but rather as a structured Being with an inner configuration of ten attributes. Evil is believed to be provoked by human sin and set right by good deeds, fulfillment of the commandments, prayer, and mystical contemplation. More esoteric Kabbalistic beliefs have included the transmigration of souls and the practice of sexual intercourse as a mirror of the union among the divine attributes. Many of these ideas are found in *The Zohar*, the leading book on Kabbalah by Moses de Leon (1250–1305). Kabbalah spread quickly, and in the sixteenth century Rabbi Isaac Luria (1534–1572) reformulated this esoteric system to emphasize messianic redemption.

Another offshoot of Kabbalah arose around an itinerant folk healer named Israel ben Eleazar (1700–1760)—more commonly called the Baal Shem Tov (bah-AHL shehm tohv), or "Master of the Good Name." This was **Hasidism**, a Jewish mystical movement that stresses joyful emotion. Hasidism soon attracted Jews in Russia, Poland, Hungary, and Romania. The message of the Hasidic masters was that God is present and directly accessible in the world, that God is best experienced and worshiped in joy, that even

A red string worn on the left wrist is a prominent sign of Kabbalah today.

© ISTOCKPHOTO.COM/CAGAN

the most evil persons and events are capable of redemption, and that each Jew has an essential role to play in making the world holy. The new Hasidic pietism drew on Kabbalah in a way that overcame its esoteric character.

Hasidism soon became established in the Jewish communities of Poland and the Ukraine. In Lithuania, Lubavich (LOOB-uh-vich) Hasidism emphasized a distinctive blend of Kabbalistic speculation and rabbinic learning. Despite Hasidism's antitraditionalist origins and history, it has ironically come to represent orthodoxy, even so-called "ultra-orthodoxy," in the modern world, especially to non-Jews.

At the end of the twentieth century, Kabbalah was popularized and spread beyond Judaism. Its psychological and social aspects were emphasized, and its Torah-related and messianic elements were muted. Although controversial among observant Jews, today there are hundreds of Kabbalah centers, conferences, books, and other sources of information about Kabbalah practice, nearly all of them catering to non-Jews.

Read a 2008 newspaper article on controversy over Kabbalah in British schools.

---

was fueled by envy, irrational suspicions, and even hatred, which led to repeated expulsions and massacres. Jews were expelled from France in 1182 and 1306, and from England in 1290. Devastating massacres occurred in Germany in 1298, wiping out 140 Jewish communities, and in 1348 to 1349, when the Black Plague was falsely attributed to Jews poisoning wells. In 1492 Spain expelled all Jews, estimated to be between 100,000 and 150,000 people. Many of them fled to temporary safety in Portugal, some of whom eventually went to The Netherlands—one of the few relatively safe havens for Jews in Europe. One reaction of European Jews to this continued persecution was the development of Jewish mystical piety, especially the Kabbalah. The Protestant Reformation in the 1500s was a mixed blessing to the Jews of northern Europe. In some places, such as The Netherlands and England, Protestant reformers treated them with some tolerance. But in Germany, the Protestant reformer Martin Luther eventually resumed some aspects of anti-Jewish sentiment—after a more tolerant start—in ways that would echo through later German history.

Hasidism [HASS-uh-dizm] Jewish mystical movement that stresses joyful emotion, which arose in the 1700s

Street scene in the medieval Jewish quarter of Lublin, Poland

PHOTO COURTESY PHOTO8.COM

nation while retaining Jewish religious faith. Just as Christians could practice their religion as citizens of different nations, so too should Jews. German-Jewish intellectual Moses Mendelssohn (MEN-dul-sohn; 1729–1786) was an influential example of those who embraced modernity while staying Jewish. He urged Jews to participate in European culture and to continue in Judaism—what he called the "double yoke" placed on them by God.

Many Jews questioned why they should shoulder a "double yoke" of being both Jewish and European—why not just assimilate completely?

10-2g Emancipation and Diversity (1800–1932)

Around 1800, under the influence of the Enlightenment, many Western European nations began to drop their restrictions on Jews. No longer did Jews have to live in their own neighborhood, be subject to the local rabbi, or dress and talk like Jews had in Europe for more than a thousand years. In less than a century, many Jews rose to become some of the leading figures in science, medicine, education, commerce, and banking. (This astonishing level of achievement continued in the twentieth century, when one-quarter of all Nobel Prize winners were Jewish.) Their **emancipation** prompted many nineteenth-century Jews to wonder why they should continue to be Jews when they could be citizens of European states. Many modern Jews chose to assimilate, which sometimes included conversion to Christianity. Some—for example, Sigmund Freud and Karl Marx—even began systems of thought, science, and government that rationalized God out of existence and opposed religion in general and particularly Judaism.

Many other Jews responded that Jewish identity was not primarily ethnic or national, but religious. One could be a loyal citizen of a European nation but still keep the Jewish religion. They urged not assimilation, but *acculturation*—that is, taking on the culture of one's

emancipation Jewish freedom from Christian and state control in Europe after 1800

Reform Movement founded by Abraham Geiger; most liberal of Jewish branches

However, many Jews in the early 1800s began to question why they should shoulder this "double yoke"—why not just assimilate completely? This questioning, and doubts about some elements of traditional Judaism that looked increasingly odd to many modern Jews, sparked controversies among mostly German Jews in the mid-1800s. The controversies eventually led to the three main branches of Judaism today—usually called "movements": Reform, Orthodox, and Conservative. The **Reform** movement, led by Abraham Geiger (1820–1874), was the first new form of Judaism to arise. Geiger wanted to change Judaism into a modern religion with patterns of worship and devotion similar to those of German Protestant Christianity. Synagogues were renamed "temples," and services were no longer conducted in Hebrew, but German. Sermons by the rabbi and music by trained choirs were introduced; candles were put at the front of remodeled synagogues that now resembled Christian churches; and the ethnic and national aspects of Judaism were no longer mentioned. Reform Judaism gave up kosher food regulations, Jewish dress and hair codes, the Yiddish language, and other traditional aspects. It ended beliefs and practices it considered not a part of the spiritual essence of Judaism. Of course, this entailed a rejection of the Talmud. The Reform movement quickly spread through much of Europe and North America.

Traditionalist Jews condemned these reforms as a betrayal of Judaism. They viewed their form of Judaism as the only legitimate continuation of Rabbinic Judaism and biblical Israel. The leader of the modern **Orthodox** movement was Samson Raphael Hirsch (hersh; 1808–1888). Hirsch urged a combination of traditional Jewish religious practices and selective appreciation of European civilization. He criticized the Reform movement for diminishing Judaism for the convenience and contentment of modern Jews. Instead, he urged the Orthodox movement to prompt Jews toward classical Judaism in a fresh and vigorous way. The Orthodox movement has several different internal groups, some of them now called (especially Hasidic groups in Israel) the "ultra-Orthodox." Because of their high birthrate and ability to keep their children in the faith, the Orthodox continue to grow in numbers in Europe and North America.

A third main branch of Judaism, originally called "Positive-Historical" in Germany, came to be known in North America as the **Conservative** movement. It was led by German-Bohemian rabbi and scholar Zecharias Frankel (FRAHN-kul; 1801–1875). It claimed the middle ground between Reform and Orthodoxy. In that sense, "moderate Judaism" would be a better name for it than "Conservative Judaism," but the latter name stuck. (In Israel and Europe today, this movement is known as **Masorti**, "traditionalist.") It opposed Reform's sweeping changes by affirming the positive value of much of past Judaism in which the voice of God could be discerned. It opposed the Orthodox movement by asserting the historical evolution of the Judaic tradition, which Orthodoxy denied with its claim that the whole Law of God—the written form that became the Bible and the oral form that became the Talmud—was revealed to Moses on Mount Sinai.

Although many European Jews modernized rapidly in the 1800s and were optimistic about the future of Judaism, a wide outbreak of hostility toward the Jews in the 1870s and 1880s cast a dark shadow on their sunny optimism. For example, in France the Dreyfus affair—in which a Jewish army officer by that name was falsely accused of crimes—stirred up wide anti-Jewish feelings. In Russia, the czar's secret police authored a vile book entitled the *Protocols of the Elders of Zion* that purported to relate how rich and powerful Jews were conspiring to take over the world. Modern anti-Semitism was a backlash against Jewish success in Europe, a sign that Jews were still considered outsiders. In earlier times, anti-Semitism had a mainly religious basis, but in modern Europe it was based on ethnicity.

In the light of this revived anti-Semitism, and in a time of rising European nationalistic movements that formed new nations such as Germany and Italy, Jewish movements sprang up, emphasizing newfound Jewish nationalism. Most important was **Zionism**, so called after an ancient Hebrew name for Jerusalem, which aimed for large Jewish emigration from Europe to Palestine. In 1897, Theodor Herzl (HURT-zuhl; 1860–1904) organized the First Zionist Congress in Basel, Switzerland, which called for an internationally recognized Jewish national home in Palestine. The Zionist movement was largely secular in orientation. With continued anti-Semitism in Europe, increasing numbers of Jewish immigrants settled in Palestine and began to set up the social infrastructure of a modern nation. The quest for a Jewish nation free from the threats of anti-Semitism was well on its way. In 1917 the British government issued the Balfour Declaration, giving

Orthodox Modern movement founded by Samson Raphael Hirsch; most conservative of Jewish branches

Conservative Movement founded by the German-Bohemian rabbi and scholar Zecharias Frankel, claiming the middle ground between Reform and Orthodoxy

Masorti [mah-SOHR-tee] "Traditionalist," name of Conservative movement in Europe and Israel

Zionism [ZY-on-izm] Modern organization promoting large Jewish immigration into Palestine

A modern Reform synagogue

© RON ZMIRI/SHUTTERSTOCK.COM

British support for a national home for the Jewish people in Palestine.

"A land without a people for a people without a land." —Zionist slogan

The Zionist slogan was "a land without a people for a people without a land," but the Jewish settlers there found that Palestine wasn't really a land without a people. Arabs in the hundreds of thousands, both Muslims and Christians, were living in Palestine when Zionist settlement began, and their ancestors had been living in that small territory for more than a thousand years. Moreover, Palestinians were culturally advanced among the various Arab groups, and still are today. As the numbers of Jewish settlers increased, friction grew with the Arab population. Freedom for European Jews would come at the expense of a future conflict between Israeli Jews and Arabs, in which they would be locked in a long struggle for a land they both considered holy. Islam had been tolerant of Judaism for 1,300 years but now became rather intolerant, largely because of long-standing Muslim resistance to non-Muslims taking their holy land. Several wars were fought between Israel and its Arab neighbors from 1948 through today, all of them won by Israel, sometimes at a high cost (see Map 10.2). A few peace treaties have been signed, but the conflict continues. Jewish settlement in Israel grew quickly after the events of World War II, especially after Germany's extermination of the majority of European Jews. We now turn to a brief examination of this horrific story.

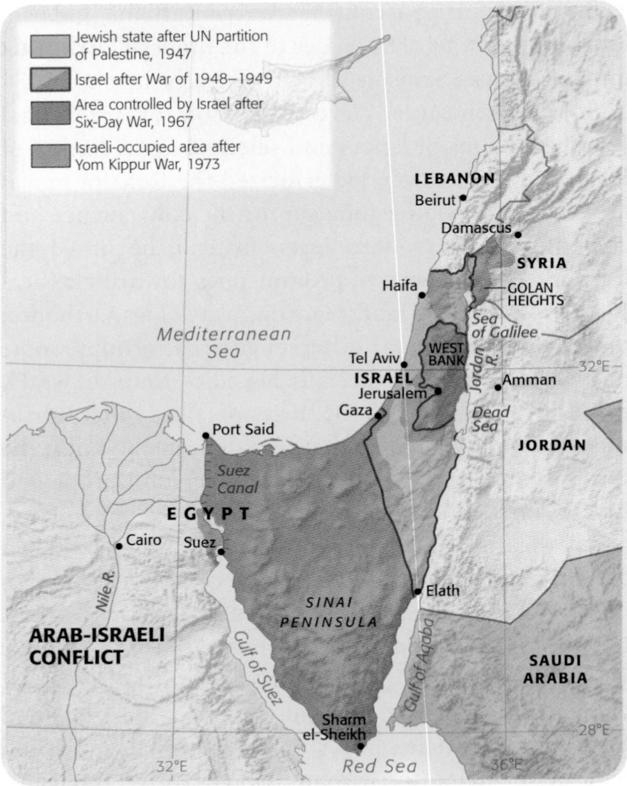

Map 10.2
Arab-Israeli Conflict, 1947–Present
By Egyptian-Israeli agreements of 1975 and 1979, Israel withdrew from the Sinai in 1982. By 1981 Israel annexed the Golan Heights in Syria. Through negotiations between Israel and the PLO, the West Bank and the Gaza Strip were placed under Palestinian self-rule, and Israeli troops were withdrawn in 1994. In 1994 Israel and Jordan signed an agreement opening their borders and normalizing their relations.

10-2h The Holocaust and Its Aftermath (1932–Present)

Adolf Hitler and his Nazi Party won office in the 1932 German national elections, and in 1933 Hitler quickly moved toward totalitarian power with a variety of repressive measures. Some of these pursued Nazi ideology to "purify" Germany through a series of anti-Semitic laws gradually introduced between 1933 and 1938. Germans who had just one grandparent who was Jewish by ethnicity— on a synagogue roll, for example, or a member of a secular Jewish organization—were deemed to be Jewish, whether or not they thought of themselves as Jewish.

Jews had to wear a yellow star in public for identification. Marriage and sexual relations between Jews and so-called Aryan Germans were banned, and by 1938 all German Jews had been stripped of their citizenship, civil rights, and some from their professional jobs. Some Jews fled as these laws were passed, but the majority stayed, hoping that each new law would be the last.

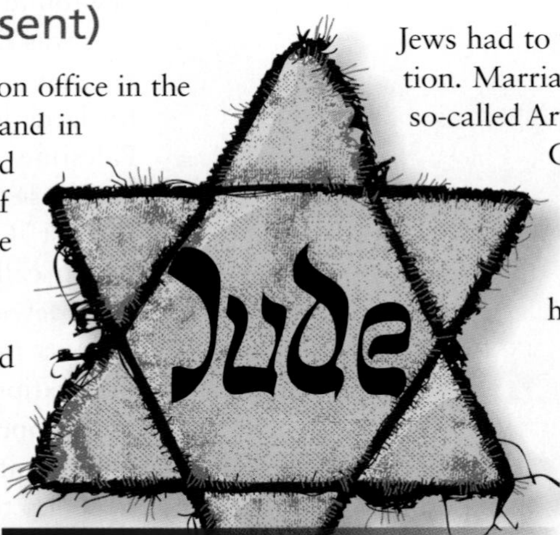

Badge worn by Jews in Nazi Germany. Jude (pronounced YOO-deh) is German for "Jew."

The Nazi aim in the "Final Solution" was to make not only Germany, but all of Europe, "Jew-free."

These hopes were in vain. When World War II began in 1939, Hitler ordered a "Final Solution" of the "Jewish Question." The term **Holocaust** (a term from Jewish ritual literally meaning a "completely burned" sacrifice) came after the war, used to describe the Nazi genocide of Jews and other groups; the Hebrew term **Shoah**, "destruction," is also used. When Germany invaded Poland, "special assignment groups" of German troops held mass executions of hundreds of thousands of Jews who lived in villages and towns in newly conquered territory. But this soon proved "inefficient." In 1942, the German government erected concentration camps in western Germany and occupied Poland, after the model of the first camp in Dachau. The purpose of these camps was not to "concentrate" Jews, but to kill them with all the efficiency of state-run mass murder. Jews from Germany and Poland were brought by train to be killed by poison gas or to work to death as slave laborers in adjoining factories. Then Jews from every other nation in Nazi-occupied Europe—especially Russia, Hungary, France, and The Netherlands—were hunted down and brought by train to the camps. The Nazi aim of the "Final Solution" was to make not only Germany, but all of Europe, "Jew-free." Approximately six million Jews perished in this Holocaust/Shoah, nearly three-quarters of Europe's Jewish population.

Relatively few Germans dared—or cared—to risk death by opposing the actions of their government. Among the famous examples of those that did are Roman Catholic industrialist Oskar Schindler, who protected 1,200 Jewish workers from death, and Protestant theologian Dietrich Bonhoeffer (BAHN-haw-fuhr), who spoke out against anti-Semitism and Nazi control of German churches. Bonhoeffer also participated in a failed plot to kill Hitler; the Nazis hanged him shortly before the war ended. When Schindler died in 1974, he was buried with great honors in Jerusalem.

Visit a website devoted to Oskar Schindler.

The Holocaust brought a crisis of faith to Judaism like no event before it. To adapt Jacob Neusner's phrase, it was an "exile" from which "return" was extremely difficult. Orthodox Jews in general explained the Holocaust as punishment for recent Jewish sins, as a test of faith, or even as an opportunity to die for the faith. For many other Jews, it shook the foundations of Judaism. Some Jews, such as Richard Rubenstein, said that the only possible valid response to the Holocaust was the rejection of God. If God could allow the Holocaust, then there was no God. Many Jews agreed with this, and the abandonment of traditional beliefs and practices of Jewish religion that had begun in the Jewish emancipation accelerated. On the other hand, Emil Fackenheim and others insisted that the Holocaust did *not* show that God was dead. To reject Judaism's God, Fackenheim said, was to aid Hitler in the accomplishment of his evil, even demonic goal to destroy Judaism.

Whatever the best response to the Holocaust—not yet a settled question in Judaism—the field of religious studies has given it a large and important place in teaching and research. Holocaust museums have sprung up in several major North American cities. Popular literature and film have also dealt extensively with the Holocaust. *The Diary of Anne Frank*, authored by the Dutch Jewish teenager who wrote about her life in hiding, has become required reading in secondary schools all over the world. The works of Holocaust survivors such as Elie Wiesel (EHL-ee vee-ZEHL), particularly his moving novel *Night*, are widely read. Hollywood films on the Holocaust—*Schindler's List*, *Sophie's Choice*, *Life Is Beautiful*, and many others—have portrayed this sad part of recent history in especially powerful ways.

Holocaust [HAUL-oh-cost] Nazi genocide of Jews and other groups in World War II

Shoah [SHOW-uh] "Destruction," Hebrew term for the Holocaust

Watch an interview with Elie Wiesel on the relationship of the Holocaust to other genocides.

Watch an introduction to Yad Vashem, the Israeli national museum of the Holocaust.

Liam Neeson (center) as Oskar Schindler in Schindler's List, walking past his Jewish workers, whom he rescued

© UNIVERSAL/COURTESY EVERETT COLLECTION

Learning Outcome 10-3

Outline the essential teachings of Judaism in your own words.

10-3 Essential Teachings of Judaism

A Jewish woman enters her home in Los Angeles. Just before she goes through her front door, she looks at a small box fastened to the right frame of the door. It contains a small scroll with three short passages from the Hebrew Bible, especially the key words of Deuteronomy 6:4–9: "Take to heart these instructions.... Recite them when you stay at home and when you are away, when you lie down and when you get up.... Inscribe them on the doorposts of your house and on your gates." She touches this box reverently as a reminder to remember God and keep God's teachings within her home. This little ritual act displays a key characteristic of Judaism: that it is a religion of action more than a religion of reflection.

Judaism as a whole has no official statement of its essential teachings. Unlike many other religions, it has rarely argued over doctrine to the point of division. The closest it came to a confession was the *Thirteen Articles* of Maimonides, but this was never widely accepted as a formal statement of Jewish teaching, in its time or later. Persons are Jewish whether they hold to a system of traditional Jewish teachings, have simple beliefs associated with rituals such as the Passover meal, or don't embrace any traditional Jewish teachings at all. This situation arises largely because actions in accordance with the Torah, not beliefs, are the most important aspect of Jewish religious life. Today, *Jewish* describes a people and a culture as well as a religion, so some who call themselves Jewish have little interest in any Jewish religious practices and even less in the teachings of Judaism.

Read the *Thirteen Articles* of Maimonides.

Tanak [TAH-nahk] Name for the Hebrew Bible, an acronym formed from the first letters of Torah (the law), Nevi'im (the prophets), and Kethuvim (the writings)

henotheism Belief in one God while accepting that other gods may exist

10-3a Foundation of Jewish Teachings: The Tanak

The foundation of Jewish teaching and ethics is the Jewish Bible, commonly called the **Tanak**. This name is an acronym formed from the first letters of the three divisions of the Bible: the Torah (instruction, law); the second division, called the Nevi'im (prophets); and the third, the Kethuvim (writings). The Jewish scriptures arose over a period of more than a thousand years, and the Tanak was finalized only in the first century C.E. Even before this finalization, a translation into Greek had been made in second century B.C.E. Egypt for Jews who had lived so long in the Diaspora that they had lost their knowledge of the Hebrew language. In the consolidation of Judaism that occurred after the Jewish revolt against Rome in 66–70 C.E., the status of this Greek translation, called the *Septuagint* (sep-TOO-uh-jint), fell. Soon only the Hebrew Bible was used in synagogues, even though many Jews could not understand it.

Even more important than the particular documents of the Bible is the authority that Jews have traditionally invested in the biblical canon. It is said to be the written revelation of God—containing God's very words. The Bible is especially authoritative in expressing what God expects the Jewish people to do in response to the divine self-revelation. It conveys and shapes the faith and action of Jews through all times. Jews have debated the meaning of the Bible, have often strongly disagreed about it, and in modern times have studied it with modern scholarly methods, but a majority of Jews accept the Bible as their special book in some significant sense. The Jewish use of their scriptural canon has deeply influenced the formation, contents, and use of scripture in Christianity and Islam.

Examine a chart of the structure of the Hebrew Bible.

Despite the lack of primary emphasis on teaching, the Bible and Talmud contain a great deal of teaching about God, humanity, and the meaning of life. Jewish history has seen significant theological and mystical inquiry into religious concepts. We'll consider three main teachings: one God, the chosen people, and life after death. (We'll also consider other foundational teachings—the position in the Torah on obedience to God's will and the concept of *ethical monotheism*—in the section "Essential Jewish Ethics" below.)

10-3b One God

Judaism teaches monotheism, meaning that Jews believe that only one God exists. Hebrew and Israelite religion acknowledged the possible existence of other gods, but only one God for Israel. This **henotheism**—the belief in one God while accepting that other gods may exist—seems to have been prevalent in ancient

Israel. For example, Canaanite gods were worshiped at Israelite holy places shortly after Israelite settlement in their promised land, King David named some of his children after Canaanite gods, and Solomon built a shrine to a Canaanite fertility goddess outside Jerusalem.

Full, formal monotheism seems to have come during the Babylonian exile in the 500s B.C.E. As we saw above, the return from Babylon featured a strict enforcement of monotheism, and Judaism has continued in it ever since. Israel's God is eternal, holy, all knowing, all present, all powerful. God is a divine being, not a principle or a force. God guides not only those who know him, but also the nations and human history. God is transcendent, far above the world and human ability to comprehend God; but God is immanent as well, present in the world and in each human being. Because God is holy and just, God punishes humans for their disobedience, particularly those who know the Torah; but because God is merciful, God forgives and renews relationships.

How individual Jews choose to relate to God has varied in different times and places. Some have related to God by studying and keeping the Torah, by formal worship in the two Temples and in synagogues, with piety and emotion, and occasionally even with mysticism. An important part of Jewish piety relating to monotheism is the **Shema**, a basic statement of faith from Deuteronomy 6 that begins "Hear, O Israel: The Lord our God is One." Some Jews today even relate to God by denying God's existence, but ironically this too has become a Jewish option.

Listen to a recitation of the Shema.

Judaism's names for God are an important aspect of its teaching about God. The holiest name of God, as God revealed it to Moses in the book of Exodus, is YHWH. This name seems to be built on the Hebrew verb *to be* and means either "I am" or "I will be." YHWH is sometimes referred to as the *tetragrammaton* (TEH-trah-GRAM-mah-tahn), from the Greek word for "four lettered." When vowels were added to written Hebrew in the Middle Ages, this name was considered too holy to be changed, so we don't know its original pronunciation. The common word *Jehovah* (jeh-HOH-vuh), however, is

Observant Jews wear kippahs out of reverence for God.
© EDUARDO RAMIREZ SANCHEZ/SHUTTERSTOCK.COM

Shema [sheh-MAH, or shmah] Basic statement of faith from Deuteronomy 6 that begins "Hear, O Israel: The Lord our God is One"

incorrect as a vocalization. A more grammatically correct spelling and pronunciation, one used by scholars, is *Yahweh* (YAH-weh; one often hears YAH-way as well). Nevertheless, this discussion is irrelevant to most Jews, because they don't pronounce God's name. When the Torah is read aloud, *Adonai* (ad-oh-NAI), meaning "Lord," is read in place of YHWH. This practice is reflected in many English translations, including in the Christian Bible, in which YHWH is rendered as "Lord." Jews demonstrate their reverence for God in a simple way, by wearing a skullcap called a *kippah* (KIHP-uh) or *yarmulke* (YAHR-muhl-kuh, sometimes YAH-mah-kuh).

Many traditionalist Jews also refer to God as *Hashem* (hah-SHEHM), "the Name," understanding that God, not just God's name, is meant. The prohibition against pronouncing God's name expresses a profound human reverence for God. Many modern Orthodox Jews and some Conservative Jews carry this reverence for God's name one step further. They refrain from writing the word *God*, replacing it instead with *G-d*. Other branches of modern Judaism do not follow them in this practice, saying that *God* is a generic noun, not a biblical name.

The tetragrammaton, or name for God in Hebrew, YHWH (Hebrew reads from right to left)
© ANASTAZZO/ISTOCK.COM

10-3c The Jews as God's Chosen People

Religions that believe in gods have seen themselves as having a special relationship with their gods, a relationship that makes them "chosen" or otherwise special. The Jews believe that they are God's "chosen people," chosen to be in a covenant with God. They didn't choose God; God chose them. The Jewish idea of being chosen is first found in the Torah and is elaborated in later books of the Tanak. This status carries both responsibilities and blessings, as described in the biblical accounts of the covenants with God.

According to the Tanak, Israel's character as the chosen people goes all the way back to Abraham and the eternal covenant God made with him: "I will establish my covenant between me and you and your descendants after you in their generations, for an everlasting covenant, to be God to you and your descendants after you" (Genesis 17:7). Being chosen as God's people brings a call to be holy and a realization of how amazing this is: "For you are a holy people to YHWH your God, and God has chosen you to be his treasured people from all the nations that are on the face of the earth" (Deuteronomy 14:2). This choice is grounded in God's love and faithfulness to the covenant promises made to Abraham, not on Israel's own qualities: "The Lord did not set his love upon you or choose you because you were more in number than any people, for you were the fewest of all people. It was because the Lord loved you, and because he would keep the oath which he had sworn to your ancestors" (Deuteronomy 7:7–8).

> Jews throughout history have found that being God's chosen people is mostly a blessing, but sometimes a mixed blessing that brings trouble.

The "flip side" of this chosen status is demanding, even ominous at times. Alongside the positive aspects, there is the necessity of obedience: "If you will obey my voice indeed, and keep my covenant, then you shall be a peculiar treasure unto me above all people" (Exodus 19:5). The obligation, even threat, that this demand for obedience entails is emphasized by the prophet Amos: "You only have I singled out of all the families of the earth; therefore will I punish you for all your iniquities" (Amos 3:2). Despite their status as a part of the chosen people, the ten tribes of the Israelites were wiped away in 721 B.C.E. because they disobeyed God continually. Jews throughout history have found their belief in being God's chosen people mostly a blessing, but sometimes a mixed blessing that brings troubles with both God and other people. A wry reflection about this mixed blessing is in the musical *Fiddler on the Roof*, when Tevye (the main character), beset by difficulties, prays, "I know we are the chosen people. But once in a while, can't you choose someone else?"

Throughout its history, Judaism has usually linked being the "chosen people" with a mission or purpose, such as being a "light to the nations," a "blessing to the nations," or a "kingdom of priests" between God and the world. This special duty derives from the covenant God made with Abraham and which was renewed at the giving of the Torah on Mount Sinai. Through the long history of Judaism and Israelite religion before it, the idea of being God's chosen people sustained many Jews throughout military defeat and exile, discrimination, persecution, even the Holocaust. In modern times, more-secular Jews have understood it to mean that their human abilities should be put to use for the good of all humankind. Even among secularized Jews there is a continuing feeling for the special status in having

Jewish clothing, hairstyles, and the hidden sign of circumcision have helped to define Jewish status as a chosen people. Here a young Orthodox Jew stands behind his father in Jerusalem.

©ISTOCKPHOTO.COM/LUOMAN

a Jewish heritage. British historian Paul Johnson sums it up well: He once wrote that historians cannot deal well with the religious claim that God actually chose the Jews and guided their history, but it can be affirmed that "The Jews believed that they were a special people with such unanimity and passion, and over so long a span, that they became one."[3]

10-3d Life after Death?

As the Hebrew Bible book of Job (johb) puts it, "If mortals die, will they live again?" (Job 14:14). World religions address this question, because clarity on the issues of life after death means a great deal to how they think about life *before* death. However, the Tanak doesn't say much on this subject, and Judaism as a whole today doesn't dwell on it. This may seem surprising to non-Jews, because the sacred texts of Christianity and Islam—both of which have their foundations in Judaism—speak often about life after death. But with Judaism's focus on actions more than on beliefs, it is actually to be expected that it not speculate about the world to come. Because many religions, including Judaism's sister faiths of Christianity and Islam, rely in part on fear of the fires of hell and the hope of heaven to motivate good conduct in their adherents, it is remarkable that Judaism, with its strong emphasis on morality, hasn't usually done the same.

An early common theme in the Bible is that death means joining one's ancestors in the land of the dead—being "gathered to one's people" (Genesis 25:8, 25:17, 35:29, 49:33; Deuteronomy 42:50). Another image emphasizes the reality of mortality. God made humans from the dust of the ground, and because of their sins they die and return to dust (Genesis 3:19). Jews take this literally: They regularly today use wooden coffins that over time allow the body to rejoin the ground. The predominant biblical image of the afterlife is *Sheol* (SHEE-ohl), which is similar to the Greek conception of Hades. Sheol is a shadowy underworld, a land of darkness and silence (Psalms 88:13, 115:17; Job 10:21, 22). Good

and evil people alike go to Sheol, and God isn't present there. These early biblical descriptions of death indicate a belief that the person continues to exist in some way after death, but not with a full or happy life. Much later in the biblical tradition the concept arises of the **resurrection** of the dead—or divine raising to eternal life—and a final judgment leading to either a blessed or a damned life. Daniel 12:2 declares, "And many of them that sleep in the dust of the earth shall awake, some to everlasting life and some to reproaches and everlasting abhorrence."

When rabbinical Judaism—based largely on the earlier Pharisees—took over, belief in resurrection was near universal in Judaism all the way to the time of the Jewish Enlightenment in 1800. The resurrection is one of the *Thirteen Articles* by Maimonides, and a prayer said regularly in traditionalist synagogues from medieval times through today affirms the resurrection. One early rabbi, Hiyya ben Joseph, suggested that the dead will travel through the ground and rise up in Jerusalem; the unrighteous will be naked and ashamed, and the righteous will be clothed and happy (Babylonian Talmud, Ketubot 111b). The hope of being raised in Jerusalem has led to large cemeteries there, especially on the Mount of Olives. Despite belief in a divine judgment that separates those whose deeds are on balance good from those whose deeds are not, some rabbis held that a middle group of people

resurrection Raising of the bodies of the dead to eternal life, usually followed by divine judgment

[3] Paul Johnson, *A History of the Jews* (New York: Harper and Row, 1987), 587.

Jewish cemetery on the Mount of Olives, facing the former site of the Temple

© YOSEFER/SHUTTERSTOCK.COM

of more mixed accomplishments will go into hell for an eleven-month period of purification and then enter heaven (Babylonian Talmud, Rosh Hashanah 16b-17a, Eduyot 2.10). This belief is probably connected to the Jewish practice of eleven months of mourning deceased loved ones.

Most Jews have believed that one need not be Jewish to enter heaven. Because God judges actions and not beliefs, all those who do what God commands will be rewarded. Maimonides, for example, wrote that all good people of the world will be blessed in the next world. Those who are "righteous among the Gentiles" (non-Jews) by virtue of their deeds, even if they belong to a different religion, will enter heaven. Heaven is typically called the "Garden of Eden," a place of joy and peace that recaptures the original home of humanity on earth. The Babylonian Talmud's imagery of heaven includes sitting at banquet tables (Taanit 25a), enjoying lavish banquets (Baba Batra 75a), and even enjoying heavenly sex with spouses (Berachot 57b). A few rabbis didn't like this imagery and held that there will be no eating, drinking, or sex in heaven—or if there is, they won't be quite so enjoyable. Instead, the blessed will enjoy heaven in a purely spiritual way (Babylonian Talmud, Berachot 17a). For example, despite his affirmation of the resurrection in the *Thirteen Articles*, Maimonides held that there is no material substance in heaven at all, only souls of the righteous without bodies (Mishneh Torah, Repentance 8). This purely spiritual view of heaven never became a mainstream Jewish teaching, because Judaism had long held that soul and body belong together in this world and the next. Both Islam and Christianity give much more importance to the teaching of resurrection and eternal life.

> "I don't believe in [an afterlife]. I believe this is it, and I believe it's the best way to live." —Natalie Portman

As stated above, this Talmudic teaching on the afterlife prevailed in virtually all of Judaism from about 400 to 1800 C.E. Today, Orthodox Jewish groups still teach the resurrection of the dead, judgment by God, and life in heaven or hell. Reform Judaism, on the other hand, rejected these doctrines as binding. Instead, its members are allowed to form their own opinions on life after death. The general view in the Reform movement, drawn from Enlightenment ideas, is that even if there is existence after death, we can't know much about it here, so it shouldn't play a large role in how people live. Human immortality, Reform Jews hold, is realized in one's children and the spiritual legacy one leaves behind. As a result, many Reform Jews and secular Jews

have no belief in life after death. For example, when the Israeli-American actress Natalie Portman—who was raised "Jewish but not religious"—was asked about her concept of the afterlife, she said, "I don't believe in that. I believe this [life] is it, and I believe it's the best way to live." The Conservative movement, between Orthodoxy and Reform, holds to the continued importance of the main lines of traditional teachings on this topic, but notes its historical conditioning and interprets its more vivid imagery as symbolic.

10-4 Essential Jewish Ethics

In Grand Rapids, Michigan, a short controversy breaks out in the press over the religious implications of a museum exhibit called "Bodies Revealed." This exhibit, which has played in several other North American cities, shows fourteen full human bodies and "hundreds of organs" in various states of dissection. The museum's website says it has anticipated the controversy that has followed the exhibition as it travels, so it has consulted ethical and religious experts about bringing the exhibit to town. Although it is popular, with excellent ticket sales, some controversy is aired publicly. An articulate examination is in a newspaper column by a local rabbi, David Krishef. Rabbi Krishef examines the good that can come from the exhibit, but, he asks, at what cost? He raises the traditional Jewish moral command to honor the bodies of the dead, not to display them to the public for profit, entertainment, or even education.

Read about the "Bodies Revealed" exhibit.

The moral life of the Jewish people today, of all branches, rests on biblical foundations. God created the world as a good place, to reflect God's own glory and goodness. God created the world as a place for human culture in all its fullness. When human beings rebelled against God, God went in search of them, calling Abraham to live in covenant with God. But God not only searches and redeems humans, he also commands them to follow his way. For the rabbis of antiquity and the Middle Ages, and for Orthodox and a majority of Conservatives today, the moral code of the Bible is composed of laws that demand obedience—they are indeed commandments, not general moral guidelines. In their understanding, God didn't give the "Ten Suggestions."

> *God didn't give the "Ten Suggestions."*

10-4a Ethics in the Image of God

Jewish morality and ethics rest on the foundation of ethical monotheism. Not only is God one and the only God, but God is perfectly right and righteous. Holiness is at the center of God's nature; God is good, just, and compassionate. The people God put in the good world he made are created to live in conformity with God's nature and will. The Torah given by God enables people to know more exactly what God's will is, but a basic notion of God's will is written in every human heart. In contrast with other religions of the ancient Near East, evil is not built into the structure of the universe, but rather is the product of human choices. Humans are free moral agents.

A fundamental Jewish teaching shared by nearly all Jews today (except those who reject the existence of God, of course) is that human beings are created in the "image of God." Israelites and Jews never took this to mean that humans somehow physically look like God, because God is a spirit and invisible to the human eye. Although the Bible doesn't explain the "image of God" in detail, Jews have interpreted it to mean that humans can think rationally and have a moral sense to know what is right. Because humans are created in God's image, they have the ability to know and even act like God. The "image of God" is related to the human mind and spirit, but it means that humans are like God, not that a part of them *is* God.

> *The effect of the good impulse and the evil impulse is like having an angel on one shoulder and a devil on the other, each urging a particular course of action.*

The early rabbis taught that God built two moral impulses into each human being: the "good impulse"

called the *yetzer hatov* (YAY-tser ha-TOHV) and the "evil impulse," the *yetzer hara* (YAY-tser ha-RAH). The good impulse is the moral conscience that reminds a person of God's law and creates an urge to follow it. The evil impulse is the urge to satisfy one's own needs and desires. Despite its name, there's nothing intrinsically evil about the evil impulse, because God created it and it's a part of human life. The "evil" impulse, acting with the good impulse, drives us to eat, drink, procreate, and make a living—all necessary and good things. However, it can easily lead to sin when not held in check and balanced by the good impulse, and this is why it is called "evil." Eating, drinking, procreating, and making a living can be taken to extremes and can destroy human life. The competing effect of the good impulse and the evil impulse is like having an angel on one shoulder and a devil on the other, each urging a particular course of action. Some rabbis have been uncomfortable about talk of a created "evil" impulse and have preferred to speak of one impulse that can be used in two different ways.

10-4b The Torah

The Torah, the first five books of the Bible—but in a wider sense the whole teaching and law of Judaism—is this religion's paramount text. It contains stories and commandments that teach about life and death. The rabbis enumerated 613 commandments (*mitzvot*): 248 positive commandments ("You shalls") and 365 negative commandments ("You shall nots"). Moreover, all the commandments are held to be binding and more or less equal. Some Jews in the modern age would make a distinction between the "moral law" and the "ceremonial" and "ritual law." This concept isn't found in the Bible and Talmud, but history seems to have ratified it, because some of the 613 commands cannot be fulfilled now that the Jewish temple is gone. All commandments come from God, the ancient and medieval rabbis said,

The Ten Commandments in Hebrew, in their shorter form. Writing on stone suggests the permanence and seriousness of the commandments.

halakhah [hah-luh-KAH] "Walk" of life, the way of moral obedience to God

so all are binding forever. Today, all Jews consider the Ten Commandments to be the leading commandments in the Torah, but not all Jews adhere to the 613 mitzvot; this is the basis of one of the main differences between the different branches of Judaism.

The Ten Commandments run as follows, with short explanations in brackets:

1. I am the Lord your God [not a commandment in grammatical form, but the basis of the people's relationship with God].

2. You shall not recognize any as god beside Me [the root of monotheism].

3. You shall not take the Name of the Lord your God in vain [God's name, symbolic of God's essence, must be respected].

4. Remember the day of Sabbath, to keep it holy [the Sabbath is a day of rest and rededication to God].

5. Honor your father and your mother [parents are to be respected as long as they live].

6. You shall not murder [not all killing is murder, but unlawful killing is].

7. You shall not commit adultery [breaking marriage vows breaks marriage].

8. You shall not steal [other people's property is to be respected].

9. Do not give false testimony against your neighbor [lying in legal settings undermines justice].

10. You shall not covet the possessions of others [desiring to have things that others have].

The rest of the Torah's legal material is based on these Ten Commandments. The rabbis of the ancient world compiled the Mishnah and the Gemara, finally combining them into the Talmud, expanding on these commandments and bringing them into every aspect of the life of the Jewish people. Judaism's emphasis on justice and love in community, rather than on just the letter of the law, has enabled it to keep to its moral tradition while adapting to changing circumstances in life.

10-4c General Jewish Ethics

Besides these Torah-based commands that originate with the Hebrew Bible, the biblical tradition also has broad legal injunctions, wisdom narratives with moral lessons, and prophetic teachings. These other teachings became important in the first millennium B.C.E., although the Torah commands remain central and foundational. In modern times, as the Torah commands became problematic for many Jews, the more-general ethical principles became paramount for them.

The biblical prophets exhorted their audiences to lead a life that honored their covenant with God. They pointed primarily to obedience to the Torah, but they also spoke of more-general moral duties: kindness to the needy, benevolence, faith, relief for the suffering, a peace-loving disposition, and a humble spirit. Civic loyalty and obedience, even to a foreign ruler, is urged as a duty (Jeremiah 29:7). This was also important in later times as Jews lived under non-Jewish governments. What the prophets viewed as the end-time is uncertain, but the moral vision was clear: It will be one of peace and righteousness (Isaiah 2:2).

In early rabbinic Judaism, the oral Torah both interpreted the Bible and delved afresh into many other ethical topics. Jewish morality, encompassing both commandments and general ethics, is known to Jews today as **halakhah**, literally "walk" of life—God has a way for the chosen people to walk in.

The best-loved and most influential rabbinic text on ethics is the Mishnah tractate of Pirke Avot (PEER-kay ah-VOHT), the "Sayings of the Fathers," often translated as "Ethics of the Fathers." The Pirke Avot traces the transmission of the oral Torah from Moses to the second century C.E., when the Mishnah was compiled. Throughout this work, the word *Torah* refers especially to the oral Torah, a "fence around the [written] law," the body of legal opinions developed by the rabbis and codified in the Mishnah. The idea behind this "fence" is that by keeping it one would also be keeping the written Torah that it protects.

Read a selection from the Pirke Avot.

10-4d Modern Jewish Ethics

In the modern period, Jewish ethics sprouted many offshoots—due to developments in modern secular ethics and to the formation of Jewish branches—each of which required clarity on ethical teachings. The nineteenth-century and early twentieth-century Reform movement promoted the idea of Judaism as pure ethical monotheism. Since about 1900, liberal Reform and Reconstructionist rabbis have fostered novel approaches to Jewish ethics—in the work of Eugene Borowitz, for example. Also during this time, Orthodox rabbis have often engaged in applied ethics by interpreting the Talmud for bioethics: end-of-life issues, in vitro fertilization, genetic therapy, and other topics.

Knowing the scriptures is an important basis of Jewish morality.

An influential work of Jewish social ethics is *I and Thou* by Martin Buber (BOO-buhr; 1878–1965). In this profound work, which is reputed to have changed the lives of many of its readers, Buber uses two pairs of words to describe two fundamentally different types of relationships between one's self and the world: "I-It" and "I-Thou." For I-It relationships, the "It" refers to other people as objects. It objectifies and devalues them. In other words, the "I" looks upon others as "Its," not as people like oneself. Buber held that many human problems are caused by I-It attitudes. By contrast, the "I" in an I-Thou relationship doesn't objectify any "It" but has a living, mature relationship with others. It recognizes that the "Thou" is a whole world of experience within one person, just as one's "I" is. Buber taught that God is the "eternal Thou," known by both direct encounter with God and indirect encounter with God as one develops I-Thou relationships with other people.

Read about how the different Jewish branches approach the moral issues relating to homosexuality.

Watch a report on Jewish rabbis working for greater Israeli justice on the West Bank.

Learning Outcome 10-5

Summarize Jewish worship, the Sabbath and major festivals, and life-cycle rituals.

10-5 Jewish Worship and Ritual

In London, a prominent Jewish rabbi criticizes pop singer Madonna's ritual practice of Kabbalah. Rabbi Yitzchak Schochet of London's Mill Hill Synagogue strongly objects to Madonna's use of Kabbalah, arguing that it tarnishes Judaism when people who don't observe Jewish law engage in Jewish mysticism. Rabbi Schochet and many other traditional, observant Jews are particularly upset by the tattoo on Madonna's right shoulder of the ancient Hebrew name for God, which a majority of Jews regard as so holy that they don't use it. (They forbid permanent tattoos as well, so this is a double fault.) Madonna's interest in Kabbalah began with her 1998 *Ray of Light* album, was strengthened by her 2007 visit to the Kabbalah center in Jerusalem, and continues today. Public fascination with her use of the Kabbalah also remains strong, and she has become the leading celebrity voice of Kabbalah.

Watch an interview with Madonna on the Kabbalah.

Because Judaism is a religion of practice, it has a full set of rituals for synagogue worship, home practices, and community-based religious festivals. We'll begin with synagogue worship, then consider the Sabbath and the main festivals; finally, we'll look at the major life-cycle rituals of circumcision, bar/bat mitzvah, and funerals.

10-5a Worship in the Synagogue

The main synagogue service takes place on either Friday evening or Saturday morning, both of which fall on the Sabbath day. In Orthodox synagogues, males and females sit separately; in Conservative and Reform, they may sit together. A **minyan**, or minimum number of men necessary to have a service (usually ten), is required. We've already discussed, in "The Jewish Present as Shaped by Its Past," language and music differences between these three branches. But the three branches all share the same basic structure of service:

minyan [MIHN-yahn] Minimum number of men necessary to have a service (usually ten)

gathering into the main synagogue room; hymns and prayers often led by a cantor, or singer; and readings from scripture.

In synagogue worship, the readings themselves are very musical. The worship leader chants the words in Hebrew employing traditional Hebrew melodies. The place where the Torah scrolls are kept is the **ark**, a reference to the Ark of the Covenant. It is a special closet or recess in the synagogue wall on the side nearest Jerusalem and is usually the focal point of the synagogue. The scrolls themselves are typically covered with richly embroidered cloth, and the upper ends of the wooden rollers are adorned with gold and silver decorations. Their use follows a prescribed ritual:

- When a scroll is removed from the ark during the service, everyone in the synagogue stands and a special song is often sung.

- The scroll is placed on a reading desk.

- The readers use a special pointer, often made of solid silver, to keep track of their place in the text and avoid touching the scroll with their hands.

- When the reading is complete, the scroll is rolled up, its covers are put back on, and it is returned to the ark with great solemnity.

Then the rabbi sometimes preaches a short sermon based on the texts that were read, especially the Torah reading.

10-5b The Sabbath

One of the Ten Commandments orders that the **Sabbath** (seventh) day of the week be kept holy. This day begins at sunset on Friday and concludes on sunset on Saturday. Sabbath usually starts off at home, with a festive meal for which the whole family is present. The ritual lighting of the Sabbath candles precedes the meal. At least eighteen minutes before sundown on Friday, the mother and daughters light the candles, usually on the dining table, to welcome the Sabbath. In many modern Jewish households the candle blessing is performed together as a family. After the candles are lit, this blessing is recited

Reading the Torah scroll in a synagogue

© ISTOCKPHOTO.COM/GEORGE CORBIN

over them: "Blessed are You, Eternal One our God, Ruler of the Universe, who makes us holy with mitzvot [commandments] and gives us this mitzvah [commandment] of lighting the Sabbath lights."

The command goes on to say that no work may be done on the Sabbath. This rest from work is connected to both the creation of the world and the giving of the Torah. The Talmud interprets this strictly; that is why traditional Jews have tended to live within walking distance of the synagogue, because to walk too far is considered work.

10-5c Jewish Annual Festivals

The Jewish year has several annual festivals. Most of them have both a historical reference and a contemporary meaning, to build faith and obedience in those who celebrate them. We can consider them quickly here. **Rosh Hashanah** is the Jewish New Year, in September or October, depending on how the Jewish lunar calendar matches the solar calendar. It begins a ten-day solemn period of repentance and self-examination. The period ends on **Yom Kippur**, the "Day of Atonement,"

A Jewish mother and daughter light the Sabbath candles.

© NOAM ARMONN/SHUTTERSTOCK.COM

deals with kosher: what foods can and cannot be eaten, and how those foods must be prepared and consumed. Contrary to popular opinion, rabbis don't "bless" food to make it kosher, but they do inspect it and its processing to assure kosher consumers that the food is kosher. All sorts of ethnic foods can be kosher; in fact, kosher Chinese restaurants can often be found in Jewish neighborhoods.

Leviticus 11 gives a list of clean and unclean foods, and the Talmud treats them in detail. The types of unclean animals specified are (1) four-footed animals that don't chew the cud and have a split hoof (pigs, for example); (2) meat-eating birds; (3) insects with wings; (4) water animals without fins and scales, for example shrimp; and (5) small creeping ("swarming") animals. In order to be kosher, acceptable animals must be killed as humanely as possible and prepared for sale in a clean way. Also, kosher food must be served and eaten in a kosher way (for example, no combination of dairy products and meat in cooking or serving). In general, raw vegetables are always kosher, and so are cooked vegetables as long as they are cooked and eaten correctly.

Kosher rules are observed at all times, but additional kosher restrictions come during Passover. Some foods that are kosher for year-round use are not kosher for Passover, because they have leaven in them. A bagel, for example, can be kosher for regular use but is certainly not kosher for Passover.

Kosher food is so closely linked with Jewish identity that the misconception has arisen that it's only for Jews. In point of fact, in 2009 nearly 85 percent of kosher meat sales were to non-Jews who appreciated the quality of the meat and its healthfulness as compared to nonkosher meat. (If you like hot dogs, for example, and are concerned more about taste

which is the holiest day in the year. *Sukkot* (SOOK-koht) is the festival of "tabernacles" or "booths," a seven-day harvest celebration linked to the wandering of the Hebrews after the Exodus; people often live in special outdoor huts during this time. **Passover** celebrates the escape of the Hebrews from Egyptian slavery. A special meal called the **seder**, with various foods including unleavened bread (*matzoh*), is the highlight. Hanukkah we have explained above. *Purim* (POOR-eem), "lots," recalls the Queen Esther story in which Persian Jews were saved from genocide when the drawing of lots exposed that evil plan. Costumes and plays, as well as special foods, are featured. Finally, *Shavuot* (SHAHV-oo-oht), meaning "weeks," comes fifty days after Passover; it celebrates the giving of the Torah.

10-5d Kosher Food

Kosher means "fitting or proper," not (as it is often understood) "pure" or "clean." A body of ritual Jewish law

Seder plate with special Passover foods

© BLUEEYES/SHUTTERSTOCK.COM

Even though its beef may be kosher, the cheese on this burger makes it nonkosher.

© GENA73/SHUTTERSTOCK.COM

and health than about price, a kosher hot dog is for you.) In 2010, kosher food was served for the first time at the Super Bowl, and it nearly sold out.

Read about the rising popularity of kosher food among non-Jews in the United States.

10-5e Circumcision, the Sign of the Covenant

Circumcision is the most significant life-cycle ritual in Judaism and probably the one rite universally observed among Jews. Circumcision (from the Latin for "cut around") involves surgically removing the foreskin of the penis. Its common name among Jews is **bris milah**, Yiddish for "covenant of circumcision," and is usually called "bris" for short. Secular Jews who observe no other part of Judaism usually circumcise their male children; to be Jewish in any meaningful way is to be circumcised. Orthodox Jews affirm the Talmudic view that a person of Jewish descent who is not circumcised will not enter heaven. A few Reform and Reconstructionist leaders oppose circumcision today, but they're in the extreme minority.

As we have already seen, the commandment to circumcise is given first in Genesis 17:10–14 as an essential part of God's covenant with Abraham. According to God's command to Abraham, circumcision is performed only on males, as the sign of the covenant and membership in God's people. Some Reform Jews argue that circumcision is sexist, so they have a "naming ceremony" for baby girls, with much of the circumcision ritual except for the actual cutting. Circumcision is often perceived by Reform and Conservative Jews to be a hygienic measure. Orthodox Jews disagree and correctly point out that this rationale isn't found in the Torah. Instead, circumcision is a religious measure: It is an outward physical sign of the eternal covenant between God and the Jewish people.

bris milah [brihs MIL-luh] Formal name for circumcision, Yiddish for "covenant of circumcision"; usually called "bris" for short

mohel [MOI-uhl, rhymes with *oil*] Jewish man who officiates at a circumcision

bar mitzvah [bahr MITZ-vuh] "Son of the commandment," the assumption of responsibility before God for keeping the Torah

bat (bas) mitzvah [baht (bahs) MITZ-vuh] "Daughter of the commandment," the assumption of responsibility before God for keeping the Torah

Circumcision is done not for any health benefits, but because God commands it.

Circumcision is performed on the eighth day of a boy's life. If this falls on the Sabbath, circumcision is still done then, even though the drawing of blood is ordinarily forbidden as work. The circumcision is performed in a home or synagogue by a **mohel**, a respected Jewish man educated in the relevant Jewish laws, skilled in hygienic practices, and possessed of a steady hand. While the cutting is done, an honored man holds the baby still on his lap. Blessings of God are recited, and a drop of wine is placed in the baby's mouth. He is then given a formal Hebrew name. As with most Jewish rituals, circumcision is a joyous, celebrative occasion (except for the baby, of course) and is followed by refreshments or more often a festive meal.

10-5f Bar Mitzvah and Bat Mitzvah

A Jewish young man becomes a **bar mitzvah**, which literally means "son of the commandment," in a coming-of-age ceremony. A young woman becomes a **bat (or bas) mitzvah**, "daughter of the commandment." The singular *mitzvah* ("commandment") is used here even though the Torah as a whole is meant. Although these terms literally refer only to adult standing in the Jewish community, they are also commonly taken to mean the ceremonies themselves—for example in the expression that someone is "having a bar mitzvah." In Reform and Conservative Judaism, the ritual for females is the same as for males. In all Orthodox practice, women are not permitted to participate in rituals such as these, so a female's ceremony is usually little more than a modest party to mark her thirteenth birthday, if it is held at all.

What does it mean to become a bar/bat mitzvah? In Jewish law, children are not obligated to obey the Torah, although they are encouraged to do so. (Like any religion passed through the generations, Judaism raises its children in the faith, as the Shema commands. Moreover, historic Jewish teaching knows nothing of the modern concept of "teenage" years between childhood and adulthood; when one comes near to puberty, one is an adult.) When they are at an "age of understanding" to know the difference between right and wrong and choose between them—traditionally thirteen—children become obligated in God's sight to obey the Torah. The bar/bat mitzvah ceremony marks the beginning of that obligation, but

some months. The father traditionally recites a blessing thanking God that his child has become an adult. The often-elaborate postceremony parties that are commonplace today in North America arose around 1900 among more-prosperous Jews.

Watch a demo from a company that specializes in filming bar mitzvahs.

10-5g Marriage

Judaism strongly encourages marriage and family life. If asked what the first commandment in the Torah is, an observant Jew will reply, "Be fruitful and multiply" (Genesis 1:28), which is indeed God's first command, given to the whole human race. Among Ashkenazi Jews, monogamy has been the rule since the 900s C.E. Among Sephardic Jews, whose rules reflect the Jewish Bible and Talmud more closely on this point and have been influenced by the Muslim context, polygamy was permitted until the 1900s, but still wasn't common. For both groups, Jews married only Jews. But in the past century, intermarriage has become more common. This has posed a problem for Reform and Conservative Jews, because Jewish identity is traced through the mother, not the father, and intermarriage leads more often to assimilation of the Jewish spouse to the Gentile world than it does to the conversion of the non-Jewish spouse to Judaism. Lately, Reform Jews have urged, and sometimes instituted, either matrilineal or patrilineal descent for membership in the Jewish people.

Jewish marriage has engagement (sometimes preceded by the work of matchmakers), rings, a vow or a document certifying marriage obligations, and a grand celebration. Ceremonies are often held outdoors or in hotels, not in the synagogue, as long as there is a rabbi to officiate and a canopy. But the Jewish ceremony has something unique. As the last part of the wedding, the groom crushes under his foot a glass wrapped in a cloth, a reminder in a time of great joy of the sorrow that came to Judaism when the Temple of Jerusalem was destroyed in 70 C.E. Then there are loud cries of "Mazel tov!" (MAH-zuhl tahv)—literally "Good luck," but in celebratory situations with more a nuance of "Congratulations"—and the wedding reception begins.

10-5h Funeral Rituals

Jewish practices relating to death and mourning have had two purposes: primarily to comfort the mourners and secondarily to help, as much as possible and

At a bar mitzvah ceremony, a young man carries the Torah scroll with pride and joy.

© GORDON SWANSON/SHUTTERSTOCK.COM

it doesn't create it. Now the young people gradually begin to assume the privileges and responsibilities of Jewish adults. They help to lead religious services, count in a minyan, enter binding contracts, and may even marry (although marriages are not carried out until later).

The bar/bat mitzvah is an innovation of the past few centuries, to mark the passage into Jewish adulthood in a ritual way. In its earliest, basic form, it is the celebrant's first participation in leading a service. During a Sabbath service or a weekday service, the young person is called up to the Torah scroll to recite a blessing over the weekly reading. The common practice today for one becoming a bar/bat mitzvah is to do more than the blessing. The celebrant learns the entire Torah reading for the day in its chanted form and recites it during the service. He or she sometimes reads the entire weekly Torah portion, leads part of the service, or leads the congregation in certain important prayers. The celebrant is also generally required to make a short speech, which traditionally begins with "Today I am a man/woman." All this requires a good deal of training by the rabbi, often over

appropriate, the deceased into the next world. In what follows, we will give a description of long-established Jewish practices that go back hundreds, sometimes thousands, of years. Some variations to this pattern will be found among Conservative/Masorti Jews today, and more among the Reform.

After a person dies, burial must be carried out in less than forty-eight hours. The body is never left alone. In the past, Jewish communities had an organization to care for the dead; these societies are now making something of a comeback as a replacement for more-conventional funeral home arrangements. Autopsies are forbidden as a desecration of the body, but they are permitted where civil authorities require it. Embalming the body is also forbidden as a desecration, and organ donation is likewise not condoned. However, some contemporary Jewish ethicists have argued that organ donation is permitted, even meritorious, if the recipient's body is buried at death.

Both the coffin and the body's clothes are simple, so that all people are equal in death. The upper body is wrapped in a prayer shawl with its fringes cut short. People never view the body; open-casket ceremonies are forbidden by Jewish law. The body must not be cremated or put in a mausoleum, but buried in the earth. Coffins must be made of wood and must rest directly in the earth. Some Orthodox groups go so far as to poke holes in the bottom of coffins to facilitate the process of "dust to dust."

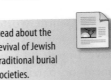

Read about the revival of Jewish traditional burial societies.

Jewish mourning practices have periods of decreasing intensity. When a person first hears of the death of a close relative, it is traditional to express the initial grief by tearing one's clothing, or sometimes a piece of cloth that is then worn on one's clothing. During the first two days after death, the family is usually left alone to allow for the full expression of their grief. The next period of mourning is known as **shiva**, the Hebrew word for "seven," because it lasts seven days, beginning on the day of burial. This process is often called "sitting shiva." Shiva is observed by the entire family of the deceased in the deceased's home. The family wears the clothing they had on when they tore it in mourning. Mourners sit on low stools or on the floor. They don't wear leather shoes; shave their faces or cut their hair; wear cosmetics; work; or do things for comfort, entertainment, or pleasure.

After shiva, lighter mourning of eleven months continues for the immediate family. *Kaddish* (KAH-dish), a prayer of faith and petition, is to be said every day. After the period is complete, the family of the deceased is not permitted to continue formal mourning. Jewish law requires that a tombstone be prepared. Many Jewish communities delay putting it up until the end of the extended mourning period. Where this custom is followed, a formal unveiling ceremony for the tombstone is usually held at the cemetery.

Read suggestions for making a good shiva visit.

shiva [SHIHV-uh]
Hebrew word for "seven"; the period of mourning that lasts seven days, beginning on the day of burial

Learning Outcome 10-6

Outline the main features of Judaism around the world today, especially in Israel and North America.

10-6 Judaism around the World Today

On a Friday night in Chicago, a Jewish family gathers in their home to welcome the Sabbath with a traditional ritual meal. As the sun is just about to set, the wife, assisted by her daughter, lights two Sabbath candles on the dining room table. It has been set for dinner, and on its white tablecloth are a wine cup and two loaves of challah (soft braided bread), covered with a special cloth. The father blesses each of his children and then recites a prayer of blessing over the wine, remembering how God rested on the seventh day of creation and hallowed the Sabbath day. Everyone around the table has a sip of the wine, and then all leave the table to wash their hands ritually. Gathered around the table again, they recite a blessing of God for the gift of food. Each receives a slice of the bread to eat, and the main meal begins. At the end of the meal, the family sings special Sabbath songs, and the meal is concluded with a prayer. This Sabbath ritual is so meaningful in Judaism that both Orthodox and Conservative families in North America practice it in much the same way. It is even making something of a comeback in Reform Judaism.

In 2010, the world Jewish population was estimated at about 13.5 million, 0.2 percent of the total world population. About 42 percent of all Jews reside in Israel and about 42 percent in North America. Approximately 8 percent are in Europe, and the remainder are scattered widely in smaller communities in South America, Asia, and Africa. The Jewish Diaspora today, both inside and outside North America, has all the dynamism and diversity that Judaism has in Israel.

10-6a Judaism in Israel

The Orthodox movement is the only branch of Judaism legally recognized in Israel. Until about 2000, only Orthodox Jews could serve on religious councils. Today, only Orthodox rabbis may perform marriages and conversions and grant divorce in Israel. Many Orthodox men were exempt from military service until 2012, when the Israeli Supreme Court struck down the law that exempted them from service, but their numbers in the military are still small. Some Orthodox scholars receive lifelong stipends from the government in order to devote themselves to full-time Torah study. Non-Orthodox Israelis increasingly bristle at this preferential treatment.

Most Israelis today don't formally identify with the three main movements. Instead, they describe themselves in terms of their degree of observance. More than half of all Israelis call themselves "secular." About 15 to 20 percent describe themselves as "Orthodox." The rest in the wide middle are "traditionally observant." However, the traditionalists (Masorti) and even the secularists of Israel tend to be more observant than are their counterparts in Europe and North America. For example, many secularists in Israel observe some traditional practices, such as lighting Sabbath candles on Friday evening, limiting their activities on the Sabbath day of rest, having a full Passover home ritual, or keeping some Jewish dietary laws (avoiding pork, for example). These practices are nearly nonexistent among American Jews who call themselves "secular." An Israeli quip on this combination of secularism and observance runs, "Most Israelis don't belong to a synagogue, but the synagogue they don't belong to is Orthodox."

> "Most Israelis don't belong to a synagogue, but the synagogue they don't belong to is Orthodox."—Israeli quip

10-6b Judaism in North America

Jews have lived in North America from the early 1600s, with Dutch Jews of Sephardic origins settling first in New Amsterdam (modern New York City). For two hundred years, the majority of North American Jews were Sephardics. The first American synagogue was established in 1677 in Rhode Island, a colony that was a center of religious toleration. Although they usually couldn't hold office or even vote, Sephardic Jews became active in their civic communities in the 1790s. Until 1830, Charleston, South Carolina, had the largest

The oldest synagogue in North America, the Sephardic congregation in Newport, Rhode Island, dates to 1677; this building is from 1763.

© ISTOCKPHOTO.COM/PETER SPIRO

Jewish community in North America. Large-scale Jewish immigration, however, didn't take place until the mid-1800s, when Ashkenazi Jews from Germany arrived in the United States, primarily becoming merchants and shop owners. By 1880, around 250,000 Jews lived in the United States. Aviva Ben-Ur, in his recent book *Sephardic Jews in America*, tells the story of how Ashkenazis marginalized and ignored Sephardics, a practice that persists even today.[4]

Jewish immigration to North America increased sharply in the early 1880s, driven mainly by persecution in Russia and Eastern Europe. Most of the newer immigrants spoke Yiddish and were religiously observant Ashkenazis from the poor rural areas of these lands. They came to America seeking freedom and a better life. Over 2 million Jews arrived between about 1880 and 1924, when new U.S. laws all but ended immigration from Eastern Europe. Many settled in the New York metropolitan area, particularly the Lower East Side of Manhattan, eventually establishing one of the world's major Jewish population centers.

Around 1900, newly arrived Jews began to build many synagogues and community associations. American Jewish leaders urged speedy integration into the wider American culture, which a large majority of Jews quickly accomplished. After World War II, in which nearly half a million American Jewish men

---

[4] Aviva Ben-Ur, *Sephardic Jews in America* (New York: NYU Press, 2012).

fought against Germany and Japan, younger Jewish families joined the American trend of settling in new suburbs. There they became increasingly integrated into American culture as previous anti-Semitic discrimination lessened. For example, in the 1950s many leading universities and colleges began to drop their quota systems that held Jewish enrollment to very small levels. Enrollment in Jewish religious schools doubled between 1945 and 1955, and synagogue affiliation jumped from only 20 percent of Jews in 1930 to 60 percent in 1960. Reform and Conservative congregations experienced rapid growth. In the 1970s and 1980s, waves of Jewish immigrants from Russia largely joined the mainstream American Jewish community. However, most of these new arrivals had been secularized by generations of Soviet Communist rule and anti-Semitic pressures.

Today, approximately 5.5 million of the world's 13.5 million Jews live in North America. Three major movements are found in North America: Reform, Conservative, and Orthodox. A fourth movement, the Reconstructionist, is more liberal than Reform and is substantially smaller than the other three. Orthodoxy is comprised of different groups: the modern Orthodox, who have integrated into modern North American society while strictly keeping the Jewish law from the Talmud; Hasidic Jews, who live in their own, separate neighborhoods and dress distinctively; and the Yeshiva Orthodox. They all believe that God gave Moses the whole Torah, including both the "written Torah" that became the first five books of the Bible and the "oral Torah," an oral tradition interpreting the written Torah that became the basis of the Talmud. The Orthodox believe that the Torah contains 613 mitzvoth (commands), binding upon Jews but not upon non-Jews. A survey of American Jews in 2000 found that 10 percent identify themselves as Orthodox. The Orthodox tend to have large families and resist assimilation, so their overall numbers are growing.

Reform Judaism doesn't believe that the Torah is divinely written or inspired. It views the entire Bible as a record of Jewish religious experience. Reform Jews don't believe in the observance of many traditional commandments, but they attempt to preserve much of what they consider the spiritual essentials of Judaism, along with some selected Jewish practices and cultural aspects. A recent survey found that 35 percent of American Jews identify themselves as Reform. Approximately nine hundred Reform synagogues are found in North America today.

Hear a lighthearted take on American Jewish identity, "The Chanuka Song" by Adam Sandler.

Visit the website of Reform Judaism.

Conservative Judaism's efforts to mediate between the Orthodox and Reform have been well received in North America. The Conservative movement holds that the main teachings of Jewish scriptures and the Talmud come from God but have a human component. It believes that Judaism can hold true to its historic roots but can also adapt to modern life. Because Conservative Judaism occupies the ground between Orthodoxy and Reform, there's a great diversity in the Conservative movement. Twenty-six percent of American Jews identify themselves as Conservative, and the approximately 750 Conservative synagogues in the world today are predominantly in North America.

Visit the website of Conservative Judaism.

All told, the varieties of Judaism in North America strive, in their widely diverse ways, to continue the mission of God's people to be a "light to the nations."

Study Tools 10

Ready to study? In the book you can:

- Review Learning Outcome answers and glossary terms with the tear-out Chapter Review card.

Or you can go online to CourseMate, at www.cengagebrain.com, for these resources:

- Chapter quizzes to prepare for tests
- Interactive flashcards of all glossary terms
- A timeline of key events in the chapter
- An eBook with introductions, interactive quizzes, and live links for all web resources in the chapter

CHAPTER 11

Encountering Christianity: The Way of Jesus Christ

BONNIE VAN VOORST © CENGAGE LEARNING

Learning Outcomes

After studying this chapter, you will be able to do the following:

11-1 Explain the meaning of *Christianity* and related terms.

11-2 Trace how the main periods of Christianity's history have shaped its present.

11-3 Outline in your own words essential Christian teachings as found in the Nicene Creed.

11-4 Describe the main features of Christian ethics.

11-5 Summarize Christian worship and other rituals.

11-6 Explain the variety of Christianity around the world today, especially in the Southern Hemisphere and in North America.

Study Tools

After you read this chapter, go to the Study Tools at the end of the chapter, page 293.

"I am the Way, the Truth, and the Life."—Jesus Christ, in the Gospel of John

Your Visit to St. Peter's in Rome

As a part of a visit to Italy, you spend a day in Vatican City, the world's smallest nation, which serves as the headquarters of the Roman Catholic Church. The center of Vatican City is St. Peter's Basilica, where the pope presides. You've seen pictures of this building, and you've seen snippets on television of religious services performed there, so now you're eager to see it for yourself.

Your tour guide gives you some advice the night before your visit: "You should expect the church to be full of visitors, as it is almost every day. Not only is St. Peter's the center of the Roman Catholic faith, it's also a historical building and an important part of art history. Neither men nor women can wear anything that shows their shoulders, stomach, or any leg above the knees. There are guards at the church entrance, and they're experts at spotting the tricks that some people use to enter without appropriate clothing."

Stepping inside St. Peter's Basilica, you see that the grandness of the building itself is stunning. Seeing it from the outside has given you no indication of how large and impressive it really is. Like many of the world's important religious sites, the grandeur of this place and what it means to believers—in this case Roman Catholic Christians—brings you a deep sense of respect. Many people pause after entering the front door to take it all in. On the right you see Michelangelo's life-size sculpture of Mary the mother of Jesus holding the body of her dead son in her arms after his crucifixion.

Front of St. Peter's Basilica, Rome

What Do YOU Think?

Its universal spread shows that Christianity is the most culturally adaptable religion in the world.

Strongly Disagree				Strongly Agree		
1	2	3	4	5	6	7

So many people want to see it that it takes several minutes to work your way to the front of the group. It shows an artistic genius that can only be marveled at, but it also shows the profound Christian faith of Michelangelo.

Explore St. Peter's Basilica by way of Google Earth™.

Watch an introduction to St. Peter's and other Roman churches.

The natural light coming from above illuminates the church and spreads a subdued radiance all around, especially under the dome. Looking up at the dome, you see the large letters giving in Latin the words of Jesus in the Gospel of Matthew (16:18–19), which the Catholic Church has always considered the foundation of its organization: "You are Peter, and on this rock I will build my church. I will give you the keys of the kingdom of heaven."

After you go up to the outside of the dome to take in the magnificent view of Rome, you take a guided tour of the tomb of St. Peter, led by a priest from the Vatican archaeology office. It's a few stories below the main altar of the church, what in the first century C.E. was a cemetery on Vatican Hill, outside the city of Rome.

 Mosaic portrait in Hagia Sophia Church, Istanbul, Turkey, of Jesus Christ enthroned in heaven. His halo contains a cross, and the Greek lettering is an abbreviation of "Jesus Christ."

259

Christ Literally, "anointed one," or prophet

You walk down an excavated street, past expensive mausoleums, toward the traditional grave of Peter. When you reach it, your guide shows pictures of what it used to look like—very simple and modest. You realize that, for all the grandeur of the building above, the foundation of it all is the grave of a humble fisherman who was killed near this spot for his faith in Jesus Christ.

Christianity is a monotheistic religion based on the first-century C.E. life, death, and resurrection of Jesus of Nazareth in Galilee. Christians believe that Jesus is the Son of God and the savior of the world, and that his teaching shows how to live for God and others. Christianity began as a prophetic reform movement within Judaism, led by Jesus, in the first century C.E., but it quickly moved out into the wider world after Jesus's departure. It has been from the first a strongly missionary faith, eager to spread itself and make converts, and it has become the largest religion in the world. Geographically the most widely diffused of all faiths—the only religion to be found on all continents and in every nation, for example—it has about 2.2 billion adherents today. Christianity has been a major influence in the shaping of Western civilization, and since around 1500 it has increasingly shaped the rest of the world. The majority of Christians now live in the Southern Hemisphere. Christianity's three largest groups are the Roman Catholic Church (larger than the other two groups together), the Eastern Orthodox churches, and the Protestant churches. In your study of Christianity, you'll encounter these unique features:

- Christianity is centered on a person, Jesus Christ. But it is also strongly concerned with teaching and doctrine—more so than Judaism and Islam, the other Abrahamic monotheisms.

- Because Christianity is centered on Jesus, it takes seriously his teachings as recorded in the New Testament. But Christianity is also shaped by the church's later teaching about Jesus, which raises the question: What is the relationship of the teaching *of* Jesus to Christian teaching *about* Jesus?

- Christianity shares much with Judaism and Islam, but with some key differences. It teaches that the one God exists in three persons—the Father, the Son, and the Holy Spirit—a mystery and a paradox. However, modern scholars have placed Christianity firmly among the monotheistic religions of the world.

- When seen from the outside, Christianity appears to be quite unified. However, when seen from the inside, it seems very diverse, even fragmented, with an estimated nine thousand different church groups. We'll discuss the variety of Christianity throughout this chapter, but especially in the last section, "Christianity around the World Today."

Learning Outcome 11-1

Explain the meaning of *Christianity* and related terms.

11-1 Names

The name **Christ** originated in the ancient Greek word *Christos* (KRIHS-toss), literally "anointed one." This word is in turn the Greek equivalent of the Hebrew word *messiah* (meh-SIGH-uh), one anointed as a king or prophet. The earliest Christians came to believe that Jesus was the promised messiah who would bring God's blessings to Israel. When the church moved into the Greek-speaking world, the term *Christ* was attached to the personal name *Jesus* to produce the longer name by which he is known to Christians, *Jesus Christ*. It's frequently thought that *Jesus* is his first name and that *Christ* is something of a last name, but that's incorrect.

> *"Christians" was a name given by others, probably as a derogatory term that means "those Christ people."*

Christianity, the religion based on Jesus Christ's life and teaching, is built from *Christians*, those who belong to the religious movement based on Christ. As related by the first-century book of early church history, the Acts of the Apostles, the first Christians themselves had called their movement within Judaism "the Way," by which they meant the "Way of Jesus"; they called themselves "followers of the Way." *Christians* was a name given to them by others, probably as a derogatory term that meant something like "those Christ people." But adherents soon accepted *Christians* as accurate and meaningful. They transformed this put-down into an honorable name used by Christians in every time and place since then.

The term *Christendom* is sometimes used in connection with Christianity. It typically refers today to those nations of the world in which Christianity is the recognized, predominant religion, whether it is the

Symbols of Christianity

The fish was an early informal symbol of Christianity. It was connected to one of Jesus's miracles, multiplying bread and fish to feed a crowd. Later, the five letters in the Greek word for *fish*, transliterated into English as *ichthus* (ick-THOOS), became an acronym for "Jesus Christ, God's Son, Savior." The fish (Fig. 11.1) is still popular today as a symbol of Christianity, especially among Protestants; one can often see it in jewelry and on bumper stickers.

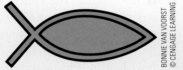

Figure 11.1 The fish

BONNIE VAN VOORST © CENGAGE LEARNING

The cross on which Jesus died is the predominant symbol of Christianity, but it didn't appear as a symbol (Fig. 11.2) until sometime in the 300s. It was a fearsome image of death by torture for people in the Roman Empire, which may have delayed its adoption as a symbol. Once it became possible to symbolize Christianity with the cross, this quickly became the universal symbol. The cross symbolizes the

Figure 11.2 The cross

BONNIE VAN VOORST © CENGAGE LEARNING

whole of the faith, but it specifically represents Jesus's death, which Christians typically believe is the sacrificial basis of their salvation from sin. Many kinds of symbolic crosses have developed over time. Some have specific religious meaning, and others are culturally associated with certain groups—the Celtic cross with Irish Roman Catholic Christianity, for example, or the Russian cross with Orthodox Christianity.

The simplest and most-common Christian cross is the Latin cross with its extended vertical beam, pictured here. The empty Latin cross, usually favored by Protestants, suggests the **resurrection** of the crucified Jesus, when his dead body was made eternally alive by the power of God. The **crucifix**, a Latin cross with a representation of the body of Jesus on it, favored by Catholic and Orthodox churches and some Protestants, is a reminder of Christ's sacrifice. The Greek cross, with arms of equal length, is just as ancient as the Latin cross and is found particularly in Eastern Orthodox Christianity. The ritual action of using one's right hand (even for left-handers) to make the sign of the cross on one's head and torso in prayer and formal worship is a common ritual act for a majority of Christians.

---

official religion of these nations or not. This term has now fallen into disuse, and in some circles even disfavor, but it is seen in older literature.

Learning Outcome 11-2

Trace how the main periods of Christianity's history have shaped its present.

11-2 The Christian Present as Shaped by Its Past

In New York City, a college student who wants to train to be a priest in the Orthodox Church in North America visits his bishop, the regional leader of this church, to inquire about education and expectations for ordination. After a pleasant conversation about his background and intent, the bishop offers the requirements. The student is surprised by the first and last items mentioned: grow a beard, finish college, and get married—preferably in that order. With these things accomplished, the student can enter a theological seminary (graduate school) to prepare more fully for the priesthood. As the student will soon learn as he travels toward becoming a priest, these expectations are a part of the ancient tradition for almost all Eastern Orthodox clergy.

Today's Christianity has been shaped by a long and significant history. Christianity is built on the foundation of Judaism and uses Jewish words and concepts, but over the first few centuries C.E. it became a separate religion and started drawing on Greek vocabulary to express its more complex teachings. From the death and resurrection of Jesus until today, his teachings have spread throughout the world. This section will relate the high points of this story and introduce the teachings, rituals, and diverse groups of Christianity along the way.

resurrection Dead body made eternally alive by the power of God

crucifix Latin cross with a representation of the body of Jesus on it

11-2a The Life, Death, and Resurrection of Jesus Christ (ca. 4 B.C.E.–30 C.E.)

The primary sources for knowledge of Jesus are the four **Gospels**—Matthew, Mark, Luke, and John. (When the term "gospel"—meaning "good news"—refers to an ancient book about Jesus, it will be capitalized here; when it refers to the message of Christianity, it will not be capitalized.) These four Gospels are found in the **New Testament**. A number of other sources written in the early 100s, notably the Gospel of Thomas, contain a few stories about Jesus and many more sayings attributed to him. The material about him in ancient non-Christian sources, both Jewish and Roman, does not add substantially to our knowledge of Jesus.

The chronology of the life of Jesus is slightly uncertain in its details. Matthew places his birth at least two years before Herod the Great's death late in 5 to 4 B.C.E. Luke connects his birth with a Roman census that probably occurred in 6 to 7 C.E. Historians generally incline to Matthew's dating and place Jesus's birth around 4 B.C.E. The church, following the Gospel of John, usually supposes that Jesus had a public ministry of three years, but Matthew, Mark, and Luke may portray a one-year ministry. Jesus's death during the rule of Pontius Pilate, the Roman governor of Judaea from 26 to 36 C.E., is placed around the years 29 to 30.

Explore the PBS site for "From Jesus to Christ."

When John the Baptizer, the fiery Jewish prophet who preached repentance and baptism in view of God's coming rule, baptized Jesus, it marked the beginning of his public ministry. Jesus taught in vivid **parables** (short stories about some aspect of life in the rule of God) and performed miraculous healings. He traveled through Galilee and became a popular prophetic figure. He gathered twelve male Jewish followers whom he called *disciples*, or "students"; the church later called them **apostles**, those "sent out" by Christ to be missionary leaders in the church. Women, both married and unmarried, were also a prominent part of his movement, highly unusual for the time. Jesus's attitude toward some aspects of the observance of Jewish law—especially as the strict law-keeping groups understood it—generated conflict with groups such as the Pharisees. The Pharisees believed in strict Sabbath rest and not associating closely with "sinners" or with women. The ruling Jewish authorities also began to suspect Jesus, but he probably didn't reach the attention of the Roman rulers.

Watch a clip from *Jesus of Nazareth*, showing Jesus giving controversial teaching and healing in a synagogue.

A triumphal entry into Jerusalem at Passover time was the prelude to a final crisis. After a last supper with his twelve closest disciples, he was betrayed by one of them, Judas Iscariot. Jesus was arrested by the Jewish temple authorities and tried by the Sanhedrin (Jewish council) and then by Pilate, who condemned him to death by crucifixion, being nailed to a cross to die an agonizing death. Christians everywhere believe that three days after his death, God raised Jesus from the dead to live eternally. The earliest church believed that sometime after the resurrection—the Gospels differ on the precise timing—the risen Jesus ascended to heaven, to stay in power there until his return at the end of time.

Jesus preached the imminent coming of God's kingdom (or full rule) to the earth and said that it has both a future and a present reality. His teachings and miracles pointed to and explained this kingdom. His disciples recognized him at some point in his ministry or shortly after it as the Messiah, although the Gospels indicate that Jesus did not often call himself that. He was mainly called "prophet" and "teacher." Jesus characteristically used the term *Son of Man* (though mysteriously in the third person) when talking about his own suffering and death, and at other times when referring to his role as God's agent of judgment at the end of time. This title is derived from Daniel 7:13 in the Jewish Bible, where "one like a son of man" first represents the oppressed people of God and then ascends to heaven to be vindicated by God.

> *Jesus called social and religious outcasts to repentance and faith, healed their diseases, and restored them to membership in the people of Israel.*

Gospel [GAHS-puhl] Early Christian book telling the "good news" of the story of Jesus

New Testament The Christian scriptural canon consisting of twenty-seven documents

parable Short story about some aspect of life in the rule of God

apostles Those "sent out" by Christ to be missionary leaders in the church

Jesus was critical of both Jewish and (implicitly) Greco-Roman society, saying that they fell far short of God's rule. Jesus encouraged the poor and oppressed, but rejected violent revolution. To Jesus, the social and religious outcasts of society (lepers, criminals, prostitutes, Jews who collected taxes for Rome, and others) were the special objects of God's love. He called them to repentance and faith, healed their diseases of mind and body, and restored them to membership in the people of Israel. Jesus taught that God desires the salvation (divine forgiveness leading to a restored relationship with God and the people of God) of the marginalized more than the righteousness of those who constantly obey God, a teaching that has proven a continual challenge for the church. Jesus embraced some outsiders including the Samaritans, whom most other Jews regarded as terrible people. (We'll consider the teaching of Jesus more fully later, in "Christian Ethics.")

Modern scholarship has delved fully into the Gospel accounts. Christianity has attracted a good deal of learned analysis by a variety of academic methods, and scholars have made research into the historical Jesus the largest single enterprise in religious study. What academics call "the quest for the historical Jesus" has been going strong for more than two centuries and shows no sign of lessening. In general, scholars agree on the main lines of Jesus's life and teaching as given above. They are divided, however, over other issues:

- *Did Jesus intend to found a church?* Jesus gathered a community of followers around himself. This community continued after his time, regarding itself as the special gathering of God's people. But many scholars doubt that Jesus intended to begin the organization that was later called the "church," with its formal organization.

- *Did Jesus intend his message to be addressed to Jews only?* In the Gospels, Gentiles (the Jewish term for non-Jews) appear only occasionally, but often in a positive light. Jesus's choice of twelve Jewish men as his closest disciples is an indication that his movement was mainly an inner-Jewish thing. Because welcoming Gentiles into the church caused such intense debate less than ten years after Jesus's departure, it's clear that Jesus probably didn't address this matter.

- *How did Jesus understand his relation to the coming of the kingdom of God?* Scholars disagree about whether Jesus merely proclaimed the kingdom/rule of God or whether he embodied it,

A pilgrim kneels at the Stone of Unction, the place where tradition says the body of Jesus was washed before his burial, in the Church of the Holy Sepulcher (tomb) in Jerusalem.

© KAVRAM/SHUTTERSTOCK.COM

or something in between. To what extent did the events of his life, death, and resurrection make the kingdom/rule of God a reality for his followers?

Some Christians today criticize Paul for his socially conservative statements, but in his own time he was criticized for being too liberal.

11-2b The Earliest Church (30–100 C.E.)

The earliest church in Jerusalem was initially composed of those Jews who had followed Jesus during his ministry, perhaps one hundred people in all. They saw themselves as a continuing reform movement within Judaism. In a few days after Jesus's departure

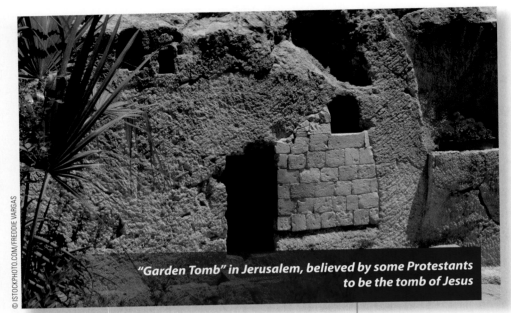
"Garden Tomb" in Jerusalem, believed by some Protestants to be the tomb of Jesus

letters to his churches, we know a good deal about Paul. He didn't write so much about Jesus's earthly life and teaching, but made the crucifixion and resurrection of Jesus the center of his proclamation. The crucifixion of Jesus was the supreme redemptive act, a self-sacrifice for the sin of humankind. Salvation is a gift of grace, and in baptism the Holy Spirit comes to transform the new Christian. Paul linked this doctrine of **justification** by faith with his strong view that Christ brings liberation from the Mosaic Law, especially for Gentiles. Justification brings freedom, not from parts of the Mosaic Law such as the Ten Commandments as a whole, but from parts that particularly mark Jewish identity—for example, keeping Jewish food regulations, observing the last day of the week for mandatory rest, and especially being circumcised. This created difficulties at Jerusalem, where many followers of Jesus wanted to see the heritage of Judaism continued. Once this struggle was settled, the radical character of Paul's doctrine of justification began to be forgotten in the church, where salvation became a matter of both faith and obedience to God's law.

See a BBC video on the life of Paul.

See a report on the significance of Paul produced by travel expert Rick Steves.

from earth, the early church experienced on the Jewish feast of Pentecost an outpouring of the Spirit of God to empower it for its continued ministry.

Saul—or as he was known when his missionary journeys began, Paul—was a Pharisee who violently persecuted the earliest church. Born at Tarsus (TAR-suhs) in southern Asia Minor (present-day Turkey), he had come to Jerusalem as a student of famous Rabbi Gamaliel and had tried to suppress a Christian group called by Luke the "Hellenists," who were led by Stephen, the first Christian to be killed for the faith. While on the road to Damascus to persecute the followers of Jesus, Paul was suddenly, dramatically converted to faith in Christ. In this conversion, or soon afterward, he came to a conviction that the Christian message must be spread among the Gentiles, without the additional requirement that they become Jews. Paul was a controversial figure throughout his career. Although he is criticized today by some for his conservative statements about women and slaves, in his own time he was criticized for being far too inclusivist, even liberal. He gained recognition in the Jerusalem church of Gentile converts. He saw clearly that the mission of the church to all humanity, implicit in the death and resurrection of Christ, meant a break with many of the rabbinical traditions in which he had previously lived. Paul worked tirelessly as a missionary, founded dozens of churches in strategically located cities, and became known as "the Apostle to the Gentiles."

Because of the preservation of several of his

justification Salvation as being made right with God by faith, for Paul a gift of God

The four New Testament Gospels record a special commission of Jesus to Peter as the leader among the twelve disciples, but Peter's life can only be partially reconstructed. He was a key leader in the earliest Jerusalem church until James, a close relative of Jesus, became its leader. We know from Paul's letters that Peter did missionary work in the Gentile world. Two letters in the New Testament bear his name, but many scholars are doubtful about their authorship by Peter—especially the second letter. According to early tradition, Peter died in Nero's persecution in 64 C.E., probably at the same time as Paul was killed. Later traditions say that he was crucified, at his request, upside down, because he wasn't worthy to die the same way that Jesus did. Peter was probably buried in a cemetery on Vatican Hill, across the Tiber River in the outskirts of Rome; later, the Roman emperor Constantine would build a large church on the site, a church that was replaced by the present St. Peter's Basilica. Rome had the bones of Peter and Paul, which helped to ensure its leading role in the Western church.

11-2c The Ancient Period (100–500 C.E.)

Although Christian tradition focuses on Peter and Paul, it is certain that many other missionaries also contributed to the growth of Christianity by planting churches. Some churches, prominently that at Rome, seem to have begun without any formal mission effort. By 100 C.E., Christianity had established itself in every large and midsize city in the eastern half of the Roman Empire (see Map 11.1). In the next two centuries, Christian churches were founded throughout the whole Roman Empire and even beyond it. These were all *house churches*, groups of Christians who met in private homes ("church" here refers to an association of people, not a building). Ancient Christianity experienced rapid growth for a variety of reasons:

- The struggle over whether to allow Gentiles to join the church without converting to Judaism was quickly settled in the affirmative for the majority of the earliest churches.

- Much of church life was dedicated to making converts and assimilating them into the close-knit social structure of the Christian community.

- Christianity offered things that many people in the ancient world were seeking: a purpose for living greater than what Roman religion and philosophy could provide, happiness in this world, the promise of eternal life, a higher religious standing for women and slaves, and a loving social-support network.

- Unlike other religions in the Roman world, Christianity made a broad appeal to people of all ethnicities, classes, and genders, which gave it a wide field for conversion and growth.

- A common New Testament **canon** arose rapidly. Although the entire 27-book New Testament official list was not finalized until the middle 300s, by the year 100 most Christians agreed on the four Gospels and the letters of Paul and John.

As Christianity spread among Gentiles, it continued to grow out of its early status as a Jewish group. By the end of the first century, many Jewish leaders began to decree that Jews confessing Jesus to be the Messiah should be expelled from synagogues. As Christians began to outnumber Jews in some cities, Christian pressure on Jews began, only to increase in 313 when the state persecution of Christianity ended. Thus began a bitter legacy of Christian anti-Semitism, prejudice against the Jewish people that has haunted the Western world through our own time. Christianity did not invent anti-Semitism—it was hundreds of years old by the time Christianity was born—but it added its own twist to it. The church understood itself, and was understood by Jews, to be Gentile. By around 400 C.E., historians generally agree today, the separation between Judaism and Christianity was complete. Judaism and Christianity are sister faiths, but like many family feuds, their conflict has been intense and sad. However, Christianity remains built on the foundation of Judaism. They share much of the same Bible, monotheism, a moral code, and similar patterns of worship.

canon Official list of the twenty-seven books of the New Testament

martyrdom Death of Christians for the faith, especially as an act of witness to others

Watch a BBC video on the origins of Roman Catholicism.

Take a tour of the oldest house-church in the world, in Dura-Europos, Syria.

> *Judaism and Christianity are sister faiths, but like many family feuds, their ongoing conflict has been intense and sad.*

As Christianity grew, it also challenged the Roman Empire. During the first century, this challenge was muted. But at the end of the first century, with the outbreak of imperial persecutions of Christians, Christianity challenged the legitimacy of the empire and the Roman religious ideology with which it was allied. Christians believed—and acted on the belief—that Jesus, not Caesar, is the Lord of this world. This led to even more Roman persecutions and the **martyrdom** of Christians. Persecution was sporadic but often fierce, especially in the late 200s, in an effort at times to kill off all Christians. Romans also countered Christianity in an informal, popular way by charging that Christians practiced secret cannibalism, were sexually immoral, and were intolerant of others, among other claims.

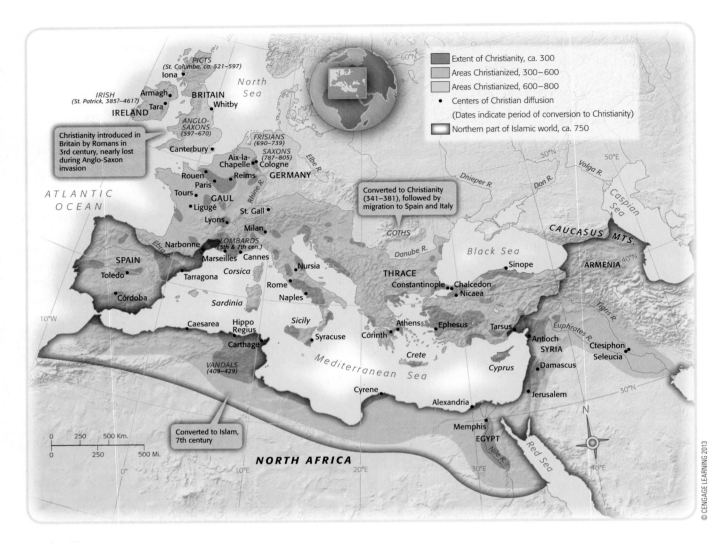

Map 11.1
The Spread of Christianity to about 800 C.E.
Christianity arose in Palestine in the first century C.E. and gradually gained footholds in parts of western Asia, North Africa, and southern Europe by 300 C.E. Over the next five centuries, Christianity became the dominant religion in much of Western and Central Europe, and expanded its influence in western Asia and North Africa. By about 750, Islam had conquered much of the Middle East and all of North Africa and Spain, and many Christians in these areas converted to Islam.

Map legend:
- Extent of Christianity, ca. 300
- Areas Christianized, 300–600
- Areas Christianized, 600–800
- • Centers of Christian diffusion (Dates indicate period of conversion to Christianity)
- Northern part of Islamic world, ca. 750

However, Roman persecution didn't stem the rise of Christianity. As one church leader at this time remarked, "The blood of the martyrs is the seed of the church."

> Some groups in the church were labeled "heretical" because they were too doctrinally conservative or morally rigorous—too "Christian" for other Christians.

The church was also challenged from within by **heresy**, the church's characterization of organized internal opposition. As in most new religions, it took time for diversity to arise and become controversial. Some alternative churches arose in the second century, and in some areas they outnumbered what was becoming mainstream Christianity. The movement known as **Gnosticism** or Gnostic Christianity believed that this material world is evil and hostile to the good. As Christianity defined itself in the second century against Judaism, Roman imperial religion, Gnosticism,

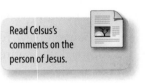

Read Celsus's comments on the person of Jesus.

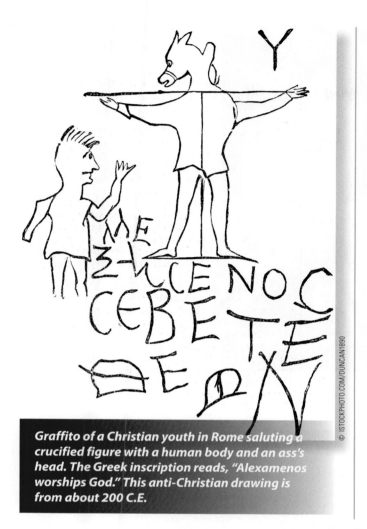

Graffito of a Christian youth in Rome saluting a crucified figure with a human body and an ass's head. The Greek inscription reads, "Alexamenos worships God." This anti-Christian drawing is from about 200 C.E.

© ISTOCKPHOTO.COM/DUNCAN1890

France. Irenaeus defined heresy as a significant departure from the Bible and the rule of faith, a move away from the center of the faith in Jesus Christ.

Emperor Constantine's toleration of Christianity in 312 ushered in a new era in the faith, one that many historians view as lasting until the twentieth century. This era featured the close association of church and state, often called **Constantinianism**. Constantine and later emperors saw religious unity and peace as important for their rule; there was one God, one Church, and one Emperor. By moving his capital to Constantinople in northern Asia Minor, Emperor Constantine created a new culture that attempted to preserve the best of ancient Greece and Rome and yet transform it through the Christian faith. The Eastern Orthodox branch of Christianity, and the many nations it has shaped, is the continuation of this effort.

heresy The church's characterization of organized internal opposition

Gnosticism Religious movement that believed this world is evil because it is material

orthodoxy Emphasis on correct teaching of the essentials of the faith and (to a lesser extent) moral practice

Constantinianism [CON-stan-TIN-ee-uhn-IZ-uhm] Close association of church and state, named after Constantine, for the promotion of religious and civil unity

monasticism Christian monks and nuns living in community

and other movements, **orthodoxy** gradually arose, with its emphasis on correct teaching of the essentials of the faith and (to a lesser extent) correct moral practice. This effort to achieve and preserve correct teaching has characterized much of Christianity ever since. Gnosticism and other dissenting groups within ancient Christianity used to be viewed and studied as corruptions of divine truths, but today historians study them more objectively as alternative forms of Christianity. Some "heretics" were given this label because they were more doctrinally conservative and morally rigorous than the mainstream church— too "Christian" for other Christians. An effective opponent of heresy was Irenaeus, the second-century bishop of Lyon, in modern-day

Read a selection of Irenaeus's attack on Gnosticism.

Finally, this period saw the beginnings of Christian **monasticism** in the 200s. It was modeled on scriptural examples and ideals, including the life of Jesus, but monasticism isn't mentioned in the Bible or based on a direct Jewish precedent. Those living the monastic life are known by the generic terms *monks* and *nuns*. Monks began by living alone, at first in the Egyptian desert. As more people took on the lives of monks, they started to come together and form communities, usually living by the threefold vow of poverty, chastity, and obedience. When the great persecutions ceased with Constantine, the rigorous self-denials of monasticism, such as celibacy (no sexual activity), were seen as a substitute for martyrdom. Monastics generally dwell in a monastery (monks) or a

The head of a statue of Constantine, more than four feet tall, suggests his importance in Roman history.

© ISTOCKPHOTO.COM/PIXELBARON

convent (nuns). Monks became the bearers of civilization in the Western church. They preserved the Christian Bible and the literary as well as some of the scientific heritage of Rome, which otherwise would have perished for lack of manuscript copying and study. Unlike the first Christian monks, these worked in their monasteries and convents as a part of their monastic calling, to support themselves. By the Middle Ages, many Catholic monasteries enjoyed vast properties, wealth, and social power.

Explore Christianity in late antiquity.

Nun in traditional clothing praying the rosary

11-2d Byzantine, Medieval, and Renaissance Christianity (500–1500)

The Eastern Roman Empire, also called the Byzantine Empire, with its capital of Constantinople, lasted for more than a thousand years from its creation by Constantine in 330 to the Turkish Muslim conquest in 1453. The traditional power of Byzantine emperors over the church was curtailed after the **Iconoclastic Controversy** that began in 726. This controversy was caused by the attempt of some emperors to remove the two-dimensional pictures of Jesus and the saints from churches, ending the veneration of these *icons* during worship. The emperors' iconoclasm was in part an effort to cope with Islam's attack on Christianity for what it called the idolatrous use of images. In both Eastern Orthodox and Roman Catholic Christianity, worship is offered only to God, with veneration for the saints. Muslims rejected this distinction. Leading monks and several empresses resisted the emperors and their allies in the church, and icons were eventually restored. The controversy over images cemented their place as an essential element of the Eastern Orthodox identity. Today,

Iconoclastic Controversy [eye-con-oh-CLASS-tick] Struggle in Eastern Orthodoxy over removing icons from churches

iconostasis [eye-con-oh-STAH-sis] Screen or wall of icons at the front of Eastern Orthodox churches, between the people and the altar

every Orthodox church has an **iconostasis**, a screen or wall of icons, between the people and the altar. To the Orthodox, icons represent the reality of God's presence in the person of Jesus Christ and the importance for the church of the saints in heaven. When the controversy ended in 843, the power of the church to direct its own doctrine and worship was strengthened. The controversy also strengthened the tendency of Eastern Orthodoxy to define itself by its worship and devotion rather than, as in Western Christianity (both Roman Catholicism and the Protestantism to arise later), by institution and doctrine.

Easter devotion using icon

> *Eastern Orthodox missionaries preserved indigenous cultures to a degree that Roman Catholic missionaries didn't.*

Byzantine Christianity also carried out missionary activity, especially to its north. The peoples of what are now Bulgaria, Russia, and Moravia were converted to Christianity in the 800s, residents of Hungary in the 900s, and those of Poland in the 900s to the 1100s. Orthodox missions tried to preserve indigenous cultures. Missionaries translated the Bible and the rituals of the church into the language of the peoples. In the Catholic West, Latin was the main language of the church and the only language of the Bible. Slavic Orthodoxy, particularly in Russia, which thought of itself as "the third Rome," was to carry on the Christian heritage of Byzantium when the eastern Roman Empire finally fell to Muslim forces in 1453.

In the Latin West, the bishop of Rome, the **pope**, set the tone for the continuing development of Christianity. By the end of the ancient period of the religion, the popes had already asserted their leadership over much of Christendom. When the western Roman Empire fell in the fifth century, the pope came to be the main embodiment of faith and cultural unity for Western Europe. Over time the **papacy**, the office of the pope and his authority, extended its spiritual and even political power over many of the European states. Gradually, the influence of the papacy spread across the entire western half of the European continent. At the same time, the Western church's relations with the Eastern Orthodox Church worsened, until the two formally split in 1054 over doctrinal, cultural, and political issues. This division still endures today. Many Christians suppose that the Catholic-Protestant split in Western Christianity is the worse, but the split between East and West is earlier and in some ways more difficult to overcome.

Medieval Christianity in the West expressed itself not only through the papacy, bishops, and priests, but also through monks and friars. Medieval

> Read about the reasons why the East and West split.

reformers within the Catholic Church, such as Bernard of Clairvaux and Pope Gregory VII, were **friars** (members of the new monastic orders that arose in the twelfth century, as opposed to the monks in the older orders). The theologians who systematized and developed Christian doctrine in the high Middle Ages, such as Anselm of Canterbury, England, and Thomas Aquinas (ah-KWIGH-nuhs), were monastics. In his major work from 1265 to 1273, Aquinas made a comprehensive overview of Christian theology, from the vantage point of the ancient Greek philosopher Aristotle's newly rediscovered thinking, and became the most influential theologian in Roman Catholicism from that point on. Some of the new movements preached the gospel to the people in churches and outdoors. Through this reform, the life of the whole Catholic Church was enriched and renewed. Another feature of the later Middle Ages was the building of cathedrals, usually one in each large city throughout Europe, in the new Gothic style that seemed to soar to heaven.

Both Eastern and Western Christianity were forced during this period to come to grips with the rising power of Islam. From its beginning in 622, Islam spread rapidly in the Middle East (see pages 300–303). Soon, almost all the Middle East and North Africa were Islamic. Christian minorities lived somewhat peaceably under Islamic rule, protected by Islamic law, but they dwindled in number. Islam continued to press on the Byzantine Empire until, in 1453, Constantinople itself became a Muslim city and its cathedral, the Church of Holy Wisdom (Greek: *Hagia Sophia*), became a mosque. The main confrontation of Western Christianity with Islam was to be in the long period of the Crusades (1095–1350), when Catholic forces from all over Europe retook Palestine from the Muslims, an effort that eventually failed and damaged Muslim–Christian relations through today.

> **pope** Bishop of Rome, the head of the Roman Catholic Church
>
> **papacy** [PAYP-uh-see] Office of the pope and his authority
>
> **friar** Member of the new monastic orders that arose in the twelfth century, as opposed to the monks in the older orders

> Explore Byzantine Christianity.

> Explore Roman Christianity in the Middle Ages.

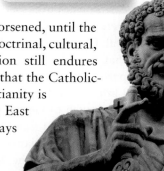

Statue of St. Peter holding the keys to the kingdom, symbolic of papal authority

© MATTIA MAZZUCCHELLI/SHUTTERSTOCK.COM

At the end of the Middle Ages, around 1400, life in Western Christianity began to experience renewal in the Renaissance, the "rebirth" of classical Greco-Roman cultural ideals in art, architecture, philosophy, and literature. Some Renaissance scholars called the church back "to the foundations" of the New Testament and the ancient church. The Renaissance examined institutions and teachings, not trusting in tradition for tradition's sake or authority for authority's sake, as had largely been the case in the Middle Ages. It promoted a more human-centered view of life—usually a Christian humanism, but sometimes not—in place of the medieval heaven-centered view. Renaissance art, for example, more realistically portrayed saints and ordinary people on earth. The Christian humanism of Desiderius Erasmus (DEH-sih-DAIR-ee-uhs er-ASS-muhs) of Rotterdam (1466–1536), the leading figure of the Northern Renaissance, prodded the church (both Protestant and Catholic) into self-examination and eventual reform. But not every aspect of the Renaissance would prove to be positive. For example, it hastened the rise of nationalism and ended the medieval Catholic ideal of a Europe united by a common faith.

11-2e Reformation in the Western Church (1500–1600)

Movements for the reform of church teaching and practice were prevalent in the later Middle Ages. This reform usually expressed itself *through* the other traditional structures of the Catholic Church. Where occasionally reform expressed itself *outside* or even *against* the Catholic Church—as for example in the cases of John Wycliffe (WIHK-liff; 1329–1384) and his movement in England, and John Hus (huhs; 1373–1415) in Bohemia—it was declared heretical and stamped out by force.

The **Magisterial Reformation**, or mainstream reform, began with Martin Luther (LOO-thur). He led an effective reform movement against the structure of the traditional church. Luther (1483–1546) was an Augustinian friar, a priest, and a professor at Wittenberg University in central Germany. Like all would-be reformers before him, Luther initially saw himself as a loyal son of the Catholic Church. In 1517, he called for a public debate over reform issues by posting his Ninety-Five Theses (propositions) on the door of the castle church in Wittenberg. The immediate complaint Luther had was the selling of indulgences to raise funds for the new St. Peter's Basilica in Rome. These were certificates securing the forgiveness of punishment in **purgatory**, the fiery place where believers' sins are burned away after death before they can enter heaven. He found the idea of buying and selling salvation unbiblical, corrupt, and even ludicrous.

Luther soon found himself so at odds with the Roman Catholic Church that he moved to create an alternative church that he called the Evangelical (characterized by the gospel of Christ) Church; after his death, others began to call it the Lutheran Church. Popes, bishops, monks, and nuns were done away with in this church. He envisioned Germany—and probably other nations as well—as having its own, more indigenous forms of Christianity. He translated the Bible into German, put hymns and worship into the language of the people, and reformed the Mass. Evangelical Christians were urged to receive Holy Communion every week, in contrast to the once-a-year Catholic practice in the Middle Ages. Luther and his followers moved to put the gospel, the essential religious message of Jesus Christ, at the center of Christianity. Luther saw the center of Christianity in the doctrine of salvation by faith alone. He also stressed the central role of God's love and grace, the sole authority of the Bible over the Church, and the role of the individual Christian's conscience. Over time, faith took precedence over moral activity in Protestantism, and still has precedence today. Reformers devalued the role of the saints and denied their power to intercede with God for Christians on earth or in purgatory. When Luther and his movement were protected and then promoted by the rulers of several German states, Protestantism gained a foothold that would enable it to endure and spread to other parts of Germany. By 1600, the Lutheran reform had taken over much of Germany and all of Scandinavia (see Map 11.2).

Watch a BBC report on Martin Luther.

What historians call the **Radical Reformation** arose in tandem with the Magisterial Reformation. Conrad Grebel (GRAY-buhl) and the Swiss Brethren movement insisted that the mainstream reform of Luther and others was inconsistent and halfhearted. They argued for

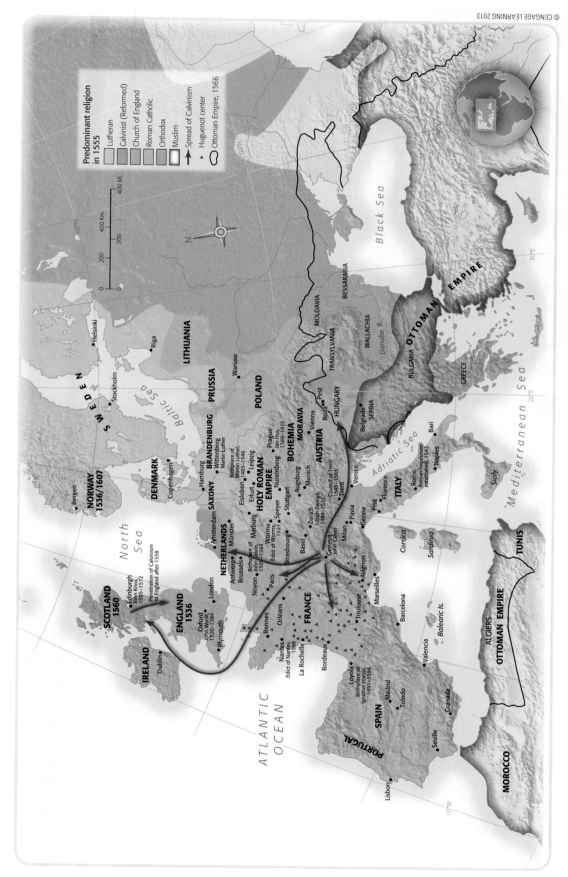

© CENGAGE LEARNING 2013

Predominant religion in 1555
- Lutheran
- Calvinist (Reformed)
- Church of England
- Roman Catholic
- Orthodox
- Muslim
- ▲ Huguenot center
- ⟶ Spread of Calvinism
- ◯ Ottoman Empire, 1566

Map 11.2

Reformation Europe

The Protestant Reformation reshaped Europe's religious landscape in the 1500s and early 1600s. By the mid-1550s, some form of Protestantism had become dominant in much of northern continental Europe, England, and Scotland. Catholicism remained predominant in the southern half of Western Europe and in parts of Eastern Europe. Catholics in Europe felt pressure from the Islamic Ottoman Empire, but Muslim rulers protected Protestants under their rule in Hungary and Transylvania.

THE CHRISTIAN PRESENT AS SHAPED BY ITS PAST   **271**

Martin Luther

1483-1983 USA 20c

© MARKAUMARK/SHUTTERSTOCK.COM

what they saw as pure "New Testament Christianity," including:

- Baptism of adult believers only, after a conversion experience
- Complete separation of the church from the civil government
- Pacifism, with refusal to be drafted for warfare
- Common ownership of some property
- Strict church enforcement of Christian morality among church members

They soon became known as **Anabaptists**, "rebaptizers," but over time the name was simplified to *Baptists*. In the 1520s, the movement spread through Switzerland and later found a home in many Protestant lands. Eventually, the Baptists became a widespread Protestant church, even extending their influence to lands such as Russia, where other Protestant churches could not penetrate. The Anabaptists that later became Baptists kept their major emphasis on

Anabaptists

"Rebaptizers," members of the Radical Reformation group that accepted only adult baptism

the baptism of believing adults only; other Anabaptist groups that became Mennonites and the Amish have preserved pacifism and detachment from civil authority in addition to baptism of believers.

The Reformed (Calvinist) branch of Protestantism was, like the Anabaptists, born in the political world of the Swiss city-republics. (All Protestant churches were "reformed" from Roman Catholicism, and the movement is called the Reformation, but the churches born of the Calvinist branch of the Reformation have in particular called themselves the "Reformed Church.") Huldreich Zwingli (HUHLD-righk TSVING-lee) began the Reformed movement in Zurich, but in the next three decades it shifted to Berne, Basel, and especially French-speaking Geneva. There, Frenchman John Calvin (1509–1564), who had studied law and theology at the University of Paris, reformed the city to Protestant ideals. He stressed (in addition to Luther's main ideas) such teachings as the sovereignty of God over all life and human responsibility to live out one's Christian calling in everyday life. Calvin carried out social reforms that became common in the Western world, such as levying a tax to support free compulsory public education for all children. Geneva became a haven for persecuted Protestants from many places in Europe.

Like Luther, Calvin wrote prolifically, and soon his ideas for reform spread widely. He was known especially as a systematizer and promoter of Protestant Christianity. His book *The Institutes [Foundations] of the Christian Religion* soon became the most influential book of Protestantism. Calvin's influence in the Reformed movement was so great that it also became known in later centuries as *Calvinism*. Calvinist churches were found by the end of the century not only in Switzerland, but also in France (where Calvinists were called Huguenots [HYOO-guh-nots]), Scotland, The Netherlands, Germany, and Hungary.

> *The name Puritan has come to mean "killjoy" or even "self-righteous," but Puritanism wasn't like that.*

Reformation came to England by way of politics. In the 1520s, King Henry VIII opposed the pope over the king's right to divorce and remarry. In 1529, Henry began forming a Church of England under his control, which was to become a "middle way" between Catholics and Protestants, especially in worship and organization. Its doctrine eventually was closer to the teaching of the Reformers than to that of Rome. Henry's daughter Mary tried to bring England back to the Roman Church by a variety of means, some so violent that they earned her the name "Bloody Mary," but by the reign of Henry's younger daughter, Elizabeth I, the Church of England was firmly established. English monarchs were made the head of the Church of England and "Defender of the Faith," which explains why in 2011 the wedding of Prince William (the presumptive eventual heir to the throne) and Katherine Middleton was held in formal Anglican style, officiated by the head of the Anglican Church.

Spanish mission in Santa Barbara, California. Today, an active parish church meets in its chapel (right), and the mission is one of the largest tourist attractions in Santa Barbara.

© ISTOCKPHOTO.COM/S. GREG PANOSIAN

In 1620, the Reformed movement came to America via the English Protestants called **Puritans**—so called because they wanted to purify the Church of England from its continuing Roman Catholic elements. The name *Puritan* has come to mean "killjoy" or even "self-righteous," but Puritanism wasn't like that. Of all religious groups, the Puritans were to have the largest influence on the development of American government. As David Hall says in *A Reforming People* (2011), Puritanism was a daring and successful reform movement in the English-speaking world during early modern times.[1]

The **Catholic Reform** was in the past called the Counter-Reformation, and that term is still used by some. When his initial measures against Protestants didn't prove effective, the pope finally called a council of bishops and theologians in 1545 at Trent, Italy, to consider church reform. Widespread reforms of Catholic Church life emerged from Trent, and many of the more-glaring abuses were removed. With the help of the new Jesuit order, these reforms were carried out in nations and regions that were still predominantly Roman Catholic. Even there the reforms of Trent were subject to national policy; for example, France rejected them as too conservative and intrusive, and Spain—which often viewed itself as more Catholic than the

pope—resisted them as too liberal. For areas that had already become Protestant, about half of Europe above the Alps, the reforms of Trent were "too little, too late." Once nations became Protestant, they didn't return to Rome. Other parts of the Catholic Reformation were a revival of mysticism, especially in Spain, and a new focus on the system of Thomas Aquinas as a mighty fortress against Protestant thought. In all, the Roman Church emerged from the 1500s severely chastened in numbers and political influence, but strengthened in spirit.

Meanwhile, events in the New World were proving a bright spot in the fortunes of Roman Catholicism. When Spain and later Portugal explored and then colonized the New World in the Western Hemisphere, Roman Catholic missionaries accompanied them. They conquered together "for God and for gold." The indigenous peoples of Central and South America were quickly brought into the Christian faith. Spanish cultural, military, and religious outposts called *missions* were constructed; then thousands of churches were built for the indigenous peoples; and eventually monasteries and nunneries were established for them. A few priests and bishops protested the high cost of colonization to the indigenous peoples, even founding a "Jesuit state" in what is now Peru (a story told in the acclaimed 1985 film *The Mission*), but to no avail. Although the Roman Church lost many lands in Europe to Protestantism in the 1500s, it gained much in the Americas, where Catholicism is still strong.

Take a virtual tour of the Santa Barbara Mission.

See a preview of the Hollywood film *The Mission*.

Puritans English Protestants who wanted to purify the Church of England from its continuing Roman Catholic elements

Catholic Reform Movement called the Counter-Reformation, spurred on by the 1545 Council of Trent

---

[1] David D. Hall, *A Reforming People: Puritanism and the Transformation of Public Life in New England* (New York: Knopf, 2011).

11-2f The Early Modern Period (1600–1900)

Because of the settled and more tolerant situation after the "wars of religion" ended around 1648, each Protestant church and the Roman Catholic Church occupied its own parts of Europe, and Protestant teachings were articulated more fully. *Confessionalism*, named for the doctrinal statements called "confessions" issued by the various Reformation churches, brought a drive for doctrinal correctness as an important aspect of church life. *Scholasticism* stressed the rational explanation and defense of the various Protestant belief systems.

The reaction against arid confessionalism and scholasticism wasn't slow in coming. When the several dimensions of religion that we saw in Chapter 1 are reduced to just a few, reaction will set in. **Pietism** arose in the last half of the seventeenth century, born with Philip Jakob Spener's (SPAY-ner) *Pious Considerations* in 1675. Spener rebelled against the Protestant orthodoxy of his day, which he viewed as sterile and lifeless. He proposed a continuing Reformation to bring the goals of Luther to fulfillment: personal Bible study, mutual correction and encouragement in Christian living, spiritual growth for all laity, and stress on emotional dimensions of faith. Pietists formed separate churches in many Lutheran and Reformed nations. The leadership of the Lutheran churches tried to suppress Pietism, but it soon became a major movement. Like Anabaptist churches before them, Pietism led to *gathered churches*, not the state churches to which nearly all citizens belonged. English Puritanism also had its pietist aspects, and the Methodist movement that emerged from the Church of England was pietist as well. Even in the Roman Catholic Church, the Jansenist movement in France and then in North America promoted personal piety and holy living among the laity.

In the 1700s, Pietism took on the major goal of counteracting the influence on Christianity of the Enlightenment, the period of secularization of culture led by reason and not faith. The Enlightenment's rationalism and "free thinking" were easier for the church to deal with when they were aggressively atheistic, as in the French Revolution. But when the Enlightenment led to more-subtle changes in the church itself, such as the introduction of modern historical sciences and their application to the Bible and theology, the effect on Christianity was profound.

Pietism [PIGH-uh-tiz-um] Protestant movement stressing individual piety, in knowledge and emotion

Especially in Protestant faculties of German universities, the acceptance of these new methods of scholarship led some to question the Christian faith. The concurrent discovery of other religions, in particular the ancient religions of Asia, gave rise to a questioning of the uniqueness and absoluteness of Christianity, something that continues today. The Enlightenment's effort to separate church and state, and the ideas of religious toleration and the freedom associated with it, would succeed throughout Western and Northern Europe, but most fully in the United States. Constantinianism was rapidly losing ground.

The nineteenth century saw the challenge of secular reason continue. Historical scholarship, particularly the historical study of the Bible, continued to chip away at some of the old certainties of the Christian faith. Even more challenging to traditional belief were discoveries in natural science. The work of evolutionary biologist Charles Darwin called into question ancient Christian beliefs in the special creation of humanity in the image of God. Although Protestant churches were more directly and immediately affected by the Enlightenment and its heirs, which produced both secularism outside the church and doctrinal change inside, Roman Catholicism later saw its effects in the Catholic *Modernist* movement. Not until the twentieth century would Catholic, Protestant, and (to a lesser extent) Eastern Orthodox churches come to grips with the challenges of modern knowledge.

Despite these challenges, nineteenth-century Christianity was broadly optimistic about the prospects of the Christian religion. The largest cause for optimism was the powerful missionary movement that flourished in the 1800s and continues somewhat lessened today. The Protestant and Roman Catholic churches of the West set out to evangelize the entire world, or at least the large parts of it not yet exposed to the gospel. (The Orthodox Church didn't participate significantly in this missionary movement.) In 1800, fewer than one in four people in the world were Christian; by 1900, one in three were Christian. Although the missionary and the colonial/commercial agents marched together, as they had often done in the past, especially in the New World, the nineteenth century saw the beginning of their separation. Christianity finally became the global religion that "catholic" implies.

Read a selection from the 1898 *Women's Bible* by Elizabeth Cady Stanton, an influential early feminist.

Watch a preview of *Amazing Grace*, the story of Anglican William Wilberforce's attack on slavery in the British Empire.

11-2g Modern Christianity (1900–Present)

The optimistic hope present in Western culture and the church at the end of the 1800s went largely unfulfilled. The new era was one of severe crisis and challenge. The carnage of World War I (1914–1918), the worldwide pandemic of influenza, and then global economic depression began the movement away from cultural optimism. Then the rise of aggressive, totalitarian regimes, first in Russia and then in Italy and Germany, led to the horrors of World War II

Assertive, even confrontational, efforts to spread the faith are typical of fundamentalism, as shown by this street sign.

(1939–1945), with its massive civilian casualties and the Holocaust. Even the end of the war brought with it the new uncertainties of nuclear weapons and the Cold War. All these events were to shake Christian optimism to its roots in much of Protestantism and in parts of Catholicism. The result for some was a loss of faith, but for others a rethinking of the essence of Christianity. In the United States, **fundamentalism** arose to oppose liberalization of church doctrine. Fundamentalism features a strictly literal interpretation of the Bible, an insistence on the truth of certain key Christian teachings (the "fundamentals" from which the movement takes its name), and an aggressive attitude toward Christian liberalism specifically and toward unbelief generally.

This impulse against liberalism in the 1900s was shared by others who were in no way fundamentalist. Swiss theologian Karl Barth (bart, 1886–1968), who was to become the leading Christian theologian of the century, turned away from liberal, optimistic Protestantism to reassert the transcendent power of a faith that cannot be shaped by human culture. The movement that Barth sparked came to be called "neo-orthodoxy," a new assertion in modern times of traditional Christian theology, especially in its Protestant form. (It has no formal relationship with Eastern Orthodoxy, however.) After World War II, this movement came to the English-speaking world and had a direct effect on its theology and life, as it still has today. Liberal, progressive theology has continued in some parts of Protestantism, especially in the mainstream **denominations**—Protestant churches united

under a single name and organization, such as the Episcopal Church or the United Methodist Church—although liberalism is reduced in size and chastened in spirit from its heyday around 1900.

While the theological reassessment occurred, a movement for greater unity among the churches came into prominence. **Ecumenism**, a movement for greater understanding and cooperation among Christian denominations, had been planted and nurtured in the mission fields of the various Protestant churches, where missionaries learned to minimize their denominational differences and cooperate in the face of a non-Christian environment. In the twentieth century, the National Council of Churches in the United States and the World Council of Churches would be the institutional bearers of this movement. Ecumenism has changed how theologians conceptualize the faith, how the different Christian churches relate to each other, and how grassroots Christians live out their faith in worship and daily life. This

fundamentalism
Movement in reaction to Protestant liberalism, featuring strictly literal interpretation of the Bible and an insistence on the truth of certain "fundamental" Christian teachings

denominations
Protestant churches united under a single name and organization

ecumenism [eh-KYOO-men-iz-uhm] Movement for greater understanding and cooperation among Christian churches

spirit of ecumenism also affected the Eastern Orthodox churches throughout the world; they've participated fully in the ecumenical movement from the start.

Read the ecumenical agreement between the Roman Catholic Church and the Lutheran churches.

> *Never before had any church changed itself so quickly and deeply as the Roman Catholic Church did after Vatican II.*

At the same time, a new movement for reform was gathering in the Roman Catholic Church that would prove to be the most important Christian event of the twentieth century. Catholicism had been insulated from dealing with modern challenges (science, secularism, religious toleration, and so on) by its sheer size and its church structure. But when Pope John XXIII convened the **Second Vatican Council** from 1962 to 1966, fresh, strong winds of reform blew through the church. In Vatican II, the Catholic Church

Pope Francis greets the crowds in St. Peter's Square before leading them in prayer.

© ALESSANDRA BENEDETTI/ALESSANDRA BENEDETTI/CORBIS

- recognized the status and role of the laity as essential to the church;
- reformed worship by putting the Mass in national languages and increasing lay participation;
- moved the altar from the front wall of the church and had the priest face the people as the Mass was said;
- opened ecumenical dialogue with Protestants and the Orthodox, affirming that they were in some way legitimate Christians;
- affirmed for the first time religious liberty and toleration for all people;
- took a new, more balanced view of non-Christian faiths, especially Judaism.

Second Vatican Council Council from 1962 to 1966, leading to reform in the Catholic Church

Never before had any church changed itself so quickly and deeply as the Roman Catholic Church did after Vatican II. Many Roman Catholics today don't remember the way the Church was before Vatican II, and it's hard for them to imagine a form of Catholic Church life that had existed from the 1500s to the 1960s. The Catholic Church continues to change, recently with the resignation of Pope Benedict XVI in 2013 for reasons of infirmity, the first time in more than five hundred years that a pope has resigned from his office. Only time will tell if this sets a precedent for later popes. Benedict was replaced by Jorge Bergoglio (HOHR-hay ber-GOH-lee-oh), the archbishop of Buenos Aires, Argentina, who took the name Francis, after St. Francis of Assisi. This marked two "firsts" for the Catholic Church: the first Jesuit to become pope, and the first pope from the Western Hemisphere.

View a CBS News interview on the election of Pope Francis.

Two liberation movements in North American Christianity have become increasingly important in the modern period. (We'll deal with the charismatic movement, the "Global South" phenomenon, and evangelicalism on pages 289–292.) First, *feminism* has stressed the full emancipation of women. It recognizes that the church by its teaching and practice has held women down and tried to make second-class Christians of them. Some feminists have urged rejection of Christianity, arguing that it is hopelessly patriarchal. Most feminists in Christianity take a more moderate approach, trying to recover the biblical roots of feminism, stressing the (admittedly few) women who have played significant roles in Christian tradition, and working toward full liberation of women within the various Christian churches. This latter approach still represents the mainstream of Christian feminism, and it will continue to be a potent force for years to come, in culture in general and in the church specifically. As

Read about the debate over women bishops in the Church of England.

Read an article on feminism in the American Protestant Church.

Watch a BBC report on the Catholic Church's pushback against feminist demands.

the movement progresses, it is loosening its European-North American orientation and will likely make more of an impact in the churches of Asia, Africa, and Latin America.

A second current movement is **liberation theology**, the heart of which is not theology, but practice. This movement stresses the active Christian mission of delivering the oppressed from evil social structures and situations. Using a combination of Marxist social analysis and Christianity, this movement was born in Roman Catholic theological circles in Latin America. Some trace its roots all the way back to the "Jesuit state" in Peru, mentioned earlier on page 273. But it has spread widely and been applied to several different situations: women's liberation, black liberation, Hispanic liberation, and now gay liberation. The latter has been particularly problematic in mainline Protestant churches and in the worldwide Anglican community, which some observers think may be breaking apart over it. (The African American civil rights movement in the 1950s and 1960s came before black liberation theology, but much of the Christian aspect of this continuing movement is now related to liberation theology.) These new applications of liberation theology are still powerful influences in much of world Christianity, especially in the West, but the original form of political-social liberation theology in South America is waning.

The Trinity Knot, of Celtic Christian origin, symbolizes the Father, Son, and Holy Spirit as one. The crown of thorns tied into it is a symbol of the suffering of Christ.

© ISTOCKPHOTO.COM/RICHARD SEARS

Learning Objective 11-3

Outline in your own words essential Christian teachings as found in the Nicene Creed.

11-3 Christian Teachings as Reflected in the Nicene Creed

Christian believers in Seoul, South Korea, gather at the Yoido Full Gospel Church, at 1 million members the largest single Christian congregation in the world. This church, which belongs to the Assemblies of God denomination, has back-to-back services held from dawn to dusk to accommodate the numbers. Protestant Christianity—both mainstream and independent—has grown so strong in South Korea that its churches have begun to send Korean missionaries to other parts of the world. The Yoido congregation's size is emblematic of the worldwide growth and power of Pentecostal, Holy Spirit–centered Christianity.

Watch a BBC report on the Yoido church. ▶ ⟩⟩⟩

Christian teaching is founded on the doctrine of the **Trinity**, one God in three Persons—the Father, Son, and Holy Spirit. Christians believe that Jesus was the **incarnation** (coming in human form) of the eternal Son of God. As both human and divine, Jesus suffered, died, was buried, and was resurrected from the dead to open heaven to those who believe in him. Jesus founded a community of his followers; after his bodily ascension to heaven, the church carried on the organized, human dimensions of Jesus's work by the power and direction of the Holy Spirit. Jesus rules and reigns with God the Father until he will return to defeat evil, judge all humans (living and dead), and grant eternal life to his followers.

The **Nicene Creed**, known by its revised form as the Nicene-Constantinopolitan Creed, completed in 381, is the leading Christian statement of belief. **Creeds** (from the Latin *credo*, "I believe") are formal statements of belief meant to be binding on the church (see "A Closer Look: The Nicene-Constantinopolitan Creed"). All Catholic and Eastern Orthodox doctrine is formally rooted in creeds, as well as that of churches originating in the Lutheran and Reformed branches of the Reformation. A precursor of the Nicene Creed, the **Apostles' Creed**, is often

liberation theology Movement that stresses the active Christian mission of delivering the oppressed from evil social structures and situations

Trinity Christian teaching of one God in three equal persons—the Father, Son, and Holy Spirit

incarnation The eternal Son of God becoming human in the one person of Jesus Christ

Nicene Creed [nigh-SEEN] Most influential of all Christian statements of belief; completed in 381

creed Formal statement of belief meant to be binding on the church

Apostles' Creed Short creed often recited in Protestant churches

The Nicene-Constantinopolitan Creed, 381 C.E.

Several English versions of the Nicene-Constantinopolitan Creed have been used in the last fifty years or so. Here is the "Ecumenical Version" of 1975, the form used by most Protestant churches and the Eastern Orthodox Churches. (The Orthodox do not say "and the Son" in the sentence that begins "We believe in the Holy Spirit.") The Roman Catholic Church uses a slightly different version, from its recent *Third Roman Missal*, including a shift to "I believe."

> We believe in one God, the Father, the Almighty maker of heaven and earth, of all that is, seen and unseen.
> We believe in one Lord, Jesus Christ, the only Son of God, eternally begotten of the Father,
> God from God, Light from Light, true God from true God, begotten, not made, of one Being with the Father.
> Through him all things were made.
> For us men and for our salvation
> he came down from heaven:
> by the power of the Holy Spirit
> he became incarnate from the Virgin Mary, and was made man.
> For our sake he was crucified under Pontius Pilate;
> he suffered death and was buried.
> On the third day he rose again in accordance with the Scriptures;
> he ascended into heaven and is seated at the right hand of the Father.
> He will come again in glory to judge the living and the dead, and his kingdom will have no end.
> We believe in the Holy Spirit, the Lord, the giver of Life, who proceeds from the Father and the Son.
> With the Father and the Son he is worshiped and glorified.
> He has spoken through the Prophets.
> We believe in one holy catholic and apostolic Church.
> We acknowledge one baptism for the forgiveness of sins.
> We look for the resurrection of the dead, and the life of the world to come. Amen.

recited in Protestant churches. Even more-independent Protestant churches that reject the idea of creeds believe the doctrines taught in the Nicene Creed. Moreover, changes in Christian teaching in the history of the church are changes originating *from* the Nicene Creed. In what follows, we'll discuss Christian teaching in terms of this creed, under the main headings of Father, Son, and Holy Spirit. We'll also deal briefly in this discussion with later Christian formulation and use of these teachings.

11-3a God the Father

Christianity's teaching about God the Father is unproblematic, and the Christian tradition has rarely had to debate it. Much of the first article of the Nicene Creed is drawn directly from Jewish belief about God that was settled long before Jesus. God is all powerful ("Almighty") in heaven and on earth. God is the creator ("maker") of heaven and earth, not only of "all things seen" on the earth, but also all things "unseen" to humans (things in heaven). Nothing is outside of God's power. That God is the creator of all physical and spiritual reality—and that God would become human in Jesus—strongly implies that the world is a good, or at least a redeemable, place. Behind this teaching about God lie other key Jewish ideas. God is a living being, the "I am who I am" in Exodus 3:14, not a force or a principle. Christians believe that God the Father is a personal being just as fully as Jesus is a person. The decisive aspect of creation is that God fashioned humans in God's own image. This special position of humans makes them coworkers with God in the continuation and care of creation. The incarnation of God in the human being Jesus is the ultimate validation of the worth of human life.

What's new in the Christian teaching about God lies in the first thing the Nicene Creed says about God: that God is *the Father*. God was known metaphorically as a father to Israel in Judaism, but this wasn't a main understanding of God. In Christianity, God is first and foremost the Christian's *Father*, but this relationship derives from and is built on Jesus's special relationship to God. Jesus regularly calls God "Father," especially in the prayer that he taught his disciples, known variously as the "Our Father" or the "Lord's Prayer." Jesus used the Aramaic word *abba* (AH-bah) for God; it was usually employed by children for their earthly father and expresses childlike trust in, and intimacy with, one's father. This father–son relationship that Jesus had with God is a model for the relationship that Christians have with God.

According to the account of his baptism, Jesus understood his sonship when a voice from heaven said, "This is my beloved Son, with whom I am well pleased" (Matthew 3:17). In the Gospel of John, this sonship constitutes the basis for the self-awareness of Jesus: "I and the Father are one" (John 10:30). Although scholars disagree on whether Jesus actually said things like this, Christians believe it is an authentic insight into who Jesus really is. In Jesus Christ, God the Father was revealed more fully to humans, and worked in and through Jesus for the salvation of the world. Some Christians today dislike the term *Father* for its apparent gender reference and its use of human fathers—who are often flawed and sometimes abusive—to explain God. However, the fact that Christian teaching understands the human relationship with God to be based on Jesus's relationship with God helps to ameliorate the weakness of this metaphor.

11-3b God the Son

The fullest section of the Nicene Creed, as with Christian statements of belief in general, is the center part that deals with Jesus Christ. Teachings about Jesus go back to the faith experiences of the first disciples. The early church experienced the incarnated Son of God in the person of Jesus, although the Gospels are clear that his disciples didn't fully recognize this, much less spread this message on their own, until after Jesus's resurrection. Jesus is the crucified and exalted Lord, and the Son of God. He sits at the right hand of the Father and will return in glory to bring in the Father's rule. Jesus has become the center of belief and devotion for Christians. However, as we saw above, Jesus is an enigmatic figure, and the church's teaching about him can't easily be reduced to a series of simple sentences.

From the beginning of the church, different interpretations of Jesus have existed, and it took several centuries for the church to fully articulate its understanding. The author of the Gospel of Mark, for example, seems to understand Jesus as the man upon whom the Holy Spirit descends when he is baptized in the Jordan River and about whom the voice of God declares from the heavens, "You are my beloved son" (Mark 1:11). In Matthew and Luke, Jesus's special identity begins at his conception in the womb of the Virgin Mary (see "A Closer Look"). The teaching in Mark's Gospel, and to a lesser extent in Matthew and Luke, provided the foundation for one of two early schools of thought concerning the person of Christ.

These two "schools," or types of theology, dominated the ancient church's teaching on Jesus Christ.

Piety toward the death of Jesus is shown in different ways; here a man kisses a crucifix in devotion.

© ISTOCKPHOTO.COM/SILVIA BORATTI

Approaches to that derived from the theological school of Antioch in Syria start from the humanity of Jesus and see his divinity as joined to him by God through the Holy Spirit. In other words, Jesus's status as God's Son is founded on his humanity. This view is common among many modern Christians—both Protestants and Roman Catholics—in the Western world, who stress his humanity while also affirming that God was in him in a special way. Another view, adopted by the school of Alexandria, is a leading theme of the Gospel of John. This Gospel regards Jesus Christ primarily as the eternal Son of God become human. Here, his divinity is first and foundational, and the humanity of Jesus is joined to it. The divinity is understood as the result of the descent of the divine Logos—a preexistent heavenly being who is the Son of God—into the world. This view is common today among traditional Roman Catholics, doctrinally conservative Protestants, and most Eastern Orthodox. Both the Antiochene and Alexandrian schools had a wide sphere of influence in the ancient church, not only among the clergy, but also among the monks and the laity.

The Nicene Creed affirms that Jesus Christ is "the only Son of God, eternally begotten of the Father." In other words, the divine nature in Jesus is God's eternal Son. The Creed stresses this divine nature in Jesus by poetic repetitions: Jesus Christ is "God from God, Light from Light, true God from true God." In his divine being, he is "of one Being with the Father," not a different, lesser kind of god "made" (created) by the Father. The Creed goes on to link the Son of God to God the Father by stating the Son's role in creation—"Through him all things were made"—just as it affirmed earlier that the Father made all things. Then the Creed talks at more length about the incarnation: "For us men [humans] and for our salvation, he came down from heaven, by the power of the Holy Spirit he became incarnate from the Virgin Mary, and was made man." Eastern Orthodoxy has stressed more than Western Christianity the meaning of the incarnation for the salvation of humankind; Western Christians stress the meaning of the death and resurrection of Jesus for salvation.

Then the Creed skips to the end of Jesus's life and emphasizes the reality of his redemptive suffering: "For our sake he was crucified under Pontius Pilate; He suffered death and was buried. On the third day He rose again in accordance with the Scriptures." Exactly *how* Jesus's death saves humans is often debated: Is it a sacrifice, a defeat of evil (Christ as victor), a moral example, or all of these and more? Without belief that Jesus "rose again" in resurrection, it is clear from the New Testament accounts, his movement would have ended and Jesus would soon have disappeared into the mists of time. The final part of the Creed's section on Jesus speaks about his present and future: "He ascended into heaven and is seated on the right hand of the Father;

He will come again in glory to judge the living and the dead, and his kingdom will have no end." That Jesus sits on the Father's "right hand" refers to his present reign with God the Father. The rest of this section of the Creed affirms the standard Christian expectation that Jesus will return "in glory" at the end of human history to bring God's eternal reign to earth.

11-3c God the Holy Spirit

The Holy Spirit is a challenging topic in Christian teaching. To begin with, the name "Holy Spirit" doesn't evoke for us meanings such as "Father" and "Son" do. It has been harder for Christians to conceive of the Holy Spirit as a divine person in the same way as they think of the Father and the Son. (Feminists, however, hold that this is a good thing and point to the feminine aspects of the Spirit.) The foundational view of the Holy Spirit is sketched in the next section of the Nicene Creed: "We believe in the Holy Spirit, the Lord, the giver of Life, who proceeds from the Father and the Son. With the Father and the Son he is worshiped and glorified. He has spoken through the prophets." (Historians are divided about whether the wording that follows this—about the church, baptism, and the rest—is a part of the section on the Holy Spirit.)

The Creed ties the Spirit to God the Father and God the Son in a variety of ways. The Spirit is called "Lord," the term Christians regularly use for the Father and the Son. Next, the Spirit is called "the giver of Life," which refers not only to a role at creation, but especially to giving life to believers now and eternally. The next phrase has been problematic between the Eastern and Western churches. Originally, the Creed said that the Spirit "proceeds from the Father," just as Jesus (in parallel) is "begotten" by the Father, but in the Middle Ages the Catholic Church added "and the Son," which Protestant churches later shared. This was a huge point of contention between the East and the West, and one of the causes for their formal split in 1054. Some Western churches omit it today, or put it in brackets. Next, the Creed says that the Spirit is "worshiped and glorified," a sign of certain divine status.

The last thing said about the Holy Spirit, that the Spirit "has spoken through the prophets," is a powerful and problematic statement about the Spirit. Although the Holy Spirit is said in the New Testament to mediate the presence of Jesus to the church and explain his words, essentially a conserving task, the Spirit also is powerful, uncontrollable, and unpredictable. Prophetic speech in the Spirit is challenging to the church. Every movement for change in church history has appealed

Jesus as the Good Shepherd is a common image of salvation and spiritual guidance in Christ.

© NANCY BAUER/SHUTTERSTOCK.COM

The Doctrine of the Virgin Mary

The teaching that the Virgin Mary is the "mother/bearer of God," or **Theotokos**, is closely connected to the incarnation. As the church wrestled with articulating its belief in the identity of Jesus, the mother of the Son of God gained a special place within the church. To a significant degree, this was in an effort to understand the nature of Jesus, not to "promote" his mother.

Historians see the expansion of the veneration of the Virgin Mary as the "Mother of God," and the formation of doctrines explaining this, as one of the most remarkable occurrences in the ancient church after about 100 C.E. The New Testament offers only scanty points of departure for this development. Although she has a prominent place in the narratives of the Nativity, Mary soon disappears behind the figure of Jesus. His family, including his mother—who thought he was mentally disturbed (Mark 3:21)—opposed his ministry. All the Gospels stress the fact that Jesus separated himself from his family, and only the Gospels of Matthew and Luke mention the virginal conception. The Gospel of John mentions the "mother of Jesus" in a positive light, but not by name. Both Roman Catholics and the Orthodox believe that Mary was a life-long virgin; this serves as an example of dedication to God, even of celibacy. The vast majority of Protestants believe that she was virginal only until the birth of Jesus, and then had other children with Joseph by natural means.

Despite her earlier doubts, Mary was present as a believer in the earliest church, and in the early 100s the doctrine of the virginal conception of Jesus spread widely in Christianity, where it was put together with the doctrine of the incarnation. The doctrine of the virginal conception found its way into all Christian creeds, as did mention of the Virgin Mary herself. Veneration of Mary (not worship) spread widely in the West and the East, and by medieval times many churches had special chapels dedicated to the Virgin Mary. (In England they can still be found in many Anglican churches, where they are known as the "Lady Chapel.") Mary became the Queen of Heaven and the chief intercessor for the church on earth. She received increasing prayer (the "Hail Mary") and devotion, especially in times

of great distress such as the Black Plague in the 1400s. Devotion to Mary was "throttled back" somewhat after the Catholic Reform, and it was never as strong in the Orthodox churches as in Roman Catholicism. In recent times, veneration of Mary has been promoted by certain popes, especially John Paul II (pope from 1978 to 2005).

In sum, Christian devotion to Mary has been steady and persistent for most Roman Catholic and Eastern Orthodox Christians, and for some Anglicans as well. For Protestants, however, this devotion to the Virgin ended during the Reformation, and many liberal Protestants today no longer believe in the virginal conception of Jesus.

Modern painting in Byzantine style of Mary and the child Jesus. This Mother and Child artistic theme speaks deeply to Christians about the humanity of Jesus Christ, whatever they may believe about Mary.

to the authority and leading of the Holy Spirit. Opposition to the mainstream church—through appeal to the Spirit—was found in Montanism (MAHN-tuh-nihz-um) around 150 C.E. This movement saw itself as the fulfillment of the promise of the coming of the Spirit on the first church. Joachim of Fiore in Italy began a movement against the institutional church in the 1200s. He promised the beginning of the period of the Holy Spirit, in which the institutional papal church

Theotokos [thee-AH-toh-koss] Virgin Mary as the "mother/bearer of God"

God the Father, Son, and Holy Spirit in St. Nicholas Church, Amsterdam, The Netherlands

then mentions the importance of "one baptism" for salvation but makes no mention of the Eucharist or any other church ritual. Baptism has from the first Christian generation been the ritual of initiation into the Christian faith; the experience of baptism and the instruction that surrounds it give guidance for the moral and spiritual life of the Christian. The Creed closes with an affirmation of "the resurrection of the dead, and the life of the world to come." Although the Creed doesn't mention him explicitly at this point, Jesus is the center of resurrection and life, just as he was the first to rise from the dead. He will return in glory to fully bring in God's reign, and the "world to come" will be present with its full life. This traditional Christian teaching about the end of the world—the return of Christ, resurrection, and judgment with eternal reward and eternal punishment—has been widely believed in the history of Christianity, but in modern times many Protestants and some Roman Catholics have called it into doubt, preferring to think of an open human future.

Getting back now to the continuing controversy over Christ's nature that the Nicene Council did not fully settle, a new council at **Chalcedon** (451) finally ended the argument between Antioch and Alexandria by drawing from each. It declared, "We all unanimously teach…one and the same Son, our Lord Jesus Christ, perfect in deity and perfect in humanity…in two natures, without being mixed, transmuted, divided, or separated…. The identity of each nature is preserved and concurs into one person and being." At Nicea and Chalcedon, the church affirmed a paradox, and continues to do so today: First, Jesus is fully human and fully divine, God and humanity perfectly present in one person. Second, Jesus Christ is completely human, not only in his historical life, but also after his resurrection and through all eternity. As Paul wrote, "The whole fullness of deity dwells bodily" in him (Colossians 2:9). The genius of the Nicene and Chalcedonian Creeds is that they hold that the mystery of the person of Jesus Christ could be grasped in a decisive, authoritative formula: two natures in one person.

would be replaced by a community of charismatic figures, all filled with the Spirit. This was put down, but it stimulated a number of revolutionary movements in the medieval church. Sixteenth-century reformer Thomas Müntzer (MOONT-zer) defended his revolution against the princes and church officials by claiming a new coming of the Spirit. In the twentieth century through today, the widespread charismatic movement has centered on the recovery of the experience of the Holy Spirit.

11-3d The Conclusion of the Nicene Creed: Church, Baptism, and Christian Hope

Finally, the Nicene Creed affirms, "We believe in one holy catholic and apostolic Church. We acknowledge one baptism for the forgiveness of sins. We look for the resurrection of the dead, and the life of the world to come." Belief "in the Church" affirms that the Church—which is holy, catholic, and apostolic—is a divine part of God's plan for human salvation. Ancient Christians believed that it is the continuing body founded by Jesus. The Creed

Chalcedon [KAL-seh-don] Council in 451 that defined the relationship of the human and divine natures of Christ

11-4 Christian Ethics: Following the Way of Jesus Christ

A new translation of the New Testament published by the American branch of Oxford University Press causes a stir around the world. Titled the *Inclusive Bible*, it features "thoroughly non-sexist" wording. Some critics deride it as the "politically correct version" and a dangerous innovation. However, students of Christianity recognize that this type of translation has a rich pedigree in America. It can trace its roots to the influential, and even more controversial, *Women's Bible* of 1898, a seminal work in the foundation of the feminist movement. The publication of the *Inclusive Bible* touches an important contemporary moral theme in Christianity: the place of women in the faith.

As an "ethical monotheism," the Christian religion is based on its view of God. God's self-revelation shows God to be both radically good and radically loving. Christians must worship God but also must live their entire lives according to God's will. Jesus affirmed that the main point of this obedience is to love God and to love one's neighbor (Matthew 22:37–39).

11-4a Foundations in the Ten Commandments, the Sermon on the Mount, and the Letters of Paul

Christian ethical teaching has two main biblical foundations: the Ten Commandments (Exodus 20:1–17; Deuteronomy 5:6–21) and the Sermon on the Mount (Matthew 5–7). The Ten Commandments (see above, page 248) remain valid for Christians, although God's laws have been broadened by Jesus Christ. The "first table" of the Law calls on Christians to worship only God, not to worship images, and to keep the Sabbath day holy. This Sabbath was changed to Sunday, the day of the Lord's resurrection, when Christians around the world gather in the morning for worship. The "second table" of the Law tells Christians to honor parents and abstain from murder, adultery, theft, false witness, and coveting.

The Sermon on the Mount opens with the Beatitudes (or statements of blessings), which contain implicit moral directions (Matthew 5:1–12). Jesus declared that the powers of the imminent Kingdom of God would enable his followers to witness the world about this kingdom even to be the "light of the world" (5:14–16). Jesus upheld the value of the Law of Moses for his followers, but radicalized it in a variety of ways. He pointed to the necessity of controlling one's thoughts and emotions, not just one's actions; Jesus called anger murderous and lust adulterous (5:21–22, 27–28). Doing what is right proceeds from the inner person, and thus is not a sham or a hypocritical action. The repeated warnings against hypocrisy in the Sermon on the Mount are primarily warnings to Jesus's followers, not attacks on others. Jesus commanded his followers to "be perfect, as your heavenly Father is perfect" (5:48). Human perfection is expressed in what Christian tradition calls the "Golden Rule," a summary of the ethics of the whole Jewish Bible: "In everything do to others as you would have them do to you." Christians have believed that taking the "hard way" (7:13–14) is possible by virtue of the divine gift of the Holy Spirit. Jesus knew that this "hard way" would not be easy for his followers and that they would fail in parts of it every day, as indicated in the daily prayer that he taught them in the Sermon on the Mount, which contains a request for divine forgiveness for one's sins (6:12).

Watch a film re-creation of the Sermon on the Mount.

As stated above, Jesus affirmed the summary of God's will given in Judaism: to "love the Lord your God" with all your being and to "love your neighbor as yourself." This love is possible because of Jesus's life, death, and resurrection. When the Christian commandment of love was connected to Christ's person and work, the demand of love for the neighbor became a "new commandment": "A new commandment I give to you, that you love one another; even as I have loved you, that you also love one another" (John 13:34). The followers of Jesus are to have this love: "By this all men will know that you are my disciples, if you have love for one another" (John 13:35). All this might imply that Christian love is given only or mostly to other Christians, but the Christian commandment of love has never been limited to fellow Christians. On the contrary, the Christian ethic crossed social and religious barriers and saw a neighbor in every suffering human being, especially the innocent and helpless. This is why, for example, Christians in the ancient world rescued infants left in remote places or garbage dumps to die.

Identification with the death of Jesus is foundational in Christian ethics.

© ISTOCKPHOTO.COM/FRANKLIN LUGENBEEL

resurrection of Jesus. For Paul, the *indicative* (who Christians are by virtue of God's action) serves to ground the *imperatives* of moral attitude and behavior. The believer has "died with Christ" in baptism and will be "raised with Christ" at the end of time, and in the meantime must "walk in newness of life." The moral dimension of the Christian faith is a struggle; in an image drawn from clothing, one must constantly "put on Christ" and "put off" sin and self-centeredness. The presence of the Spirit in the individual and in the church gives both direction and empowerment for spiritual living. Summing up his ethic, Paul says, "I appeal to you therefore, brothers and sisters, by the mercies of God, to present your bodies as a living sacrifice, holy and acceptable to God, which is your reasonable service. Do not be conformed to this world, but be transformed by the renewal of your mind, that you may prove what is the will of God, what is good, and acceptable, and perfect" (Romans 12:1–2).

11-4b The Enactment of Moral Life in the Church

Christian social ethics are foundational for the community of the faithful. As the church took in all sorts of people, certain occupations were deemed incompatible with a Christian life of love toward others. Thieves, brothel keepers and prostitutes, workers in pagan temples, actors, charioteers, gladiators, soldiers, magicians, astrologers, and fortune-tellers could not keep their trades when they became Christians. (Slave owning, however, was still mostly tolerated, and the church often allowed slaves who were forced to engage in these forbidden trades to be church members.) Moral instruction for **catechumens**, those preparing for baptism, and many ancient sermons reveal that preachers regularly explained Christian morality and urged their audiences to keep it.

Jesus himself explicated his understanding of the commandment of love in the parable of the Good Samaritan, who followed the commandment of love and helped a person in need whom a Jewish priest and a Levite had chosen to ignore (Luke 10:29–37).

The Apostle Paul often drew on the Ten Commandments to shape the moral life of Christians. Because his churches were made up mainly of Gentiles, they needed basic instruction in the Jewish basis of morality. Paul's letters also stress the moral virtues of the Christian life: trust in God, hope in the future God will bring, peace in one's heart and in the church, and especially love for all people. More than any other New Testament author, Paul grounds the ethical life of the Christian in the life, death, and

In the Middle Ages and Byzantine times, moral instruction centered on the Ten Commandments, the Beatitudes, and the lists of virtues and vices drawn from the New Testament. The ritual act of reconciliation (as it is now called), in which individuals confessed their sins in the "confessional" to a priest in order to receive direction and assurance of forgiveness, helped to shape

catechumen [KAT-uh-KYOO-men] Individual preparing for baptism in a period of doctrinal and moral instruction

© ISTOCKPHOTO.COM/AMANDA ROHDE

individual character and conduct. At least in the West, people leaving church in the Middle Ages would typically see a painting of the Last Judgment over the doors, to remind them of the rewards of doing good and the penalty for evil.

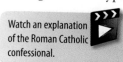
Watch an explanation of the Roman Catholic confessional.

Besides this inner-church sphere of morality, the "conversion of the empire" in the 300s permitted bishops to begin influencing the personal and political affairs of government and the wider life of society. Soon **canon law**—the legal system that codifies ethical, organizational, and other matters in the Roman Catholic Church—arose to guide the overall moral life of the church. Canon law is still today an important foundation of moral reflection and decision making by priests and bishops in the Church of Rome. In the Protestant churches, different patterns of social ethics emerged, based more directly on the Bible. A powerful and controversial explanation of Protestant ethics is Max Weber's book *The Protestant Ethic and the Spirit of Capitalism*, which argued for a strong relationship between Protestant (specifically, Calvinist) morality and the development of modern capitalism in the West.

Read a summary of *The Protestant Ethic and the Spirit of Capitalism* by Max Weber.

Modern times have seen a decline in the direct institutional role of the churches in society, as church leaders can no longer directly influence rulers with whom they share authority. Instead, church leaders advise the shaping of public laws and policies, seeking to guide not only the members of their churches, but also the whole common life of nations. In Roman Catholicism, this has occurred at the global level through the so-called social encyclicals of popes from Leo XIII in 1891 to today. These teaching documents deal with a variety of topics in social ethics, and almost every pope has issued them. At times, they have been highly controversial, as when Pope Paul VI in 1968 used an encyclical (*Humanae Vitae*, "On Human Life") to forbid the use of all artificial birth control among Roman Catholics. In Eastern Orthodoxy, the fall of Communist rule has presented particular problems and opportunities to help guide public life. Protestant denominations have typically made pronouncements and initiated programs on their own and through ecumenical agencies to which they belong.

The World Council of Churches, a fellowship of Christian churches founded in 1948, has created "middle axioms" (the notion of a "just society," for example, or "the care of creation"), which were intended as common ground on which Christian churches and governments could meet for discussion and action. Now, they are common ground for cooperating with people of other religions, especially today on environmental issues. The rise of Christian social organizations such as Church World Service, Catholic Relief Services, Bread for the World, World Vision, Habitat for Humanity, and many others is particularly notable. In the developing world, Christian organizations are among the largest nongovernmental organizations working for human and social development. Individual Christians have also had an impact here—for example, the lead singer of the rock band U2, Bono, advocates tirelessly for justice for Africa. He has become known for his advocacy of justice as well as for his music.

Watch an interview with Bono on Christianity's role in combating AIDS in Africa.

Bono inspects a water project in Rwanda in 2012.

© AFRICA 24 MEDIA/RICCARDO GANGALE/AFRICA MEDIA ONLINE/GLOW IMAGES

Summarize Christian worship and other rituals.

11-5 Christian Worship and Ritual

In Rome, the Congregation for Divine Worship, the Roman Catholic department responsible for guiding the Church's religious services, presents to Pope John Paul II a report entitled "Authentic Liturgy." It states that language used in the Mass must avoid many of the features of inclusive language, because they obscure the meaning of the text. For example, where the original language of Scripture or the Mass book says "brothers," expressions such as "brothers and sisters" or "friends" may not be used. The document stirs up a controversy in European and North American Catholic churches, which have gotten used to more-inclusive language. This controversy is an example of how issues of inclusive/ exclusive language have become important in contemporary churches, both Roman Catholic and Protestant.

sacrament Ritual believed to be a special means of grace

liturgy Literally, "work of the people" in worship; pattern of worship in Christian churches

Read "Authentic Liturgy."

In this section, we'll discuss the rise of Christian worship in history. Christian worship emerged from, and then gradually separated from, the worship practices of Judaism. The Acts of the Apostles relates that the first Christian believers worshiped in the Jerusalem temple, as Jesus had; they worshiped in Jewish synagogues as well. But the earliest church also had its own meetings for worship (see "A Closer Look: An Ancient Christian Service"). After Constantine, worship and the church buildings in which it was held became more formal. The Roman Catholic Church built itself around seven **sacraments**, rituals believed to be a special means of grace, and the Eastern Orthodox Church made the worship in its various branches more unified. In the Protestant Reformation and Catholic Reform, and again in Vatican II, worship was reformed by being made more the work of the people, the **liturgy**. Since around 1950, the ecumenical movement has brought more of a consensus of worship style and content.

11-5a Christian Worship before Constantine

Christian worship and ritual varies widely throughout the world, but its common foundation can be traced to the first centuries of the church and before this to the Jewish synagogues. As in the worship of the synagogue, public prayer and praise to God are a constant in the church. So too are the reading and explanation

A Closer Look:

An Ancient Christian Service

As a part of his defense of Christianity in sections 65–66 of his *Apology*, Justin briefly describes a Christian service from about 150. This is the earliest description of Christian worship that we have. It has the same basic elements and almost exactly the same order as almost all Christian worship since: gathering as a community, reading of scripture, prayer, sermon, Holy Communion, and dismissal. Singing hymns isn't mentioned here, but we know from other sources that it was common.

After thus washing [baptizing] the one who has been convinced and signified his assent, we lead him to those who are called brothers, where they are assembled. The memoirs of the apostles or the writings of the apostles are read, as long as time permits. When the reader has ceased, the presiding leader instructs and exhorts us to imitate these good things. Then we rise together and pray. We pray that

we may be made worthy, having learned the truth, to be found good citizens and keepers of what is commanded, so that we may be saved with eternal salvation. On finishing the prayers we greet each other with a kiss.

Then bread and a cup of wine mixed with water are brought to the one presiding. Taking them, he gives praise and glory to the Father of the universe through the name of the Son and the Holy Spirit, and offers thanksgiving at some length that we have been deemed worthy to receive these things from him. When he has finished the prayers and the thanksgiving, the whole congregation assents by saying, "Amen." Those whom we call deacons [assistants] then give a portion of the consecrated bread and wine to all those present, and they take it to the absent.

of a portion of Scripture. Christian churches, especially in the eastern half of the Roman Empire, adapted the **lectionary** system of the Jewish synagogues and added readings from the New Testament. Changes from synagogue worship were introduced as well. The weekly day for worship went from the Jewish Sabbath on the last day of the week to Sunday.

Baptism replaced circumcision as the main rite of initiation into the faith, and it was preceded by instruction and fasting. Persons about to be baptized renounced evil, and after they declared their faith, they went into the water. They then received by anointing with oil and by the laying on of hands the gift of the Holy Spirit, the same Spirit who had descended on Jesus at his baptism. Only the baptized were admitted to the Eucharist, and weekly participation in this ritual meal took the place of both the Passover meal and Jewish sacrifices. Baptism has been the rite of entry, but the Eucharist is the regular ritual of food for the body and soul.

11-5b Worship after Constantine

After Christianity was permitted and then became official in the 300s, worship became more elaborate. Formal church buildings were erected, and church officials dressed for worship in special vestments modeled after Roman government garb. The church developed a liturgical calendar with seasons of self-denial, such as Advent and Lent, and seasons of celebration, such as Christmas and Easter.

> *The basilica type of building was used by Christians for the first church buildings, and has been the most common pattern for churches since.*

Before about 350 C.E., worship was typically in private homes. (A religion almost constantly persecuted by the government isn't able to put up its own buildings.) The service was held in the largest room of the house, usually the central atrium in a middle- or upper-class house. When church buildings became common around 350, they were designed for the community. The rectangular **basilica** with a long nave (main area for the congregation) and an apse (semicircular area at the front), which had been used for Roman law courts, was particularly suitable for Christian worship. This architectural layout of the church building has been the most common pattern of church buildings ever since. Many Byzantine churches had mosaic pictures on their floors. Old Testament/Jewish heroes of faith also appear in the earliest Christian art in both the East and West. The artists adapted conventional pagan forms: the shepherd carrying a sheep, the praying person with hands uplifted, and various birds and animals. Symbols of the Eucharist and baptism were especially common. The exteriors of these churches were simple, but inside they were often richly ornamented with marble and mosaic. The decoration was designed to represent the angels and saints in heaven with whom the church on earth was joining for worship—saints whose presence was suggested by icons in the East and statues, paintings, and then stained glass in the West. The oldest church buildings to survive largely intact are from early medieval and early Byzantine times: Hagia Sophia at Constantinople (which became a mosque and is now a museum) and San Vitale at Ravenna in

lectionary Systematic schedule of reading the Bible in worship

basilica [bah-SIHL-ih-kuh] Building with a long rectangular area for the congregation and a semicircular area at the front for clergy

Iconostasis of an Orthodox Church in Russia

© ANDREWS KOTURANOV/SHUTTERSTOCK

Italy. Worship in churches became more impressive and formal for a greatly enlarged and now official religion, but much of the earlier intimacy that was a part of house churches was necessarily lost.

In the early Middle Ages, Catholic worship became centered on the sacraments and has stayed focused on them ever since. These are, the *Catholic Catechism* says, "efficacious signs of grace, instituted by Christ and entrusted to the Church, by which divine life is dispensed." The sacraments are necessary for salvation, because they were instituted by Christ as the means through which God communicates grace. Christ bestows a particular grace through each sacrament, such as baptism's joining one to Christ and the Church, confession/reconciliation's forgiveness of sins and amendment of life, and the Eucharist's feeding of body and soul with the mystical food of Jesus's body and blood. A sacrament works *ex opere operato* (ehks OH-puh-reh OH-puh-RAH-toh), Latin for "by the working of the work." In other words, they are effective just by being administered, regardless of the personal holiness of the one administering them. However, the holiness of the recipient *does* make a difference; lack of a proper spiritual attitude can thwart the effectiveness of the sacrament. These seven sacraments are known today as baptism, confirmation, the Eucharist, reconciliation, anointing of the sick, ordination (to holy orders), and marriage. The Eastern Orthodox Church also has seven sacraments but hasn't organized its worship so fully around them.

Other worship practices also began in post-Constantinian times. One of the more significant was the **cult of the saints**, the veneration of saints in shrines, churches, and other places. (This "cult" has no connection with the more modern use of the word to designate some new religious movements.) Shrines were erected in honor of local holy men and women, especially those Christians who had worked miracles and those who had suffered for the faith. Usually shrines were found in churches and contained a relic or the entire body of the saint. Until modern times, many Christian saints weren't recognized by the whole church but were known and venerated regionally. The saints were recognized as intercessors with God for the faithful on earth and were thought to be vehicles for God's miraculous power. The shrines became the focus of religious pilgrimage. Many popular shrines today are dedicated to the Virgin Mary, particularly in the places where she is believed to have appeared: Lourdes, France; Medjugorje in Bosnia and Herzegovina; and Guadalupe, Mexico.

The pattern of the Eucharistic liturgy was basically set by the year 400, but different forms existed in different areas. Especially varied was the main, long prayer of Holy Communion, which the Orthodox called *anaphora* (uh-NAH-fohr-uh), or "offering," and the Romans called *canon*, "prescribed form" (to be distinguished from the canon of the Bible and canon law). The canon of the Latin Mass in the 500s was basically similar to the form it has kept through today. (Most Protestant forms for Holy Communion were adapted from the Roman Catholic version.) Earlier beliefs that Jesus Christ was somehow present in the celebration of Holy Communion, especially in the bread and wine, were greatly developed in the Middle Ages. The Roman Church officially adopted the teaching of **transubstantiation**—that the bread and wine were changed in all but appearance into the substance of Christ's body. Music also became elaborate after Constantine, with chanting in Gregorian style of Psalms, hymns, and service music, as well as plainsong with several voices unaccompanied by instruments. Eastern Orthodox chanting, like the liturgy in general,

Roman Catholic pilgrims stream into the site in Lourdes, France, dedicated to the Virgin Mary.

was richer, more sonorous, and more soaring than Gregorian plainsong.

The Protestant Reformation carried out an immediate reform of worship, along with theology. In general, the Lutheran churches kept some distinctly Roman Catholic features such as crucifixes and altars, the Calvinist churches kept a few (kneeling in services, baptismal fonts), and the Anabaptist churches discarded everything they didn't find in the Bible. In general, the worship found in churches of the Baptist tradition is *nonliturgical*, not bound to a set form of worship or rituals—embracing spontaneous, informal prayer rather than written prayer, for example—but other Protestant churches tend to be *liturgical*, with set forms. Worship in the Church of England remained the most Catholic of all the breakaway churches.

All Protestant churches from the Reformation through today share a few important new features of worship. First, the Bible was restored to what the Reformers considered a more central place. Preaching the Bible in sermons was emphasized, as was private reading of the Bible in homes. Second, the sacraments were generally reduced to the two that had been founded by Jesus: baptism and Holy Communion. Many Reformers made frequent communion the rule for all laity, and denied the Roman Catholic doctrine of transubstantiation in favor of other understandings of the spiritual meaning of communion. Third, all services were put completely into the language of the people, and the liturgy again became literally the "work of the people." Music, especially hymn singing, was done by the people as well as by trained musicians. The Catholic Reform in the 1500s and Vatican II in the 1960s brought the Roman Church into line with many of these changes, but its theology remained the same.

> Some observers have estimated that between one-fourth and one-third of all Christians today "speak in tongues."

In the years since the Reformation, Christian worship has become more diverse. The strongest impact on worship has been the **charismatic movement** stressing supernatural "gifts of the Holy Spirit," a movement also known as **Pentecostalism**. These two names are a bit tricky: *Charismatic* usually refers to groups inside the Roman Catholic, Orthodox, and mainline Protestant churches. *Pentecostal* usually refers to Protestant churches such as the Assemblies of God where these practices are the norm, whether they have "Pentecostal" in their formal name or not. "Gifts of the Holy Spirit" are called *charismata* in Greek. These gifts are used primarily in worship. The modern Pentecostal movement began in 1906 in an African American church in Los Angeles. Over time it has moved into mainstream Protestantism and Roman Catholicism as well. Today, the charismatic movement has spread throughout the Christian world. "Speaking in tongues"—an emotional outpouring of prayer in human sounds but in no human language—is its primary activity, but others are often seen as well: interpretation of tongues, prophecy, healing, and so forth. The charismatic movement has often been divisive and controversial when it appears in non-Pentecostalist denominations, but it has brought new life and an emphasis on spirituality. Some observers have estimated that between one-fourth and one-third of all Christians—about 600 million people—are charismatics.

11-5c The Liturgical Year

The **liturgical year**, also known as the **church year**, is the pattern of liturgical seasons that determines when holy days are to be observed, which portions

charismatic movement (Pentecostalism) Modern Christian movement stressing use of supernatural "gifts of the Holy Spirit"

liturgical (church) year Pattern of liturgical seasons that determines when holy days are to be observed

Reading the Bible regularly is a distinctive practice for many Christians.

of Scripture are to be read, and the special themes of purpose of worship. Distinct liturgical colors usually mark different seasons of the year. The dates of the festivals vary somewhat between Orthodox, Roman Catholic, and Protestant churches, though the sequence and purpose are generally the same.

The extent to which the liturgical year with its feasts and festivals are celebrated also varies between churches. In the Roman Catholic Church and in the Orthodox churches, the church year is rigorously observed. In general, Protestant churches observe far fewer holy days than do Catholic and Orthodox churches. The broad seasons of the year are observed in mainline Protestant churches, but many evangelical, fundamentalist, and/or Pentecostalist churches today largely ignore the main church year, celebrating only a few holy days such as Christmas and Easter.

The church year begins with Advent, the four-week period of preparation for Christmas Day and the usually two-week Christmas period that follows Christmas Day. The short season of Epiphany in January marks the manifestation of Christ to the world. Next is the season of Lent, a forty-day season of preparation for Easter, often with special devotions and acts of self-denial. Easter Day and the Easter season following it celebrate the resurrection of Jesus. After the feast of Pentecost, a long period of "ordinary time" without a specific seasonal focus extends to the beginning of Advent in December.

Learning Outcome 11-6

Explain the variety of Christianity around the world today, especially in the Southern Hemisphere and in North America.

11-6 Christianity around the World Today

A group of Old Order Amish has met in a home for worship in Lancaster County, Pennsylvania. As their horses and buggies wait outside, they conduct a two-hour service of hymns, prayers, scripture readings, and sermon—all in their own "Pennsylvania Dutch" language, which is actually a Swiss dialect of German. No cleric conducts the service, for

in their religious life the men are all equal. Their worship and lifestyle continues the same pattern of "coming out from the world and being separate" that their Anabaptist ancestors practiced at the dawn of the Reformation. The Amish have been oppressed in many parts of the world, but they've found a happy haven in the United States and Canada, where they are widely respected for their consistent witness for pacifism.

11-6a Christianity in the Global South

Religion scholars today are nearly unanimous that the single most important area for the future of Christianity is outside the areas of its historic strength. In its past, Christianity has been strongest in the Northern Hemisphere, especially in Europe and North America. Now, Christianity is shifting its "center of gravity" to the Southern Hemisphere, where most Christians live and where Christianity is growing quickly even as the number and cultural influence of Christians in the Northern Hemisphere declines. An unmistakable sign of the increasing importance of Christianity in the Southern Hemisphere is the election of the archbishop of Buenos Aires, Argentina, as pope in 2013.

These **Global South Christians**, with their more traditional interpretations of the Bible and the creeds, sometimes present a challenge to older churches. For example, the African Independent Churches, a dynamic adaptation of Christianity by European mission churches in Africa, is now spreading to North America. To cite another example, the Anglican churches in Africa—where more people in Uganda or Nigeria attend Anglican religious services on a typical Sunday than in all of Great Britain—strongly oppose efforts by the Church of England and the Episcopal Church in the United States to approve of same-sex relationships and ordain gay and lesbian clergy. Mark Noll has written in his *The New Shape of World Christianity* that Global South Christians are less concerned about historic patterns of church government and doctrine (things important in the North) as they are about spiritual warfare between good and evil today and the continuing gulf between the wealthy North and the "Majority World."[2]

Visit the website of the Redeemed Christian Church of God, an African Independent church now found in several U.S. cities.

---

[2] Mark Noll, *The New Shape of World Christianity: How American Experience Reflects Global Faith* (Downers Grove, IL: IVP Academic, 2009).

In Europe, Christianity is steadily declining in numbers and influence, contributing to the relative strength of the Global South churches. In many European nations, fewer than ten percent of the population attends church services on even an occasional basis, and many church buildings are being converted to secular use. Many universities that for centuries offered degrees in theology for the training of clergy have now dropped them; in The Netherlands, for example, only four universities now offer theological education, down from eight as recently as 1975. In those nations that have established state churches, the formal ties with the churches are loosening. In the United Kingdom, Prince Charles, the heir to the crown, has stated that he wishes to be called "Defender of Faith," not "Defender of the Faith." Although Christianity in Europe is being marginalized, religion as a whole is not: For example, several Western European nations are facing the difficult challenges of a rising Muslim population.

11-6b Christianity in North America

Christianity is the largest religion in the United States, with 78 percent of those polled identifying themselves as Christian in 2009. About 62 percent reported that they were members of a church congregation. With around 240 million Christians, the United States has the largest Christian population on earth. In Canada, the church has slightly less of a presence, but more than 60 percent of Canadians identify themselves as Christians. As a result of immigration, widespread importation of European (and now African and Asian) churches, and new denominations springing up in the United States, Christianity is more internally diverse—for better and for worse—in North America than anywhere else in the world. This poses a challenge and an opportunity for the study of Christianity.

Protestant denominations together account for about 50 percent of North Americans, Roman Catholicism about 25 percent, and Eastern Orthodox less than 1 percent. Roman Catholics are by far the largest single church group, and the Roman Catholic Church in the United States is growing in size with Hispanic immigration. The Eastern Orthodox population is relatively tiny, making up only about 0.04 percent of North Americans—due largely to smaller immigration from Eastern Orthodox nations, recent difficulties in "Americanization," and the

Read a summary of the Hartford Institute for Religion Research's study of Orthodoxy in America.

persistence of twenty-six different ethnic-based denominations within Orthodoxy.

Christianity came to the Americas when it was first colonized by Europeans, beginning in the 1500s. The vast majority of colonists were Christians, and over time a majority of Native Americans became Christians as well. Today, most Christian congregations are mainline Protestant, evangelical Protestant, or Roman Catholic, or they belong to the various denominations of Eastern Orthodoxy. Sociologists of religion distinguish the *mainline* Protestant churches (defined below) from the *evangelical* Protestant churches. The authoritative Association of Religion Data Archives (ARDA) estimates 26 million members of mainline churches versus about 40 million members of evangelical Protestant churches. Good evidence suggests a sizeable shift in membership from mainline denominations to evangelical churches since about 1950. Then, Protestant Christians tended to belong to mainline churches, and evangelical churches were comparatively smaller.

11-6c The Different Churches: Roman Catholic and Protestant

At the time the United States was founded, only a small fraction of the U.S. population was Roman Catholic, generally in Maryland. As we saw above, the number of Roman Catholics has grown dramatically in recent years. The United States now has the fourth-largest Catholic population in the world. The Church's main national body is the United States Conference of Catholic Bishops, made up of all bishops and archbishops of the United States, although each bishop has independent power in his own diocese and is responsible only to the pope. Many other nations have a Roman Catholic *primate*, or lead bishop, but there is no primate for the United States.

Although Protestantism is divided into mainline and evangelical groups, as we saw above, the distinction between them is not easy to maintain. **Mainline** Protestant denominations are those brought to North America by their historic immigrant groups. The largest are the Episcopal (English, from the Anglican Church), Presbyterian (Scottish), Methodist (English and Welsh), and Lutheran (Scandinavian and German) denominations. They are generally more open to new ideas and social changes than are evangelical Protestants and Roman Catholics.

mainline Protestant denominations brought to North America by their historic immigrant groups

Evangelicalism The modern movement that seeks to spread the gospel of Jesus Christ, giving people an opportunity to convert

Restorationism Belief that first-century Christianity is the purest form of the faith and that it should be restored

> The experience of conversion that evangelicals see as necessary for salvation is called being "born again."

Evangelicalism is the modern movement that seeks to spread the gospel of Jesus Christ, giving people an opportunity to convert. The experience of conversion that evangelicals see as necessary for salvation is called being "born again." They have a strong sense of the presence and direction of God in their lives, as explored in a recent, highly praised book by Tanya Luhrmann of Stanford University, *When God Talks Back*.[3] Although it became strong in the past two centuries, evangelicalism has roots that reach into the earliest decades of the Reformation. It arose with the Anabaptist movement in the 1500s, moved into the mainstream Reformation with Pietism in the 1700s, and became stronger in the late 1800s, especially as a result of the world mission movement of the time. A famous evangelical of the twentieth century is Southern Baptist (U.S.) evangelist Billy Graham, who held mass meetings that ended with a call to come forward to "accept Christ as your personal Lord and Savior" and be "born again." There is a good deal of variety in evangelicalism. Evangelicals tend to be politically conservative, but an increasing number today—especially younger evangelicals—are politically moderate or liberal. Probably the most influential modern voice in the evangelical movement was C. S. Lewis (1898–1963), the University of Oxford professor of

For example, they've been increasingly open to the ordination of women and to equality in church and society for gay and lesbian persons. Mainline churches belong to organizations such as the National Council of Churches and the World Council of Churches. Mainline Protestant groups were dominant in North America for more than two centuries, up until the 1960s.

medieval literature and Anglican who ironically did not call himself an "evangelical" but did have a powerful conversion experience as an adult. Lewis wrote popular religious works such as *Mere Christianity* and *The Screwtape Letters*, which are still best sellers for their clear, creative presentation of the faith. He also wrote the popular children's novels *The Chronicles of Narnia*, which are full of traditional Christian themes but not overtly Christian.

The black church—or, more commonly today, African American church—in North America are those churches that are mainly African American in membership. Most African American congregations belong to African American denominations such as the National Baptist Convention or a variety of other Baptist or Methodist groups, although some black congregations belong to predominantly white denominations. Freed slaves in the South, and especially in the North, formed the first black congregations before 1800. After slavery ended, African Americans continued in separate congregations and denominations, with communities and styles of worship that were distinct from those of their white counterparts. They continued a unique, powerful form of Christianity that adapted African religious practices in preaching, music, and congregational life. For example, matriarchal traditions from Africa have led to some women having a much higher status, even authority, in African American churches than is found in white churches. Many African American congregations have "mother boards" composed of older women who are real power brokers in their churches. Segregation of the races discouraged and, especially in the South, prevented African Americans from belonging to the same churches as whites, thus helping to preserve the distinctive patterns of African American Christianity.

African Americans continued to form separate congregations and denominations during the 1900s. This separation continues today despite the decline of segregation and the rising occurrence of integrated worship. African American churches are usually the centers of their communities, opening schools in the early years after the Civil War and pursuing other social welfare efforts. As a result, they have founded strong community organizations and provided spiritual and political leadership, especially during the civil rights movement, seen clearly in the leadership of African American Baptist pastor Martin Luther King Jr.

Another broad trend in North American Protestantism is **Restorationism**. This refers to the belief held by various groups that the Christianity of the first century C.E. is the purest form of the faith

---

[3] Tanya Luhrmann, *When God Talks Back: Understanding the American Evangelical Relationship with God* (New York: Vintage, 2012).

Minister and choir, important parts of the African American church

and that it can and should be restored. (It was a strong impulse in the United States in the 1800s.) Such groups typically claim that their group is that restoration. They teach that restoration is necessary because other Christians before them introduced defects into the Christian faith or lost a vital element of genuine Christianity. Restorationist denominations include the Christian Church (Disciples of Christ) and the Churches of Christ. Several other groups that shared the Restorationist impulse eventually became new religious movements. The Church of Jesus Christ of Latter-day Saints founded by Joseph Smith, more commonly called the Mormons, is notable. Visitors to the Mormon headquarters in Salt Lake City, Utah, can view the hour-long movie *Joseph Smith: Prophet of the Restoration*. Another major Restorationist religion is the Jehovah's Witnesses. It's estimated that in the United States 1.9 million adults are Jehovah's Witnesses. Like the LDS church, the Jehovah's Witnesses church rejects many teachings of the Nicene Creed and views itself as the only true church. In conclusion, despite the seemingly fractured life of Christianity in the world today, Christianity remains a growing, vibrant religion around the globe.

Examine the results of a recent survey that analyzes North American Christians by types and levels of belief and practice.

Study Tools 11

Ready to study? In the book you can:

- Review Learning Outcome answers and glossary terms with the tear-out Chapter Review card.

Or you can go online to CourseMate, at www.cengagebrain.com, for these resources:

- Chapter quizzes to prepare for tests
- Interactive flashcards of all glossary terms
- A timeline of events for this chapter
- An eBook with introductions, interactive quizzes, and live links for all web resources in the chapter

CHAPTER 12

Encountering Islam: The Straight Path of the One God

BONNIE VAN VOORST © CENGAGE LEARNING

Learning Outcomes

After studying this chapter, you will be able to do the following:

12-1 Explain *Islam* and related terms.

12-2 Outline how the main periods of Islamic history have shaped its present, especially different Muslim groups.

12-3 Give the essential elements of Islamic teachings in your own words.

12-4 Explain Muslim ethics, especially in diet, dress, and marriage.

12-5 Explain the ways Muslims worship, especially the Five Pillars.

12-6 Explain the main aspects of Muslim life around the world today, especially in Europe and North America.

Study Tools

After you read this chapter, go to the Study Tools at the end of the chapter, page 331.

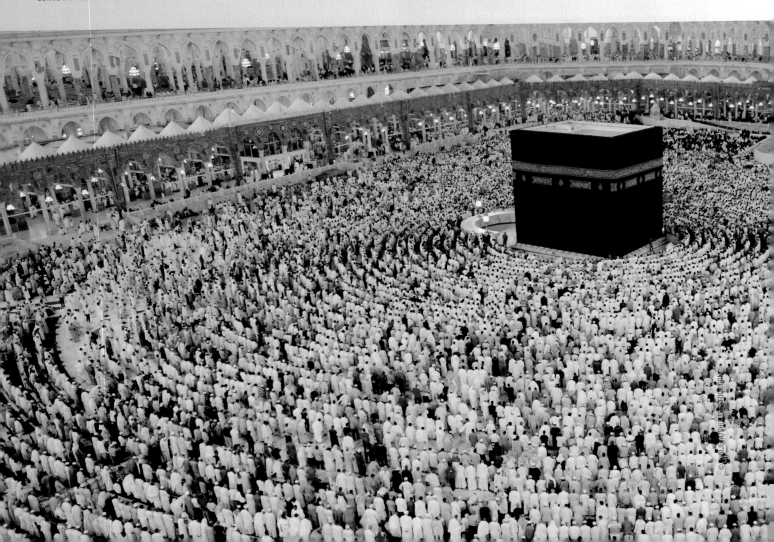

"There is no god but God, and Muhammad is God's prophet."
—Main statement of belief in Islam

Your Visit to Mecca

Imagine, if you will, your visit to Mecca (MEHK-uh), Saudi Arabia, during the Month of Pilgrimage. (Unless you are a Muslim, you cannot actually visit Mecca, so your "visit" here must be done with respectful imagination.) Your emotions run high as you come within sight of Mecca. You've looked forward to this trip as long as you can remember, and now you're there, at the very center—geographically and spiritually—of Islam. With Muslims all participating in the pilgrimage together, you feel a strong sense of Muslim unity.

Before you enter Mecca, you must be physically and spiritually clean. If you're a man, you shave your head, take off your outer clothes, and put on over your underwear two large triangular pieces of linen. Everyone dresses in these, whether rich or poor, royal or commoner. If you're a woman, you bathe and wear a traditional Muslim full-body veil, but you don't shave your hair. You also stay in women's groups apart from men for your activities on the pilgrimage. From now on, until you begin the journey home, you'll strictly observe all ritual restrictions in how you dress, act, speak, and eat. But you know all this beforehand, and you're still looking forward to it. In fact, these rules heighten your appreciation of how special this trip is.

Next, you walk seven times around the cube-shaped shrine at the open-air center of the Grand Mosque. This brings you closer to the shrine with each circle, so the walk isn't at all tiring for you. It ends when you touch the sacred stone, a meteorite embedded in the shrine by Abraham himself about three thousand years ago. As you circle, you notice all the different races and nationalities present.

After you touch the sacred stone, you run seven times back and forth between two hills, just as Abraham's wife Hagar ran between them until an angel gave her water from the Zamzam well. These two hills are now inside the Grand Mosque and are connected by a long hallway. You know

that this area has been the site of a few deadly stampedes in the past, but you realize that you have no fear of one as you pass through, because all is in the hands of God. Then you drink water from Zamzam before leaving this area.

Next, you move with all the other pilgrims out of the city of Mecca. You gather on the Plain of Arafat near the Mount of Mercy. From the afternoon prayer until the sunset prayer, the pilgrims "stand in the presence of Allah" by praying, meditating, and reading the Qur'an, the holy scripture of Islam. An older friend told you that this afternoon would be the high point of your pilgrimage, and he was right. That evening, you walk back to the village of Mina, where all of the pilgrims live in a huge tent city for three days. Sheep and goats are slaughtered in the evening as offerings to God, then roasted and eaten in happy feasts. These sacrifices commemorate Abraham sacrificing an animal to God instead of his son Ishmael.

The next day, you throw small stones at three pillars representing the devil. Every pilgrim is supposed to do this, symbolizing your rejection of evil, a life-long task. Then you go back into Mecca and walk in the Grand Mosque one more time; your pilgrimage is complete. You return home to find that some of your friends half-teasingly call you *Hajji*, the new name given informally to people who make the pilgrimage—*Hajj* in Arabic. This makes you smile, but you know that this new name points to a deeper truth: No one who goes on the pilgrimage will ever be the same again.

 Visit Mecca by way of Google Earth™.

 Muslims walk around the cube-shaped shrine at the center of the Grand Mosque in Mecca during the Month of Pilgrimage.

This sign over the Saudi Arabian highway to Mecca (in Arabic, Makkah) shows that Mecca is closed to non-Muslims.

عرفات مكة المكرمة
للمسلمين فقط
Arafat Makkah
Muslims only

جـــدة
اتجاه اجباري
لغير المسلمين
Jeddah Obligatory
for non muslims

View a PBS video on Islam in contemporary Indonesia.

Islam is the world's second-most populous religion, after Christianity. It has about 1.3 billion followers, almost one out of every five people. Islam is now present in virtually every part of the world. About 8 million Muslims live in North America and around 15 million in Europe. Although Islam is traditionally associated with the Middle East, the largest Muslim populations are in south Asia: Indonesia, Malaysia, Bangladesh, Pakistan, and India. Indonesia has the largest number of Muslims—around 200 million—of any country in the world. Large Muslim populations are also found in central Asia, including China. In the aftermath of recent events involving violence done in the name of Islam, careful and unbiased study of Islam has become more challenging for North American students than in the past. However, it is all the more necessary. As you begin your study of Islam, these particular puzzlements may emerge:

- Islam seems to be centered on Muhammad (moo-HAHM-id) and his teaching. Whenever Muslims mention his name they say, "Peace be upon him," and Muhammad is now the most common first name in the world. Muslims honor Muhammad and are usually quick to defend him. However, Muhammad isn't at the heart of Muslim devotion, or even near it. Muslims believe that he was only the human conduit of God's revelations.

- Islam is a deeply spiritual religion centered on the one God, but it is equally a religiously shaped way of life for a community of people. From its founding, Islam has preferred to function as both a religion and a state, and in twenty-five nations of the world—in the Middle East, North Africa, and south Asia—it is the official state religion.

- Islam has spread throughout the world and has adapted to many cultures, but wherever it goes it still carries on key elements of its Arab origins. For example, all Muslims who own a Qur'an are expected to have one with the Arabic text alongside a modern translation if they can't read Arabic, and Muslims typically have an Arabic first name.

- Some Muslims today seem to speak for all of Islam, but no one really can because of its diversity. For example, Muslim leaders in some nations

This mosque in Singapore shows a combination of Arab and south Asian styles.

enforce laws in the name of Islam that all women wear a veil that covers their whole body when they are in public, but Muslim women in other nations are free to go out in regular clothing, with their hair covered by a scarf and their face fully visible.

- Many non-Muslims today think that Islam is a violent religion, but the vast majority of Muslims don't engage in violence for their faith—today or in the past. This misconception is especially prevalent in nations that have been the objects of recent attacks by terrorists claiming to act in the name of Islam.

Read an introduction to Islam for Westerners by the Saudi Arabian government.

> Muslims understand the name of their religion as submission to God, not peace with God.

Learning Outcome 12-1

Explain *Islam* and related terms.

12-1 The Name *Islam*

Muhammad and his first followers referred to their movement as **Islam**, "submission," always understood as submission to God. They came to be known as **Muslims**, which means "submitters." (The older spelling *Moslem* is still found, and is not incorrect, but *Muslim* is now preferred.) Explanations of the word *Islam* today, even by some Muslims, sometimes imply that it comes from the Arabic word for "peace," *salam* (sah-LAHM). *Salam* is indeed related to *Islam*, but it is a different word. Although Muslims see peace as coming from submission to God, the great majority of Muslims correctly understand the name of their religion as *submission* to God, not *peace* with God.

The term *Mohammedanism* for Islam came about when Christians wrongly supposed that followers of Muhammad named themselves after him, just as Christians were named after Jesus Christ. You may see this term in older literature, but you should avoid using it. You may also see the current term **Islamist** for

Muslim radicals, particularly those who espouse violence in the name of Islam. We'll consider the validity of this term later in this chapter, but for now you should know that it covers only a very small proportion of Muslims.

Islam [ihz-LAHM] "Submission" to God

Muslim [MUHZ-lim] "Submitter," follower of Islam

Islamist Recent term for Muslim radicals

Learning Outcome 12-2

Outline how the main periods of Islamic history have shaped its present, especially different Muslim groups.

12-2 Islam Today as Shaped by Its Past

A film depicting the life of the Prophet Muhammad began production in 2009. In keeping with Muslim tradition, however, the face and voice of the Prophet won't be seen or heard on screen. *The Messenger of Peace* is a remake of *The Message* from 1977. Producer Oscar Zoghbi, who worked on *The Message*, said that his team had great respect for the original film and that this latest project will employ modern film techniques in its renewal of the original film's message. The mistaken belief that actor Anthony Quinn was portraying Muhammad in the 1977 film sparked protests by Muslims in the West, some of them violent, and harmed commercial prospects for the film. With the risk of similar misunderstandings lessened by careful publicity in the Muslim world, work on the new film goes forward, but slowly and carefully. At the beginning of 2013, its release had still not been announced.

Read a newspaper account of planning for the film *The Messenger of Peace*.

12-2a Arabia at the Time of Muhammad (500s C.E.)

Arabian religion of the sixth century C.E. had many gods, and Muslims refer to it as the "age of ignorance." Mecca, the largest city in the Arabian Peninsula, was a regional center of this religion, and many pilgrims visited its shrines. Pilgrims entering Mecca first saw statues of the three beautiful daughters of Allah, one of the high gods of traditional Arab religion. They visited a

A Closer Look:

The Symbol of Islam?

This chapter opens with a representation of the crescent and star, said by many to be a symbol of Islam. Because Islam is typically against religious images and pictures, whether worshiped or not, it hasn't officially adopted pictorial symbols for itself. The crescent-and-star symbol is featured prominently on the flags of several countries in the Islamic world. It's often thought to be an Islamic symbol from the first centuries of Islam, but it first appeared as the symbol of the Ottoman Empire that governed much of Islam from about 1300 to 1920, not of Islam as a whole. Thus, it's no more than five hundred years old. The Ottoman

Figure 12.1
Crescent and star

BONNIE VAN VOORST
© CENGAGE LEARNING

flag had the crescent-and-star symbol, which has since become associated with Islam itself. (The culinary legend that the popular crescent roll, or "croissant," was invented in Vienna to celebrate the European defeat of the Ottoman siege of that city in 1683 has no solid historical evidence behind it.)

Crescents without a star are often found at the top of mosques, where they remind Muslims of God's rule over creation, and in particular of the importance of the moon in the Muslim religious calendar—which is based on the phases of the moon, not the sun. Also, the crescent and star are carved as a symbol of Islam into the gravestones of Muslims in the U.S. armed forces buried in U.S. military cemeteries. But on the whole, Islam has no official symbol.

---

hanifs [hah-NEEFS]
"Pious ones," pre-Islamic Arabian monotheists

cube-shaped shrine dedicated to the god Hubal and drank from a sacred well. Although religious practices were important in Mecca, social life in the tribes shaped the key values of pre-Islamic Arabia much more than did religion. One scholar has called pre-Islamic Arabia's way of life a "tribal humanism."[1] Arabs honored loyalty to one's kin, bravery in battle, and protection of the weak. But they had no strong religious values that could challenge tribal values and little belief in any meaningful afterlife.

Pre-Islamic Arabia also had no religious or social resources to deal with rising social inequities. In the generation before the beginning of Islam, unprecedented wealth from international commerce

Read a geographic sketch of the Arabian Peninsula.

was pouring into Mecca, which had come to control the international trade that passed through the Arabian Peninsula, mostly by camel caravans. This new wealth produced new social divisions, and it brought more cross-cultural interaction throughout the peninsula. Jews, Christians, and Zoroastrians lived there in significant numbers along with the Arab majority, particularly in the north. A small group of Arab monotheists, the **hanifs**, or "pious ones," was devoted to the worship of Allah, the one and only God.

Camel caravans were important for lucrative Meccan trade, and camels are referred to often in Islamic scripture and tradition.

© SHUTTERSTOCK.COM/TANATAT

---

[1] W. Montgomery Watt, *Muhammad: Prophet and Statesman* (New York: Oxford University Press, 1974), 51.

12-2b The Life and Work of Muhammad (ca. 570–632)

Muhammad Ibn ("son of") Abdullah was the founder of Islam. Historians disagree about how much his ideas arose out of older religions, as well as about the factors that contributed to the rapid expansion of Arab rule and Islamic religion. But what follows here is mostly agreed on. Muhammad was born around 570 C.E. in Mecca, into a relatively humble family of the Quraysh (KUR-aish) tribe that controlled Mecca. He was orphaned as a boy and raised by relatives. They couldn't afford schooling for Muhammad, so he worked as a camel driver and then a caravan manager. His scant financial resources meant that he wasn't able to marry at the usual age.

Eventually, he came to work for a wealthy widow engaged in trade, Khadija (kah-DEE-juh). When she suggested marriage to him, he agreed, even though she was fifteen years older than he. Muhammad and Khadija were devoted exclusively to each other; while she lived, he didn't take another wife. They had six children together, four girls and two boys, but the boys died in childhood, a situation that has influenced Islam through today, as we'll see later in this chapter. Muhammad prospered and became a wealthy merchant, and his extensive travel for business brought him into contact with Jews, Christians, and Zoroastrians as well as hanifs and believers in many gods. Much current scholarship suggests that this contact likely helped shape his own faith as he began to doubt his own inherited religion, although traditional Muslim teaching maintains that Muhammad obtained monotheism from Allah. His humble origins as the son of a poor widow, then as an orphan, and finally as a happy husband to Khadija are no doubt related to Muhammad's strong concern, as expressed in the Qur'an, that the treatment of widows, orphans, and wives be significantly improved.

In 610 C.E., Muhammad was meditating continually for days and nights in a cave outside Mecca. There he saw visions that came in a dream-like state and revealed the word of God to him. When he fell into a trance, the angel Gabriel, known to Jews and Christians from the Bible, spoke to him. Muhammad heard Gabriel's voice outside himself and sometimes inside. "Recite!" the angel commanded (Qur'an 96), and Muhammad submitted to this command, reciting Gabriel's words to others. In a short time, the uncertain seeker of truth became a bold prophet. He had been transformed by submitting to the one true God who spoke to him, and in his submission he found freedom and courage. According to Islamic tradition, Muhammad received his first revelation from Gabriel the night of the twenty-seventh day of the month of **Ramadan**, and the month-long fast all Muslims undertake for Ramadan celebrates the giving of the revelations.

Muhammad's early prophetic message to the Meccans had two main themes. First, only one God exists, **Allah** (Arabic for "the God"), who commands people to believe in this one God and to submit to God's holy will. Second, a day of judgment will certainly come, when those who have submitted to God will be rewarded forever, and those who haven't will be punished eternally. Other themes of the early revelations include generosity to the poor, widows, and orphans; the presence and goodness of God in the natural world; and the prophetic call of Muhammad himself. This message shows clearly that Islam from its beginning is in the line of the Abrahamic monotheisms, Judaism and Christianity.

Khadija and other members of Muhammad's immediate family believed him, but as Muhammad began his public proclamations (probably around 613), some Meccans became hostile to him. However, Muhammad did gain some followers outside his family, and in ten years the number of Muslims numbered in the thousands. Most of them were relatively young and of lower social status. The tribal leaders in Mecca looked on Muslims as social deviants whose denial of the traditional gods and growing numbers threatened the economic foundations of the city. They ridiculed Muhammad as a lunatic, "only a poet" inventing his own revelations (Qur'an 52:30–49). They pointed out that Muhammad worked no miracles and offered no other supernatural signs of his prophetic calling. Muhammad responded by saying that the revelations themselves were a supernatural

> **Ramadan** [RAHM-uh-dahn] Month of fasting and commemoration of the giving of the Qur'an
>
> **Allah** [AHL-lah] "The God" in Arabic

Read about the call of Muhammad in the Qur'an.

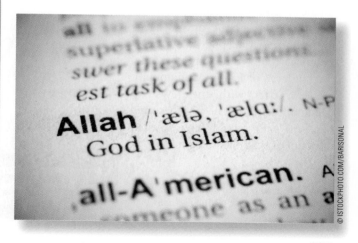

Hijra [HIHJ-ruh] "Flight" of Muslims from Mecca to Medina in 622 C.E.

umma [OOM-uh] Organized Muslim community

sign. His "Night Journey" to Jerusalem later on was a supernatural event that served to bolster his credibility, and his ascent into heaven from the rock on the Jewish Temple Mount would lead to the building of the Dome of the Rock mosque on that site. But persecution escalated, and after the death of both his uncle and Khadija in 619, Muhammad's position in Mecca deteriorated.

Read about the Night Journey.

> "In Medinah, Muhammad became a prophet-statesman, the founder of a political order ... that would change the history of the world."—Daniel Peterson.

In 622 C.E., the Prophet and his followers fled Mecca for Medina (then called Yathrib), about two hundred miles to the north. This relocation is called the **Hijra**, "flight," and is used to mark year 1 A.H. ("in the year of the flight") on the Islamic calendar, much as Christians traditionally use A.D., "in the year of our Lord (Jesus)." The Muslims were welcomed in Medina, and Muhammad was soon in charge of the fractious town. Muhammad would live in Medina for the rest of his life. There, Islam developed into a well-organized religious-political community called the **umma**, a complete way of life for its followers. As Daniel Peterson remarks, "Muhammad became a prophet-statesman, the founder of a political order and eventually of an empire that would change the history of the world. And Islam took on a political dimension that it has never abandoned."[2] Principles of a legal system came in divine revelations given at Medina, as did details about prayer, fasting, charity, and pilgrimage, key practices that would later become the "pillars" of Islam. Muhammad made a pact with the Jews of Medina; they didn't need to become Muslims and would have a rich measure of religious freedom.

The Muslims organized armed raids on Meccan caravans to punish them for their hostility. These raids continued until the Muslim military victory over Mecca in the Battle of Badr (BAHD-er) in 624 C.E. The booty from this battle greatly increased the financial strength of the Muslims, and Muhammad gained great respect in Arabia; the battle proved to be a turning point in the fortunes of Islam. Judaism gradually declined in Medina, and hundreds of Medinan Jews were killed and the rest expelled between 624 and 627, after a failed Jewish attempt to assassinate Muhammad. This led to a more powerful dependence on Arabian religious practices reformed for Islamic use, particularly the religious system of the Quraysh tribe. For example, Muslims were no longer to pray facing Jerusalem, but rather toward Mecca (see Qur'an 2:142). The first Muslim pilgrimage to Mecca occurred in 629; pilgrimage to Jerusalem fell in importance. And the month-long Ramadan fast replaced the ten-day fast connected with the Jewish Day of Atonement.

Many Arab tribes in the region came into Islam while Muhammad controlled Medina, acknowledging his leadership. When the army he commanded got Mecca to surrender without a fight in 630, Muhammad immediately removed all idolatrous images from the city. He left only the sacred cubic building and its holy stone that was believed to have come directly from God. He kept Mecca as the destination for Muslim pilgrimage and maintained some of its religious sites, for example the sacred well. Muhammad raised armies to conquer the important northern regions of the Arabian Peninsula, taking on the Christian Byzantine Empire in the process. By the time Muhammad died in Medina two years later, in 632, he ruled nearly all the Arabian Peninsula. Islam had established itself permanently in this area, and it had become a rapidly growing religion (see Map 12.1).

[2] Daniel Peterson, *Muhammad, Prophet of God* (Grand Rapids, MI: Eerdmans, 2007), 91.

Muhammad returns to Mecca. In Muslim art from Persia and Turkey, Muhammad's face is sometimes pictured, contrary to Muslim convention.

© BETTMANN/CORBIS

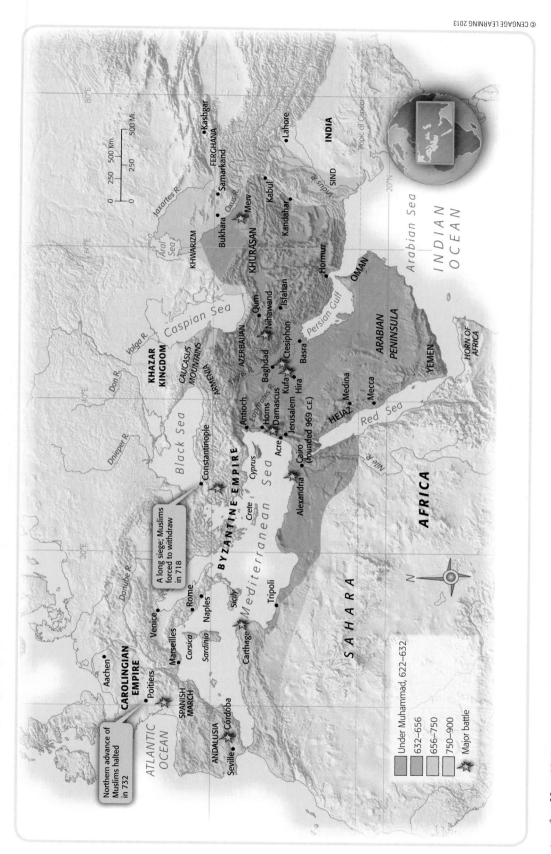

Map 12.1
Expansion of Islam to 900 C.E.

The Arabs rapidly conquered much of western Asia, North Africa, and Spain, in the process expanding Islam into the conquered territories. By 900 their empire included all the Mediterranean islands, and stretched from Morocco and Spain in the west to western India and central Asia.

ISLAM TODAY AS SHAPED BY ITS PAST   **301**

12-2c Islam Immediately Following the Death of Muhammad (632–661)

The pressing issue at Muhammad's death was who would succeed him as leader of the Islamic movement, and the way it was settled affects Islam through today. For whatever reason, Muhammad hadn't publicly designated a successor. Muslims needed to select a leader of the faith who would be the **caliph**, the "representative" or "successor" of Muhammad. This successor would not receive new revelations from Gabriel or change Islam in major ways, but would lead the community in its political and religious life. In the Arab culture of the times such leadership would usually stay in the family, but Muhammad had no surviving son, so the leading choice from his family was his cousin Ali (ah-LEE), who was also his son-in-law due to his marriage to Muhammad's daughter Fatima (FAH-tih-muh). Ali had always been enthusiastic for Islam, and Ali claimed that Muhammad had privately designated him as his successor. However, many contested Ali's fitness to rule.

A majority consensus arose among Muhammad's most powerful followers that Abu Bakr (AB-oo BAHK-uhr), Muhammad's father-in-law, would be Muhammad's successor. He was an early believer and one of Islam's main military leaders. Abu Bakr soon took over the leadership of Islam, due to three factors: his power base in the Muslim military forces; the need to squelch defections from Islam by several Arab tribes when Muhammad died; and his connection to the Prophet by way of Muhammad's favorite wife, A'isha (AH-ee-shah), who was Abu Bakr's daughter. Naturally, Ali's supporters objected to this, and the seeds of division were sown. The groups that grew from these seeds are the **Shi'as** or **Shi'ites**, "followers" or "party" (of Ali), and the **Sunnis**, the "people of the tradition," who formed the majority of Muslims. We'll discuss these two groups in more depth at the end of this history section.

caliph [kah-LEEF] "Representative" or "successor" of Muhammad; ruler of Muslim community

Shi'as [SHEE-uhs] or **Shi'ites** [SHEE-ights] "Party" or "followers" of Ali, the group that holds that Muhammad's true successors descended from his son-in-law Ali

Sunnis [SOON-eez] "People of the tradition," the majority of Muslims

Rightly Guided Caliphs First four caliphs, with special divine guidance

> The pressing issue at Muhammad's death was who would succeed him, and how it was settled affects Islam through today.

The rejection of Ali's leadership happened two more times: when Abu Bakr died and was replaced as caliph by Umar in 634, and again when Uthman, a member of the Umayyad (oo-MY-ahd) tribe, became caliph in 644 when Umar was assassinated. Ali's supporters grew increasingly bitter about these rejections. The caliphate seemed to be moving further and further from Muhammad's family. Despite this conflict, Islam continued to spread by Arab military conquest and follow-up Muslim missionary activity. In an action that would influence all of Islam to come, Uthman gathered all of Muhammad's revelations and issued an authoritative edition of the Qur'an. Muhammad himself had not committed any of the revelations to writing, much less overseen that process. Instead, his followers had recorded his prophetic recitations on parchment, palm leaves, and even pieces of wood. Uthman gathered these, along with the collections that already existed. He kept what he knew to be authentic and destroyed the rest. The Qur'an emerged as we have it today, and Muslims believe that it perfectly reflects Gabriel's revelations to Muhammad.

 Watch a BBC report on the spread of Islam.

After Uthman was assassinated by rebels in 656, Ali finally became caliph, the last of what Muslims call the **Rightly Guided Caliphs**—that is, the first four caliphs whom God directed to be faithful in ways other caliphs have not been. However, a leader of the Umayyad tribe soon claimed the caliphate. Hostilities between Ali and the Umayyads increased, and their armies faced off in 661. When Ali tried to compromise and avoid war, some of his followers killed him. War did break out, and the Sunnis were triumphant over the Shi'as. Sunnis had become the majority tradition of Muslims, in fact as well as in name.

12-2d Islam from the Umayyads until Today (661–Present)

The subsequent history of Islam can be concisely traced by means of its dynasties and its geographic growth. Sunni leadership belonged to the Umayyad tribe for about one hundred years (661–750). The Umayyad Islamic Empire included nearly all the Middle East, Persia (modern-day

Iran), Egypt, North Africa, and Spain. The largest of the empires this area had seen since the fall of Rome in the fifth century C.E., it remained largely united for two centuries after Muhammad's death. However, the Umayyad rulers and their courts were lax in devotion to Islam, and their drinking of alcohol and their marital infidelities offended pious Muslims, who often revolted.

They were replaced by the Abbasid (ah-BASS-id) dynasty, which had a long rule, from 750 to 1258. Islam spread farther into Africa and Asia; this was the second main period in the expansion of Islam. Many Muslims consider the Abbasid period to be the high point of Islamic history, particularly in such fields as art, science, philosophy, and Muslim theology. Muslim lands enjoyed a higher degree of civilization than that of most Europeans during Abbasid times. They preserved much of the science, medicine, and mathematics of the ancient Mediterranean world, and they made important contributions of their own to these fields. Abbasid rule saw Islam strengthen as a religion, with greater equality between Arab and non-Arab Muslims. Muslim belief and practices grew wider and deeper in the Arab empire. By the 900s, religious schools known as **madrasas** began to appear, usually headed by a well-known scholar of religion or religious law. Thousands of these schools can be found today all over the Muslim world. In 1285, invading Mongols, who had recently been converted from Buddhism to Islam, ended Abbasid rule. Arab control of Islam was permanently ended, and Islam was hurt both politically and culturally. Islamic law and philosophy, for example, were never the same again. However, between 1285 and 1550, Muslim territory doubled in size.

In Egypt, Abbasid rule yielded to the Shi'a Fatimid kingdom (919–1171). The end of wider Abbasid rule started when the Seljuk (SEL-jook) Turks took power in the eleventh century. The Turks—a name for a wide family of tribes and peoples—had long been residents of central Asia, but around 900 C.E. some of them migrated

Modern, idealized image of a Crusader

© ALGOL/SHUTTERSTOCK.COM

"The most persistent mistake Westerners make about Islam today is to think of it as monolithic."—Rodney Stark

into the northern parts of the Middle East. As they migrated, they came into contact with Islam and converted to it. The Turks took over Arab Muslim rule as they moved. They lost possession of Palestine during the **Crusades**, when Catholic military forces from Europe invaded to take control of the "Holy Land" where Christianity was born. *Crusade* comes from the Latin word for "cross," and Crusaders typically wore this symbol of Christianity on their clothing and shields, replacing the symbols of their own European states. The Crusader state was never large and was ended by the second dynasty of Turks, the Mamluks (MAM-luhks). Because Christian nations were able to hold a key part of the Muslim homeland—including their holy city of Jerusalem—for more than a century, a negative impression toward Christianity was strengthened in Islam, one that continues today. This explains why Muslims who oppose the presence of Western military personnel in Muslim lands sometimes call them "Crusaders."

In 1453, Muslims finally conquered Constantinople and renamed it Istanbul; the last Christian empire in the Middle East had finally fallen, and many of its churches were converted to mosques. For example, the former Christian Church of Holy Wisdom (Hagia Sophia) in Istanbul, Turkey, was made into a mosque. Turkish Muslim control spread eastward into India, where from 1526 until 1858 the Mughal (MOO-gahl) dynasty of Turkish Muslims ruled the largest part of the Indian subcontinent. (Our word *mogul*, meaning a powerful leader such as a Hollywood "movie mogul," comes from *Mughal*.) When the early modern age began to dawn in the 1600s, Islam reached the height of its power in three main empires: the Sunni Ottoman Turks in the Middle East, North Africa, and much of southeastern Europe; the Shi'a Safavids in Iran; and the Sunni Mughals in India.

Read a BBC article on Muslim Spain.

madrasa [muh-DRAH-suh] Muslim religious school

Crusades Christian military expeditions to take control of Palestine

The Church of Holy Wisdom in Istanbul was made into a mosque and is now a state museum.

with democratization, as European colonization after World War I held back that process. The popular uprisings in several Arab nations from 2010 through the present, called the **Arab Spring**, demand an end to autocratic rule and a measure of democracy, but they have also resulted in civil turmoil and the increased power of radical Islamic groups. Oxford University scholar Tariq Ramadan has recently written that the Arab Spring will face several challenges to establishing civil, democratic societies. Chief among them is what role Islam will play, and whether "Islamist" and secular movements can coexist.[3] Despite these challenges, Islam is firmly established throughout North Africa, the Middle East, and both central and south Asia (see Map 12.2).

After the Mamluks lost their rule, the Ottoman Turks took over the vast empire of Islam and became the longest-lived Islamic dynasty (1300–1923). It collapsed after its defeat in World War I, when it was on the side of Germany and Austria-Hungary. For the first time, the main Muslim empire had fallen to external powers. Something new to Islam was imposed on it by the victors: Instead of one Islamic empire, there were now many Muslim nation-states, nearly all of them officially Muslim. Turkey, under its leader Mustafa Kemal (muh-STAHF-uh keh-MAHL), known as Ataturk ("Father of the Turks"), became the first and still today the only officially secular nation with a predominantly Muslim population. It remains so today not without difficulties, as some religiously conservative Muslims attempt to make it officially Muslim. Since 1923, Muslims in the nation-states have struggled to preserve Islam as an umma within their borders. They have also struggled

Arab Spring Popular uprisings in Arab nations from 2010 through today, which demand an end to autocratic rule and a measure of democracy

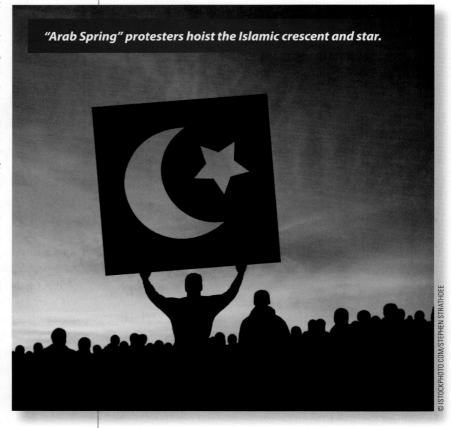

"Arab Spring" protesters hoist the Islamic crescent and star.

---

[3] Tariq Ramadan, *Islam and the Arab Awakening* (New York: Oxford University Press, 2012).

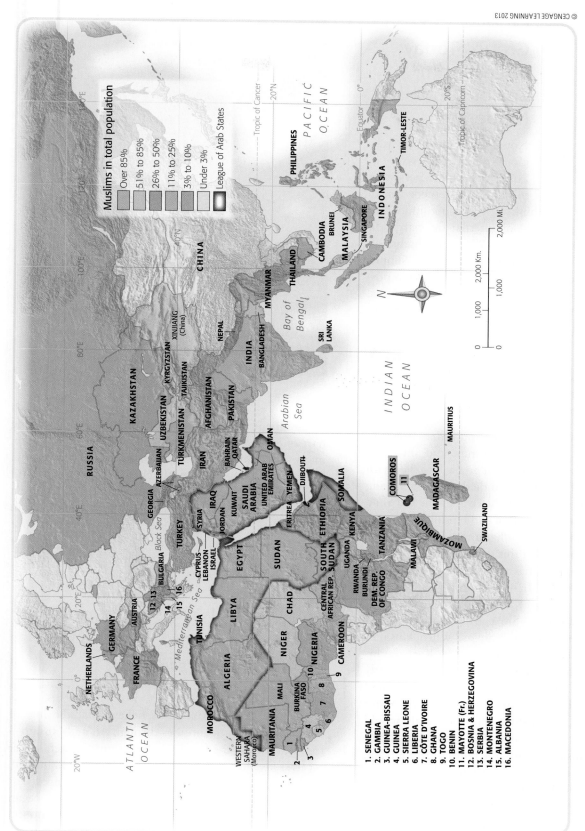

Muslims in total population

- Over 85%
- 51% to 85%
- 26% to 50%
- 11% to 25%
- 3% to 10%
- Under 3%
- League of Arab States

PACIFIC OCEAN

Tropic of Cancer

20°N

Equator 0°

20°S

Tropic of Capricorn

PHILIPPINES

INDONESIA

TIMOR-LESTE

CAMBODIA

BRUNEI

MALAYSIA

SINGAPORE

CHINA

XINJIANG (China)

KAZAKHSTAN

KYRGYZSTAN

TAJIKISTAN

TURKMENISTAN

UZBEKISTAN

AZERBAIJAN

GEORGIA

RUSSIA

MYANMAR

THAILAND

Bay of Bengal

SRI LANKA

NEPAL

BANGLADESH

INDIA

PAKISTAN

AFGHANISTAN

IRAN

BAHRAIN

QATAR

OMAN

Arabian Sea

INDIAN OCEAN

MAURITIUS

MADAGASCAR

COMOROS

11

SWAZILAND

MOZAMBIQUE

MALAWI

TANZANIA

KENYA

SOMALIA

ETHIOPIA

SOUTH SUDAN

UGANDA

RWANDA

BURUNDI

DEM. REP. OF CONGO

CENTRAL AFRICAN REP.

SUDAN

EGYPT

DJIBOUTI

ERITREA

YEMEN

SAUDI ARABIA

UNITED ARAB EMIRATES

KUWAIT

IRAQ

SYRIA

JORDAN

ISRAEL

LEBANON

CYPRUS

TURKEY

Black Sea

BULGARIA

GREECE

Mediterranean Sea

TUNISIA

LIBYA

CHAD

NIGER

NIGERIA

CAMEROON

MALI

BURKINA FASO

MAURITANIA

WESTERN SAHARA (Morocco)

MOROCCO

ALGERIA

NETHERLANDS

GERMANY

AUSTRIA

FRANCE

ATLANTIC OCEAN

20°W

0°

20°E

40°E

60°E

80°E

100°E

120°E

140°E

40°N

12 13

14

15 16

1

2

3

4

5

6

7

8

9

10

N

0   1,000   2,000 Km.

0   1,000   2,000 Mi.

1. SENEGAL
2. GAMBIA
3. GUINEA-BISSAU
4. GUINEA
5. SIERRA LEONE
6. LIBERIA
7. CÔTE D'IVOIRE
8. GHANA
9. TOGO
10. BENIN
11. MAYOTTE (Fr.)
12. BOSNIA & HERZEGOVINA
13. SERBIA
14. MONTENEGRO
15. ALBANIA
16. MACEDONIA

Map 12.2
The Islamic World Today

The Islamic world includes not only the Middle East—western Asia and North Africa—but also countries with Muslim majorities in sub-Saharan Africa, central Asia, and south and Southeast Asia. Sunnis predominate in most of the Islamic world; Shi'as predominate in Iran and form sizeable minorities in Iraq and Lebanon. In addition, Muslims live in most other Eastern Hemisphere nations and in the Americas, where they make up under 3 percent of the population.

12-2e Diverse Muslim Groups Today: Mainstream, Zealous, and Moderate

Noted sociologist of religion Rodney Stark wrote in 2008, "The most persistent mistake Westerners make about Islam today is to think of it as monolithic."[4] In fact, Islam has a good deal of internal diversity, and often strongly opposing factions. We begin discussion of contemporary groups with the mainstream: Sunnis, Shi'as (whom we've met above, but who are so important that they require fuller treatment here), and Sufis. Then we'll consider the more zealous groups in Sunni Islam: the Wahhabis, the Muslim Brotherhood, and the Taliban. Finally, we'll consider moderate Muslim movements. Along the way, we'll take a closer look at the term *Islamic fundamentalism*.

Read a National Geographic report on unity and diversity in Islam.

Sunnis and Shi'as. The most important diversity within Islam is the split between Sunnis and Shi'as. As we saw above, the roots of this split go back to the death of Muhammad. When Caliph Ali died in 661, a lasting formal split developed between the rival Sunni and Shi'a groups. Ali had two sons, Hassan and Husain, who were of course the grandsons of Muhammad. Shi'as claimed then, and still do today, that this descent made them the rightful caliphs. Hassan gave up his claim due to illness and died soon afterwards. In 680, Husain's army battled the Sunnis near the town of Karbala in present-day Iraq. But the Sunnis cut off the Shi'a army from its water supply and then destroyed the Shi'as. When Husain's severed head was thrown over the wall of Karbala, his supporters in the town put it on a lance and reverently carried it around with deep mourning. Shi'a would continue in Islam as a separate group averaging about 10 to 15 percent of all Muslims, but never again would Shi'as challenge Sunnis for control of Islam as a whole.

The day of Husain's death, the tenth of Muharram, is observed by Shi'as as a day of mourning—called **Ashura**, "the tenth." Husain's death is now viewed as martyrdom, a holy death, for the true form of Islam;

Ruholla Khomeini, head Shi'ite imam and leader of the Iranian Revolution in 1979, pictured on Iranian currency.

© YURIY BOYKO/SHUTTERSTOCK.COM

commitment to martyrdom for Islam became a leading part of Shi'a. In mass processions still held on Ashura, many Shi'a men connect with Husain's martyrdom by lashing themselves with chains and whips until their blood flows. It was on Ashura in 1979 that Shi'a radicals in the capital of Iran stormed the American embassy and held its personnel hostage, in violation of international law, for more than a year—an event that still casts a dark shadow on U.S.–Iranian relations.

> *Shi'as and Sunnis have typically lived, worked, and worshiped apart from each other.*

As we saw above, Shi'as believe that the line of Islamic leadership continues through Ali and Husain—that is, through the family of Muhammad. Each leader receives, as Shi'as claim Ali received from Muhammad, a direct designation of succession from his predecessor and a supernatural knowledge of Islam to be an effective leader. The Arabic term for "leader" is **imam**, a general term that carries different (and sometimes confusing) meanings; for example, it is also the term

---

[4] Rodney Stark, *Discovering God: The Origins of the Great Religions and the Evolution of Belief* (New York: HarperOne, 2008), 378.

for the leader of a Sunni mosque. Shi'as typically view their imam's interpretation of Islam as perfect and fully authoritative. Sometimes they even view the imam as unusually holy, even saintly; this is especially true for regional or national imams. All this makes for powerful religious leaders in Shi'a—more so than in Sunni groups. Shi'as revere and make pilgrimage to other holy places in addition to Mecca, such as the tombs of the imams, particularly those of Ali and Husain.

Shi'as and Sunnis have typically lived and worshiped apart from each other. Shi'as have their own territories where they predominate, and beyond this they tend to be minorities in many Sunni nations. Where Sunnis and Shi'as are found in the same cities, they prefer to live in different neighborhoods. They usually don't intermarry or go into business with each other, and they have their own mosques and leaders. Shi'as have five additional pillars—besides the Five Pillars common to all Muslims that we'll consider below—stressing Shi'a doctrines and practices, and slight differences in their formal prayers.

Shi'a history is a story of continual internal splits. Shi'a sects are still wary of one another. (One of the features of splinter groups in religion is that they're often beset by internal splintering; in other words, splitters keep splitting.) Three main groups account for the majority of Shi'as today, but each has its own subgroups. The three groups are named by how many original imams they recognize.

- The *Twelvers*, also known as *Imamites*, recognize twelve imams in the line of succession from Muhammad. The twelfth imam vanished when he was five years old and is still living in a hidden cave. He'll return near the end of time as the **Mahdi**, "the one guided" by God, and establish worldwide Shi'a rule. Twelvers are the majority of Shi'as today; they make up most Iranian and Iraqi Shi'as, and they are present in Lebanon as well.

- The *Seveners*, or *Ismailites*, are found today in India, Pakistan, and east Africa. Some Seveners believe that the seventh imam, Ismail, was Allah in human form, a notion that all other Muslims regard as heretical. Ismailites claim that Ismail will return as the Mahdi. The Fatimid dynasty in Egypt was from the Seveners. Also from the Seveners were the Hashishin (ha-SHEESH-een), who used hashish to induce visions before killing others for hire. (Our word *assassin* comes from this group.) The current leader of the largest group of Seveners is Prince Karim Aga Khan IV, the forty-ninth Ismaili imam, who traces his lineage to Muhammad through Fatima.

- The *Fivers*, or *Zaidites*, are a small sect of Shi'as found mostly in Yemen. Their fifth imam is Zaid, who began a different line of succession that eventually died out. He is now living in concealment. Fivers tend to be less hostile to Sunnis, but in the past decade they've engaged in armed rebellion against the Sunni government of Yemen.

The Sunnis and Shi'as comprise the two main divisions in Islam, but other Muslim groups have brought further Muslim diversity. Despite their relatively small size, these latter groups have exerted a significant influence within Islam and are still important in Islam today. We'll consider them in chronological order.

Sufis. Islam typically emphasizes the practice of religion, not thinking or feeling it. Submitting to God's will in one's actions is most important. However, Islam developed a mystical tradition to find deeper spiritual power within its religious teachings and practices. Islamic mystics are **Sufis**, a word for the woolen garments worn by the first Muslim mystics. Sufism arose in the 700s and is still found among both Sunnis and Shi'as. It has spread Islam on the peripheries of the Muslim world. Within Islamic lands it has spread deeper religious commitment among the lower classes, particularly in "folk Islam" in Africa and central Asia. Sufism is also very popular today in Pakistan. In its long history, it has organized into several "orders" or "brotherhoods," among whom are the Medlevi (mehd-LEHV-ee) order.

> *Sufis pursue a mystical quest for a direct, ecstatic experience of God.*

Sufis pursue a direct, loving, and ecstatic experience of God, usually to narrow the gap between God and humans. Poetry, music, and dancing are important in this mystical quest. At first Muslim authorities viewed Sufism with suspicion, until it became apparent that Sufis did indeed follow key Muslim practices. Sufism was allowed to continue, but many Muslims viewed the notion of human beings becoming literally one with God as idolatrous. (A factor in this suspicion, beyond the doctrinal element, could

Mahdi [MAH-dee] "The one guided" by God, hidden Shi'a imam who will return to establish worldwide Shi'a rule

Sufis [SOO-feez] Followers of Islamic mystical movement Sufism

have been the influence of passages in the Qur'an about Muhammad's struggle with religious poets in Medina and Mecca.) All Muslims expect to be close to God after the final judgment, but only the Sufis see achieving a mystical closeness—not to mention oneness—with God in this life as possible. The most influential Sufi by far is Jalal al-Din Rumi (jah-LAL al-DIHN ROO-mee), the thirteenth-century Persian poet of mystical love who has been called the most popular poet in America today, even among non-Muslims. Sufism produced the "whirling dervishes," who seek ecstasy in their dance; they have attained religious and cultural fame today.

Watch a BBC video on the whirling dervishes.

According to some proponents of Sufism in the Western world, Sufi ideas developed prior to our modern "organized" religions and are universal in nature, a system of mysticism that is employable by people of many faiths. They point to verses in Rumi's poetry, such as this one from "One Song":

> All religions, all this singing, one song
> The differences are just illusion and vanity.
> Sunlight looks different on this wall than it does on
>   that wall
> and different on this other one,
> but it is still one light.

However, Sufis themselves typically reject the notion of Sufism without Islam. Despite the words of Rumi, "I am neither Christian, nor Jew, nor Zoroastrian, nor Muslim," Sufism has been, and probably will remain, an inner-Islamic movement.

Wahhabis. From its very beginnings, Islam has seen movements that strive for strict purity and zeal. In more recent times, one such group, the **Wahhabi** reform movement in Sunni Islam, was begun by Muhammad al-Wahhab (al-wah-HAHB) in the late 1700s. Wahhab was shocked by what he regarded as widespread corruption in Islam. He despised Sufism because he thought that it mixed Islam and Hindu pantheism, and he disapproved of many Shi'a popular practices as well. For example, the tombs of prominent Shi'a and Sufi Muslims became places to venerate them in order to gain spiritual power. Wahhab considered this idolatry, the most serious sin in Islam. His message of reform was summed up in the cry "Back to the Book [the Qur'an] and the Tradition [sunna] of the Prophet!" He adhered to a conservative method of Qur'anic interpretation that avoided all innovations.

In time, Wahhab gained the support of powerful tribal ruler Ibn Sa'ud (EE-bin sah-OOD). Together they began to cleanse the Arabian Peninsula of anything they considered detrimental to pure Islam. They sacked the Shi'a shrines in what is today Iraq and destroyed Sufi settlements in the Arabian Peninsula. (The 2009 destruction of a historic Sufi shrine in Peshawar, Pakistan, by militant Sunnis is an echo of Wahhabi opposition to Sufism.) After Wahhab's death in 1792, his movement made uncertain progress in the 1800s, because the Ottoman rulers occasionally cracked down on new religious groups that they saw as a challenge to their authority and religious moderation.

A Wahhabi state was finally established in the 1920s, when the Sa'ud family became rulers of the new nation of Saudi Arabia. Practices that Wahhabis considered idolatrous were strongly punished: consumption of any alcohol, veneration of saints at their tombs, playing of secular music, possession of anything deemed pornographic, or the formal presence of any

Sufi dancers, "whirling dervishes," of the Medlevi order

other religions. Muslim religious law became the law of Saudi Arabia, and is strictly enforced. The so-called religious police (formally called the "Commission for the Promotion of Virtue and the Prevention of Vices") patrol public areas to enforce this law, particularly on women's dress and conduct, but this has been easing a bit since 2001. The Western press often calls Wahhabism "puritanical," but that's a term from Protestant Christian history that ill fits this Islamic movement. Wahhabism's strong convictions are carried out not in religious thought or theory (Sunni, Shi'a), or even in emotional dimensions of submission to God (Sufi), but in daily practice. Sunnis in the world today don't typically live under Wahhabi requirements. However, Saudi Arabia is the most influential nation in the Muslim world, for its holy cities of Mecca and Medina and its vast oil wealth, so the way it practices Islam has become widely known and influential.

The Muslim Brotherhood. When the Ottoman Empire collapsed around 1920, the Muslim world was left for the first time without a caliph. This vacuum in religious leadership, coupled with new colonial control of many Middle Eastern nations by European powers under the direction of the League of Nations, led to a rise of conservative movements in several large Muslim nations. One of the earliest and most influential—the **Muslim Brotherhood**—was launched in Egypt by the charismatic Hassan al-Banna in 1929. Opposed to corruption, the lax practice of Islam, and Westernization in Egyptian government and life, the Brotherhood worked for purely Islamic legal systems in Egypt. Since then, the movement has spread to several other Sunni Muslim countries.

Sometimes the Brotherhood's actions are violent, and many Arab governments view the movement as undermining their rule. The Muslim Brotherhood is often said to be the beginning of organized "Islamic fundamentalism" (see "A Closer Look: 'Islamic Fundamentalism'?") with "political" dimensions, but that distinction should probably belong to Wahhabism. It is true, however, that Muslim Brotherhood members have taken very conservative stances; for example, in Kuwait they have recently opposed laws giving women the right to vote. In early 2011, the Muslim Brotherhood played a key role in toppling the rule of Egyptian president Hosni Mubarak (HOHS-nee moo-BAHR-ahk), and Egypt moved toward conservative Muslim rule under president Mohamed Morsi (MOHR-see) until the Egyptian military ousted him in 2013. Observers anticipate the Brotherhood's continued role in political change in other Middle Eastern nations.

The Taliban. The latest movement important for understanding Islam today is the **Taliban**, "students" of the Qur'an. (We'll consider a related group, al-Qaeda, below.) They draw members from many Sunni Islamic countries. The Taliban was influenced by the Wahhabi movement during the successful Muslim struggle to drive the Soviet Union out of the Muslim nation of Afghanistan in the 1980s. In the 1990s, the Taliban was able to gain control of Afghanistan. The first Taliban home page on the World Wide Web invited Muslims to contribute money to what they called the "first truly Islamic state in history." The Taliban gained opposition in the West for repressive measures against Afghani women, such as ending all education except homeschooling for females of any age and prohibiting women from working outside their homes. Like some Muslims before them who were also zealous for Islam, the Taliban considers those Muslims who don't adhere to their strict attitudes and standards of behavior to be false Muslims and enemies of Islam. Their means for bringing about their ideals have often been brutally violent, and as of this writing they continue their military struggle to regain rule in Afghanistan. Their strong belief has made them tenacious fighters.

Moderate Muslim Movements. It might seem to you from this treatment of Muslim groups that Islam has only gotten more conservative in the last century or so. This would be a mistake. In recent times, Muslim modernism tried to revive what it considered the original form of Islam by determining the meaning of their scriptures. Some historical methods new to Islam but well known in Europe were introduced to attempt to recover the original meaning of the Qur'an. For example, Indian Muslim scholar M. Azad (1888–1958) argued that one must study Arabian culture at the time of Muhammad to understand what the Qur'an originally meant. This liberalizing movement was generally confined to the more Westernized upper classes, and it didn't get much traction.

Since 2001, a small but vocal group of Muslims has been trying to move Islam to the center, and some even call themselves "Progressives." Omid Safi, a professor at the University of North Carolina at Chapel Hill who wrote *Progressive Muslims: On Justice, Gender, and Pluralism*, opposes (along with moderates)

Muslim Brotherhood
Conservative religious and political movement founded in 1929

Taliban [TAHL-ih-bahn] "Students" of the Qur'an, a radical Sunni group in Afghanistan

A Closer Look:

"Islamic Fundamentalism"?

Deciding what to call the phenomenon commonly known as "Islamic fundamentalism" isn't easy. This term became popular after the Iranian Revolution in 1979 as a description of the resurgent Shi'a movement. It was used first by Westerners, especially American journalists, often unaware that they were applying to Muslims a term used for certain American Protestant Christians. Sometimes other contemporary groups are labeled "Islamic fundamentalists," for example the Taliban, al-Qaeda, the Wahhabis, and the Muslim Brotherhood.

The term *Islamism* is found today in the press and in scholarly writing. It avoids the weaknesses of *Islamic fundamentalism* and has the appeal of one-word simplicity. However, *Islamism* is an oddly constructed word, and the suffix *-ism* can be pejorative. Some groups labeled "Islamists" maintain that they are simply faithful Muslims—that they follow Islam, not "Islamism"—and that their political convictions are an expression of their religious belief in the Islamic way of life.

Read a short essay on growing dissatisfaction with the term *Islamist*.

Salafi refers to the movement of Muslims who model their faith on their understanding of the *Salaf* ("predecessors" or "ancestors"), the earliest Muslims. A modern Sunni Islamic movement related to Wahhabism, Salafism is rapidly gaining popularity. Salafism is connected today with the literalist, strict practice of Islam. In Egypt, the Salafist movement is even more conservative than the Muslim Brotherhood, and has become its main political opponent.

Political Islam is occasionally used today for this movement's effort to reunite the "political" and the "religious," but as we've seen, Islam traditionally strives to do this and has in fact done so in most of its history. *Activist Islam* is accurate enough but is vague and wrongly implies that mainstream Islam isn't really "active." In *militant Islam*, we must distinguish between those who use violence and those who don't. Even among the first group, a distinction must be drawn between those who use violence according to traditional rules of jihad and those who use it outside jihad (a term discussed in an upcoming section).

Radical Islam is perhaps the best of these options, although it isn't without its own problems. *Radical* is vaguer than the terms above, and it can have a pejorative connotation. On the positive side, it has the connotation of both "going to the root" and going all the way with what "radicals" believe God wants.

Wahhabism, the Taliban, and all other radical Islamic groups.[5] Another example of progressive Islam is Sisters in Islam, a Malaysian group founded in the 1980s by the politically connected professor Zainab Anwar. Sisters in Islam promotes an Islamic vision of freedom, justice, and equality for women. Taking their cues from the ministry of Muhammad, who reformed the conditions of the poor and women, they urge further reform. Progressive Muslims typically claim that after Muhammad died a conservative wave swept over Islam and that his reforms were effectively frozen when they should have continued. They view themselves as carrying on in the spirit and message of Muhammad.

Salafi [suh-LAH-fee]
Sunni movement promoting strict practice of Islam

An important part of this moderating movement is the liberation of Muslim women. The status of Muslim women has been a persistently difficult issue, both within Islam and in the wider world. Traditionally, Islam sees gender differences as given by God. The Qur'an says, "Men have authority over women because God has made the one superior to the other, and because men spend their wealth to maintain women" (4:34). It also affirms that "Women shall with justice have rights similar to those exercised against them, although men have a status above women" (2:228). Moderates and progressives struggle to give women a greater measure of freedom: to wear a head covering or not, to have an opportunity for a full education equal to that of men, to vote and participate in politics, and to attain other freedoms. Their progress is slow, and they encounter opposition in parts of the Muslim world, but they are not discouraged.

Watch a video by Irshad Manji, a prominent Muslim feminist.

[5] Omid Safi, *Progressive Muslims: On Justice, Gender, and Pluralism* (New York: OneWorld, 2003).

Give the essential elements of Islamic teachings in your own words.

12-3 Essential Teachings

California's Orange County has a thriving mosque. Yassir Fazaga keeps an eye on the American calendar to provide a connection for his weekly Friday sermon as the imam. Around Valentine's Day, he talks about how the Qur'an endorses romantic love within certain moral boundaries. "My main objective is to make Islam relevant," said Fazaga, who was born in east Africa, went to high school in Orange County, and attended college and a religious training school in Virginia. As the first generation of American-born Muslims begins to graduate from American colleges in significant numbers, some mosques are beginning to seek native-born leaders who can teach not just about the main, central teachings of Islam, but also about religious and social issues that are relevant to Muslim young people here (such as dating, marriage, and drugs). So one of the challenges facing Islam in North America is to obtain imams who can lead Muslim communities in the North American context.

12-3a God Is One

Muslims consider the teaching that there is only one God to be the basis and the center of their religion. The Arabic word *Allah* doesn't refer only to the God of Islam. It is the common, generic Arabic word for God—any God—and when Muslims talk in Arabic about the God of Jews, Christians, and Zoroastrians, *Allah* is the word they use.

Because Muslims forbid anything that encourages idolatry, they don't make images or pictures of God or even of Muhammad.

The roots of Muhammad's understanding of Allah lie in monotheism. God is an eternal, spiritual being; God is not a force, but a divine person. The Qur'an sees Islam as carrying on this true monotheistic religion that Judaism and Christianity have mostly abandoned. Islam has a strict, absolute form of monotheism, because God is seen as one and one only. Therefore, Muslims reject all forms of polytheism as false religions, and other gods as false. Like Muhammad, they urge others to follow only the one God. Muhammad considered the "fatherhood" of Allah—which he associated with the sexual procreation of a son or the "daughters of Allah," taught in pre-Islamic Arabian religion—as idolatrous. Muslim monotheism led to opposing the Christian doctrine of Jesus as the Son of God. The Qur'an says, "God is One, the eternal God. He begot no one, nor was He begotten" (112:1–3). In Islam, idolatry (*shirk*), acknowledging other gods besides the one and only God, is considered the worst sin.

Read the Qur'an on God's oneness.

Muslims forbid idolatry so strongly that they forbid anything that encourages it or even makes it possible. Therefore, they don't make images or pictures of God. If Muhammad is depicted at all, his face is omitted. (A few schools of Muslim art in the past have ignored this.) Strict Muslims today object to any representational art forms as a temptation to idolatry. This has led to mosques being decorated only with colorful geometric patterns, which are said to reflect the order and beauty of the creation as a whole, not of God. These patterns can be strikingly beautiful and inspiring. When the author of this book went for the first time into the Dome of the Rock mosque in Jerusalem, it impressed him as one of the most beautiful buildings he had ever seen.

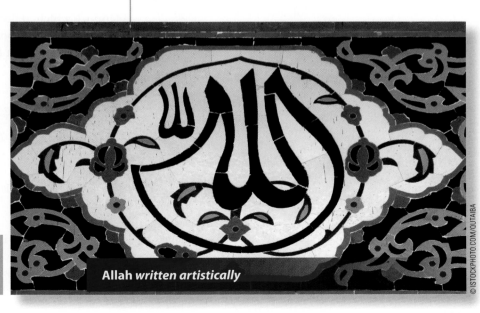

Allah *written artistically*

ⒸISTOCKPHOTO.COM/QUTAIBA

Noniconic art in a mosque in Isfahan, Iran

three other archangels and a large company of ordinary angels. As in Judaism and Christianity, angels are the messengers carrying divine revelation to humans. There are also many **jinn**, "spirits" (related to our word *genie*). In the Qur'an they say about themselves, "Some of us are Muslims and some are wrongdoers" (72:14). Evil jinn are led by the devil, a spirit who rebelled against God when humans were created. Muslims must be on guard against the jinn, because they can cause not only physical but spiritual harm, by luring believers away from Allah. Some Westerners misunderstand jinn as ghosts, spirits of deceased humans, but they are non-human spirits who have fallen into evil and often tempt humans to do wrong.

Many Muslim believers have a lively sense of the good and evil forces of the jinn. For example, in 2012 hundreds of Saudi teenagers raided an abandoned hospital in Riyadh to drive out evil jinn thought to "haunt" it, and the authorities had to intervene to stop the mayhem. Although the Qur'an and official Muslim teachings focus on belief and practices that draw the believer's focus to God alone, some Muslims practice Islam primarily to keep evil spirits at bay and bring the blessing of good spirits. Many Islamic teachers are laboring today, as Sufis did in the past, to raise all Muslims to a fuller understanding of monotheism—an understanding that the focus of one's faith should not be on spirits, but on the God who controls good and evil spirits.

12-3c The Qur'an

Muslims believe that the angel Gabriel divinely revealed to Muhammad the Qur'an, the perfect copy of an eternal, heavenly book. The name *Qur'an* means "recitation," which reflects the main origin and use of this scripture, oral communication—first from Gabriel to Muhammad, then from Muhammad to his followers.

> *Televised contests of Qur'anic recitation are as popular in Muslim lands as shows such as "American Idol" are in North America.*

jinn [jihn] Spirits, both good and evil

surah [SOO-ruh] Chapter of the Qur'an

Verses from the Qur'an are also used in decorating mosques and homes.

God is unique in essence and attributes, infinite, and the creator and sustainer of all that exists. "His are the beautiful names," ninety-nine in all; these names are scattered throughout the Qur'an, but they are compiled in a later tradition. Moreover, God is beyond all human thought and understanding. God can be described, but not known in any comprehensive way. God is all powerful, and Muslims typically believe that all that happens in the world, good or evil, happens within the plan and control of God. Muslims use the phrase *enshallah* (en-SHAHL-ah), "if God wills it," whenever they talk about the future; in fact, it's probably the most commonly used Arabic expression.

12-3b Angels and Spirits

God created angels and spirits to serve God and the human beings created later. Muhammad received the Qur'an through the archangel Gabriel. Islam recognizes

The Qur'an is divided into 114 chapters called **surahs**, and each chapter is divided into verses. Because the Qur'an is viewed by Muslims as the successor and fulfillment of the Jewish and Christian scriptures, it is

Even mass-produced modern Qur'an covers suggest the high regard Muslims have for their scripture.

legitimate to compare their relative sizes: The Qur'an is about two-thirds the size of the New Testament and half the size of the Jewish Bible. The chapters are arranged by length, from longer chapters to shorter ones. The shorter, older chapters focus on the basic themes of one God and future judgment; the longer, later ones contain many detailed instructions for the Islamic community as well as references to biblical history. Unlike the Jewish and Christian Bibles, the Qur'an gives virtually no historical narratives; it's almost all teaching and commands. It begins with **al-Fatihah**, "the Opening," Chapter 1, a beautifully resonant prayer that is recited at prayer times. This chapter comes close to providing a summary of Islam:

> In the name of God, the Most Gracious, the Most Merciful. All praise and thanks be to God, the Lord of the Worlds, the Most Gracious, the Most Merciful, the only Lord of the Day of Judgment. You alone we worship, and You alone we ask for help. Guide us on the Straight Way, the Way of those on whom you have bestowed your grace, not of those who incur your anger or those who have gone astray.

The Qur'an itself is said to exist only in Arabic, the language in which it was revealed by Muhammad to others. (Whether Gabriel communicated it in Arabic or in a more supernatural way to Muhammad, who then understood it in Arabic, has been

an open question to many Muslim leaders; many Muslims assume that Gabriel spoke in Arabic.) Muslims believe that all translations of the Qur'an involve some distortion of meaning, so no translation can be the authentic, perfect Qur'an. Where translations are used, many printed Qur'ans have the original Arabic text on facing pages. Muslim schoolchildren memorize large sections of the Qur'an in Arabic, even if Arabic isn't their main language. Imams are required to memorize all of it. Recitation of the Qur'an is an art form, with fame and sometimes riches going to those who are talented in the art. Many Muslim nations televise contests of Qur'anic recitations, and the level of excitement for these television shows approaches that in North America for shows such as *American Idol*.

View a recitation by a young girl in a Qur'an contest.

The Qur'an contains many references to people and stories in the Jewish and Christian Bibles. We meet in the Qur'an figures such as Adam and Eve, Noah, Abraham, Moses, Jesus, and Mary, all of whom are considered Muslims and "prophets" in the prophetic line that culminates in Muhammad. Muslims believe that Gabriel spoke these biblical references to Muhammad during the revelations of Qur'anic content, thus accounting for the differences in these accounts between the Bible and the Qur'an. However, non-Muslim

Arab Muslim girl reads the Qur'an

Wooden placards decorated with Qur'anic verses for sale in a Moroccan bazaar

to be the Mahdi. He will come shortly before the end of time and the final judgment; his work is to rid the world of injustice as a preparation for the end. In the early 2000s, the main Shi'a paramilitary force in Iraq was called the Mahdi Army, but without any direct implication that the powerful Shi'a imam leading it was the Mahdi. The Mahdi idea has even appeared in Sunni circles at times, which is a bit odd, because the Sunni view is that Muhammad was the final prophet, and this leaves no room for a Mahdi.

12-3e "People of the Book": Jews, Christians, and Zoroastrians

scholars typically hold that Muhammad probably heard these stories first from his Jewish and Christian contacts.

Read the Qur'an on the Qur'an.

12-3d Prophets

The Qur'an states that God has revealed the divine will at key points in human history through prophets. All the prophets, including Muhammad, call for the same response: submission to the will of God and preparation for an impending judgment. Most of the twenty-five prophets mentioned in the Qur'an are well-known figures in Judaism and Christianity. (The Qur'an also names three other prophets—Hud, Shu'aib, and Salih (7:66-93)—who may have been leading figures in the monotheistic tradition leading to Islam.) Although Jews and Christians claim many of the prophets as their own, Muslims view them as Islamic prophets who teach submission to God. They didn't come to found Judaism, Christianity, or the hanif tradition as different religions—Muhammad is the culmination and conclusion of the entire line of prophets.

Despite this emphasis on Muhammad as the culmination of the prophets, some Muslims look for one more prophetic figure to come, the Mahdi. As stated above, Shi'as expect the last in the line of imams

People of the Book
Christians, Jews, and Zoroastrians, whose scriptures are related to the Qur'an

Some in the line of Muslim prophets gave books to their people: Zarathustra wrote down his message for Zoroastrians; Moses recorded the law and David composed the Psalms, for the Jews; Jesus taught the Gospels to Christians. Muslim call these groups **People of the Book**. This expression doesn't refer, as is sometimes said, to all people who have sacred books in their religions—after all, many religions have sacred books—but only to people whose sacred book(s) Muslims view as in a line of religious development with *the* Book, the Qur'an. Some passages in the Qur'an even suggest that "people of the book" who follow their religions carefully will enter heaven along with Muslims.

Muhammad gave these "people of the book" privileges not available to others under his rule. After Muslim forces conquered their nations—their status didn't protect them from attack—they weren't forced to choose between conversion to Islam and death, as people of other religions usually were. They had to pay an extra tax and were subject to greater government oversight, but they were allowed to practice their religions among themselves. As long as they respected Muslim rule in their lands, these communities were tolerated; but if they didn't obey, especially if they turned rebellious, they were subject to annihilation. They didn't have the right to seek or even accept converts from Islam, build new houses of worship, or sometimes even repair old ones. They didn't have what North Americans would call "freedom of religion," but they weren't violently persecuted minorities either. Over time, most of the Jewish,

Christian, and Zoroastrian communities shrank to shadows of their earlier sizes in the Middle East and North Africa, as second-class status, pressure for conversion to Islam, and migration out of the Islamic empire took their tolls. In the past sixty years or so, there has been a great migration to Israel of Jews living in Arab lands and, in the past twenty years, a steady migration of Arab Christians from Palestine and Iraq to the United States.

 Read the Qur'an on Jews and Christians.

12-3f Final Judgment

The Qur'an's teaching on the judgment is simple and sobering (20:100–127; 18:101–104; 23:105–115). On a day known only to God, a heavenly trumpet will sound, and all the dead will rise from their graves with eternal bodies to meet their Maker. Everyone will be given a book in which is recorded all the deeds he or she has done in life. Angels will put the books of the wicked in their left hand, a symbol of divine disapproval, but the righteous will receive their book in their right hand. The righteous can then enter heaven, but the wicked go straight to hell.

God will judge people by how they submitted to God's will. Saying that one is a follower of Islam won't save anyone at the judgment; living in an obedient way is the important thing. In fact, the Qur'an states that severe punishments are in store for hypocrites who claim to be Muslims but haven't lived by Islam. To other Muslims who sincerely believe in God and try to do what God has revealed, God is "most gracious" and "most merciful." God gives special consideration to those who die in warfare or other struggle for Islam; they go to heaven, with great blessings. Literalist interpretation of this belief is used by a few radical Muslim groups today to recruit poor young men—those who seem to have little prospect for blessings on earth—for suicide missions as "martyrs." Muslims trust that God will forgive the occasional sins of otherwise obedient people. For hypocrites and unbelievers, including those of other religions who know of God but haven't submitted to God, there is no forgiveness.

Islam focused from the first on heaven as an eternal reward for those who submit to God's will and on hell as an eternal punishment for those who don't. Heaven and hell are pictured in the Qur'an as places with physical and spiritual aspects (56:1–56). Heaven is a place of beautiful gardens, cool waters, plentiful food, wine that doesn't intoxicate, and the beautiful virginal women called *houris* (HOO-rees) whom God has created as rewards for righteous men. Hell is a place of physical and spiritual pain, complete with darkness, fire, and boiling filth. Although Muslims differ on how these descriptions of heaven and hell are to be interpreted—and most interpret them quite literally—all observant Muslims believe that heaven and hell are real. Muslims are motivated to submit to God by the attractive promises about heaven and fearsome warnings about hell that reach all the way back to Muhammad.

Learning Objective 12-4

Explain Muslim ethics, especially in diet, dress, and marriage.

12-4 Islamic Ethics

A young married woman in Jiddah, Saudi Arabia, tuned into a twice-weekly broadcast of the *Oprah Winfrey Show* until it stopped in 2011. "I feel that Oprah truly understands me," she told an American visitor. "She gives me energy and hope for my life." This Saudi woman isn't alone; Saudi women under thirty watched *Oprah* more than any other television show. They were drawn by Oprah's welcoming personality, modest dress, and helpfulness in dealing with personal and family issues similar to some of those faced by Muslim women in Saudi Arabia. Government censors usually saw nothing subversive in the *Oprah* show, but its segments dealing with forbidden practices, such as drinking alcohol or same-sex love, were not allowed to enter the nation.

A Muslim's whole life is a submitting to God's revealed way of behavior. Muslims believe that every person is born with an equal inclination toward God and doing what is good. Faith is a matter of knowing God and submitting to God's way. According to Muslim moral thought, all actions fall into one of three categories. The first are good actions that are required, such as the Five Pillars of Islam that we'll consider in the next section. The second category includes evil actions explicitly prohibited, such as idolatry, immorality, and theft. The third are neutral matters that are permitted and left up to the discretion of the believer. Before considering the Five Pillars, we must first discuss a variety of other Muslim practices: foundations in the hadith and the Shari'a; modesty in dress; marriage and gender relations; and jihad, the struggle for the faith.

Muslims are obligated to commend what is good and reprimand evil.

Muslim pilgrims toss pebbles at pillars to "stone the devil," symbolizing their rejection of evil.

12-4a The Hadith

The Qur'an is the main source of Muslim practices by which believers submit to God. For any issues that are undefined in the Qur'an, the Prophet's life and informal sayings are the authoritative sources. These traditions are called the **hadith**, and they were vigorously collected and evaluated in the first generations of Islam after Muhammad's death. The hadith point to Muhammad's life and teaching—as distinct from God's teaching through Muhammad as found in the Qur'an—as indications of how Muslims should act. The Qur'an itself says relatively little about the actions of Muhammad, so this further interpretive aid came to be viewed as necessary as a context through which to interpret the more difficult material in the Qur'an.

The hadith include many sayings that are attributed to Muhammad. These may be used to clarify the revelation of the Qur'an, and thus their authority comes close to that of the Qur'an itself. Among the hadith are various stories, including Muhammad's important Night Journey from Mecca to Jerusalem and back to Mecca, as well as his ascent to heaven while in Jerusalem to receive revelations.

hadith [huh-DEETH] "Traditions," a traditional report recording a saying or action of Muhammad

Shari'a [shah-REE-uh] "Way, path," formal system of traditional Islamic law

fatwa Religious ruling by an imam urging a particular action by Muslims

Read a hadith.

12-4b Shari'a

If you've already heard of the **Shari'a**, traditional Islamic law enforced in many Muslim lands, it may have been in reports about the stoning of women convicted of adultery or the cutting off of thieves' hands. These sensationalist reports, although generally true, give an incomplete and misleading impression of Muslim law. Shari'a developed to guide the implementation of Qur'anic and hadith interpretation. Two hundred years after Islam's founding, its central institution was Shari'a law. Shari'a deals with many aspects of day-to-day life, including politics, business, family life, sexuality, hygiene, and social issues. Many people today might consider it a civil and criminal law shaped by a religion, but Muslims don't make that distinction. They believe that Shari'a is simply God's law for the regulation of all Muslim life. Four different schools of Shari'a arose in Sunni Islam between 750 and 850, and still exist today. These aren't schools of theology that differ in belief or practice, because the four Sunni schools hold to the same basic Muslim beliefs and practices. Rather, they are distinct ways of defining morals and practices in precise and technical legal terms. A part of Muslim law is the **fatwa**, a religious ruling by an imam trained in Shari'a urging a particular course of action for Muslims that may or may not be binding on them.

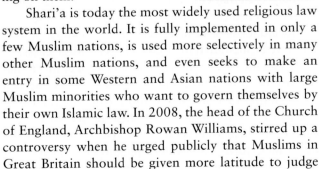

Watch an expert in Shari'a explain its place in Islam.

Shari'a is today the most widely used religious law system in the world. It is fully implemented in only a few Muslim nations, is used more selectively in many other Muslim nations, and even seeks to make an entry in some Western and Asian nations with large Muslim minorities who want to govern themselves by their own Islamic law. In 2008, the head of the Church of England, Archbishop Rowan Williams, stirred up a controversy when he urged publicly that Muslims in Great Britain should be given more latitude to judge themselves according to Shari'a. Informal Shari'a courts already operate in the Muslim communities of Great Britain, dealing with marital conflicts and divorce. That same year in France, where relations between the secular government and observant French Muslims can be difficult, a nationwide political dispute broke out when a French court upheld a Shari'a-based annulment of the marriage of two Muslims after the groom discovered on their wedding night that his bride wasn't a virgin.

12-4c Diet and Other Regulations

Only **halal** ("permitted") foods may be eaten by Muslims. One can see restaurants and fast-food outlets in the Muslim world that advertise this concept—for example the popular Halal Fried Chicken chain, HFC for short. Foods that are **haram**, "forbidden," may not be eaten. Consuming pork or products with even a small amount of pork mixed in them is particularly forbidden. The Qur'an also prohibits the drinking of wine (2:219); this is taken to mean that all alcoholic drinks and even food cooked with alcohol are haram.

Other behaviors and practices are haram as well. Muslims must not gamble or charge interest on loans. Banks in more-moderate Muslim nations don't observe this prohibition on interest; banks in stricter Muslim nations do. An interesting case on haram is the current controversy over whether smoking tobacco—a widespread practice in the Arab part of the Muslim world—should now be forbidden. Some Muslims argue that it should be forbidden as something that is harmful to the body that God has created. Others argue that what the Qur'an, hadith, and Shari'a don't expressly prohibit should be accepted. "Islam has so few permitted vices," some Muslims say with a smile, "so

the ones it has should be kept." In general, Muslims must "commend what is good and reprimand evil." This applies to matters of dress for both men and women (see "A Closer Look: Muslim Dress").

halal [huh-LAHL] "Permitted" foods and actions

haram [huh-RAHM] "Forbidden" foods and actions

12-4d Marriage and the Status of Women

The status of women in Islam is determined by its view of marriage, not by its view of gender or gender relationships in themselves. Marriage is customary for all Muslims; parents typically arrange it while children are young, although women often can refuse engagements to men they don't like. Some Muslim parents living in North America will travel back to their Middle Eastern homelands in order to find suitable matches for their children. The Qur'an says that a man may have up to four wives at one time as long as he provides for them equally and with separate living quarters, but the vast majority of Muslim men have only one wife.

The Qur'an also says that the limitation on the number of wives didn't apply to Muhammad (33:50–52). His multiple marriages, to nine wives after the death of Khadija, and the move to Mecca are thought to be a part of his special calling as the Prophet. Some were entered into for political reasons, but an effort to obtain a son may have figured into these multiple marriages as well. Muhammad's marriage to A'isha, Abu Bakr's nine-year-old daughter whom we have already met, was controversial because of her young age, and his marriage to Zainab, the ex-wife of Muhammad's adopted son Zaid, was controversial because of the closeness of the family relation. Because the life of Muhammad can be viewed as normative for Muslims, the Qur'an and later Muslim tradition are careful to say when these practices apply to other Muslims and when they don't.

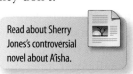

Read about Sherry Jones's controversial novel about A'isha.

Muslim diversity in New York City

© JFEINSTEIN/DREAMSTIME.COM

Muslim Dress for Women and Men

No specific types of clothing are pre-scribed for Muslims. The Qur'an and hadith don't lay down requirements for dress, probably because Arab ways of dress were a given in the first decades of Islam. In line with Semitic cultures, all Muslims are required to dress modestly. You may have encountered the view of Muslim modesty common in the West: women in robes and veils with only their eyes visible. In some Middle Eastern cultures, such a covering over other clothes is the required Islamic mode of dress for women. For example, in the 1980s the Shi'a government of Iran required full-body veiling of Muslim women out in public. This garment, called the *chador* (shah-DOHR) in Iran, is referred to as the *burkah* (BUR-kuh) in most places. In the 1990s, the Taliban government of Afghanistan imposed it on all Muslim women there, and some Afghani women still wear it today.

Figure 12.2 Woman in burkah

Many Muslims argue correctly that the Qur'an, hadith, and Shari'a don't say that a woman must be completely shrouded, and they disagree with this added requirement. The Qur'an does require that a woman should dress in a way that conceals her physical beauty from men (24:31). Muslims typically interpret this requirement by saying that a woman's body, including her arms and legs, should be fully clothed. Her face may be visible, but her hair needs to be covered at least with a *hijab* (hih-JAHB), a scarf placed around the head, the most common form of modest dress in the Muslim world. These rules don't apply in the home; among her immediate family a woman is unveiled and with no hijab, but still modest. They also don't apply where only women are present, such as in all-female areas. For example,

Egypt's Mediterranean coast has some all-female beaches for Muslim women who want to follow religious expectations and still wear Western-style swimming suits, to "have fun and not sin." Although wearing the hijab is controversial in many nations, Leila Ahmed of Harvard University showed in her prize-winning book, *A Quiet Revolution: The Veil's Resurgence from the Middle East to America*,[6] that the surge of Muslim women wearing the hijab is not due to conservative, patriarchal forms of Islam, but is mainly a symbol of religious activism and a way for women to assert their identity.

Figure 12.3 The hijab

Muslim men must dress modestly as well. Their body must be clothed in a way that doesn't draw attention to their shape. In general, Muslim men don't expose their skin above their elbows or knees, and they're usually clothed to their ankles. (You'd rarely, if ever, see a Muslim man shirtless in public.) A head covering for men, such as a turban or cap, is a part of men's dress in many Islamic lands, but this is more cultural than religious.

Figure 12.4 Muslim man in cap

---

[6] Leila Ahmed, *A Quiet Revolution: The Veil's Resurgence from the Middle East to America* (New Haven: Yale University Press, 2012).

Divorce is relatively simple for a man to obtain in most Muslim nations today; women can divorce their husbands only with difficulty. The Shari'a states that a man can divorce his wife by saying "I divorce you" in front of other male witnesses at three different times, usually over a period of three months. (You may hear that a Muslim husband can say "I divorce you" three times in one moment for a divorce to be effective, but that isn't correct.) Divorce is not to be undertaken trivially. A hadith states that divorce is "hateful in the sight of God." However, the Qur'an fully and carefully provides for it (2:228–242; 115:1–7).

Of course, Muslim nations that don't follow the Shari'a fully have other procedures for divorce that follow Muslim tradition more loosely. If there are children in the marriage, they are typically in the main custody of the man after the divorce. Early Islamic law gave Muslim women significant new rights in marriage and divorce. A man must provide adequate alimony for his ex-wife as long as she lives, but there is usually no expectation that an ex-wife must be supported in "the manner to which she has become accustomed," as divorce laws in the Western world sometimes say.

Read "Thinking through Western Questions about Islam and Women."

12-4e Jihad

Jihad means "struggle" for God and Islam. Many people think that Islam expanded in its first centuries through methods that were mostly military struggle, not religious. Recent activities by terrorists ostensibly acting in the name of Islam have reinforced this stereotype. On the other hand, many Muslims and non-Muslims say that Islam is a religion of peace and that jihad refers to peaceful struggle to be better Muslims. As Stephen Prothero remarks, "This crucial conversation rarely advances beyond a ping-pong match of clichés."[7] So let's go deeper into this difficult issue.

The great majority of Muslims today want to be seen as tolerant toward others. "There must be no compulsion in religion," says an often-quoted verse in the Qur'an (2:256). Muslims frequently—and correctly—point out that many Qur'anic passages about jihad refer to spiritual striving within individual Muslims. A hadith calls this the "greater jihad," and military conflict the "lesser jihad." The basic meaning of jihad for most Muslims is the struggle against one's own evil to fully submit to Allah. It also refers to groups of Muslims who struggle to improve the state of Islam. Nevertheless, jihad as military action is important in the Qur'an. Muslim scripture repeatedly commands Muslims to take up arms and fight when necessary on behalf of the Islamic community (for example, 2:190; 8:38; 9:29; 22:39–41), and it treats jihad as military struggle more often than nonmilitary. Muhammad

> *"This crucial conversation [about war and peace in Islam] rarely advances beyond a ping-pong match of clichés."*
> —Stephen Prothero

himself strongly criticized those who implied that spiritual struggle substituted for military struggle. Military action is commanded "even though it may be hateful to you" (2:216). This struggle is usually directed against opposing military forces, but it includes deadly action against people of other religions in Islamic lands when they resist Muslim rule. Muslim warriors in conflicts with a religious dimension are often called *mujahedeen* (moo-JAH-huh-DEEN), "those who engage in jihad." Today in the West they are frequently called "jihadists," but this is usually pejorative.

jihad [jee-HAHD]
"Struggle," both personal, inner struggle and armed struggle for Islam

The basic principles of the military aspect of jihad were drawn up by Abu Bakr from the Qur'an and the practice of Muhammad, and expanded later by others. Although the "rules for jihad" vary somewhat in history and today, here are the main common points:

- Violence shouldn't be used to advance the cause of Islam. An Islamic country may never initiate conflict against another state or people for religious reasons only.

- Suicide in warfare is often seen as evil. It usurps the power of God alone to determine life and death, even in battle. The Qur'an makes a blanket prohibition of suicide (4:29) but doesn't explicitly apply it to warfare, so some Muslims disagree with its application there.

- If another nation acts aggressively against an Islamic country, that country is justified in using military force to defend itself. Muslims must publicly and formally declare war in a *fatwa* (ruling by a recognized Muslim leader) before any military action can commence.

- All noncombatants—women and children, the sick and the elderly, and enemy soldiers who surrender—are to be spared and treated well.

- If a Muslim or non-Muslim country uses physical or legal force to repress the free exercise of Islam, those actions constitute hostility to Islam. It would then be appropriate, even a requirement, for Islamic nations to liberate the oppressed Muslims by force of arms.

---

[7] Stephen Prothero, *God Is Not One* (New York: HarperOne, 2010), 26.

- Jihad can be waged against other Muslim nations who are thought to have departed from the faith. For example, Ayatollah Khomeini, the Shi'a religious leader of Iran, declared its 1980s war against Sunni-ruled Iraq to be a jihad and Iranian soldiers who died in it, martyrs.

- Once a country is Islamic, it may not be allowed to go back into non-Muslim rule, as this would be an action against Islam. Jihad must be waged to bring it back to Islam. This is why many Muslims today don't recognize the nation of Israel as legitimate.

Usually there was little resistance to the spread of Islam in its first centuries, due to the strength of the Muslim forces and the cultural conditions in the lands they conquered. Whole regions welcomed the advancing Muslims, eager for them to replace the hated Byzantine rulers. Most Christians and Jews welcomed the Muslim armies, expecting and receiving basically respectful treatment. In several Muslim areas, a sizeable Christian and Jewish population continued for centuries. For example, in Egypt the Coptic Christian group was a majority of the population for more than a thousand years, but over time with steady pressure and sometimes persecution Islam reduced the Copts to a small minority, around 10 percent today. They have come under renewed pressure, sometimes violent, with the 2012 rise of the Muslim Brotherhood in the Egyptian government. As we saw above, peoples not "of the book" were converted to Islam by force if necessary. The Muslim armies marched on, annexing an enormous amount of territory in a very short time. Nearly the entire Middle East came into the Islamic rule in about thirty years, and by one hundred years it stretched from the Atlantic coast of North Africa to modern Afghanistan. This was one of the fastest imperial expansions in history.

Watch a National Geographic report on the war in Darfur, Sudan, as religion-related genocide.

Five Pillars of Islam Sunni practice of confession of faith, prayer, fasting, almsgiving, and pilgrimage to Mecca

We should end our discussion of this challenging topic by saying this: Despite all the attention justifiably paid to it today in some parts of Islam and especially in the Western world, jihad is not one of Islam's central practices. It isn't a pillar, nor is it one of the key doctrinal teachings. But to understand Islam in the world today, one must understand jihad well.

Muslim engaged in armed jihad

© OLEG ZABIELIN/SHUTTERSTOCK.COM

Learning Outcome 12-5

Explain the ways Muslims worship, especially the Five Pillars.

12-5 Worship: The Five Pillars of Islam

In Dearborn, Michigan, home to one of the largest Muslim populations in North America, Hussein Elhaf prepares for the annual month-long fast observed by Muslims around the world. Hussein's family owns a restaurant with a mainly Muslim clientele, so he works around food during the month of Ramadan, but he will eat and drink only between sunset and sunrise, when eating and drinking are permitted. The restaurant serves food during daylight hours in Ramadan for non-Muslim customers, and it is crowded with Muslims taking their main meal of the day from sunset until 11:00 PM. Fasting while working with food and drink all day won't be a struggle for him, he says; in fact, "it strengthens my faith and brings me closer to God."

The study and practice of religion in our time have reaffirmed the importance of core religious practices of worship: stating one's beliefs, prayer, giving of one's wealth, occasional fasting, and others. The core practices of Islam are all related to worship and form what Muslims call the **Five Pillars of Islam**. (Shi'as generally recognize ten pillars, with particularly Shi'a additions in the second group of five.) The notion that Islam has "pillars" is not in the Qur'an or the hadith, although Muslims view it as faithful to what the Qur'an and hadith say about these five obligations. The pillars—of the worship of God on which Islam is built—are essential but not exhaustive.

12-5a Confession of Faith

> The first part of the Islamic confession can be said sincerely by a monotheist in any religion; the second, only by Muslims.

The first pillar is built on the foundational rock of Islam. Although we've said that Islam is primarily a religion of action, not of belief, the first pillar is indeed a statement of belief. The **shahada** is the "confession" of Islam; here, "confession" means a formal statement of faith, not a confession of sin. It runs: "There is no god but God, and Muhammad is God's prophet." Its Arabic form is resonantly poetic: *La ilaha illa Allah, Muhammad rasul Allah* (lah ih-LAH-ha ihl-lah AHL-lah, moo-HAHM-id rah-SOOL AHL-lah). This confession is among the shortest of any world religion that has formal confessions. The shahada isn't found in the Qur'an in this exact form, but its two parts are often repeated there separately. Sometimes the shahada is translated "There is no god but Allah." But in Arabic, its second and fourth words are *Allah*, so "There is no god but God" is a better translation.

A monotheist in any religion can sincerely recite the first part of the confession. The second part connects monotheism to the Islamic faith. Saying "Muhammad is God's prophet" entails submission to all God's commandments as given through Muhammad. He is the *rasul*, the final prophet and messenger who speaks God's words definitively. The shahada encompasses the key points of a Muslim's life. Newborn babies hear it whispered to them. Those who convert to Islam repeat this confession as their own. Those who say the formal prayers repeat it every time they pray. The last words of dying Muslims are the shahada; if they are unable to speak, someone else says it for them.

12-5b Prayer

Prayer is the main, regular form of Muslim worship, so we will treat it more fully than the other pillars. Each observant Muslim says the ritual prayers called **salat** five times a day: at sunrise, at noon, in midafternoon, at sunset, and one hour after sunset. Prayers must be performed wherever one finds oneself at the hours of prayer. A **mosque** (from *masjid*, "place of prostration") is a building for prayer. Each mosque typically has a tower, called a **minaret**. The minaret traditionally has a balcony from which the *muezzin*, or "caller," summons the people to prayer. Today in Muslim lands, this task is often done through loudspeakers on the minaret. The most common pattern of the call to prayer goes like this:

God is great. [said 4 times]
I bear witness that there is no god but God. [2 times]
I bear witness that Muhammad is the prophet of God. [2 times]
Make haste to prayer. [2 times]
Make haste to success. [2 times]
God is great. [2 times]
There is no god but God. [1 time]

shahada [shah-hah-DAH] Fundamental confession of faith: "There is no god but God, and Muhammad is God's prophet"

salat [sah-LAHT] Ritual Muslim prayers recited five times a day

mosque [mahsk] Building for formal Muslim worship

minaret [mihn-uh-REHT] Tower on a mosque from which the call to prayer is made

Inside a mosque in Morocco

© POSZTOS [COLORLAB.HU]/SHUTTERSTOCK.COM

The main part of the mosque is the prayer hall, an open room often with abstract decoration on the ceiling or walls. It has no pictures, statuary, incense, altars, or marked-off areas as are found in the sanctuaries of other world religions. To enter a prayer hall, worshipers must remove their shoes and wash. Then they get in straight lines facing a niche at the front of the prayer hall. This indicates the direction toward Mecca, or the **qiblah**, to which prayer and the whole service is oriented. The straight rows also signify to Muslims the equality of all people before God. Mosques typically have a pulpit at which the imam preaches a sermon at the Friday noon service, and one often sees a few copies of the Qur'an on wooden stands for reading.

Take a Google Earth™ tour of some important historic mosques.

The prayer itself then begins. The sequence of salat is tightly structured in both words and actions; personal, spontaneous prayer is not a part of salat. Just before the prayer time, the muezzin or his recorded voice gives the official call to prayer in a melodic chant that can be heard throughout the neighborhood. Visitors in Muslim countries often notice the public call to prayer. (When the author was studying in Amman, Jordan, as a college student, he was startled awake by the dawn call to prayer on a loudspeaker next door to the rooftop where he was sleeping.)

As stated above, Muslims prepare for prayer by ritual washing. Hands, feet, eyes, ears, nose, and mouth are rinsed three times with water. When women pray in the mosque, they are out of the men's sight, in back of them or in a separate room. The reason for the segregation of the sexes is said to be the preservation of the dignity of women. Because a part of the prayer ritual is to bow and prostrate oneself, it would be unseemly in traditional Muslim cultures for men to line up alongside or behind women in this position. If a man were to touch a woman in the mosque, even accidentally, he would have to then go out and ritually wash again.

Watch an explanation of Muslim prayer.

Salat is a formal ritual with both postures and recitation. All the people in the prayer hall follow the words and actions together, giving a sense of unity. The imam at the front leads the process. People begin the prayer standing upright and cup

qiblah [KIB-luh]
Direction toward which Muslims face during prayer

their ears with their hands, showing God that they are present and listening. The first chapter of the Qur'an is spoken as a prayer, followed by other prescribed words. One's body is active in prayer: bowing, standing, kneeling, prostrating oneself while kneeling with forehead to the ground, kneeling, prostrating, and standing again. These actions remind Muslims in a physical way of their submission to God. The prayers are uttered in a quiet, humble voice, but in contrast the changes of posture are indicated by the leader's louder call of "Allah." Depending on the number of repetitions, daily prayers take approximately five to ten minutes to perform. On Friday afternoons, special prayer services in the mosque feature a sermon preached by the imam. This whole service, which is typically the best-attended service of the week, lasts between thirty and sixty minutes. It was after Friday noon prayers in the first months of 2011 that worshipers poured out into the streets to demand change from unresponsive, authoritarian governments in many Arab nations during the beginning of the "Arab Spring."

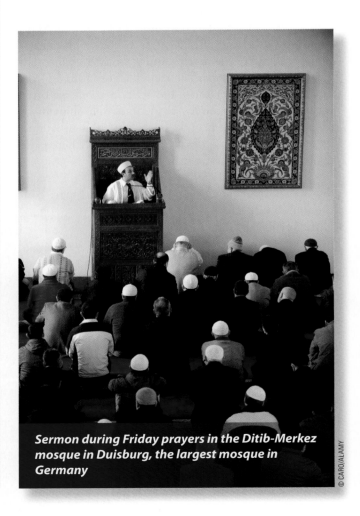

Sermon during Friday prayers in the Ditib-Merkez mosque in Duisburg, the largest mosque in Germany

© CARO/ALAMY

12-5c Fasting

In commemoration of Muhammad receiving the Qur'an, Muslims are required to observe fasting, called in Arabic **sawm**, during daylight hours throughout the month of Ramadan. This is designed to cultivate greater submission to God. Not a bit of food or drink may be taken for the entire daylight hours. (Some particularly pious Muslims won't even swallow their own saliva.) Sexual intercourse during the daylight is also forbidden, as are some types of amusement. Eating, drinking, and sex are permissible in the morning while it is still dark and after sunset. Because leap days are not inserted into the Muslim lunar calendar, Ramadan moves through the seasons. When it falls in winter, fasting is comparatively easy. But when Ramadan falls in the longer, hot days of summer—and most Muslims live in tropical or subtropical lands—it calls for much more effort.

Fasting in Ramadan is done in a humane way, as are all Muslim pillars. Infants and young children are excused from the fast, but many students in school observe it. The hunger produced can be a challenge to learning. People who are sick, those infirm from old age, and soldiers on active duty may fast when they are better able to do so. When it is impossible to make up the fast, one may substitute a significant act of mercy or charity. When the month of Ramadan is finished, Muslims celebrate the Eid-al-Fitr festival with a special service in the mosque. Families feast together during the day and exchange gifts in decorated homes.

12-5d Almsgiving

The Qur'an urges all Muslims to give generously to the poor, such as orphans and widows (for example, 2:43), but as with the other four items that became traditional pillars, it doesn't lay down specific requirements. The Shari'a made this generosity a formal obligation with specific rules, and it has become so important that it is the fourth pillar of Islam, called **zakat**, "almsgiving" or "charity." Although it is an obligation, Muslims are expected to be generous from the heart, out of liberality. In most Islamic lands it is a monetary obligation collected by a representative of the umma, often a department of the government. It is then distributed to poor families, widows and orphans, stranded travelers, and others in need. In addition, it can be used in jihad for the defense and support of Muslims under threat.

> *Muslims are expected to be generous from the heart, out of liberality.*

In places such as Europe and North America, zakat is based on voluntary giving to the mosque or an Islamic charity. The rate for zakat in all parts of the world is not large, especially when compared to the system of tithing (10 percent of income) that it resembles, laid down in the Jewish Bible. Zakat is one-fortieth (2.5 percent) of the value of one's assets, not counting necessary personal possessions such as homes, animals, vehicles, or clothing. Because every observant Muslim gives zakat, it generates large sums of money in the international Muslim community. Zakat has provided Islamic countries with the resources for comprehensive programs of social support and development that are unique among world religions and reinforce solidarity among Muslims of different classes. It is the principal way in which Muslim lands promote a fuller measure of social justice.

12-5e Pilgrimage

The last of the Five Pillars of Islam is pilgrimage to Mecca. A Muslim is required to participate in the official pilgrimage to Mecca, called the **hajj**, at least once in his or her lifetime. This requirement applies to both men and women, but traditionally the great majority of pilgrims are men. As with the other pillars, it is imposed humanely: In this case, one who is unable to make the pilgrimage may designate someone else to do it on his or her behalf. The last month of the Muslim calendar, called al-Hajj, is the official period of pilgrimage. Muslims can go to Mecca at other times when it isn't so crowded, but these visits are not considered a hajj. Muhammad at first had his followers pray facing Jerusalem, and some Muslims did pilgrimages to Jerusalem as well. After his conflict with the Jews of Medina, he made Mecca, and particularly the Kaaba in

sawm [sahwm]
Ritual fasting done during daylight hours throughout the month of Ramadan

zakat [zah-KAHT]
"Almsgiving" or "charity"; mandatory contribution of one-fortieth of one's income to support Islam

hajj [hahj] Pilgrimage to Mecca

Dome of the Rock mosque in Jerusalem

prominent rock now inside the mosque. The first mosque on this temple hill was built slightly before the Dome of the Rock and was known as Al-Aqsa (ahl-AHK-suh), "the farthest" mosque from Mecca at the time it was built. Shi'as have their own holy places of pilgrimage, including Qom in Iran and Karbala in Iraq. They also make the hajj to Mecca, but sometimes violence has erupted between Sunnis and Shi'as during the hajj. Muslims have designated other centers of pilgrimage, but no other place comes close to Mecca in importance. A man who has journeyed to Mecca on the hajj receives an additional, honorary personal name, **Hajji**. The importance of the hajj for Islam and the world has been well summarized by Robert Bianchi, who as a Muslim made the hajj himself: "Creating a global community seems less daunting after making a pilgrimage, especially one that stirs us—physically and spiritually—in a single pot with all humanity."[8]

Hajji [HAHJ-ee] "Pilgrim," additional personal name given to a man who has taken the hajj

the Grand Mosque there, the geographic center of Islam. (For an account of activities during the hajj, see the section that begins this chapter, "Your Visit to Mecca.")

Watch a CNN introduction to the hajj.

> *"Creating a global community seems less daunting after making a pilgrimage, especially one that stirs us—physically and spiritually—in a single pot with all humanity."*
> —Robert Bianchi

Other cities are centers of other pilgrimage for some Muslims. Medina is the second-holiest city in Islam, especially because it was the home of Muhammad for the second part of his prophetic career and the place where he is buried. The Dome of the Rock mosque in Jerusalem, which Muslims call the "Noble Sanctuary," was built in the seventh century. Muhammad made his ascent to heaven during his lifetime from a

Tents for hajj pilgrims on the Plains of Mina outside Mecca

8 Robert R. Bianchi, *Guests of God: Pilgrimage and Politics in the Islamic World* (New York: Oxford University Press, 2004), 272.

Learning Outcome 12-6

Explain the main aspects of Muslim life around the world today, especially in Europe and North America.

12-6 Islam around the World Today

Chicago's Mosque Maryam is host to Louis Farrakhan, leader of the Nation of Islam. He strongly defends the late Libyan leader Muammar Qaddafi against military attacks begun in 2011 by the United States and other NATO nations in support of a rebellion against Qaddafi. The Nation of Islam is one of North America's oldest African American Muslim groups. Calling him a brother in Islam who has been supportive of the cause of the Nation of Islam, Farrakhan asks, "What kind of brother would I be if a man has been that way to me, and to us, and when he's in trouble I refuse to raise my voice in his defense?" Although this is greeted with cheers by his followers in the mosque, other observers wonder if these controversial, attention-grabbing statements are not an effort to regain strength for Farrakhan's faltering movement. The Nation of Islam has, according to many experts, lost about half of its membership to more traditional Muslim groups since around 1995, when it was able to rally a huge crowd for its Million Man March on Washington, D.C.

Islam has typically been spread by near-continuous, intentional movement from Arabia and other historic points to the farthest reaches of the world. China has a substantial Muslim population in its western and northern sections (see "A Closer Look: Difficulties of the Hajj for Muslims in Western China"). Europe has a large Muslim population, to the extent that Islam is the second-largest religion in Europe after Christianity. Muslim Europeans are mostly immigrants since the Second World War, but a native Muslim population in the Balkans has existed for centuries, because that area was under the long-term control of the Ottoman Empire. In North America, however, the picture is more mixed. Some slaves brought here from Africa were probably Muslims—estimates range widely from 5 percent to almost 50 percent—but they were unable to maintain their faith through the generations due to the harsh conditions of slavery and their owners' insistence that slaves share their masters' Christian religion. In the early twentieth century, a new "Black Muslim" movement grew in North American soil.

12-6a Islam in Europe

Europe has around 13 million Muslim residents today. France has the largest number of Muslims in Western Europe, with 6 to 7 million Muslims making up 8 to 10 percent of its population. Most French Muslims come from the former French colonies in North Africa. France is followed by Germany; most of its 4.5 million Muslims are Turkish "guest workers" who do unskilled labor. The United Kingdom has 2.7 million Muslims from its former empire, and Italy has 1.5 million from Africa. Aside from Turkey (most of which lies outside Europe geographically but which is in the process of becoming a member of the European Union), the only European nation to have a majority of Muslims is Albania. Bosnia and Macedonia, also in the Balkans, have large Muslim minorities.

A series of violent events by radical Muslims has taken place in the past decade or so: the murder of Dutch filmmaker Theo van Gogh for perceived insults to Islam; the 2004 Madrid train bombings; the controversy over Danish cartoons picturing Muhammad, with attempts to kill the cartoonist; and numerous terrorist attacks in the UK, especially the July 7, 2005, bombings of London's mass-transportation system. Since these events, scrutiny of European Muslims and controversy over their place in European society has grown exponentially. Just as important for Muslim life in Europe today are matters of Muslim identity and respect, especially the wearing of the hijab. The French prohibition of Muslim head scarves in schools and other public buildings is particularly controversial. In general, European Muslims are not as integrated into wider national life as North American Muslims are.

12-6b Muslim Migration to North America

From about 1950, millions of Muslims immigrated to North America from various nations in the Middle East, and some from British Commonwealth lands in south Asia have come to Canada. Some smaller immigration had occurred before 1950, but Muslims generally entered after that year. They can be found in virtually every city in North America, with more substantial numbers in large cities on the East and West Coasts. The proportion of Sunnis to Shi'as in North America is about the same as in the wider Muslim world—about 85 percent to 15 percent. Dearborn, Michigan, a suburb of Detroit, has the largest population of Muslims outside metropolitan New York City. Canada has Muslims in every major city, with larger numbers in the cities of

Difficulties of the Hajj for Muslims in Western China

In the province of Xinjiang (zin-JYAHNG) in northwestern China, practicing Muslims from the Uighur (WEE-guhr) ethnic group of Turkic peoples have a challenging time participating in the pilgrimage to Mecca. Communist Party authorities there want to discourage Muslims from going to Mecca, thinking that they may be exposed to more-radical forms of Islam and would return to form separatist movements in Xinjiang.

Uighur Muslims are prohibited from arranging their own trips for the hajj, either individually or in groups. To be among the fortunate few who receive permission for a government-approved hajj, one must pay a deposit of $6,000, refunded upon one's return, and about $4,000 for the trip. Relatively few Chinese Muslims in the province can afford such an expense; the large cost ensures that only a few thousand who can afford it will go on the hajj. Communist Party rules also state that applicants must be fifty to seventy years old, have a clean criminal record, and "love the country." The trips are led by imams deemed most loyal to the Chinese government.

The regional Communist Party restricts Islam in other ways as well. All students and government workers are required to eat and drink during the daylight hours of Ramadan; fasting is prohibited. Prayer in public is also forbidden. Workers in government and government-controlled businesses aren't allowed to attend services in mosques; women in businesses are forbidden to wear head scarves. No Muslims may teach the faith in private, Arabic is taught only in government schools, and all Qur'ans must be the government-approved version. Although this government control is ostensibly to keep down religious opposition to Communist rule, many people are convinced that it is doing exactly the opposite. Western human-rights groups and some Muslim nations have been sharply critical of these policies.

Uighurs at Friday noon prayers

© PETE NIESEN/SHUTTERSTOCK.COM

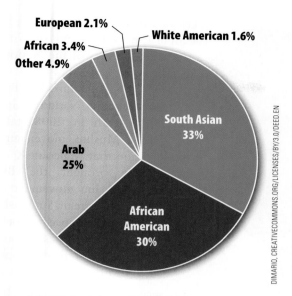

European 2.1%

African 3.4%

Other 4.9%

White American 1.6%

South Asian 33%

Arab 25%

African American 30%

DIMARIO, CREATIVECOMMONS.ORG/LICENSES/BY/3.0/DEED.EN

Figure 12.5 Ethnicity of Muslims in the United States, 2012

Ontario, Alberta, and British Columbia. Today there are 6 to 7 million Muslims in North America with origins in other nations, most from the Middle East. The majority have no formal affiliation to a mosque (in lands that are officially Muslim, one doesn't "belong to a mosque"), but they are nonetheless practicing Muslims.

Our knowledge of Muslims in the United States is a bit imprecise, because the U.S. Census does not collect information about religious affiliation. However, scientific surveys have filled in much of this gap. A 2007 Pew Research Center survey of Muslim Americans found that about two-thirds are foreign born and have immigrated since 1980. A second generation of Muslims is now arising in the United States, facing the same sort of intergenerational issues that other immigrant groups have faced. Of the one-third of Muslim Americans born in the United States, the majority are converts and African American. In 2005, about 100,000 people from Islamic countries—most of them Muslims—became permanent residents of the United States, more than in any single year since 1980. A majority of these are on a path to citizenship. As a result of immigration since the 1950s, Islam in North America now more closely reflects the global diversity of Islam than at any time in the past.

> *Muslims in North America are more educated and affluent than other Americans.*

A recent survey by the Zogby polling company showed that Muslims are prospering in the United States. They are significantly more educated than the national average, with incomes to match. Some 60 percent of them hold at least one academic degree, and about 40 percent have an income over $75,000. As stated above, compared to European Muslims, North American Muslims are more assimilated into wider cultural life. The United States and Canada have largely extended to Muslims the same rights to practice religion that they have extended to others. U.S. Muslims practice the pillars of Islam with little need for adaptation, although observing afternoon prayers has occasionally been problematic for Muslims working in businesses and factories. Some have worked for improved relations between Muslim and non-Muslim Americans. Many scholars have held out the hope that North American Muslims might show other Muslims how they can lead faithful religious lives in a predominantly non-Muslim environment.

Nation of Islam "Black Muslim" movement in North America begun by W.D. Fard and now led by Louis Farrakhan.

See an interview with Imam Zaid Shakir, a leading U.S. Muslim.

12-6c The Nation of Islam and the American Society of Muslims

About one-third of North American Muslims today are African Americans who have joined either mainstream Islam or a sectarian Islamic movement. The largest sectarian group is the Black Muslim movement. In 1930, Elijah Poole, an African American living in Detroit, met W. D. Fard, a man of either Iranian or Turkish descent who preached Islam as the only true religion for African Americans. Poole converted to this movement, changing his name to Elijah Muhammad. He effectively spread Fard's teachings, and their movement grew rapidly. Fard disappeared in 1934, and Elijah Muhammad took over. The movement then became known as "The Lost-Found Nation of Islam in the Wilderness of North America," or the **Nation of Islam** for short, and spread to many urban areas in the northern United States. Its appeal to prisoners was especially potent, and still is today. Its five main teachings are as follows:

- W. D. Fard is an incarnation of God, and Elijah Muhammad is God's prophet.

- African Americans are descended from a tribe called Shabazz, the ancient pre-Islamic inhabitants of Mecca; they are by nature good.

- White people are evil and oppressive, the creation of an evil scientist named Yakub.

- Black people ought to recapture their African Muslim roots by submitting to the Five Pillars of Islam and opposing white oppression.

- Black people who submit to God will rule the world, and white people will get the punishment they so richly deserve.

Several obvious differences exist between these Nation of Islam teachings and the teachings of other Muslims. Other Muslims sharply reject the ideas of an incarnation of God in any human and a new prophet equal to Muhammad; they view both as idolatry. Moreover, race-based beliefs are not a legitimate part of Islam. On the other hand, the Nation of Islam appreciates Islamic practices such as the Five Pillars. Despite being largely ignored—or considered heretical—by the rest of the Islamic world, the Nation of Islam became a potent force in the African American community in the United States. It gave hope for a better life to many oppressed people, with resources to fight against drug abuse, poverty, and racism. But it had a race-based message that was problematic for fellow North Americans and for the rest of Islam.

In 1960, a Muslim led a significant change in the Nation of Islam. Malcolm X (born Malcolm Little) went to Mecca on pilgrimage and saw a harmony between peoples of different races. This experience, along with his growing disillusionment with Elijah Muhammad, gave him a new vision for African American Muslims: God did not want one race to rule another race, but for all races to live together in harmony. He began a new organization of Muslims not based on racial hostility. Malcolm's new message was appealing to many African

Malcolm X, American Muslim reformer, in 1964

LIBRARY OF CONGRESS, U.S. NEWS & WORLD REPORT MAGAZINE COLLECTION, LC-U9-11695-FRAME #5

American Muslims, and it survived his death in 1965 at the hands of two disgruntled members of the Nation of Islam.

Warith Muhammad, Elijah's son, then led the Nation of Islam until his death in 2008, taking the Black Muslim movement in the direction that Malcolm X had begun. He brought the Black Muslim movement into mainstream Sunni Islam. He renounced all beliefs that Sunnis considered heretical, adopting authentically Muslim beliefs and practices. Muhammad began cooperating with worldwide Islam. He permitted American Muslims in his movement to participate in politics and vote, and he abolished the paramilitary wing of the Nation of Islam. This movement has had three names, currently the **American Society of Muslims**. These changes resulted in his movement receiving large amounts of Arab financial support. Islamic centers then spread throughout the United States, serving new immigrants from the Arab world and African American Muslims.

This reform produced an almost-immediate reaction. In 1978, Louis Farrakhan (FAIR-uh-kahn) moved some African American Muslims back to a revived Nation of Islam. Farrakhan occasionally used strong rhetoric, especially against Jews. He continued the efforts to free African Americans from white economic power, as well as educational and private-policing activities to keep their neighborhoods free from drugs and drug-related crimes. Farrakhan's movement is based in Chicago, but three other groups claiming to be the authentic Nation of Islam are based in Baltimore, Detroit, and Atlanta. Today, most African American Muslims belong not to these Nation of Islam groups but to the American Society of Muslims, where they are mainstream Sunnis. Despite its small size relative to the American Society of Muslims and the fact that it is much smaller now than before 1960, the Nation of Islam is an active and occasionally vocal part of American religious life today.

American Society of Muslims American Muslim reform movement founded by Malcolm X, with mainstream Sunni features

12-6d Muslim Life in the United States after 9/11

On September 11, 2001, **al-Qaeda** ("the base" of jihad), an organization of radical Muslims based in Afghanistan, launched coordinated attacks on the United States. That morning, nineteen members of al-Qaeda from various Middle Eastern nations who had been living in "sleeper cells" in the United States hijacked four large commercial passenger airliners soon after they took off from airports in the eastern United States. The hijackers crashed two of the airplanes into the main towers of the World Trade Center in New York City, causing both towers to collapse unexpectedly about two hours later. They crashed a third airplane into the Pentagon, the U.S. military headquarters in Washington, D.C. The fourth plane crashed into a field in western Pennsylvania when its passengers and crew bravely tried to retake control of the plane as it was heading east, probably to another prominent target in Washington, D.C. Excluding the hijackers, 2,974 people died; another 24 are missing and presumed dead; and several thousand were injured. The great majority of deaths and injuries were of civilians, including citizens of over ninety different nations who worked in the World Trade Center.

> *Osama Bin Laden recorded messages in the cadences of the Qur'an, and liked to be photographed living in caves as Muhammad once did.*

What is this al-Qaeda organization? Osama bin Laden (oh-SAM-uh bin LAHD-en, 1957–2011) founded it to oppose with violence those he saw as a threat to true Islam. A Saudi Arabian banished from his land for extremism, he took up residence with the other leaders of his movement in Afghanistan, where al-Qaeda secretly bankrolled the Taliban government. He mounted first verbal and then physical attacks against

*An issue of Louis Farrakhan's newspaper, **The Final Call***

© JEFFREY BLACKLER/ALAMY

a variety of targets, with strong, religiously based opposition to the influence of Western nations in Muslim nations and opposition to the presence of the Jewish state of Israel. Bin Laden typically spoke in taped addresses in the poetic cadences of the Qur'an, and he liked to be photographed living in caves as Muhammad once did. Al-Qaeda brought something new to Islam: continual attacks on non-Muslims. Al-Qaeda and its splinter groups have carried out dozens of other attacks from the 1990s until today, on civilian targets in both Western and Muslim nations (especially England, Spain, Saudi Arabia, India, Indonesia, and various east African countries), attacks designed to terrorize their people and influence government policy. The victims have been Muslims as much as Westerners or native Christians or Jews. A group related to al-Qaeda took control of the northern half of Mali, and ran it with strict enforcement of Shari'a until it was ousted by French forces in 2013. As a predominantly Sunni movement, however, al-Qaeda has gathered only a little support from Shi'as, and even the majority of Sunnis in the world do not approve of it.

The attacks on September 11, 2001, deeply shocked not only the United States, but also other nations of the world. The United States responded by leading a broad coalition of international military forces in invading Afghanistan to depose the Taliban and destroy the home base of the al-Qaeda network. The hunt for Osama bin Laden lasted ten years after that, ending with his 2011 death in a U.S. military raid on his hideout in Pakistan. The 2001 federal "Patriot Act" gave the U.S. government far greater powers than previously permitted in gathering intelligence on suspected terrorists in America and around the world. Many other nations also increased their antiterrorism efforts and stepped up military preparations. Muslim organizations in the United States were swift to

al-Qaeda [al KIGH-duh] "The base" (of jihad), contemporary terrorist movement begun by Osama bin Laden

Palestinian Muslims in Gaza protest the killing of Osama bin Laden. They carry a sign with images of bin Laden and the burning World Trade Center.

condemn the attacks on 9/11 and called upon Muslim Americans to help the victims. In addition to large donations of funds, many Islamic organizations held blood drives and provided medical assistance, food, and housing for victims of 9/11. Some Muslim groups in the United States have even worked effectively with law enforcement agencies to identify North American Muslims who may be fostering violence.

One result of 9/11 has been a rise in anti-Muslim prejudice and actions by some American citizens who suppose that most Muslims are active or potential

A Closer Look:

Muslim Views of Islamic-Western Conflict

The largest study of public opinion in the Muslim world was completed by the Gallup organization in 2007, and was published as *Who Speaks for Islam? What a Billion Muslims Really Think.*[9] It is based on six years of research and more than fifty thousand interviews of Muslims in more than thirty-five nations that are officially Muslim, predominantly Muslim, or have sizable Muslim populations. This study carefully surveyed around 90 percent of the world's Muslim community—the "billion Muslims" of the title—about their attitudes to the conflict, perceived and real, between Islam and the West. It also collected comparative data from the U.S. population as a whole.

The results of this study, as outlined by the publisher, may surprise you:

- Muslims and Americans are equally likely to reject attacks on civilians as morally wrong in all circumstances.

- Large majorities of Muslims would guarantee free speech if it were up to them to write a new constitution.

- Large majorities of Muslims say that religious leaders should have no direct role in drafting laws or governing.

- Muslims state that what they least admire about the West is its perceived moral decay and breakdown of traditional values. Ironically, this is identical to what Americans themselves say when asked this question.

- Muslims say they want prosperity and security, and see conflict and violence as harming that goal.

- Muslims say that Westerners can improve relations with their societies by changing their negative, stereotyped views toward Muslims and by learning to respect Islam.

The research suggests that Muslims and non-Muslim Americans have more in common than what they may think. But as authors Esposito and Mogahed caution, most Muslims do not live in democratic societies where their opinions are taken seriously, and anti-Muslim voices in the United States continue to have an outsized influence on U.S. public opinion. They conclude, "Until and unless decision makers listen directly to the people and gain an accurate understanding of this conflict, extremists on all sides will continue to gain ground."

---

[9] John Esposito and Dalia Mogahed, *Who Speaks for Islam? What a Billion Muslims Really Think* (New York: Gallup Press, 2007).

terrorists, or aid terrorists. (Other Western nations—including Germany, France, and Britain—have even stronger popular prejudice against Muslims that goes far back before 9/11.) This is upsetting to American Muslims, particularly because the 9/11 attacks were the work of foreign Muslims who came to this country to carry out attacks (see "A Closer Look: Muslim Views of Islamic-Western Conflict"). The al-Qaeda network has sometimes obtained help from ordinary Muslims in Europe. Also, the latest troubling trend in Europe and Asia is that some Muslims born and raised in non-Muslim nations are now launching their own terror attacks in looser connection with al-Qaeda, as they did in the 2005 attacks by suicide bombers on the London mass-transport system. India is particularly plagued with violence from native Muslim groups, some related to al-Qaeda and some not. So far, there have been only a few cases of this homegrown violence in North America, although 2009 did see an uptick with at least two dozen U.S. residents charged with terrorism-related crimes. In 2013 two Muslims born in the Russian area of Chechnya bombed the Boston Marathon, resulting in three deaths and dozens of serious injuries.

More widely troubling to many American Muslims has been the systematic monitoring of Muslim individuals and institutions. The New York City police department's active spying on mosques in New York City and even in some neighboring states provoked strong criticism from Muslims and many others when it was revealed in 2012. The U.S. government has especially investigated those Muslim charitable organizations that distribute abroad the funds raised from American Muslims, some of it from zakat. Although some funds have indeed gone into the shadowy network of terror, the vast majority of funds do not, and many American Muslims are disturbed over this perceived interference in their exercise of a pillar of their religion. However, Muslims in the United States and Canada are increasingly working with religious and civic organizations for better Muslim relations with the wider public. They are hopeful that relations are in fact improving, although the progress isn't always steady. (A setback of sorts came in 2010 with the conflict over building a mosque near the site of the al-Qaeda attacks on New York City and ensuing threats by a few non-Muslim Americans to burn the Qur'an in opposition to Islam.) Another, constructive reaction to the 9/11 attacks and their aftermath has been an increase in the study of Islam in colleges and universities—of which you are now a part.

Read a widely reprinted newspaper story, "American Muslims Ask, Will We Ever Belong?"

Read the story of a young Arab American man from Alabama who became a "jihadist."

Watch a video about the conversion to Islam of Hispanics in Los Angeles.

Study Tools 12

Ready to study? In the book you can:

- Review Learning Outcome answers and glossary terms with the tear-out Chapter Review card.

Or you can go online to CourseMate, at www.cengagebrain.com, for these resources:

- Chapter quizzes to prepare for tests
- Interactive flashcards of all glossary terms
- A timeline of events for this chapter
- An eBook with introductions, interactive quizzes, and live links for all web resources in the chapter

CHAPTER 13

Encountering New Religious Movements: Modern Ways to Alternative Meanings

BONNIE VAN VOORST © CENGAGE LEARNING

Learning Outcomes

After studying this chapter, you will be able to do the following:

13-1 Evaluate the different names for new religious movements.

13-2 Summarize the common features of new religious movements.

13-3 Survey the distribution of new religious movements in the world today.

13-4 State and explain the teachings and practices of Falun Gong.

13-5 State and explain the history, teachings, and practices of the Church of Jesus Christ of Latter-day Saints.

13-6 State and explain the teachings and practices of Scientology.

Study Tools

After you read this chapter, go to the Study Tools at the end of the chapter, page 358.

©JSTOCK PHOTO.COM/STEVE GEER

Many NRMs are controversial, but several world religions today were also controversial when they were new.

Your Visit to Temple Square, Salt Lake City, Utah

The Church of Jesus Christ of Latter-day Saints (LDS), whose members are popularly called the Mormons, is headquartered in Salt Lake City. Temple Square is named for the main LDS temple that majestically stands there. The other church buildings are impressive as well, and are all near Temple Square. Lest you think that the LDS church is only interested in spiritual things, you notice that next to Temple Square is the billion-dollar City Creek Center mall owned by the LDS church that opened in 2012, complete with high-end stores and restaurants, business offices, and condominiums.

The granite temple with its spires soars over the downtown. Only LDS members in good standing can go inside an LDS temple (and this lends a mysterious air to it). The opportunity is the high point of any Latter-day Saint's visit to Salt Lake City, but there is still plenty to do for non-Mormons. The LDS church has always been intent on spreading its faith, so it has built several other impressive buildings where non-Mormons can learn more about the LDS church. There are two visitor centers where you can pick up literature and see exhibits. You can experience the LDS emphasis on sacred music at the Mormon Tabernacle building—the concert hall for the world-renowned Mormon Tabernacle Choir—or take in a concert in the Assembly Hall. You could walk around the formal gardens. Just north of Temple Square is the Conference Center, where the main representative body of the LDS church meets twice a year. Non-Mormons often come away from Salt Lake City with mixed feelings on the LDS church, especially that it is both secretive and open.

Because you're interested in your genealogy, you've been looking forward to seeing the Family History Library near Temple Square. Even though you're only visiting, you can investigate your family tree in the genealogical collection housed there, the largest genealogical database in the world. Staff in the library can help you in your research, which is all done by computer. It's a little unnerving to you to hear that the LDS church has collected genealogical information from every corner of the world, perhaps for every person who has ever lived and left behind a genealogical record. But you're happy for it too, because it makes for the best genealogical searching in the world.

Finally, you walk nearby to see the Beehive House dating from 1855. It's the home of Brigham Young, the second leader of the LDS church, for whom Brigham Young University is named. Free tours are available to go through the home and see how Brigham Young and his family lived.

Take a Google Earth™ tour of LDS sites.

The academic term **new religious movements (NRMs)** denotes religious groups that arose in modern times and have sufficient size, longevity, and impact to merit academic study. (*Modern* here doesn't mean "contemporary" or even "recent," but in the modern age of history.) These movements have been studied from the first, especially by sociologists, but the term *new*

new religious movements (NRMs)
Religious groups that arose in modern times and now have sufficient size, longevity, and cultural impact to merit academic study

 Baha'i Temple in Wilmette, Illinois. Baha'i arose from Islam in the 1800s, and its temples resemble large mosques.

Temple Square in Salt Lake City, Utah

religious movements is a newcomer in the field of religious studies. Most recently published encyclopedias, handbooks, and textbooks on religion use this term and provide information about the groups to which it refers.[1] More than five hundred groups around the world today have been identified as NRMs. Each year sees the birth of dozens more religious movements, and also the death of some. This chapter will first give a general description of NRMs and briefly discuss several of them to illustrate the description. Then it will focus in more detail on three NRMs that have become significant worldwide. These three are treated here to illustrate the general description offered, which students can subsequently apply to other NRMs.

Watch an introduction to a new religious movement with Christian origins.

Some things that students often wonder about NRMs can be listed quickly here to stir thought and imagination:

- The inclusion of these groups in this chapter isn't intended to imply that they see themselves as new religious movements. Often they don't, and some even view this term as uncomplimentary. They don't usually understand themselves as a "new" movement, but as a restoration of a religion.

- Some of these NRMs are highly controversial. Many were persecuted or prosecuted in their early years by religious and civil authorities. However, several world religions were also controversial when they were new.

- World religions examined in this book usually go back so far in human history that we can't fully know about their origins. Because the study of NRMs shows us contemporary religions as they are born and begin to grow, they are fertile fields of study for scholars and students alike. Eileen Barker, who coined the term "new religious movements," said that NRMs are "interesting because you can see a whole lot of social processes going on: conversion, leaving, bureaucratization, leadership squabbles, ways in which authority is used, [and] ways in which people can change."[2]

- Because these NRM movements are contemporary, a lot of detail is available on many of them, so much that it's sometimes overwhelming. Some of this detail will be dealt with below. But students should keep their focus on the general features of NRMs as discussed and illustrated here.

The study of NRMs often proves to be a strong test of a student's impartiality and objectivity. Some of these movements are in the news and on the Web today, and not always for complimentary reasons. Careful students of religion will want to recognize any preconceived notions they may have about NRMs, and deal with them. You can make evaluations of NRMs, as of older religions, but you must earn the right to evaluate an NRM by studying it carefully first. In other words, before you conclude, "That's a weird group," you should learn about it and then try to think like one of its "insiders": What is it about this movement that makes it appealing to some?

[1] For an excellent concise overview of NRMs, see W. H. Swatus, Jr., ed., *Encyclopedia of Religion and Society* (Walnut Creek, CA: AltaMira, 1998), 328–333. For an anthology, see Michael Ashcraft and Dereck Daschke, eds., *New Religious Movements: A Documentary Reader* (New York: NYU Press, 2005).

[2] Quoted in Toby Lester, "Oh, Gods!" *The Atlantic* (February, 2002), http://theatlantic.com/magazine/archive/2002/02/oh-gods/2412/, accessed 4/25/2011.

"You can see a whole lot of social processes going on [in NRMs]: conversion, leaving, bureaucratization, leadership squabbles, ways in which authority is used, [and] ways in which people can change."—Eileen Barker

Because many religions are treated in this chapter, it has an organization that differs from that of most previous chapters. First, we'll discuss the variety of names that scholars have given to this type of religion, and then explain why this book calls them "new religious movements." Second, we'll draw out important common characteristics of NRMs. Third, we'll examine their world distribution. Finally, we'll look in some detail at three important NRMs.

Learning Outcome 13-1

Evaluate the different names for new religious movements.

13-1 Names for This Type of Religion

Naming the overall type of the religions we're dealing with in this chapter has been a challenge for scholarship. Some scholars even ask, Why it is necessary at all to give them one name, if a comprehensive name distorts them? We cannot go deeply into that complicated issue here; suffice it to say that religious studies on the whole has seen how we label these religions as important to how we think about them, so we must deal with this issue in our discussion here.

The first names that were given to this type of religion were *cults* and *sects*. These two terms overlap to some extent. **Sect** derives from the Latin term for "cut off" and refers to a new, small group that has emerged from within an established religion. Many of today's world religions began as reforming sects within a larger religion and only later grew separate. **Cult** refers to a religious group that is extreme in its dedication to its beliefs, often living communally or semi-communally under the control of an authoritarian leader. The name often carries the connotation of a dangerous religion.

Up until about 1980, these two names were commonly used in Christian churches and scholarship to denote controversial groups that had separated from Protestant churches. Although the terms have some validity, they have become so prejudicial that most religious studies scholars today don't use them to characterize new religious groups. Other, more recent terms such as **alternative religious movements** are used, sometimes in reference to more long-standing NRMs from the 1800s and early 1900s, keeping *new religious movements* for more-recent groups such as Scientology and Falun Gong. However, all NRMs, whether founded in the 1800s or in 2013, present alternative religious meanings, as the subtitle of this chapter suggests. The term **marginal religious movements** is also used to refer to new religious groups. But this may prompt you to ask, *Alternative* and *marginal* to what? Some of these movements are so large that they can't be considered marginal—for example, the LDS church, perhaps the fastest-growing religious group in the world, or Falun Gong. A final term for this type of religion is **emergent religions**, which highlights their contemporary origin and ongoing development. They are "emerging" in our time.

Gradually, scholars of religion and sociologists settled on the term *new religious movements*, which we have defined above. Although it been generally accepted by religion scholars, it has been criticized for three reasons. First, how does this term distinguish NRMs from reform movements in established religions (as Buddhism and Christianity started), especially before the reform movements become a separate religion? Second, even though it looks neutral, it has occasionally been used with a put-down tone. Third, to call them "religious movements" may imply that they are not full-fledged religions, which they usually are.

sect New, small group that has emerged from an established or larger religion

cult Religion or religious sect that is extremist and under the control of an authoritarian leader

alternative religious movements One current name for NRMs, especially for the long-standing NRMs from the 1800s and early 1900s

marginal religious movements Another current name for NRMs, suggesting that they are less important than world religions

emergent religions Another current name for NRMs, highlighting their contemporary origin and ongoing development

Despite these questions, the term *new religious movements* is widely used today. "New" is ambiguous, of course, but these movements are indeed "new" compared to the ancient origins of other religions. A consensus among religion scholars takes "new" to mean within the last two centuries or so. *Nova Religio*, the premier scholarly journal for the study of NRMs, covers them from 1800 to the present. The term *new religious movements* holds out the nuanced understanding that in time some of today's NRMs may become regarded as established religions.

Examine the home page of *Nova Religio*.

13-2 Common Features of New Religious Movements

> Many NRMs *are rooted in ancient traditions, but they arise in the modern world and address modern concerns.*

Although there's a great deal of diversity among NRMs, they have a number of common features. First, NRMs are *founded by a single powerful leader*. This is true of all the NRMs named in this chapter. The founder is often believed to have extraordinary, even supernatural, powers or insights. He or she is skilled at organizing and guiding a movement. If the NRM is based in a literate culture, the leader typically writes authoritative literature that, as the group's sacred scripture, guides the movement when the founder dies.

Second, NRMs can *spring up quickly and disappear quickly*. Because they are founded by a single person, they emerge quickly, in contrast to many older religions that developed over generations,

even centuries, under multiple leaders. Sociologists estimate that more than thirty NRMs begin in the United States annually, but many of them don't last for more than a decade, some of them even less. At times, NRMs disappear in violent tragedy, as we'll discuss below. Those that survive often face a threat when their founder dies. When an NRM is able to last for centuries, it loses *new* and *movement* and becomes known simply as a religion.

Third, NRMs *start small but can become international movements*. Established world religions usually started small as well, but this is the rule with all NRMs. Some NRMs from the 1800s that survived are strong in numbers today: the Church of Jesus Christ of Latter-day Saints, the Jehovah's Witness church, and others. Even more-recent movements such as Falun Gong can quickly gain an international following and become worldwide religious movements. No study of world religions is complete without a consideration of NRMs.

Fourth, most NRMs are *tightly organized*. Because they are controlled from the top, and because they understand themselves as countercultural movements, NRMs often make strong demands of their followers. Members live for the group and the group directs their lives. NRMs can become substitutes for one's family and friends. This emotionally intense religious life with alternative views of marriage and family life is the main reason why some NRMs are popularly known as "cults." When NRMs encounter opposition, their organization becomes even tighter.

Fifth, NRMs are *religious responses to the modern world*. Other world religions come from the past, often from ancient times. NRMs are not only new in the sense of recent. Although many NRMs claim to

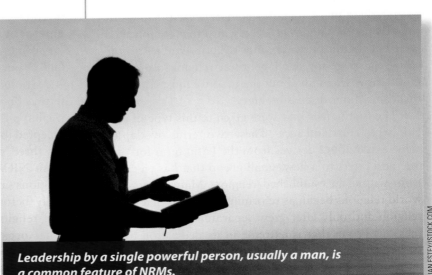

Leadership by a single powerful person, usually a man, is a common feature of NRMs.

© JUAN ESTEY/ISTOCK.COM

be rooted in older traditions, they arise in the modern world and address modern concerns in new ways. NRMs are often more media-savvy than established world religions. For example, the Church of Scientology has all its scriptures in electronic form, and has probably the most sophisticated website of any religious group. Moreover, many NRMs incorporate scientific understandings, real or claimed, into their teachings and practices that older religions do not. NRMs are responses to various aspects of modern life: loss of religious meaning, religious and cultural pluralism, and the scientific worldview. Because the overall number of NRMs and the numbers of believers in them are increasing, NRMs are obviously making an effective appeal in the modern world.

Finally, NRMs are usually *countercultural* in their response to the modern world. They move against the mainstream currents of society, especially as societies have been shaped by the dominant historic religions. This countercultural quality often makes them controversial in a whole culture, not just with established or traditional religions in that culture. To illustrate, the Unification Church and Scientology are often accused of disrupting traditional family ties of their new members. The Latter-day Saints movement encountered wide cultural opposition in the 1800s for its espousal of polygamy, and pockets of polygamy among non-LDS Mormons still make headlines today.

Learning Outcome 13-3

Survey the distribution of new religious movements in the world today.

13-3 New Religious Movements in the World Today: A Survey

Many people in the Western world suppose that new religious movements are primarily a Western thing and aren't found in other areas of the world. Nothing could be further from the truth. As this section will show, NRMs are spread throughout the world as widely as the older, established religions are.

13-3a NRMs Founded in the Western World

NRMs in the West are widely diverse. Most of them come from Christianity, the dominant religion in the West, but many don't. The following survey organizes this diversity into certain categories, but an NRM can often be classified into more than one category.

Some NRMs are shaped by **apocalyptic** belief that the world will end soon and God will bring a new, perfect society in place of the old one. Many world religions also have apocalyptic features. However, modern Christian apocalypticism, especially **millenarianism**—a belief in some forms of Protestantism that Christ will establish and lead a thousand-year reign of peace on earth—has been a foundation of many NRMs in the West. Even in Asia, a millenarian impulse for a golden age on this earth occasionally surfaces, with or without Christian influence.

Two of the earliest significant NRMs in the United States were the Seventh-Day Adventists and the Jehovah's Witnesses. William Miller (1782–1849) prophesied that Christ would come to earth to establish his kingdom in 1843 or 1844. The failure of his prediction didn't deter many of his followers, who still today believe in the imminent return of Jesus. The Seventh-Day Adventist Church was started by one of

apocalyptic [uh-POC-uh-LIP-tick] Belief that the world will end soon and God will bring a new, perfect society in place of the old one

millenarianism [MILL-en-AIR-ee-uhn-iz-uhm] Belief in a thousand-year reign of peace on earth near the end of time

The nearness of the end of time is a key teaching of apocalyptic.

© ISTOCKPHOTO.COM/DNY59

New Age Eclectic beliefs and practices that aim to bring the individual to a state of higher consciousness

People's Temple Utopian NRM led by Jim Jones that ended in mass murder in Guyana in 1978

Branch Davidian Apocalyptic NRM led by David Koresh that ended in fire in Waco, Texas, in 1993

Miller's followers, Ellen G. White (1827–1915). As their name implies, they keep to Saturday as their day of worship and rest, and look forward to the coming (advent) of Christ. The Jehovah's Witnesses, begun by Charles Taze Russell (1852–1916), also hold millenarian views. Members of this international movement recognize no human government and are in other ways aggressively countercultural. The Jehovah's Witnesses suffered greatly in World War II, when they were targeted in the Holocaust for refusing to recognize the authority of the Nazi government. The Latter-day Saints ("saints living in the latter days" of human history) movement begun by Joseph Smith also drew some of its energy from apocalypticism. These three NRMs have actively spread their message and are found throughout the world today.

> The aim of New Age groups is to bring the individual to a state of higher consciousness.

The utopian impulse in millenarianism also underlies the **New Age** movement that arose in the 1970s and 1980s outside the Christian tradition. It has touches of various Asian and indigenous religions. This is an eclectic group of beliefs and practices: crystal healing, "channeling" spirits, shamanism, veneration of the Earth, and ritual techniques. The aim of New Age groups is to bring the individual to a state of higher consciousness. They believe that the world has entered, or is about to enter, a spiritual millennium of more-fulfilling spiritual life. Scholars disagree whether New Age is a genuine movement, largely because it is so eclectic.

Apocalyptic movements can sometimes turn violent, and this happened with a prominent NRM in the 1970s. A magnetic Christian minister named Jim Jones moved many members of his large, prominent congregation called the **People's Temple** from San Francisco to Guyana, in South America. He tried to build a utopian commune on "apostolic socialism," a version of Christianity inclined to liberation theology,

which was strong in South America at the time. Jones became increasingly dictatorial and erratic, even naming his settlement Jonestown. In 1978, a U.S. congressman from San Francisco and some relatives of church members visited the group's settlement along with a television news crew and began to leave with an unfavorable report. Most of them were killed, and Jones then induced his followers to kill themselves by drinking a powdered drink laced with cyanide rather than see their community broken up. (This is the origin of the expression "drink the Kool-Aid," meaning to accept something detrimental unthinkingly. In light of the tragedy from which it comes, this expression is insensitive, to say the least.) Those who didn't willingly drink the poison were forced to drink it or were killed by other means. In all, 913 persons—about equal numbers of men, women, and children—died at Jonestown.

Read more about the Jonestown tragedy.

Watch news coverage of Jonestown.

Tragedy also befell the **Branch Davidian** (dah-VID-ee-uhn) NRM in 1993. The group, originating in the Seventh-Day Adventist Church but independent from its control, first settled in a compound near Waco, Texas, in 1935. Vernon Howell, who renamed himself David Koresh (koh-REHSH), became the leader of the group in 1987. He identified himself as an apocalyptic figure from the New Testament book of Revelation. Allegations of sexual abuse of children and the founding of a gun business in the compound attracted the suspicion of state and federal authorities. When federal authorities assaulted the compound to end a long standoff, a fire killed Koresh and some eighty followers, and the Branch Davidian movement died with them.

13-3b Asian NRMs in the West

As we saw in our study of Hinduism and Buddhism, the teachings of these religions appeared in Europe and the United States in the 1800s and began to influence Western intellectuals. The most influential of these teachings were those of Hindu Vedantic beliefs, especially the idea that the universe participates in a single divine spiritual reality. North Americans started a few NRMs with Vedantic teachings in the 1800s, most prominently the Theosophical Society founded by Helena Petrovna Blavatsky. These groups brought Hindu concepts into a combination of traditional and nontraditional Western religious teachings and practices.

By the end of the nineteenth century, the first Hindu groups took root in the United States when

Indian gurus brought them over. Because the beliefs were presented in language Westerners appreciated, these NRMs were stronger in the West than in India, where they were often marginalized. Vivekananda (VIV-uh-kah-NAHN-duh; 1864–1902), a prominent Indian philosopher, founded the **Vedanta Society** in New York City on the doctrines of his teacher, Ramakrishna. This NRM appealed to many prominent artists of the time. With centers around the world, the Vedanta Society holds that all religions teach the same basic truth but that Vedanta articulates the truth best. Vivekananda and the Vedanta Society were instrumental in raising Hinduism to the status of a world religion.

In 1968, the Beatles and their wives studied in India with the Maharishi Mahesh Yogi (center background). Seated left to right on the red platform are Ringo Starr and Maureen Starkey, Jane Asher and Paul McCartney, George Harrison and Patti Boyd, and Cynthia and John Lennon.

© HULTON ARCHIVE/GETTY IMAGES

Another teacher from India, Paramahansa Yogananda (PAR-uh-mah-HAN-suh YOH-guh-NAHN-duh; 1893–1952), established the **Self-Realization Fellowship** in Los Angeles in 1920 and was the first to teach yoga to Americans. Adapting Hindu practices of mental, physical, and spiritual self-control and self-realization, Yogananda explained yoga in scientific, not religious, terms, which helped to reach a larger audience. Like Vivekananda, Yogananda promoted an inclusive approach and said that the founders of other religions had taught the same system. More than five hundred Self-Realization Fellowship societies are found today around the world.

Although these Hindu movements introduced Hinduism to North America, it was only in the 1960s and 1970s that Asian NRMs became popular here. In 1959, Maharishi Mahesh Yogi (MA-hah-REESH-ee MA-hesh YOH-gee; 1914–2008) began **Transcendental Meditation**, widely known as **TM** for short, in North America. TM was presented as a scientifically sound way to obtain both personal and world peace; like the Self-Realization Fellowship, TM promoted yoga and meditation as a nonreligious system. TM's system of so-called Vedantic science featured meditation, often with yoga, on a special mantra given to a follower by the guru. This is similar to long-standing Hindu practice. The Maharishi drew millions of practitioners to TM, even though most of them didn't formally join his movement, and he was influential in spreading yoga in North America. The fame of his movement increased when it attracted celebrities such as American film star Mia Farrow and director David Lynch, American architect R. Buckminster Fuller, and especially the Beatles and other pop music stars.

The **Rajneesh International Foundation** is also from India. This NRM was founded by Bhagwan Shree Rajneesh (1931–1990), who developed a Westernized Tantrism that stressed its psychological and sexual aspects. Also called Acharya Rajneesh and Osho, and more informally the "sex guru," Rajneesh taught a system of "dynamic meditation." Unlike other meditation, which is quiet and still, "dynamic meditation" featured screaming and dancing, even physical violence and sexual intercourse, the latter sometimes in public. Of all Indian groups that came to North America, this one was the most widely known as a "cult," for its strongly countercultural practices and the flamboyant lifestyle of its founder.

This treatment of Hindu NRMs isn't meant to imply that the only presence of Hinduism and Buddhism in North America is by way of NRMs. As we saw in the

Vedanta Society
Hindu NRM founded by Vivekananda promoting Vedantic Hinduism

Self-Realization Fellowship Hindu NRM founded by Paramahansa Yogananda promoting Vedanta and yoga

Transcendental Meditation (TM) Hindu NRM founded by Maharishi Mahesh Yogi

Rajneesh International Foundation Hindu NRM founded by Bhagwan Shree Rajneesh on "dynamic meditation"

concluding sections of the chapters on these two religions, they've been introduced into North America and Europe with little change to their traditional forms, particularly through the immigration of Hindus and Buddhists. The forms of these religions found in North American NRMs can depart significantly from their mainstream manifestations. For example, in India one would not often see the emphasis many Hindu NRMs put on leadership of a mass movement by a guru, explicit religious universalism as a key teaching, and the secular or scientific nature of religious teachings and techniques such as yoga and meditation. The modern appeal of science leads us to the next group of Western NRMs.

The headquarters church of Christian Science, the First Church of Christ, Scientist, in Boston

© ISTOCKPHOTO.COM/DENIS JR. TANGNEY

13-3c "Scientific" NRMs: Christian Science and UFO Groups

Some NRMs claim to reveal scientific truths that haven't yet been acknowledged by the public or even discovered by scientists. These NRMs draw on the most powerful authority in the modern world: science.

The founder of the **Christian Science Church**, Mary Baker Eddy (1821–1910), was a prolific writer, like many founders of NRMs. Although NRMs sometimes consider everything their founders wrote to be scriptural, the Christian Science Church has named only one of Eddy's writings scriptural—her 1875 *Science and Health with Key to the Scriptures*. The title of the book accurately suggests its content: a "science" that uses prayer, Christian scripture, and Eddy's book itself to heal body, mind, and spirit. This science involves a view that the mind is the source of health and sickness; to cure the mind leads to cures in the body. Until around 2005 when it began to moderate its stance, the Christian Science Church had completely rejected medical science and treatment. It is still headquartered in Boston today, and its local churches spread throughout North America have "reading rooms" for the general public.

Christian Science Church Scientific NRM founded by Mary Baker Eddy on spiritual healing of disease

UFO groups Type of scientific NRMs holding that human salvation will come from extraterrestrial beings

> UFO groups developed teachings of space aliens who will bring advanced knowledge and spiritual wisdom.

UFO groups, also called the "contact [with space aliens] movement," represent another type of a scientific NRM, although one quite different from Christian Science. That they may look to outsiders more like "science fiction" than "science" is largely unimportant. These movements from the 1950s and 1960s came at a time when North American popular culture spread fear about space aliens coming to earth—a fear many historians believe to be related to the threat of nuclear war that was widely felt at the time. In contrast to the alarmist reports, however, UFO NRMs looked to space aliens for blessings. Adapting some religions' stories of the coming of beings from heaven, UFO groups teach about space aliens who bring scientific knowledge and spiritual wisdom. Beginning in the 1950s, groups such as Understanding Inc. argued that UFOs carried beings who would promote peace and happiness throughout the whole world. The Amalgamated Flying Saucer Clubs of America and the yoga-employing Aetherius Society believed that space aliens will bring salvation to the world. This "salvation" consists of superior technical and psychological knowledge that makes possible a blessed age, not the revelation of more-traditional religious truths.

The UFO groups founded in the twentieth century tend to be in decline, with one exception. The **Raëlians** is a UFO group now headquartered in Quebec, with about 55,000 members worldwide. It was established in 1973 by Raël, a French race-car driver and sports journalist whose given name was Claude Vorilhon (b. 1946). Raël states that in December of 1973 he was abducted to a "flying saucer," as spaceships from other worlds were widely called at the time. There he met a four-foot tall extraterrestrial with human features, with whom Raël had conversations for one week. Raël was told that humans originated in a genetic manipulation by the Elohim—a word the Bible (according to the extraterrestrial) mistranslates as "God" and really means "those who came from the sky." Humans are descended from these beings from the sky, and knowledge of this leads to enlightenment. Raël, whose name supposedly means "messenger of Elohim," has also formed a company called Clonaid to develop cloning of human beings. Clonaid created a world-wide stir in 2002 when it claimed that it had successfully cloned a human being named "Eve." This led to renewed debates over the ethics of human cloning, but soon the debate shifted to whether the whole announcement was a fraud.

Watch a BBC report on a UFO NRM.

Another UFO group was the small **Heaven's Gate** movement founded in Texas in the 1970s by Marshall Applewhite. Applewhite (who called himself "Do") professed that he and his wife ("Ti") were beings from another world at an "evolutionary level above human." Claiming to have already appeared on earth as Jesus, Applewhite argued that the "kingdom of heaven" that Jesus taught was a real place with highly evolved beings from another world. The "Garden of Eden" in the biblical book of Genesis was the whole earth, where human beings had been "planted" by the otherworldly beings. Applewhite organized communal living for his group of "plants" in a new "garden." He taught that the "plants" could evolve into "members of the level above human," but they had to discard their humanity, including sexuality. In response, some Heaven's Gate followers castrated themselves. Such self-mutilation foreshadowed worse violence to come. In 1996, the group settled near San Diego, California, where it supported itself by creating websites for Internet users. Most people who came in contact with the group thought they were harmless eccentrics, but in March of 1997 Applewhite revealed that the Hale-Bopp comet was bringing a spaceship in its tail. The "mature plants" would

Examine the 1997 Heaven's Gate website.

be transplanted into this spaceship before the "garden was spaded over" and the earth was destroyed. Led by Applewhite, the thirty-nine Heaven's Gate members committed suicide to free their spirits for transportation to the aliens' spaceship. The Heaven's Gate movement perished with them.

As we've seen from the examples above, these UFO-oriented NRMs can express traditional religious themes in the language of science, science fiction, and biological evolution. As space-alien fervor has waned in North America with the ending of the Cold War, other types of scientific NRMs have become popular. The Church of Scientology expresses its teachings in the language of modern psychology. We'll consider the Scientology movement more fully below, but now we turn our attention to NRMs based on beliefs about nature.

13-3d Nature NRMs: Neo-Paganism, Wicca, and Druidry

Most nature NRMs are antiscientific. They oppose the alienation of humans from nature that they see in science and technology, and they advance the "re-enchantment" of nature. They seek to return to the meaningful patterns of the natural world. Their use of magic, spells, potions, and other ritual devices to pursue their personal goals intentionally opposes modern science and technology. Neo-pagan NRMs are found particularly in Western Europe, but are present in North America as well. Some neo-pagan groups, such as the Druids (DROO-ids), claim to be the ancient pagan religion of Europe that was suppressed by Christianity (see "A Closer Look: Druidry Gains Official Status"). Although "pagan" might seem pejorative, these groups proudly embrace it. Other groups take the name **Wicca**, the NRM of modern witchcraft. Wicca draws on religious implications of ideas in today's ecology movement and in feminism. Made up predominantly of women, Wicca groups typically center on a Goddess and a "female principle," which they see as the leading force of nature. Like other nature NRMs, they aim to re-enchant and re-personalize the world, reclaiming it from the wrongs that science has inflicted on it.

Watch a BBC report on current Wicca.

Raëlians [rye-EHL-ee-uhnz] UFO NRM established in 1973 by Raël (Claude Vorilhon)

Heaven's Gate UFO NRM established in the 1970s by Marshall Applewhite

Wicca [WIHK-kuh] Nature NRM of modern witchcraft

A Closer Look:

Druidry Gains Official Status

Druidry, the pagan worship that its current practitioners claim has existed for thousands of years, in 2010 gained recognition by the British government as a bona fide religion after a four-year process. The Charity Commission, established to oversee charities in England and Wales, and the body that determines whether movements qualify under British law as religions, ruled that the Druids' worship of spirits in nature is a religious activity. The Charity Commission didn't have to rule on how ancient this movement actually is, only its present status as a religion.

Current membership in the Druid Network totals about 350 dues-paying members, although the BBC claimed in 2005 that Druidry is practiced by as many as ten thousand people in the United Kingdom. Druidry has eight annual festivals, including rites on the summer solstice amid the ancient stone monoliths at Stonehenge.

Watch a BBC report on the Druids at Stonehenge.

Modern Druids carry out a summer solstice ceremony at Stonehenge in England.

© ISTOCKPHOTO.COM/ROBERT TOMLINSON

13-3e NRMs in Asia

New religious movements in Asia today began after 1850, and they reflect the colonial impact of the West on that region. Arising in this environment, they were either in opposition to Western religion and culture or in some sort of blended agreement with it. When they were against Western imperialism, these NRMs reinvented older Asian traditions; when they agreed with parts of it, they blended Western and Asian religions. Both types of NRMs helped Asian cultures adapt to growing Westernization there, in colonial and postcolonial times.

NRMs in China arose at the end of the first Opium War in 1842. Western imperialism, poverty in southern China, and the work of the first Protestant missionaries were a part of the mix that occasioned Chinese NRMs. The most important of these NRMs was the Taiping Tianguo (tigh-PING TEE-ahn-GWOH), the Heavenly Kingdom of the Great Peace. This NRM combined evangelical Christianity, Confucianism, and various popular Daoist traditions. Guided by its powerful leader, Hong Xiuquan (hong zyoo-KWAHN), the Heavenly Kingdom of the Great Peace established a religious state, which its follower saw as a kingdom on earth and in heaven. At first it controlled several provinces in southern China, and then moved into the center of the country. It threatened the stability of China until it was put down in 1865.

The emperor legalized Western Christian missionary work in China in 1858, and many types of Protestant messages and churches then spread through China. One effect of this was the rise of indigenous churches that were independent of foreign control. These were typically Pentecostal and other evangelical groups; mainline Christian denominations didn't spawn independent churches so readily.

Some of China's NRMs grew out of popular Daoism, and predated the Opium Wars. New Daoist groups had been arising regularly for almost two thousand years, and the coming of Westerners didn't change this. One large NRM, which evolved out of the White Lotus millenarian tradition is the eclectic Yiguan (yee-GWAHN) Dao, the Unity School. "Spirit writing" done in a shamanic trance provides moral direction for the group. Another spirit-writing group, the

Zhihui (ZHEE-wee) Tang, the Compassion Sect, began in Taiwan in 1949.

By far the most significant type of NRM to arise recently in China relates to **Qi Gong**, or "Energy Working," an ancient practice combining physical exercise and meditation. In the 1980s and 1990s, China experienced a rebirth of traditional exercise practices with a religious basis. These encourage health by energizing the flow of cosmic qi ("vital force") in one's body. Tai Qi (Tai Chi) is the best known of the meditational exercises. Qi Gong masters gained popularity and founded movements throughout China by displaying their extraordinary abilities. Many NRMs arose from these Qi Gong activities. The best-known Qi Gong group is Falun Gong, which began in 1992; we'll consider this movement more fully below. Religion in China today is growing rapidly, and NRMs are playing a significant part.

> Read a report on the resurgence of religion today in officially atheist China.

> Japan has proportionally more NRMs and people in them than any other nation today.

In Japan, the rapid changes in the 1800s saw the rise of many religious organizations, which scholars of Japan have termed **new religions**. In the wider field of international religious studies, they are usually seen as NRMs. Most Japanese new religions have their roots in Buddhism, some in Shinto, and a few in Confucianism; they tend to be eclectic, blending these three in unique ways. The perceived empty formalism and lack of vitality in the older traditions, particularly Shinto and traditional Buddhism, has given space for new Japanese religions to arise, with their vitality and dynamism. Like many NRMs worldwide, the new religions of Japan draw on lay participation, with followers spreading the faiths and running the organizations. It's safe to say that Japan, despite its modern, increasingly secular society, has proportionately more NRMs and people in them than any other nation today. Here, of course, we can mention only a few.

The earliest of the Japanese new religions include Tenrikyo (ten-REEK-yoh) and Konkokyo (kon-KOHK-yoh). Gedatsu-kai (geh-DAHT-suh-kai), a blend of Shinto, Buddhism, and Confucianism, developed before World War II. The postwar period saw many new groups appear, including the Dancing Religion and also Johrei (JOH-ray), a self-help movement based on Christianity.

The most infamous of the Japanese new religions was the apocalyptic group **Aum Shinrikyo**. Founded in 1987 by Chizuo Matsumoto (chih-ZOO-oh MAHT-soo-MOH-toh), its teachings combined Asian religions and Christianity. Aum Shinrikyo launched a 1995 nerve-gas attack on the Tokyo subway system in which twelve people died and more than fifty were seriously injured. The group later renamed itself Aleph, the first letter of the Hebrew alphabet, and tried to regroup without its founder, but it has almost completely disbanded. Two of its members evaded arrest until 2012. Five Aum Shinrikyo members are now serving life sentences for the attack and thirteen have been sentenced to death, including Matsumoto.

The largest Japanese NRM is **Soka-Gakkai**, the Value Creation Society. This Buddhist group claims more than 6 million members today. Founded in 1930, it was disbanded by the Japanese government during

Qi Gong [chee gong] "Energy Working," ancient Chinese tradition of spiritual and physical exercise

new religions Characteristic name in scholarship for NRMs in Japan

Aum Shinrikyo [ohm shin-REEK-yoh] Apocalyptic Japanese NRM founded in 1987 by Matsumoto

Soka-Gakkai [SOH-kah-GAHK-kigh] Largest Japanese NRM, founded in 1930 as an offshoot of Nichiren Buddhism

The Yin Yang symbol stands for an invisible rolling ball in the Tai Chi exercise called "Wave Hands Like Clouds."

© ISTOCKPHOTO.COM/SONGSPECKELS

Unification Church
NRM from Korea founded by Sun Myung Moon, a blend of Christianity and Asian religions

True Parents In Unification, the late Sun Myung Moon and his wife, who can lead humanity to perfection

World War II for its opposition to the war, but it was refounded in 1946. It grew rapidly in the 1950s, and in 1964 it founded the Clean Government political party. Its teachings draw from Nichiren, a thirteenth-century Japanese Buddhist, but it is independent enough from Buddhism to merit recognition as an NRM. Soka-Gakkai emphasizes beauty and goodness, and is known for its main ritual practice of chanting praise to its main scripture, the *Lotus Sutra*.

The largest NRM to emerge from Korea is the **Unification Church**, the unofficial name of the Holy Spirit Association for the Unification of World Christianity. Because of its rapid growth and now nearly worldwide reach, we will treat it more fully than other groups. The Unification Church began in South Korea with the work of Sun Myung Moon (1920–2012), formerly a Korean Presbyterian, in 1954. The church has sparked controversy almost wherever it has spread, and its members are often mocked as "Moonies." Moon related a vision, while a teenager, in which God charged him with completing Jesus Christ's work. Because of Adam and Eve's failure to obey God, their selfish love has damaged human life, and God tried to restore his original plan for humanity in the life of Jesus. Although Jesus was the First Messiah and should have brought full salvation to humanity, he didn't marry and have children, so he failed to complete his divine mission. The Unification Church openly called Moon the Second Messiah who would complete Jesus's mission.

As the parents of an "ideal" family, Moon and his second wife Hak Ja Han expected Unification Church members to follow their example in marriage and thus help to bring the world to perfection. This invested special significance in the mass weddings for which the church became well known. The emphasis on family originates in Confucianism, where marriage and family are central to religion and life. Moon's own task as "Lord of the Second Coming" was to continue the unfinished work of Jesus Christ and, in a perfect marriage and family, to fulfill God's original plan of creation. Moon's second marriage

Watch a brief statement of basic Unification beliefs.

Read an excerpt from the *Divine Principle* on salvation through the True Family.

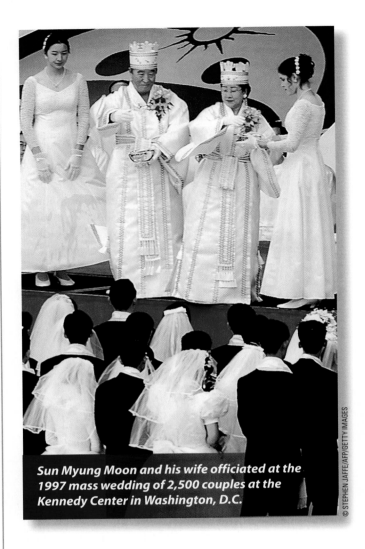

Sun Myung Moon and his wife officiated at the 1997 mass wedding of 2,500 couples at the Kennedy Center in Washington, D.C.

© STEPHEN JAFFE/AFP/GETTY IMAGES

in 1960 marked the beginning of a new age. The **True Parents**, Moon and his wife, could realize perfection and lead humanity to a perfect state, in order to build God's ideal world on earth. Strong anticommunism and political conservatism are also found in the Unification movement.

In the late 1950s, the Unification Church came to North America. In the 1970s, it worked especially for the conversion of college students and used means that proved controversial. Some parents protested their children's membership in the communal-living groups that Unification operated, membership that brought a severing of family ties. This controversy led to U.S. congressional hearings, and in 1982 Moon was convicted of tax evasion and spent a few years in federal prison. Many mainline Protestant church leaders saw Moon's prosecution as persecution, even though they disagreed with his adaptation of Christianity. The Unification Church kept growing, however, and soon emerged from these troubles with a worldwide base. The church now is in more than one hundred countries, but reliable membership numbers are hard to come by. Its influence is extended by a dozen or so church-funded organizations without its name (called "front groups" by the church's opponents)—for example the Professor's World Peace Academy, the International Conference on the Unity of the Sciences, and the International Federation for World Peace. The church also owns media companies such as the conservative *Washington Times* newspaper and United Press International (UPI), a news-distribution company. Since Sun Myung Moon died in 2012, students of NRMs are watching the Unification Church closely to see how well it turns over leadership to a new generation.

In Vietnam, Cao Dai (cow digh), a syncretistic religion, became a social force with considerable political power from 1945 to 1954. Its political power is reduced in now-Communist Vietnam, but as a religion it is still strong. Cao Dai attempts to create a perfect synthesis of world religions, combining Christianity, Buddhism, Islam, Confucianism, Hinduism, Daoism, and shamanism. The Cao Dai faithful must detach themselves from material possessions to cultivate their spirits.

Cao Dai monks inside Holy See Temple, Tay Ninh, Vietnam

© DENIS ROZAN/SHUTTERSTOCK.COM

They worship one God, the most prominent spirits, and their ancestors. Cao Dai also uses spiritual mediums in its worship, a practice that derives from Daoism and shamanism. These mediums offer guidance from those in the spirit world, departed family members, and other wise individuals.

Learning Outcome 13-4

State and explain the teachings and practices of Falun Gong.

13-4 An NRM from Asia: Falun Gong

Falun Gong, "Practice of the Wheel of Dharma," is a controversial NRM begun by Li Hongzhi (lee hong-ZHER) in 1992. Falun Gong is the common name in the West and in China, but its adherents more frequently call it Falun Dafa. The essence of this NRM is to achieve mental and spiritual renewal by way of physical and mental exercises, as well as some mystical teachings. The teachings of Falun Gong tap into Buddhism, popular and religious Daoism, Confucianism, and even New Age movements. Li teaches meditation techniques and physical exercises that encourage mental and spiritual renewal. Falun Gong exploded on the world scene in 1999 with a large, sudden demonstration in Beijing against the Chinese government, which has since denounced Falun Gong as a "falsehood" and an "evil cult." In the government's view, it does not deserve governmental toleration as a religion. As Fenggang Yang has written in his recent book *Religion in China: Survival and Revival under Communist Rule*, the authorities claim they are justified in eradicating Falun Gong and similar groups in China.[3] The Communist government has suppressed this group through today with both prosecution and persecution, just as the emperors of China before it suppressed religious groups that were seen as a threat to their rule.

Watch the "exercise video" introduction to Falun Gong at its website.

Falun Gong [FAH-loon gong] "Practice of the Wheel of Dharma," a Chinese NRM founded by Li Hongzhi in 1992

---

[3] Fenggang Yang, *Religion in China: Survival and Revival under Communist Rule* (New York: Oxford University Press, 2012), p. 26.

13-4a History

Qi Gong, as we saw above, is based on beliefs and practices that go back to the dawn of Chinese civilization. Practitioners in China have long represented these techniques as nonreligious, in an effort to evade the government prohibition of independent, unapproved religious activity. In the twentieth century, when Qi Gong appeared in China as a distinct qi school, its new practitioners taught that it was rooted in religion. Chief among them was Li Hongzhi (1951–present), who worked as a police officer and in private security before he founded Falun Gong.

Li, already a Qi Gong teacher with Buddhist and Daoist credentials, began promoting his own version of Qi Gong in 1992. He synthesized traditional techniques with Buddhist and Daoist concepts about self-development. His book *Zhuan Falun*, or *Turning the Wheel of the Law*, teaches a path to enlightenment and salvation through meditation and morality. After publishing *Zhuan Falun*, Li stated that he had completed his work in China. He began to travel internationally to spread his movement. Li became an American citizen in 1997 and a resident of New York City in 1998.

Falun Gong became popular in the West in the 1990s, in part because some Falun Gong followers claimed to have been healed of various diseases. Membership in the new movement grew rapidly. Li himself claimed around 100 million Falun Gong followers worldwide; this is no doubt an exaggeration, but practitioners do number in the millions.

In China, however, the government became increasingly wary of Falun Gong's continued growth. Government officials feared that Li's movement could inspire a revolutionary challenge to public order and especially to Communist Party rule. In 1999 more than ten thousand Falun Gong members protested in Beijing against being labeled a "superstitious cult." This massive sit-in somehow caught the Chinese government by surprise. Three months later, the president of China declared the practitioners of Falun Gong an imminent threat to the government and a rebellious movement, and launched a harsh crackdown. He detained thousands of Falun Gong practitioners, some of whom were even officials in the Chinese Communist Party. The government confiscated and destroyed as many of Li's books and cassette tapes as possible, probably in the millions. Hundreds of Falun Gong leaders are still imprisoned in China today. Falun Gong members outside China have tried to keep up pressure on the Chinese government, and have accused prison authorities of harvesting vital organs for transplant from

live or executed Falun Gong prisoners. The Chinese Communist government's actions against Falun Gong are rooted in Communist opposition to religion in general, and specifically to independent, unregulated religious activities in China. They also derive in no small measure from the Communist Party's unwillingness to give up power or share it with other groups. The actions taken against Falun Gong in China are driving it underground, but its beliefs and practices are surviving there.

Living now in the United States, Li has called for negotiation with the Chinese government to resolve the crisis over his movement. His teachings are now spread around the world by a variety of methods: books and audio recordings; a free newspaper, *The Epoch Times*, which has an online version; Chinese-language television and radio networks; and a Chinese New Year entertainment it sponsors in major cities around the world.

13-4b Teaching and Practice

Falun Gong's scripture, *Zhuan Falun*, is the main book of its founder. It contains a series of lectures, indicating the origin of the book in Li's efforts to spread his teaching, beginning in the 1990s. It was first published in 1995, soon after the founding of the movement. The chapters in the book preserve the feel of lectures to live audiences. *Zhuan Falun* has already been translated into

BONNIE VAN VOORST © CENGAGE LEARNING

Figure 13.1 The symbol of Falun Gong prominently features the turning wheel.

forty languages. Although the Falun Gong movement doesn't explicitly describe *Zhuan Falun* as scripture—for example, by calling it a sutra (the formal Buddhist name for a scriptural writing) or venerating it in ceremonies—it is clear nonetheless that the movement regards it as such. *Zhuan Falun* is organized into nine "lectures" or "talks." These nine teachings discuss all the basics of Falun Gong theory and practice. A good deal of treatment is given to the relationship of Falun Gong practice with that of other traditional Buddhist teachings and with Daoism.

In Buddhism, *wheel* is the "wheel of law" or "wheel of dharma," but in Falun Gong the "wheel" is the bodily center of one's energy. Li locates this center in the abdomen and teaches that one can activate it by "cultivating and practicing" exercises; he also claims to be able to install his wheel in others. Most Qi Gong groups tend to be inclusive in spirit, but Falun Gong maintains that Li alone has established the correct exercises. The spiritual discipline he teaches, the "cultivation Mind-Nature," is essential to their success.

In a twist on the teachings of UFO religious movements, Li has said that demonic space aliens are now undermining life on earth. Since 1900, these aliens have controlled scientists and world leaders. Opponents of Falun Gong ridicule this as bizarre, and they regard reliance on Falun Gong as a hazard to health. Chinese medical authorities claim that 1,400 Falun Gong practitioners have died from refusing to seek modern medical care. The controversy between the Chinese government and Falun Gong appears set to continue for at least the near future, especially if this movement keeps gaining strength and stature in the world.

> Read a short excerpt from *Zhuan Falun* on Falun Gong teachings.

A public Falun Gong meditation session in Warsaw, Poland. The sign gives the three key concepts of Falun Gong: truth, compassion, and tolerance.

13-5 A North American NRM: The Church of Jesus Christ of Latter-day Saints

The Church of Jesus Christ of Latter-day Saints (LDS) is one of several churches originating in a movement begun by Joseph Smith Jr. (1805–1844) in New York State in 1830. The name **Mormon**, often used for these churches, is from the *Book of Mormon*, published by Smith in that year. Mormonism differs from the Christianity it separated from by its teachings about God, family life, continuing revelation, and missionary work. The mission work has been largely effective in making the LDS church the fastest-growing NRM in the world, with 14 million members. Most of them are outside North America, with about a third in Latin America.

13-5a History

Mormons believe that in 1827 an angel named Moroni (moh-ROHN-igh) appeared to Smith and told him about engraved golden plates (see Fig. 13.2). Using what he called "seer stones," Smith translated them from their "Reformed Egyptian" language as the *Book of Mormon*. The Mormon after whom this book is named was an ancient American prophet who authored the book written on the plates. The *Book of Mormon* tells the story of ancient Israelites who sailed to America centuries before Jesus Christ, led by prophets. Smith's new religion originated in a setting of great fervor of competing American Protestant denominations in the early 1800s; the area of upstate New York where Smith lived was even known as the "burned-over district" for its frequent emotional

Mormon [MOHR-muhn] Member of a church from the movement started by Joseph Smith; also used to describe their churches revivals. Mormonism departed from them in its proclamation that, in Joseph Smith's work, God restored the "true church" and reestablished the true faith from which all Christianity had strayed since the first century C.E.

Examine a chart of the origins of various Mormon churches.

This new church was millennialist, and Smith hoped to establish God's kingdom in the western United States. Smith received revelations of both new and traditional teachings from the *Book of Mormon*, and also received practical help from Moroni. He and his followers soon began their westward trek by moving to Kirtland, Ohio. In Jackson County, Missouri, where Zion was to be established, Smith formed his followers into a communalistic society. Growing tensions with slave-owning Missourians, who thought that the Mormons opposed slavery, resulted in armed clashes. Most Mormons fled Missouri for western

Joseph Smith's boyhood home in Manchester, New York, where some of the translation of the Book of Mormon *was done.*

©ISTOCKPHOTO.COM/ELDON GRIFFIN

Council of the Twelve Apostles In LDS, the highest ruling body

BONNIE VAN VOORST © CENGAGE LEARNING

Figure 13.2 A statue of the Angel Moroni is found on LDS temples. An angel blowing a trumpet to the world is a common apocalyptic image in Christianity.

Illinois in 1839. There Smith built a new city, Nauvoo. Mormon success in business and politics provoked persecution once again. Increasing rumors about secret polygamy by Smith and other top Mormon leaders began to circulate—rumors that later turned out to be true. Smith's strong repression of some Mormon dissidents intensified non-Mormon hostility and led to his arrest. Joseph Smith and his brother Hyrum were jailed in Carthage, Illinois, near Nauvoo, and they were killed by a mob that took over the jail on June 27, 1844.

A **Council of the Twelve Apostles** then assumed the leadership of the church, and still leads it today. Mormons overwhelmingly favored Brigham Young as Smith's successor. When increasing violence made the Mormons' life in Nauvoo difficult, Young led a 1,100-mile trek to what is now Utah in 1846 to 1847. The Mormons aimed to establish a territory in Utah where they could live by themselves and practice their religion without opposition from local and state governments. (At the time, Utah was technically a part of Mexico, and out of U.S. control.) Young established more than three hundred settlements in Utah and adjacent areas. Seeking to bolster his numbers and strength, Young sent missionaries throughout North America and to Great Britain. They urged their converts to move to Utah. In all, about eighty thousand Mormon pioneers travelled west in wagon trains, in handcarts, or on foot by 1869.

Despite the difficulties of life around Salt Lake, the pioneers made a prosperous life for themselves, empowered by their faith. Utah's first request for statehood in 1849 was denied; later applications for statehood were blocked by the church's announcement in 1852 of its practice of polygamy, which Mormons call **plural marriage**. As mentioned previously, it had been practiced secretly by Joseph Smith and by a few other leading Mormons during the church's time in Nauvoo (and since), but in the 1850s plural marriage became a key doctrine and practice of the LDS movement as a whole. As Young and the U.S. government argued over polygamy, and as Mormons continued to press for their own church-directed government during the 1850s, tensions boiled over. In 1857, a group of Mormons murdered all the men, women, and children of a wagon train moving through the Mountain Meadows, Utah, area. In response to this massacre and other conflicts with federal authorities, U.S. president James Buchanan threatened to dispatch the U. S. Army to suppress the Mormon "rebellion" and set up a non-Mormon government in the territory.

Troubles over polygamy continued until 1890, when the president of the LDS church, Wilford Woodruff, announced with great anguish the church's abandonment of plural marriage. This and other changes led to the 1896 admission of Utah as a state, with Young as its first governor. However, Woodruff's decree applied only to the United States, and polygamy continued for decades in the LDS settlements in Mexico and even in remote places in the American West. Although it caused wrenching problems for Mormons at the time, the LDS church's renunciation of polygamy is probably a main cause of its increasing strength during the 1900s; those Mormon groups that chose to keep it have had smaller growth. The church grew rapidly through the traditionally large families that Mormons have, and after World War II the practice of sending young Mormons out as missionaries led to exponential growth. At any given moment, the LDS church has around forty thousand missionaries active around the world. The church's appeal throughout the world was greatly enhanced when in 1978 it dropped its racist teachings of the 1800s and allowed Africans and members of the African diaspora to become full-fledged members of the LDS church. The LDS church gained a great deal of publicity in 2012, when Mitt Romney, a Mormon from a prominent family in the church, was the Republican nominee for president of the United States.

In the diverging paths of Mormonism, more than 150 different independent groups have arisen. They follow new prophets, practice polygamy, or keep various practices abandoned by the main LDS church.

- Some Mormons rejected Brigham Young's leadership and remained in the Midwest. The largest of these groups—which Joseph Smith's widow Emma and Joseph Smith III (1860–1914) joined—formed the **Reorganized Church of Jesus Christ of Latter-day Saints** under Smith's leadership in 1852. The Reorganized Church eventually settled in Independence, Missouri, which LDS leaders had once called the location of Zion. For many decades the descendants of Joseph Smith III led the church. In the 1990s, they renamed themselves by the more mainstream-Protestant-sounding name of "Community of Christ." They number around 250,000 members and keep only the *Book of Mormon* as their scripture besides the Bible.

- Another Mormon group moved to Independence and purchased the Temple Lot, the site chosen by Smith for the main Mormon temple. This purchase was opposed by the Reorganized Church, whose headquarters were right next door.

- In 1847, James Strang founded a polygamous community of about three thousand Mormons on Beaver Island in northern Lake Michigan. He proclaimed himself its prophet and king, and his following grew to as many as twelve thousand in the Upper Midwest. The movement ended in violence a few years later; King James was killed, and his followers scattered.

- Among the Latter-day Saints factions to emerge in the twentieth century were groups that defiantly kept to polygamy. The first such group was established in Arizona in 1902. Other polygamist settlements were established in Mexico, Canada, and even in Salt Lake City. These groups are estimated at around thirty thousand people in all today. The largest single group committed to the continuation of plural marriage calls itself the **Fundamentalist Church of Jesus Christ of Latter-day Saints (FLDS)**. This church suffered a blow in 2011 when their leader, Warren

plural marriage
Mormon term for polygamy

Reorganized Church of Jesus Christ of Latter-day Saints
Historic name for the Mormon denomination now called Community of Christ

Fundamentalist Church of Jesus Christ of Latter-day Saints (FLDS) Sectarian Mormon group that still practices plural marriage

Jeffs, was convicted for sexual assault of two underage (twelve- and fifteen-year-old) wives and sent to prison.

Despite these splits, the LDS church has always been far larger than all other Mormon groups combined, comprising at least 90 percent of Mormons in the world.

Watch a report on a contemporary polygamist Mormon group in Canada.

13-5b Scripture

The Church of Jesus Christ of Latter-day Saints has a four-part scripture. The *Book of Mormon* is the leading part, and it is from this title that the followers of the movement came to be known as "Mormons." (At first this was a put-down name given by Smith's opponents outside his movement, but gradually accepted in the LDS church; it is also the only instance among world religions of a faith being named from the name of its scripture.) It was first published in 1830 at Grandin Press in Palmyra, New York. A second, shorter scripture is the *Pearl of Great Price*; the third scripture is *The Doctrine and Covenants*, which contains the continuing revelation of God's word through Latter-day Saints prophets, especially Joseph Smith. In addition to this "second canon" of scripture, the Latter-day Saints church has a "first canon" of the Christian Bible, the King James Version of 1611, the fourth LDS scripture.

The contents of LDS scriptures are quite complex. They record a story of ancient American peoples descended from ancient Hebrews who left Judah and sailed to North America around 600 B.C.E., and the appearance in the first century C.E. of the resurrected Jesus Christ to these Americans. This purported record ends around 400 C.E. The *Book of Mormon* has fifteen main parts, known, with one exception, as books. Like the Bible, these books are subdivided into chapters and verses. Mormons believe that the *Book of Mormon* is based on writings appearing on four groups of metal plates: gold plates of Nephi (NEE-figh), Mormon, and Ether; and brass plates that, according to founder Joseph Smith, people fleeing Jerusalem in 600 B.C.E. brought to the Americas. In 421 C.E., Moroni, the last of the Nephite prophets, is believed to have sealed the sacred plates and hidden them by divine instruction. Smith said that in 1823 this same Moroni visited him as a resurrected prophet and directed him to the sacred plates. He reported that he translated the writing on the plates into English, and he published them in 1830. The plates themselves, Mormons believe, were returned to Moroni and then hidden away for all time.

The second Latter-day Saints scripture, *Pearl of Great Price*, was first compiled in 1851 by Franklin Richards, then a member of the church's Council of the Twelve Apostles and in charge of LDS missions in Great Britain. Richards intended this book to increase circulation of Joseph Smith's testimony among Latter-day Saints. *Pearl of Great Price* quickly received wide acceptance, especially in mission fields, and became a scripture of the church by the action of its First Presidency (highest official body) in 1880.

> *Ironically, the Book of Mormon is more similar to mainstream Protestant Christian teaching than are later official church writings and teachings.*

The third Latter-day Saints scripture, *Doctrine and Covenants*, has 138 sections, plus two "official declarations." It contains revelations on doctrines and community life—some narrative, some theological,

Book of Mormon *first edition (1830) with a printing plate. It was published with a large initial print run of 5,000 copies.*

and some legal—from 1823 until 1978. The declarations deal with two controversial topics: the ending of polygamy and the admission of blacks to the priesthood. Although the LDS church has an "open" canon, and thus could add an entirely new scriptural book if it decided to do so, its well-established practice is to add any new material to the *Doctrine and Covenants*.

Ironically, the *Book of Mormon* tends to be more similar to mainstream Protestant Christian teaching than are later official church writings and teachings. This is even true of some controversial doctrines that have set the Latter-day Saints apart from other Christians. For example, the *Book of Mormon* promotes monogamy and discourages (but does not forbid) polygamy (see Jacob 2:27, 30), but the *Doctrine and Covenants* preserves both the approval of polygamy (section 132.37–38, 52, 61–62) and the official disapproval of it ("Official Declaration 1"). Although opponents of the church point to more than three thousand alleged changes to the *Book of Mormon* since its initial publication, the majority of these are corrections and updates of spelling and grammar. In essence, this important book remains the same today as its first edition.

13-5c Teachings

Many LDS teachings are similar to Protestant ones, but its distinctive doctrines make it an NRM in its beliefs as well as its organization. LDS members believe that their religion restores true teaching as well as organization and practices. Their official list of key doctrines, the **Articles of Faith**, teaches belief in God, the eternal Father; in Jesus Christ, God's Son; and in the Holy Spirit. But LDS teaches that these three are distinct divine beings rather than united in a single deity, as in mainstream Christian teaching. God was once similar to a human but became divine, as all righteous Mormons also hope to do after death. Mormons believe that Christ came to earth to bring salvation, but they maintain that salvation comes by one's own deeds as well as by the grace of God in Christ. This Mormon belief reflects cultural optimism in the 1800s as to basic human goodness and potential, even for self-salvation. Mormons also stress the importance of faith, repentance, and

LDS missionary in typical clothing

© ISTOCKPHOTO.COM/JASON LUGO

carrying out the key practices of the church, including baptism by immersion. They administer the Lord's Supper weekly as a memorial of Jesus's death, but use water instead of wine. They attend Sunday services regularly and **tithe**—give one-tenth of all their income to the church—faithfully. With the increasing size of the LDS Church and rising prosperity of its members, this tithe has brought in vast wealth.

Mormons teach that the faithful may become gods themselves after death. Every human being, except for a few who reject God after coming to know him, will receive a happy afterlife. When Christ returns, he will establish a thousand-year kingdom on the earth. After this period, the earth will be a heavenly, blessed place, and the truly righteous will live on it. Others will live forever in less-significant kingdoms, happy but not so blessed.

Read the Articles of Faith of the LDS church.

13-5d Institutions, Practices, and Structure of the LDS Church

The LDS church ignores the distinctions between clergy and laity that are found in most branches of Christianity. It uses Christian-clergy terms such as "priest," but this always applies in LDS to lay members. At age twelve, "worthy males" (a term that until 1978 did not apply to Africans and African Americans) can enter the "Aaronic priesthood" as deacons; they are teachers at age fourteen and "priests" at sixteen. At eighteen, they can enter the "Melchizedek priesthood" as elders and may become leaders of local churches. In general, middle-aged LDS men have local and regional authority; national and international authority goes to men of proven ability in their retirement years. (This is why pictures of top LDS leaders always feature old men.) Many Latter-day Saints do missionary work. Single young men aged eighteen to twenty-one undertake a two-year proselytizing mission. Single young women nineteen and older serve for eighteen

Articles of Faith Short statement of the main LDS beliefs

tithe Giving one-tenth of all income to the church, mandatory for LDS members

months. This is voluntary, but many young "Saints" participate in it. They may serve in this country or in a foreign land. Some older married couples also serve as missionaries for eighteen months. This extensive missionary work is the main reason why the LDS church is probably the most rapidly spreading NRM in the world. It has also helped to give young Saints a remarkably important role in the church.

Baptism, a ritual of initiation and obedience, is considered necessary for salvation. It is administered to LDS children at age eight and to adult converts. Mormon proxy baptism is more famous for being undertaken by substitution for those who have died outside the Mormon religion. This is more widely known as **baptism for the dead**, and it is sometimes misunderstood by non-Mormons as "baptism *of* the dead." The Mormons' commitment to compiling genealogies springs from their concern for bringing their ancestors who have died into the fullness of blessing. Although many people today think of this mainly as a genealogical resource, the information is used for religious purposes, to identify candidates for baptism by proxy. In 2010, after some Jewish groups protested, the LDS church changed its policies, especially to prevent the names of Jews who had died in the Holocaust from being used in baptism.

Ceremonies of baptism, **endowment** (a ritual in which blessings and knowledge are imparted to adult Mormons in good standing), and the **sealing** of families (assuring their unity in time and eternity) all occur in the temple. In the endowment, Mormons are washed and anointed with oil. Then they see a dramatized story of creation, the fall of humanity into sin, and God's bringing of salvation to the world.

In general, Mormon moral expectations flow from the New Testament and are much the same as in mainstream Christian churches. In addition, Mormons have their own practices. The use of alcohol and tobacco is forbidden, as is coffee, tea, and other drinks with caffeine. Mormons promote education and have a strong work ethic. Their outer clothing must always be modest. A **temple garment**, often called simply *garments*, is a type of white underwear worn by members of the LDS church after they have gone through the endowment ceremony in the temple. LDS members receive their first temple garments during the washing and anointing part of this ceremony. An observant Mormon wears temple garments day and night; any endowed adult must wear them to enter an LDS temple. The undergarments remind those who wear them of the sacred covenants made in temple ceremonies. Today, the temple garment is worn as a rule by LDS members and by members of most Mormon fundamentalist churches, but optionally by more-liberal Mormon groups like the Community of Christ.

Read about Mormon clothing expectations on a church website.

The LDS church is structured in top-down order as follows. At the worldwide level, headquartered of course in Salt Lake City, is the First Presidency, a group of three men, including the church president (who is viewed as a prophet) and two members of the Council of the Twelve Apostles. Next is the Council of the Twelve Apostles itself, and then the First Quorum of Seventy. These men have primary spiritual and organizational leadership in the LDS church. They also administer the church's extensive properties, businesses, and relief programs. All world church leaders are "sustained in office" by a vote at the twice-yearly General Conference, which is open to public observation. At the regional level, individual churches are gathered into **stakes** of four thousand to five thousand members, under the leadership of a stake president. At the local level is the local church—called a **ward**—with no more than a few hundred members, under a bishop. Presidents and bishops are men who hold the Melchizedek priesthood, but as we said above, they are not "clergy" in the wider Christian sense, nor do they have a theological education. The religious life of the individual Mormon centers on the ward; the ward organizes weekly worship, sponsors social activities, collects tithes, and administers the local levels of the LDS church's extensive social welfare plans. With this ward activity, individual Mormons do their part to make the Church of Jesus Christ of Latter-day Saints a powerful faith.

13-6 The Church of Scientology

Scientology was born in the 1950s from the thoughts of L. Ronald Hubbard (1911–1986). Hubbard said that he aimed to understand mental and emotional problems and propose a way to end them. His initial focus was almost completely psychological, but after a few years he broadened his thinking to a more explicitly religious approach, and called it Scientology. He established the Church of Scientology in 1954, and today it is a strong—and strongly controversial—new religious movement.

Visit the sophisticated official website of the Church of Scientology.

13-6a L. Ron Hubbard's Life and Teachings

Hubbard was an undergraduate at George Washington University from 1930 to 1932 but dropped out, as he later said, to pursue more pressing personal interests. In 1933 he married and began a successful career as a short-feature writer. His output included western fiction, horror stories, and especially science fiction. He also became interested in seafaring, and was something of an adventurer. In 1940 and 1941, he obtained licenses as a master of power and sailing vessels. Nautical themes and terms would later have a large place in Scientology.

During World War II, Hubbard entered the U.S. Navy and served in naval intelligence. At the end of the war he was treated at a naval hospital in Oakland, California. This seems to have been the catalyst for his thinking on the human mind, and he began searching for a "science of the mind." His ideas first appeared in his book *The Original Thesis* (1948) and were further developed in *Dianetics: The Modern Science of Mental Health* (1950). Although *Dianetics* is by far the most important of Scientology literature, all Hubbard's publications on Scientology became the official scriptures of the church.

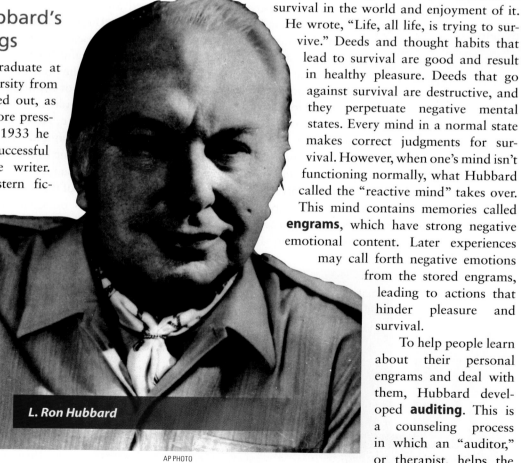

L. Ron Hubbard

AP PHOTO

Scientology
Psychologically oriented NRM founded by L. Ron Hubbard

engram In Scientology, image of past experience stored in the mind that hinders full functioning

auditing In Scientology, one-on-one counseling in which a client is helped to deal with his or her engrams

Watch a trailer for *The Master*, ostensibly based on L. Ron Hubbard.

Hubbard believed that the world is overall a good place and that the goal of human existence is survival in the world and enjoyment of it. He wrote, "Life, all life, is trying to survive." Deeds and thought habits that lead to survival are good and result in healthy pleasure. Deeds that go against survival are destructive, and they perpetuate negative mental states. Every mind in a normal state makes correct judgments for survival. However, when one's mind isn't functioning normally, what Hubbard called the "reactive mind" takes over. This mind contains memories called **engrams**, which have strong negative emotional content. Later experiences may call forth negative emotions from the stored engrams, leading to actions that hinder pleasure and survival.

To help people learn about their personal engrams and deal with them, Hubbard developed **auditing**. This is a counseling process in which an "auditor," or therapist, helps the

E-meter Electrical instrument used in Scientology auditing for identification of engrams

clear In Scientology, fully functioning state of the mind when it is rid of engrams

thetan [THAY-tan] In Scientology, spiritual entity that can exist apart from the body, the true self of every person

MEST In Scientology, matter, energy, space, and time, which form the physical universe and trap thetans

Operating Thetan Levels at which a Scientologist lives as a fully conscious, well-functioning thetan

dynamics In Scientology, the drive for survival that encompasses eight aspects

client deal with his or her engrams. A key part of auditing is the **E-meter**, a device that measures a very small electrical current that is said to pass through a person being audited. The auditor uses E-meter readings to identify engrams, and then talks out these engrams with the person being audited. The goal of auditing is to free the mind of engrams; when that is accomplished, the individual is said to be **clear**. Much of the income of Scientology comes from the fees for these auditing sessions.

What moved Hubbard to develop Dianetics into a religion was, among other things, his experience of "exteriorization." This is when the individual consciousness senses that it has left the body. His own exteriorization encouraged Hubbard to realize that the real spiritual self—what he called the **thetan**—is a being distinct from the body. The thetan is the true self of every person, but most people never know this. Thetans have inhabited many other bodies before coming into their present bodies, a concept similar to reincarnation. This emphasis on the thetan led to a religion that shares elements with some Asian religions, without embracing them. But it was incompatible with the teaching of Christian

churches. Even though Scientology is a church and has some of the trappings of Christianity such as crosses and church services (adapted for Scientology), it has never claimed to be Christian. In other words, for Hubbard and Scientologists today, *church* means simply "religious organization."

Hubbard wrote that the original Cause (loosely understood as God) created thetans billions of years ago, just before the universe began. The Cause created thetans first, and their interaction with each other gave rise to **MEST** (matter, energy, space, and time); and thus the physical universe came into existence. In time, all thetans became trapped in MEST, but they eventually lost the knowledge of who they were. After wandering through the universe, they finally came to earth.

Scientology maintains, against some controversy, that it enables people to know how engrams inhibit them from fully living as thetans. As stated above, Hubbard believed that freeing the individual from mental and emotional error is the fundamental purpose of religion. The main goal of all religion, he said, has been the salvation of the human spirit, but only Scientology knows how this salvation can be realized. The most sacred and secret doctrines of Scientology are about the **Operating Thetan** (OT) levels, at which one lives as a fully conscious, well-functioning thetan freed from their engrams and MEST. In the Operating Thetan, the spirit controls the body and can act independently of it.

In his habit of continually developing his teachings, Hubbard later identified more significant teachings, beyond the thetan. He named these **dynamics**, or drive for survival. When auditing begins, the individual first learns the dynamic of individual survival, and then the three larger dynamics: the family, the nation, and all humans. Much of the social-betterment efforts of Scientology flow from these three larger dynamics. Four other dynamics were developed to include even larger entities—animals, the physical side of the universe in MEST, the spiritual side of the universe composed of thetans, and finally infinity or God. The eight-pointed cross (Fig. 13.3), now the official symbol of Scientology, symbolizes these eight dynamics.

Examine an interactive Scientology timeline.

Finally, we should treat more fully Scientology's beliefs about God. Individual Scientologists experience God as the highest dynamic, but Scientology asks them to reach their own conclusions about who—or what—God is.

© ISTOCKPHOTO.COM/BARTONIA

A Scientology E-meter

Figure 13.3 The eight-pointed cross symbolizes the eight dynamics of Scientology, with no reference to the death of Jesus Christ.

Nevertheless, what the individual Scientologist believes about God is important. As Hubbard wrote, "It is an empirical observation that men without a strong and lasting faith in a Supreme Being are less capable, less ethical and less valuable to themselves and society." Despite this affirmation of an idea that is much contested today—that one needs a God to be good—Scientology does not specify any teachings about God, but aims to realize individual potential. Scientology is a psychological, not a theological, religion.

13-6b Organization of the Church

Hubbard always kept a firm hand on the rudder of Scientology. Soon after its founding, he started an initiative to attract Hollywood celebrities to its ranks. (See "A Closer Look: Scientology and Celebrities.") He resigned from his formal leadership of the church in 1966 in order to go to sea and discover the Operating Thetan levels and write the training materials to enable members of the church to reach them. He established a society of highly dedicated church members to whom he delegated these new teachings. He called this society the Flag Service Organization. Headquartered in Clearwater, Florida, at the Fort Harrison Hotel, now owned by the church, it provides instruction for the highest OT levels. The allied Flag Ship Service Organization, quartered on the ship Freewinds, conducts on-board training in the highest level of OT, stage VIII. Contents of the OT training is only for church members who have paid for, and successfully completed, the basic auditing to rid themselves of engrams, thus allowing them to perfect themselves as Operating Thetans.

A well-known part of Scientology is the **Sea Organization** (which Scientologists typically call *Sea Org* for short), established in 1968. Its approximately six thousand members work in the central offices of the Church of Scientology as well as in individual churches; they are considered the most dedicated of Scientologists. They sign agreements to serve in the Sea Org through thousands of lives and millions of years. Its members do not actually work for the Sea Org itself, but for the local church or office where they are employed, and receive a weekly allowance.

Scientology functions mainly through its local churches, but unlike local churches in Christianity, they are organized on a business model. Local churches are semi-independent corporations franchised to use Scientology materials, teach the religion, and conduct auditing and counseling. A church member who has become "clear" by auditing and wants to become an Operating Thetan gets instruction at one of the OT training centers. As stated above, the majority of the church's income comes from auditing sessions and instruction to reach OT levels. Administration of local Scientology churches and missions is carried out by the Church of Scientology International. The Religious Technology Center (RTC) of the Church of Scientology has final authority for the religion. It owns and cares for the manuscripts, recordings, and publications of L. Ron Hubbard—the Scientology scriptures. It also grants to local Scientology churches and regional organizations the legal permission to operate. The RTC also ensures that the church's procedures are followed, that franchises are carried out legally and faithfully, and that its "spiritual technology" (such as the E-meter) is used properly.

To meet what it described as an increasing worldwide need for Scientology, the church launched a program in 2012 to transform all local Scientology churches into what L. Ron Hubbard is said to have called "Ideal Organizations." An "Ideal Organization"

Sea Organization
Group of full-time church workers who assist national and local Scientology organizations

church offers all the programs of Scientology to its members and at the same time reaches out to the community in which it is located with social-improvement programs. Scientologists typically see themselves as uniquely qualified and obligated to provide effective service to others. This "Ideal Organization" effort shows two important aspects of Scientology today: It reaches back to its deceased founder to claim guidance for new initiatives, and it shares a wider contemporary religious impulse in North America to make religion more relevant and helpful in public life.

In the 1970s, Scientology spread throughout Europe; Hubbard's writings and course materials were translated into many languages. Following the 1980s fall of Communist governments in Eastern Europe, it also spread quickly there. Today, the Church of Scientology operates in more than 150 countries, but it remains controversial. We will examine this controversy next.

A Closer Look:

Scientology and Celebrities

Scientology has always sought to attract celebrities in art, music, and especially film. Already in 1955, shortly after Scientology was founded, L. Ron Hubbard began "Project Celebrity" to work for the conversion of prominent actors and musicians. Hubbard believed that celebrities are "special people" who have power to shape public opinion about Scientology and attract others to it. Today Scientology operates "Celebrity Centers" in Los Angeles, Nashville, and Paris, luxurious facilities that cater to celebrities. This effort to bring celebrities into the church has been highly successful.

Why would Scientology be attractive to celebrities? Perhaps the best explanation comes from Hugh B. Urban, a professor of religious studies at Ohio State University and author of one of the few academic books on Scientology, *The Church of Scientology: A History of a New Religion*.[4] After stating on a Beliefnet.com blog that the first reason is Scientology's targeting of celebrities, Urban goes on to say:

> [Scientology is] a religion that fits pretty well with a celebrity kind of personality. It's very individualistic. It celebrates your individual identity as ultimately divine. It claims to give you ultimate power over your own mind, self, destiny, so I think it fits well with an actor personality. . . . These aren't people who need more wealth, but what they do need, or often want at least, is some kind of spiritual validation for their wealth and

Scientologist and film star John Travolta speaks at a new Scientology Center in St. Petersburg, Florida.

lifestyle, and Scientology is a religion that says it's OK to be wealthy, it's OK to be famous; in fact, that's a sign of your spiritual development.[5]

Among the most well-known celebrity Scientologists are John Travolta, Kirstie Alley, Nancy Cartwright (the voice of Bart Simpson), Jason Lee, Giovanni Ribisi, Jenna Elfman, Anne Archer, and musicians Chick Corea and the late Isaac Hayes. Probably the best-known Scientology celebrity is Tom Cruise. If you don't recognize some of these names, it's because Scientology works to convert celebrities who are at or approaching what the church considers their prime; therefore, new and rising stars in the world of music and movies, whom you may know, are not often found in its ranks.

---

[4] Hugh B. Urban, *The Church of Scientology: A History of a New Religion* (Princeton: Princeton University Press, 2013).

[5] Quoted from Beliefnet.com, http://www.beliefnet.com/Faiths/Scientology/Mind-Over-Matter.aspx?p=4, accessed 1/14/2013.

13-6c Controversy and Present Status

Scientology has always been controversial. When Hubbard introduced Dianetics as a "mental therapy," physicians and psychiatrists charged that it involved practicing medicine without a license. They also disputed Dianetics's understanding of the human mind. Scientologists responded that psychiatrists deny the spiritual side of human life. Thus began what would prove to be a long conflict with the American Psychiatric Association (APA). The church developed a strong opposition to medicines used to treat mental illness, claiming they did more harm than good. Conflict with the APA, including a campaign against the popular drug Prozac, has been carried on by a special organization in the church called the Citizens' Commission on Human Rights.

Another dimension of conflict is opposition to Scientology by the federal government. In 1958, the U.S. Internal Revenue Service began investigating Scientology churches for possible violations of Federal tax laws. U.S. Food and Drug Administration agents searched the local church in Washington, D.C., in 1963 and took its E-meters, charging that they were unapproved medical appliances. These actions by the U.S. government also led to action against the church in both Australia and the United Kingdom. In response, the church created the Guardian's Office in 1966 to vigorously defend Scientology, usually by going on the offensive against its opponents. (Scientology does not usually "turn the other cheek.") The Guardian's Office filed lawsuits against publications the church considered libelous. In the 1970s it began a worldwide operation to gather information on opposition to the church. Frustrated by the U.S. government's refusal to release information about its investigations of Scientology, some leaders in the Guardian's Office approved a plan to infiltrate or break into various federal agencies. As a result, agents of the Guardian's Office were arrested in 1979 and convicted of a variety of crimes. After its own investigation, the church expelled those who broke the law, and the office was disbanded. However, the church still takes an active role in dealing with its opponents.

> *In recent years, anti-Scientology groups have led many protests and demonstrations at Scientology locations.*

In 1993 the church finally gained recognition as a religious organization and the tax-exempt status that went with it. The church saw this as recognition that it is a genuine religion. Nevertheless, Scientology faces continuing controversy and challenges. Several former members have strongly criticized the church, charging it with deceiving its members financially, harrying journalists, and acting vindictively against those who try to leave the church. Scientology is under pressure in Germany and France. In 1997 and again in 2007, Germany's domestic intelligence agency investigated the church. Some Germans hold that Scientology is a totalitarian organization, forbidden under the country's postwar constitution. The German government even proposed in the 1990s that a symbol of Scientology be put on Scientologists' identity papers, which understandably raised a storm of protest because of the use of identity marks for some groups during the Hitler era. In

Read a hard-hitting press article from *Time* magazine against Scientology.

Watch an interview with a woman who left the Sea Organization of Scientology.

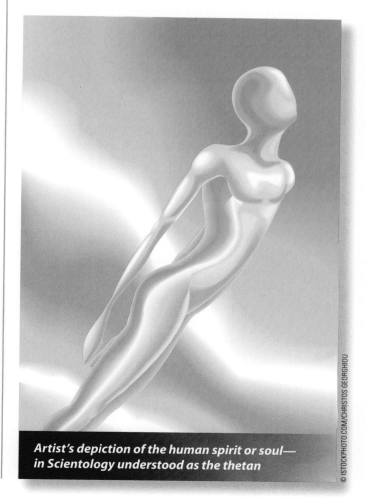

Artist's depiction of the human spirit or soul— in Scientology understood as the thetan

© ISTOCKPHOTO.COM/CHRISTOS GEORGHIOU

2009, a French court convicted Scientology officials of fraud but did not suspend the church's activities there. Scientologists regard these actions as a violation of their religious liberty.

Opposition to Scientology continues today. An increasing number of former Scientologists, a few of them high placed in the church, have gone public to oppose it. The church responds by calling them "suppressive persons," or "suppressives" for short. Especially vexing to the church has been the posting of secret, copyrighted materials for the Operating Thetan levels. In recent years, hundreds of protests and demonstrations have been held at Scientology locations in North America and Europe by anti-Scientology groups.

To conclude this chapter, we can state that NRMs, for all their wide diversity, are a religious response to modern life: pluralism; the influence of science, especially the rise of psychology and psychotherapy; a rising value placed on nature and the environment; and secularization. They are also efforts to find alternatives to the mainstream religious traditions. Although a few NRMs have come to tragic ends and some have faded away quickly, many have provided meaning in life to those who have not obtained it elsewhere. Some will eventually become part of "mainstream" religions. Even now, NRMs increase the diversity and vitality of the world's religions.

> Watch a statement by Scientologists explaining the appeal of their beliefs and practices.

Study Tools 13

Ready to study? In the book you can:

- Review Learning Outcome answers and glossary terms with the tear-out Chapter Review card.

Or you can go online to CourseMate, at www.cengagebrain.com, for these resources:

- Chapter quizzes to prepare for tests
- Interactive flashcards of all glossary terms
- A timeline of key events for this chapter
- An eBook with introductions, interactive quizzes, and live links for all web resources in the chapter

Index

Entries in boldface are key terms.

A

Abbasids, 303
Aboriginals, 33, 36, 38, 42, 43
Abraham
    in Islam, 295, 313
    in Judaism, 229–230, 232, 238, 244, 246, 252
Abu Bakr, 302, 317, 319
Adam, 256, 313, 344
Adi Granth, 140, 143, 144, 145
Africa, 9, 16, 19
    Christianity in, 266, 269, 277, 285, 290, 292
    Hinduism in, 65, 72, 90
    indigenous religions in, 32, 34–40, 42, 43, 44, 46, 53, 55, 56, 58, 59
    Islam in, 296, 301, 303, 304, 305, 307, 311, 315, 320, 325
    Jainism in, 104
    Judaism in, 229, 236, 254
    Sikhism in, 144
    Zoroastrianism in, 210, 214, 222
African Americans, 292, 327, 328, 351
Agni, 65, 67
Agnihotra, 67
agnosticism, 22
ahimsa, 72, 97, 104, 107
Ahura Mazda, 207, 209–212, 216–220, 222, 223, 225
ajiva, 102, 104
Albanese, Catherine, 35
alcohol, 53, 133, 139, 148, 201, 303, 308, 315, 317, 352
Aleichem, Sholom, 236
Ali, 302, 306, 307
Allah, 13, 295, 297–299, 307, 311, 312, 319, 321, 322
alms, 105
alternative religious movements, 335
Amaterasu, 194, 196, 197, 198, 201
American Indian, 36, 40, 53. *See also* Native Americans.
American Society of Muslims, 328
Amesha Spentas, 218
amrit, 151
Amritsar (India), 139, 143, 145, 148, 149, 150, 152, 154
Anabaptists, 272. *See also* Baptists; Radical Reformation.
Analects, 168, 170, 171, 178, 180, 185
anatta, 126
ancestor(s)
    in indigenous religions, 33, 34, 37, 44, 54, 56, 58, 61

in Confucianism and Daoism, 172, 173, 179, 182, 184
Anglican Church. *See* Church of England.
Angra Mainyu, 211, 216, 217, 218, 219
anicca, 125
animals
    in Buddhism, 119
    in Christianity, 287
    in Daoism and Confucianism, 161, 162, 173, 178, 179, 182
    in Hinduism, 64, 80, 88, 92
    in indigenous religions, 31, 33, 45, 50, 60
    in Islam, 323
    in Jainism, 101, 103, 104, 105
    in Judaism, 251
    in new religious movements, 354
    in Shinto, 191, 200
    in Zoroastrianism, 207, 211
animism, 32–33
anthropology, 17, 18, 19, 20, 33, 34
anti-Semitism, 235, 239, 241, 265
Anwar, Zainab, 310
apocalyptic, 337, 338, 343, 348
apostle(s)
Apostles' Creed
Applewhite, Marshall, 341
Aquinas, Thomas, 269, 273
Arab(s), 23, 39, 42
    and Islam, 296–300, 302–304, 309, 313, 315, 317, 318, 322, 328, 331
    and Judaism, 236, 240
    and Zoroastrianism, 207, 215
Arabia, 295, 297, 298, 300, 308, 309, 315, 325, 329
Arab Spring, 304
architecture, 3, 4, 13, 192, 270. *See also* Art.
Ark of the Covenant, 231
ark (in Jewish synagogues), 250
Armstrong, Karen, 6
art, arts, 4, 5, 9, 10, 13, 19. *See also* Architecture.
    in Buddhism, 113, 124
    in Christianity, 259, 270, 275, 287
    in Confucianism and Daoism, 165, 166, 168, 171, 187
    in indigenous religions, 43, 58
    in Islam, 300, 303, 311, 312, 313, 317
    in Jainism, 99
    in new religious movements, 356
    in Shinto, 192
    in Sikhism, 152

artha, 83
Articles of Faith, 351
Aryans, 15, 67, 68, 70, 216, 240. *See also* Indo-Europeans.
asceticism, 97, 98, 99, 113, 148
Ashkenazi, 236, 253, 255
Ashoka, 70, 117
ashram, 95
Ashura, 306
Asia
    Buddhism in, 111–119, 127, 131–136
    Christianity in, 264, 266, 267, 274, 277
    Confucianism, and Daoism in, 158, 159, 166, 185, 187
    Hinduism in, 65–67, 69, 90
    indigenous religions in, 35, 42
    Islam in, 296, 301, 303–305, 307, 325, 331
    Judaism in, 254
    new religious movements in, 337, 342, 345
    Shinto in, 194, 195, 197
    Sikhism in, 152, 153, 154
    Zoroastrianism in, 210, 212, 213, 216, 224
assimilation, 51–52, 53, 136, 153, 155, 238, 253, 256
Ataturk, Kemal, 304
atheism, 22
atman, 69, 77, 89, 126
auditing (Scientology), 353, 354, 355
Aum Shinrikyo, 343
Avesta, 213, 216, 220, 222
Axial Age, 210
Azad, M., 309

B

Baal Shem Tov, 237
babalawo, 57
Babylonian Talmud, 235–236, 238, 239, 242, 245–248, 250–251, 253, 256
Balfour Declaration, 239
baptism
    in Christianity, 262, 264, 272, 278, 280, 282, 284, 287–289
    in Latter-day Saint Church, 351, 352
    in Sikhism, 151
baptism for the dead, 352
Baptists, 289, 292. *See also* Anabaptists.
bar mitzvah, bat/bas mitzvah, 249, 252, 253

Baron Samedi, 60
Barr, James, 208
Barth, Karl, 275
basilica, 287
Battle Hymn of the Tiger Mother
    (Chua), 178
Bellah, Robert, 6
Benedict XVI, Pope, 23, 276
Beneke, Stephen, 25
benevolence, 248
Ben-Ur, Aviva, 255
Bhagavad Gita, 70, 71, 72, 73, 74, 76,
    88, 92
bhakti, 71, 89
Bianchi, Robert, 324
Bible, 28. *See also* Scripture; Canon.
    and Islam, 299, 313, 323
    and new religious movements, 341,
        349, 350
    and Zoroastrianism, 208
    Christian, 262, 265, 267–270,
        274–275, 283, 285, 287,
        288–290
    Jewish, 230–234, 239, 242, 243, 245,
        247, 248, 253, 256
bindi, 84, 85
birth, 15, 18, 19, 27
    in Buddhism, 113, 114,
    in Christianity, 262, 281, 285
    in Confucianism and Daoism,
        177, 180
    in Hinduism, 69, 74, 81, 85
    in indigenous religions, 42, 44, 49, 57
    in Jainism, 102
    in Judaism, 234
    in Shinto, 196
    in Sikhism, 152
    in Zoroastrianism, 210, 212
bishop, 261, 267, 269, 291, 352
Black Elk, 50, 52, 53
Blavatsky, Helena, 134, 338
Bodhi Tree, 115
Bodhidharma, 119, 120, 121
bodhisattva, 119, 122
Bonhoeffer, Dietrich, 241
Bono, 285
Book of Mormon, 27, 347, 348, 349,
    350, 351
de Botton, Alain, 22
Bowker, John, 5
Boyce, Mary, 208
Brahman, 66, 69, 75, 76, 77, 78, 89, 123
Brahmanas, 68
Brahmins (caste), 68, 72, 79, 80
Branch Davidian, 338
bris milah, 252. *See also* Circumcision.
Buber, Martin, 249
buddha, 112, 113, 119, 122
Buddha, the (Gautama) 3, 7, 20, 24
    in Buddhism, 111–121, 123, 125–130,
        132, 134, 136, 137
    in Jainism, 98
    in Shinto, 191, 193, 196
Buddhism, Buddhists, 3, 4, 6, 7, 11, 13,
    14, 16, 18, 23, 24, 27, 28
    around the world today, 132–136

    and Confucianism and Daoism, 158,
        163, 166, 167, 169, 171, 173, 176,
        179, 181, 183–185
    ethics, 126–128
    and Hinduism, 66, 69, 70, 89
    history, 113–123
    and indigenous religions, 42, 54
    and Jainism, 95, 102, 103, 105
    name, 112–113
    and new religious movements, 335,
        338–340, 343–347
    ritual and meditation, 128–132
    and Shinto, 190–194, 196–199,
        201–205
    symbol, 113
    teachings, 123–128
Buddhist Catechism, 134
burial. *See also* Funeral, death, cremation.
    in Buddhism, 132
    in Christianity, 263
    in Confucianism and Daoism, 161,
        183, 184
    in Hinduism, 88
    in indigenous religions, 46, 60
    in Judaism, 254
    in Shinto, 20
    in Zoroastrianism, 223

C

caliph, 302, 309
Calvin, John, 272
canon. *See also* Scripture.
    in Buddhism, 117, 120, 128
    in Christianity, 262, 265
    in Confucianism and Daoism, 163,
        165–167, 170
    in Jainism, 99
    in Judaism, 242
    in new religious movement, 350, 351
canon law, 285, 288
Cao Dai, 345
caste
    in Buddhism, 114, 127
    in Hinduism, 65, 70, 72, 73, 75–77,
        79–83, 86, 88, 90–92
    in Jainism, 98, 107
    in Sikhism, 147, 148, 149, 153
catechumen, 284
Catholic Church, 259, 260, 268–282,
    285, 286, 288–291
Catholic Reform, 273, 281, 286, 289
celibacy, celibate. *See also* Sex.
    in Buddhism, 127
    in Christianity, 267, 281
    in Hinduism, 72, 82
    in Jainism, 105
    in Zoroastrianism, 217, 220
chador, 318
Chalcedon, 282
charismatic movement. *See also*
    Pentecostalism. 13, 231, 276, 282,
    289, 309
chaur, 149, 150

child, children, 8, 17, 20, 22, 23
    in Buddhism, 117, 126, 137
    in Christianity, 272, 278, 281, 292
    in Confucianism and Daoism, 168,
        171, 178, 179, 181, 183
    in Hinduism, 68, 79, 80, 82, 83, 85,
        88, 91
    in indigenous religions, 37, 44, 52,
        54, 57
    in Islam, 299, 317, 319, 323
    in Judaism, 239, 243, 246, 252,
        253, 254
    in new religious movements, 338, 344,
        349, 352
    in Shinto, 196, 200,
    in Sikhism, 147, 148, 149, 151, 154
    in Zoroastrianism, 214, 219, 220,
        223, 224
Chinvat Bridge, 218
Christ, 27. *See also* Jesus.
    in Christianity, 258–262, 264, 267,
        268, 270, 277, 278–284, 288, 290,
        292, 293
    in Islam, 297
    in new religious movements, 332, 333,
        336–338, 340, 344, 347, 349,
        350–352, 355
Christendom, 260, 269
Christian Science Church, 27, 340
Christianity, Christians, 4, 6, 9, 12–16,
    19–21, 23–28
    around the world today, 290–293
    and Buddhism, 127, 133, 134, 136
    and Confucianism and Daoism, 167,
        170, 171, 173, 184
    ethics, 283–285
    and Hinduism, 70, 72
    history, 261–276
    and indigenous religions, 37, 42, 43,
        45, 46, 50, 53, 54, 55, 56, 57,
        59, 61
    and Islam, 296–300, 303, 310–312,
        314, 315, 320, 325
    and Judaism, 228, 230, 234, 235, 236,
        238, 242, 243, 245, 246
    name, 260
    and new religious movements, 335,
        337, 338, 341–345, 347, 348, 351,
        354, 355
    and Shinto, 194
    and Sikhism, 147, 151
    symbol, 261
    teaching, 277–282
    worship and ritual, 286–289
    and Zoroastrianism, 208, 213, 216
Chua, Amy, 178
Church of England, 272, 273, 274, 276,
    289, 290, 291, 316
Church of Jesus Christ of Latter-day
    Saints, 27, 293, 332, 333, 336. *See
    also* Mormons.
    history, 347–350
    institution, practices, and structure,
        351–352
    scripture, 350–351
    teachings, 351

circumcision, 230, 231, 234, 244, 249, 252, 287
city gods, 175
civil religion, 18
clear (Scientology), 347, 354, 355
confession, 19, 145, 219, 242, 288, 320, 321
confessionalism, 274
Confucianism, Confucianists, 6, 7, 16
   around the world today, 185–186
   and Buddhism, 119, 132
   ethics, 179–181
   history, 161–163, 167–171
   names, 159–160
   and new religious movements, 342, 343, 344, 345
   ritual and worship, 182–184
   and Shinto, 190, 192, 193, 194, 198
   symbol, 160
   teaching 172–173, 177–178
Confucian Centers, 185
Confucius, 7, 9, 158–161, 163, 165, 167–171, 174, 177–186
Conservative (Judaism), 239
Constantine, 264, 267, 268, 286, 287, 288
Constantinianism, 267, 274
cosmogonic myth, 43
Council of the Twelve Apostles, 348
covenant (Judaism), 230–233, 244, 246, 248, 252
create, creation, 11, 26. *See also* Earth, World
   and Buddhism, 125, 126
   and Christianity, 268, 270, 274, 278, 280, 283, 285
   and Hinduism, 65, 66, 67, 74, 75, 76
   and indigenous religions, 34, 43, 49, 54, 56
   and Islam, 298, 311, 328
   and Jainism, 101
   and Judaism, 230, 250, 253, 254
   and new religious movements, 344, 345, 352
   and Shinto, 192, 194, 199
   and Sikhism, 145, 146
   and Zoroastrianism, 216, 218
creed, 190, 217, 277, 278
cremation. *See also* Death, Funeral.
   in Buddhism, 115, 116, 132
   in Confucianism and Daoism, 183
   in Hinduism, 64, 83, 88, 90
   in Sikhism, 141, 143
   in Zoroastrianism, 207
cross (symbol), 259, 261, 262, 298, 303, 354, 355
crucifix, 261, 279
Cruise, Tom, 27, 356
Crusades, 24, 269, 303
cult, 23, 27, 59, 60, 91, 169, 288, 335, 336, 339, 345, 346
cult of the saints, 288
cult religion, 59
cultural anthropology, 18
cultural intelligence, 10
Cultural Revolution (China), 167, 171
Custer, George, 52
Cyrus Cylinder, 211

D

daevas, 217
Dalai Lama, 121, 122, 123, 133, 136, 171
Dalits, 77, 79, 80, 81, 88, 127
Dao, 159, 160, 165, 170, 172–174, 176–179, 181, 184, 187, 342
Daode Jing, 159, 163, 164, 166, 172, 174, 176, 178, 179, 185, 187
Daoism, Daoists, 7, 16, 27
   around the world today, 185–187
   and Buddhism, 119, 132
   ethics, 179
   history, 161–167, 170–172
   name, 159
   and new religious movements, 342, 345, 347
   ritual and worship, 181–184
   and Shinto, 190, 192, 194
   symbol, 160
   teachings, 172–177
Daozang, 165, 166, 167, 170
Darbar Sahib (Harmandir Sahib), 143
Dasam Granth, 144
David (Israelite king), 229, 231, 232, 243, 246
Day of Atonement, 234, 250, 300
De, 172
death, 5, 9, 10, 11, 13, 17. *See also* Funeral.
   in Buddhism, 113, 114, 116, 119, 123, 126, 128–130, 132
   in Christianity, 260, 261, 262, 263, 270, 278–280, 283, 284
   in Confucianism and Daoism, 170, 174, 175, 177, 181, 183, 184
   in Hinduism, 64, 66, 69, 71, 72, 74, 75, 77, 83–85, 88, 90
   in indigenous religions, 44–46, 49, 50–52, 54, 60
   in Islam, 300, 302, 303, 306, 308, 314, 316–319, 328, 329
   in Jainism, 97, 98, 101–103, 107, 108
   in Judaism, 232, 234, 241, 242, 245, 246, 247, 253, 254
   in new religious movements, 334, 343, 351, 355
   in Shinto, 194, 200, 204
   in Sikhism, 142, 143, 144, 151, 152
   in Zoroastrianism, 218–219, 222–223
Deloria, Vine, 39
denominations, 275, 278, 285, 289, 291, 292, 293, 342, 347
dharani, 131
dharma, 76, 77, 78, 80, 83, 116, 123, 127, 129, 347
dharmachakra, 113
dhoti, 84
Dianetics, 353, 354, 357
diaspora, 91, 152, 153, 233, 242, 254
Digambar, 98, 99, 100, 101, 106, 107
divination, 45, 57, 58, 119, 161, 162, 172, 182
divorce, 85, 255, 272, 316, 318, 319

Diwali, 88, 108, 152
Doctrine and Covenants, 350, 351
Dravidians, 66
Druidry, Druids, 341, 342
dualism, 160, 206, 216, 217, 218
dukkah, 126
Durkheim, Emile, 6, 18
Dyer, Wayne, 187
dynamics, 354–355

E

Earth, 3, 4, 20, 22, 26. *See also* Create, Creation; World.
   in Buddhism, 112
   in Confucianism and Daoism, 174
   in Hinduism, 63
   in indigenous religions, 36, 40, 46, 56, 57
   in Islam, 295
   in Jainism, 99
   in Judaism, 230
   in new religious movements, 322, 333, 338
   in Shinto, 191
   in Zoroastrianism, 207, 218
ecology, 3, 10, 26, 133, 200, 341
ecumenism, 275, 276
Eddy, Mary Baker, 340
Eightfold Path. *See* Noble Eightfold Path.
Ek Onkar, 146
Eliade, Mircea, 12, 45
Elizabeth I, 273
ema, 190, 202
emancipation, 230, 238, 241, 276
emergent religions, 335
E-meter, 354, 355, 357
endowment, 352
engram, 353
Enlightenment, 14, 22, 25, 114, 115, 245, 246, 274
Essenes, 234
etiological myth, 43
Eucharist, 282, 287, 288
evangelical, 22, 276, 290, 291, 292, 342
Evangelicalism, 276, 292
Eve, 313, 341, 344
exoticism, 60–61, 134
Ezra, 233

F

Fackenheim, Emile, 24
faith of kindred marriage, 220
Falun Gong, 4, 23, 24, 27, 171, 332, 335, 336, 343, 345–347
faravahar, 209, 216
Farrakhan, Louis, 325, 327, 328, 329
fast, fasting, 7. *See also* Food.
   in Buddhism, 115, 127
   in Christianity, 287
   in Hinduism, 51

fast, fasting (*continued*)
    in Islam, 299, 300, 317, 320, 323, 326
    in Jainism, 90, 95, 103, 108
    in Zoroastrianism, 217
al-Fatihah, 313
fatwa, 316
feminism, feminist, 20, 133, 274, 276,
    283, 341
feng shui, 162, 172, 183
fire temple, 215, 220, 221
First Nations (Canada), 36
First Temple Period (Israelite), 229, 230,
    231, 232
Five Ks, 141, 147, 148, 151
Five Pillars of Islam, 320–324
food, 12. *See also* Vegetarianism.
    in Buddhism, 111, 116, 128, 137
    in Christianity, 264, 287, 288
    in Confucianism and Daoism,
        177, 183
    in Hinduism, 72, 74, 81, 86, 88,
        90, 92
    in Islam, 315, 317, 320, 323, 330
    in Jainism, 105–107
    in Judaism, 238, 251–252, 254
    in Shinto, 189, 200, 203, 204
    in Sikhism, 139, 140, 147, 150, 151
    in Zoroastrianism, 207, 224
Forbidden City (Beijing), 157–158
forest-dweller stage, 82
forgiveness, 19, 108, 219, 263, 270, 278,
    282–284, 288, 315
Four Books, 169, 170
Four Noble Truths, 11, 116, 123,
    125–126
Four Passing Sights, 114–115
Francis, Pope, 276
Frank, Anne, 241
Freud, Sigmund, 6, 17, 238
friar, 269, 270
fundamentalism, 73, 275, 306, 309, 310
**Fundamentalist Church of Jesus Christ
    of Latter-Day Saints (FLDS)**,
    349–350
funeral. *See also* Death; Cremation.
    in Buddhism, 116, 132
    in Confucianism and Daoism, 169,
        181, 183
    in Hinduism, 64, 72, 83, 85, 88, 90
    in indigenous religions, 49
    in Judaism, 254
    in Shinto, 200, 204
    in Sikhism, 146, 149, 151
    in Zoroastrianism, 207, 210, 213,
        219, 223

G

gaccchas, 100
Gandhi, Mohandas, 63, 72, 73, 104, 145
Gathas, 210, 219
Geertz, Clifford, 19, 20
genocide, 37, 241, 251, 320

genre, 61, 71
Gentiles, 246, 263, 264, 265, 284
Gere, Richard 136
Ghadar, 153, 154
ghetto, 236
ghost dance, 52, 53
Global South Christians, 276, 290–291
Gnosticism, 266, 267
Gobind, Guru, 140, 143, 144, 151, 152
Goodstein, Laurie, 4
Gospel, 259, 262, 263, 277, 279, 281
government, 4, 9, 10, 22, 23, 24, 25
    in Buddhism, 121, 122, 131, 133, 134
    in Christianity, 272, 273, 285, 287, 290
    in Confucianism and Daoism, 158,
        161, 164, 165, 167, 168, 169,
        170, 171, 174, 177, 185, 186
    in Hinduism, 73, 78, 80, 83, 85
    in indigenous religions, 42, 51, 52, 53
    in Islam, 297, 307, 309, 314, 317,
        318, 320, 322, 323, 326, 329, 331
    in Judaism, 231, 235, 238, 239, 241,
        248, 255
    in new religious movements, 338, 342,
        343, 345–349, 356, 357
    in Shinto, 192, 193, 194, 195
    in Sikhism, 140, 145, 148
    in Zoroastrianism, 224
granthi, 150
Grebel, Conrad, 270
gris-gris, 60
gurdwara, 147, 149, 150, 151, 153, 155
Gurmat, 140
guru
    in Buddhism, 122
    in Hinduism, 78, 81, 87
    in new religious movements, 339, 340
    in Sikhism, 140, 142–146, 149, 152
Guru Granth, 140, 141, 143, 144, 146,
    148, 149, 150, 151, 152, 153, 154

H

hadith, 315, 316, 317, 318, 319, 320, 321
hajj, 323, 324, 326
hajji, 324
halakhah, 248
halal, 317
Hall, David D., 273
Hamer, Dean, 21
hanifs, 298
Hanukkah, 229, 234, 251
haoma, 222
haram, 317
Harmandir Sahib, 143
Hasidism, 237
heaven
    in Buddhism, 119, 123
    in Christianity, 259, 262, 268, 269,
        270, 277, 278, 280, 287
    in Hinduism, 67, 85, 88
    in Islam, 300, 314, 315, 316, 324
    in Jainism, 97, 101, 102, 103

    in Judaism, 245, 246, 252
    in new religious movements, 340,
        341, 342
    in Zoroastrianism, 208, 211, 218, 219
Heaven's Gate, 341
Hebrews, 229, 251, 350
hell
    in Buddhism, 119, 123, 126
    in Islam, 315
    in Jainism, 102, 103
    in Judaism, 245, 246
    in Zoroastrianism, 208, 211, 218, 219
henotheism, 242
Henry VIII, 272
heresy, 266, 267
Heschel, Abraham, 232
Hijra, 300
Hinayana, 117
Hinduism, Hindus, 6, 7, 12, 13, 14, 16,
    20, 23, 24, 26, 27
    around the world today, 89–91
    and Buddhism, 112–115, 118, 123,
        124, 126, 127
    ethics, 78–84
    history, 65–73
    and indigenous religions, 32, 35
    and Islam, 308
    and Jainism, 95, 97–100, 102–104,
        107, 109
    name, 65
    new religious movements,
        338–340, 345
    rituals, 85–89
    and Sikhism, 139–141, 144–149,
        151, 152
    symbol, 66
    teachings, 74–78
    and Zoroastrianism, 211, 214, 217,
        219, 220
Hindutva, 73
Hirata, 194
historical-critical method, 15
history of religions school, 15
Hitchens, Christopher, 22
Hitler, Adolf, 240, 241, 357
Holocaust, 24, 230, 240–241, 244, 275,
    338, 352
Holy Spirit, 260, 264, 277–283, 286,
    287, 289, 344, 351
honden, 201
householder stage, 82
Hubbard, L. Ron, 13, 353–357
Husain, 306, 307
husband, 56, 71–72, 76, 83, 85, 92, 147,
    172, 179, 181, 192, 204, 299,
    318. *See also* Wife.
hymn, 67, 79, 80, 143, 151, 289

I

Iconoclastic Controversy, 268
iconostasis, 268
idol, 86, 100, 107

Ifa, 57
imam, 306, 307, 311, 314, 316, 322
immortality, 151, 167, 177, 209, 246
indigenous religion, 9
    and Buddhism, 118
    challenges to study, 36–38
    common features, 38–45
    names, 32–35
    and new religious movements, 338
    and Shinto, 190
Indo-European, 67, 153, 211
Indra, 67
Indus Valley civilization, 66
insight meditation, 131
Ise Shrine, 194
Islam, Muslim, 4, 6, 9, 7, 8, 11, 12, 14,
    16, 19, 20–24, 26, 27
    around the world today, 325–330
    and Buddhism, 118
    and Christianity, 260, 266, 268, 269,
      271, 291
    and Confucianism and Daoism, 171,
      173, 187
    ethics, 315–319
    and Hinduism, 32, 37, 42, 46, 55, 65,
      72, 73, 89
    history, 297–310
    and Jainism, 99, 100
    and Judaism, 228, 233, 235, 236, 240,
      242, 245, 246, 253
    name, 297
    and new religious movements, 333, 345
    and Sikhism, 139–141, 143–147, 149,
      153–155
    symbol, 298
    teachings, 311–315
    worship: the Five Pillars, 320–324
    and Zoroastrianism, 207, 208, 213,
      214, 215, 216, 222
Islamist, 297, 310
Israel, 226–234, 237, 239, 240, 242–
    244, 254, 255, 260, 262, 263, 278
    and Islam, 315, 320, 329
Israelis, 229, 255
Israelites, 228–231, 235, 244, 247, 347
iyalawo, 57
Izanagi, 192
Izanami, 192

J

Jade Emperor, 174, 175, 186
JAINA, 10
Jainism, Jains, 6
    around the world today 108–109
    ethics, 104–105
    and Hinduism, 66, 69, 70, 72
    history, 96–100
    name, 96
    ritual and worship 106–108
    and Sikhism, 152
    teachings, 101–103
    and Zoroastrianism, 220

James, William, 15, 17, 18
jati, 79, 81
Jenkins, Philip, 15
Jensen, Lionel, 160
Jerusalem, 12
    in Christianity, 262, 263, 264, 286
    in Islam, 300, 303, 311, 316, 323, 324
    in Judaism, 227–229, 231–234, 239,
      241, 243–245, 249, 250, 253,
Jesus, 7, 8, 27. *See also* Christ.
    in Christianity, 258–268, 270,
      277–284, 286–290, 292, 293
    in Confucianism and Daoism,
      167, 187
    in Hinduism, 72
    in Islam, 297, 300, 311, 313, 314
    in Judaism, 234
    in new religious movements, 332, 333,
      336, 337, 341, 344, 347, 349,
      350–352, 355
    in Zoroastrianism, 208
jihad, 310, 315, 319, 320, 323, 329
Jina, 96, 106, 107
jing, 162
jinn, 312
jiva, 77, 102, 104
Johnson, Paul, 245
Judaism, Jews, 6, 13, 23
    around the world today, 254–256
    and Christianity, 260, 261, 263–266,
      276, 278, 283, 286
    ethics, 246–248
    history, 230–241
    and Islam, 299, 300, 311, 312, 314
    name, 228
    symbols, 229
    teachings, 242–245
    worship and ritual, 249–253
    and Zoroastrianism, 208, 211, 216
judgment, 5, 28
    in Christianity, 262, 282
    in Islam, 299, 308, 313, 314, 315
    in Judaism, 245, 246
    in Zoroastrianism, 208, 211, 218–219
Jung, Carl, 17
junzi, 181
justification, 264

K

Kabbalah, 236
kahuna, 54, 55
kalpa, 102
kama, 83
kami, 189, 191, 192, 193, 195, 196, 197,
    198, 199, 200, 201, 202, 203, 204
kamidana, 203
kamikaze, 197
Kami no michi, 191
kapu, 54, 55
karma
    in Buddhism, 123–124, 127–128,
      131–132

    in Hinduism, 77, 78, 83, 85, 88, 89
    in Jainism, 95, 101–105, 107, 108
Kehoe, Alice, 33–34
Keown, Damien, 114
Kethuvim, 242
Kevalin, 103
Khadija, 299, 300, 317
Khalsa, 144, 145, 146, 147, 148, 150,
    151, 154
khanda, 141
Khomeini, Ruholla, 306, 320
kirtan, 149, 150
koan, 120, 121
Kohn, Lydia, 159, 186
Kojiki, 192, 194 , 198
kosher, 236, 238, 251, 252
Kshatriyas, 80
Kuly, Lisa, 202
Kumbha Mela, 87
kusti, 222

L

laity, 13
Lakota religion, 30, 32, 36, 38, 42, 43
    basic features, 49–50
    culture and religions, 51–52
    name and location, 46–48
    rituals, 50–51
lama, 121
langar, 148, 151, 154, 155
Laozi, 163, 164, 166, 174, 178
Laveau, Marie, 60, 61
Laws of Manu, 71
lectionary, 287
letter, 23, 24, 149, 151, 248, 264, 343
letters, 66, 151, 242, 259, 261, 264,
    265, 284
Lewis, James and Sarah, 15
Li Hongzhi, 345, 346
liberation theology, 277, 338
life-cycle ritual, 19
lingam, 74, 75, 86
Little Big Horn, 52
liturgical (church) year, 289
liturgy, 215, 286, 288, 289
loa, 59, 60
Love, Velma, 57
Luhrmann, Tanya, 292
Luther, Martin, 237, 270, 272, 274, 292

M

Maccabean Revolt, 234
Madonna (pop singer), 249
magi, 221, 222
Magisterial Reformation, 270
Mahavira, 96, 97, 98, 99, 106, 108
Mahayana, 27, 118–120, 122, 124, 126,
    128–131, 174, 194, 198, 199

Mahdi, 307, 314
Maimonides, 236, 242, 245, 246
mainline (Christianity), 291
Malcolm X, 328
Malina, Bruce, 19
manaism, 33
mandala, 125
Mandate of Heaven, 168, 170
mantra, 72, 78, 89, 91, 107, 131, 339
Mao Zedong, 167, 171
marginal religious movements, 335
marriage, 11
    in Buddhism, 123, 127
    in Christianity, 288
    in Hinduism, 74, 78, 79, 81, 82, 85, 91
    in Islam, 294, 299, 302, 311, 315, 317, 319
    in Jainism, 105
    in Judaism, 248, 253
    in new religious movements, 336, 344, 349
    in Shinto, 192
    in Sikhism, 148, 149, 151
    in Zoroastrianism, 218, 220
martial arts, 124, 152, 165, 166
martyrdom, 265, 267, 306
Marx, Karl, 6, 18, 238
Mary (mother of Jesus), 208, 259, 273, 278, 279, 280, 281, 288, 313, 340
Masorti, 239
Maspero, Henri, 185
Massacre at Wounded Knee, 53
Mazdayasnian religion, 210
Mazu, 174, 175, 186
Mecca, 12, 141, 295–300, 307–309, 316, 317, 320, 322–324, 326–328. See also Hajj.
meditation, 4, 7, 12, 17, 18
    in Buddhism, 111, 112, 113, 115, 116, 119, 120, 126, 128–136
    in Confucianism and Daoism, 165, 167, 177, 181
    in Hinduism, 66, 67, 68, 69, 72, 78, 82, 85, 89, 91
    in Jainism, 95, 103, 104, 105, 106, 107, 108
    in new religious movements, 339, 340, 343, 345, 346, 347
    in Sikhism, 142, 146, 150
Meiji Restoration, 195
Mencius, 169, 170, 185
menorah, 229
Messiah, 262, 265, 344
MEST, 354
Middle Path, 110, 113, 115
miko, 191, 202, 203
millenarianism, 337, 338
minaret, 321
minyan, 249
Mishnah, 235, 248
mohel, 252
moksha, 77, 78, 82, 83, 88, 103
Momaday, N. Scott, 36
monasticism, 100, 116, 127, 128, 267
money, 9, 10; see also Poor, Rich.
    in Buddhism, 127, 128

in Confucianism and Daoism, 161, 176, 183, 184
    in Hinduism, 60
    in Islam, 309, 323
    in Jainism, 87, 99
    in Judaism, 236
    in Shinto, 202
    in Sikhism, 139, 153
monk (s), 3, 11, 13, 24
    in Buddhism, 111–114, 116–128, 130–136
    in Christianity, 267–270, 279, 289
    in Daoism, 167, 183, 186
    in Jainism, 94–99, 101, 103–109
    in new religious movements, 345
    in Shinto, 202
monotheism, 7, 17, 42, 206, 211, 214, 217, 219, 227, 228, 242, 243, 247, 248, 265, 283, 299, 311, 312, 321
Montanism, 281
Moon, Sung Myung, 344, 345
Mormon(s), 27, 333, 347–352
Moses, 17, 231, 236, 237, 238, 239, 243, 248, 256, 283, 313, 314
mosque, 13, 73, 144, 269, 287, 296, 300, 303, 304, 306, 311, 312, 321–325, 327, 331
mudra, 129
Muhammad, 7, 295–300, 302, 303, 306–317, 319, 321, 323–325, 327–329
Müller, Max, 10, 15, 185
murti, 86
Muslim Brotherhood, 306, 309, 310, 320
myth, 12, 15, 33, 43, 54–56, 59, 192, 200

N

Nair, Mira 92
Nam, 146
Namokar Mantra, 107
Nanak, 140, 141, 142, 143, 144, 146, 149, 152
Nasr, Seyyed Hossein, 26
Nation of Islam, 325, 327, 328
Native American Church, 50–51
Native Americans, 26, 31, 34, 35, 36, 42, 49, 50, 52, 53, 291
nature religion, 35
navjote, 222
Nayar, Kamala Elizabeth, 153
Neo-Confucianism, 169
Neo-Daoism, 166
Neusner, Jacob, 232, 233, 241
New Age, 10, 35, 338, 345
new religions, 343
new religious movements (NRMs), 4, 9, 12, 18, 27, 28, 140, 195, 288, 293
    common features, 336–337

names, 335
    survey of world NRMs today, 337–344
New Testament, 19, 260, 262, 264, 265, 270, 272, 280–281, 283, 284, 287, 313, 338, 352
Newberg, Andrew, 18
Nguyen, Bich Minh 137
Nicene Creed, 258, 277–280, 282, 293
Nichiren, 120, 121, 131, 343, 344
Nihongi, 192, 194, 198
nirvana, 95, 103, 113, 116, 119, 123–125, 128–131
Noble Eightfold Path, 113, 116, 123–126
noble savages, 37
Noll, Mark, 290
Nova Religio, 335, 336
Nowruz or Noruz, 222
NRM(s). See New Religious Movements.
nun(s), 18, 20
    in Buddhism, 112, 116, 126, 127, 133, 137
    in Christianity, 267, 268, 270
    in Jainism, 94–97, 98, 100, 101, 103–107

O

Ogun, 55
Olcott, Henry Steel, 134, 136
Old Testament, 287
Olorun, 55, 59
Om (Aum), 65, 66, 75, 78, 120
omikuji, 202–203
Operating Thetan, 354, 355, 358
oracle bones, 162, 182
oral tradition, 20, 21, 67, 234, 256
orisha, 55–56
Orthodox (Judaism), 237, 274
orthodoxy (Christianity), 267
Otto, Rudolf, 6
outcastes, 64, 70, 73, 79, 80

P

Pan-Indian movement, 40, 50
Panth, 140
parable, 262
parinirvana, 116
paritta, 131
parshad, 150, 151
Parshvanatha, 97
Parsis, 210, 214, 215, 221
Paryusana, 108
Passover, 242, 251, 255, 262, 287
patet, 222
patriarchs, 230
patriarchy, 20
Paul, Apostle, 6, 130, 208, 245, 263–265, 281–286

peace, 6, 10, 14. *See also* Nivana; War.
  in Buddhism, 111, 122, 123, 124, 126
  in Christianity, 267, 284
  in Confucianism and Daoism, 178, 186
  in Hinduism, 64, 89
  in Islam, 295, 297, 319
  in Jainism, 103, 106, 107
  in Judaism, 240, 246, 248
  in new religious movements, 337, 339, 340
  in Shinto, 197, 199
  in Sikhism, 143, 146, 149
Pearl of Great Price, 350
Pentecostalism, 289. *See also* Charismatic movement.
People of the Book, 214, 314
People's Temple, 338
Persian Empire, 210, 211, 212, 213, 233
Peter, Apostle, 255, 259, 260, 264, 265, 269, 270, 276
Peterson, Daniel, 300
peyote, 37, 40, 46, 50, 51
Pharisees, 234, 235, 245, 262
phenomenology of religion, 21
Pietism, 274, 292
pilgrimage, pilgrim, 12
  in Buddhism, 128, 133
  in Christianity, 263, 288
  in Confucianism and Daoism, 175
  in Hinduism, 63, 85, 86, 87
  in Islam, 295, 300, 307, 316, 320, 323, 324, 326, 328
  in Jainism, 101
  in Shinto, 204
  in Sikhism, 142, 149
  in Zoroastrianism, 207, 208
Pinyin, 159. *See also* Wade-Giles.
Pirsig, Robert, 135
plural marriage, 349
pluralism, 18, 25, 26, 91, 205, 337, 358
polytheism, 7, 17, 23, 211, 311
poor, poverty. *See also* Money; Rich.
  in Buddhism, 124
  in Christianity, 263, 267
  in Confucianism and Daoism, 178
  in Hinduism, 72, 73, 77, 79, 82
  in indigenous religions, 35, 53, 60, 61
  in Islam, 295, 299, 310, 315, 323, 328
  in Judaism, 231, 232, 255
  in Sikhism, 139
pope, 23, 24, 259, 269, 272, 273, 276, 281, 285, 290, 291
Portman, Natalie, 246
possession cult, 59–60
prayer, 4, 12, 13, 18
  in Buddhism, 116, 117, 122, 130, 131
  in Christianity, 261, 276, 278, 281, 283, 286, 288, 289
  in Confucianism and Daoism, 157
  in Hinduism, 63, 67, 68, 72, 74, 76
  in indigenous religions, 40, 54
  in Islam, 295, 300, 306, 313, 320–323
  in Jainism, 95, 107, 108
  in Judaism, 227, 231, 237, 245, 254

in Shinto, 189, 190, 198–199, 200–202, 204
  in Sikhism, 150, 151
precept (Buddhism), 126–127
preunderstanding, 2, 4, 5
priest(s), 10, 13, 23
  in Christianity, 259, 261, 269, 270, 273, 276, 284, 285
  in Confucianism and Daoism, 179, 185, 186
  in Hinduism, 64, 65, 67–69, 72, 79, 85, 86, 88, 90, 91, 92
  in indigenous religions, 45, 54, 55, 57, 58, 59, 60
  in Judaism, 234, 244
  in Shinto, 189, 191, 192, 196, 197, 199, 202, 203, 204
  in Zoroastrianism, 207, 208, 210, 212, 215, 218, 220, 221, 222
primitive religion, 32
private religion, 7
prophets, 231, 232, 242, 248, 280, 313, 314, 347, 349, 350
Prothero, Stephen, 4, 9, 25, 158, 159, 319
puja, 84, 85, 86, 87, 100, 144
Pure Land, 119, 120
purgatory, 270
Puritans, 273
purity, 54, 69, 86, 107, 126, 147, 189, 192, 200, 208, 222, 223, 308

Q

al-Qaeda, 310, 329, 331; *see also* Bin Laden.
qi, 172, 176, 177, 183, 187, 343, 346
Qi Gong, 343, 346, 347
qiblah, 322
Qufu, 167, 168, 182

R

rabbis, 18, 230, 235, 236, 245–249, 251, 255
Radical Reformation, 270, 272
Raëlians, 341
Rajneesh International Foundation, 339
Ramadan (Muslim month), 299, 300, 320, 323, 326
Ramadan, Tariq, 304
rebirth
  in Buddhism, 113, 114, 123, 126, 127, 132
  in Christianity, 270
  in Hinduism, 64, 66, 69, 77, 83, 87
  in indigenous religions, 46, 50, 54
  in new religious movements, 343
Reform
reincarnation, 4
  in Buddhism, 113, 122, 123, 124, 126, 132

in Hinduism, 69, 71, 72, 76, 77, 78, 83, 88
  in indigenous religions, 55
  in Jainism, 95, 97, 98, 101, 102, 103, 104, 105, 106, 107, 108
  in Scientology, 354
  in Sikhism, 141, 146
religion
  definition, 5–8
  dimensions of, 10–13
  preunderstanding, 4–5
  reasons for study, 8–10
  special issues in studying, 21–28
  ways of study, 14–21
religious studies, 10, 14, 15, 18–20, 21, 26, 27, 32, 241, 334, 335, 343, 356
ren, 36, 180, 200
Reorganized Church of Jesus Christ of Latter-day Saints, 349
Restorationism (Christianity), 292
resurrection
  in Christianity, 260–264, 278–280, 282–284, 290
  in Judaism, 245, 246
  in Zoroastrianism, 208, 218, 223
rich, riches, 15. *See also* Money; Poor.
  in Buddhism, 124
  in Christianity, 283
  in Confucianism and Daoism, 178, 187
  in Hinduism, 77
  in indigenous religions, 40, 47, 61
  in Islam, 295, 300, 313
  in Judaism, 231, 239
  in Sikhism, 145
Rightly Guided Caliphs, 302
Rinzai, 120, 121
rishi, 67
ritual, 12, 13, 15, 19, 20, 21, 24
  in Buddhism, 122, 128, 131
  in Christianity, 261, 282, 284, 286, 287
  in Confucianism and Daoism, 168–170, 173, 175, 177, 181, 184
  in Hinduism, 65, 67, 72, 74, 78, 79, 83, 87, 88
  in indigenous religions, 31, 32, 33, 38, 40, 44, 45, 46, 50, 51, 54–57, 59, 60, 61
  in Islam, 295, 321, 322
  in Jainism, 100, 101, 106, 108
  in Judaism, 227, 230, 236, 241, 242, 247, 250–255
  in new religious movements, 338, 341, 344, 352
  in Shinto, 191, 192, 196, 199–205
  in Sikhism, 141, 149, 151
  in Zoroastrianism, 208, 209, 212, 214, 215, 217, 218, 220, 222, 223
Roman Catholic Church. *See* Catholic Church.

Rosh Hashanah, 250
Rousseau, Jean-Jacques, 37
Rubenstein, Richard, 241
Rumi, 308

S

Sabbath
    in Christianity, 262, 283, 287
    in Judaism, 234, 248–255
sacraments, 286, 288, 289
Sacred Court, 143, 145, 148, 152
sacred pipe, 50
sadhus, 70
Safi, Omid, 309–310
Salafi, 310
salat, 321, 322
Saman Suttam, 101
samsara, 77, 123, 124
sangha, 116
Sant, 141
Santoshi Ma, 20, 74
sannyasin stage, 82
Saso, Michael, 185
Sassanian Empire, 210, 211, 213, 214
sawm, 323
Schindler, Oscar, 241
*Science and Health with Key to the
    Scriptures*, 340
Scientology, 13, 23, 27, 28, 332, 335,
    337, 341
    controversy and present status,
        357–358
    history and teaching, 353–355
    organization, 355–357
scripture, 27. *See also* Canon.
    in Buddhism, 116, 117, 120, 125,
        128, 131
    in Christianity, 286, 290
    in Confucianism and Daoism, 159,
        163, 167, 172, 182, 183
    in Hinduism, 64, 67, 70, 76
    in Islam, 295, 298, 312, 313, 319
    in Jainism, 98, 100, 101, 102, 103,
        106, 108
    in Judaism, 242, 250
    in new religious movements, 336, 340,
        344, 346, 347, 349, 350
    in Sikhism, 139, 140, 141, 142, 143,
        145, 149, 150, 151
    in Zoroastrianism, 213, 216
sealing, 352
Sea Organization, 355
Second Temple Period (Jewish), 230,
    233, 234
Second Vatican Council, 276
sect, 27, 98, 100, 101, 135, 141, 195,
    307, 335
secularism, 8, 9, 25, 133, 255, 274, 276
secularization hypothesis, 9
seder, 251
Self-Realization Fellowship, 339

semi-historical myth, 43–44
Sephardic, 236, 253, 255
Sermon on the Mount, 283
sex, sexuality, 10, 19. *See also* Celibacy.
    in Buddhism, 123, 127
    in Christianity, 290
    in Hinduism, 64, 83
    in Islam, 315, 316, 323
    in Judaism, 246
    in new religious movements, 339, 341
shahada, 321
Shakyamuni, 114
shaman, 19, 31, 33–34, 45, 54
shamanism, 33
Shari'a, 316
Shema, 243, 252
Shi'as (Shi'ites), 302, 303, 305–310, 314,
    318, 320, 324, 325, 329
Shinto, 6
    around the world today, 204–205
    and Buddhism, 131
    ethics, 199–200
    history, 191–197
    and indigenous religions, 34, 42
    names, 190–191
    and new religious movements, 343
    ritual, 200–204
    symbol, 193
    teachings, 198–199
shoah, 241
shrine
    in Hinduism, 63, 66, 70, 74, 83, 85,
        87, 88, 90, 91
    in indigenous religions, 54, 56
    in Islam, 295, 297, 298, 308
    in Judaism, 231, 243
    in Shinto, 189–193, 195–204
Shudras, 80, 81
Shvetambar, 98, 99, 100, 101, 106
Singh, Pashaura, 153
Sikhism, Sikh, 23, 24
    around the world today, 152–155
    ethics, 147–148
    and Hinduism, 84
    history, 140–144
    name, 140
    ritual and worship, 149–152
    symbol, 141
    teachings, 145–147
Sisters in Islam, 310
Shi'a, Shi'ites, 302–303, 305–310, 314,
    318, 320, 324, 325, 329
shiva, 254
slave, 57, 60, 161, 230, 241, 348
small-scale religion, 34
Smith, Joseph Jr., 338, 347–350
sociology, 18
Soka-Gakkai, 343–344
soma, 67, 68
Soto, 120
soul, 7. *See also* Spirit.
    in Buddhism, 123, 125, 126, 132
    in Christianity, 287, 288
    in Confucianism and Daoism,
        183, 187

in Hinduism, 64, 66, 68, 69, 72, 75,
    76, 77, 78, 83, 88, 90, 92
in indigenous religions, 32, 55, 60
in Jainism, 95, 97, 98, 101, 102, 103,
    104, 107, 108
in new religious movements, 357
in Shinto, 199, 204
in Sikhism, 140, 141, 143, 146, 149
in Zoroastrianism, 209, 217, 218,
    223, 246
spirit, 8, 19. *See also* Soul.
    in Buddhism, 119, 122, 132
    in Christianity, 273, 275, 276
    in Confucianism and Daoism, 160,
        173, 174, 176, 177, 182,
        183, 184
    in Hinduism, 69, 73, 78
    in indigenous religions, 32, 33, 45, 49,
        50, 51, 56, 57, 60
    in Islam, 310, 312
    in Judaism, 247, 248
    in new religious movements, 340, 342,
        345, 347, 354, 357
    in Shinto, 191, 200, 204
    in Zoroastrianism, 209, 216, 217
St. Peter's Basilica, 259, 265, 270
stake, 352
Star of David, 13, 229
Stark, Rodney, 11, 303, 306
Sthanakvasi, 100
Stroumsa, Guy, 14–15
student stage, 81
stupa, 132
Sufis, 306, 307, 308, 312
sun dance, 51
Sun Myung Moon, 344, 345
Sunnis, 302, 305–309, 324, 325, 328, 329
surah, 312
sutra, 117, 121, 347
suttee, 85
Suzuki, D. T., 135
swastika, 66
sweat lodge, 37, 40, 50
synagogue, 229, 235, 236, 239, 240, 249,
    250, 252, 253, 255, 256, 262,
    286, 287

T

Taiji, 160
Taiping Rebellion, 167
Taliban, 24, 154, 155, 306, 309–310,
    318, 329
Tanak, 242, 244, 245
Tantras, 71, 72, 75
Tathagata, 115
temple, 3, 12
    in Buddhism, 111–113, 120, 128, 129,
        131, 132
    in Christianity, 262, 286
    in Confucianism and Daoism, 157,
        167, 168, 171, 175, 181–184, 186

in Hinduism, 61, 63, 70, 72, 74, 77, 84–86, 90
in Jainism, 95, 98–101, 103, 107–109
in Judaism, 227, 229, 231, 232, 233, 235, 247
in new religious movements, 324, 333, 349, 352
in Shinto, 194, 203
in Sikhism, 139, 140, 143, 144, 147, 148, 149, 150
in Zoroastrianism, 207, 211, 215, 220, 221, 224
temple garment, 352
Ten Commandments, 231, 247, 248, 250, 264, 283, 284
tetragrammaton, 243
theology, 14, 269, 272, 274, 275, 277, 279, 289, 291, 303, 316, 338
Theotokos, 281. *See also* Mary.
Theravada, 116, 117, 118, 119, 124, 126, 127, 128, 130, 131, 133, 134, 137
Thetan, 354, 355, 358
Three Characteristics of Existence, 125
Three Refuges, 116
Thus Spoke Zarathustra, 224–225
Tian, 173
Tibet, 4, 42, 78, 112, 113, 118, 119, 121–123, 131–133, 136
Tipitaka, 117
Tirthankara, 96, 97, 98, 108
tithe, 351
tolerance, 22, 23, 25, 26, 122, 141, 216, 237
Torah, 231, 233–237, 242–244, 246–248, 250–253, 255, 256
torii, 193, 201
totemism, 32, 33, 34
tower of silence, 213, 223
trance meditation, 130
Transcendental Meditation (TM), 91, 339
transubstantiation, 288
Trent, Council of, 273
trickster, 45, 56
Trikaya, 118
Trinity, 277
True Parents, 344
Tsubaki, 189, 190, 204, 205
Turner, Victor, 20
Twin Spirits, 217
Tylor, Edward B., 33

U

UFO groups, 340
umma, 300, 304, 323
Unification Church, 27, 337, 344–345
Upanishads, 69, 70, 72, 91
Urban, Hugh B., 356

V

Vaishyas, 80
Vajrayana, 121
vak lao, 150
Varanasi, 63, 64, 87, 88
varna, 79, 80, 81
Vedas, 65, 67, 70, 72, 75, 76
Vedanta Society, 339
vegetarianism, 92, 101, 105, 109, 116, 179. *See also* food.
Vinaya Pitaka, 117
Vishnu, 71, 74, 75, 76, 78, 86
vision quest, 40, 49, 50
Vivekananda, 90, 91, 339
Vodou, 32, 37, 46, 55
   divinities, 59
   groups, 59
   location and name, 58
   political influence in Haiti, 61
   spell rituals, 60
   worship, 59

W

Wade-Giles, 159, 162, 163, 164, 173, 174, 181
Waheguru, 146
Wahhabi, 308, 309
Wakan Tanka, 49, 50, 51
Wakanpi, 49
war, 10, 23, 24. *See also* Peace.
   in Buddhism, 135
   in Christianity, 275
   in Hinduism, 67, 72
   in Islam, 302, 319, 320
   in Judaism, 241
   in new religious movements, 340, 344, 353
   in Shinto, 195, 196, 197, 198
   in Sikhism, 155
ward, 352
Watt, W. Montgomery, 298
White, 10, 49, 50, 53, 134, 165, 166, 167, 328, 338, 342
White, Lynn, 26
Whitehead, Alfred North, 14
Wicca, 341
Wiesel, Elie, 241
wife, wives. *See also* Woman; Husband.
   in Confucianism and Daoism, 179
   in Hinduism, 74, 75, 76, 78, 83, 85, 92
   in Islam, 295, 299, 302, 317, 318, 319, 330
   in Jainism, 108
   in Judaism, 230, 254
   in new religious movements, 341, 344, 350
   in Shinto, 192
   in Sikhism, 153
   in Zoroastrianism, 218

Wilson, Edward, 22
woman, women, 19, 20, 21, 22, 23. *See also* Wife.
   in Buddhism, 123, 131, 133
   in Christianity, 259, 262, 264, 265, 276, 277, 283, 288, 292
   in Confucianism and Daoism, 168, 181
   in Hinduism, 64, 65, 71, 72, 74–78, 80–86, 88, 90, 92
   in indigenous religions, 49, 53
   in Islam, 295, 297, 309, 310, 315, 316–319, 322, 323, 326
   in Jainism, 95, 98, 103, 106, 108
   in Judaism, 227, 231, 242, 252, 253
   in new religious movements, 338, 341, 349, 351, 357
   in Shinto, 191, 192, 200, 202, 204
   in Sikhism, 139, 145, 147, 148, 150
   in Zoroastrianism, 209, 214–216, 218, 219, 221–223
Woods, Tiger, 136
World, 2, 5, 8, 14, 15, 16, 19, 21, 23, 25, 26. *See also* Creation; Earth.
   in Buddhism, 132, 133, 134, 135
   in Christianity, 260, 273, 274, 275, 285, 290, 292
   in Confucianism and Daoism, 157, 158, 159, 166, 167, 185, 186
   in Hinduism, 69, 89, 90
   in indigenous religions, 35, 45, 56, 58
   in Islam, 304, 305, 309, 324, 325, 329, 330
   in Jainism, 102, 108
   in Judaism, 240, 241, 245, 254, 255
   in new religious movements, 334, 337, 338, 343, 344, 345, 349, 353
   in Shinto, 191, 194, 195, 197, 198, 204
   in Sikhism, 152, 154
World Council of Churches, 275, 285, 292
wu wei, 176, 178, 179, 184

X

xiao, 179, 180, 181

Y

Yang, Fenggang, 167, 345
Yasna, 215, 217, 219, 222
Yasukuni, 195
Yi Jing, 162, 172, 182
yin-yang, 160, 162, 172, 184

yoga, 13, 69, 71, 72, 78, 82, 83, 85, 89, 91, 109, 111, 146, 339, 340
Yom Kippur, 250
yoni, 75, 76, 86
Yoruba religion, 30, 32, 37, 42
    gods, 55–57
    religious specialists, 57
    spirits of the ancestors, 58
Young, Brigham, 333, 348, 349

Z

Zainab, 310, 317
zakat, 323
Zarathustra, 208, 209, 210, 211, 214, 215, 216, 217, 219, 224, 225, 314
Zarathushtrian Assembly, 216, 225
zazen, 120
Zen, 24, 111, 112, 119–121, 124, 131, 133, 135, 137

zhong, 181
Zionism, 239
zombie, 37, 59, 60
Zoroastrianism, Zoroastrians
    and Hinduism, 65
    and Islam, 298, 299, 308, 311, 314, 315
    and Judaism, 233
Zoroastrian Studies Association, 216
Zwingli, Huldreich, 272

With the growth in eReader usage among students, this edition features a new numbering system for major headings that we recommend you use instead of page numbers when creating assignments.

This edition also features an increased number of glossary terms and definitions, as well as seventeen new BBC videos on religious life and issues today. Specific chapter-by-chapter changes follow.

Chapter 1

- Section "Your Preunderstanding of Religion" has been moved to the front of the chapter

- More attention given to the history of the discipline, with fuller consideration of the methods and work of prominent scholars who have influenced the rise of religious studies as an academic discipline

- Expanded coverage of various views on atheism

Chapter 2

- New chapter opening: "Your Visit to the Petroglyph National Monument"

- New "A Closer Look" on Polynesian religion in Hawaii

Chapter 3

- Coverage of the caste system heavily edited for simplicity and clarity

- Inclusion of *suttee* as a glossary term with full definition

- New section on Hindu festivals and holidays

- Newly expanded concluding section on Hinduism around the world today, including North America

Chapter 4

- New linked primary source reading on Mahavira's enlightenment

- Details of the lives of monks and nuns added

- Newly expanded concluding section on Hinduism around the world today, including North America

Chapter 5

- Clarification of concept of "Pure Land" Buddhism

- New primary source reading on a possible female Dalai Lama

- New scripture reading on the Four Noble Truths

- New section-opening story on President Barack Obama's 2012 visit to Southeast Asia

- Section on Buddhism in modern Asia moved to new concluding section at end of chapter

- Newly expanded concluding section on Buddhism around the world today, including North America

Chapter 6

- New primary source reading from the *Guru Granth*

- Newly expanded concluding section on Sikhism around the world today, including North America

Chapter 7

- New primary source reading on the dao

- Newly expanded concluding section on Daoism and Confucianism around the world today, including North America

Chapter 8

- Newly expanded concluding section on Shinto in the world today

Chapter 9

- Newly expanded concluding section on Zoroastrianism in the world today

Chapter 10

- New "A Closer Look" on the Kabbalah

- Newly expanded concluding section on Judaism in the world today, especially in Israel and North America

Chapter 11

- New section on the liturgical year

- Newly expanded concluding section on Christianity in the world today, beyond North America

Chapter 12

- New "A Closer Look" on Muslim views of Islamic-Western conflict

- Updated discussion of the meaning of wearing the hijab

- Newly expanded concluding section on Islam in the world today, especially Europe and North America

Chapter 13

- Common features of NRMs revised and streamlined

- New "A Closer Look" on celebrity Scientologists

What's Inside

Key topics in this chapter: "preunderstanding" and the study of religion; defining *religion*; why we study religion; six different dimensions of religion: cognitive, ethical, ritual, institutional, aesthetic, and emotional; the branches in the study of religion: theology and religious studies; the other academic disciplines involved in the study of religion: history, psychology, sociology, cultural anthropology, women's studies, and biology; special issues in the study of religion today: tolerance and intolerance, violence, pluralism, ecology, and new religious movements

Learning Outcomes

1-1   State and explain your own "preunderstanding" of religion.

1-2   State and explain the definition of *religion* used in this book.

1-3   Give your own answer to the question "Why study religion?"

1-4   List and describe the six different dimensions of religion.

1-5   Discuss how the various academic disciplines contribute to the study of religion.

1-6   Explain the special issues in the study of religion today.

Chapter 1 Outline

Your Visit to the Hsi Lai Temple in Southern California

1-1 Coming to Grips with Your Preunderstanding of Religion

1-1a What Is Preunderstanding?

1-1b Your Preunderstanding of Religion

1-2 What Is Religion?

1-2a Defining *Religion*

1-2b Notable Definitions of *Religion*

1-2c The Definition Used in This Book

1-3 Why Study Religion?

1-3a Studying the Persistence of Religion in the Modern World

1-3b What the Academic Study of Religion Can Offer You

1-4 Dimensions of Religion

1-4a The Cognitive Dimension

1-4b The Ethical Dimension

1-4c The Ritual Dimension

1-4d The Institutional Dimension

1-4e The Aesthetic Dimension

1-4f The Emotional Dimension

1-5 Ways of Studying Religion

1-5a Theology and Religious Studies

1-5b History

1-5c Psychology

1-5d Sociology

1-5e Cultural Anthropology

1-5f Women's Studies

1-5g Biology

1-5h Conclusions about Methods of Studying Religion

1-6 Special Issues in the Study of Religion Today

1-6a Tolerance and Intolerance

1-6b Violence

1-6c Pluralism

1-6d Religion and Ecological Crisis

1-6e New Religious Movements

Terms

preunderstanding (p. 5)

religion (p. 6)

monotheism (p. 7)

polytheism (p. 7)

private religion (p. 7)

secularism (p. 8)

secularization hypothesis (p. 9)

cultural intelligence (p. 10)

ritual (p. 12)

pilgrimage (p. 12)

myth (p. 12)

new religious movements (NRMs) (p. 12)

laity (p. 13)

theology (p. 14)

religious studies (p. 14)

historical-critical method (p. 15)

history of religions school (p. 15)

sociology (p. 18)

civil religion (p. 18)

cultural anthropology (p. 18)

shaman (p. 19)

life-cycle ritual (p. 19)

feminism (p. 20)

patriarchy (p. 20)

phenomenology of religion (p. 21)

atheism (p. 22)

agnosticism (p. 22)

tolerance (p. 22)

pluralism (p. 25)

Discussion Questions

1. The "What Do YOU Think?" at the beginning of this chapter asked your opinion about the statement "Most Americans with a religious faith don't know much about it." In what ways is this statement true, and in what ways is it not? Explain your answer.

2. Explain and critique this statement by Peter Berger: "The process of comparing multiple conflicting beliefs in world religions requires a 'methodological atheism.' "

3. Some have labeled Andrew Newberg's work not neuroscience, but "neurotheology." Taking into account what this chapter says about the difference between theology and religious studies, do you think this is an accurate or helpful term?

4. Which one of the definitions on page 6 is the most appealing to you? The least appealing? Why?

5. Assess this provocative declaration by University of Chicago religion professor Jonathan Z. Smith: "Religion is solely the creation of the scholar's study."

6. In his book *Religious Literacy*, Stephen Prothero suggests that every American high school should teach a required course on the Christian Bible and another one on world religions. What to you are the pros and cons of this suggestion?

7. What way of studying religion seems the most important to you? The least important? Why?

8. The ancient Roman philosopher Terrence once wrote, "I am a human, and nothing human is alien to me." What might this proverb mean for your study of world religions?

Religion in Film: Suggestions for Viewing and Discussion Questions

Religulous, directed by Larry Charles, written by and starring Bill Maher, is rated R. It is a scathing attack on all religion in general, particularly religion that is politically to the right of Maher. Although it contains some scurrilous statements and ad hominem arguments, his film is a good summary of current popular critiques of religious belief and practice. It might not be easy for you to watch if you are religious. Watch it with an open mind, and then consider these questions: What are the main objections to religion in this film? In your opinion, is it fair overall?

Beyond the Class

A selection of materials is in the Instructor's Manual and PowerLecture.

What's Inside

Key topics in this chapter: the different names used for this type of religion; the special challenges students and scholars alike face in studying indigenous religions; the common features of indigenous religions; the main features of Lakota (North America), Yoruba (west Africa) and Vodou (Haiti) religions.

Learning Outcomes

2-1   State and evaluate the different names for indigenous religions.

2-2   Explain in your own words the challenges to the study of indigenous religions.

2-3   Discuss the common features of indigenous religions.

2-4   State and explain the main features of Lakota religion.

2-5   State and explain the main features of Yoruba religion.

2-6   State and explain the main features of Vodou religion.

Chapter 2 Outline

Your Visit to the Petroglyph National Monument, New Mexico

2-1   Names for This Type of Religion

2-1a   Traditional Religion

2-1b   Primitive Religion

2-1c   Animism and Totemism

2-1d   Manaism

2-1e   Shamanism

2-1f   Small-Scale Religions

2-1g   Nature Religion

2-1h   Indigenous Religions

2-2   Challenges to Study

2-2a   Lack of Written Sources

2-2b   Difficulty Discerning Continuity and Discontinuity

2-2c   Mainstream Guilt

2-2d   Misrepresentations in Popular Culture

2-2e   Misuse of Indigenous Rituals

2-3   Common Features of Indigenous Religions

2-3a   The Importance of Place

2-3b   Global Distribution

2-3c   Many Gods and Spirits

2-3d   Influenced by Other Cultures

2-3e   Based on Orality, Story, and Myth

2-3f   Oriented More to Practice Than to Belief

2-3g   In-Group Based

2-3h   The Goodness of the World

2-3i   The Role of Religious Specialists

2-3j   Continuing Vitality

2-4   A Native American Religion: Lakota

2-4a   Name and Location

2-4b   Basic Features of Lakota Religion

2-4c   Lakota Rituals

2-4d   Culture and Religion

2-5   An African Religion: Yoruba

2-5a   High God and Other Gods

2-5b   Religious Specialists

2-5c   Spirits of the Ancestors

2-6   An Afro-Caribbean Religion: Vodou

2-6a   Location and Name

2-6b   Divinities

2-6c   Groups

2-6d   Worship

2-6e   Spell and Counter-Spell Rituals

2-6f   Political Influence in Haiti

Terms

primitive (primal) religion (p. 32)

animism (p. 32)

totemism [TOHT-em-iz-uhm] (p. 33)

manaism [MAH-nah-iz-uhm] (p. 33)

shamanism (p. 33)

small-scale religion (p. 34)

nature religion (p. 35)

indigenous religion (p. 35)

First Nations (p. 36)

Aboriginals [AB-oh-RIHJ-ih-nahls] (p. 36)

genocide (p. 37)

noble savages (p. 37)

Pan-Indian movement (p. 40)

cosmogonic myth (p. 43)

etiological myth (p. 43)

semi-historical myth (p. 43)

trickster (p. 45)

Wakan Tanka [WAHK-ahn THAHN-kuh] (p. 49)

Wakanpi [wah-KAHN-pee] (p. 49)

vision quest (p. 50)

sacred pipe (p. 50)

sweat lodge (p. 50)

peyote [pay-YOHT-ee] (p. 50)

Native American Church (p. 50)

sun dance (p. 51)

assimilation (p. 51)

Little Big Horn (p. 52)

ghost dance (p. 52)

Massacre at Wounded Knee (p. 53)

kahuna [kah-HOO-nuh] (p. 54)

kapu [KAH-poo] (p. 54)

Olorun [OHL-oh-ruhn] (p. 55)

orisha [ohr-EE-shuh] (p. 55)

Ogun [OH-guhn] (p. 55)

babalawo [BUB-uh-LAH-woh] (p. 57)

iyalawo [EE-yah-LAH-woh] (p. 57)

Ifa [EE-fuh] (p. 57)

loa [LOH-uh] (p. 59)

cult religion (p. 59)

possession cult (p. 59)

Baron Samedi [sah-MEHD-ee] (p. 60)

gris-gris [gree-gree] (p. 60)

exoticism [egg-ZOT-uh-siz-uhm] (p. 60)

Discussion Questions

1. The "What Do YOU Think?" at the beginning of this chapter asked your opinion about the statement "Native American religions still have something significant to offer people of other religions or people of no religion." In what ways is this statement true, and in what ways is it not? Explain your answer.

2. In what sense are indigenous religions "world religions," and in what sense are they not?

3. Rank in order, beginning with the best, the names for this type of religion. Then answer this question: Why did I put them in this order?

4. What is the most difficult challenge to you in studying this type of religion?

5. What is the present state of Lakota culture and religion, in terms of strengths and weaknesses?

6. What, in your estimation, are the most important things to know about Yoruba religion and culture?

7. How might the recent interest in zombies reflect a continuing, mainstream North American fascination with Vodou?

Indigenous Religions in Film: Suggestions for Viewing and Discussion Questions

Avatar (2009, rated PG-13), written and directed by James Cameron, is the story of struggle between natives on another planet and American corporate interests. Its visual appeal was more widely praised than its story line. *Avatar* gives a rich treatment of indigenous religion.

Questions: How does this film understand and explain the notion of an "avatar"? Why is the main character so attracted to indigenous culture that he becomes a part of it? How are the main parts of the indigenous religion depicted here similar to the main parts studied in this chapter? What happens at the end of the film that is strikingly different from the way other stories of this type typically end?

Dances with Wolves, 1990, directed by and starring Kevin Costner, is the fictional story of a U.S. Army officer who becomes a Lakota Indian. This film won the Academy Award for Best Picture of the year.

Questions: Why is the main character so attracted to indigenous culture that he becomes a part of it? What in this picture of Lakota life is, in your opinion, idealized? What is realistic? Explain your responses. How are the main parts of the indigenous religion depicted here similar to the main parts studied in this chapter?

The Mission (1986, rated PG), directed by Roland Joffe, is a study in indigenous-colonial interaction, as eighteenth-century Jesuit missionaries protect a remote South American tribe in danger of falling under the rule of pro-slavery Portugal.

Questions: When the emissary says, "Sometimes a surgeon has to cut off a limb to save the patient," what does he mean by it? Do you agree? Had you been one of the Jesuit priests, what would have been your choice? What does the sad ending of this film say about what happens overall in interactions between indigenous peoples and colonists?

Apocalypto (2006, rated R), written and directed by Mel Gibson: Like many films by Gibson, it is drenched in bloody violence. As the Mayan kingdom in Central America faces decline, its rulers insist that the key to survival is to build more temples and offer more human sacrifices. Jaguar Paw, a young man captured for sacrifice, flees to avoid this fate.

Questions: What to you is the meaning of the title of this film, drawn as it is from Jewish and Christian religions? How does this film portray the interaction of a large-scale Native American empire and small-scale tribes? How might the portrayal of violence in this film distort ancient Central American religion, as some film critics have suggested? Discuss in particular the depiction of human sacrifice in this film.

Beyond the Class

A selection of materials is in the Instructor's Manual and PowerLecture.

What's Inside

Key topics in this chapter: the diversity and unity of Hinduism; the history of Hinduism as this explains its diversity today; key Hindu teachings on gods and religious concepts; Hindu ethics and ways of life; Hindu worship and ritual; Hindu life around the world and in North America today

Learning Outcomes

3-1 Explain what *Hinduism* means and its strengths and weaknesses as a name.

3-2 Explain how the main periods of Hinduism's history have shaped its present, especially its unity and diversity.

3-3 Outline the essentials of Hindu teachings in your own words.

3-4 Relate Hindu ethics to the essential Hindu teachings.

3-5 Outline the ways Hindus worship, at home and in temples.

3-6 State the main aspects of Hindu life around the world today, especially in North America.

Chapter 3 Outline

Your Visit to Varanasi, India

3-1 The Name *Hinduism*

3-2 The Hindu Present as Shaped by Its Past

3-2a The Vedic Period (1500–600 B.C.E.)

3-2b The Upanishadic Period (600–400 B.C.E.)

3-2c The Classical Period (400 B.C.E.–600 C.E.)

3-2d The Devotional Period (600 C.E.–Present)

3-3 Essential Hindu Teachings

3-3a Main Deities in the Three Devotional Movements

3-3b Hindu Doctrinal Concepts

3-4 Hindu Ethics and Ways of Life

3-4a The Caste System

3-4b The Four Stages of a Man's Life

3-4c The Four Goals of Life

3-4d The Lives of Hindu Women

3-5 Hindu Rituals

3-5a Images

3-5b Worship in the Temple and the Home

3-5c Pilgrimage

3-5d Festivals and Holidays

3-5e Funerals

3-5f Yoga

3-6 Hinduism around the World Today

3-6a Hinduism in South Asia and Africa

3-6b Hinduism in the West

3-6c Hindu Migration and Life in North America

Discussion Questions

1. The "What Do YOU Think?" at the beginning of this chapter asked your opinion about the statement "Hinduism is mostly about escaping this material world." In what ways is this statement true, and in what ways is it not? Explain your answer.

Terms

Om (Aum) [OHM] (p. 66)

swastika [SWAHS-tee-kuh] (p. 66)

Indus Valley civilization (p. 66)

Dravidians [druh-VID-ee-uhnz] (p. 66)

Aryans [AIR-ee-unzs] (p. 67)

Vedas [VAY-duhs] (p. 67)

Agnihotra [AHG-nee-HOH-trah] (p. 67)

rishi [REE-shee] (p. 67)

Upanishads [oo-PAHN-ih-shahds] (p. 69)

Brahman [BRAH-muhn] (p. 69)

atman [AHT-muhn] (p. 69)

reincarnation (p. 69)

yoga [YOH-guh] (p. 69)

sadhus [SAH-doos] (p. 70)

Bhagavad Gita [BAH-guh-vahd GEE-tuh] (p. 70)

Laws of Manu [MAH-new] (p. 71)

bhakti [BAHK-tee] (p. 71)

Tantras [TAHN-truhs] (p. 71)

mantra [MAHN-truh] (p. 72)

Hindutva [hihn-DOOT-vah] (p. 73)

lingam [LING-gahm] (p. 74)

yoni [YOH-nee] (p. 75)

dharma [DAHR-muh] (p. 76)

samsara [sahm-SAH-ruh] (p. 77)

jiva [JEE-vuh] (p. 77)

karma [KAHR-muh] (p. 77)

moksha [MOHK-shuh] (p. 77)

caste [kast] (p. 79)

varna [VAHR-nuh] (p. 79)

outcastes (p. 79)

Brahmins [BRAH-munz] (p. 79)

Kshatriyas [kshuh-TREE-yuhz] (p. 80)

Vaishyas [VIGH-shuhs] (p. 80)

Shudras [SHOO-druhs] (p. 80)

Dalits [DAHL-its] (p. 80)

jati [JAH-tee] (p. 81)

student stage (p. 81)

householder stage (p. 82)

forest-dweller stage (p. 82)

sannyasin [sahn-YAH-sin] **stage** (p. 82)

artha [AHR-thuh] (p. 83)

kama [KAH-muh] (p. 83)

bindi [BIHN-dee] (p. 84)

suttee [suh-TEE] (p. 85)

puja [POO-juh] (p. 85)

murti [MUHR-tee] (p. 86)

Kumbha Mela [KOOM-buh MEHL-uh] (p. 87)

Transcendental Meditation (TM) (p. 91)

diaspora [dee-ASS-pohr-uh] (p. 91)

2. What makes it possible for Hinduism to tolerate so much internal diversity?

3. Radhakrishnan, a former president of India, said that "Hinduism is more a culture than a creed." What are the strengths and weaknesses of this statement?

4. Give in your own words a critique of Sharon Stone's comments about karma given in the "Closer Look" box in section 3-3b.

5. How does the caste system undergird the main teachings of Hinduism? What is your take on the rightness of this system, first from a Hindu and then a non-Hindu point of view?

6. Explain how this definition of happiness by Mohandas Gandhi is related to Hinduism: "Happiness is when what you think, what you say, and what you do are in harmony."

7. What do you find to be the major strengths and weaknesses of the Hindu notion of karma and reincarnation? How might a Hindu reply to your answer?

8. Explain the dissemination Hinduism in the world today, and then give your opinion of the future of Hinduism in North America.

Hinduism in Film: Suggestions for Viewing and Discussion Questions

The Indian film industry is second in size only to that of the United States. However, it has not produced many English-language films that deal with Hinduism. *The Mahabharata* (1989, not rated), directed by Peter Brooks, is a short version of the lengthy stage play done by the Brooklyn Academy of Music and has a short section on the *Bhagavad Gita*.

Questions: How is the teaching of the *Gita* summarized in this film? How effectively, in your opinion, is the enlightenment of the main character portrayed?

Sita Sings the Blues by Nina Paley (2008, not rated) is an animated retelling of parts of the *Ramayana* from a woman's perspective; it is available free of charge on the web.

Questions: Does the filmmaker protect the original intent of the story, or has she changed the story and themes? How effectively does this film adapt the story of the original *Ramayana* by adding the filmmaker's personal story?

For a treatment of the history of modern India, see *Gandhi* (1982, rated PG), directed by Richard Attenborough and starring Ben Kingsley; this film won eight Academy Awards.

Questions: How did Gandhi motivate people to follow him, and would these same techniques work today in India and elsewhere? Some people have said that Gandhi's type of nonresistance only works if the governments one resists have a conscience. What do you think? Explain the following saying by Gandhi and relate it to situations today: "An eye for an eye only makes the whole world blind."

Set in the time of Gandhi is *Water* (2005, not rated, in Hindi with English subtitles) by Deepa Mehta, the riveting story of widowed women and girls confined to an ashram for the rest of their lives.

Questions: The lead character in the film asks, "What happens when our conscience conflicts with our faith?" What do her faith and conscience say, and how does she answer that question? Has the United States had any similar problems regarding widows in the past? Have these problems been fully corrected?

Finally, *Slumdog Millionaire*, directed by Danny Boyle, is a 2008 blockbuster with several Academy Awards. It tells the story of a Muslim boy in Mumbai, India, who "strikes it rich" with the Indian version of the television show *Who Wants to Be a Millionaire*.

Questions: What does the title mean? How do the contrasts within it provide a summary of the film? Compare and contrast the pivotal choices or decisions made by Jamal and Salim: How do their choices affect their respective paths in life or "destinies"? How are those who have money and power glamorized and criticized in this film?

What's Inside

Key topics in this chapter: the meaning of *Jainism* and related words; how the history of Jainism has shaped its present form; basic Jain teachings; the main ethical precepts for laypeople as well as monks and nuns; Jain worship and meditation; Jain life around the world today.

Learning Outcomes

4-1   Explain the meaning of *Jainism* and related terms.

4-2   Summarize how the main periods of Jainism's history have shaped its present.

4-3   Outline the essential Jain teachings in your own words.

4-4   State the main ethical precepts of Jainism for monks/nuns and laity, and relate them to Jain teachings.

4-5   Outline the way Jains worship and practice other rituals.

4-6   Explain the main aspects of Jain life around the world today, especially in North America.

Chapter 4 Outline

Your Visit with Jain Nuns

4-1   The Name *Jainism*

4-2   The Jain Present as Shaped by Its Past

4-2a Founding and the First Thousand Years (600 B.C.E.–ca. 400 C.E.)

4-2b The Next Thousand Years (600–1600)

4-2c Early Modern Times through Today (1600–Present)

4-3   Essential Jain Teachings

4-3a No Gods

4-3b Time and the World

4-3c Jiva and Ajiva

4-3d Karma and Liberation

4-3e Theories of Knowledge

4-4   Ethics: The Five Cardinal Virtues

4-4a Do No Harm; Speak the Truth

4-4b Do Not Steal; Do Not Be Possessive

4-4c Be Chaste

4-5   Jain Ritual and Worship

4-5a The Life of Monks and Nuns

4-5b Life of the Laity in Worship and Devotion

4-5c Two Jain Festivals

4-6   Jainism around the World Today

4-6a Jainism in the West

4-6b Jainism in North America

Terms

Jina [JEE-nuh] (p. 96)

Jains [jines] (p. 96)

Mahavira [MAH-hah-VEER-ruh] (p. 96)

asceticism [ah-SET-uh-SIHZ-uhm] (p. 97)

reincarnation (p. 97)

Parshvanatha [parsh-VAHN-ah-thuh] (p. 97)

Tirthankaras [tuhr-TAHN-kah-ruhz] (p. 97)

Shvetambar [shveht-AHM-bahr] (p. 98)

Digambar [die-GAM-bahr] (p. 98)

gacchas [GOTCH-uhs] (p. 100)

Sthanakvasi [STHAHN-ahk-VAH-see] (p. 100)

Saman Suttam [SAH-muhn SOOT-ahm] (p. 101)

kalpa [CALL-puh] (p. 102)

jiva [JEE-vuh] (p. 102)

ajiva [AH-jee-vuh] (p. 102)

karma [KAR-muh] (p. 103)

moksha [MOHK-shah] (p. 103)

nirvana [near-VAH-nuh] (p. 103)

kevalin [keh-VAHL-in] (p. 103)

ahimsa [ah-HIM-zuh] (p. 104)

Namokar Mantra [NAHM-oh-cahr MAHN-truh] (p. 107)

Paryusana [PAR-yoo-SAHN-uh] (p. 108)

Diwali [dee-WALL-ee] (p. 108)

JAINA (p. 109)

Discussion Questions

1. The "What Do YOU Think?" at the beginning of this chapter asked your opinion about the statement "The most important Jain teaching in the world today is nonviolence as a way of life." In what ways is this statement true, and in what ways is it not? Explain your answer.

2. Why and how has ahimsa played such a large role in Jainism?

3. What are some of the basic similarities and differences between Jainism and Buddhism?

4. Explain the rise of different Jain groups and sects, and how Jainism is now working to overcome some of these differences.

5. What are some of the main features of Jainism in North America today?

6. Give a reflection on this statement: "When Jainism's large contribution to the world is compared to its relatively small numbers, it may not be an exaggeration to say that person for person Jainism is one of the most powerful religions in the world."

7. Explain this irony, that the religious principles and practices that help Jains detach themselves from the world are the same things that have brought them material success.

Beyond the Class

A selection of materials is in the Instructor's Manual and PowerLecture.

What's Inside

Key topics in this chapter: the meaning of *Buddhism* and related terms; how the history of Buddhism's founding and growth has shaped its present form; basic Buddhist teachings such as the Four Noble Truths and the Eightfold Path; the main ethical precepts for laypeople, as well as for monks and nuns; Buddhist ritual and meditation; Buddhist life around the world today, with special attention to North America.

Learning Outcomes

5-1   Explain the meaning of *Buddhism* and related terms.

5-2   Summarize how Buddhism was founded and developed into what it is today.

5-3   Outline the essential Buddhist teachings.

5-4   State the main ethical precepts of Buddhism for both monastics and laypeople.

5-5   Discuss the way Buddhists worship and meditate.

5.6   State the main features of Buddhist life around the world today, especially in North America.

Chapter 5 Outline

Your Visit to a Zen Retreat Center

5-1   The Name *Buddhism*

5-2   Buddhism Today as Shaped by Its Past

5-2a Gautama's Road to Enlightenment

5-2b Achievement of Enlightenment

5-2c India, Sri Lanka, and Theravada

5-2d The Rise of Mahayana: China and Japan

5-2e Tibet and the Diamond Vehicle

5-3   Essential Buddhist Teachings

5-3a The Four Noble Truths

5-3b The Noble Eightfold Path

5-3c The Three Characteristics of Existence

5-4   Buddhist Ethics for Monastics and Laypeople

5-4a General Buddhist Morality

5-4b The Five Precepts

5-4c Other Precepts and Moral Rules

5-5   Buddhist Ritual and Meditation

5-5a Temples

5-5b Images of the Buddha

5-5c Prayer and Meditation

5-5d Protective Rituals

5-5e Funeral Rituals

5-6   Buddhism around the World Today

5-6a Buddhism in Modern Asia

5-6b Buddhism Comes to the Western World

5-6c Early Buddhist Immigration to North America

5-6d The Next Wave of Buddhist Immigration

5-6e Conclusion

Discussion Questions

1. The "What Do YOU Think?" question at the beginning of this chapter asked your opinion about the statement "The most important aspect of Buddhism today is meditation to bring inner peace." Now that you have encountered Buddhism in this chapter, what is your opinion on this statement, and why?

Terms

Buddhism [BUHD-ihz-um] (p. 112)

buddha [BUH-dah] (p. 112)

dharmachakra [DAHR-muh-CHAHK-ruh] (p. 113)

Middle Path (p. 113)

Shakyamuni [SHAK-yah-MOO-nee] (p. 114)

Four Passing Sights (p. 114)

Bodhi Tree [BOH-dee] (p. 115)

Tathagata [tah-THAH-gah-tuh] (p. 115)

sangha [SAHN-guh] (p. 116)

Three Refuges (p. 116)

parinirvana [PAHR-ee-near-VAHN-uh] (p. 116)

Hinayana [HIN-ah-YAHN-uh] (p. 117)

Theravada [THAIR-uh-VAHD-uh] (p. 117)

sutra [SOO-truh; Pali: *Sutta*] (p. 117)

Tipitaka [TIH-pee-TAH-kuh] (p. 117)

Mahayana [MAH-hah-YAHN-uh] (p. 118)

Trikaya [trih-KIGH-yuh] (p. 118)

bodhisattva [BOHD-hee-SAHT-vuh] (p. 119)

Zen (p. 119)

koan [KOH-an] (p. 120)

zazen [ZAH-zehn] (p. 120)

Dalai Lama [DAHL-eye (not "dolly") LAH-muh] (p. 121)

Vajrayana [VAHJ-ruh-YAH-nuh] (p. 121)

lama [LAH-muh] (p. 121)

dharma [DAHR-muh] (p. 123)

karma [KAR-muh] (p. 123)

samsara [sam-SAR-uh] (p. 123)

nirvana [neer-VAH-nuh] (p. 123)

Four Noble Truths (p. 123)

Noble Eightfold Path (p. 125)

Three Characteristics of Existence (p. 125)

anicca [uh-NEEK-uh] (p. 125)

mandala [MAHN-dah-luh] (p. 125)

dukkha [DUHK-uh] (p. 126)

anatta [ah-NAHT-uh] (p. 126)

precept (p. 126)

mudra [MOOD-ruh] (p. 129)

trance meditation (p. 130)

insight meditation (p. 131)

paritta [puh-REET-uh] (p. 131)

dharani [duh-RAHN-ee] (p. 131)

mantra [MAHN-truh] (p. 131)

stupa [STOO-pah] (p. 132)

2. Explain why the life and experience of Siddhartha Gautama is exemplary for Buddhists today.

3. What are the differences and similarities between the lives of Buddhist monks and nuns, and those of laypeople?

4. Explain the Four Noble Truths and the Eightfold Path, as much as possible in your own words.

5. Explain the Dalai Lama's often-repeated statement "My religion is very simple—my religion is kindness."

6. Some claim that Buddhism is a "world denying" religion, too negative about the human condition and the future. To what extent might that be accurate?

7. What are some of the main features of Buddhism in North America today?

8. Why and how did Zen become the most influential form of Buddhism in North America? Discuss both religious and cultural factors.

9. Do you think that "celebrity Buddhism" is a fair name for what it claims to describe? Why or why not?

Buddhism in Film: Suggestions for Viewing and Discussion Questions

Although the life of Gautama Buddha has great meaning as a narrative for Buddhists and for many other people, no feature film has been made of his life. Martin Meissonier's 2001 film *Life of Buddha* is a blend of documentary and drama.

Questions: How effective do you think this film's blend of drama and documentary is? What did viewing this film contribute to your knowledge of the life of Gautama Buddha?

Little Buddha (1993, rated PG), directed by Bernardo Bertolucci and starring Keanu Reeves in the title role, tells the story of the Buddha in tandem with a search for a new Tibetan leader, one that leads to the United States.

Questions: How effective, in your opinion, is the tandem narration of the story of Buddha and that of a new Tibetan lama? What did you learn about the Buddha and Tibetan Buddhism that you didn't know before?

Two films made in 1997 and rated PG-13 tell the story of the current Dalai Lama. The better one, from both cinematic and religious studies points of view, is *Kundun*, directed by Martin Scorsese. The other is *Seven Years in Tibet*, directed by Jean-Jacque Annaud.

Questions for *Kundun*: In the meeting between Chairman Mao and the Dalai Lama, Mao says, "Religion is poison." What does he mean by this? What compelled the Dalai Lama to flee Tibet for India? Explain this statement given as advice to the Dalai Lama: "Nonviolence means cooperation when possible, resistance when not."

Questions for *Seven Years in Tibet*: What is the European political context for the main character spending seven years in Tibet? What perspective do you get on Tibetan Buddhism? How does this film compare with *Kundun*, in your opinion?

What's Love Got to Do with It (1993, directed by Brian Gibson and starring Angela Bassett and Laurence Fishburne, rated R) is the story of singer Tina Turner and her conversion to the Sokka Gakkai sect of Nichiren Buddhism.

Questions: What leads Tina Turner to convert to Buddhism, according to this film? How does Buddhism help her to cope with the problems in her life, particularly spousal abuse?

Beyond the Class

A selection of materials is in the Instructor's Manual and PowerLecture.

What's Inside

Key topics in this chapter: the meaning of *Sikhism* and related terms *Sikh*, *Gurmat*, and *Panth*; key formative events in Sikhism, especially the ten founding gurus, formation of the Khalsa, and Sikh life in the British Empire and in independent India; essential Sikh teaching of monotheism, devotion to the one God, and release from reincarnation; the main ethical principals in Sikhism, especially equality in caste and personal moral rules; the way Sikhs worship in the gurdwara; and Sikh life around the world and in North America today, especially the challenges of discrimination and diversity.

Learning Outcomes

6-1   Explain the meaning of *Sikhism* and related terms.

6-2   Summarize how Sikhism developed over time, especially its founding by the ten gurus and its life in the British Empire through the present.

6-3   Explain the essential Sikh teachings.

6-4   State and discuss the main ethical precepts of Sikhism.

6-5   Outline the way Sikhs worship and practice other rituals, especially life-cycle rituals.

6-6   Summarize the main features of Sikh life around the world today, especially in North America.

Chapter 6 Outline

Your Visit to a Sikh Temple

6-1   The Name *Sikhism*

6-2   Sikhism Today as Shaped by Its Past: Two Key Periods

6-2a   The Ten Gurus

6-2b   Sikhism from British Rule until Today

6-3   Essential Sikh Teachings

6-3a   The One God

6-3b   Devotion to God

6-4   Key Sikh Ethics

6-4a   Rejection of Hindu Caste

6-4b   Other Rules of Morality

6-5   Sikh Ritual and Worship

6-5a   The Gurdwara

6-5b   The Langar

6-5c   Sikh Life-Cycle Rituals

6-5d   Other Festivals

6-6   Sikhism around the World Today

6-6a   The Sikh Diaspora

6-6b   The First Wave of Immigration to North America (1900–1940)

6-6c   Second and Third Waves to North America (1965–Present)

6-6d   Sikhism in Post-9/11America

Terms

Sikh [seek] (p. 140)

Panth [pahnth] (p. 140)

Gurmat [GOOR-maht] (p. 140)

Guru Granth [GOO-roo GRAHNTH] (p. 140)

khanda [KAHN-duh] (p. 141)

Sant [sahnt] (p. 141)

Darbar Sahib (Harmandir Sahib) [HAR-mahn-dear SAH-ihb] (p. 143)

Khalsa [KALL-suh] (p. 144)

Dasam Granth [DAH-sum grahnth] (p. 144)

Waheguru [VAH-heh-GUHR-oo] (p. 146)

Ek Onkar [ehk ON-kahr] (p. 146)

Nam [nahm] (p. 146)

Five Ks (p. 147)

langar [LAHN-gar] (p. 148)

gurdwara [guhr-DWAHR-uh] (p. 149)

chaur [chowr] (p. 149)

kirtan [KEER-tahn] (p. 149)

vak lao [vahk low] (p. 150)

granthi [GRAHN-thee] (p. 150)

parshad [PAHR-shahd] (p. 150)

Discussion Questions

1. In the "What Do YOU Think" section at the beginning of this chapter, you were asked to give your opinion on the statement "Sikhism is just a combination of Hinduism and Islam." Now that you have finished reading this chapter, what is your opinion?

2. Discuss this statement: "Sikhism is perhaps more than any other religion in the world a 'religion of the book.'"

3. How is Sikhism similar to Hinduism and Islam? How is it distinct?

4. Explain how and why Sikhism went from a pacifistic religion to a militant one.

5. What effects have the events of 1984 in Amritsar had on Sikhism, then and now?

6. State and explain the Five Ks—with "kudos" to you if you can give the Sikh terms!

7. What is the layout of the typical gurdwara, and what are the main parts of the service?

Sikhism in Film: Suggestions for Viewing and Discussion Questions

One recent film giving good insight into contemporary Sikhs in the Western world is *Bend It Like Beckham* (2002, directed by Gurinder Chadra, rated PG-13), the story of how the daughter (played by Parminder Nagra) of strict Sikhs living in London is attracted to soccer (football).

Questions: How well is this serious topic treated as comedy? What are the differences, if any, between Sikh religious practices and Punjabi cultural practices? What does this film say about the challenges and opportunities of living in the Sikh diaspora, especially for young females?

More serious is the 2008 drama *Ocean of Pearls*, directed by Sarab Neelam. When Amrit Singh, played by Omid Abtahi, sees his dreams of becoming chief of surgery at a prestigious transplant center disappear because of his traditional Sikh appearance, he cuts his hair. When his other compromises result in the death of a patient, Amrit reexamines Sikh traditions.

Questions: Why is Amrit so driven to achieve professional success? Why and how do people misunderstand his Sikh religion? How does his religious and cultural assimilation lead to a personal crisis, and how does he resolve it? What does this film say about the challenges and opportunities of living in the Sikh diaspora?

Beyond the Class

A selection of materials is in the Instructor's Manual and PowerLecture.

What's Inside

Key topics in this chapter: the meaning of *Daoism* and *Confucianism*; how Daoism and Confucianism developed over time into what they are today; the essential teachings of Daoism and Confucianism; the main ethical precepts of Daoism and Confucianism; the way Daoists and Confucianists worship and practice other rituals; Daoist and Confucian life around the world today, especially in North America.

Learning Outcomes

7-1   Explain the names *Daoism* and *Confucianism* and related terms.

7-2   Outline how Daoism and Confucianism developed over time into what they are today, especially in relationship to each other.

7-3   Explain the essential teachings of Daoism and Confucianism, especially their similarities and differences.

7-4   Paraphrase in your own words the main ethical principles of Daoism and Confucianism.

7-5   Outline the way Daoists and Confucianists worship and practice other rituals.

7-6   Summarize the main features of Daoism and Confucianism around the world today, especially in North America.

Chapter 7 Outline

7-1   **The Names *Daoism* and *Confucianism***

7-2   **Daoism and Confucianism Today as Shaped by Their Past**

7-2a   China before the Birth of Confucianism and Daoism (ca. 3000–500 B.C.E.)

7-2b   The Origins of Daoism (ca. 500 B.C.E.–200 C.E.)

7-2c   Daoism from 200 C.E. to 1664 C.E.

7-2d   The Near-Destruction of Daoism (1644–1980)

7-2e   Confucius and the Origins of Confucianism (551–479 B.C.E.)

7-2f   The Rise of Confucianism and Neo-Confucianism (ca. 350 B.C.E.–1200 C.E.)

7-2g   The Modern Period of Daoism and Confucianism (1912–Present)

7-3   **Essential Daoist and Confucian Teachings**

7-3a   Ancient Teachings Common to Daoism and Confucianism

7-3b   Daoist Teachings on the Dao

7-3c   Chinese Traditional Deities

7-3d   Daoist Teaching of Wu Wei

7-3e   Daoist Views of Qi

7-3f   The Daoist Quest for Immortality

7-3g   Confucian Reformulations of Ancient Teachings

7-4   **Daoist and Confucian Ethics**

7-4a   Daoist Ethics

7-4b   Confucian Ethics

7-5   **Ritual and Worship**

7-5a   Daoist Temples and Worship

7-5b   Confucian Temples and Worship

7-5c   The Traditional Chinese Funeral

7-5d   A Final Comparison of Daoism and Confucianism

7-6   **Daoism and Confucianism around the World Today**

7-6a   Daoism and Confucianism in the West

7-6b   Confucianism in North America

7-6c   Daoism in North America

Terms

Daoism [DOW-ihz-um] (p. 159)

Confucianism [kun-FYOO-shuhn-ihz-um] (p. 159)

yin-yang [yihn-yahng] (p. 160)

Taiji [TIGH-jee] (p. 160)

oracle bones (p. 162)

feng shui [FUNG shway] (p. 162)

jing (p. 162)

Yi Jing [yee jing] (p. 162)

Heaven (p. 163)

Daozang [DOW-zhahng] (p. 165)

Neo-Daoism (p. 166)

Mandate of Heaven (p. 168)

Neo-Confucianism (p. 169)

Dao [dow] (p. 172)

de [duh] (p. 172)

qi [chee] (p. 172)

Tian [tee-AHN] (p. 173)

city gods (p. 175)

wu wei [woo way] (p. 176)

xiao [show; rhymes with *now*] (p. 179)

ren (p. 180)

zhong (p. 181)

junzi [JUHN-tzoo] (p. 181)

Confucius Centers (p. 185)

Discussion Questions

1. The "What Do YOU Think?" at the beginning of this chapter asked your opinion about the statement "The two main religious and ethical systems of China, Daoism and Confucianism, are trying to reach the same goal by different means." Now that you have studied this chapter, in what ways is this statement true, and in what ways is it not? Explain your answer.

2. How well does Wayne Dyer's advice "Stop striving, start arriving," explain the Daoist concept of wu wei?

3. Give your critique of the following statement: "In Chinese religion, Confucianism is the yang, and Daoism the yin."

4. Critique this statement: "In Daoism, following the Way entails becoming more like nature; in Confucianism, it entails becoming more human."

5. Discuss the possible futures of Daoism and Confucianism in Asia and the West.

6. Explain why Confucius would probably not have wanted what we call "Confucianism" to be named after him.

7. Suppose someone said to you, "Confucianism isn't a religion—it's just a cultural and ethical heritage." How could you answer this statement, based on what you have learned in this chapter?

Daoism and Confucianism in Film: Suggestions for Viewing and Discussion Questions

Confucius (2010, rated PG-13; in Mandarin, with English subtitles), directed by Mei Hu and starring action-film actor Chow Yun-fat, is a retelling of the story of Confucius.

Questions: Why was this film controversial, in both the casting of Chow Yun-fat as Confucius and in the portrayal of the life of Confucius? What insights do you get on Confucius and his times from this film?

The Last Emperor (1987, rated PG-13), directed by Bernardo Bertolucci, tells the story of Pu Yi, China's final monarch; it was filmed in part in the Forbidden City in Beijing. See the "director's cut" DVD for a fuller story that carries the life of Pu Yi through Communist "reeducation" camps.

Questions: How does this film show Confucian ideas of government? What might this film have to say about the possible transition from Communist rule to another form of government?

Raise the Red Lantern (1998, rated PG), directed by Zhang Yimou, deals with the life of a traditional Chinese family in 1920.

Questions: How does this film portray the difficulties posed by second and third marriages in China? How are the "family values" of Confucianism reflected here?

The Joy Luck Club (1993, rated R), based on the novel by Amy Tan, tells the story of challenging relationships between Chinese immigrant mothers and their adult Chinese American daughters.

Questions: What relational "issues" do mothers and daughters have with each other? How might this illustrate not just the first and second generations of Chinese immigrants, but also those of all immigrants?

Crouching Tiger, Hidden Dragon (2000, directed by Ang Lee; in Mandarin, with English subtitles) shows the connection between Daoism and martial arts. This film, which won four Academy Awards including Best Foreign Film, draws on the Wudang Daoist School of meditation and martial arts, although this is not made explicit in the film.

Questions: How much of the portrayal of martial arts is realistic, in your opinion, and how much is not? How do Daoism and Buddhism relate to these martial arts?

Koyaanisqatsi ("Life Out of Balance," 1982, directed by Godfrey Reggio) has a more avant-garde presentation of Daoist themes. Without any characters or conventional plot, this film uses music and film photography to depict the balance in nature that humans should study and adapt to—a key Daoist teaching.

Questions: What impressions do you get about the Dao from this film? How does it present the balance of human life and nature?

Beyond the Class

A selection of materials is in the Instructor's Manual and PowerLecture.

What's Inside

Key topics in this chapter: the meaning of *Shinto* and related words; how the history of Shinto has shaped its present form; basic Shinto teachings; the main ethical precepts; Shinto worship and meditation; Shinto life in the world today.

Learning Outcomes

8-1 Explain the meaning of *Shinto* and *Kami no michi.*

8-2 Summarize how the four main periods of Shinto's history have shaped its present.

8-3 Outline essential Shinto teachings in your own words.

8-4 Describe the main features of Shinto ethics.

8-5 Outline Shinto worship and other rituals, and explain why they play a leading role in Shinto.

8-6 Explain why the practice of Shinto in North America today is so small.

Chapter 8 Outline

Your Visit to the Tsubaki Shinto Shrine in Granite Falls, Washington

8-1 Names

8-2 The Shinto Present as Shaped by Its Past

8-2a Before the Arrival of Buddhism (to 600 C.E.)

8-2b Shinto and Buddhism Together in Japan (600–1850)

8-2c The Meiji Period (1850–1945)

8-2d Shinto in Recent Times (1945–Present)

8-3 Shinto Teachings

8-3a The Kami

8-3b Characteristics of Other Shinto Teachings

8-4 Shinto Ethics

8-4a General Characteristics

8-4b Purity

8-5 Shinto Ritual

8-5a The Shinto Shrine

8-5b The Shinto Priesthood

8-5c Prayer Plaques and Fortunes

8-5d The Wedding Ceremony

8-5e The Home Shrine

8-5f The Shinto Funeral

8-6 Shinto around the World Today

Terms

Shinto [SHIN-toh] (p. 190)

Kami no michi [KAH-mee noh MEE-chee] (p. 191)

kami [KAH-mee] (p. 191)

miko [MEE-koh] (p. 191)

Izanagi [EE-zah-NAH-gee (hard g)] (p. 192)

Izanami [EE-zah-NAH-mee] (p. 192)

Kojiki [koh-JEE-kee] (p. 192)

Nihongi [nee-HAWN-gee (hard g)] (p. 192)

torii [TOH-ree-ee] (p. 193)

Amaterasu [ah-MAH-tehr-AH-soo] (p. 194)

Ise Shrine [EE-say] (p. 194)

Yasukuni [YAS-soo-KOO-nee] (p. 195)

kamikaze [KAHM-ih-KAHZ-ee] (p. 197)

honden [HAHN-den] (p. 201)

ema [AY-muh] (p. 202)

omikuji [OH-mee-KOO-jee] (p. 202)

kamidana [KAH-mee-DAH-nuh] (p. 203)

Discussion Questions

1. The "What Do YOU Think?" question at the beginning of this chapter asked your opinion about the statement "The Shinto religion explains the Japanese 'love affair' with robots and robotics." Now that you have finished this chapter, what do you think about this?

2. How do the basic Shinto teachings as outlined above illustrate that ritual is more important in Shinto than doctrine?

3. Explain why a better understanding of *Shinto* might be "the way of the kami" rather than "the way of the gods."

4. Why do Japanese myths place so much emphasis on the creation of Japan and so little on the creation of the world?

5. Why is the Shinto ritual performed at the Yasukuni Shrine controversial in Japan and even more controversial in China and South Korea?

6. In your opinion, what might the future of Shinto be?

Shinto in Film: Suggestions for Viewing and Discussion Questions

The best recent film that portrays Japan's religion and culture is *The Last Samurai* (2003, rated R), directed by Edward Zwick. Tom Cruise plays an eighteenth-century American military adviser who, after being captured in battle, embraces the samurai culture he was hired to destroy. The film begins with a brief retelling of the creation myth from the *Kojiki* and reflects its feeling for the land and peoples of Japan. The film also illustrates well the interplay between Buddhist tendencies to pacifism and Shinto militarism.

Questions: How does this film portray Buddhism's traditional pacifism? What Shinto "spin" is put on this film by its opening citation of the *Kojiki* creation myth? How can Shinto be seen in the traditional Japanese cultural elements shown in the film? How might the samurai-warrior ethic, portrayed sympathetically here, have had a resurgence in the twentieth century?

Beyond the Class

A selection of materials is in the Instructor's Manual and PowerLecture.

What's Inside

Key topics in this chapter: the meaning of *Zoroastrianism* and related words; key formative events in the history of Zoroastrianism; essential Zoroastrian teachings of monotheism and moral dualism; the main ethical principles in Zoroastrianism; the way Zoroastrians worship; and Zoroastrian life in the world today, with particular attention to North America.

Learning Outcomes

9-1 Explain the meaning of *Zoroastrianism* and related terms.

9-2 Outline how Zoroastrianism developed over time into what it is today.

9-3 Explain the essential Zoroastrian teachings of monotheism and moral dualism.

9-4 State the main ethical precepts of Zoroastrianism.

9-5 Outline the way Zoroastrians worship and observe rituals.

9-6 State the main features of Zoroastrian life around the world today, especially in North America.

Chapter 9 Outline

Your Visit to Yazd, Iran

9-1 Names for Zoroastrianism and Zoroastrians

9-2 Zoroastrianism as Shaped by Its Past

9-2a The Birth of Zoroastrianism (ca. 630–550 B.C.E.)

9-2b The Spread of Zoroastrianism in the Persian and Sassanian Empires (550 B.C.E.–650 C.E.)

9-2c The Coming of Islam and the Zoroastrian Dispersion (650 C.E.–Present)

9-3 Essential Zoroastrian Teachings: Monotheism and Moral Dualism

9-3a The One God, Ahura Mazda

9-3b The Spirit of Destruction, Angra Mainyu

9-3c Moral Dualism

9-3d Supernatural Intermediaries

9-3e Judgment and the Final Victory of Ahura Mazda

9-4 Zoroastrian Ethics

9-4a Zoroastrian General Morality

9-4b A Current Ethical and Social Issue: Marriage and Children

9-5 Zoroastrian Rituals

9-5a Fires in the Fire Temple

9-5b Interior Plan of the Fire Temple

9-5c Worship

9-5d Priesthood

9-5e Other Rituals

9-5f Funeral Rituals

9-6 Zoroastrianism around the World Today

Discussion Questions

1. In the "What Do YOU Think?" feature at the beginning of this chapter, you were asked to consider the statement "The belief that the world is locked in a cosmic struggle between good and evil, as Zoroastrians hold, makes for a powerful faith." Now that you've finished the chapter, what do you think about this, and why?

Terms

Zarathustra [ZAHR-uh-THOOS-truh] (p. 209)

faravahar [FAHR-uh-VAH-har] (p. 209)

Mazdayasnian religion [MAHZ-duh-YAHZ-nee-uhn] (p. 210)

Ahura Mazda [ah-HOOR-uh MAHZ-duh] (p. 210)

Parsis [PAR-seez] (p. 210)

Axial Age (p. 210)

Cyrus Cylinder (p. 211)

Avesta [ah-VEHS-tuh] (p. 213)

tower of silence (p. 213)

Zarathushtrian Assembly (p. 216)

Zoroastrian Studies Association (p. 216)

Angra Mainyu [AHN-gruh MIGHN-yoo] (p. 217)

dualism (p. 217)

Twin Spirits (p. 217)

daevas [DIGH-vuhs] (p. 217)

Amesha Spentas [uh-MAY-shuh SPEN-tuhz] (p. 218)

Chinvat Bridge [CHIN-vaht] (p. 218)

faith of kindred marriage (p. 220)

fire temple (p. 220)

magi [MAY-jigh] (p. 221)

haoma [HO-mah] (p. 222)

navjote [nahv-JOH-tee] (p. 222)

kusti [KOOS-tee] (p. 222)

patet [PAH-teht] (p. 222)

Nowruz or Noruz [NOH-rooz] (p. 222)

2. In what sense can the Zoroastrian belief in many supernatural beings but only one God be compared to Christian and Islamic belief in one God and many angels, archangels, and demons, as well as the devil?

3. How does Zoroastrianism answer one of the perennial questions of many religions: How can one reconcile the imperfections of the world with the existence of a good God who created and sustains it?

4. The Parsis are often called "the Jews of India." Explain this expression.

5. What might Zoroastrian monotheism and the heritage of tolerance toward other religions and ethnic groups say about the belief today, held by some, that monotheism is intolerant?

Beyond the Class

A selection of materials is in the Instructor's Manual and PowerLecture.

What's Inside

Key topics in this chapter: the meaning of *Judaism* and related terms; key formative events in the history of Judaism, especially the rise of Jewish diversity; essential Jewish teachings of monotheism, creation, the chosen people, and life after death; the main ethics of Judaism, especially the commands of the Torah and more-general ethical principles; the ways Jews worship, celebrate festivals and the Sabbath, and observe life-cycle rituals; Jewish life around the world today, particularly in Israel and North America.

Learning Outcomes

10-1   Explain the meaning of *Judaism* and related terms.

10-2   Summarize how the main periods of Judaism's history have shaped its present.

10-3   Outline the essential teachings of Judaism in your own words.

10-4   Describe the main features of Jewish ethics.

10-5   Summarize Jewish worship, the Sabbath and major festivals, and life-cycle rituals.

10-6   Outline the main features of Judaism around the world today, especially in Israel and North America.

Chapter 10 Outline

Your Visit to the Western Wall in Jerusalem

10-1   The Name *Judaism* and Related Terms

10-2   The Jewish Present as Shaped by Its Past

10-2a   From the Creation to Abraham (ca. 2000 B.C.E.)

10-2b   The Emergence of Ancient Israel (ca. 1200–950 B.C.E.)

10-2c   The First Temple Period (950–586 B.C.E.)

10-2d   The Second Temple Period (539 B.C.E.–70 C.E.)

10-2e   Revolts and Rabbis (70 C.E.–ca. 650)

10-2f   Jews under Islamic and Christian Rule (ca. 650–1800)

10-2g   Emancipation and Diversity (1800–1932)

10-2h   The Holocaust and Its Aftermath (1932–Present)

10-3   Essential Teachings of Judaism

10-3a   Foundation of Jewish Teachings: The Tanak

10-3b   One God

10-3c   The Jews as God's Chosen People

10-3d   Life after Death?

10-4   Essential Jewish Ethics

10-4a   Ethics in the Image of God

10-4b   The Torah

10-4c   General Jewish Ethics

10-4d   Modern Jewish Ethics

10-5   Jewish Worship and Ritual

10-5a   Worship in the Synagogue

10-5b   The Sabbath

10-5c   Jewish Annual Festivals

10-5d   Kosher Food

10-5e   Circumcision, the Sign of the Covenant

10-5f   Bar Mitzvah and Bat Mitzvah

10-5g   Marriage

10-5h   Funeral Rituals

10-6   Judaism around the World Today

10-6a   Judaism in Israel

10-6b   Judaism in North America

Terms

Judaism [JOO-dee-ihz-um] (p. 228)

Hebrews [HEE-brewz] (p. 229)

Israelites [IHZ-ray-ehl-ights] (p. 229)

Israelis [ihz-RAIL-eez] (p. 229)

menorah [men-OHR-uh] (p. 229)

Star of David (p. 229)

patriarchs [PAY-tree-arks] (p. 230)

covenant [CUH-veh-nent] (p. 230)

circumcision (p. 230)

Torah [TOHR-uh] (p.231)

Ark of the Covenant (p. 231)

First Temple Period (p. 231)

prophets (p. 231)

Second Temple Period (p. 233)

Diaspora [dee-ASS-pohr-uh] (p. 233)

Pharisees [FAIR-uh-seez] (p. 234)

Essenes [ESS-eenz] (p. 234)

Maccabean Revolt [MAK-uh-BEE-uhn] (p. 234)

Hanukkah [HAHN-uh-kuh] (p. 234)

rabbis [RAB-ighs] (p. 235)

synagogue [SIN-uh-gawg] (p. 235)

anti-Semitism [SEHM-ih-TIHZ-um] (p. 235)

Babylonian Talmud [TALL-mood] (p. 236)

Sephardic [seh-FAR-dik] (p. 236)

Kabbalah [KAHB-uh-luh] (p. 236)

Ashkenazi [ASH-kuh-NAHZ-ee] (p. 236)

ghetto (p. 236)

Hasidism [HASS-uh-dizm] (p. 237)

emancipation (p. 238)

Reform (p. 238)

Orthodox (p. 239)

Conservative (p. 239)

Masorti [mah-SOHR-tee] (p. 239)

Zionism [ZY-on-izm] (p. 239)

Holocaust [HAUL-oh-caust] (p. 241)

Shoah [SHOW-uh] (p. 241)

Tanak [TAH-nahk] (p. 242)

henotheism (p. 242)

Shema [sheh-MAH, or shmah] (p. 243)

resurrection (p. 245)

halakhah [hah-luh-KAH] (p. 248)

minyan [MIHN-yahn] (p. 249)

ark (p. 250)

Sabbath (p. 250)

Rosh Hashanah [rohsh ha-SHAH-nah] (p. 250)

Yom Kippur [yohm kip-PUHR] (p. 250)

Passover (p. 251)

seder [SAY-duhr] (p. 251)

kosher [KOH-sher] (p. 251)

bris milah [brihs MIL-luh] (p. 252)

mohel [MOI-uhl, rhymes with *oil*] (p. 252)

bar mitzvah [bahr MITZ-vuh] (p. 252)

bat (bas) mitzvah [baht (bahs) MITZ-vuh] (p. 252)

shiva [SHIHV-uh] (p. 254)

Discussion Questions

1. In the "What Do YOU Think?" at the beginning of this chapter, you were asked to consider the statement "Judaism is the best example in world religions of 'ethical monotheism.'" Now that you've finished the chapter, what do you think about this, and why?

2. What are the main commonalities of the three major Jewish movements (Orthodox, Conservative, and Reform)? What are their main differences?

3. What is accurate and inaccurate in the term "ultra-Orthodox"?

4. How does keeping the law of God relate to being a member of the chosen people of God?

5. How does the term *ethical monotheism* relate to the teachings and practices of Judaism?

6. What does it mean to be "Jewish but not religious"?

7. Describe the situation of Judaism in the modern state of Israel.

Judaism in Film: Suggestions for Viewing and Discussion Questions

Hollywood hasn't made major films based directly on the Hebrew Jewish Bible/Old Testament for more than fifty years, despite the grand narratives of the Bible that are seemingly tailor-made for film. One exception is the acclaimed animated film *Prince of Egypt* (1998, directed by Brenda Chapman), the story of Moses and the Exodus.

Questions: How closely does the *Prince of Egypt* film follow the biblical account, in your opinion?

The Holocaust has so shaped recent Jewish life that it and other contemporary Jewish events have received the lion's share of attention in film (*Schindler's List*, *Sophie's Choice*, *A Beautiful Life*, and other movies).

Questions on *Schindler's List*: How realistically does this film present the motives of Oskar Schindler? Some have called him a "saint"—would you? Why do you think actions such as his were comparatively rare in the Holocaust?

A more recent treatment of a contemporary topic is *Trembling Before G-d [God]*, directed by Simcha Dubowski (2001). This prize-winning documentary film deals with Jews from Orthodox backgrounds who are dealing with their same-sex orientation and with the traditional biblical reaction to it by other Orthodox Jews.

Questions: How sensitive is this film to the concerns of same-sex Jews? To heterosexual Jews maintaining the traditional Jewish view on this topic?

Beyond the Class

A selection of materials is in the Instructor's Manual and PowerLecture.

What's Inside

Key topics in this chapter: the meaning of *Christianity* and related words; how the history of Christianity has shaped its present form; basic Christian teachings; the main ethical teachings of Christianity; Christian worship and ritual; Christianity around the world today, especially in the Southern Hemisphere and North America.

Learning Outcomes

11-1   Explain the meaning of *Christianity* and related terms.

11-2   Trace how the main periods of Christianity's history have shaped its present.

11-3   Outline in your own words essential Christian teachings as found in the Nicene Creed.

11-4   Describe the main features of Christian ethics.

11-5   Summarize Christian worship and other rituals.

11-6   Explain the variety of Christianity around the world today, especially in the Southern Hemisphere and in North America.

Chapter 11 Outline

Your Visit to St. Peter's in Rome

11-1   Names

11-2   The Christian Present as Shaped by Its Past

11-2a The Life, Death, and Resurrection of Jesus Christ (ca. 4 B.C.E.–33 C.E.)

11-2b The Earliest Church (30–100 C.E.)

11-2c The Ancient Period (100–500 C.E.)

11-2d Byzantine, Medieval, and Renaissance Christianity (500–1500)

11-2e Reformation in the Western Church (1500–1600)

11-2f The Early Modern Period (1600–1900)

11-2g Modern Christianity (1900–Present)

11-3   Christian Teachings as Reflected in the Nicene Creed

11-3a God the Father

11-3b God the Son

11-3c God the Holy Spirit

11-3d The Conclusion of the Nicene Creed: Church, Baptism, and Christian Hope

11-4   Christian Ethics: Following the Way of Jesus Christ

11-4a Foundations in the Ten Commandments, the Sermon on the Mount, and the Letters of Paul

11-4b The Enactment of Moral Life in the Church

11-5   Christian Worship and Ritual

11-5a Christian Worship before Constantine

11-5b Worship after Constantine

11-5c The Liturgical Year

11-6   Christianity around the World Today

11-6a Christianity in the Global South

11-6b Christianity in North America

11-6c The Different Churches: Roman Catholic and Protestant

Terms

Christ (p. 260)

resurrection (p. 261)

crucifix (p. 261)

Gospel [GAHS-puhl] (p. 262)

New Testament (p. 262)

parable (p. 262)

apostles (p. 262)

justification (p. 264)

canon (p. 265)

martyrdom (p. 265)

heresy (p. 266)

Gnosticism (p. 266)

orthodoxy (p. 267)

Constantinianism [CON-stan-TIN-ee-uhn-iz-uhm] (p. 267)

monasticism (p. 267)

Iconoclastic Controversy [eye-CON-oh-CLASS-tick] (p. 268)

iconostasis [eye-CON-oh-STAH-sis] (p. 268)

pope (p. 269)

papacy [PAYP-uh-see] (p. 269)

friar (p. 269)

Magisterial Reformation (p. 270)

purgatory (p. 270)

Radical Reformation (p. 270)

Anabaptists (p. 272)

Puritans (p. 273)

Catholic Reform (p. 273)

Pietism [PIGH-uh-tiz-um] (p. 274)

fundamentalism (p. 275)

denominations (p. 275)

ecumenism [eh-KYOO-men-iz-uhm] (p. 275)

Second Vatican Council (p. 276)

liberation theology (p. 277)

Trinity (p. 277)

incarnation (p. 277)

Nicene Creed [nigh-SEEN] (p. 277)

creed (p. 277)

Apostles' Creed (p. 277)

Theotokos [thee-AH-toh-koss] (p. 281)

Chalcedon [KAL-seh-don] (p. 282)

catechumen [KAT-uh-KYOO-men] (p. 284)

canon law (p. 285)

sacrament (p. 286)

liturgy (p. 286)

lectionary (p. 287)

basilica [bah-SIHL-ih-kuh] (p. 287)

cult of the saints (p. 288)

transubstantiation (p. 288)

charismatic movement (Pentecostalism) (p. 289)

liturgical (church) year (p. 289)

Global South Christians (p. 290)

mainline (p. 291)

Evangelicalism (p. 292)

Restorationism (p. 292)

Discussion Questions

1. In the "What Do YOU Think?" feature at the beginning of this chapter, you were asked your opinion about the statement " Its universal spread shows that Christianity is the most culturally adaptable religion in the world." In what ways is this statement true, and in what ways is it not? Explain your answer.

2. Discuss this provocative comment by a Jewish scholar on the relationship of Judaism and Christianity: "Christianity is Judaism's gift to the non-Jewish world."

3. Aside from the life of Jesus, what period of the church discussed here do you think is most important for Christianity? Why?

4. What were the main issues that the Protestant Reformers were concerned about?

5. How is the Jewish conception of God different from the Christian teaching about God the Father?

6. Explain why Jesus Christ is thought by Christians to be Lord and Savior.

7. Explain the similarities and differences between Christian ethics and Jewish ethics.

8. Despite obvious differences in music style, level of formality, and so on, how is most Christian worship similar? What are the deeper differences?

9. Is Christianity more internally fractured than other major religions such as Buddhism or Islam? Explain your answer.

Christianity in Film: Suggestions for Viewing and Discussion Questions

Of all major world religions, Christianity is the most fully, if not always the most artistically, represented in feature films. *The Gospel According to St. Matthew* (1964, unrated), directed by Pier Paolo Pasolini, is the most cinematically artistic.

Questions: What view of Jesus comes through in this film? How accurate is it as a retelling of the Gospel of Matthew?

The Passion of the Christ (2004, rated R), directed by Mel Gibson, is a controversial, thought-provoking depiction of the death of Jesus.

Questions: What do you think caused such a stir about this film? Do you think it is accurate as a retelling of the death of Jesus? How does the film suggest his resurrection?

For a taste of apocalyptic style in the New Testament and in modern film, see *The Seventh Seal* (1958, unrated), one of the classics of world cinema, directed by Ingmar Bergman.

Questions: What are the apocalyptic elements of this film? How does it draw on Christian themes?

Also of interest to students of Christianity is *Jesus of Montreal* (1989, rated R), directed by Denys Arcand, in which a Montreal theater troupe puts on a controversial passion play and begins to experience suffering akin to that of Jesus.

Question: How does this film relate Jesus's suffering to the troubles of the modern actors?

Babette's Feast (1987, not rated but suitable for all audiences, in Danish with English subtitles), directed by Gabriel Axel, is a story of frugality and prodigality that won the 1987 Academy Award for best foreign film.

Questions: How does this film show the beauty of God's grace in the Christian view? The extravagance?

Beyond the Class

A selection of materials is in the Instructor's Manual and PowerLecture.

What's Inside

Key topics in this chapter: the name "Islam"; the beginning and growth of Islam, and its different groups; the essential teachings of Islam; Islam as a way of life; the Five Pillars of worship; Muslim life around the world today, especially in Europe and North America.

Learning Outcomes

12-1 Explain *Islam* and related terms.

12-2 Outline how the main periods of Islamic history have shaped its present, especially the different Muslim groups.

12-3 Give the essential elements of Islamic teachings in your own words.

12-4 Explain Muslim ethics, especially in diet, dress, and marriage.

12-5 Explain the ways Muslims worship, especially the Five Pillars.

12-6 Explain the main aspects of Muslim life around the world today, especially in Europe and North America.

Chapter 12 Outline

Your Visit to Mecca

12-1 The Name *Islam*

12-2 Islam Today as Shaped by Its Past

12-2a Arabia at the Time of Muhammad (500s C.E.)

12-2b The Life and Work of Muhammad (ca. 570–632)

12-2c Islam Immediately Following the Death of Muhammad (632–661)

12-2d Islam from the Umayyads until Today (661–Present)

12-2e Diverse Muslim Groups Today: Mainstream, Zealous, and Moderate

12-3 Essential Teachings

12-3a God Is One

12-3b Angels and Spirits

12-3c The Qur'an

12-3d Prophets

12-3e "People of the Book": Jews, Christians, and Zoroastrians

12-3f Final Judgment

12-4 Islamic Ethics

12-4a The Hadith

12-4b Shari'a

12-4c Diet and Other Regulations

12-4d Marriage and the Status of Women

12-4e Jihad

12-5 Worship: The Five Pillars of Islam

12-5a Confession of Faith

12-5b Prayer

12-5c Fasting

12-5d Almsgiving

12-5e Pilgrimage

12-6 Islam around the World Today

12-6a Islam in Europe

12-6b Muslim Migration to North America

12-6c The Nation of Islam and the American Society of Muslims

12-6d Muslim Life in the United States after 9/11

Discussion Questions

1. In the "What Do YOU Think?" feature at the beginning of this chapter, you were asked your opinion about the statement "Islam is mostly a religion of peace." In what ways is this statement true, and in what ways is it not? Explain your answer.

Terms

Islam [ihz-LAHM] (p. 297)

Muslim [MUHZ-lim] (p. 297)

Islamist (p. 297)

hanifs [hah-NEEFS] (p. 298)

Ramadan [RAHM-uh-dahn] (p. 299)

Allah [AHL-lah] (p. 299)

Hijra [HIHJ-ruh] (p. 300)

umma [OOM-uh] (p. 300)

caliph [kah-LEEF] (p. 302)

Shi'as [SHEE-uhs] or **Shi'ites** [SHEE-ights] (p. 302)

Sunnis [SOON-eez] (p. 302)

Rightly Guided Caliphs (p. 302)

madrasa [muh-DRAH-suh] (p. 303)

Crusades (p. 303)

Arab Spring (p. 304)

Ashura [uh-SHOOR-uh] (p. 306)

imam [IHM-ahm] (p. 306)

Mahdi [MAH-dee] (p. 307)

Sufis [SOO-feez] (p. 307)

Wahhabi [wah-HAH-bee] (p. 308)

Muslim Brotherhood (p. 309)

Taliban [TAHL-ih-bahn] (p. 309)

Salafi [suh-LAH-fee] (p. 300)

jinn [jihn] (p. 312)

surah [SOO-ruh] (p. 312)

al-Fatihah [al-fah-TEE-huh] (p. 313)

People of the Book (p. 314)

hadith [huh-DEETH] (p. 316)

Shari'a [shah-REE-uh] (p. 316)

fatwa (p. 316)

halal (huh-LAHL) (p. 317)

haram [huh-RAHM] (p. 317)

jihad [jee-HAHD] (p. 319)

Five Pillars of Islam (p. 320)

shahada [shah-hah-DAH] (p. 321)

salat [sah-LAHT] (p. 321)

mosque [mahsk] (p. 321)

minaret [mihn-uh-REHT] (p. 321)

qiblah [KIB-luh] (p. 322)

sawm [sahwm] (p. 323)

zakat [zah-KAHT] (p. 323)

hajj [hahj] (p. 323)

Hajji [HAHJ-ee] (p. 324)

Nation of Islam (p. 327)

American Society of Muslims (p. 328)

al-Qaeda [al KIGH-duh] (p. 329)

2. How did the Sunni and Shi'a groups arise, and how do their differences today relate to their origins?

3. How did Islam come to Africa and south Asia?

4. Name the main Muslim groups today and the issues on which they agree and disagree.

5. What special opportunities and difficulties do you see in studying Islam in our post-9/11 situation?

6. In what ways is Islam especially Arabic, and in what ways is it not?

7. Explain the statement "Islam is a religion of the book."

8. How does Islamic monotheism relate to monotheism in Judaism and Christianity?

9. How, and how well, does almsgiving function to promote compassion and social justice in Islam?

10. Give your choice of a term for modern militant Islam, and explain why.

11. Why do you think the remake of the 1976 film *The Message* is now titled *The Messenger of Peace*?

12. Comment on the 2008 statement by Madeline Albright, U.S. secretary of state in the 1990s: "I know there are some who would like to engage with Muslim communities without bringing religion into the conversation. But to them I say, 'Good luck!'"

Islam in Film: Suggestions for Viewing and Discussion Questions

Significant but of mixed cinematic value is *The Message* (1976, rated PG), directed by Moustapha Akkad, the story of Muhammad (without depicting him directly) and early Islam. Production work began in 2008 for a remake of this film, tentatively entitled *The Messenger of Peace*.

Questions: How well does this film depict Muhammad without showing his face? "Messenger of Peace" is not a common Muslim title for Muhammad. Why do you think the filmmakers are using it for the remake? What overall portrait of the birth of Islam emerges from the original film?

An excellent film on the history of Islam in America is *Malcolm X* (1992, rated PG-13), directed by Spike Lee and starring Denzel Washington.

Questions: How does this film show the "conversion" of Malcolm X to mainstream Islam during his pilgrimage to Mecca? What is the appeal of both mainstream Islam and the Nation of Islam to African Americans, according to this film?

Persepolis (2007, rated PG-13), an animated film directed and written by Vincent Paronnaud and Marjane Satrapi, is an acclaimed coming-of-age story about an outspoken Iranian girl. It begins near the time of the Islamic Revolution in Iran, which it presents unfavorably.

Questions: How do the personality and views of the main character in this film shape her view of Islam in Iran? What is the meaning of the film's title? How does this film express the unhappiness of many young Iranians with religious and social conditions in their country?

Kite Runner (2007, rated PG-13), directed by Marc Foster and based on a novel by Kaled Hosseini, is the powerful story of an Afghani expatriate who goes back to Taliban-controlled Afghanistan to bring out the child of a friend.

Questions: How does this film portray the strength of mind and courage of the main character? How accurate is the depiction of Taliban rule, in your opinion?

Arusi Persian Wedding (2008), directed by Marjan Tehrani, is a documentary about Iranian Americans who travel back to Iran to be married, with good treatment of the social, political, and religious contexts of modern Iran.

Questions: What are the challenges facing Iranian Americans who go back to Iran for marriage? How might this film throw light on the experiences of people of other religions who go back to their homelands for engagement and/or marriage?

What's Inside

Key topics in this chapter: the different names used for this type of religion; the common features of new religious movements; the distribution of new religious movements in the world today; the main features of Falun Gong, the Church of Jesus Christ of Latter-day Saints, and the Church of Scientology.

Learning Outcomes

13-1   Evaluate the different names for new religious movements.

13-2   Summarize the common features of new religious movements.

13-3   Survey the distribution of new religious movements in the world today.

13-4   State and explain the teachings and practices of Falun Gong.

13-5   State and explain the history, teachings, and practices of the Church of Jesus Christ of Latter-day Saints.

13-6   State and explain the teachings and practices of Scientology.

Chapter 13 Outline

Your Visit to Temple Square, Salt Lake City, Utah

13-1   Names for This Type of Religion

13-2   Common Features of New Religious Movements

13-3   New Religious Movements in the World Today: A Survey

13-3a   NRMs Founded in the Western World

13-3b   Asian NRMs in the West

13-3c   "Scientific" NRMs: Christian Science and UFO Groups

13-3d   Nature NRMs: Neo-Paganism, Wicca, and Druidry

13-3e   NRMs in Asia

13-4   An NRM from Asia: Falun Gong

13-4a   History

13-4b   Teaching and Practice

13-5   A North American NRM: The Church of Jesus Christ of Latter-day Saints

13-5a   History

13-5b   Scripture

13-5c   Teachings

13-5d   Institutions, Practices, and Structure of the LDS Church

13-6   The Church of Scientology

13-6a   L. Ron Hubbard's Life and Teachings

13-6b   Organization of the Church

13-6c   Controversy and Present Status

Discussion Questions

1. In the "What Do YOU Think?" feature at the beginning of this chapter, you were asked your opinion about the statement "New religious movements are often dangerous organizations." In what ways is this statement true, and in what ways is it not? Explain your answer.

2. How adequate is the term *new religious movement*, in your view? What are its strengths and weaknesses?

3. What similarities and differences can you draw between Falun Gong and Buddhism?

Terms

new religious movements (NRMs) (p. 333)

sect (p. 335)

cult (p. 335)

alternative religious movements (p. 335)

marginal religious movements (p. 335)

emergent religions (p. 335)

apocalyptic [uh-POC-uh-LIP-tick] (p. 337)

millenarianism [MILL-en-AIR-ee-uhn-iz-uhm] (p. 337)

New Age (p. 338)

People's Temple (p. 338)

Branch Davidian (p. 338)

Vedanta Society (p. 339)

Self-Realization Fellowship (p. 339)

Transcendental Meditation (TM) (p. 339)

Rajneesh International Foundation (p. 339)

Christian Science Church (p. 340)

UFO groups (p. 340)

Raëlians [rye-EHL-ee-uhnz] (p. 341)

Heaven's Gate (p. 341)

Wicca [WIHK-kuh] (p. 341)

Qi Gong [chee gong] (p. 343)

new religions (p. 343)

Aum Shinrikyo [ohm shin-REEK-yoh] (p. 343)

Soka-Gakkai [SOH-kah-GAHK-kigh] (p. 343)

Unification Church (p. 344)

True Parents (p. 344)

Falun Gong [FAH-loon gong] (p. 345)

Mormon [MOHR-muhn] (p. 347)

Council of the Twelve Apostles (p. 348)

plural marriage (p. 349)

Reorganized Church of Jesus Christ of Latter-day Saints (p. 349)

Fundamentalist Church of Jesus Christ of Latter-day Saints (FLDS) (p. 349)

Articles of Faith (p. 351)

tithe (p. 351)

baptism for the dead (p. 352)

endowment (p. 352)

sealing (p. 352)

temple garment (p. 352)

stake (p. 352)

ward (p. 352)

Scientology (p. 353)

engram (p. 353)

auditing (p. 353)

E-meter (p. 354)

clear (p. 354)

thetan [THAY-tan] (p. 354)

MEST (p. 354)

Operating Thetan (p. 354)

dynamics (p. 354)

Sea Organization (p. 355)

4. Critique this statement: "The LDS church is, among all world religions or NRMs, the most American."

5. The Church of Jesus Christ of Latter-day Saints has given the Book of Mormon an unofficial subtitle: "Another Testament of Jesus Christ." What do you think was the church's reason for doing so?

6. Would you say that the Unification Church is a Christian church? Why or why not?

7. At what point do NRMs cease being "new religious movements" and begin being "religions"? Explain your answer, using the example of a traditional religion such as Christianity, Islam, or Buddhism.

8. What is the most difficult challenge to you in studying this type of religion? Why?

New Religious Movements in Film: Suggestions for Viewing and Discussion Questions

Perhaps because of their controversial nature, the stories of new religious movements are not often captured in feature films. One exception can be found in connection with the Latter-day Saints church, which has a motion-picture operation loosely related to the church (nicknamed "Molly-wood"). *God's Army* (2000, rated PG), directed by Richard Dutcher, tells the story of four young LDS missionaries as they encounter various problems and opportunities in their work and their lives.

Questions: What are some of the main LDS teachings and practices highlighted in this film? What did you learn about the work of Mormon missionaries? What are some of the challenges facing Mormon missionaries today?

The Book of Mormon Movie (volume 1; 2004, rated PG), directed by Gary Rogers, tells of roughly the first half of the Book of Mormon. The portrayal of this book is selective but literal. Viewers—including Mormons—accustomed to typical Hollywood production values may be disappointed with the cinematic quality of the film, but it is worthwhile watching as an example of Mormons explaining their scriptures through the medium of film. Volume 2 of *The Book of Mormon Movie*, titled *Zarahemia*, was released in 2008.

Questions: What key insights into Mormonism can be derived from these films? Why do you think the LDS church has invested so much money and effort into making them? What is your own conclusion about the "production values" in the films? Do they help or hinder your own viewing?

The Master (2012, rated R), directed by Paul Thomas Anderson, stars Joaquin Phoenix, Philip Seymour Hoffman, and Amy Adams—all of whom received Academy Award nominations for their performances. Freddie Quell (Phoenix), a psychologically troubled World War II veteran struggling to adjust to civilian life, meets Lancaster Dodd (Hoffman), a leader of a movement known as "The Cause," and joins it. He travels with Dodd to spread The Cause's teachings. Although this film draws on several sources, most film critics conclude that it draws mainly on the story of Scientology founder L. Ron Hubbard.

Questions: What does this film say about the leaders of NRMs? How does the teaching of The Cause help Freddie with his problems, and how does it not? What is your own conclusion about whether this film may be a portrayal of L. Ron Hubbard?

Beyond the Class

A selection of materials is in the Instructor's Manual and PowerLecture.